THE AMERICAN PEOPLE

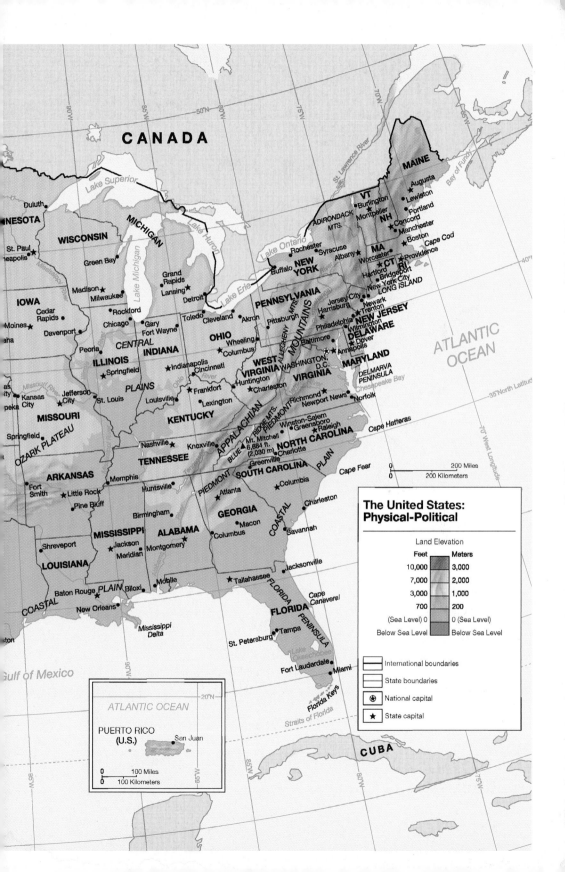

CANADA

Lake Superior

Duluth

MINNESOTA

St. Paul
neapolis

WISCONSIN

Green Bay

Madison
Milwaukee

MICHIGAN

Lake Huron

Lake Michigan

Grand
Rapids
Lansing

Detroit

Lake Ontario

Rochester
Syracuse

Buffalo

NEW
YORK

ADIRONDACK
MTS.

VT
Burlington
Montpelier

NH
Concord
Manchester

MAINE

Augusta
Lewiston
Portland

Bay of Fundy

St. Lawrence River

Albany

MA
Worcester
Hartford
CT
Bridgeport

Boston

Cape Cod

Providence
RI

IOWA

Cedar
Rapids

Rockford

Chicago
Gary
Fort Wayne

Toledo
Cleveland
Akron

PENNSYLVANIA

Pittsburgh

New York City
LONG ISLAND

Moines
Davenport

aha

Peoria

CENTRAL

ILLINOIS

Springfield

INDIANA

Indianapolis
Cincinnati

OHIO

Wheeling

Columbus

ALLEGHENY MTS.

Harrisburg

Jersey City
Newark
Trenton

Philadelphia

NEW JERSEY

DELAWARE

Dover

as
ity
peka City

Kansas
City

Jefferson
City

St. Louis

PLAINS

MISSOURI

Springfield

OZARK PLATEAU

Louisville

Frankfort

KENTUCKY

Lexington

Ohio River

WEST
VIRGINIA

Huntington

Charleston

WASHINGTON
D.C.

Baltimore

Annapolis

MARYLAND

VIRGINIA

Richmond

Newport News

Norfolk

DELMARVA
PENINSULA

Chesapeake Bay

ATLANTIC
OCEAN

Nashville

Knoxville

APPALACHIAN

BLUE RIDGE MTS.

Mt. Mitchell
6,684 ft.
(2,030 m)

PIEDMONT

Winston-Salem
Greensboro

Raleigh

Cape Hatteras

ARKANSAS

Fort
Smith

Little Rock

Pine Bluff

Memphis

TENNESSEE

Huntsville

PIEDMONT

Charlotte

Greenville

SOUTH CAROLINA

NORTH CAROLINA

Cape Fear

COASTAL
PLAIN

0   200 Miles
0   200 Kilometers

MISSISSIPPI

Shreveport

Jackson
Meridian

ALABAMA

Montgomery

Birmingham

GEORGIA

Macon

Columbus

Atlanta

Columbia

Charleston

Savannah

COASTAL

The United States:
Physical-Political

Land Elevation

Feet	Meters
10,000	3,000
7,000	2,000
3,000	1,000
700	200
(Sea Level) 0	0 (Sea Level)
Below Sea Level	Below Sea Level

LOUISIANA

Baton Rouge
PLAIN
Biloxi

Mobile

Tallahassee

Jacksonville

FLORIDA

International boundaries

State boundaries

COASTAL

ston

New Orleans

Mississippi
Delta

Tallahassee

Cape
Canaveral

FLORIDA
PENINSULA

National capital

State capital

Gulf of Mexico

St. Petersburg
Tampa

Lake
Okeechobee

Fort Lauderdale
Miami

Florida Keys

Straits of Florida

ATLANTIC OCEAN

PUERTO RICO
(U.S.)

San Juan

0   100 Miles
0   100 Kilometers

CUBA

THE AMERICAN PEOPLE

Creating a Nation and a Society

Concise Sixth Edition

Volume II   **Since 1865**

Gary B. Nash
University of California,
Los Angeles
General Editor

Julie Roy Jeffrey
Goucher College
General Editor

John R. Howe
University of Minnesota

Allan M. Winkler
Miami University

Allen F. Davis
Temple University

Charlene Mires
Villanova University

Peter J. Frederick
Wabash College

Carla Gardina Pestana
Miami University

PEARSON
Longman

New York   San Francisco   Boston
London   Toronto   Sydney   Tokyo   Singapore   Madrid
Mexico City   Munich   Paris   Cape Town   Hong Kong   Montréal

Executive Editor: Michael Boezi
Editorial Assistant: Vanessa Gennarelli
Executive Marketing Manager: Sue Westmoreland
Assistant Development Manager: David B. Kear
Supplements Editor: Brian Belardi
Media Supplements Editor: Melissa Edwards
Production Manager: Eric Jorgensen
Project Coordination, Text Design, and Electronic Page Makeup: Elm Street Publishing
    Services, Inc.
Senior Cover Design Manager/Cover Designer: Nancy Danahy
Cover Illustration/Photo: Digital Vision/Getty Images, Inc.
Photo Researcher: Julie Tesser
Manufacturing Buyer: Roy Pickering
Printer and Binder: Courier Corporation
Cover Printer: Phoenix Color Corp.

Library of Congress Cataloging-in-Publication Data
The American people: creating a nation and a society/general editors, Gary B. Nash,
  Julie Roy Jeffrey; with John R. Howe ... [et al.].—Concise 6th ed.
     p. cm.
  Includes bibliographical references and index.
  ISBN 978-0-205-56843-7
  1. United States History—History.   I. Nash, Gary B.   II. Jeffrey, Julie Roy.   III. Howe,
  John R.
  E178.1.A49355 2008
  973—dc22

                                                                    2007023088

Please visit us at www.ablongman.com

ISBN 10: 0-205-56843-2; ISBN 13: 978-0-205-56843-7 (Combined Volume)
ISBN 10: 0-205-57246-4; ISBN 13: 978-0-205-57246-5 (Volume One)
ISBN 10: 0-205-57247-2; ISBN 13: 978-0-205-57247-2 (Volume Two)

1 2 3 4 5 6 7 8 9 10—CRK—10 09 08 07

Brief Contents

Detailed Contents   ix
Features   xiii
  Recovering the Past
  How Others See Us
  Maps
Preface   xvii
Supplements   xxv
About the Authors   xxix

16   The Union Reconstructed   481

PART FOUR **An Industrializing People, 1865–1900   511**

17   The Realities of Rural America   511
18   The Rise of Smokestack America   540
19   Politics and Reform   572
20   Becoming a World Power   599

PART FIVE **A Modernizing People, 1900–1945   628**

21   The Progressives Confront Industrial Capitalism   628
22   The Great War   661
23   Affluence and Anxiety   691
24   The Great Depression and the New Deal   720
25   World War II   753

PART SIX **A Resilient People, 1945–2006   785**

26   Postwar America at Home, 1945–1960   785
27   Chills and Fever During the Cold War, 1945–1960   819
28   Reform and Rebellion in the Turbulent Sixties, 1960–1969   851
29   Disorder and Discontent, 1969–1980   883
30   The Revival of Conservatism, 1980–1992   917
31   The Post-Cold War World, 1992–2006   948

Appendix   A-1
Index   I-1
World Map   M-2

Detailed Contents

Features   xiii
   Recovering the Past
   How Others See Us
   Maps
Preface   xvii
Supplements   xxv
About the Authors   xxix

16 **The Union Reconstructed   481**

   The Bittersweet Aftermath of War   482

   National Reconstruction Politics   487

   RECOVERING THE PAST *Novels   490*

   The Lives of Freedpeople   494

   Reconstruction in the Southern States   501

   Conclusion: A Mixed Legacy   508

PART FOUR An Industrializing People, 1865–1900   511

17 **The Realities of Rural America   511**

   Modernizing Agriculture   513

   The West   515

   Resolving the Native American Question   522

   HOW OTHERS SEE US *Red Cloud, Speech to the U.S. Secretary of the Interior, 1870   523*

   RECOVERING THE PAST *Magazines   524*

   The New South   528

   Farm Protest   535

   Conclusion: Farming in the Industrial Age   538

18 **The Rise of Smokestack America   540**

   The Texture of Industrial Progress   541

   Urban Expansion in the Industrial Age   547

   The Industrial City, 1880–1900   550

   The Life of the Middle Class   553

   HOW OTHERS SEE US *Herbert Spencer, "The Americans"   554*

   Industrial Work and the Laboring Class   556

   Capital Versus Labor   561

   Conclusion: The Complexity of Industrial Capitalism   570

19 Politics and Reform   572

Politics in the Gilded Age   573

Middle-Class Reform   578

Politics in the Pivotal 1890s   586

Conclusion: Looking Forward   596

20 Becoming a World Power   599

Steps Toward Empire   600

Expansionism in the 1890s   604

War in Cuba and the Philippines   607

Theodore Roosevelt's Energetic Diplomacy   614

RECOVERING THE PAST *Political Cartoons   616*

Conclusion: The Responsibilities of Power   625

PART FIVE A Modernizing People, 1900–1945   628

21 The Progressives Confront Industrial Capitalism   628

The Social Justice Movement   630

RECOVERING THE PAST *Documentary Photographs   634*

The Worker in the Progressive Era   640

Reform in the Cities and States   644

Theodore Roosevelt and the Square Deal   647

Woodrow Wilson and the New Freedom   655

Conclusion: The Limits of Progressivism   658

22 The Great War   661

The Early War Years   662

The United States Enters the War   668

The Military Experience   673

RECOVERING THE PAST *Government Propaganda   676*

Domestic Impact of the War   680

Planning for Peace   684

Conclusion: The Divided Legacy of the Great War   688

23 Affluence and Anxiety   691

Postwar Problems   692

A Prospering Economy   696

HOW OTHERS SEE US *Luigi Barzini, Jr., An Italian Student Falls in Love with the United States   697*

Hopes Raised, Promises Deferred   700

The Business of Politics   710

Conclusion: A New Era of Prosperity and Problems   716

24 The Great Depression and the New Deal   720

The Great Depression   721

Roosevelt and the First New Deal   726

One Hundred Days   728

The Second New Deal   734

The Last Years of the New Deal   740

The Other Side of the 1930s   743

HOW OTHERS SEE US *Georges Duhamel, A French Writer Visits the United States and Finds Nothing to Admire*   745

RECOVERING THE PAST *The Movies*   746

Conclusion: The Mixed Legacy of the Great Depression and the New Deal   750

25 World War II   753

The Twisting Road to War   754

The Home Front   761

The Social Impact of the War   767

A War of Diplomats and Generals   771

HOW OTHERS SEE US *Yamaoka Michiko, On the Ground at Hiroshima*   780

Conclusion: Peace, Prosperity, and International Responsibilities   782

PART SIX A Resilient People, 1945–2006   785

26 Postwar America at Home, 1945–1960   785

Economic Boom   787

Demographic and Technological Shifts   794

Consensus and Conformity   799

Origins of the Welfare State   803

The Other America   809

Conclusion: Qualms amid Affluence   816

27 Chills and Fever During the Cold War, 1945–1960   819

Origins of the Cold War   821

Containing the Soviet Union   824

HOW OTHERS SEE US *A West German Poster on the Marshall Plan*   826

Containment in Asia, the Middle East, and Latin America   830

Atomic Weapons and the Cold War   837

The Cold War at Home   841

RECOVERING THE PAST *Public Opinion Polls*   844

Conclusion: The Cold War in Perspective   848

28 Reform and Rebellion in the Turbulent Sixties, 1960–1969   851

John F. Kennedy: The Camelot Years   853

RECOVERING THE PAST *Television*   856

Lyndon B. Johnson and the Great Society   861

Continuing Confrontations with Communists   870

War in Vietnam and Turmoil at Home   873

Conclusion: Political and Social Upheaval   880

29 Disorder and Discontent, 1969–1980   883

The Decline of Liberalism   885

The Ongoing Effort in Vietnam   892

Constitutional Conflict and Its Consequences   895

HOW OTHERS SEE US *French and German Posters on the American War in Vietnam*   896

The Continuing Quest for Social Reform   902

RECOVERING THE PAST *Popular Music*   906

Conclusion: Sorting Out the Pieces   914

30 The Revival of Conservatism, 1980–1992   917

The Conservative Transformation   919

An End to Social Reform   927

Economic and Demographic Change   933

Foreign Policy and the End of the Cold War   939

Conclusion: Conservatism in Context   945

31 The Post–Cold War World, 1992–2006   948

The Changing Face of the American People   950

RECOVERING THE PAST *Autobiography*   952

Economic and Social Change   956

Democratic Revival   966

The Second Bush Presidency   969

Foreign Policy in the Post–Cold War World   973

HOW OTHERS SEE US *Elfriede Jelinek, "No New Wars"*   974

Conclusion: The Recent Past in Perspective   979

Appendix   A-1

Index   I-1

World Map   M-2

Features

RECOVERING THE PAST

Novels   490

Magazines   524

Political Cartoons   616

Documentary Photographs   634

Government Propaganda   676

The Movies   746

Public Opinion Polls   844

Television   856

Popular Music   906

Autobiography   952

HOW OTHERS SEE US

Red Cloud, Speech to the U.S. Secretary of the Interior, 1870   523

Herbert Spencer, "The Americans"   554

Luigi Barzini, Jr., An Italian Student Falls in Love with the United States   697

Georges Duhamel, A French Writer Visits the United States and Finds Nothing to
     Admire   745

Yamaoka Michiko, On the Ground at Hiroshima   780

A West German Poster on the Marshall Plan   826

French and German Posters on the American War in Vietnam   896

Elfriede Jelinek, "No New Wars"   974

Maps

The United States   ii

The Return of Conservative Democratic Control in Southern States During
   Reconstruction   501

The Natural Environment of the West   517

Native Americans, 1850–1896   527

Migration to the United States, 1860–1910   549

The Presidential Election of 1896   593

United States Territorial Expansion to 1900   605

United States Involvement in Central America and the Caribbean,
   1898–1939   619

United States Involvement in the Pacific and Eastern Asia,
   1898–1909   621

Woman Suffrage Before the Nineteenth Amendment   636

The Great War in Europe and the Middle East   663

Europe and the Near East After World War I   685

Mexican Population, 1930   704

The Tennessee Valley Authority   732

World War II: Pacific Theater   773

World War II: European and North African Theaters   774

U.S. Interstate Highway System   789

Independence in Africa   810

Cold War Europe in 1950   827

The Korean War   832

The Berlin Wall   871

The Vietnam War   874

The Yom Kippur War of 1973   888

The Fall of Communism   942

Portrait of a Nation   955

World Map   M2-M3

Preface

The Yoruba people of West Africa have an old saying: "However far the stream flows, it never forgets its source." Why, we wonder, do such ancient societies as the Yoruba find history so important, while modern American students question its relevance? This book aims to end such skepticism about the usefulness of history.

As we begin the twenty-first century in an ethnically and culturally diverse society caught up in an interdependent global system, history is of central importance in preparing us to exercise our rights and responsibilities as a free people. Studying history cannot make good citizens, but without a knowledge of history, we cannot understand the choices before us and think wisely about them. Lacking a collective memory of the past, we lapse into a kind of amnesia, unaware of the human condition and the long struggles of men and women everywhere to deal with the problems of their day and to create a better society. Unfurnished with historical knowledge, we deprive ourselves of knowing about the huge range of approaches people have taken to political, economic, and social life; to solving problems; and to surmounting the obstacles in their way.

History has a deeper, even more fundamental importance: the cultivation of the private person whose self-knowledge and self-respect provide the foundation for a life of dignity and fulfillment. Historical memory is the key to self-identity: to seeing one's place in the long stream of time, in the story of humankind.

When we study our own history, we see a rich and extraordinarily complex human story. This country, whose written history began with a convergence of Native Americans, Europeans, and Africans, has always been a nation of diverse peoples—a magnificent mosaic of cultures, religions, and skin shades. This book explores how American society assumed its present shape and developed its present forms of government; how as a nation we have conducted our foreign affairs and managed our economy; how science and technology and religion and reform have changed our lives; how as individuals and in groups we have lived, worked, loved, married, raised families, voted, argued, protested, and struggled to fulfill our dreams and the noble ideals of the American experiment.

Several ways of making the past understandable distinguish this book from traditional textbooks. The coverage of public events such as presidential elections, diplomatic treaties, and economic legislation is integrated with the private human stories that pervade them. Within a chronological framework, we have woven together our history as a nation, as a people, and as a society. When, for example, national political events are discussed, we analyze their impact on social and economic life at the state and local levels. Wars are described not only as they unfolded on the battlefield and in the salons of diplomats but also on the home front, where they have been history's greatest motor of social change. The interaction of ordinary and extraordinary Americans runs as a theme throughout this book.

Above all, we have tried to show the "humanness" of our history as it is revealed in people's everyday lives. Throughout these pages, we have often used the words of unnoticed Americans to capture the authentic human voices of those who participated in and responded to epic events such as war, slavery, industrialization, and reform movements.

GOALS AND THEMES OF THE BOOK

Our primary goal is to provide students with a rich, balanced, and thought-provoking treatment of the American past. By this we mean a history that treats the lives and experiences of Americans of all national origins and cultural backgrounds, at all levels of society, and in all regions of the country. It also means a history that seeks connections between the many factors—political, economic, technological, social, religious, intellectual, and biological—that have molded and remolded American society over four centuries. Finally, it means a history that encourages students to think about how we have all inherited a complex past filled with both notable achievements and thorny problems. The only history befitting a democratic nation is one that inspires students to initiate a frank and searching dialogue with their past.

To speak of a dialogue about the past presumes that history is interpretive rather than an agreed-upon account of what happened in the past and why history unfolded as it did. Students should understand that historians are continually reinterpreting the past. New interpretations may result from the discovery of new evidence, but more often they emerge because historians reevaluate old evidence in the light of new ideas that spring from the times in which they write and from their personal views of the world.

Through this book, we also hope to promote class discussions, which can be organized around six recurring themes basic to the American historical experience:

1. **The peopling of America**   How has this nation been peopled, from the first inhabitants to the many groups that arrived in slavery or servitude during the colonial period to the voluntary immigrants of today? How have these waves of newcomers contributed to and reshaped the American cultural mosaic? To what extent have different immigrant groups both assimilated into American culture and also preserved elements of their ethnic, racial, and religious heritages? How have the tensions between cultural assimilation and cultural preservation been played out, in the past and today?
2. **The development of American democracy**   To what extent have Americans developed a stable, democratic political system flexible enough to address the wholesale changes occurring in the last two centuries? To what degree has this political system been consistent with the principles of our nation's founding?
3. **Environmental, economic, and technological change**   How have environmental, economic, scientific, and technological changes affected the American landscape, attitudes toward nature, work, family life, leisure, sexual behavior, the division of wealth, and community relations in the United States?
4. **Religion and reform in American life**   What role has American religion played in the development of the nation? How have religion and religious values affected social change in our history? Whatever their varied sources, how have the recurring reform movements in our history dealt with economic, political, and social problems in attempting to square the ideals and realities of American life?
5. **America and the world**   In what ways have global events and trends had an impact on the shape and character of American life? How has the United

States affected the rest of the world? To what extent has the United States served as a model for other peoples, as an interventionist savior of other nations around the globe, and as an interfering expansionist in the affairs of other nations?

6. **Diversity, values, and American dreams** In the pursuit of American dreams, how have American beliefs and values changed over time? How have they varied between different groups: women and men; Americans of many colors and cultures; people of different regions, religions, sexual orientations, ages, and classes?

In writing a history that revolves around these themes, we have tried to convey two dynamics that operate in all societies. First, we observe people continuously adjusting to new developments, such as industrialization and urbanization, over which they seemingly have little control; we realize that people are not paralyzed by history but are the fundamental creators of it. They retain the ability, individually and collectively, to shape the world in which they live and thus in considerable degree to control their own lives. Second, we emphasize the connections that always exist among social, political, economic, and cultural events.

STRUCTURE OF THE BOOK

The chapters of this book are grouped into six parts that relate to major periods in American history. The titles for each part suggest a major theme that helps to characterize the period.

Each chapter has a clear structure, beginning with a chapter outline and then a personal story, called *American Stories*, recalling the experience of an ordinary or lesser-known American. Chapter 3, for example, is introduced with an account of the life of Anthony Johnson, who came to Virginia as a slave but who along with his wife, Mary, managed to gain his freedom. This brief anecdote introduces the overarching themes and major concepts of the chapter, in this case the tri-racial character of American society, the gradual tightening of racial slavery, and the instability of late seventeenth century colonial life. In addition, *American Stories* launches the chapter by engaging the student with a human account, suggesting that history was shaped by ordinary as well as extraordinary people. Following the personal story and easily identifiable by its visual separation from the anecdote and the body of the chapter, a *brief chapter overview* links the story and its themes to the text.

We aim to facilitate an exciting engagement with history for students in other ways as well. Every chapter ends with pedagogical features to reinforce and expand the presentation. A *timeline* reviews the major events and developments covered in the chapter. The *conclusion* briefly summarizes the chapter's main concepts and developments, revisits the individual described in *American Stories*, and serves as a bridge to the following chapter. *Questions for Review and Reflection* provide an opportunity to think about the chapter's major themes and their relation to the larger questions the text raises. An annotated section of suggested Web sites, *Discovering U.S. History Online*, offers students electronic resources relating to chapter content and themes and suggestions for further reading. *Fiction and Film* provides an annotated selection of historical novels and films. In addition, each map, figure, and table has been chosen to relate clearly to the narrative. *Captions* are specially written to help students understand and interpret these visual materials.

THE CONCISE SIXTH EDITION

This Concise Sixth Edition is condensed from the very successful comprehensive Seventh Edition of *The American People*, with its balance of political, social, and economic history. While we have eliminated detail and extra examples and have compressed the text, we have retained the interpretive connections and the "humanness" of history—the presentation of history as revealed through the lives of ordinary as well as extraordinary Americans and the interplay of social and political factors.

Continued Features

The Concise Sixth Edition continues the format and more compact size of the previous brief editions. The four-color design enhances the value of the maps and graphs and gives the book a vibrant appearance. This makes the book accessible, easy to read, and convenient for students to carry to and from class.

This edition contains one of the most popular features of *The American People*: the two-page sections entitled *Recovering the Past*. The RTPs, as the authors affectionately call them, introduce students to the fascinating variety of evidence—ranging from novels, political cartoons, and diaries to houses and popular music—that historians have learned to employ in reconstructing the past. Each RTP gives basic information about the source and its use by historians and then raises questions—called *Reflecting on the Past*—for students to consider as they study the example reproduced for their inspection.

In this edition, we have provided an international framework so students will think across international boundaries and understand the ways in which our history intersects with the world. Rather than developing a separate discussion of global events, we have woven an international narrative into our analysis of the American past. Chapter 13, for example, discusses the international context for American expansionism. Many maps underscore the international dimension of the text.

New Features

New to this edition and included in each section of the textbook are brief passages or, on occasion, illustrations such as posters or cartoons from non-Americans, commenting on **How Others See Us**. This feature is in keeping with our aim of putting American history into a global context and illustrating that those outside the United States (and often the "outsiders" within) sometimes know us better than we know ourselves.

Also new in the text are **review questions** at the end of each chapter. These questions not only help students identify, recall, and think about the major themes of the chapter but also encourage them to connect chapter themes to the book's large themes and questions.

Chapter Changes

Chapter-by-chapter changes include the following:

- *Chapter 3* contains the new feature, *How Others See Us*. In this case, the commentator is a traveler who describes New England, including its social structure and the presence of witches.
- *Chapter 4* also includes *How Others See Us*. Here a visitor analyzes Pennsylvania and includes his belief that exposure to British officers has improved its tone.
- *Chapter 7* reveals the attitudes of several English commentators after the Revolution in *How Others See Us*.
- *Chapter 9* has a new RTP focusing on federal census returns and what they can reveal. The chapter also contains insightful comments from an English-woman visiting the United States early in the nineteenth century for the feature *How Others See Us*.
- *Chapter 10* contains selections from Alexis de Tocqueville's visit to the United States in 1830, with his impression of American agriculture for *How Others See Us*.
- *Chapter 13* features the comments of a Mexican military officer as he observed American settlers in Texas in the feature *How Others See Us*.
- *Chapter 17* shows the Indian as outside observer in *How Others See Us*. Here Red Cloud's comments to the U.S. Secretary of the Interior in 1870 have been included.
- *Chapter 18* provides a different angle to understanding American industrial development with the comments of an English intellectual who argued that American businessmen worked too hard. His comments appear in *How Others See Us*.
- *Chapter 23* contains *How Others See Us* that provides the perspective of an Italian student who studied at Columbia University in the 1920s.
- *Chapter 24* has a new introductory vignette that focuses on how young people viewed the Great Depression and the Civilian Conservation Corps.
- *Chapter 25*'s *How Others See Us* feature shows the experience of a young Japanese high school student who experienced the atom bomb explosion at Hiroshima.
- *Chapter 27* uses a West German poster on the Marshall Plan for *How Others See Us*.
- *Chapter 29* also uses posters, in this case French and German posters during the Vietnam War, for *How Others See Us*.
- *Chapter 31* takes the text up through the midterm elections of 2006 and provides coverage of the Iraq War. In addition, it also contains *How Others See Us* with the views of a European opponent to that war.

Our aim has been to write a balanced and vivid history of the development of the American nation and its society. We have also tried to provide the support materials necessary to make teaching and learning enjoyable and rewarding. The reader will be the judge of our success. We welcome your comments.

ACKNOWLEDGMENTS

Over the years, as new editions of this text were being developed, many of our colleagues read and critiqued the various drafts of the manuscript. For their thoughtful evaluations and constructive suggestions, the authors wish to express their gratitude to the following reviewers:

Richard H. Abbott, Eastern Michigan University; John Alexander, University of Cincinnati; Kenneth G. Alfers, Mountain View College; Terry Alford, Northern Virginia Community College; Donna Alvah, St. Lawrence University; Gregg Andrews, Southwest Texas State University; Robert Asher, University of Connecticut at Storrs; Patrick Ashwood, Hawkeye Community College; Arthur H. Auten, University of Hartford; Harry Baker, University of Arkansas at Little Rock; L. Diane Barnes, Youngstown State University; Michael Batinski, Southern Illinois University; Gary Bell, Sam Houston State University; Virginia Bellows, Tulsa Junior College; Spencer Bennett, Siena Heights College; Jackie R. Booker, Western Connecticut State University; Linda J. Borish, Western Michigan University; James Bradford, Texas A&M University; Thomas A. Britten, Briar Cliff College; Neal Brooks, Essex Community College; Jeffrey P. Brown, New Mexico State University; Dickson D. Bruce, Jr., University of California, Irvine; David Brundage, University of California, Santa Cruz; Steven J. Bucklin, University of South Dakota; Colin Calloway, Dartmouth University; D'Ann Campbell, Indiana University; Jane Censer, George Mason University; Vincent A. Clark, Johnson County Community College; Neil Clough, North Seattle Community College; Stacy A. Cordery, Monmouth College; Matthew Ware Coulter, Collin County Community College; A. Glenn Crothers, Indiana University Southeast; David Culbert, Louisiana State University; Jolane Culhane, Western New Mexico University; Mark T. Dalhouse, Northeast Missouri State University; Bruce Dierenfield, Canisius College; John Dittmer, DePauw University; Gordon Dodds, Portland State University; Richard Donley, Eastern Washington University; Dennis B. Downey, Millersville University; Robert Downtain, Tarrant County Community College; Robert C. Duncan, Western Oklahoma State College; Keith Edgerton, Montana State University at Billings; Trace Etienne-Gray, Southwest Texas State University; Robert Farrar, Spokane Falls Community College; Bernard Friedman, Indiana University–Purdue University at Indianapolis; Kathryn H. Fuller, Virginia Commonwealth University; Bruce Glasrud, California State University, Hayward; Brian Gordon, St. Louis Community College; Barbara Green, Wright State University; Richard Griswold del Castillo, San Diego State University; Carol Gruber, William Paterson College; Gretchen Grufman, Dominican University; Stephen A. Harmon, Pittsburgh State University; Thomas D. Hamm, Earlham College; Colonel William L. Harris, The Citadel Military College; Robert Haws, University of Mississippi; Jerrold Hirsch, Northeast Missouri State University; Frederick Hoxie, University of Illinois; John S. Hughes, University of Texas; Link Hullar, Kingwood College; Carol Sue Humphrey, Oklahoma Baptist University; Donald M. Jacobs, Northeastern University; Delores Janiewski, University of Idaho; David Johnson, Portland State University; Richard Kern, University of Findlay; Robert J. Kolesar, John Carroll University; Monte Lewis, Cisco Junior College; Xaio-bing Li, University of Central Oklahoma; William Link, University of North Carolina at Greensboro; Patricia M. Lisella, Iona College; Jeff Livingston, California State University, Chico; Ronald Lora, University of Toledo; Paul K. Longmore, San Francisco State University; Rita Loos, Framingham State College; George M. Lubick, Northern Arizona University; Suzanne Marshall, Jacksonville State University; John C. Massman, St. Cloud State University; Vernon Mattson, University of Nevada at Las Vegas; Joanne Maypole, Front Range Community College; Delove Nason McBroome, Humboldt State University; Arthur McCoole, Cuyamaca College; John McCormick, Delaware County Community College; George W. McDaniel, St. Ambrose University; David H. McGee, Central Virginia Community College; Sylvia McGrath, Stephen F. Austin University; James E. McMillan, Denison University; Otis L. Miller, Belleville Area College; Walter Miszczenko, Boise State University; Norma Mitchell, Troy State University; Gerald F. Moran, University of Michigan at Dearborn; William G. Morris, Midland College; Marian Morton, John Carroll University; Ting Ni, St. Mary's University; Roger Nichols, University of Arizona; Elizabeth Neumeyer, Kellogg Community College; Paul Palmer, Texas A&M University; Albert Parker, Riverside City College; Judith Parsons, Sul Ross State University; Carla Pestana, Ohio State University; Neva Peters, Tarrant County Community College; James Prickett, Santa Monica Community College; Noel Pugash, University of New Mexico; Juan Gomez-Quiñones, University of California, Los Angeles; George Rable, Anderson College; Joseph P. Reidy, Howard University; Leonard Riforgiato, Pennsylvania State University; Randy Roberts, Purdue University; Mary Robertson, Armstrong State University; David Robson, John Carroll University; Robert G. Rockwell, Mt. San Jacinto College; David E. Ruth, Pennsylvania State University; Judd Sage, Northern Virginia Community College; A. J. Scopino, Jr., Central Connecticut State University; Sylvia Sebesta, San Antonio College; Phil Schaeffer, Olympic College; Herbert Shapiro, University of Cincinnati; David R. Shibley, Santa Monica Community College; Ellen Shockro, Pasadena City College; Nancy Shoemaker, University of Connecticut; Bradley Skelcher, Delaware State University; Kathryn Kish Sklar, State University of New York at Binghamton; James Smith, Virginia State University; John Snetsinger, California Polytechnic State University at San Luis Obispo; Jo Snider, Southwest Texas State University; Randi Storch, State University of New York at Cortland; Stephen Strausberg, University of Arkansas; Katherine Scott Sturdevant, Pikes Peak Community College; Nan M. Sumner-Mack, Hawaii Community College; Cynthia Taylor, Santa Rosa Junior College; Thomas Tefft, Citrus College;

John A. Trickel, Richland College; Donna Van Raaphorst, Cuyahoga Community College; Morris Vogel, Temple University; Michael Wade, Appalachian State University; Jackie Walker, James Madison University; E. Sue Wamsley, University of Akron; Paul B. Weinstein, University of Akron-Wayne College; Joan Welker, Prince George's Community College; Michael Welsh, University of Northern Colorado; Seth Wigderson, University of Maine at Augusta; Kenneth H. Williams, Alcorn State University; Nelson E. Woodard, California State University, Fullerton; Mitch Yamasaki, Chaminade University; and Charles Zappia, San Diego Mesa College.

GARY B. NASH

JULIE ROY JEFFREY

SUPPLEMENTS FOR INSTRUCTORS AND STUDENTS

For Qualified College Adopters

Name of Supplement	Available in Print	Available Online	Instructor or Student Supplement	Description
Instructor's Resource Center (IRC)		✓	Instructor Supplement	Web site for downloading relevant supplements. Password protected. Please contact your local Pearson representative for an access code. *www.ablongman.com/irc*
MyHistoryLab		✓	Both	With the best of Longman's multimedia solutions for history in one easy-to-use place, MyHistory-Lab offers students and instructors a state-of-the-art interactive instructional solution for your U.S. History survey course. Built around a complete e-book version of this text, MyHistoryLab provides numerous study aids, review materials, and activities to make the study of history an enjoyable learning experience. Icons in the e-book link directly to relevant materials in context, many of which are assignable. MyHistoryLab includes several hundred primary source documents, videos, images and maps, all with accompanying analysis questions. It also includes a History Bookshelf with 50 of the most commonly assigned books in U.S. history courses and a History Toolkit with guided tutorials and helpful links. MyHistoryLab is flexible and easy-to-use as a supplement to a traditional lecture course or to administer a completely online course. *www.myhistorylab.com*
MyHistoryKit for American History		✓	Both	Online package of study materials, gradable quizzes and over 1,000 primary sources organized generically by typical American History themes to support your U.S. history survey text. Access code required. *www.myhistorykit.com*
American History Study Site		✓	Both	Online package of practice tests, Web links and flashcards organized generically by major history topics to support your U.S. history survey text. Open access. *www.longmanamericanhistory.com*
Instructor's Manual	✓	✓	Instructor Supplement	Each chapter includes a chapter overview, lecture supplements, and questions for class discussion. Text specific.
Test Bank	✓	✓	Instructor Supplement	Contains thousands of conceptual, objective, and essay questions. Text specific.
Computerized Test Bank	✓	✓	Instructor Supplement	Includes all items in the printed test bank. Questions can be edited, and tests can be printed in several different formats. Text specific.

(continued)

For Qualified College Adopters

Name of Supplement	Available in Print	Available Online	Instructor or Student Supplement	Description
PowerPoint Presentation		✓	Instructor Supplement	Designed to accompany the comprehensive version of *The American People*, these slides contain an outline of each chapter of the text and full-color images of maps and figures. *www.ablongman.com/irc*
Digital Transparency Masters		✓	Instructor Supplement	Designed to accompany the comprehensive version of *The American People*, these digital transparency masters are available exclusively on the Instructor's Resource Center. Text specific. *www.ablongman.com/irc*
Comprehensive American History Digital Transparency Masters		✓	Instructor Supplement	Vast collection of American history transparency masters. Available exclusively on the Instructor's Resource Center. *www.ablongman.com/irc*
Discovering American History Through Maps and Views Digital Transparency Masters		✓	Instructor Supplement	Set of 140 full-color digital transparency masters includes cartographic and pictorial maps, views, and photos, urban plans, building diagrams, and works of art. Available exclusively on the Instructor's Resource Center. *www.ablogman.com/irc*
History Digital Media Archive	CD		Instructor Supplement	Contains electronic images, interactive and static maps, and video. Available on CD only.
Visual Archives of American History, Updated Edition	CD		Instructor Supplement	Contains dozens of narrated vignettes and videos as well as hundreds of photos and illustrations. Available on CD only.
Study Guide	✓		Student Supplement	Contains chapter overviews, learning objectives, identifications, mapping exercises, multiple-choice and essay questions, and critical thinking exercises. Available in two volumes. Text specific.
VangoNotes		✓	Student Supplement	Downloadable MP3 audio topic reviews. Includes major themes, key terms, practice tests, and rapid reviews. *www.vangonotes.com*
Study Card for American History	✓		Student Supplement	Distills course information down to the basics, helping students quickly master the fundamentals and prepare for exams.
Research Navigator Guide	✓	✓	Student Supplement	A book that contains an access code to EBSCO ContentSelect, *New York Times*, and "Best of the Web."
Longman American History Atlas	✓		Both	100 full color maps.
Mapping America: A Guide to Historical Geography	✓		Student Supplement	18 exercises explore the role of geography in history.
Voices of *The American People*	✓		Student Supplement	Two volume collection of primary sources, organized to correspond to the table of contents of *The American People*.

For Qualified College Adopters

Name of Supplement	Available in Print	Available Online	Instructor or Student Supplement	Description
America Through the Eyes of Its People	✓		Student Supplement	Two-volume comprehensive anthology of primary sources expertly balances social and political history and includes up-to-date narrative material.
American History Timeline	✓		Student Supplement	Gives students a chronological context to help them understand important political, social, economic, cultural, and technology events.
Sources of the African-American Past	✓		Student Supplement	This collection of primary sources covers key themes in the African-American experience.
Women and the National Experience	✓		Student Supplement	Primary source reader contains both classic and unusual documents describing the history of women in the United States.
Reading the American West	✓		Student Supplement	Primary sources in the history of the American West.
A Short Guide to Writing About History	✓		Student Supplement	Teaches students to write cogent history papers.
American History Firsthand: Working with Primary Sources	✓		Student Supplement	Two-volume collection of looseleaf reproduced primary sources exposes students to archival research.
Longman–Penguin Putnam Inc. Value Packs	✓		Student Supplement	Variety of Penguin Putnam texts are available at discounted prices when bundled with *The American People*. Complete list of available titles at ***www.ablongman.com/penguin***.
Library of American Biography Series	✓		Student Supplement	Renowned series of biographies that focus on figures who had a significant impact on American history. Complete list of available titles at ***www.ablongman.com/html/lab***.

Gary B. Nash received his Ph.D. from Princeton University. He is currently Director of the National Center for History in the Schools at the University of California, Los Angeles, where he teaches colonial and revolutionary American history. Among the books Nash has authored are *Quakers and Politics: Pennsylvania, 1681–1726* (1968); *Red, White, and Black: The Peoples of Early America* (1974, 1982, 1992, 2000); *The Urban Crucible: Social Change, Political Consciousness, and the Origins of the American Revolution* (1979); *Forging Freedom: The Formation of Philadelphia's Black Community, 1720–1840* (1988); *First City: Philadelphia and the Forging of Historical Memory* (2002); and *The Unknown American Revolution: The Unruly Birth of Democracy and the Struggle to Create America* (2005). A former president of the Organization of American Historians, his scholarship is especially concerned with the role of common people in the making of history. He wrote Part One and served as a general editor of this book.

Julie Roy Jeffrey earned her Ph.D. in history from Rice University. Since then she has taught at Goucher College. Honored as an outstanding teacher, Jeffrey has been involved in faculty development activities and curriculum evaluation. She was Fulbright Chair in American Studies at the University of Southern Denmark, 1999–2000 and John Adams Chair of American History at the University of Utrecht, The Netherlands, 2006. Jeffrey's major publications include *Education for Children of the Poor* (1978); *Frontier Women: The Trans-Mississippi West, 1840–1880* (1979, 1997); *Converting the West: A Biography of Narcissa Whitman* (1991); *The Great Silent Army of Abolitionism: Ordinary Women in the Antislavery Movement* (1998) and *Abolitionists Remember* (forthcoming 2008). She collaborated with Peter Frederick on *American History Firsthand*, two volumes (2002, 2007). She is the author of many articles on the lives and perceptions of nineteenth-century women. Her research continues to focus on abolitionism as well as on history and film. She wrote Parts Three and Four in collaboration with Peter Frederick and acted as a general editor of this book.

John R. Howe received his Ph.D. from Yale University. At the University of Minnesota, he has taught the U.S. history survey and courses on the American revolutionary era and the early republic. His major publications include *The Changing Political Thought of John Adams* (1966), *From the Revolution Through the Age of Jackson* (1973), *The Role of Ideology in the American Revolution* (1977), and *Language and Political Meaning in Revolutionary America* (2003). His present research deals with the social politics of verbal discourse in late eighteenth- and early nineteenth-century Boston. He has received a Woodrow Wilson Graduate Fellowship, a John Simon Guggenheim Fellowship, and a Research Fellowship from the Charles Warren Center for Studies in American History. Howe wrote Part Two of this book.

Peter J. Frederick received his Ph.D. in history from the University of California, Berkeley. His career of innovative teaching began at California State University, Hayward, in the 1960s and continued at Wabash College (1970–2004) and Carleton College (1992–1994). He also served as distinguished Professor of American History and Culture at Heritage University on the Yakama Nation reservation in Washington between 2004 and 2006. Recognized nationally as a distinguished teacher and for his many articles and workshops on teaching and learning, Frederick was awarded the Eugene Asher Award for Excellence in Teaching by the AHA in 2000. He has also written several articles on life-writing and a book, *Knights of the Golden Rule: The Intellectual as Christian Social Reformer in the 1890s.* With Julie Jeffrey, he recently published *American History Firsthand.* He coordinated and edited all the "Recovering the Past" sections and coauthored Parts Three and Four.

Allen F. Davis earned his Ph.D. from the University of Wisconsin. A former president of the American Studies Association, he is a professor emeritus at Temple University and editor of *Conflict and Consensus in American History* (9th ed., 1997). He is the author of *Spearheads for Reform: The Social Settlements and the Progressive Movement* (1967); *American Heroine: The Life and Legend of Jane Addams* (1973); and *Postcards from Vermont: A Social History* (2002). He is coauthor of *Still Philadelphia* (1983); *Philadelphia Stories* (1987); and *One Hundred Years at Hull-House* (1990). Davis wrote Part Five of this book.

Allan M. Winkler received his Ph.D. from Yale University. He has taught at Yale and the University of Oregon, and he is now Distinguished Professor of History at Miami University of Ohio. An award-winning teacher, he has also published extensively about the recent past. His books include *The Politics of Propaganda: The Office of War Information, 1942–1945* (1978); *Home Front U.S.A.: America During World War II* (1986, 2000); *Life Under a Cloud: American Anxiety About the Atom* (1993, 1999); *The Cold War: A History in Documents* (2000), and *Franklin D. Roosevelt and the Making of Modern America* (2006). His research centers on the connections between public policy and popular mood in modern American history. Winkler wrote Part Six of this book.

Charlene Mires earned her Ph.D. in history at Temple University. At Villanova University, she teaches courses in nineteenth- and twentieth-century U.S. history, public history, and material culture. She is the author of *Independence Hall in American Memory* (2002) and serves as editor of the Pennsylvania History Studies Series for the Pennsylvania Historical Association. A former journalist, she was a co-recipient of the Pulitzer Prize for general local news reporting with other staff members of the Fort Wayne (Indiana) *News-Sentinel.* She has contributed to Part Five of *The American People.*

Carla Gardina Pestana received her Ph.D. from the University of California at Los Angeles. She taught at Ohio State University, where she served as a Lilly Teaching Fellow and launched an innovative on-demand publishing project. Currently she holds the W. E. Smith Professorship in History at Miami University.

Her publications include *Liberty of Conscience and the Growth of Religious Diversity in Early America* (1986), *Quakers and Baptists in Colonial Massachusetts* (1991), and *The English Atlantic in an Age of Revolution, 1640–1661* (2004). She is also the co-editor, with Sharon V. Salinger, of *Inequality in Early America* (1999). At present, she is completing a book on religion in the British Atlantic world to 1830 for classroom use. She has contributed to Part One of *The American People.*

CHAPTER 16

CHAPTER 16

The Union Reconstructed

CHAPTER OUTLINE

- The Bittersweet Aftermath of War
- National Reconstruction Politics
- The Lives of Freedpeople
- Reconstruction in the Southern States
- Conclusion: A Mixed Legacy

American Stories

Blacks and Whites Redefine Their Dreams and Relationships

In April 1864, a year before Lincoln's assassination, Robert Allston died, leaving his wife Adele and his daughter Elizabeth to manage their many rice plantations. With Union troops moving through coastal South Carolina in the winter of 1864–1865, Elizabeth's sorrow turned to "terror" as Union soldiers arrived and searched for liquor, firearms, and valuables. The women fled. Later, Yankee troops encouraged the Allston slaves to take furniture, food, and other goods from the Big House. Before they left, the Union soldiers gave the keys to the crop barns to the semifree blacks.

After the war, Adele Allston swore allegiance to the United States and secured a written order for the newly freed African Americans to relinquish those keys. She and Elizabeth returned in the summer of 1865 to reclaim the plantations and reassert white authority. She was assured that although the blacks had guns, "no outrage has been committed against the Whites except in the matter of property." But property was the issue. Possession of the keys to the barns, Elizabeth wrote, would be the "test case" of whether former masters or former slaves would control land, labor, and its fruits, as well as the subtle aspects of interpersonal relations.

Nervously, Adele and Elizabeth Allston confronted their ex-slaves at their old home. To their surprise, a pleasant reunion took place as the Allston women greeted the blacks by name and caught up on their lives. A trusted black foreman handed over the keys to the barns. This harmonious scene was repeated elsewhere.

But at one plantation, the Allston women met defiant and armed African Americans, who ominously lined both sides of the road as the carriage arrived. An old black driver, Uncle Jacob, was unsure whether to yield the keys to the barns full of rice and corn, put there by slave labor. Mrs. Allston insisted. As Uncle Jacob hesitated, an angry young man shouted: "If you give up the key, blood'll flow." Uncle Jacob slowly slipped the keys back into his pocket.

The African Americans sang freedom songs and brandished hoes, pitchforks, and guns to discourage anyone from going to town for help. Two blacks, however, slipped away to find some Union officers. The Allstons spent the night safely, if restlessly, in their house. Early the next morning, they were awakened by a knock at the unlocked front door. There stood Uncle Jacob. Silently, he gave back the keys.

The story of the keys reveals most of the essential human ingredients of the Reconstruction era. Defeated southern whites were determined to resume control of both land and labor. The law and federal enforcement generally supported property owners. The Allston women were friendly to the blacks in a maternal way and insisted on restoring prewar deference in black–white relations. Adele and Elizabeth, in short, both feared and cared about their former slaves.

The African American freedpeople likewise revealed mixed feelings toward their former owners: anger, loyalty, love, resentment, and pride. They paid respect to the Allstons but not to their property and crops. They wanted not revenge, but economic independence and freedom.

Northerners played a most revealing role. Union soldiers, literally and symbolically, gave the keys of freedom to the freed men and women but did not stay around long enough to guarantee that freedom. Despite initially encouraging blacks to plunder the master's house and seize the crops, in the crucial encounter after the war, northern officials had disappeared. Understanding the limits of northern help, Uncle Jacob ended up handing the keys to land and liberty back to his former owner. The blacks realized that if they wanted to ensure their freedom, they had to do it themselves.

This chapter describes what happened to the conflicting goals and dreams of three groups as they sought to redefine new social, economic, and political relationships during the postwar Reconstruction era. Amid vast devastation and bitter race and class divisions, Civil War survivors sought to put their lives back together. Victorious but variously motivated northern officials, defeated but defiant southern planters, and impoverished but hopeful African Americans could not all fulfill their conflicting goals, yet each had to try. Reconstruction would be divisive, leaving a mixed legacy of human gains and losses.

THE BITTERSWEET AFTERMATH OF WAR

IMAGE

Abraham Lincoln—Portrait (April 10, 1865)

"There are sad changes in store for both races," the daughter of a Georgia planter wrote in the summer of 1865. To understand the bittersweet nature of Reconstruction, we must look at the state of the nation after the assassination of President Lincoln.

The United States in April 1865

Constitutionally, the "Union" faced a crisis in April 1865. What was the status of the 11 former Confederate states? The North had denied the South's constitutional right to secede but needed four years of war and more than 600,000 deaths to win the point. Lincoln's official position had been that the southern states had never left the Union and were only "out of their proper relation" with the United

The United States in 1865: Crises at the End of the Civil War

Given the enormous casualties, costs, and crises of the immediate aftermath of the Civil War, what attitudes, goals, dreams, and behaviors would you predict for white southerners, white northerners, and black freedpeople?

Military Casualties

360,000 Union soldiers dead
260,000 Confederate soldiers dead
620,000 Total dead
375,000 Seriously wounded and maimed
995,000 Casualties nationwide in a total male population of 15 million (nearly 1 in 15)

Physical and Economic Crises

The South devastated; its railroads, industry, and some major cities in ruins; its fields and livestock wasted

Constitutional Crisis

Eleven former Confederate states not a part of the Union, their status unclear and future states uncertain

Political Crisis

Republican party (entirely of the North) dominant in Congress; a former Democratic slaveholder from Tennessee, Andrew Johnson, in the presidency

Social Crisis

Nearly 4 million freedpeople throughout the South facing challenges of survival and freedom, along with thousands of hungry demobilized white southern soldiers and displaced white families

Psychological Crisis

Incalculable stores of resentment, bitterness, anger, and despair throughout North and South

States. The president, therefore, as commander in chief, had the authority to decide how to set relations right again. Lincoln's congressional opponents retorted that the ex-Confederate states were now "conquered provinces" and that Congress should resolve the constitutional issues and direct Reconstruction.

Politically, differences between Congress and the White House over Reconstruction mirrored a wider struggle between the two branches of the national government. During war, as has usually been the case, the executive branch assumed broad powers. Many believed, however, that Lincoln had far exceeded his constitutional authority, and his successor, Andrew Johnson, was worse. Would Congress reassert its authority?

In April 1865, the Republican party ruled nearly unchecked. Republicans had made immense achievements in the eyes of the northern public: winning the war, preserving the Union, and freeing the slaves. They had enacted sweeping economic programs on behalf of free labor and free enterprise. But the party remained an uneasy grouping of former Whigs, Know-Nothings, Unionist Democrats, and antislavery idealists.

The Democrats were in shambles. Republicans depicted southern Democrats as rebels, murderers, and traitors, and they blasted northern Democrats as weak-willed, disloyal, and opposed to economic growth and progress. Nevertheless, in the election of 1864, needing to show that the war was a bipartisan effort, the Republicans nominated a Tennessee Unionist Democrat, Andrew Johnson, as Lincoln's vice president. Now the tactless Johnson headed the government.

Economically, the United States in the spring of 1865 presented stark contrasts. Northern cities and railroads hummed with productive activity; southern cities and railroads lay in ruins. Southern financial institutions were bankrupt; northern banks flourished. Mechanizing northern farms were more productive than ever; southern farms and plantations, especially those along Sherman's march, resembled a "howling waste." The widespread devastation in the South affected southern attitudes. As a later southern writer explained, "If this war had smashed the Southern world, it had left the essential Southern mind and will ... entirely unshaken." Many white southerners braced to resist Reconstruction and restore their former life and institutions; others, the minority who had remained quietly loyal to the Union, sought reconciliation.

AUDIO

Free at Last

Socially, nearly 4 million newly freedpeople faced the challenges of freedom. After initial joy and celebration in jubilee songs, freedmen and freedwomen quickly realized their continuing dependence on former owners. A Mississippi woman said:

> I used to think if I could be free I should be the happiest of anybody in the world. But when my master come to me, and says, Lizzie, you is free! it seems like I was in a kind of daze. And when I would wake up in the morning I would think to myself, Is I free? Hasn't I got to get up before day light and go into the field of work?

For Lizzie, and 4 million other blacks, everything—and nothing—had changed.

Hopes Among the Freedpeople

Throughout the South in the summer of 1865, optimism surged through the old slave quarters. The slavery chain, however, broke slowly, link by link. After Union troops swept through an area, "we'd begin celebratin'," one man said, but Confederate soldiers would follow, or master and overseer would return and "tell us to go back to work." The freedmen and women learned, therefore, not to rejoice too quickly or openly.

IMAGE

Freedmen at Rest on a Levee

Gradually, though, African Americans began to test the reality of freedom. Typically, their first step was to leave the plantation, if only for a few hours or days. "If I stay here I'll never know I am free," said a South Carolina woman who went to work as a cook in a nearby town. Some freedpeople cut their ties entirely—returning to an earlier master, or, more often, going into towns and cities to find jobs, schools, churches, and association with other blacks, safe from whippings and retaliation.

Many blacks left the plantation in search of a spouse, parent, or child sold away years before. Advertisements detailing these sorrowful searches filled African American newspapers. For those who found a spouse or who had been living together in slave marriages, freedom meant getting married legally, some-

Consequences of War This 1867 engraving shows two southern women and their children soon after the Civil War. In what ways are they similar and in what ways different? Is there a basis for sisterhood bonds? What separates them, if anything? From *Frank Leslie's Illustrated Newspaper*, February 23, 1867. *(The Granger Collection, New York)*

times in mass ceremonies common in the first months of emancipation. Legal marriage was important morally, but it also established the legitimacy of children and meant access to land titles and other economic opportunities. Marriage brought special burdens for black women, who assumed the double role of housekeeper and breadwinner. Their determination to create a traditional family life and care for their children resulted in the withdrawal of women from plantation field labor.

Freedpeople also demonstrated their new status by choosing surnames. Names connoting independence, such as Washington, were common. Revealing their mixed feelings toward their former masters, some would adopt their master's name while others would pick "any big name 'ceptin' their master's." Emancipation changed black manners around whites as well. Masks fell, and expressions of deference—tipping a hat, stepping aside, calling whites "master" or "ma'am"—diminished. For African Americans, these changes were necessary expressions of selfhood, proving that race relations had changed; whites, however, saw such behaviors as "insolence" and "insubordination."

The freedpeople made education a priority. A Mississippi farmer vowed to "give my children a chance to go to school, for I consider education next best ting to liberty." One traveler through the South counted "at least five hundred" schools "taught by colored people." Other than a persisting desire for education, the primary goal for most freedpeople was getting land. "All I want is to git to own fo' or five acres ob land, dat I can build me a little house on and call my home," a Mississippi black said. Through a combination of educational and economic independence, basic American means of controlling one's own life, labor, and land, freedpeople like Lizzie would make sure that emancipation was real.

During the war, some Union generals had put liberated slaves in charge of confiscated and abandoned lands. In the Sea Islands of South Carolina and Georgia, blacks had been working 40-acre plots of land and harvesting their own crops for several years. Farther inland, freedmen who received land were the former slaves of the Cherokee and the Creek. Some blacks held title to these lands. Northern philanthropists had organized others to grow cotton for the Treasury Department to prove the superiority of free labor. In Mississippi, thousands of ex-slaves worked 40-acre tracts on leased lands that ironically had formerly been owned by Jefferson Davis. In this highly successful experiment, they made profits sufficient to repay the government for initial costs, then lost the land to Davis's brother.

Many freedmen expected a new economic order as fair payment for their years of involuntary work. "Give us our own land," said one, "and we take care ourselves; but widout land, de ole massas can hire us or starve us, as dey please." Freedmen had every expectation that "forty acres and a mule" had been promised. Once they obtained land, family unity, and education, some looked forward to civil rights and the vote—along with protection from vengeful defeated Confederates.

The White South's Fearful Response

White southerners had equally strong dreams and expectations. Middle-class (yeoman) farmers and poor whites stood beside rich planters in bread lines, all hoping to regain land and livelihood. White southerners responded with feelings of outrage, loss, and injustice. Said one man, "My pa paid his own money for our niggers; and that's not all they've robbed us of. They have taken our horses and cattle and sheep and everything."

A dominant emotion was fear. The entire structure of southern society was shaken, and the semblance of racial peace and order that slavery had provided was shattered. Having lost control of all that was familiar, whites feared everything—from losing their cheap labor to having blacks sit next to them on trains. Ironically, given the rape of black women during slavery, southern whites' worst fears were of rape and revenge. African American "impudence," some thought, would lead to legal intermarriage and "Africanization," the destruction of the purity of the white race. African American Union soldiers seemed especially ominous. These fears were greatly exaggerated, as demobilization of black soldiers came quickly, and rape and violence by blacks against whites was extremely rare.

Believing their world turned upside down, the former planter aristocracy tried to set it right again. To reestablish white dominance, southern legislatures passed "Black Codes" in the first year after the war. Many of the codes granted freedmen the right to marry, sue and be sued, testify in court, and hold property. But these rights were qualified. Complicated passages explained under exactly what circumstances blacks could testify against whites, own property (mostly they could not), or exercise other rights of free people. Forbidden rights were racial intermarriage, bearing arms, possessing alcoholic beverages, sitting on trains (except in baggage compart-

DOCUMENT

The Mississippi Black Code (1865)

The End of Slavery? The Black Codes, widespread violence against freedpeople, and President Johnson's veto of the civil rights bill gave rise to the sardonic title "Slavery Is Dead?" in this Thomas Nast cartoon. What do you see in the two scenes? Describe the two images of justice. What is Nast saying?
(Courtesy of the Newberry Library, Chicago)

ments), being on city streets at night, or congregating in large groups. Many of the qualified rights guaranteed by the Black Codes were only passed to induce the federal government to withdraw its remaining troops from the South. This was a crucial issue, for in many places marauding whites were terrorizing virtually defenseless African Americans.

Key provisions of the Black Codes regulated freedpeople's economic status. "Vagrancy" laws provided that any blacks not "lawfully employed" (by a white employer) could be arrested, jailed, fined, or hired out to a man who would assume responsibility for their debts and behavior. The codes regulated black laborers' work contracts with white landowners, including severe penalties for leaving before the yearly contract was fulfilled. A Kentucky newspaper was blunt: "The tune ... will not be 'forty acres and a mule,' but ... 'work nigger or starve.'"

NATIONAL RECONSTRUCTION POLITICS

The Black Codes directly challenged the national government in 1865. Would it use its power in the South to uphold the codes, white property rights, and racial intimidation, or to defend the liberties of freedpeople? Although the primary drama of Reconstruction pitted white landowners against African American freedmen over land and labor in the South, in the background of these local struggles lurked the debate over Reconstruction policy among politicians in Washington. This dual drama would extend well into the twentieth century.

Presidential Reconstruction by Proclamation

After initially demanding that the defeated Confederates be punished for treason, President Johnson adopted a more lenient policy. On May 29, 1865, he issued two proclamations setting forth his Reconstruction program. Like Lincoln's, it rested on the claim that the southern states had never left the Union.

Johnson's first proclamation continued Lincoln's policies by offering "amnesty and pardon, with restoration of all rights of property" to most former Confederates who would swear allegiance to the Constitution and the Union. Johnson revealed his Jacksonian hostility to "aristocratic" planters by exempting ex–Confederate government leaders and rebels with taxable property valued over $20,000. They could, however, apply for individual pardons, which Johnson granted to nearly all applicants.

In his second proclamation, Johnson accepted the reconstructed government of North Carolina and prescribed the steps by which other southern states could reestablish state governments. First, the president would appoint a provisional governor, who would call a state convention representing those "who are loyal to the United States," including persons who took the oath of allegiance or were otherwise pardoned. The convention must ratify the Thirteenth Amendment, which abolished slavery; void secession; repudiate Confederate debts; and elect new state officials and members of Congress.

Under Johnson's plan, all southern states completed Reconstruction and sent representatives to Congress, which convened in December 1865. Defiant southern voters elected dozens of former officers and legislators of the Confederacy, including a few not yet pardoned. Some state conventions hedged on ratifying the Thirteenth Amendment, and some asserted former owners' right to compensation for lost slave property. No state convention provided for black suffrage, and most did nothing to guarantee civil rights, schooling, or economic protection for the freedmen. Eight months after Appomattox, the southern states were back in the Union, freedpeople were working for former masters, and the new president was firmly in charge. Reconstruction seemed to be over.

Congressional Reconstruction by Amendment

Late in 1865, northern leaders painfully saw that almost none of their moral or political postwar goals were being fulfilled and that the Republicans were likely to lose their political power. Would Democrats and the South gain by postwar elections what they had lost by civil war?

Congressional Republicans, led by Congressman Thaddeus Stevens of Pennsylvania and Senator Charles Sumner of Massachusetts, decided to set their own policies for Reconstruction. Although labeled "radicals," the vast majority of Republicans were moderates on the economic and political rights of freedmen.

Rejecting Johnson's position that the South had already been reconstructed, Congress exercised its constitutional authority to decide on its own membership.

Reconstruction Amendments

What three basic rights were guaranteed in these three amendments? What patterns do you see? How well were the dreams of the freedpeople fulfilled? Was that fulfillment immediate or deferred? For how long?

Substance	Outcome of Ratification Process	Final Implementation and Enforcement
Thirteenth Amendment—Passed by Congress January 1865		
Prohibited slavery in the United States	Ratified by 27 states, including 8 southern states, by December 1865	Immediate, although economic freedom came by degrees
Fourteenth Amendment—Passed by Congress June 1866		
(1) Defined equal national citizenship; (2) reduced state representation in Congress proportional to number of disfranchised voters; (3) denied former Confederates the right to hold office	Rejected by 12 southern and border states by February 1867; Congress made readmission depend on ratification; ratified in July 1868	Civil Rights Act of 1964
Fifteenth Amendment—Passed by Congress February 1869		
Prohibited denial of vote because of race, color, or previous servitude	Ratification by Virginia, Texas, Mississippi, and Georgia required for readmission; ratified in March 1870	Voting Rights Act of 1965

It refused to seat the new senators and representatives from the old Confederate states. It also established the Joint Committee on Reconstruction to investigate conditions in the South. Its report documented white resistance, disorder, and the appalling treatment and conditions of freedpeople.

Congress passed a civil rights bill in 1866 to protect the fragile rights of African Americans and extended for two more years the Freedmen's Bureau, an agency providing emergency assistance at the end of the war. Johnson vetoed both bills and called his congressional opponents "traitors." His actions drove moderates into the radical camp, and Congress passed both bills over his veto—both, however, watered down by weakening the power of enforcement. Southern courts regularly disallowed black testimony against whites, acquitted whites of violence, and sentenced blacks to compulsory labor.

In such a climate, southern racial violence erupted. In a typical outbreak, in May 1866, white mobs in Memphis, encouraged by local police, rampaged for over 40 hours of terror, killing, beating, robbing, and raping virtually helpless African American residents and burning houses, schools, and churches. Forty-eight people, all but two of them black, died. The local Union army commander took his time restoring order, arguing that his troops had "hated Negroes too." A congressional inquiry concluded that Memphis blacks had "no protection from the law whatever."

RECOVERING THE PAST

We usually read novels, short stories, and other forms of imaginary literature for pleasure, for the enjoyment of plot, style, symbolism, and character development. "Classic" novels such as *Moby Dick, Huckleberry Finn, The Great Gatsby, The Invisible Man,* and *Beloved,* for example, are not only written well, but also explore timeless questions of good and evil, of innocence and knowledge, of noble dreams fulfilled and shattered. We enjoy novels because we often find ourselves identifying with one of the major characters. Through that person's problems, joys, relationships, and search for identity, we gain insights about our own.

Even though they may be historically untrue, we can also read novels as historical sources, for they reveal much about the attitudes, dreams, fears, and ordinary everyday experiences of human beings in a particular period. In addition, they show how people responded to the major events of that era. The novelist, like the historian, is a product of time and place and has an interpretive point of view. Consider the two novels about Reconstruction quoted here. Neither is reputed for great literary merit, yet both reveal much about the various interpretations and impassioned attitudes of the post–Civil War era. *A Fool's Errand* was written by Albion Tourgée, a northerner; *The Clansman,* by Thomas Dixon, Jr., a southerner.

Tourgée was a young northern teacher and lawyer who fought with the Union army and moved to North Carolina after the war to begin a legal career. He became a judge and was an active Republican, supporting black suffrage and helping to shape the new state constitution. Because he boldly criticized the Ku Klux Klan, his life was threatened many times. When he left North Carolina in 1879, he published an autobiographical novel about his experiences as a judge challenging the Klan's campaign of violence and intimidation against the freedpeople.

The "fool's errand" in the novel is that of the northern veteran, Comfort Servosse, who, like Tourgée, seeks to fulfill humane goals on behalf of both blacks and whites in post–Civil War North Carolina. His efforts are thwarted, however, by threats, intimidation, a campaign of violent "outrages" against Republican leaders in the county, and a lack of support from Congress. Historians have verified the accuracy of many of the events in Tourgée's novel. While exposing the brutality of the Klan, Tourgée features loyal southern Unionists, respectable planters ashamed of Klan violence, and even guilt-ridden poor white Klansmen who try to protect or warn intended victims.

In the year of Tourgée's death, 1905, another North Carolinian published a novel with a very different analysis of Reconstruction and its fate. Thomas Dixon, Jr., was a lawyer, state legislator, Baptist minister, pro-Klan lecturer, and novelist. *The Clansman,* subtitled *A Historical Romance of the Ku Klux Klan,* reflects turn-of-the-century attitudes most white southerners still had about Republican rule during Reconstruction. According to Dixon, a power-crazed, vindictive, radical Congress, led by scheming Austin Stoneman (Thaddeus Stevens), sought to impose corrupt carpetbagger and brutal black rule on a helpless South. Only through the inspired leadership of the Ku Klux Klan was the South saved from the horrors of rape and revenge.

Dixon dedicated *The Clansman* to his uncle, a Grand Titan of the Klan in North Carolina during the time when two crucial counties were being transformed from Republican to Democratic through intimidation and terror. No such violence shows up in Dixon's novel. When the novel was made the basis of D. W. Griffith's film classic, *Birth of a Nation* in 1915, its attitudes were firmly implanted on the twentieth-century American mind.

Both novels convey Reconstruction attitudes toward the freedpeople. Both create clearly defined heroes and villains. Both include exciting chase scenes, narrow escapes, daring rescues, and tragic deaths. Both include romantic subplots. Yet the two novels are strikingly different.

A Fool's Errand,
Albion Tourgée (1879)

When the second Christmas came, Metta wrote again to her sister:

"The feeling is terribly bitter against Comfort on account of his course towards the colored people. There is quite a village of them on the lower end of the plantation. They have a church, a sabbath school, and are to have next year a school. You can not imagine how kind they have been to us, and how much they are attached to Comfort. ... I got Comfort to go with me to one of their prayer-meetings a few nights ago. I had heard a great deal about them, but had never attended one before. It was strangely weird. There were, perhaps, fifty present, mostly middle-aged men and women. They were singing in soft, low monotone, interspersed with prolonged exclamatory notes, a sort of rude hymn, which I was surprised to know was one of their old songs in slave times. How the chorus came to be endured in those days I can not imagine. It was—

'Free! free! free, my Lord, free!
An' we walks de hebben-ly way!

"A few looked around as we came in and seated ourselves; and Uncle Jerry, the saint of the settlement, came forward on his staves, and said, in his soft voice,

"Ev'nin', Kunnel! Sarvant, Missuss! Will you walk up, an' hev seats in front?'

"We told him we had just looked in, and might go in a short time; so we would stay in the back part of the audience.

"Uncle Jerry can not read nor write; but he is a man of strange intelligence and power. Unable to do work of any account, he is the faithful friend, monitor, and director of others. He has a house and piece of land, all paid for, a good horse and cow, and, with the aid of his wife and two boys, made a fine crop this season. He is one of the most promising colored men in the settlement: so Comfort says, at least. Everybody seems to have great respect for his character. I don't know how many people I have heard speak of his religion. Mr. Savage used to say he had rather hear him pray than any other man on earth. He was much prized by his master, even after he was disabled, on account of his faithfulness and character."

The Clansman,
Thomas Dixon, Jr. (1905)

At noon Ben and Phil strolled to the polling-place to watch the progress of the first election under Negro rule. The Square was jammed with shouting, jostling, perspiring negroes, men, women, and children. The day was warm, and the African odour was supreme even in the open air. ...

The negroes, under the drill of the League and the Freedman's Bureau, protected by the bayonet, were voting to enfranchise themselves, disfranchise their former masters, ratify a new constitution, and elect a legislature to do their will. Old Aleck was a candidate for the House, chief poll-holder, and seemed to be in charge of the movements of the voters outside the booth as well as inside. He appeared to be omnipresent, and his self-importance was a sight Phil had never dreamed. He could not keep his eyes off him. ...

[Aleck] was a born African orator, undoubtedly descended from a long line of savage spell-binders, whose eloquence in the palaver houses of the jungle had made them native leaders. His thin spindle-shanks supported an oblong, protruding stomach, resembling an elderly monkey's, which seemed so heavy it swayed his back to carry it.

The animal vivacity of his small eyes and the flexibility of his eyebrows, which he worked up and down rapidly with every change of countenance, expressed his eager desires.

He was already mellow with liquor, and was dressed in an old army uniform and cap, with two horse-pistols buckled around his waist. On a strap hanging from his shoulder were strung a half-dozen tin canteens filled with whiskey.

REFLECTING ON THE PAST   Even in these brief excerpts, what differences of style and attitude do you see in the depictions of Uncle Jerry and Old Aleck? What emotional responses do you have to these passages? How do you think late nineteenth-century and early twentieth-century Americans might have responded?

A month later, Congress sent to the states for ratification the Fourteenth Amendment, the single most significant act of the Reconstruction era. The first section of the amendment promised permanent constitutional protection of the civil rights of blacks by defining them as citizens. States were prohibited from depriving "any person of life, liberty, or property, without due process of law," and citizens were guaranteed the "equal protection of the laws." Section 2 granted black male suffrage in the South, inserting the word "male" into the Constitution for the first time. Other sections of the amendment barred leaders of the Confederacy from national or state offices (except by act of Congress), repudiated the Confederate debt, and denied claims of compensation to former slave owners. Johnson urged the southern states to reject the Fourteenth Amendment, and 10 immediately did so.

The Fourteenth Amendment was the central issue of the 1866 midterm election. Johnson barnstormed the country asking voters to throw out the radical Republicans and trading insults with hecklers. Democrats north and south appealed openly to racial prejudice in attacking the Fourteenth Amendment. Republicans responded by attacking Johnson personally and freely "waved the bloody shirt," reminding voters of the Democrats' treason. Self-interest and local issues moved voters more than fiery speeches, and the Republicans won an overwhelming victory. The mandate was clear: presidential Reconstruction had not worked, and Congress could present its own.

Early in 1867, Congress passed three Reconstruction acts. The southern states were divided into five military districts, whose commanders had broad powers to

DOCUMENT

Thirteenth, Fourteenth, and Fifteenth Amendments (1864)

maintain order and protect civil and property rights. Congress also defined a new process for readmitting a state. Qualified voters—including blacks but excluding unreconstructed rebels—would elect delegates to state constitutional conventions that would write new constitutions guaranteeing black suffrage. After the new voters of the states had ratified these constitutions, elections would be held to choose governors and state legislatures. When a state ratified the Fourteenth Amendment, its representatives to Congress would be accepted, completing its readmission to the Union.

The President Impeached

Congress also restricted presidential powers and established legislative dominance over the executive branch. The Tenure of Office Act, designed to prevent Johnson from firing the outspoken Secretary of War Edwin Stanton, limited the president's appointment powers. Other measures trimmed his power as commander in chief.

Johnson responded exactly as congressional Republicans had anticipated. He vetoed the Reconstruction acts, hindered the work of Freedmen's Bureau agents, limited the activities of military commanders in the South, and removed cabinet officers and other officials sympathetic to Congress. The House Judiciary Committee charged the president with "usurpations of power" and of acting in the "interests of the great criminals" who had led the rebellion. But moderate House Republicans defeated the impeachment resolutions.

In August 1867, Johnson dismissed Stanton and asked for Senate consent. When the Senate refused, the president ordered Stanton to surrender his office, which he refused, barricading himself inside. The House quickly approved impeachment resolutions, charging the president with "high crimes and misdemeanors." The three-month trial in the Senate in 1868 featured impassioned oratory, similar to the trial of President Bill Clinton 130 years later. And, as with Clinton, evidence was skimpy that Johnson had committed any constitutional crime justifying his removal. With seven moderate Republicans joining Democrats against conviction, the effort to find the president guilty fell one vote short of the required two-thirds majority. Not until the late twentieth century (Nixon and Clinton) would an American president face removal from office through impeachment.

Moderate Republicans were fearful that by removing Johnson, they might get Ohio Senator Benjamin Wade, a leading radical Republican, as president. Wade had endorsed woman suffrage, rights for labor unions, and civil rights for African Americans in both southern and northern states. As moderate Republicans gained strength in 1868 through their support of the eventual presidential election winner, Ulysses S. Grant, radicalism lost much of its power within Republican ranks.

What Congressional Moderation Meant for Rebels, Blacks, and Women

Congress's political battle against President Johnson was not matched by an idealistic resolve on behalf of the freedpeople. State and local elections of 1867 showed that voters preferred moderate Reconstruction policies. It is important to look not only at what Congress did during Reconstruction, but also at what it did not do.

With the exception of Jefferson Davis, Congress did not imprison Confederate leaders, and only one person, the commander of the infamous Andersonville prison camp, was executed. Congress did not insist on a long probation before southern states could be readmitted. It did not reorganize southern local governments. It did not mandate a national program of education for the freedpeople. It did not confiscate and redistribute land to the freedmen. It did not prevent Johnson from taking land away from those who had gained titles during the war. It did not, except indirectly and with great reluctance, provide economic help to the new black citizens.

Congress did, however, halfheartedly grant citizenship and suffrage to freedmen, but not to freedwomen. Northerners were no more prepared than southerners to make African Americans equal citizens. Proposals to give black men the vote gained support in the North only after the presidential election of 1868, when General Grant, the supposedly invincible military hero, barely won the popular vote in several states. To ensure grateful black votes, Congressional Republicans, who had twice rejected a suffrage amendment, took another look at the idea. After a bitter fight, the Fifteenth Amendment, forbidding all states to deny the vote to anyone "on account of race, color, or previous condition of servitude," became part of the Constitution in 1870.

One casualty of the Fourteenth and Fifteenth Amendments was the goodwill of women who had worked for suffrage for two decades. They had hoped that male legislators would recognize their wartime service in support of the Union and were shocked that black males got the vote but not loyal white (or black) women. Elizabeth Cady Stanton and Susan B. Anthony, veteran suffragists and opponents of slavery, campaigned against the Fourteenth Amendment, breaking with abolitionist allies such as Frederick Douglass, who had long supported woman suffrage yet declared that this was "the Negro's hour."

When the Fifteenth Amendment was proposed, many suffragists wondered why gender was still a barrier to the right to vote. Disappointment over the suffrage issue helped split the women's movement in 1869. Anthony and Stanton continued their fight for a national amendment for woman suffrage and a long list of other rights, while other women concentrated on securing the vote state-by-state. Abandoned by radical and moderate men alike, women had few champions in Congress, and their efforts did not bear fruit for half a century.

Congress compromised the rights of African Americans as well as women. It gave blacks the vote but not land, the opposite of what they wanted first. Thaddeus Stevens argued that "forty acres ... and a hut would be more valuable ... than the ... right to vote." But Congress never seriously considered his plan to confiscate the land of the "chief rebels" and give a small portion of it, divided into 40-acre plots, to freedpeople, which would have violated deeply held beliefs of the Republican party and the American people on the sacredness of private property. Moreover, northern business interests looking to develop southern industry and invest in southern land liked the prospect of a large pool of propertyless African American workers.

Congress did pass the Southern Homestead Act of 1866, making public lands available to blacks and loyal whites in five southern states. But the land was poor and inaccessible, and most black laborers were bound by contracts that prevented them from making claims before the deadline. Only about 4,000 African American families even applied for the Homestead Act lands, and fewer than 20 percent of them saw their claims completed. White claimants did little better.

THE LIVES OF FREEDPEOPLE

Union army major George Reynolds boasted late in 1865 that in the area of Mississippi under his command, he had "kept the negroes at work, and in a good state of discipline." Clinton Fisk, a well-meaning white who helped found a black college in Tennessee, told freedmen in 1866 that they could be "as free and as happy" working again for their "old master ... as any where else in the world." Such pronouncements reminded blacks of white preachers' exhortations during slavery to work hard and obey masters. Ironically, Fisk and Reynolds were agents of the Freedmen's Bureau, the agency intended to aid the black transition from slaves to freedpeople.

The Freedmen's Bureau

Never in American history has one small agency—underfinanced, understaffed, and undersupported—been given a harder task than was the Bureau of Freedmen, Refugees, and Abandoned Lands. Controlling less than 1 percent of southern lands, the Bureau's name is telling; its fate epitomizes Reconstruction.

The Freedmen's Bureau performed many essential services. It issued emergency food rations, clothed and sheltered homeless victims of the war, and established medical and hospital facilities. It provided funds to relocate thousands of freedpeople. It helped blacks search for relatives and get legally married. It represented African Americans in local civil courts to ensure that they got fair trials and learned to respect the law. Working with northern missionary aid societies and southern black churches, the Bureau became responsible for an extensive program of education, and by 1870 there were almost 250,000 pupils in 4,329 agency schools.

The Bureau's largest task was to promote African Americans' economic well-being. This included settling them on abandoned lands and getting them started with tools, seed, and draft animals, as well as arranging work contracts with white landowners. But in this area the Freedmen's Bureau, determined not to instill a new dependency, more often than not supported the needs of white landowners to find cheap labor than of blacks to become independent farmers.

Although a few agents were idealistic New Englanders eager to help freedpeople adjust to freedom, most were Union army officers more concerned with social order than social transformation. Working in a postwar climate of resentment and violence, Freedmen's Bureau agents were overworked, underpaid, spread too thin (at its peak only 900 agents were scattered across the South), and constantly harassed by local whites. Even the best-intentioned agents would have agreed with Bureau commissioner General O. O. Howard's belief in the nineteenth-century American values of self-help, minimal government interference in the marketplace, the sanctity of private property, contractual obligations, and white superiority.

On a typical day, overburdened agents would visit local courts and schools, file reports, supervise the signing of work contracts, and handle numerous complaints, most involving contract violations between whites and blacks or property and domestic disputes among blacks. A Georgia agent wrote that he was *"tired out* and *broke down.* … Every day for 6 months, day after day, I have had from 5 to 20 complaints, *generally trivial* and of no moment, yet requiring consideration & attention coming from both Black & White." To find work for freedmen, agents implored freedwomen to hold their husbands accountable as providers and often sided with white landowners by telling blacks to obey orders, trust employers, and accept disadvantageous contracts. One agent sent a man who had complained of a severe beating back to work: "Don't be sassy [and] don't be lazy when you've got work to do."

Despite numerous constraints, the agents accomplished much. In little more than two years, the Freedmen's Bureau issued 20 million rations (nearly one-third to poor whites), reunited families and resettled some 30,000 displaced war refugees, treated some 450,000 people for illness and injury, built 40 hospitals and 4,000 schools, provided books, tools, and furnishings—and even some land—to the freedmen, and occasionally protected their economic and civil rights. The great African American historian and leading black intellectual of the twentieth century, W. E. B. Du Bois, wrote that, "In a time of perfect calm, amid willing neighbors and streaming wealth," it "would have been a herculean task" for the bureau to fulfill its many purposes. But in the midst of hunger, sorrow, spite, suspicion, hate, and cruelty, "the work of any instrument of social regeneration was … foredoomed to failure." But Du Bois, reflecting the varied views of freedpeople themselves, recognized that in

DOCUMENT

Southern Skepticism of the Freedmen's Bureau (1866)

laying the foundation for black labor, future land ownership, a public school system, and recognition before courts of law, the Freedmen's Bureau was "on the whole successful beyond the dreams of thoughtful men."

Economic Freedom by Degrees

Despite the best efforts of the Freedmen's Bureau, the failure of Congress to provide the promised 40 acres and a mule forced freedmen and women into a new dependency on former masters. Blacks made some progress, however, in degrees of economic autonomy and were partly responsible, along with international economic developments, for forcing the white planter class into making major changes in southern agriculture.

First, a land-intensive system replaced the labor intensity of slavery. Land ownership was concentrated into fewer and even larger holdings than before the war. From South Carolina to Louisiana, the wealthiest tenth of the population owned about 60 percent of the real estate in the 1870s. Second, these large planters increasingly specialized in one crop, usually cotton, and were tied into the international market. This resulted in a steady drop in postwar food production (both grain and livestock). Third, one-crop farming created a new credit system whereby most farmers, black and white, were forced into dependence on local merchants for renting land, housing, seed, and farm implements and animals. These changes affected race relations and class tensions.

This new system took a few years to develop after emancipation. At first, most African Americans signed contracts with white landowners and worked in gangs as during slavery. All members of the family had to work to receive their rations. The freedpeople resented this new semiservitude, refused to sign the contracts, and sought a measure of independence working the land themselves. Freedwomen especially wanted to send their children to school rather than to apprenticeships, and insisted on "no more outdoor work," preferring small plots of land to grow vegetables rather than plantation labor.

Many blacks therefore broke contracts, ran away, engaged in work slowdowns or strikes, burned barns, and sought other means of negotiation. In the Sea Islands and rice-growing regions of coastal South Carolina and Georgia, where slaves had long held a degree of autonomy, resistance was especially strong. On the Heyward plantations, near those of the Allstons, the freedmen "refuse work at any price," a Freedman's Bureau agent reported, and the women "wish to stay in the house or the garden all the time."

Blacks' insistence on autonomy and land of their own was the major impetus for the change from the contract system to tenancy and sharecropping. Families would hitch mules to their old slave cabin and drag it to their plot, as far from the

DOCUMENT

A Sharecrop
Contract (1882)

Big House as possible. Sharecroppers received seed, fertilizer, implements, food, and clothing. In return, the landlord (or a local merchant) told them what and how much to grow, and he took a share—usually half—of the harvest. The cropper's half usually went to pay for goods bought on credit (at high interest rates) from the landlord. Thus sharecroppers remained tied to the landlord.

Tenant farmers had only slightly more independence. Before a harvest, they promised to sell their crop to a local merchant in return for renting land, tools,

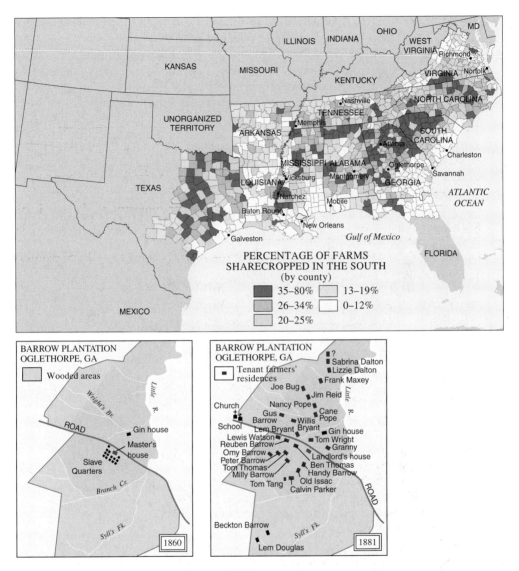

THE RISE OF TENANCY IN THE SOUTH, 1880 Although no longer slaves and after resisting labor contracts and the gang system of field labor, the freedmen (as well as many poor whites) became tenant farmers, working on shares, in the New South. The former slaves on the Barrow plantation in Georgia, for example, moved their households to individual 25- to 30-acre tenant farms, which they rented from the Barrow family in annual contracts requiring payment in cotton and other cash crops. Where was the highest percentage of tenant farms, and how do you explain it? How would you explain the low-percentage areas? What do you notice about how circumstances have changed—and not changed—on the Barrow plantation?

and other necessities. From the merchant's store they also had to buy goods on credit (at higher prices than whites paid) against the harvest. At "settling up" time, income from sale of the crop was compared to accumulated debts. It was possible, especially after an unusually bountiful season, to come out ahead and eventually to own one's own land. But tenants rarely did; in debt at the end of each year, they had to pledge the next year's crop. World cotton prices remained low, and whereas big landowners still generated profits through their large scale of operation, sharecroppers rarely made much money. When they were able to pay their debts, landowners frequently altered loan agreements. Thus peonage replaced slavery, ensuring a continuing cheap labor supply to grow cotton and other staples in the South.

Despite this bleak picture, painstaking, industrious work by African Americans helped many gradually accumulate a measure of income, personal property, and autonomy, especially in the household economy of producing eggs, butter, meat, food crops, and other staples. Debt did not necessarily mean a lack of subsistence. In Virginia, the declining tobacco crop forced white planters to sell off small parcels of land to blacks. Throughout the South, a few African Americans became independent landowners—about 3 to 4 percent by 1880, but closer to 25 percent by 1900.

White Farmers During Reconstruction

Changes in southern agriculture affected middle-class and poor white farmers as well, and planters worried about a coalition between poor black and pro-Unionist white farmers. As a Georgia farmer said in 1865, "We should tuk the land, as we did the niggers, and split it, and giv part to the niggers and part to me and t'other Union fellers." But confiscation and redistribution of land was no more likely for white farmers than for the freedmen. Whites, too, had to concentrate on growing staples, pledging their crops against high-interest credit, and facing perpetual indebtedness. In the upcountry piedmont area of Georgia, for example, the number of whites working their own land dropped from nine in ten before the Civil War to seven in ten by 1880, while cotton production doubled.

Reliance on cotton meant fewer food crops and greater dependence on merchants for provisions. In 1884, Jephta Dickson of Jackson County, Georgia, purchased over $50 worth of flour, meal, meat, syrup, peas, and corn from a local store; 25 years earlier, he had been almost completely self-sufficient. Fencing laws seriously curtailed the livelihood of poor whites raising pigs and hogs, and restrictions on hunting and fishing reduced the ability of poor whites and blacks alike to supplement incomes and diets. In the worn-out flatlands and barren mountainous regions of the South, the poverty, health, and isolation of poor whites worsened after the war. They lived a marginal existence, hunting, fishing, and growing crops that, as a North Carolinian put it, were "puny." Some became farmhands at $6 a month (with board). Others fled to low-paying jobs in cotton mills.

The cultural life of poor southern whites reflected their lowly position and their pride. Their emotional religion centered on camp meeting revivals in backwoods clearings. There, ballads and folklore told of debt, chain gangs, herbal remedies for poor health, and deeds of drinking prowess. Their quilt making and house construction reflected a marginal culture in which everything was saved and reused.

In part because their lives were so hard, poor whites clung to their belief in white superiority. Many joined the Ku Klux Klan and other southern white terror groups that emerged between 1866 and 1868. A federal officer reported, "The poorer classes of white people ... have a most intense hatred of the Negro," which expressed itself in midnight raids on teachers in black schools, Republican voters, and any black whose "impudence" caused him not to "bow and scrape to a white man, as was done formerly."

Black Self-Help Institutions

But however hard life was for poor whites, things were even worse for blacks, whose hopes slowly soured. Recalled an African American Texan, "We soon found out that freedom could make folks proud but it didn't make 'em rich." Many African American leaders realized that because white institutions could not fulfill the promises of emancipation, freedpeople would have to do it themselves.

Black community self-help survived in the churches and schools of the antebellum free Negro communities and in the "invisible" cultural institutions of the slave quarters. Emancipation brought a rapid increase in the growth of membership in African American churches. The Negro Baptist Church grew from 150,000 members in 1850 to 500,000 in 1870, while the membership of the African Methodist Episcopal Church increased fourfold in the postwar decade, from 100,000 to over 400,000 members. African American ministers continued to exert community leadership. Many led efforts to oppose discrimination, some by entering politics; over one-fifth of the black officeholders in South Carolina were ministers. Most preachers, however, focused on sin, salvation, and revivalist enthusiasm. An English visitor to the South in 1867 and 1868 noted the intensity of black "devoutness." As one woman explained: "We make noise 'bout ebery ting else ... I want to go to Heaben in de good ole way."

The freedpeople's desire for education was as strong as for religion. A school official in Virginia said that the freedmen were "down right crazy to learn." In addition to black teachers from the churches, "Yankee schoolmarms taught black children and adults." Sent by aid societies such as the American Missionary Association, these high-minded young women sought to convert blacks to Congregationalism and their version of moral behavior. In October 1865, Esther Douglass found "120 dirty, half naked perfectly wild black children" in her schoolroom near Savannah, Georgia. Eight months later, she reported that they could read, sing hymns, and repeat Bible verses and had learned "about right conduct which they tried to practice."

Such glowing reports waned as white teachers grew frustrated with crowded facilities, limited resources, local opposition, and absenteeism caused by fieldwork. In Georgia, for example, only 5 percent of black children went to school for part of any one year between 1865 and 1870, as opposed to 20 percent of white children. As white teachers left, they were increasingly replaced by blacks, who boarded with families and were more persistent and positive. Charlotte Forten, for example, noted that even after a half day's "hard toil" in the fields, her older pupils were "as bright and as anxious to learn as ever," showing "a desire for knowledge, and a capability for attaining it." Under teachers like Forten, by 1870 there was a 20 percent gain in adult literacy, a figure that, against difficult odds, continued to grow for all ages to the end of the century, when more than 1.5 million black children attended school. To train African American teachers and

Black Schoolchildren with Their Books and Teacher Along with equal civil rights and land of their own, what the freedpeople wanted most was education. Despite white opposition, one of the most positive outcomes of the Reconstruction era was education in Freedmen's Bureau schools. What do you see in this photograph? Is it sad or uplifting? Why? *(Cook Collection, Valentine Richmond History Center)*

preachers, northern philanthropists founded Howard, Atlanta, Fisk, Morehouse, and other black universities in the South after 1865.

African American schools, like churches, became community centers. They published newspapers, provided training in trades and farming, and promoted political participation and land ownership. These efforts made black schools objects of local white hostility. As a Virginia freedman told a congressional committee, in his county, anyone starting a school would be killed and blacks were "afraid to be caught with a book." In 1869, in Tennessee alone, 37 black schools were burned to the ground.

White opposition to black education and land ownership stimulated African American nationalism and separatism. In the late 1860s, Benjamin "Pap" Singleton, a former Tennessee slave, urged freedpeople to abandon politics and migrate westward. He organized a land company in 1869, purchased public property in Kansas, and in the early 1870s took several groups from Tennessee and Kentucky to establish separate black towns in the prairie state. In following years, thousands of "exodusters" from the Lower South bought some 10,000 infertile acres in Kansas. But natural and human obstacles to self-sufficiency often proved insurmountable. By the 1880s, despairing of ever finding economic independence in the United States, Singleton and other nationalists advocated emigration to Canada and Liberia. Other black leaders like Frederick Douglass continued to press for full citizenship rights within the United States.

RECONSTRUCTION IN THE SOUTHERN STATES

Douglass's confidence in the power of the ballot seemed warranted in the enthusiastic early months under the Reconstruction Acts of 1867. With President Johnson neutralized, Republican congressional leaders finally could prevail. Local Republicans, taking advantage of the inability or refusal of many southern whites to vote, overwhelmingly elected their delegates to state constitutional conventions in the fall of 1867. Guardedly optimistic and sensing the "sacred importance" of their work, black and white Republicans began creating new state governments.

MAP

Reconstruction

Republican Rule

Contrary to early pro-southern historians, southern state governments under Republican rule were not dominated by illiterate black majorities intent on "Africanizing" the South. Nor were these governments unusually corrupt or extravagant, nor did they use massive numbers of federal troops to enforce their will. By 1869, only 1,100 federal soldiers remained in Virginia, and most federal troops in Texas were guarding the frontier against Mexico and hostile Indians. Lacking strong

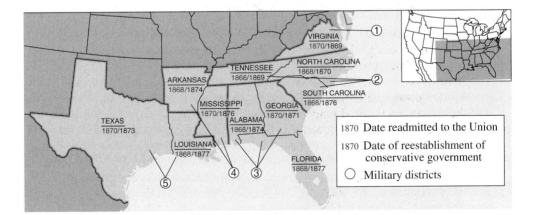

THE RETURN OF CONSERVATIVE DEMOCRATIC CONTROL IN SOUTHERN STATES DURING RECONSTRUCTION Note that the duration of Republican governments in power to implement even moderate Reconstruction programs varied from state to state. In North Carolina and Georgia, for example, Republican rule was very brief, while in Virginia it never took place at all. "Redemption," the return of conservative control, took longest in three Deep South states. How would you explain these variations among the southern states?

military backing, the new state governments faced economic distress and increasingly violent harassment.

Diverse coalitions made up the new governments elected under congressional Reconstruction. These "black and tan" governments (as opponents called them) were actually predominantly white, except for the lower house of the South Carolina legislature. Many of the new leaders were local bankers, industrialists, and others interested more in economic growth and sectional reconciliation than in radical social reforms. A second group consisted of northern Republican capitalists who headed south to invest in land, railroads, and new industries. Others included Union veterans, and missionaries and teachers inspired to work in Freedmen's Bureau schools. Such people were unfairly labeled "carpetbaggers."

Moderate African Americans made up a third group in the Republican state governments. A large percentage of black officeholders were mulattos, many of them well-educated preachers, teachers, and soldiers from the North. Others were self-educated tradesmen or representatives of the small landed class of southern blacks. In South Carolina, for example, of some 255 African American state and federal officials elected between 1868 and 1876, two-thirds were literate and one-third owned real estate; only 15 percent owned no property at all. This class composition meant that black leaders often supported policies that largely ignored the economic needs of the African American masses. Their goals fit squarely into the American republican tradition. Black leaders reminded whites that they were also southerners, seeking only, as an 1865 petition put it, "that the same laws which govern white men shall govern black men [and that] we be dealt with as others are—in equity and justice."

The primary accomplishment of Republican rule in the South was to eliminate undemocratic features from prewar state constitutions. All states provided universal male suffrage and loosened requirements for holding office. Underrepresented counties got more legislative seats. Automatic imprisonment for debt was ended, and laws were enacted to relieve poverty and care for the handicapped. Many southern states passed their first divorce laws and provisions granting property rights to married women. Lists of crimes punishable by death were shortened.

Republican governments financially and physically reconstructed the South by overhauling tax systems and approving generous railroad and other capital investment bonds. Harbors, roads, and bridges were rebuilt; hospitals and asylums were established. Most important, the Republican governments created the South's first public school systems. As in the North, these schools were largely segregated, but for the first time rich and poor, black and white alike had access to education. By the 1880s, African American school attendance increased from 5 to over 40 percent, and white from 20 to over 60 percent. All this cost money, so the Republicans also increased tax rates and state debts.

These considerable accomplishments came in the face of opposition like that expressed at a convention of Louisiana planters, which labeled the Republican leaders the "lowest and most corrupt body of men ever assembled in the South." There was some corruption, mostly in land sales, railway bonds, and construction contracts. Such graft had become a way of life in postwar American politics,

South and North. Given their lack of experience with politics, the black role... remarkable. As Du Bois put it, "There was one thing that the White South fear... more than negro dishonesty, ignorance, and incompetence, and that was negro honesty, knowledge, and efficiency."

The Republican coalition did not survive. It lasted for different periods in different states, surviving longest in the Deep South, where the black population was equal to or greater than the white. In Virginia, Republicans ruled hardly at all, joining with Democrats to encourage northern investors to rebuild shattered cities and develop industry. In South Carolina, African American leaders' unwillingness to use their power to help black laborers contributed to their loss of political control to the Democrats, and class divisions among blacks in Louisiana helped weaken the Republican regime there. But the primary reason for the return of Democrats to power was the use of violence.

Violence and "Redemption"

A southern editor said, "We must render this either a white man's government, or convert the land into a Negro man's cemetery." The Ku Klux Klan was only one of several secret organizations that forcibly drove black and white Republicans from office. Although violence was pervasive throughout the South, North Carolina and Mississippi typified the pattern.

After losing a close election in North Carolina in 1868, conservatives waged a concentrated terror campaign in several piedmont counties, areas of strong Unionist support. If the Democrats could win these counties in 1870, they would most likely win statewide. In the year before the election, several prominent Republicans were killed, including a white state senator and a leading black Union League organizer, who was hanged in the courthouse square with a sign pinned to him: "Bewar, ye guilty, both white and black." Scores of citizens were flogged, fired from their jobs, or driven in the middle of the night from burning homes and barns. The courts consistently refused to prosecute anyone for these crimes, which local papers blamed on "disgusting negroes and white Radicals." The conservative campaign worked. In the election of 1870, some 12,000 fewer Republicans voted in the two crucial counties than had voted two years earlier, and the Democrats swept back into power.

In Mississippi's state election in 1875, Democrats used similar tactics in what became known as the "Mississippi Plan." Local Democratic clubs formed armed militias, marching defiantly through black areas, breaking up Republican meetings, and provoking riots to justify killing hundreds. Armed men posted during voter registration intimidated Republicans. At the election itself, voters were either "helped" by gun-toting whites to cast a Democratic ballot or chased away. Counties that had given Republicans majorities in the thousands managed a total of less than a dozen votes in 1875!

Democrats called their victory "redemption." As conservative Democrats resumed control of each state government, Reconstruction ended. Redemption succeeded with a combination of persistent white southern resistance, including violence and coercion, and a failure of northern will.

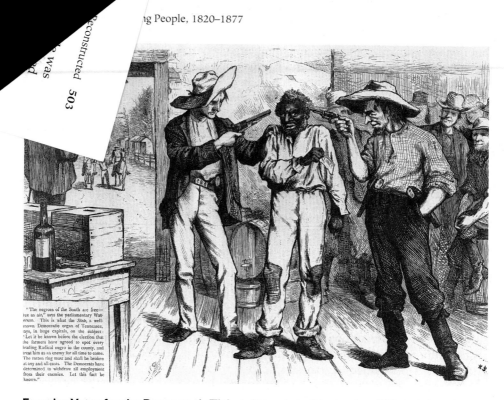

"The negroes of the South are free—free as air," says the parliamentary Waterson. This is what the *State*, a well-known Democratic organ of Tennessee, says, in huge capitals, on the subject: 'Let it be known before the election that the farmers have agreed to spot every leading Radical negro in the county, and treat him as an enemy for all time to come. The rotten ring must and shall be broken at any and all costs. The Democrats have determined to withdraw all employment from their enemies. Let this fact be known."

Ensuring Votes for the Democratic Ticket Although the Fourteenth and Fifteenth Amendments gave African American males the right to vote, almost immediately white southerners opposed to black suffrage found many illegal ways of influencing and eventually depriving them of that vote, thus returning white Democrats to office. In this cartoon, titled "Of course he wants to vote the Democratic Ticket," one of the two pistol-wielding men is saying: "You're as free as air, ain't you? Say you are, or I'll blow your black head off!" Note that another freedman is being led down the street to the polling place. Do you think he will also vote Democratic or for the party of Lincoln? *(Corbis)*

Congress and President Grant did not totally ignore southern violence. Three Force Acts, passed in 1870 and 1871, gave the president strong powers to use federal supervisors to ensure that citizens were not prevented from voting by force or fraud. The third act, also known as the Ku Klux Klan Act, declared illegal secret organizations that used disguise and coercion to deprive others of equal protection of the laws. Congress created a joint committee to investigate Klan violence, and in 1872 its report filled 13 huge volumes with horrifying testimony. Grant sent messages to Congress proclaiming the importance of the right to vote and condemning lawlessness, and dispatched additional troops to South Carolina, where violence against blacks was the worst. However, reform Republicans lost interest in defending African Americans, and regular Republicans decided that they could keep political power without black votes. In 1875, Grant's advisers told him that Republicans might lose important Ohio elections if he continued protecting African Americans, so he rejected appeals by Mississippi blacks for troops to guarantee free elections. He and the nation, Grant said, "had tired of these annual autumnal outbreaks."

The success of the Democrats' Mississippi Plan in 1875, repeated a year later in South Carolina and Louisiana, indicated that congressional reports, presidential proclamations, and the Force Acts did little to stop the reign of terror against black and white Republicans throughout the South. Despite hundreds of arrests, all-white juries refused to find whites guilty of crimes against blacks. The U.S. Supreme Court backed them in two 1874 decisions throwing out cases against whites convicted of preventing blacks from voting and declaring key parts of the Force Acts unconstitutional. Officially, the Klan's power ended, but the attitudes (and tactics) of Klansmen would continue long into the next century.

Shifting National Priorities

The American people, like their leaders, were tired of battles over the freedpeople. The easiest course was to give citizenship and the vote to African Americans, and leave them to fend for themselves. Americans of increasing ethnic diversity were primarily interested in starting families, finding work, and making money. Slovakian immigrants fired furnaces in Pittsburgh; Chinese men pounded in railroad ties for the Central Pacific over the Sierra Nevada mountains and across the Nevada desert; Yankee women taught in one-room schoolhouses in Vermont for $23 a month; Mexican *vaqueros* drove Texan cattle herds to Kansas; and Scandinavian families battled heat, locusts, and high railroad rates on farmsteads in the Dakotas.

American priorities had shifted, at both the individual and national levels. Failing to effect a smooth transition from slavery to freedom for freedpeople, northern leaders focused their efforts on accelerating and solidifying programs of economic growth and industrial and territorial expansion.

As North Carolina Klansmen convened in dark forests in 1869, the Central Pacific and Union Pacific railroads met in Utah, linking the Atlantic and the Pacific. As southern cotton production revived, northern iron and steel manufacturing and western settlement of the mining, cattle, and agricultural frontiers also surged. As black farmers haggled over work contracts with landowners in Georgia, white workers were organizing the National Labor Union in Baltimore. As Elizabeth and Adele Allston demanded the keys to their barns in the summer of 1865, the Boston Labor Reform Association was demanding that "our ... education, morals, dwellings, and the whole Social System" needed to be "reconstructed." If the South would not be reconstructed, labor relations might be.

The years between 1865 and 1875 featured not only the rise (and fall) of Republican governments in the South, but also a spectacular surge of working-class organization. Stimulated by the Civil War to improve working conditions in northern factories, trade unions, labor reform associations, and labor parties flourished, culminating in the founding of the National Labor Union in 1866. Before the depression of 1873, an estimated 300,000 to 500,000 American workers enrolled in some 1,500 trade unions, the largest such increase in the nineteenth century. This growth inevitably stirred class tensions. In 1876, hundreds of freedmen in the rice region along the Combahee River in South Carolina went on strike to protest a 40-cent-per-day wage cut, clashing with local sheriffs and white Democratic rifle clubs. A year later, also fighting wage cuts, thousands of northern railroad workers went out in a nationwide wave of strikes, clashing with police and the National Guard.

As economic relations changed, so did the Republican party. Heralded by the moderate tone of the state elections of 1867 and Grant's election in 1868, the

DOCUMENT

Trial of Susan B.
Anthony, on the
charge of Illegal
Voting, at the
Presidential
Election in
November 1872

Republicans changed from a party of moral reform to one of material interest. In the continuing struggle in American politics between "virtue and commerce," self-interest was again winning. Abandoning the Freedmen's Bureau as an inappropriate federal intervention, Republican politicians had no difficulty handing out huge grants of money and land to the railroads. As freedpeople were told to fend for themselves, the Union Pacific was getting subsidies of between $16,000 and $48,000 for each mile of track it laid. As Susan B. Anthony and other women tramped through the snows of upstate New York with petitions for women's rights, Boss Tweed and other politicians defrauded New York taxpayers of millions of dollars. As Native Americans in the Great Plains struggled to preserve the sacred Black Hills from gold prospectors protected by U.S. soldiers, corrupt government officials in the East "mined" public treasuries.

By 1869, the year financier Jay Gould almost cornered the gold market, the nation was increasingly defined by its sordid, materialistic "go-getters." President Grant's cabinet was filled with his old army cronies and rich friends to whom he owed favors. Henry Adams, descended from two former presidents, charged that Grant's administration "outraged every rule of decency." Honest himself, Grant showed poor judgment of others. The scandals of his administration touched his relatives, his cabinet, and two vice presidents. Outright graft, loose prosecution, and generally negligent administration flourished in a half dozen departments. The Whiskey Ring affair, for example, cost the public millions of dollars in tax revenues siphoned off to government officials. Gould's gold scam was aided by Grant's Treasury Department and by the president's brother-in-law.

Nor was Congress pure. Crédit Mobilier, a dummy corporation supposedly building the transcontinental railroads, received generous bonds and contracts in exchange for giving congressmen money, stock, and railroad lands. An Ohio congressman described the House of Representatives in 1873 as an "auction room where more valuable considerations were disposed of under the speaker's hammer than any place on earth."

The election of 1872 showed the public uninterested in moral issues. "Liberal" Republicans, disgusted with Grant, formed a third party calling for lower tariffs and fewer grants to railroads, civil service reform, and the removal of federal troops from the South. Their candidate, Horace Greeley, editor of the New York *Tribune,* was also nominated by the Democrats, whom he had spent much of his career condemning. But despite his wretched record, Grant easily won a second term.

The End of Reconstruction

Soon after Grant's second inauguration, a financial panic, caused by railroad mismanagement and the collapse of some eastern banks, started a terrible depression that lasted throughout the mid-1870s. In these hard times, economic issues dominated politics, further diverting attention from freedpeople. As Democrats took control of the House of Representatives in 1874 and looked toward winning the White House in 1876, politicians talked about new Grant scandals, unemployment and public works, the currency, and tariffs. No one said much about freed-

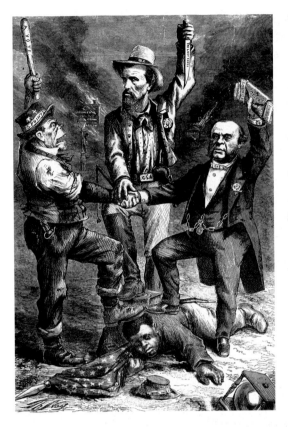

The End of Reconstruction This 1868 Thomas Nast cartoon ran under a caption quoting a Democratic party newspaper, "This is a white man's government." Describe each of the four (stereotyped) figures in this cartoon. Note the details in what each person carries in his raised (or outstretched) arm. You will see symbols of Irish workers in the "5 Points" neighborhood of New York City, the "lost cause" of the CSA, Confederate general Nathan Bedford Forrest, capitalist wealth, a Union soldier's uniform, and the ballot box. Note also the images in the background. In short, what do you see, and what does it mean? No single image better captures the story of the end of Reconstruction. (Harper's Weekly, September 5, 1868)

people. In 1875, a guilt-ridden Congress did pass Senator Charles Sumner's civil rights bill to put teeth into the Fourteenth Amendment. But the act was not enforced, and eight years later the Supreme Court declared it unconstitutional. Congressional Reconstruction, long dormant, was over. The election of 1876, closest in American history until 2000, sealed the end.

As their presidential candidate in 1876, the Republicans chose a former governor of Ohio, Rutherford B. Hayes, partly because of his reputation for honesty, partly because he had been a Union officer (a necessity for post–Civil War candidates), and partly because, as Henry Adams put it, he was "obnoxious to no one." The Democrats nominated Governor Samuel J. Tilden of New York, a well-known civil service reformer who had broken the corrupt Tweed ring.

Tilden won a popular-vote majority and appeared to have enough electoral votes for victory—except for 20 disputed electoral votes, all but one in Louisiana, South Carolina, and Florida, where some federal troops remained and where Republicans still controlled the voting apparatus despite Democratic intimidation. To settle the dispute, Congress created a commission of eight Republicans and seven Democrats who voted along party lines to give Hayes all 20 votes and a narrow electoral college victory, 185 to 184.

Outraged Democrats protested the outcome and threatened to stop the Senate from officially counting the electoral votes, preventing Hayes's inauguration. There was talk of a new civil war. But unlike the 1850s, a North–South compromise

TIMELINE

1865	Civil War ends
	Thirteenth Amendment ratified
	Freedmen's Bureau established
1865–1866	Black Codes
	Repossession of land by whites
	Ku Klux Klan formed
1867	Reconstruction acts passed over Johnson's veto
1868	Fourteenth Amendment ratified

1868–1870	Ten former Confederate states readmitted to the Union
1870	Fifteenth Amendment ratified
1876–1877	Three remaining former Confederate States of America readmitted to the Union
1880s	Tenancy and sharecropping prevail in the South
	Disfranchisement and segregation of southern blacks begins

emerged. Northern investors wanted the government to subsidize a New Orleans-to-California railroad. Southerners wanted northern dollars but not northern political influence—no social agencies, no federal enforcement of the Fourteenth and Fifteenth amendments, and no military occupation, not even the symbolic presence left in 1876.

As the March 4 inauguration date approached, the forces of mutual self-interest concluded the "compromise of 1877." On March 2, Hayes was declared president-elect. After his inauguration, he ordered the last federal troops out of the South, sending them west to fight Plains Indians, appointed a former Confederate general to his cabinet, supported federal aid for economic and railroad development in the South, and promised to let southerners handle race relations themselves. On a goodwill trip to the South, he told blacks that "your rights and interests would be safer if this great mass of intelligent white men were let alone by the general government." The message was clear: Hayes would not enforce the Fourteenth and Fifteenth Amendments, initiating a pattern of executive inaction that lasted to the 1960s. But the immediate crisis was averted, officially ending Reconstruction.

Conclusion

A Mixed Legacy

In the 12 years between Appomattox and Hayes's inauguration, victorious northern Republicans, defeated white southerners, and hopeful black freedpeople each wanted more than the others would give. Each got something. The compromise of

1877 cemented the reunion of North and South, providing new opportunities for economic development in both regions. The Republican party achieved its economic goals and generally held the White House, though not always Congress, until 1932. The ex-Confederate states came back into the Union, and southerners retained their grip on southern lands and black labor, though not without struggle and some changes. The Allstons' freedpeople refused to sign work contracts, even when offered livestock and other favors, and in 1869, Adele Allston had to sell much of her lands, albeit to whites.

In 1880, Frederick Douglass wrote: "Our Reconstruction measures were radically defective. ... To the freedmen was given the machinery of liberty, but there was denied to them the steam to put it in motion. ... The old master class ... retained the power to starve them to death, and wherever this power is held there is the power of slavery." The wonder, Douglass said, was "not that freedmen have made so little progress, but, rather, that they have made so much; not that they have been standing still, but that they have been able to stand at all."

Freedpeople had made strong gains in education and in economic and family survival. Despite sharecropping and tenancy, black laborers organized themselves to achieve a measure of autonomy and opportunity in their lives. The three great Reconstruction amendments, despite flagrant violation over the next 100 years, held out the promise that equal citizenship and political participation would yet be realized.

Questions for Review and Reflection

1. At the end of the Civil War, what were the goals and dreams of defeated southern whites, victorious northerners, and emancipated freedpeople? Can you name three for each group?

2. How did each group pursue its goals and dreams, what resources did each have, and how did they conflict with each other between 1865 and 1877?

3. What differences existed *within* each of the three major groups?

4. What were the major differences between northern presidential and congressional plans for reconstruction? In your judgment, which was more important—reconstruction politics in the North or daily life, race relations, and politics in the South?

5. What is your assessment of how well American democratic politics and values served the dreams of diverse American peoples in the postwar era?

Discovering U.S. History Online

A Documentary History of Emancipation, 1861–1867 www.inform.umd.edu/ARHU/Depts/History/Freedman/home.html
A rich collection of primary sources from the Freedom and Southern Society Project of the University of Maryland, containing superb links to nine projected volumes of collected documents.

Freedmen's Bureau Online http://freedmen'sbureau.com/
An excellent collection of Freedmen's Bureau sites, including marriage records and accounts of "murders and other outrages," as well as links to other African American and Freedmen's Bureau sites.

The Impeachment of Andrew Johnson www.andrewjohnson.com
Over 200 excerpts from contemporary issues of *Harper's Weekly* (1865–1869) provide in-depth information about Andrew Johnson and the impeachment process.

Images of African Americans from the Nineteenth Century www.digital.nypl.org/schomburg/images_aa19/
A vast collection of visual images by artists, engravers, and photographers capturing elements of African American life in the nineteenth century.

Reports on Black America, 1857–1874 www.blackhistory.harpweek.com
Fascinating text and imagery found in the pages of *Harper's Weekly* magazine.

African American Perspectives, 1818–1907 www.memory.loc.gov/ammem/aap/aaphome.html
This searchable collection is filled with links to Reconstruction topics and political speeches and manuscripts from the Federal Writers' Project interviews with ex-slaves in the 1930s.

Fiction and Film

W. E. B. Du Bois's *The Quest of the Silver Fleece* (1911) is a little-known novel by the sociologist-historian about the lives of sharecroppers during Reconstruction. Howard Fast's *Freedom Road* (1944) is a novel about the heroic but ultimately failed efforts of poor whites and blacks to unite for mutual benefit during the era. Ernest Gaines's *The Autobiography of Miss Jane Pittman* (1971), framed as an autobiography, is a gripping fictional account of a proud centenarian black woman who lived from the time of the Civil War to the era of civil rights. In *A Fool's Errand* (1879), as described in this chapter's "Recovering the Past" section, Albion Tourgée takes the viewpoint of a sympathetic white judge who helps the freedpeople in North Carolina during Reconstruction.

Margaret Walker's *Jubilee* (1966) is a black female novelist's epic version of the African American experience in the Civil War era, and Alice Randall's *The Wind Done Gone* (2001) is a parody of Margaret Mitchell's *Gone with the Wind* (1936); both follow black and white families from slavery to Reconstruction. Toni Morrison's *Beloved* (1988), an extraordinary novel set near Cincinnati in 1873 that includes flashbacks, is about the lasting traumas of slavery as black women especially seek to put their lives together and pursue their dreams of freedom. The film of the same name (1998), though slow moving, follows the time disconnections of the novel well with many moving scenes. *Birth of a Nation,* the classic 1913 film by D. W. Griffith that portrays the rise of the Ku Klux Klan as the defender of white supremacy and womanhood, is based on Thomas Dixon's *The Clansman* (1905) (also described in the "Recovering the Past" section). A quite different film portrayal is seen in Oscar Micheaux's *Within Our Gates* (1919), the first feature film by an African American, available from the Library of Congress's early American film collection.

Recommended Reading

www.ablongman.com/nash
The Companion Website has a list of recommended readings about the post–Civil War period.

The Realities of Rural America

CHAPTER OUTLINE

- Modernizing Agriculture
- The West
- Resolving the Native American Question
- The New South
- Farm Protest
- Conclusion: Farming in the Industrial Age

American Stories

Realizing Dreams: Life on the Great Plains

In 1873, Milton Leeper, his wife Hattie, and their baby Anna climbed into a wagon piled high with their possessions and set out to homestead in Boone County, Nebraska. Like others, the Leepers believed the opportunities offered by the western plains were vital to continued national health as well as individual well-being. Once on the claim, the Leepers dreamed confidently of their future. Wrote Hattie to her sister in Iowa, "I like our place the best of any around here." "When we get a fine house and 100 acres under cultivation," she added, "I wouldn't trade with any one." But Milton had broken in only 13 acres when disaster struck. Hordes of grasshoppers appeared, and the Leepers fled their claim and took refuge in the nearby town of Fremont.

There they stayed for two years. Milton worked first at a store, and then hired out to other farmers. Hattie sewed, kept a boarder, and cared for chickens and a milk cow. The family lived on the brink of poverty, but never gave up hope. "Times are hard and we have had bad luck," Hattie acknowledged, but "I am going to hold that claim ... there will [be] one gal that won't be out of a home." In 1876, the Leepers triumphantly returned to their claim with $27 to help them start over.

The grasshoppers were gone, there was enough rain, and preaching was only half a mile away. The Leepers, like others, began to prosper. Two more daughters were born. The sod house was "homely" on the outside, but plastered and cozy within. Hattie thought that the homesteaders lived "just as civilized as they would in Chicago."

Their luck did not last. Hattie died in childbirth along with her infant son. Heartbroken, Milton buried his wife and child and left the claim. The last frontier had momentarily defeated him, although he would try farming in at least four other locations before his death in 1905.

The same year that the Leepers established their Boone County homestead, another family tried their luck in a Danish settlement about 200 miles west of Omaha. Rasmus and Ane Ebbesen and their 8-year-old son, Peter, had arrived in the United States from Denmark in 1868, lured by the promise of an "abundance" of free land "for all willing to cultivate it." By 1870, they had made it as far west as Council Bluffs, Iowa. There they stopped to earn the capital they needed to begin farming. Rasmus dug ditches for the railroad, Ane worked as a cleaning woman in a local boardinghouse, and young Peter brought water to thirsty laborers digging other ditches.

Like the Leepers, the Ebbesens eagerly took up their homestead and began to cultivate the soil. Peter later recalled that the problems that the family had anticipated never materialized. Even

511

the rumors that the Sioux, "flying demons" in the settlers' eyes, were on the rampage proved false. The real obstacles facing the family were unexpected: rattlesnakes, prairie fires, grasshoppers—the latter just as devastating as they had been to the Leeper homestead. But unlike the Leepers, the Ebbesens stayed on the claim. Although the family "barely had enough" to eat, they survived the three years of grasshopper infestation.

In the following years, the Ebbesens thrived. Rasmus had almost all the original 80 acres under cultivation and purchased an additional 80 acres from the railroad. A succession of sod houses rose on the land and finally even a two-story frame house, paid for with money Peter earned teaching school. By their fifties, Rasmus and Ane could look with pride at their "luxurient and promising crop." But once more natural disaster struck, a "violent hailstorm ... which completely devastated the whole lot."

The Ebbesens were lucky, however. A banker offered to buy them out, for $1,000 under what the family calculated was the farm's "real worth." But it was enough for the purchase of a "modest" house in town. Later, there was even a "dwelling of two stories and nine rooms ... with adjacent park."

The stories of the Leepers and the Ebbesens, though different in their details and endings, hint at some of the problems confronting rural Americans in the last quarter of the nineteenth century. As a mature industrial economy transformed agriculture and shifted the balance of economic power permanently away from America's farmlands to the country's cities and factories, many farmers found it impossible to realize the traditional dream of rural independence and prosperity. Even bountiful harvests no longer guaranteed success. "We were told two years ago to go to work and raise a big crop; that was all we needed," said one farmer. "We went to work and plowed and planted; the rains fell, the sun shone, nature smiled, and we raised the big crop they told us to; and what came of it? Eight cent corn, ten cent oats, two cent beef and no price at all for butter and eggs—that's what came of it." Native Americans also discovered that changes threatened their values and dreams. As the Sioux leader Red Cloud told railroad surveyors in Wyoming, "We do not want you here. You are scaring away the buffalo."

This chapter explores several of this book's basic themes as it analyzes the agricultural transformation of the late nineteenth century. Highlighting the ways in which rural Americans—red, white, and black—joined the industrial world, it asks how diverse groups responded to new economic and social conditions. The rise of large-scale agriculture in the West, the exploitation of its natural resources, and the development of the Great Plains form a backdrop for the discussion of the impact of white settlement on western tribes and the assessment of how well native peoples were able to preserve their culture and traditions. In an analysis of the South, the efforts of whites to create a "New South" form a contrast to the underlying realities of race and cotton. Although the chapter shows that discrimination and economic peonage scarred the lives of most black southerners during this period, it also describes the rise of new black protest tactics and ideologies. Finally, the chapter highlights the ways in which agricultural problems of the late nineteenth century, which would continue to characterize much of agricultural life in the twentieth century, led American farmers to become reformers.

MODERNIZING AGRICULTURE

Between 1865 and 1900, the nation's farms more than doubled in number as Americans flocked west of the Mississippi. Farmers raised specialized crops with modern machinery and relied on railroads to speed them to market. Recognizing the new realities, one farmer explained agriculture was "a business."

While small family farms still typified American agriculture, vast mechanized operations devoted to one crop appeared, especially west of the Mississippi River. Bonanza wheat farms, established in the late 1870s on the northern plains, symbolized the trend to large-scale agriculture. Thousands of acres in size, these farms required large capital investments; corporations owned many of them. Like factories, they depended on machinery, hired hundreds of workers, and relied on efficient managers. Although bonanza farms were not typical, they dramatized the agricultural changes that were occurring everywhere on a smaller scale.

Despite their success in adapting farming to modern conditions, farmers were slipping from their dominant position in the workforce. In 1860, they represented almost 60 percent of the labor force; by 1900, less than 37 percent of employed Americans farmed. At the same time, farmers' contribution to the nation's wealth declined from one-third to one-quarter.

American Agriculture and the World

The expansion of American agriculture was tied to changing global patterns and demands. During the nineteenth century, the population of Europe exploded. While some Europeans still cultivated the land, increasing numbers abandoned farming for urban industrial work. In Britain, farmers, only 10 percent of the total workforce, could not produce nearly enough to feed the nation. Like other European countries, Great Britain imported substantial food supplies for its citizens. The growing demand prompted American farmers along with their counterparts in eastern Europe, Australia, and New Zealand to expand their operations for the European market.

In their attempts to improve crop yields and livestock, American farmers both benefited from and contributed to trends in agriculture elsewhere in the world. German scientists facilitated agricultural expansion after 1850 by developing better seeds, livestock, and chemical fertilizers. The land-grant university system in the United States, established during the Civil War, ensured research into and development of better strains of crops and animals and more effective farming methods. For their part, American farmers led the way in using farm machinery such as the horse-drawn harvester, showing farmers elsewhere in the world the way to raise bigger harvests.

A Vision of the Lackawanna Valley George Inness's *Lackawanna Valley*—with the reclining figure in the foreground, the train, and puffing smokestacks in the background—suggests that there need be no conflict between technology and agriculture. What other signs of technology besides the train can you see in this painting? *(Gift of Mrs. Huttleston Rogers, [1945.4.1] © Board of Trustees, National Gallery of Art, Washington)*

This integration into the wider world depended on improved transportation at home and abroad. Reliable, cheap transportation in the United States allowed farmers to specialize: wheat on the Great Plains, corn in the Midwest. Eastern farmers turned to vegetable, fruit, and dairy farming—or sold out. Cotton, tobacco, wheat, and rice dominated in the South, while grain, fruits, and vegetables prevailed in the Far West. The development of steamships and an ever-expanding European network of railroad systems ensured that Americans goods and products could move swiftly, efficiently, and cheaply across land and sea to distant markets.

As farmers specialized for national and international markets, their success depended increasingly on outside forces and demands. Bankers and investors, many of them European, provided the capital to improve transportation and expand operations; middlemen stored and sometimes sold produce; and railroads and steamships carried it to market. A prosperous economy at home and abroad put money into laborers' pockets for food purchases. But when several European countries banned American pork imports between 1879 and 1883, fearing trichinosis, American stock raisers suffered. As Russian, Argentinean, and Canadian farmers turned to wheat cultivation, increased competition in the world market affected the United States' chief cash crop. Moreover, the worldwide deflation of prices for crops such as wheat and corn affected all who raised these crops for the international market, including American farmers.

The Character of American Agriculture

Technological innovation played a major role in facilitating American agricultural expansion. Harvesters, binders, and other new machines, pulled by work animals, diminished much of the drudgery of farming life, making the production of crops easier, more efficient, and cheaper. Moreover, they allowed a farmer to cultivate far more land than possible with hand tools. But machinery was expensive, and many American farmers borrowed to buy it. In the decade of the 1880s, mortgage indebtedness grew two and a half times faster than agricultural wealth.

Only gradually did farmers realize the perils of their new situation. Productivity rose 40 percent between 1869 and 1899. But so large were the harvests for crops such as wheat that the domestic market could not absorb them. Foreign competition and deflation further affected steadily declining prices. In 1867, corn sold for 78 cents a bushel; by 1889, it had tumbled to 23 cents. Wheat similarly plummeted from about $2 a bushel in 1867 to only 70 cents a bushel in 1889. Cotton profits also spiraled downward, the value of a bale depreciating from $43 in 1866 to $30 in the 1890s.

Falling prices did not automatically hurt all farmers. Because the supply of money rose more slowly than productivity, all prices declined—by more than half between the end of the Civil War and 1900 (for a discussion of the money issue, see Chapter 19). Farmers were receiving less for their crops but also paying less for their purchases. But deflation may have encouraged overproduction. To make the same amount of money, many farmers believed they had to raise larger and larger crops. As they did, prices fell even lower. Furthermore, deflation increased the real value of debts. In 1888, it took 174 bushels of wheat to pay the interest on a $2,000 mortgage at 8 percent. By 1895, it took 320 bushels. Falling prices thus affected most negatively farmers in newly settled areas who borrowed heavily to finance their new operations.

THE WEST

In 1893, the young American historian Frederick Jackson Turner addressed historians gathered at Chicago's World's Fair. His message was startling. The age of the American frontier had ended, Turner declared, pointing to recent census data that suggested the disappearance of vacant land in the West. Although Turner overstated his case (for even in the twentieth century much of the West remained uninhabited), his analysis reflected rapid expansion into the trans-Mississippi West after the Civil War. Between 1870 and 1900, acreage devoted to farming tripled west of the Mississippi, while from 1880 to 1900, the western population grew at a faster rate than the nation as a whole.

The Frontier Thesis in National and Global Context

Turner considered the end of the frontier a milestone in the nation's history. The frontier had played a central role, he argued, in shaping American character and American institutions. Over the course of American history, the struggle to tame the wilderness had changed settlers from Europeans into Americans and created a rugged individualism that "promoted democracy." Turner's thesis, emphasizing the unique nature of the American experience and linking it to the frontier, won many supporters. His interpretation complemented long-held ideas about the exceptional nature of American society and character. It accorded with what many saw as a long struggle to conquer what Turner called the "wilderness."

But the American westward movement was less unusual than Turner suggested. The settlement of the trans-Mississippi West was part of a global pattern that redistributed European populations into new areas of the world. Paralleling their American counterparts, farmers, miners, and ranchers were claiming land in Argentina, Brazil, New Zealand, Australia, Canada, and South Africa. Like Americans, they argued that native occupants had failed to make the land productive, and they used their technological superiority to wrest the land from them. Around the world, many native peoples were facing domination by settler societies or retreating as far away from "civilization" as they could.

Turner's frontier scheme gave the place of honor to the frontier farmer who transformed and civilized the wilderness. Before the Civil War, however, real farmers avoided many parts of the West, especially the Great Plains, an area from 200 to 700 miles wide, extending from Canada to Texas. Much of this region, especially beyond the 98th meridian, had little rain. The absence of trees seemed to symbolize the plains' unsuitability for agriculture.

The Cattleman's West, 1860–1890

While the Great Plains initially discouraged farmers, its grasses provided the foundation for the cattle kingdom. Cattle raising dated back to Spanish mission

AUDIO

Cowboys and Cattle

days, but the commercial cattle frontier was one result of the Union's success in separating Texas from Confederate cattle markets. By war's end, millions of longhorns roamed the Texas range. The postwar burst of railroad construction allowed cattle to be turned into dollars. By the 1870s, cowboys were herding thousands of longhorns north to towns such as Abilene, Kansas, where they were loaded on trains for Chicago and Kansas City packinghouses.

Ranchers on the Great Plains bought some of the cattle and bred them with Hereford and Angus cows to create animals acclimatized to severe winters. In the late 1870s and early 1880s, huge ranches, many owned by eastern or European investors, arose from eastern Colorado to the Dakotas. These ventures paid handsomely since cattle grazed cheaply on public lands and then commanded good prices. Cowboys (a third of them Mexican and black) who herded the steers came cheap, earning paltry wages of $25 to $40 a month.

By the mid-1880s, the first phase of the cattle frontier was ending as farmers moved onto the Plains, buying and fencing public lands once used for grazing. But the arrival of farmers was only one factor in transforming the cattle frontier.

Ranchers overstocked herds in the mid-1880s and malnourished cattle weakened. Fierce blizzards followed the very hot summer of 1886. By spring, 90 percent of the cattle were dead. Frantic owners dumped their remaining animals on the market, getting $8 or even less per head.

Ranchers who survived the disaster adopted new techniques. Experimenting with new breeds, they began to fence in their herds and feed them grain during the winter. Consumers wanted tender beef rather than tough cuts from free-range animals, and these new methods satisfied the market. Ranching, like farming, was becoming a modern business.

Farmers on the Great Plains, 1865–1890s

Views of the agricultural possibilities of the Great Plains brightened after the Civil War, with railroads playing a key role in publicizing the region's potential. Now that rail lines crossed the continent, they needed customers, settlers, and freight to make a profit. Along with town boosters and land speculators, also hoping to capitalize on their investments, railroads joined in promotional campaigns. "This is the sole remaining section of paradise in the western world," promised one newspaper. Such propaganda reached beyond the United States to Scandinavians, Germans, and others. Dismissing the fear that the plains lacked adequate rainfall, promotional material assured readers that "All that is needed is to plow, plant, and attend to the crops properly; the rains are abundant." Above-average rainfall in the 1880s strengthened the case.

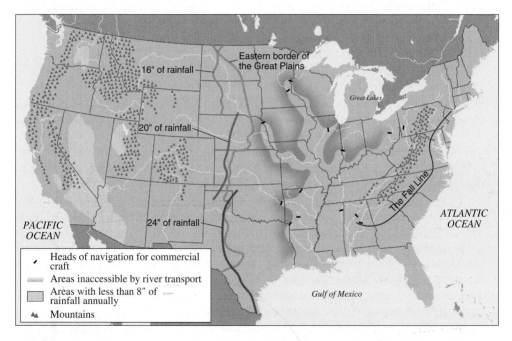

THE NATURAL ENVIRONMENT OF THE WEST Study the patterns of rainfall and the natural features of the West, including rivers and mountain ranges. What do these patterns suggest about native vegetation and the prospects for farming? What is revealed about the role of water and irrigation in the West? What difficulties facing the settlers are revealed?

Domestic Work in the West This photograph shows some of the hard physical labor involved in homesteading. How many steps were involved in doing the family laundry? The clothing of these women, probably settlers in North Dakota, identifies them as immigrants. Their presence reminds us that the West was the home of diverse peoples including Asians, European newcomers, Native Americans, black migrants, and Hispanics whose families had lived in the West for generations. *(The Fred Hulstrand History in Pictures Collection, NDSU, Fargo, ND)*

In the first boom period of settlement from 1879 to the early 1890s, tens of thousands of eager families began farming the Great Plains. The majority came from Illinois, Iowa, and Missouri. Like the Ebbesens, many others were immigrants. The largest numbers came from Germany, the British Isles, and Canada, but Scandinavians, Czechs, and Poles also arrived. Unlike many immigrating to American cities, they came in family groups and intended to stay.

Some claimed land under the Homestead Act, which granted 160 acres to any family head or adult who lived on the claim for five years or paid $1.25 an acre after six months of residence. Because homestead land was frequently less desirable, however, most settlers bought land from railroads or land companies. Start-up costs were thus higher than the Homestead Act would suggest. Although western land was cheap compared with eastern farmland, a farmer was lucky to buy a good quarter section for under $500. Machinery added another $700. Although some thought leasing rather than buying land made economic sense, many rented only because they lacked capital. In 1880, some 20 percent of the Plains farmers were tenants, and this percentage rose over time.

Late-nineteenth-century industrial innovations helped settlers overcome some natural obstacles. The shortage of timber for fencing and housing had encouraged early emigrants to go elsewhere. But in the 1870s, Joseph Glidden developed barbed wire as a cheap alternative to timber fencing. Other innovations minimized other challenges. Twine binders, which speeded up grain harvesting, reduced the threat of losing crops to the unpredictable weather. And mail-order steel windmills for pumping water from deep underground wells relieved some of the water shortages by the 1890s.

Industrial innovations, however, could not resolve all of the problems confronting settlers. Wrote one Kansas homesteader:

> I tell you Auntie no one can depend on farming for a living in this country. Henry is very industrious and this year had in over thirty acres of small grain, 8 acres of corn and about an acre of potatoes. We have sold our small grain ... and it come to $100; now deduct $27.00 for cutting, $16.00 for threshing, $19.00 for hired help ... and where is your profit. I sometimes think this a God forsaken country, the [grass]hopper hurt our corn and we have 1/2 a crop and utterly destroyed our garden. If one wants trials, let them come to Kansas.

This letter highlights the uncertainties of frontier life: high costs, market fluctuations, pests, and natural disasters. Since many Plains pioneers took up homesteads with only a few dollars in their pockets, survival often depended on how well families managed during the crucial first years.

The first boom on the Great Plains fizzled in the late 1880s and early 1890s. Falling prices cut profits; one wheat farmer reported in 1890 earnings of $41.48 and expenses of $56.00. Then a devastating drought replaced the unusual rainfall that had lured farmers west. The destitute survived on boiled weeds, a few potatoes, and a little bread and butter. Many lost their farms to creditors. Some stayed as tenants. Homesteaders like the Leepers gave up. By 1900, two-thirds of homestead farms had failed. In western Kansas, the population fell by half between 1888 and 1892, and eastward-bound wagons bore a sad epitaph: "In God We Trusted: In Kansas We Busted."

Both ranching and agriculture had a long-term impact on the region's environment. Ranchers disrupted a complex natural balance when they killed off antelope, elk, wolves, and other wildlife. As cattle on overstocked ranges devoured perennial grasses, less nutritious annual grasses sprang up and, in turn, sometimes disappeared altogether. Lands once a lush home for large herds of cattle turned into parched deserts of sagebrush, weeds, and dust. Farmers who bought steel windmills to pump water from deep underground depleted the water table level. When they removed sod to build their houses and plowed, they removed the earth's protective covering. Heavy winds, common on the prairies, could lift topsoil and carry it miles away. Deep plowing, essential for dry farming techniques introduced after the drought of the 1880s, worsened the situation. The 1930s dust bowl was the eventual outcome of such human interventions.

Cornucopia on the Pacific

Although Americans rushed West when gold was discovered in California, one father advised his son, "Plant your lands; these be your best gold fields." He was right; completion of a national railroad system made farming California's greatest asset. But California farming resembled neither the traditional picture of rural life nor the dreams of homesteaders.

Little of California's land was homesteaded or developed as family farms. When California entered the Union, speculators acquired much of the land held by Mexican ranchers and sold it at prices beyond the reach of many small farmers. Those small farmers and ranchers who existed found it hard to compete with large, mechanized operators using cheap migrant laborers, usually Mexican or Chinese. One San Joaquin Valley wheat farm was so vast that workers started plowing in the morning at one end of the 17-mile field, ate lunch at its halfway point, and camped at its end that night. By 1900, farms of 1,000 acres or more made up two-thirds of the state's farmland.

The value of much of California's agricultural land, especially the southern half of the Central Valley, depended on water. By the 1870s, water, land, and railroad companies, using the labor and expertise of Chinese workers, were building dams, headgates, and canals—at high costs that they passed on to buyers eager to acquire hitherto barren land and water rights. By 1890, over a quarter of California's farms were irrigated. The irrigation ditches symbolized the importance of both technology and the managerial attitude toward the land characterizing late-nineteenth-century agriculture.

Although grain was initially California's most valuable crop, it faced stiff competition from farmers on the Plains and abroad. Some argued that land capable of raising luscious fruits "in a climate surpassing that of Italy, is too valuable for the cultivation of simple cereals." But high railroad rates and lack of refrigeration limited the volume of fresh produce sent to market. As railroad managers in the 1880s realized the potential profit that California's produce represented, they cut rates and introduced refrigerated cars. Fruit and vegetable production rose, benefiting from the agricultural expertise of Chinese laborers, tenant farmers, and Chinese entrepreneurs. So important were their contributions that some have argued that Chinese know-how was mainly responsible for the shift to produce farming. Before long, California fruit was sold as far away as London.

The Mining West

Mining hastened rapid western growth and development. The first and best-known mining rush occurred in 1848 when gold was discovered in California, but others followed as precious metals—silver, iron, copper, coal, lead, zinc, and tin—lured thousands west to Colorado, Montana, Idaho, and Nevada as well as to states such as Minnesota. Mining discoveries were transformative events, for they attracted people and businesses west, often to places far away from agricultural settlements. Hastily built mining communities might be eyesores, but they had bustling urban characters. If and when the strike was over, however, residents abandoned the mining camps and towns as fast as they had rushed into them. The pattern of boom and bust characterized much of mining life.

The reality of late-nineteenth-century mining was nothing like the popular stereotype of the independent miner panning for gold. Retrieving minerals from rock was difficult, expensive, and dangerous, requiring a large labor force, industrial tools, and railroad links. Miners worked way below the earth's surface in poorly ventilated tunnels, with no means for removing human or animal waste. Temperatures could reach as high as 120 degrees. Accidents were part of the job that involved blasting equipment and industrial machinery. In 1884, a Montana miner drilled into an unexploded dynamite charge and lost his eyes and ear. He received no compensation, for the court decided that the accident "was the result of an unforeseen and unavoidable accident incident to the risk of mining." As the next chapter will show, in time, western miners became one of the most radical groups of industrial workers.

Exploiting Natural Resources

Mining was a big business with high costs and a basic dynamic that encouraged rapid and thorough exploitation of the earth's resources. The destruction of forests accompanied large-scale mining and the railroads that provided the links to markets. Both railroads and mining depended on wood—railroads for wooden ties, mines for shaft timber and ore reduction. In California, the California State Board of Agriculture estimated in the late 1860s that one-third of the state's forests had already disappeared.

Resources and Conflict in the West

When lumber companies cut down timber, they affected the flow of streams and destroyed the habitat supporting birds and animals. Like the activities of farmers and cattle owners, the companies stripping the earth of its forest cover were also contributing to soil erosion. The idea that the federal public lands ought to be rapidly developed supported such exploitation of natural resources. Often, in return for royalties, the government leased parts of the public domain to companies that hoped to extract valuable minerals, not to own the land permanently. In other cases, companies bought land, but not always legally. In 1878, Congress passed the Timber and Stone Act, which initially applied to Nevada, Oregon, Washington, and California. This legislation allowed the sale of 160-acre parcels of the public domain that were "unfit for cultivation" and "valuable chiefly for timber." Timber companies were quick to see the possibilities in the new law. They hired men willing to register for claims and then to turn them over to timber interests. By the end of the century, more than 3.5 million acres of the public domain had been acquired under the legislation, and most of it was in corporate hands.

The rapacious and rapid exploitation of resources combined with the increasing pace of industrialization made some Americans uneasy. Many believed that forests played a part in causing rainfall and that their destruction would have an adverse impact on the climate. Others, like John Muir, lamented the destruction of the country's great natural beauty. In 1868, Muir came upon the Great Valley of California, "all one sheet of plant gold, hazy and vanishing in the distance ... one smooth, continuous bed of honey-bloom." He soon realized, however, that a "wild, restless agriculture" and "flocks of hoofed locusts, sweeping over the ground like a fire" would destroy this vision of loveliness. Muir became a preservation champion. He played a part in the creation of Yosemite National Park in 1890, participated in a successful effort to allow President Benjamin Harrison to classify certain parts of the public domain as forest reserves (the Forest Reserve Act of 1891), and in 1892, established the Sierra Club. At the same time, conservation ideas were also emerging. Gifford Pinchot, a leading advocate of these ideas, was less interested in the preservation of the nation's wilderness areas than in careful management of its natural resources. "Conservation," he explained, "means the wise use of the earth and its resources for the lasting good of man." Both perspectives, however, were more popular in the East than in the West, where the seeming abundance of natural resources and the profit motive diminished support.

RESOLVING THE NATIVE AMERICAN QUESTION

Black Elk, an Oglala Sioux, listened to a story his father had heard from his father.

> A long time ago ... there was once a Lakota [Sioux] holy man, called Drinks Water, who dreamed what was to be; and this was long before the coming of the Wasichus [white men]. He dreamed ... that a strange race had woven a spider's web all around the Lakotas. And he said: "When this happens, you shall live in square gray houses, in a barren land, and beside those square gray houses you shall starve."

Red Cloud (Maqpeya-luta), Chief of the Oglala Sioux

So great was the wise man's sorrow that he died soon after his strange dream. But Black Elk lived to see it come true.

As farmers settled the west and became entangled in a national economy, they clashed with the Indians who lived on the land. In California, disease and violence killed 90 percent of the Native Americans in the 30 years following the gold rush. Elsewhere, the struggle among Native Americans, white settlers, the U.S. Army, government officials, and reformers was prolonged and bitter. Some tribes moved onto government reservations with little protest. But most—including the Nez Percé in the Northwest, the Apache in the Southwest, and the Plains Indians—resisted stubbornly.

Background to Hostilities

The lives of most Plains Indians revolved around the buffalo. As migration to California and Oregon increased in the 1840s and 1850s, tribal life and animal migration patterns were disrupted. Initially, the federal government tried to persuade the tribes to stay away from white wagon trains and settlements. They did not have much success.

During the Civil War, some of the eastern tribes that had relocated across the Mississippi sided with the Confederacy; others with the Union. But after the war all were "treated as traitors." The federal government callously nullified pledges and treaties, leaving Indians defenseless against incursions. As settlers pushed into Kansas, tribes there were shunted into Oklahoma.

The White Perspective

When the Civil War ended, red and white men on the Plains were already at war. In 1864, the Colorado militia massacred a band of friendly Cheyenne at Sand

How Others See Us

Red Cloud, Speech to the U.S. Secretary of the Interior, 1870

Although winning what was called the Red Cloud War of 1866–1867, the Lakota, Cheyenne, and other Plains Indians lost much of their advantage in the Fort Laramie Treaty of 1868. Torn between continuing resistance against the invading Americans and agreeing to move onto reservations, Red Cloud nevertheless continued to remind Americans of their broken treaties and promises. In 1870, he and other Sioux chiefs went to Washington, D.C., to meet with President Grant, and then to New York. Excerpts from his speech to Secretary of the Interior Jacob Cox, who was in charge of Indian affairs, follow.

The Great Father says he is good and kind to us. I don't think so. ... I come here to tell my Great Father what I do not like in my country. You are all close to my Great Father, and are a great many chiefs. The men the Great Father sends to us have no sense—no heart. What has been done in my country I did not want, did not ask for it; white people going through my country. Father, have you, or any of your friends here, got children? Do you want to raise them? Look at me; I come here with all these young men. All of them have children and want to raise them. The white children have surrounded me and have left me nothing but an island. When we first had this land we were strong, now are melting like snow on the hillside, while you are grown like spring grass. Now I have come a long distance to my Great Father's house—see if I have left any blood in his land when I go. When the white man comes in my country he leaves a trail of blood behind him. Tell the Great Father to move Fort Fetterman away and we will have no more trouble. I have two mountains in that country—the Black Hills and the Big Horn Mountain. I want the Great Father to make no roads through them. I have told these things three times; now I have come here to tell them the fourth time. ...

- *What complaints and charges against the United States does Red Cloud make? Are they fair?*
- *What contrasts does he make between his people and the Americans?*
- *Red Cloud uses the phrase "my country" to refer to both native lands and the United States. He also variously says "my Great Father" and "the Great Father." Why the confusion, the double usage? Do you think it was intentional? Why would he do that?*

Source: First Annual Report of the Board of Indian Commissioners for 1870 (Washington, D.C.: U.S. Government. Printing Office, 1871), 41.

Creek. Cheyenne, Sioux, and Arapaho soon responded in kind. The Plains wars had begun.

Although not all whites condoned this butchery, the congressional commission authorized to make peace viewed Native Americans' future narrowly. The commissioners, including the commander of the army in the West, Civil War hero William T. Sherman, accepted as fact that the West belonged to an "industrious, thrifty, and enlightened population" of whites. Native Americans, the commission believed, must relocate to western South Dakota or Oklahoma to learn white ways. Annuities, food, and clothes would ease their transition to "civilized" life.

DOCUMENT

Red Cloud's Speech (1866)

RECOVERING THE PAST

Weekly and monthly magazines constitute a rich primary source for the historian, offering a vivid picture of the issues of the day and useful insights into popular tastes and values. With advances in the publishing industry and an increasingly literate population, the number of these journals soared in the years following the Civil War. In 1865, only 700 periodicals were published. Twenty years later, there were 3,300. As the *National Magazine* grumbled, "Magazines, magazines, magazines! The newsstands are already groaning under the heavy load, and there are still more coming."

Some of these magazines were aimed at the mass market. *Frank Leslie's Illustrated Newspaper,* established in 1855, was one of the most successful. At its height, circulation reached 100,000. Making skillful use of pictures (sometimes as large as two by three feet and folded into the magazine), the weekly covered important news of the day as well as music, drama, sports, and books. Although Leslie relied more heavily on graphics and sensationalism than do modern news weeklies, his publication was a forerunner of *Newsweek* and *Time.*

Another kind of weekly magazine was aimed primarily at middle- and upper-class readers. Editors such as Edwin Lawrence Godkin of *The Nation,* with a circulation of about 30,000, hoped to influence those in positions of authority and power by providing a forum for the discussion of reform issues. In contrast, *Scribner's* revealed a more conservative, middle-of-the-road point of view. Both magazines, however, exuded a confident, progressive tone characteristic of middle-class Americans.

Harper's Weekly was one of the most important magazines designed primarily for middle- and upper-class readers. Established in 1857, this publication continued in print until 1916. The success of *Harper's Weekly,* which called itself a "family newspaper," rested on a combination of its moderate point of view and an exciting use of illustrations and cartoons touching on contemporary events. The popular cartoons of Thomas Nast appeared in this magazine. In large part because of the use of graphics, in 1872 the circulation of *Harper's Weekly* reached a peak of 160,000.

Illustrated here is a page from the January 16, 1869, issue of *Harper's Weekly.* The layout immediately suggests the importance of graphics. Most of the page is taken up with the three pictures. The top and bottom pictures are wood engravings based on drawings by Theodore R. Davis, one of *Harper's* best-known illustrator-reporters. The center picture was derived from a photograph. Davis's story on this page concerns a victory of General George Custer in the war against the Cheyenne tribe that the U.S. Army was waging that winter. Davis had been a correspondent in the West covering Custer's actions in 1867. But when news of Custer's victory arrived, Davis was back in New York. He thus drew on his imagination for the top and bottom wood engravings reproduced on the page; the center photograph was not taken during the Custer campaign.

What kind of characterization of Native Americans does Davis give in the picture at the top of the page? What view of American soldiers does he suggest? At the bottom of the page, you can see soldiers slaughtering "worthless" horses while Cheyenne teepees burn in the background. Would the average viewer have any sympathy for the plight of the Cheyenne by looking at this picture? This "victory," in fact, involved the slaughter not only of horses but also of all males over age eight.

REFLECTING ON THE PAST   The editors' decision to insert a picture that had nothing to do with the incident being reported was obviously significant. As you can see, the subject in the center illustration is a white hunter who had been killed and scalped by Indians. What kind of special relationship were the editors suggesting by placing the picture of one dead white hunter in the center of a

Harper's Weekly delivered powerful messages about the Native Americans in its choice of illustrations. *(Harper's Weekly)*

page that primarily covered a specific conflict between the Indians and the U.S. Army? How might the reader respond to the group of pictures as a whole? How do you? How does the text contribute to the overall view of the Indian–white relationship that the pictures suggest? By considering the choice of graphics and text, you can begin to discover how magazines provide insight, not only into the events of the day, but also into how the values and perspectives of nineteenth-century men and women were shaped.

At two major conferences in 1867 and 1868, chiefs listened to these drastic proposals spelling the end of traditional native life. Some agreed; others, like a Kiowa chief, insisted, "I don't want to settle. I love to roam over the prairies." In any case, the agreements were not binding because no chief had authority to speak for his tribe. For its part, the U.S. Senate dragged its feet in approving the treaties. Supplies promised to Indians who settled in the arid reserved areas failed to materialize, and wildlife proved too sparse to support them. These Indians soon drifted back to their former hunting grounds.

Sherman warned, "All who cling to their old hunting ground are hostile and will remain so till killed off." When persuasion failed, the U.S. Army went to war. "The more we can kill this year," Sherman remarked, "the less will have to be killed the next war." In 1867, he ordered General Philip Sheridan to deal with the tribes. Sheridan introduced winter campaigning, aimed at seeking out Indians who divided into small groups during the winter and exterminating them.

Completion of the transcontinental railroad in 1869 added yet another pressure for "solving" the Indian question. Transcontinental railroads wanted rights-of-way through tribal lands and needed white settlers to make their operations profitable. Few whites considered Native Americans had any right to lands they wanted.

In his 1872 annual report, the commissioner for Indian affairs, Francis Amasa Walker, addressed two fundamental questions: how to prevent Indians from blocking white migration to the Great Plains, and what to do with them over the long run. Walker suggested buying off the "savages" with promises of food and gifts, luring them onto reservations, and there imposing a "rigid reformatory discipline," necessary because Indians were "unused to manual labor." Though Walker wanted to save the Indians from destruction, he offered only one grim choice: "yield or perish."

The Tribal View

Native Americans defied such attacks on their ancient way of life. Black Elk remembered that in 1863, when he was only three, his father had his leg broken in a fierce battle with white men. "When I was older," he recalled,

> I learned what the fighting was about. ... Up on the Madison Fork the Wasichus had found much of the yellow metal that they worship and that makes them crazy, and they wanted to have a road up through our country ... but my people did not want the road. It would scare the bison and make them go away, and also it would let the other Wasichus come in like a river. They told us that they wanted only to use a little land, as much as a wagon would take between the wheels; but our people knew better.

Black Elk's father and many others soon realized fighting was their only recourse. "There was no other way to keep our country."

Broken promises fueled Indian resistance. In 1875, the government allowed gold prospectors into the Black Hills, one of the Indians' sacred places and part of the Sioux reservation. Chiefs such as Sitting Bull led the angry Sioux on the warpath. At the Battle of Little Big Horn in 1876, they vanquished the army's most famous Indian fighter, George Custer. But bravery and skill could not permanently withstand the well-supplied, well-armed, and determined U.S. Army.

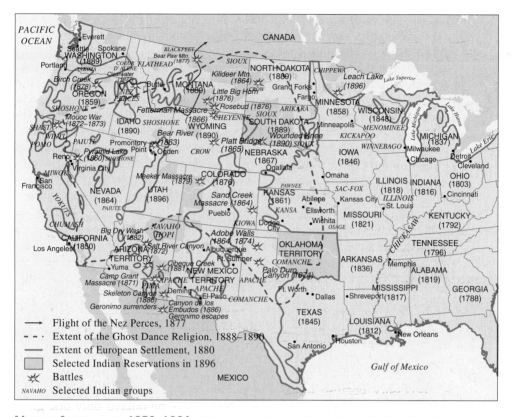

NATIVE AMERICANS, 1850–1896 This map reveals the widespread appeal of the Ghost Dance movement as well as the result of efforts to force Native Americans onto reservations.

The wholesale destruction of the buffalo that were central to Indian life contributed significantly to white victory. Plains Indians could be wasteful of buffalo when the animals were abundant, but white miners and hunters wiped out the herds. Sportsmen shot the beasts from trains. Railroad crews ate the meat. Ranchers' cattle competed for grass. And demand for buffalo bones for fertilizer and hides for robes and shoes encouraged decimation. The slaughter of 13 million animals by 1883 appears disgraceful today. Certainly, the Indians considered white men demented. "They just killed and killed because they like to do that," said one, whereas when "we hunted the bison ... [we] killed only what we needed." But the destruction pleased whites because it helped control the Indians.

The Dawes Act, 1887

Changing federal policy was aimed at ending Indian power and culture. In 1871, Congress stopped the practice, in effect since the 1790s, of treating the tribes as sovereign nations. Other measures supplemented this attempt to undermine tribal integrity and leaders. Federal authorities extended government jurisdiction to reservations and warned tribes not to gather for religious ceremonies.

The Dawes Severalty Act of 1887 pulled together the strands of federal Indian policy and set its course for the rest of the century. Believing that tribal bonds kept Indians in savagery, reformers intended to destroy them. Rather than allotting reservation lands to tribal groups, the act allowed the president to distribute these lands to individuals. The lure of private property, the framers of the bill reasoned, would undermine communal norms and encourage Indians to settle as farmers. Those who accepted allotments would become citizens and presumably shed their tribal identity. But the support of speculators for the legislation suggested another force was at work. Even if each Indian family head claimed a typical share of 160 acres, millions of "surplus" acres would remain for sale to whites. Within 20 years of the Dawes Act, Native Americans lost 60 percent of their lands. The federal government held the profits from land sales "in trust" for the "civilizing" mission.

Act of Congress, the General Allotment Act, Dawes Act (1887)

The Ghost Dance: An Indian Renewal Ritual

Sioux Ghost Dance

By the 1890s, their grim plight prepared many Native Americans for the message of Paiute prophet Wovoka. Predicting the destruction of the white race through natural disasters, Wovoka promised that Indians who performed the Ghost Dance would survive and gain new strength as their ancestors and wild game returned to life. Wovoka's ideas spread rapidly. Believers expressed their hope for change through new rituals of ghost dancing, hypnosis, and meditation.

Sioux Encampment (early 1890s)

American settlers were uneasy even though the prophet did not encourage Native Americans to harm whites. Indian agents tried to prevent ghost dances and filed hysterical reports. One agent determined that the Sioux medicine man Sitting Bull, a strenuous opponent of American expansion, was a leading troublemaker and decided to arrest him. In the confusion, Indian police killed Sitting Bull. Bands of Sioux fled the reservation with the army in swift pursuit. In late December 1890, the army caught up with them at Wounded Knee Creek. Although the Sioux had raised a flag of truce and started turning over weapons, a scuffle led to a bloody massacre. Using the most up-to-date machine guns and Hotchkiss cannons, the army killed more than 200 men, women, and children.

With such measures, white Americans defeated the western tribes. Once proud, independent, and strong, Native Americans suffered dependency, poverty, and cultural disorganization on reservations, in Indian schools, or urban slums.

THE NEW SOUTH

The trans-Mississippi West was transformed as native peoples were subdued, the Great Plains settled, and commercial agriculture helped knit the region into the larger world. Mining camps turned into industrial centers. Western cities grew at a fast pace; by 1900, nearly 40 percent of westerners lived in cities. The large number of itinerant workers who worked in mines, forests, and fields provided a flexible workforce that supported economic growth.

In contrast to this pattern, the southern economy sputtered. Of all the nation's agricultural regions, the South was the poorest. The agricultural labor force lacked efficiency, mobility, and capital for needed improvements. And while some southerners dreamed of making the agricultural South rival the industrial North, the region remained dependent on the North. Southern industrial workers were poorly paid, caught in dead-end jobs with little hope of advancement.

Postwar Southerners Face the Future

After the painful war and Reconstruction, compelling arguments for regional self-sufficiency rang out. Those wanting a "New South" argued that southern back-wardness did not stem from the war, as so many southerners wished to believe, but from southern conditions, especially the cotton-based economy. Defeat only made clearer the reality that power and wealth came from factories, machines, and cities, not cotton.

In hundreds of speeches, editorials, pamphlets, articles, and books, New South spokesmen tried to persuade fellow southerners to replace genteel prewar ideals with the ethic of hard work. Because the South was short of capital, New South advocates held out attractive investment possibilities to northern bankers and manufacturers. Several southern state governments offered tax exemptions and the cheap labor of leased convicts. Texas and Florida awarded the railroads land grants, and cities including Atlanta and Louisville mounted huge industrial exhibitions. Middle-class southerners increasingly accepted new entrepreneurial values. The most dramatic example of commitment to the New South vision may have come in 1886 when southern railroad companies, in a crash effort, relaid tracks and adjusted rolling stock to fit "standard" northern gauges.

During the late nineteenth century, northern money flowed south. In the 1880s, northerners increased investments in the cotton industry sevenfold and financed an expansion of southern railroads. Northern capital fueled southern urban expansion. The percentage of southerners living in cities rose from 7 percent in 1860 to 15 percent in 1900 (as compared to national averages of 20 and 40 percent).

Birmingham, Alabama, symbolized the New South. In 1870 it was a cornfield. The next year, two northern real estate speculators arrived, attracted by rich iron deposits. Despite cholera and the depression of the 1870s, Birmingham rapidly became the center of the southern iron and steel industry. By 1890, a total of 38,414 people lived there. Coke ovens, blast furnaces, rolling mills, iron foundries, and machine shops belched smoke. Mills and factories poured out millions of dollars of finished goods, and eight railroad lines carried them away.

Other southern cities flourished, too. Memphis prospered from its lumber industry and the manufacturing of cottonseed products, while Richmond became the country's tobacco capital even as its flour mills and iron and steel foundries continued to produce wealth. Augusta, Georgia, led the emerging textile industry of Georgia, the Carolinas, and Alabama.

The Other Side of Progress

New South enthusiasts, a small group of merchants, industrialists, and planters, bragged about their iron and textile industries and paraded statistics to prove the success of modernization. But progress was slow, and older values persisted. Even New South spokesmen romanticized the recent past, impeding full acceptance of a new economic order. Despite modernization, southern schools lagged far behind the North's.

Although new industries and signs of progress abounded, two of the new industries depended on tobacco and cotton, crops long at the center of rural life. As they had before the war, commerce and government work drove urban growth. The South's economic achievements, though not insignificant, did not improve its position in relation to the North. While southern industry grew in absolute terms, it declined in relative terms.

Moreover, the South failed to reap many of industrialization's possible benefits. The South remained an economic vassal of the North. Southern businessmen grew in number, but except for the American Tobacco Company, no great southern corporations arose. Instead, southerners worked for northern corporations, which absorbed southern businesses or dominated them financially. Profits and critical decision-making power flowed north. In many cases, southern mills and factories were allowed to handle only the early stages of processing. Northern factories finished the goods.

Individual workers in the new industries may have preferred factory life to sharecropping, but the rewards were meager. The presence of thousands of women and children in factories highlighted their husbands' and fathers' inability to earn a "family wage." As usual, women and children earned less than men. Justifying these policies, one Augusta factory president explained that child labor was "a matter of charity with us; some of them would starve if they were not given employment. ... The work we give children is very light." Actually, many children at his factory performed adults' work for children's pay.

In general, workers earned less and toiled longer in the South than elsewhere. Per capita income was the same in 1900 as in 1860—and half the national average. In North Carolina in the 1890s, workers averaged 50 cents a day, with a 70-hour week. Black workers, who made up 6 percent of the southern manufacturing force in 1890 (but were excluded from textile mills), usually had the worst jobs and the lowest wages.

Cotton Still King

Although New South advocates envisioned the South's transformation from a rural to an industrial society, they always recognized the need for agricultural change. "It's time for an agricultural revolution," proclaimed Henry Grady, the New South's most vocal spokesman. Overdependence on "King Cotton" hobbled southern agriculture by making farmers the victims of faraway market forces and an oppressive credit system. Subdivide old cotton plantations into small diversified farms, Grady urged. Raising choice produce for urban markets could result in "simply wonderful profits."

A new agricultural South with new class and economic arrangements did emerge, but not the one Grady envisioned. Despite the breakup of some plantations, large landowners were resourceful in keeping their property and dealing

with postwar conditions, as Chapter 16 showed. As they adopted new agricultural arrangements, former slaves sank into peonage.

White farmers on small and medium-size holdings fared only slightly better
than black tenants and sharecroppers. Immediately after the war, high cotton
prices tempted them to raise as much cotton as they could. Then prices began a
disastrous decline, from 11 cents a pound in 1875 to less than 5 cents in 1894. Yeoman farmers became entangled in debt. Each year, farmers bought supplies on
credit from merchants so they could plant the next year's crop and support their
families until harvest. In return, merchants demanded their exclusive business
and acquired a lien (claim) on their crops. But when farmers sold their crops at declining prices, they usually discovered that they had not earned enough to settle
with the merchant, who had charged dearly for store goods and whose annual interest rates might exceed 100 percent. Each year, thousands of farmers fell farther
behind. By 1900, over half the South's white farmers and three-quarters of its
black farmers were tenants. Tenancy increased all over rural America, but
nowhere faster than in the Deep South.

These patterns had baneful results for individual southerners and for the
South as a whole. Caught in a cycle of debt and poverty, few farmers could think
of improving techniques or diversifying crops. Desperate to pay debts, they concentrated on cotton despite falling prices. Landowners pressured tenants to raise
a market crop. Far from diversifying, farmers increasingly limited their crops. By
1880, the South was not growing enough food to feed its people adequately. Poor
nutrition contributed to chronic bad health.

The Nadir of Black Life

Grady and other New South advocates expected that their region could deal with
the race issue without the interference of any "outside power." He had few regrets
over the end of slavery, which he thought had contributed to southern economic
backwardness. Realizing that black labor would be crucial to the transformation
he sought, he advocated racial cooperation. But racial cooperation did not mean
equality. Grady assumed that blacks were inferior and therefore supported informal segregation.

By the time of Grady's death in 1889, a much harsher perspective on southern
race relations was appearing. Congressional leaders' decision in 1890 to shelve a
proposed act protecting black civil rights and the defeat of a bill giving federal assistance for educational institutions rendered black Americans vulnerable. The
traditional sponsor of freed people's rights, the Republican party, left blacks to
fend for themselves. The courts also abandoned them: in 1878, the Supreme Court
ruled unconstitutional a Louisiana statute banning discrimination in transportation. In 1882, the Court voided the Ku Klux Klan Act of 1871, finding that the civil
rights protections of the Fourteenth Amendment applied to states, not to individuals. In 1883, provisions of the Civil Rights Act of 1875 that ensured for blacks
equal rights in public places were similarly voided.

Rather than opposing these actions, northerners increasingly promoted negative stereotypes of blacks as lazy, ignorant, and childlike. Clearly blacks could

Lynching In 1896, an African American named William Bigger-staff was hanged for what was labeled the murder of a white man. The picture cannot reveal the innocence or guilt of the accused. Lynching and violence aimed at blacks became common in the late nineteenth century. What does the presence of the people in the background suggest about lynchings? *(Montana Historical Society, Helena, MT)*

hardly enjoy the same rights and freedoms as whites; they needed the paternal protection of the superior white race. Such stereotypes filled magazines and newspapers and were popularized in advertisements, cartoons, and theater.

The *Atlanta Monthly* in 1890 doubted that this "lowly variety of man" could ever be brought up to the intellectual and moral standards of whites. Other magazines opposed black suffrage as wasted on people too "ignorant, weak, lazy and incompetent" to make good use of it. *Forum* magazine suggested that "American Negroes" had "too much liberty." Only lynching and burning would deter "barbarous" rapists and other "sadly degenerated" Negroes corrupted since the Civil War by independence and too much education. Encouraged by northern public opinion, and with the blessing of Congress and the Supreme Court, southern whites sought to make blacks permanently second-class citizens.

In the political sphere, white southerners amended state constitutions to disfranchise black voters. By various legal devices—the poll tax, literacy tests, "good character" and "understanding" clauses administered by white voter registrars, and all-white primary elections—blacks lost the right to vote. The most ingenious method was the "grandfather clause," which specified that only citizens whose grandfathers were registered to vote on January 1, 1867, could cast ballots. This virtually excluded blacks. Although the Supreme Court outlawed such blatantly discriminatory laws, other constitutional changes, beginning in Mississippi in 1890 and spreading to all 11 former Confederate states by 1910, effectively eliminated the black vote.

Opinion of the Supreme Court for *Plessy v. Ferguson* (1896)

In a second tactic in the 1890s, southern state and local laws legalized segregation in public facilities. Beginning with railroads and schools, "Jim Crow" laws soon covered libraries, hotels, hospitals, prisons, theaters, parks, cemeteries, toilets, sidewalks, drinking fountains—nearly every place where blacks and whites might mingle. The Supreme Court upheld these laws in 1896 in *Plessy v. Ferguson,* ruling that "separate but equal" facilities did not violate the Fourteenth Amendment's equal protection clause. The decision opened the way for as many forms of legal segregation as southern lawmakers could devise.

Political and social discrimination made it easier to keep blacks permanently confined to agricultural and unskilled labor and dependent on whites. In 1900, nearly 84 percent of black workers nationwide either did some form of agricultural labor or had service jobs, mostly as domestic servants and in laundries. These had been the primary slave occupations. The remaining 16 percent worked in forests, sawmills, mines, and, with northward migra-

Plessy v. Ferguson (1896)

tion, in northern cities. As whites systematically excluded blacks from trades, the percentage of blacks laboring in these jobs dropped to under 10 percent, although at the end of the Civil War, at least half of all skilled craftsmen in the South had been black. Such factory work as blacks had been doing was also reduced, largely to separate poor blacks from whites and to undercut unionization. Exclusion of blacks from industry prevented them from acquiring the skills and habits that facilitated the entry of European immigrants and their children into the middle class by the mid-twentieth century.

Blacks did not accept their decline passively. In the mid-1880s, they enthusiastically joined the Knights of Labor (discussed in Chapter 18), making up at least a third of the membership in the South. But southern whites feared that the Knights' policies of racial and economic cooperation might lead to social equality. The Charleston *News and Courier* warned darkly about "mongrels and hybrids." As blacks continued to join, whites fled the organization. White violence finished it off.

Lynching and other violence against blacks increased. On February 21, 1891, the *New York Times* reported that in Texarkana, Arkansas, a mob caught a 32-year-old black man, Ed Coy, charged with raping a white woman, tied him to a stake, and burned him. As Coy pleaded his innocence to a large crowd, his alleged victim somewhat hesitatingly put the torch to his oil-soaked body. The *Times* report concluded that only by the "terrible death such as fire ... can inflict" could other blacks "be deterred from the commission of like crimes." Ed Coy was one of more than 1,400 black men lynched or burned alive during the 1890s. About a third were charged with sex crimes. The rest were accused of a variety of "crimes" related to not knowing their place: marrying or insulting a white woman, testifying in court against whites, or having a "bad reputation." Such violence operated not only to keep blacks but also white women in their "places."

Diverging Black Responses

White discrimination and exploitation nourished new protest tactics and ideologies among blacks. For years, Frederick Douglass had urged blacks to remain loyal Americans and count on the Republican party. In 1895 his dying words were allegedly "Agitate! Agitate! Agitate!"

Calls for black separatism within white America rang out. Insisting that blacks must join together to fight the rising tide of discrimination, T. Thomas Fortune in 1891 organized the Afro-American League. The League (the precursor of the NAACP) encouraged independent voting, opposed segregation and lynching, and urged the establishment of black institutions such as banks to support black businesses. In the 1890s, black leaders lobbied to make the Oklahoma Territory, recently opened to white settlement, an all-black state. Blacks founded 25 towns there, as well as in other states and even Mexico. But these attempts, like earlier ones, were short-lived.

There were more radical black voices, too. Bishop Henry McNeal Turner, a former Union soldier and prominent black leader, despaired of ever securing equal rights for American blacks. The Constitution, he said, was "a dirty rag, a cheat, a libel" that "every Negro in the land" should "spit upon." In 1894, he organized the International Migration Society to return blacks to Africa, arguing that "this country owes us forty billions of dollars" to help. He sent two boatloads of emigrants to Liberia, but this effort worked no more successfully than those earlier in the century.

Douglass had long argued that no matter how important African roots might be, blacks had been in the Americas for generations and would have to win justice and equal rights here. W. E. B. Du Bois, the first black to receive a Ph.D. from Harvard, agreed. Yet in 1900, at the first Pan-African Conference in London, he argued that blacks must lead the struggle for liberation both in Africa and in the United States. It was at this conference that Du Bois first made his prophetic comment that "the problem of the Twentieth Century" would be "the problem of the color line."

Despite such militancy, many blacks worked patiently but persistently within white society for equality and social justice. In 1887, J. C. Price formed the Citizens Equal Rights Association, which supported various petitions and direct-action campaigns to protest segregation. Other blacks boycotted segregated streetcars in southern cities. Most black Americans continued to follow the slow, moderate self-help program of Booker T. Washington, the best-known black leader in America. Born a slave, Washington had risen through hard work to become the founder in 1881 and principal of Tuskegee Institute in Alabama, which he made the nation's largest and best-known industrial training school. At Tuskegee, young blacks received a highly disciplined education in scientific agriculture and skilled trades. Washington believed that economic self-help and the familiar Puritan virtues of hard work, frugality, cleanliness, and moderation would help African Americans succeed despite racism. He spent much time traveling through the North to secure philanthropic gifts for Tuskegee, becoming a favorite of the American entrepreneurial elite, whose capitalist assumptions he shared.

In 1895, Washington delivered a speech at the Cotton States and International Exposition in Atlanta—his invitation had been a rare honor for a former slave—in which he proclaimed black loyalty to southern economic development while accepting the lowly status of southern blacks. "It is at the bottom of life we must begin, and not at the top," he declared. Although Washington worked behind the scenes for black civil rights, in Atlanta he publicly renounced black interest in the vote, civil rights, or social equality. Whites throughout the country enthusiastically acclaimed Washington's address, but many blacks considered his "Atlanta Compromise" a serious setback.

Washington has often been charged with conceding too quickly that political rights should follow rather than precede economic well-being. In 1903, Du Bois confronted Washington directly in *The Souls of Black Folk,* arguing for the "manly assertion" of a program of equal civil rights, suffrage, and higher education in the ideals of liberal learning. A trip through Dougherty County, Georgia, showed Du Bois the "forlorn and forsaken" condition of southern blacks. Although "here and there a man has raised his head above these murky waters ... a pall of debt hangs over the beautiful land." The lives of most blacks were still tied to the land of the South. To improve their lives, rural blacks would have to organize.

FARM PROTEST

During the post–Civil War period, many farmers, black and white, began to realize that only through collective action could they improve rural life. Not all were dissatisfied; midwestern farmers and those near city markets adjusted to changing economic conditions. Southern and western farmers, however, faced new problems that led to the first mass organization of farmers in American history.

The Grange in the 1860s and 1870s

The earliest effort to organize white farmers came in 1867 when Oliver Kelley founded the Order of the Patrons of Husbandry. Originally a social and cultural organization, it soon was protesting the powerlessness of the "immense helpless mob" of farmers, victims of "human vampires." The depression of the 1870s (discussed in Chapter 18) sharpened discontent. By 1875, an estimated 800,000 had joined Kelley's organization, now known as the National Grange.

The Purposes of the Grange

The Grangers recognized some, but not all, of the complex changes that had created rural problems. Some of their "reforms" attempted to bypass middlemen by establishing buying and selling cooperatives. Although many cooperatives failed, they indicated that farmers realized the need for unified action. Midwestern farmers also accused grain elevator operators of cheating them, and they pointed to the railroads, America's first big business, as the worst offenders. As Chapter 18 will show, cutthroat competition among railroad companies generally brought lower rates. But even though charges dropped nationwide, railroads often set high rates in rural areas, and their rebates to large shippers discriminated against small operators.

Advice on Keeping Children on the Farm (1881)

Farmers recognized that confronting the mighty railroads demanded cooperation with others, like western businessmen whose interests railroads also hurt, and political action. Between 1869 and 1874, businessmen and farmers successfully pressed Illinois, Iowa, Wisconsin, and Minnesota to pass so-called Granger laws (an inaccurate name, for the Grangers did not deserve complete credit for them) establishing maximum rates that railroads and grain elevators could charge. Other states set up railroad commissions to regulate railroad rates, or outlawed railroad pools, rebates, passes, and other practices that seemed to represent "unjust discrimination and distortion."

Railroad companies and grain elevators quickly challenged the new laws. In 1877, the Supreme Court upheld them in *Munn* v. *Illinois*. Even so, it soon became apparent that state commissions might control local rates but not long-haul rates. While Granger laws did not control the railroads and raised questions difficult to resolve on the local level, they established an important principle. The Supreme Court had made it clear that state legislatures could regulate businesses of a public nature such as the railroads. When the Court reversed its ruling in *Wabash* v. *Illinois* in 1886, pressure increased on Congress to continue the struggle.

The Interstate Commerce Act, 1887

In 1887, Congress responded with the Interstate Commerce Act, requiring that railroad rates be "reasonable and just," that rate schedules be made public, and that rebates and similar practices be discontinued. The act also created the first federal regulatory agency, the Interstate Commerce Commission (ICC), empowered to investigate and prosecute lawbreakers. But the legislation limited its authority to commerce crossing state lines.

Like state railroad commissions, the ICC found it hard to define a reasonable rate, and thousands of cases overwhelmed its tiny staff. The ICC could only bring offenders into the federal courts for lengthy legal proceedings. Few railroads worried about defying it. When they appeared in court four or five years later, they often won their cases from judges suspicious of new federal authority. Between 1887 and 1906, the Supreme Court decided 15 of 16 such cases in the railroads' favor.

The Southern Farmers' Alliance in the 1880s and 1890s

The Grange declined in the late 1870s as the nation recovered from depression. But farm protest did not die. Depression struck farmers once again in the late 1880s and worsened in the early 1890s. Official statistics told the familiar, dismal story of falling grain prices on the plains and prairies. The national currency shortage, which usually reached critical proportions at harvest time, helped drive agricultural prices ever lower. Debt and shipping costs, however, climbed. It sometimes cost a farmer as much as one bushel of corn to send another bushel to market. Distraught farmers again tried organization, education, and cooperation.

The Southern Farmers' Alliance became one of the most important reform organizations of the 1880s. Its ambitious organizational drive sent lecturers across the South and onto the Plains. Alliance lecturers proposed programs that would help realize their slogan: "Equal rights to all, special privileges to none." Among the Alliance's efforts were experiments with cooperatives to free farmers from the clutches of supply merchants, banks, and other credit agencies. While cooperatives often failed, the Alliance also supported legislative efforts to regulate powerful monopolies and corporations that, they believed, gouged farmers. Many Alliance members believed that increasing the money supply was critical to improving the position of farmers and supported a national banking system empowered to issue paper money. Finally, the Alliance called for a variety of measures to improve the quality of rural life. Better rural public schools, state agricultural colleges, and improvements in the status of women were all on its agenda.

By 1890, rural discontent swept more than a million farmers into the Alliance. Included in this burst of organization growth were black as well as white farmers. Organized in 1888, the Colored Farmers' Alliance recognized that farmers of both races shared common economic problems and therefore must cooperate. But many southern cotton farmers, depending on black labor, disagreed. In 1891, black cotton pickers on plantations near Memphis went on strike. Revealing the racial tensions simmering just below the surface, white posses chased the strikers and lynched 15 of them.

The Ocala Platform, 1890

DOCUMENT

Ocala Platform, 1890

In December 1890, the National Alliance gathered in Ocala, Florida, to develop a platform. Most delegates believed that the federal government had failed to address the farmers' problems. They attacked both parties as too subservient to the "will of corporation and money power."

Much of the Alliance's program was radical in the context of late-nineteenth-century political life. It called for the direct election of U.S. senators and supported lowering the tariff (a topic much debated in Congress) with the dangerous-sounding justification that prices must be reduced for the sake of the "poor of our land." The money plank went far beyond what any national legislator would consider, boldly envisioning a new banking system controlled by the federal government. The platform called for the government to take an active economic role by increasing the amount of money in circulation in the form of treasury notes and silver. More money would cause inflation and help debtors pay off loans.

The platform also called for subtreasuries (federal warehouses) in agricultural regions where farmers could store their produce at low interest rates until market prices favored selling. To tide farmers over, the federal government would lend farmers up to 80 percent of the current local price for their produce. Other demands included a graduated income tax and the regulation of transportation and communication networks—or, if regulation failed, their nationalization.

Even though a minority of farmers belonged to the Alliance, many Americans feared it. The New York *Sun* reported that the Alliance had caused a "panic" in the two major parties.

Although the Alliance was not formally in politics, it supported sympathetic candidates in the fall elections of 1890. A surprising number of them won. Alliance victories in the West hurt the Republican party enough to cause President Harrison to refer to "our election disaster." Before long, many Alliance members were pressing for an independent political party. Legislators elected with Alliance support did not necessarily bring action on issues of interest to farmers, or even respect. On the national level, no one had much interest in the Ocala platform. But

TIMELINE

1865–1867	Sioux wars on the Great Plains			Interstate Commerce Act
1869–1874	Granger laws		1890	Sioux Ghost Dance movement
1873	Financial panic triggers economic depression			Massacre at Wounded Knee
1875	Black Hills gold rush incites Sioux war			Ocala platform
1880s	"New South"			Yosemite National Park established
1884	Southern Farmers' Alliance founded		1890s	Black disfranchisement in the South
1887	Dawes Severalty Act			

among rural spokesmen, the first to realize the necessity of forming an independent third party was Georgia's Tom Watson, who also knew that success in the South would depend on unity between white and black farmers.

Conclusion

Farming in the Industrial Age

The late nineteenth century brought turbulence to rural America. The "Indian problem," which had plagued Americans for 200 years, was tragically solved for a while, but not without resistance and bloodshed. Few whites found these events troubling. Most were caught up in the challenge of responding to a fast-changing world. Believing themselves to be the backbone of the nation, white farmers brought Indian lands into cultivation, modernized their farms, and raised bumper crops. But success and a comfortable competency eluded many who were caught up in a cycle of poverty and debt. Farmers like Milton Leeper never gave up hope or farming. Others fled to cities, where they joined the industrial workforce described in the next chapter. Many turned to collective action and politics. Their actions demonstrate that they did not merely react to events but attempted to shape them.

Questions for Review and Reflection

1. Compare and contrast farming on the Great Plains with farming in California.

2. How did technology affect agriculture and mining in the West?

3. Describe the differing viewpoints of Native Americans and whites and the differing cultural values lying behind these viewpoints.

4. What were the reasons that the New South did not achieve its goals?

5. Compare and contrast the treatment of Native Americans and African Americans in this period. Are there any similarities?

6. In what ways did agricultural life in the West and South create conditions that did not mesh with the ideals of American life?

Discovering U.S. History Online

Native American Documents www.csusm.edu/projects/nadp/nadp.htm
Several documents relating to Native Americans have been transcribed, including indexed published reports of the Commissioner of Indian Affairs and the Board of Indian Commissioners for 1871, "allotment" data, and over 100 documents from the Rogue River War and Siletz Reservation.

Lynching in America www.journale.com/withoutsanctuary/index.html
This site presents a stark visual history of lynching in the South. The site includes a flash movie with narration.

The Grange Society www.indianhill.org/History/Hist018.htm
This local historical site gives an example of an agricultural society that became an increasingly "commercialized industry."

Farmers' Alliance and Colored Farmers' Alliance www.tsha.utexas.edu/handbook/online/articles/ view/FF/aaf2.html www.tsha.utexas.edu/handbook/online/articles/view/CC/aac1.html
These two articles from this online "multidisciplinary encyclopedia of Texas history" give more detail about these allied farm-protest organizations.

Fiction and Film

Willa Cather's novels *My Antonia* (1918) and *O Pioneers!* (1913) emphasize the energy and determination of farmers in the post–Civil War West as well as the presence of immigrants there. O. E. Rölvaag's *Giants in the Earth* (1927) gives a very grim picture of immigrants' adjustment to American farming life. Written in 1885 by Maria Amparo Ruiz de Burton, *The Squatter and the Don* provides insights into the views of Mexican Americans. *The Searchers* (1956), *Stagecoach* (1939), and *She Wore a Yellow Ribbon* (1949) come from the heyday of western films and reveal mid-twentieth-century (and John Wayne's) views of the late frontier. *Dances with Wolves* (1990) is Kevin Costner's indictment of the white assault on Native American life and culture that betrays the consciousness of the 1990s. *Ethnic Notions* (1987), an Emmy-winning documentary, traces the evolution of negative stereotypes of African Americans in popular culture.

Recommended Reading

www.ablongman.com/nash
The Companion Website has a list of recommended readings about the modernization of agriculture, the Second Great Removal, the New South, and farm protests.

CHAPTER 18

The Rise of Smokestack America

CHAPTER OUTLINE

- The Texture of Industrial Progress
- Urban Expansion in the Industrial Age
- The Industrial City, 1880–1900
- The Life of the Middle Class
- Industrial Work and the Laboring Class
- Capital Versus Labor
- Conclusion: The Complexity of Industrial Capitalism

American Stories

Telling His Story: O'Donnell and the Senators

By 1883, Thomas O'Donnell, an Irish immigrant, had lived in the United States for over a decade. He was 30 years old, married with two young children, and in debt for the funeral of his third child, who had died the year before. Money was scarce, for O'Donnell was a textile worker in Fall River, Massachusetts, and not well educated. "I went to work when I was young," he explained, "and have been working ever since." However, O'Donnell worked only sporadically at the mill, whose owners preferred to hire man-and-boy teams. Because O'Donnell's children were only one and three, he often saw others preferred for day work. Once, when he was passed over, he recalled, "I said to the boss ... 'what am I to do; I have got two little boys at home ... how am I to get something for them to eat; I can't get a turn when I come here. ...'" I says, "Have I got to starve; ain't I to have any work?"

O'Donnell and his family were barely getting by. He said that he had earned only $133 the previous year. Rent came to $72. The family spent $2 for a little coal, but depended on driftwood for heat. Clams were a major part of the family diet, but on some days, there was nothing to eat at all.

The children "got along very nicely all summer," but it was now November, and they were beginning to "feel quite sickly." It was hardly surprising. "One has one shoe on, a very poor one, and a slipper, that was picked up somewhere. The other has two odd shoes on, with the heel out." His wife was healthy, but not ready for winter. She had two dresses, one saved for church, and an "undershirt that she got given to her, and ... an old wrapper, which is about a mile too big for her; somebody gave it to her."

O'Donnell was testifying to a Senate committee, which was gathering testimony in Boston in 1883 on the relations between labor and capital. The senators asked him why he did not go west. "It would not cost you over $1,500," said one. The gap between the worlds of the senator and the worker could not have been more dramatic. O'Donnell replied, "Well, I never saw over a $20 bill ... if some one would give me $1,500 I will go." Asked by the senator if he had friends who could provide him with the funds, O'Donnell sadly replied no.

The senators, of course, were far better acquainted with the world of comfort and leisure than with the poverty of families like the O'Donnells. For them, the fruits of industrial progress were clear. As the United States became a world industrial leader in the years after the Civil War, its factories poured forth an abundance of ever-cheaper goods ranging from steel rails and farm reapers to mass-produced parlor sets. These were years of tremendous growth and broad economic and social change. Manufacturing replaced agriculture as the leading source of economic growth between 1860 and 1900. By 1890, a majority of the American workforce held nonagricultural jobs; over a third lived in cities. A rural nation of farmers was becoming a nation of industrial workers and city dwellers.

As O'Donnell's appearance before the senatorial committee illustrates, industrial and technological advances profoundly changed American life. For O'Donnell and others like him, the benefits of this transformation were hard to see. Although no nationwide studies of poverty existed, estimates suggest that half the American population was too poor to take advantage of the new goods of the age. Eventually, the disparity between the reality of life for families like the O'Donnells and American ideals would give rise to attempts to improve conditions for working-class Americans, but it is unlikely that O'Donnell ever profited from such efforts.

This chapter examines the new order that resulted from the maturing of the American industrial economy. Focusing on the years between 1865 and 1900, it describes the rise of heavy industry, the organization and character of the new industrial workplace, and the emergence of big business. It then examines the locus of industrial life, the fast-growing city, and its varied people, classes, and social inequities. The chapter's central theme grows out of O'Donnell's story: as the United States built up its railroads, cities, and factories, its production and profit orientation led to a maldistribution of wealth and power. Although many Americans were too exhausted by life's daily struggles to protest new inequalities, strikes and other forms of working-class resistance sought to return dignity and power to working people and to compensate them more generously for the labor they performed. The ineffectiveness of these protests points to the many obstacles confronting those who wished to change the status quo.

THE TEXTURE OF INDUSTRIAL PROGRESS

When America went to war in 1861, agriculture was its leading source of economic growth. Forty years later, manufacturing had taken its place. During these years, the production of manufactured goods outpaced population growth. Per capita income increased by over 2 percent a year. But these aggregates disguise the fact that many people won no gains at all.

◁ GOAL

Big businesses became the characteristic form of economic organization. They could raise the capital to build huge factories, acquire the most efficient machinery, hire hundreds of workers, and use the most up-to-date methods. The result was more goods at lower prices.

New regions grew in industrial importance. From New England to the Midwest lay the country's industrial heartland. New England remained a center of light industry, and the Midwest still processed natural resources. Now, however, the production of iron, steel, and transportation equipment joined older manufacturing operations there. In the Far West, manufacturers concentrated on processing the region's natural resources, but heavy industry made strides as well. In the less industrialized South, the textile industry put down roots by the 1890s.

Although many factors contributed to the dramatic rise in industrial productivity, the changing nature of the industrial sector itself explains many of the gains. Pre–Civil War manufacturers had concentrated either on producing textiles, clothing, and leather goods or on processing agricultural and natural resources. Although these enterprises remained important, heavy industry grew rapidly after the war. The manufacturing of steel, iron, and machinery, meant for other producers rather than consumers, fueled economic growth.

Technological Innovations

IMAGE

Edison with
Phonograph
(1878)—Mathew
Brady

An accelerating pace of technological change contributed to and was shaped by the industrial transformation of the late nineteenth century. Technological breakthroughs allowed more efficient production that, in turn, helped to generate new needs and further innovation. Developments in the steel industry exemplify this process and highlight the important role of entrepreneurs.

Before the Civil War, skilled workers used a slow and expensive process to produce an iron that was so soft iron train rails wore out within a few years. The need for a harder metal supported the development and introduction of new technology. The Bessemer converter transformed iron into steel by forcing air through the molten iron, thus reducing the carbon. The converter had the added advantage of reducing the need for highly paid skilled workers.

Andrew Carnegie was neither an inventor nor an engineer, but he recognized the possibilities of the new process and new ways to organize industry effectively. Steel companies like Carnegie's acquired access to both raw materials and markets and brought all stages of steel manufacturing into one mill. Output soared and prices fell. When Andrew Carnegie introduced the Bessemer process in his plant in the mid-1870s, the price of steel dropped from $100 to $50 a ton. By 1890, it cost only $12 a ton.

In turn, the production of a cheaper, stronger, more durable material than iron created new goods, new demands, and new markets, and it stimulated further technological changes. Bessemer furnaces, geared toward making steel rails, did not produce steel appropriate for building. Experimentation with the open-hearth process using high temperatures yielded steel usable by bridge builders, engineers, architects, and even designers of subways. Steel use increased dramatically, from naval vessels to screws.

The Homestead Steel Works The Homestead Steel Works, pictured here in about 1890, were located near Pittsburgh, Pennsylvania. The vast scale of the enterprise suggests the ways in which technological innovation stimulated the expansion of the steel industry in the late nineteenth century. Although the two small figures in the foreground humanize the picture, what does this picture suggest about the character of work in the steel mills? *(Courtesy of Rivers of Steel Heritage Area)*

New power sources facilitated American industry's shift to mass production and also suggest the importance of new ways of organizing research and innovation. In 1869, about half the industrial power came from water. The opening of new anthracite deposits, however, cut the cost of coal, and American industry rapidly converted to steam. By 1900, steam engines generated 80 percent of the nation's industrial energy supply. Then, electricity began to replace steam as a power source. Its development owed much to Thomas Edison, who had decided in 1878 to solve the problem of electric lighting. Rather than relying on individual creativity, Edison believed that professional collaboration fostered successful innovation. His research lab had a range of specialists and facilities that included an advanced library, a chemical lab, and eventually a glassblowing lab. From these beginnings eventually came the electric generator.

DOCUMENT

Thomas Edison, The Success of the Electric Light (1879)

Railroads: Pioneers of Big Business

Railroads were the pioneers of big business and a great modernizing force in the economy. Efficient national transportation and communications networks encouraged mass production and mass marketing and promoted new management techniques.

The creation of a national railway system was facilitated by the largesse of both federal and state governments that granted railroads lands from the public domain. Eventually, railroads received lands one and a half times the size of Texas.

Benefiting from such incentives, the first transcontinental railroad was finished in 1869. Four additional transcontinental lines and miles of feeder and branch roads were laid down in the 1870s and 1880s, with telegraph lines running alongside them.

Railroad companies were large, complicated organizations presenting both new opportunities and new problems. The costs of construction required unprecedented amounts of capital, while the numbers of workers and the operation of the business demanded new management techniques. In 1854, the Erie Railroad hired engineer and inventor Daniel McCallum to discover how to make managers and employees more accountable. McCallum realized that large organizations needed to be handled differently than small ones. The system he devised separated responsibilities and ensured a regular flow of information. Other large-scale businesses copied both the new procedures that effectively distributed work and separated management from operations and many of the ruthless techniques railroads adopted.

Unlike small businesses, railroads' high costs and heavy indebtedness encouraged aggressive business practices that could contribute to instability. Slashing workers' wages was one tactic that often led to powerful worker unrest. To meet competition, railroads might offer customers lower rates or secret rebates (cheaper fares in exchange for all of a company's business). While rivalry between railroads lowered freight rates steadily, they might result in bankruptcy. Hoping to impose some order on the railroad business in the 1870s, railroad leaders set up "pools"—informal arrangements that established uniform rates—or agreed to divide up the traffic. Yet these deals never completely succeeded. Too often, companies broke them, especially during business downturns.

Growth in Other Industries

By the last quarter of the century, the textile, metal, and machinery industries equaled the railroads in size. By 1900, more than 1,000 American factories had giant labor forces ranging between 500 and 1,000, and another 450 employed more than 1,000 workers. Big business had come of age.

Business expansion was accomplished in one of two ways (or a combination of both). Some owners such as steel magnate Andrew Carnegie integrated vertically—adding operations either before or after the production process. Even though he had introduced the most up-to-date innovations in his steel mills, Carnegie realized he needed his own sources of pig iron, coal, and coke—"backward" integration—to avoid dependence on suppliers. When Carnegie acquired steamships and railroads to transport his finished products, he was integrating "forward." Companies that integrated vertically frequently achieved economies of scale.

Other companies copied the railroads and integrated horizontally by combining similar businesses. They did not intend to control all stages of production, but rather, by monopolizing the market, hoped to eliminate competition and stabilize prices. John D. Rockefeller used horizontal integration to control the oil market. Rockefeller bought or drove out competitors of his Standard Oil of New Jersey. Although his company never achieved a complete monopoly, by 1898 it refined

84 percent of the nation's oil. While horizontal integration occasionally stimulated economies and greater profits, it was the monopolistic control over prices that boosted earnings.

In the oil business, Rockefeller observed, "the day of individual competition ... is past and gone." As giant businesses competed intensely, often cutting wages and prices, they absorbed smaller, weaker producers. Business ownership became increasingly concentrated. In 1870, 808 American iron and steel firms were operating, but by 1900, fewer than 70 were left.

As businesses grew, like the railroads, they recognized the many advantages of legal incorporation. A corporation could raise money for large-scale operations by selling stocks. Its legal identity allowed it to survive the death of original and subsequent shareholders, while the principle of limited liability protected the personal assets of both shareholders and officials. Such characteristics made investments in corporations more attractive.

Financing Postwar Growth

The economic transformations sketched here demanded huge amounts of capital and the willingness to accept financial risks. Building the railroad system cost over $1 billion by 1859 (the prewar canal system's price tag was under $2 million); after the war, another $10 billion went to complete the national railroad network. Foreign investors contributed a third of that. Americans, too, began to invest an increasing percentage of the national income.

Although savings and commercial banks continued to invest depositors' capital, investment banking houses like Morgan & Co. played a new and significant role in transferring resources to economic enterprises. Stocks, which paid dividends only if a company made a profit, were riskier investments than bonds. When J. Pierpont Morgan, a respected investment banker, began to market stocks, they caught on. The market for industrial securities expanded rapidly in the 1880s and 1890s. Although some Americans feared the powerful investment bankers and distrusted the financial market, both were integral to late-nineteenth-century economic expansion.

American Industry and the World

The industrialization of the late nineteenth century represented the second stage of the great transformation that began in eighteenth-century Great Britain. By reorganizing production, often through the use of machinery, early manufacturers turned out more and cheaper goods than at any time in human history. Innovation created the textile, mining, and metal industries and stimulated changes in transportation and communications. From Britain, industrialization spread to other European countries and the United States.

The second stage of the Industrial Revolution was marked by the application of science and technology to manufacturing and by the creation of new ways to mass-produce goods. The United States was the leader in developing techniques of mass production, while Germany excelled in using science and technology to reshape production. Technological innovations transformed German industry. As in the United States, giant firms turned out goods (especially heavy machinery and chemicals) for ever lower prices. Along with Great Britain, Germany and the United States produced two-thirds of the world's manufactured products between 1870 and 1930.

Great Britain, the world's most powerful nation during the nineteenth century, had long been its economic leader. But the balance of power began to shift as German and American businesses developed large new enterprises, introduced new ways of organizing and efficiently managing them, invested heavily in equipment, and promoted research. Great Britain lost ground, preferring traditional ways of organizing businesses rather than the new corporate structure. British manufacturing continued to be centered in older industries such as textiles, while British investors channeled their capital away from domestic industries towards investment opportunities abroad. American railroads and subways were constructed partly with the assistance of British investors.

The full impact of the changed position of the United States in the world triggered by its industrial might only became fully apparent in the twentieth century. But the importance of connections with other nations was obvious. Standard Oil sent two-thirds of the kerosene it refined to overseas markets. Firms manufacturing sewing machines, a range of office machines such as typewriters, and farm machinery came to dominate the world market. Singer Sewing Machine had a factory in Scotland in the 1880s and two decades later manufactured over 400,000 machines in Moscow, employing 2,500 workers and 300 managers. American locomotives were exported to South America, parts of Africa and Europe, the Middle East, and Asia. The Baldwin Locomotive Works of Philadelphia produced as many engines as any other locomotive company in the world.

These connections between American business and other nations meant that foreign events could affect the American economy. Furthermore, they suggested the intricate ties binding American business to other parts of the world. American industrial production contributed to the economic development of countries around the globe, while American business also competed with foreign producers. John D. Rockefeller told a congressional committee that Standard Oil "spared no expense in forcing its products into the markets of the world among people civilized and uncivilized," and that the company was "holding its market against the competition of Russia and all the many countries which are producers of oil and competitors against American oil."

An Erratic Global Economy

Affected by national and worldwide economic trends, the transformation of the economy was neither smooth nor steady. Two depressions, from 1873 to 1879 and from 1893 to 1897, surpassed the severity of pre–Civil War downturns. Collapsing land values, unsound banking practices, and changes in the money supply had caused antebellum depressions. In the larger and more interdependent late-nineteenth-century economy, depressions were industrial, intense, and accompanied by widespread unemployment, a phenomenon new to American life. They were also related to economic declines in European industrial nations.

The business cycle had a recurring rhythm. The global pattern of falling prices and fierce competition encouraged overproduction and the flooding of markets with goods. When the market was saturated, sales and profits declined and the economy spiraled downward. Owners laid off workers (who lived solely on their wages); and when workers economized on food, farm prices plummeted. Farmers, like wage workers, cut purchases. Business stagnated. Finally, the railroads were hurt. Eventually the cycle bottomed out, but millions of workers had lost jobs, thousands of businesses had gone bankrupt, and many Americans had suffered hardship.

Pollution

The business cycle worried Americans more than did widespread pollution. But by the late nineteenth century, industrial processes were polluting urban air, eastern and midwestern lakes and rivers, and creating acid soil. In Birmingham, Alabama, for example, the production of iron and steel befouled the air with smoke, soot, and ashes. Coal tar, a by-product of the process, was dumped, making the soil so acid that nothing would grow in it.

The intellectual rationale of the times stressed growth, development, and the rapid exploitation of resources. As the last chapter pointed out, some steps were taken to protect the environment. But limited actions such as setting aside forest reserves did not touch the problems created by the rise of heavy industry and rapid urban expansion.

URBAN EXPANSION IN THE INDUSTRIAL AGE

As postwar manufacturers shifted from water to steam power, most favored urban locations that offered workers, specialized services, local markets, and railroad links to raw materials and distant markets. Industry, rather than commerce or finance, fueled urban expansion between 1870 and 1900, and cities of all sizes grew. New York and Philadelphia doubled and tripled their populations. Smaller cities, especially in the industrial Midwest and the South, shared in the growth; far western cities increased explosively. In 1870, some 25 percent of Americans lived in cities; by 1900, fully 40 percent of them did.

A Growing Population

The American population grew about 2 percent a year, but cities expanded far more rapidly. Although more people were born than died in American cities, births contributed only modestly to the urban explosion. Urban families tended to have fewer children than rural ones, and the host of urban health hazards meant that the death rate for infants was twice as high in cities as in the countryside. In the 1880s, half the children born in Chicago did not live to celebrate their fifth birthdays.

The real cause of rapid urban growth was the spectacular ability of the cities to attract newcomers from the nation's small towns and farms and abroad. For rural Americans, the "push" came from agricultural modernization: farm machines were replacing human hands. The "pull" was the promise of employment. Although urban jobs were often dirty, dangerous, and exhausting, so was farm work. Furthermore, by 1890 manufacturing workers were earning hundreds of dollars more a year than farm laborers. Higher urban living costs gobbled up some of the differential between rural and urban wages but not all of it. The "gilded metropolis" also offered a host of "marvels" absent from rural life. Shops, theaters, restaurants, department stores, baseball games, and the crowds amazed and amused young people coming from towns and farms.

Southern blacks, often single and young, also joined the migratory stream into the cities. In the West and North, blacks formed only a tiny part of the population, but in southern cities they were more numerous. About 44 percent of late-nineteenth-century Atlanta's residents were black, and so were 38 percent of Nashville's. But for black Americans, cities offered few rewards and many dangers.

The New Immigration, 1880–1900

In the 40 years before the Civil War, 5 million immigrants poured into the United States; from 1860 to 1900, that volume almost tripled. Three-quarters of them stayed in the Northeast, while many of the rest settled in cities across the nation, where they soon outnumbered native-born whites.

Until 1880, three-quarters of the immigrants, so-called "old immigrants," hailed from the British Isles, Germany, and Scandinavia. Then the pattern slowly changed. By 1890, "old immigrants" composed only 60 percent of the total number of newcomers, with "new immigrants" from southern and eastern Europe making up most of the rest. Italian Catholics and eastern European Jews were most numerous, followed by Slavs (mostly Russians and Poles).

A variety of forces prompted the tide of migration. Better and cheaper transportation made the trip possible. Trains reached deep into eastern and southern Europe. Even steerage passengers on transatlantic vessels could expect a bed and communal washroom. The modernization of European economies also stimulated immigration. New agricultural techniques led landlords to consolidate their land, evicting longtime tenants. Some moved to European cities, others to Canada or South America, but the largest group headed to the United States. Artisans, their skills made obsolete by machinery, also pulled up stakes. But dissatisfaction with life at home also played a part. Especially in Russia, government persecution and the expansion of military drafts drove millions of Jews and other minorities to emigrate.

Opportunity in "golden" America was the lure. State commissioners of immigration and American railroad and steamship companies wooed potential immigrants. Friends and relatives wrote optimistic letters promising help in finding work: American cities were great places for "blast frnises and Rolen milles," explained one unskilled worker. Often letters included passage money or pictures of friends in fashionable clothes.

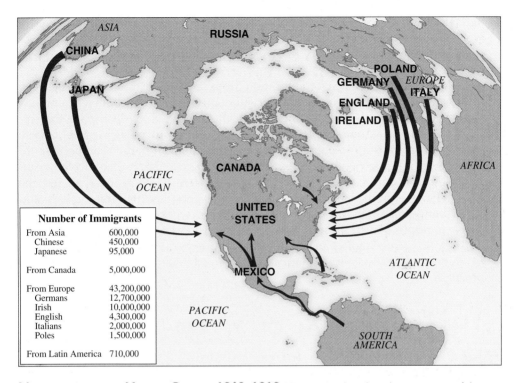

Number of Immigrants	
From Asia	600,000
Chinese	450,000
Japanese	95,000
From Canada	5,000,000
From Europe	43,200,000
Germans	12,700,000
Irish	10,000,000
English	4,300,000
Italians	2,000,000
Poles	1,500,000
From Latin America	710,000

MIGRATION TO THE UNITED STATES, 1860–1910 This map makes clear the many parts of the world that sent population to the United States. Many of those who came were dislodged by economic changes in their home countries. ■ **Reflecting on the Past** What were the most important short-term consequences of these migratory streams? What have been the long-term consequences?

Like rural and small-town Americans, Europeans came primarily to work. Most were young, single men with few skills. Jews, however, came most often in family groups, and women predominated among the Irish. When times were good and American industry needed unskilled laborers, migration was heavy. In bad times, the numbers fell off. Immigrants hoped to earn enough money in America to realize ambitions at home, and as many as a third eventually went back.

Although the greatest influx of Mexicans would come in the twentieth century, Mexican laborers also migrated to the United States. Like Europe, Mexico was modernizing. Overpopulation and new land policies uprooted many inhabitants, while the construction of a 900-mile railroad from central Mexico to the Texas border facilitated migration. Many Mexicans ended up in the Southwest and West, often working on railroads and in mines.

Overpopulation, turmoil, unemployment, and crop failures brought Asians, mostly from south China, to the "Land of the Golden Mountains." Although only 264,000 Chinese came to the United States between 1860 and 1900, they constituted a significant minority on the West Coast. Most were unskilled male contract laborers, away from wives and families for years. They held some of the worst jobs in the West. They worked in mining and

DOCUMENT

William B. Farwell, The Chinese at Home and Abroad (1885)

agriculture, on railroad and levee construction, and labored in factory and laundry work. To serve them, contractors brought in Chinese women to serve as prostitutes. Virtually enslaved, few of these women could pay off the costs of their passage or escape brothel life.

IMAGE

Chinese-Americans
in California

MAP

Foreign-Born
Population, 1890

The importance of migration from Europe, Mexico, and Asia can hardly be overestimated. Immigrants contributed to the country's rapid urbanization and provided much of the labor needed to accomplish the economic transformation of the late nineteenth century. Their presence also helped transform American society. The American population became far more heterogeneous in terms of ethnicity and religion than any other industrial nation. Since most immigrants were workers, they altered the character of the laboring class. Differences between immigrant groups and between immigrants and American workers weakened immigrants' ability to respond to employers with one voice. The presence of those who spoke little or no English and had values and experiences very different from those of native-born Americans challenged American ideals, beliefs, and practices.

THE INDUSTRIAL CITY, 1880–1900

VIDEO

A 1901 Fire
Department

Late-nineteenth-century industrial cities had new physical and social arrangements. Slums (nothing new) grew disturbingly, but grand mansions, handsome business and industrial buildings, impressive civic monuments, parks, and acres of substantial middle-class homes also characterized urban life.

By the last quarter of the nineteenth century, the jumbled arrangements of the antebellum city based upon the necessity of walking to work disappeared. Central business districts emerged, where many worked but few lived. Nearby were areas of light manufacturing and wholesale activity with housing for workers. Beyond lay middle-class residential areas. Then came the suburbs with their "pure air, peacefulness, quietude, and natural scenery." Scattered throughout were pockets of industrial activity surrounded by crowded working-class housing.

The new pattern, still characteristic of American cities today, reversed the early nineteenth-century urban form, in which the most desirable housing was in the heart of the city. The new living arrangements were also more segregated by race and class than those in the preindustrial walking city.

Transportation improvements enormously affected the development of American cities. The first improvement was modest, a slow horse-drawn omnibus, accommodating only 10 to 12 passengers. High fares meant most people walked to work and lived nearby. In the 1850s, many cities introduced faster and bigger horse railways, allowing the city to expand outward about four miles. The fare, however, limited ridership to the prosperous classes. Cable cars, trolleys, and subways after 1880 further extended city boundaries, enabling the middle class to escape grimy industrial districts.

Neighborhoods and Neighborhood Life

Working-class neighborhoods clustered near the center of most industrial cities. Here lived newcomers from rural America and crowds of foreigners. Ethnic groups frequently crowded together near industries requiring their labor. Although such neighborhoods often had an ethnic flavor, they were not ghettos. Immigrants and native-born Americans often lived in the same neighborhoods, on the same streets, and even in the same houses.

Working-class neighborhoods were often what we would call slums. Many workers occupied buildings once housing middle- and upper-class residents, now subdivided to squeeze people in. Others jammed into tenements, built to hold as many families as possible. Outdoor privies, often shared by several families, were the rule. Water came from hydrants, and women had to carry it inside. Such indoor fixtures as existed frequently poured waste directly into unpaved alleys. Refuse piles stank in the summer and froze in the winter. Even when people kept their own living quarters clean, the outside environment was unsanitary. It was no surprise that urban death rates were so high. Not till the turn of the century did the public health movement begin to improve such conditions.

Working-class living conditions, however, were far from uniform. Skilled workers might rent and furnish comfortable quarters. A few owned their homes. Unskilled and semiskilled workers were not so fortunate. Yet, despite the often drab circumstances, working families succeeded in creating a sense of community. A wide range of institutions and associations came to life. Religious and ethnic associations helped immigrants feel at home. Jews gathered in their synagogues, Hebrew schools, and Hebrew- and Yiddish-speaking literary groups. Germans had their family saloons and their educational and singing societies. Irish associational life focused around the parish church, its Irish priest, clubs, and activities. In Irish nationalist organizations, in ward politics, and in Irish saloons, men met, socialized, drank, and talked politics. These types of organizations provided companionship, although they also separated those involved in them from native-born Americans and other ethnic groups.

Black Americans faced the worst living conditions in the city, in segregated black neighborhoods in the North and in back alleys and small streets in the South. They, too, created a rich religious and associational life. Rapidly growing black churches retained the emotional exuberance of slave religion. Black members of mainline Protestant denominations established separate branches, and the African Methodist Episcopal Church mushroomed. Some urban blacks rose into the middle class despite heavy odds.

Beyond working-class neighborhoods and pockets of black housing lay streets with the middle-class houses for clerks, shopkeepers, bookkeepers, salesmen, and small tradesmen. Separate spaces for cooking and laundry work kept unpleasant tasks away from other living areas. Many houses boasted new gas lighting and bathrooms. Neighborhoods were cleaner than in the inner city because residents could pay for municipal services.

On the fringes of the city lived the substantial middle class and the rich, who sped between downtown offices and their suburban homes by public

Lower East Side, New York Here is a picture of life on Hester Street on New York's Lower East Side. Study the photograph to see what it reveals about living conditions in the city. What indications are there of commercial activity? Why are there so many women on the street and so few men? What is suggested about children? What impression does the picture give of city services to this poor neighborhood? *(New York City views, Milstein Division of U.S. History, Local History & Genealogy, The New York Public Library/Art Resource, NY)*

transportation. For example, Robert Work, a modestly successful merchant, moved his family to a $5,500 house in West Philadelphia in 1865 and commuted more than four miles to work. In 1880, his household contained two servants, two boarders, his wife, and their eldest son. The Works' house had running hot and cold water, indoor bathrooms, central heating, and other up-to-date conveniences. Upstairs, comfortable bedrooms provided a maximum of privacy for family members. The live-in servants, who did most of the housework, were mostly restricted to kitchen, pantry, and attic bedrooms.

The Social Geography of the Cities

DOCUMENT

Charles Loring Brace, The Dangerous Classes of New York (1872)

Industrial cities sorted people by class, occupation, and race. Physical distances between upper- and middle-class neighborhoods and working-class areas eliminated or distorted firsthand knowledge of other people and bred social disapproval. While middle-class newspapers criticized "crowds of idlers, who, day and night, infect Main Street," often the "idlers" were men unable to find work. A working-class woman's response to visitors who were attacking the use of alcohol captures the critical view from the bottom of society. "When the rich stopped drinking, it would be time to speak to the poor about it."

THE LIFE OF THE MIDDLE CLASS

For middle-class Americans, there was much to value in the new age. Between 1865 and 1890, average middle-class income rose about 30 percent. By 1900, fully 36 percent of urban families owned their homes.

Industrial expansion raised living standards for increasing numbers of Americans. They were able to purchase dozens of products, manufactured, packaged, and promoted in an explosion of technological inventions and shrewd marketing techniques. Among still-familiar products and brands invented or mass-produced for the first time in the 1890s were Jell-O, Wesson oil, the Hershey bar, Aunt Jemima pancake mix, and Coca-Cola.

More leisure time and greater access to consumer goods signaled industrialism's power to transform the lives of middle-class Americans. Plentiful immigrant servant girls relieved urban middle-class wives of many housekeeping chores, and smaller families lightened the burdens of motherhood. New department stores began to appear in the central business districts in the 1870s, feeding women's desire for material possessions and revolutionizing retailing. Shopping for home furnishings and clothes became integral to many middle-class women's lives.

New Freedoms for Middle-Class Women

As many middle-class women acquired leisure time and enhanced purchasing power, they also won new freedoms. Several states granted women more property rights in marriage, adding to their growing sense of independence. Casting off confining crinolines, they now wore a shirtwaist blouse and ankle-length skirt that was more comfortable for working, school, and sports. The "new woman" was celebrated as *Life* magazine's attractively active, slightly rebellious "Gibson girl."

Using their new freedom, women joined organizations of all kinds—literary societies, charity groups, reform clubs. There they gained organizational experience, awareness of their talents, and contact with people and problems outside

HOW OTHERS SEE US

Herbert Spencer, "The Americans"

Herbert Spencer was an English intellectual who adapted Charles Darwin's theory of the survival of the fittest to human society. These remarks come from a speech he made at a New York dinner during his visit to this country in 1882.

> Everywhere I have been struck with the number of faces which told in strong lines of the burdens that had to be borne. I have been struck, too, with the large proportion of gray-haired men; and inquiries have brought out the fact, that with you the hair begins to turn some ten years earlier than with us. Moreover, in every circle I have met men who had themselves suffered from nervous collapse due to stress of business, or named friends who had either killed themselves by overwork, or had been permanently incapacitated, or wasted long periods in endeavors to recover health. I do but echo the opinion of all the observant persons I have spoken to that immense injury is being done by this high-pressure life—the physique is being undermined.... Beyond these immediate mischiefs there are remoter mischiefs. Exclusive devotion to work has the result that amusements cease to please; and, when relaxation becomes imperative, life becomes dreary from lack of its sole interest—the interest in business. The remark current in England, that, when the American travels, his aim is to do the greatest amount of sight-seeing in the shortest time, I find current here also."

■ *What social class is Spencer talking about? How do his comments reflect the values of English society? How seriously should we take them?*

Source: Herbert Spencer, "The Americans," *Living Age*, v. 41 (1883), 327–328.

---

their traditional family roles. The depression of 1893 stimulated many women to investigate slum and factory conditions, and some began even earlier. Jane Addams, who told her college classmates in 1881 to lead lives "filled with good works and honest toil," went on to found Hull House, a famous social settlement.

Job opportunities for these educated middle-class women were generally limited to the social services and teaching. Still regarded as a suitable female occupation, teaching was a highly demanding but poorly paying field that grew as urban schools expanded under the pressure of a burgeoning population. By the 1890s, the willingness of middle-class women to work for low pay opened up new forms of employment in office work, nursing, and department stores. But moving up to high-status jobs proved difficult, even for middle-class women.

After the Civil War, educational opportunities for women expanded. New women's colleges offered programs similar to those at competitive men's colleges, while midwestern and western state schools dropped prohibitions against women. In 1890, some 13 percent of all college graduates were women; by 1900, nearly 20 percent were. Higher education prepared middle-class women both for conventional female roles and work and public service. A few courageous graduates overcame many barriers to enter the professions. By the early twentieth century, the number of women professionals (including teachers) was increasing at three times the rate for men.

One reason for the greater independence of American women was that they were having fewer babies. This was especially true of educated women. In 1900, nearly one married woman in five was childless. Advances in birth control technology (the modern diaphragm was developed in 1880) helped make new patterns possible. But decreasing family size and an increase in the divorce rate (1 out of 12 marriages in 1905) also fueled male responses. Arguments against the new woman intensified as many men reaffirmed Victorian stereotypes of "woman's sphere." Male campaigns against prostitution and for sex hygiene also suggested they feared female passions might weaken male vigor.

Male Mobility and the Success Ethic

The postwar economy opened up many new opportunities for middle-class men. As the lower ranks of the white-collar world became more specialized, the number of middle-class jobs increased.

Because these new careers required more education, the educational system expanded. Public high schools increased from 160 in 1870 to 6,000 in 1900. By that year, most states and territories had compulsory school attendance laws. Enrollments in colleges and universities nearly doubled, from 53,000 in 1870 to 101,000 in 1900. Universities gained a new stature in American life. Land-grant state colleges expanded, and philanthropists established research universities such as Johns Hopkins, Stanford, and the University of Chicago.

These developments led to greater specialization and professionalism. By the 1890s, government licensing and the rise of professional schools helped to give the word *career* its modern meaning. No longer were tradesmen likely to read up on medicine in their spare time and become doctors. Organizations such as the American Medical Association and the American Bar Association were regulating and professionalizing membership.

The need for lawyers, bankers, architects, and insurance agents to serve business and industry expanded opportunities. Large companies required many more managers, while the growing public sector provided new positions in social services and government. Young professionals with graduate training in the social sciences filled many of them.

The social ethic of the age stressed that economic rewards were available to anyone who fervently sought them. It was endlessly pointed out, for example, that John D. Rockefeller had raised turkeys as a boy. Horatio Alger's rags-to-riches novels were read by millions. A typical one told the story of a shoeshine-boy-turned-office-boy who decided to "learn the business and grow up 'spectable.'" Good fortune intervened when he rescued a girl who had tumbled into the harbor. His reward was a position as a clerk in her father's counting house. Virtuous habits were crucial for Alger's heroes, although success often depended as much on luck as on pluck.

Unlimited and equal opportunity for upward advancement in America has never been as easy as the "bootstraps" ethic maintains. But the persistence of the success myth owes something to the fact that many Americans, particularly those who began well, did rise rapidly. Native-born, middle-class whites tended to have the skills, resources, and connections that opened up the most desirable jobs. The typical big businessman was an Anglo-Saxon Protestant from a middle- or upper-class family whose father was most likely in business, banking, or commerce.

INDUSTRIAL WORK AND THE LABORING CLASS

David Lawlor, an Irish immigrant who came to the United States in 1872, might have agreed with the bootstraps ethic. As a child, he worked in textile mills and read Horatio Alger. Like Alger's heroes, he went to night school and rose in the business world, eventually becoming an advertising executive. But his success was exceptional. Most working-class Americans labored long hours, in unpleasant or dangerous conditions, for meager wages. As industrialization transformed work, traditional opportunities for mobility and security eluded many working-class Americans.

The Impact of Ethnic Diversity

Late-nineteenth-century immigrants formed 20 percent of the labor force and over 40 percent of laborers in the manufacturing and extractive industries. They tended to settle in cities and made up more than half the working-class population. The fact that more than half the urban industrial class was foreign, unskilled, and often unable to speak English influenced industrial work, urban life, labor protest, and local politics. Immigrants often had little in common with native-born workers or even with one another.

There were many gradations within the working class. Atop the working-class hierarchy, native-born Protestant whites held most of the well-paying skilled jobs. Their occupations bore the mark of late-nineteenth-century industrialism: machinists, iron puddlers and rollers, engineers, foremen, conductors, carpenters, plumbers, mechanics, and printers. Skilled northern European immigrants filled most middle-rank positions. Often they had held similar jobs in their homelands. Jews, who had tailoring experience, became the backbone of the garment industry (where they faced little competition because American male workers considered it unmanly to work on women's clothes). But most "new immigrants" from southern and central Europe lacked urban industrial experience. They got the unskilled, dirty jobs near the bottom of the occupational ladder: relining blast furnaces, carrying raw materials or finished products, or cleaning up. Often, they were day laborers on the docks, ditchdiggers, or construction workers. Hiring was often done on a daily basis, usually arranged through middlemen such as the Italian *padrone*. Unskilled work seldom gave much job stability or paid much money.

At the bottom, blacks occupied the most marginal positions as janitors, servants, porters, and laborers. Racial discrimination generally kept them from industrial jobs, even though their occupational background differed little from that of rural white immigrants. There were always plenty of whites eager to work, so it was not necessary to hire blacks except occasionally as scabs during a strike.

The Changing Nature of Work

Big business and mechanization changed the size and shape of the workforce and the nature of work. More and more Americans were wage earners rather than independent artisans. The number of manufacturing workers doubled between 1880 and 1900, with the fastest expansion in the unskilled and semiskilled ranks.

But skilled workers were still needed. New positions, as in steam fitting and structural ironwork, appeared as industries expanded and changed. Increasingly, though, older skills grew obsolete. And all skilled workers faced the possibility that technical advances would eliminate their favored status or that employers would eat away at their jobs by having unskilled helpers take over parts of them.

Work Settings and Experiences

A majority of American manufacturing workers now labored not in shops but in factories dominated by the unceasing rhythms of machinery. Industrial jobs became increasingly specialized and monotonous. Even skilled workers did not produce a complete product, and the range of their skills narrowed. Those still toiling in small shops and basement, loft, or tenement sweatshops shared the monotony and the relentless pressure to produce—volume, not hours, determined pay.

The organization of work kept workers apart. In large factories, workers were divided into small work groups often defined by ethnicity, and the entire workforce rarely mingled. Those paid by the piece competed in speed, agility, and output.

What workers shared in common was a very long working day—usually 10 hours a day, six days a week—and unhealthy, dangerous, and uncomfortable workplaces. A few states passed laws to regulate work conditions, but enforcement was spotty, and owners were unconcerned with workers' health or safety. Women bent over sewing machines developed digestive illnesses and curved spines. In some mines, workers labored in temperatures above 120 degrees, handled dynamite, and died in cave-ins caused by inadequate timber supports. When new drilling machinery was introduced, the air was filled with tiny particles that caused lung disease. Accident rates in the United States far exceeded those of Europe's industrial nations. Nationwide, nearly 25 percent of the men reaching the age of 20 in 1880 would not live to see 44, compared with 7 percent today. The law placed the burden of avoiding accidents on workers, who were expected to quit if they thought conditions unsafe.

Still, industrial work provided some personal benefits. New arrangements helped humanize the workplace. Workers who found jobs through family and friends then worked with them. In most industries, the foreman controlled day-to-day activities. He chose workers from crowds at the gate, fired unsatisfactory ones, selected appropriate materials and equipment, and determined the order and pace of production. Himself a worker, he might sympathize with subordinates. Yet he could also be authoritarian and harsh, especially if his workers were unskilled or belonged to another ethnic group.

The Worker's Share in Industrial Progress

The huge fortunes accumulated by Andrew Carnegie and John D. Rockefeller during the late nineteenth century dramatized the pattern of wealth concentration that began in the early period of industrialization. In 1890, the top 1 percent of American families possessed over a quarter of the wealth, and the top 10 percent owned about 73 percent. But what of the workers who tended machines that created industrial wealth? Working-class Americans made up the largest segment of the labor force (more than 50 percent), so their experience reveals important facets of the American social and economic system and American values.

Statistics tell an important part of the story. Industry still needed skilled workers and paid them well. Average real wages rose more than 50 percent between 1860 and 1900. Skilled manufacturing workers, about a tenth of the nonagricultural working class in the late nineteenth century, saw their wages rise by about 74 percent. But wages for the unskilled increased by only 31 percent—a substantial differential that widened as the century drew to a close.

On the whole, the working class accrued solid benefits in the late nineteenth century, even if its share of total wealth did not increase. American workers had more material comforts than their European counterparts. But the general picture conceals realities of working-class economic life. A U.S. Bureau of Labor study in 1889 reveals great disparities of income: a young girl in a silk mill made $130 a year; a laborer earned $384 a year; a carpenter took home $686. The carpenter's family lived comfortably in a four-room house, usually breakfasting on meat or eggs, hotcakes, butter, cake, and coffee. The silk worker and the laborer generally ate bread and butter for two of their three daily meals.

For workers without steady employment, rising real wages meant little. Workers, especially unskilled ones, often found work only sporadically. When times were slow or conditions depressed, as they were from 1873 to 1879 and 1893 to 1897, employers, especially in small firms, laid off skilled and unskilled workers alike and reduced wages. Even in a good year like 1890, one out of every five men outside of agriculture had been unemployed at least a month. Workers were left to fend for themselves because unemployment insurance did not exist. One woman grimly recalled, "If the factory shuts down without warning, as it did last year for six weeks, we have a growing expense with nothing to counterbalance." Occasionally, kindhearted employers offered assistance in hard times, but it was rarely enough.

The Family Economy

Although nineteenth-century ideology pictured men as breadwinners, many working-class married men could not earn enough to support their families alone. In the nineteenth century, married women did not usually take outside employment, although they contributed to family income by taking in sewing, laundry, and boarders. In 1890, only 3.3 percent of married women were in the paid labor force. A working-class family's standard of living thus often depended on the work of children. The laborer whose annual earnings amounted to only $384 depended on his 13-year-old son, not his wife, to earn an extra $196, critical to the family's welfare. In 1880, one-fifth of the nation's children between the ages of 10 and 14 held jobs.

Child labor was closely linked to a father's income, which in turn depended on skill, ethnic background, and occupation. Immigrant families more frequently sent their young children out to work (and also had more children) than native-born families. Middle-class reformers who sentimentalized childhood disapproved of parents who put their children to work. "Father never attended school, and thinks his children will have sufficient schooling before they reach their tenth year, thinks no advantage will be gained from longer attendance at school, so children will be put to work as soon as able," said one. Such a father condemned his children to future poverty, reformers believed. Actually, sending children to work was a means of handling the immediate threat of poverty, of financing the education of one of the children, or even of ensuring that children stayed near their family.

Children Working in Coal Mine— Lewis Hine Photo

Women at Work

Many more young people over the age of 14 were working for wages than was the case for children. Half of all Philadelphia's students had quit school by that age. Daughters as well as sons were expected to take jobs, although young women from immigrant families were more likely to work than young American women. By 1900, nearly 20 percent of American women were in the labor force.

Massachusetts Bureau of Statistics of Labor, from *The Working Girls of Boston* (1884)

Discrimination, present from women's earliest days in the workforce, persisted. An experienced female factory worker might be paid $5 or $6 a week, whereas an unskilled male laborer could make about $8. Still, factory jobs were desirable because they often paid better than other kinds of work open to women.

Employment opportunities for women were limited, and ethnic taboos and cultural traditions helped shape choices. About a quarter of working women secured factory jobs. Italian and Jewish women (whose cultural backgrounds virtually forbade their going into domestic service) clustered in the garment industry, and Poles and Slavs went into textiles, food processing, and meatpacking. In some industries, such as textiles, women composed an important segment of the workforce. With the introduction of the typewriter, other sorts of employment opportunities opened up. By 1900, nearly all typists were female. Specialized skills such as stenography also meant more office work for working-class young women, while big department stores needed scores of clerks to wait on middle-class shoppers. But about 40 percent of working-class women, especially those from Irish, Scandinavian, or black families, were maids, cooks, laundresses, and nurses.

Domestic service was arduous, and domestics could not count on much sympathy from their employers. "Do not think it necessary to give a hired girl as good a room as that used by members of the family," said one lady of the house. "She should sleep near the kitchen and not go up the front stairs or through the front hall to reach her room." A servant received room and board plus $2 to $5 a week. The fact that so many women took such work speaks clearly of their limited opportunities.

Domestic Servants   Wearing their best clothes, these domestics pose for the camera. What do the women appear to be holding and why? In what room does the picture appear to have been taken? Although there is no way to ascertain the background of these young women, a majority of domestic servants were Irish or Irish American. Domestic work was often exhausting and provided little privacy or free time, but many women were attracted by the opportunity to live in a middle-class home and have regular meals. In addition, domestic work often paid better than factory work. Still, some young women avoided service, explaining that "it's freedom that we want when the day's work is done." *(Historical Society of Wisconsin)*

The difficult situation facing working women drove some, like Rose Haggerty, into prostitution. Burdened with a widowed and sickly mother and four young brothers and sisters, at 14 Rose started work at a New York paper bag factory. She earned $10 a month, of which $6 went for rent. Her fortunes improved when a friend helped her buy a sewing machine. Rose then sewed shirts at home, often working as many as 14 hours a day to support her family. Suddenly, the piecework rate for shirts was slashed in half. Rose contemplated suicide. But when a sailor offered her money for spending the night with him, she realized that she had an alternative. Prostitution meant food, rent, and heat for her family. "Let God Almighty judge who's to blame most," the 20-year-old Rose reflected, "I that was driven, or them that drove me to the pass I'm in."

Prostitution appears to have increased in the late nineteenth century, although there is no way of knowing the actual numbers of women involved. Probably most single women accepted the respectable jobs open to them. They tolerated discrimination and low wages because their families depended on their contributions. They also knew that when they married, they would probably leave the paid workforce forever.

Marriage hardly ended women's work, however. Like colonial families, late-nineteenth-century working-class families operated as economic units. The unpaid domestic labor and management skills of working-class wives were critical to family survival. With husbands away for 10 to 11 hours a day, women bore the burden of caring for children and doing all domestic chores, made more difficult by the lack of conveniences and urban services. As managers of family resources, married women bore significant responsibilities. What American families had once produced for themselves now had to be bought. It was the working-class wife's job to scour secondhand shops for cheap clothes and to practice the small domestic economies that were crucial for survival.

Women also supplemented family income by taking in work. Jewish and Italian women frequently did piecework and sewing at home. In the Northeast and the Midwest, between 10 and 40 percent of all working-class families kept boarders. Immigrant families, in particular, often made ends meet by taking single young countrymen into their homes. The added chores (providing meals and clean laundry), the need to juggle work schedules, and the sacrifice of privacy were disadvantages outweighed by the extra income boarders provided.

Black women's working lives reflected the obstacles African Americans faced in late-nineteenth-century cities. Although few married white women (about 7 percent) worked outside the home, many black women did. In southern cities in 1880, about three-quarters of single black women and one-third of married black women worked outside the home. Because industrial employers would not hire black women, most served as domestics or laundresses. The high percentage of married black women in the labor force reflected the marginal wages their husbands earned. But it may also be explained partly by the lesson learned during slavery that children could thrive without the constant attention of their mothers.

CAPITAL VERSUS LABOR

Class conflict colored late-nineteenth-century industrial life. Although workers welcomed the progress the factory made possible, many rejected their employers' values, which emphasized individual gain at the expense of collective good. While owners reaped most of the profits, workers were becoming wage slaves. Fashioning their arguments from their republican legacy, workers claimed that the degradation of the country's citizen laborers threatened to undermine the republic itself.

On-the-Job Protests

Workers and employers struggled over control of the workplace. Many workers staunchly resisted unsatisfactory working conditions. They resented being "like any other piece of machinery, to be made to do the maximum amount of work with the minimum expenditure of fuel." Because skilled workers had indispensable practical knowledge, they were well positioned to direct on-the-job actions. Sometimes they tried to control critical work decisions or to humanize work.

Cigar makers clung to their custom of having one worker read to others as they performed their tedious chores.

Workers also sought to control the pace of production. Too many goods meant an inhuman work pace and might result in overproduction, massive lay-offs, and a reduction in piecework prices. So an experienced worker might whisper to a new hand, "See here, young fellow, you're working too fast. You'll spoil our job for us if you don't go slower."

Absenteeism, drunkenness at work, and general inefficiency—all widespread—contained elements of protest. In three industrial firms in the late nineteenth century, one-quarter of the workers stayed home at least one day a week. Some lost days were due to layoffs, but not all. The efforts of employers to impose stiff fines on absent workers suggested their frustration with uncooperative employees.

To a surprising extent, workers made the final protest by quitting their jobs altogether. Most employers responded by penalizing workers who left without sufficient notice—to little avail. A Massachusetts labor study in 1878 found that although two-thirds of them had the same occupation for more than 10 years, only 15 percent of the workers surveyed held the same job. A similar rate of turnover occurred in the industrial workforce in the early twentieth century. Workers unmistakably and clearly voted with their feet.

Strike Activity After 1876

The most direct and strenuous attempts to change conditions in the workplace came in the form of thousands of strikes punctuating the late nineteenth century. In 1877, railroad workers staged the first and bloodiest nationwide industrial strike of the nineteenth century. The immediate cause was the railroad owners' decision to reduce wages. But the rapid spread of the strike all over the country, as well as the violence of the strikers, who destroyed railroad property and kept trains idle, indicated more fundamental discontent.

An erratic economy, high unemployment, and the lack of job security all fed the conflagration. More than 100 people died before federal troops ended the strike. The frenzied response of the propertied class, which saw the strike as the beginning of revolution and applauded military intervention, forecast the pattern of later conflicts. Time and time again, middle- and upper-class Americans would turn to state power to crush labor activism.

A wave of confrontations followed the strike of 1877. Between 1881 and 1905, there were 36,757 strikes involving over 6 million workers, three times the strike activity in France. Such numbers show widespread working-class discontent, involving more than just those at the very bottom. Strikes, as well as sabotage and violence, were most often linked to demands for higher wages and shorter hours.

Nineteenth-century strike activity underwent important changes as the consciousness of American workers expanded. In the period of early industrialization, discontented laborers rioted in their neighborhoods rather than at their workplaces. Between 1845 and the Civil War, however, strikes for higher wages began to replace neighborhood brawls. Workers, angry though they were at their employers, had little sense that the strike might force employers to improve working conditions. In the post–Civil War period, collective actions at the workplace spread. Local and national unions played a more important role in organizing protest, conducting 60 percent of the strikes between 1881 and 1905. Coordination between strikers in different companies improved. Finally, wages among the most highly unionized workers became less of an issue. Workers sought more humane conditions. By the early 1890s, over one-fifth of strikes involved workplace rules.

Labor Organizing, 1865–1900

Civil War experience colored postwar labor organizing. As one working-class song pointed out, workers had borne the brunt of that struggle. "You gave your son to the war/ The rich man loaned his gold/ And the rich man's son is happy to-day,/ And yours is under the mold." Workers who had fought to save the Union argued that wartime sacrifices justified efforts for justice and equality in the workplace.

Labor leaders quickly realized the need for national as well as local organizations to protect the laboring class against "despotic employers." In 1866, several craft unions and reform groups formed the National Labor Union (NLU). Claiming 300,000 members by the early 1870s, the organization supported a range of causes including temperance, women's rights, and the establishment of cooperatives to bring the "wealth of the land" into "the hands of those who produce it."

MAP

Organizing American Labor in the Late Nineteenth Century

The call for an eight-hour day reveals some of the basic assumptions of the organized labor movement. Few workers saw employers as a hostile class or wanted to destroy the economic system. But they did believe bosses were often tyrants whose demands for their time threatened to turn citizens into slaves. The eight-hour day would curb the power of owners and allow workers the time to cultivate the qualities necessary for republican citizenship.

Many of the NLU's specific goals survived, although the organization did not. An unsuccessful attempt to create a political party and the depression of 1873 decimated the NLU. Survival and job searches took precedence over union causes.

The Knights of Labor and the AFL

As the depression wound down, a new mass organization, the Noble and Holy Order of the Knights of Labor, rose to prominence. Founded as a secret society in 1869, the order became public and national when Terence V. Powderly was elected Grand Master Workman in 1879. The Knights of Labor sought "to secure to the workers the full enjoyment of the wealth they create." Because the industrial system denied workers their fair share as producers, the Knights of Labor proposed a cooperative system of production paralleling the existing system. Cooperative efforts would provide workers with the economic independence necessary for citizenship, and an eight-hour day would allow them time for moral, intellectual, and political pursuits.

The Knights of Labor was open to all American "producers," defined as all contributing members of society—skilled and unskilled, black and white, men

Labor Unrest This depiction of working-class unrest appeared in
Harper's Weekly in 1894. Why does the artist give a prominent place to the
National Guardsmen and the destruction wrought during the trouble?
Contrast the individualized guardsmen with the faceless mob in the back-
ground and draw some general conclusions about the artist's choices and
intent. *(The Granger Collection, New York)*

and women, even merchants and manufacturers. Only the idle and the corrupt
(gamblers, saloon keepers, speculators, bankers, lawyers) were excluded. Many
shopkeepers joined, advertising themselves as a "friend of the workingman."
This inclusive membership policy provided the organization with the potential
power of great numbers. The organization grew in spurts, attracting miners between 1874 and 1879, skilled urban tradesmen between 1879 and 1885, and unskilled workers thereafter.

Although Powderly frowned on strikes, the organization reaped the benefit of
grassroots strike activity. Local struggles proliferated after 1883. In 1884, unorgan-
ized workers of the Union Pacific Railroad walked off the job when management
announced a wage cut. Within two days, the company caved in, and the men
joined the Knights. The next year, a successful strike against the Missouri Pacific
Railroad brought in another wave of members. Then, in 1886, the Haymarket Riot
in Chicago caused such a growth in labor militancy that in that single year the
membership of the Knights of Labor ballooned from 100,000 to 700,000.

The "riot" at Haymarket was, in fact, a peaceful protest meeting connected
with a lockout at the McCormick Reaper Works. When the Chicago police arrived
to disperse the crowd, a bomb exploded. Seven policemen died. Although no one
knows who planted the bomb, eight anarchists were tried and convicted. Three
were executed, one committed suicide, and the others served prison terms.

Labor agitation and turbulence spilled over into politics. In 1884 and 1885, the
Knights lobbied for a national contract labor law that would require work con-

tracts and state laws outlawing convict labor. The organization also pressed successfully for the creation of a federal Department of Labor. As new members poured in, however, direct political action became increasingly attractive. Despite many local successes, no national labor party emerged. But in the 1890s, the Knights cooperated with the Populists' attempt to reshape American politics and society.

The Knights could not sustain momentum. Alerted by the Haymarket Riot, employers were determined to break the organization. A strike against Jay Gould's southwestern railroad system in 1886 collapsed. Consumer and producer cooperatives fizzled; the policy of accepting both black and white workers led to strife and discord in the South. The two major parties co-opted labor politicians. Furthermore, national leaders also failed. Powderly could neither unify his diverse following nor control militants opposing him. By 1890, membership plummeted to 100,000, although the Knights continued to play a role well into the 1890s.

The American Federation of Labor (AFL), founded in 1886, became the nation's dominant union in the 1890s. The history of the Knights pointed up the problems of a national union that admitted all who worked for wages, but officially rejected strikes in favor of the ballot box and arbitration. The leader of the AFL, Samuel Gompers, had a different notion of effective worker organization. He was convinced that skilled workers should put their specific occupational interests first, so that they could control the supply of skilled labor and keep wages up.

Gompers organized the AFL as a federation of skilled trades—cigar makers, iron molders, ironworkers, carpenters, and others—each one autonomous, yet linked through an executive council to work together for prolabor national legislation and mutual support during boycott and strike actions. He repudiated dreams of a cooperative commonwealth or of ending the wage system, instead focusing on immediate "bread and butter" issues—higher wages, shorter hours, industrial safety, and the right to organize. Although Gompers rejected direct political action as a means of obtaining labor's goals, he believed in the value of the strike. A shrewd organizer, he knew from bitter experience the importance of dues high enough to sustain a strike fund through a long, tough fight.

Under Gompers's leadership, the AFL grew from 140,000 in 1886 to nearly 1 million by 1900. Although his notion of a labor organization was elitist, he steered his union through a series of crises, fending off challenges from socialists on his left and corporate opposition to strikes on his right. But there was no room in his organization for the unskilled or for blacks. The AFL did make a brief, halfhearted attempt to unionize women in 1892, but men resented women as coworkers and preferred them to stay in the home. The AFL agreed. In 1900, the International Ladies' Garment Workers Union (ILGWU) was established. Although women were its backbone, men dominated the leadership.

Working-Class Setbacks

Despite the growth of working-class organizations, workers lost many battles. Some of the more spectacular clashes reveal why working-class activism often failed and why so many workers lived precariously.

In 1892, silver miners in Coeur d'Alene, Idaho, struck when their employers installed machine drills in the mines, reduced skilled workers to shovelmen, and cut wages. The owners, supported by state militiamen and the federal government, successfully broke the strike by using scabs, but not without fighting. Several hundred union men were eventually tried and found guilty of a wide variety of charges. Out of the defeat emerged the Western Federation of Miners (WFM), whose chief goal was an eight-hour law for miners.

The Coeur d'Alene struggle set the pattern for many subsequent strikes. Mine owners fought strikes by shutting off credit to union men, hiring strikebreakers and armed guards, and infiltrating unions with spies. Violence was frequent, usually ending with the arrival of state militia, arrests or intimidation, legal action, and blacklisting. Despite this, the WFM won as many strikes as it lost.

The Homestead and Pullman Strikes of 1892 and 1894

Labor's worst setback came in 1892 at the Homestead steel mills near Pittsburgh. Carnegie had purchased the Homestead plant and put Henry Clay Frick in charge. Together, they wanted to break the union that threatened to extend its organization of the steel industry. After three months of stalemated negotiations over a new wage contract, Frick issued an ultimatum. Workers must accept wage cuts or be replaced. Frick barricaded the entire plant and hired 300 armed Pinkerton guards. As they arrived on July 6, they and armed steelworkers fought a day-long gun battle. Several men on both sides were killed, and the Pinkertons retreated. Then, at Frick's request, the governor of Pennsylvania sent 8,000 troops to crush the strike and the union. Two and a half weeks later, a New York anarchist tried to assassinate Frick.

The Homestead strike dramatized the lengths to which both labor and capital would go. Eugene Debs, for many years an ardent organizer of railroad workers, wrote, "If the year 1892 taught the workingmen any lesson worthy of heed, it was that the capitalist class, like a devilfish, had grasped them with its tentacles and was dragging them down to fathomless depths of degradation."

Debs saw 1893 as the year in which organized labor would "escape the prehensile clutch of these monsters." Instead, 1893 brought a serious depression and more setbacks for labor. Undaunted, Debs combined several of the separate railroad brotherhoods into a united American Railway Union (ARU). Within a year, over 150,000 railroadmen joined the ARU, and Debs won a strike against the Great Northern Railroad, which had attempted to slash wages.

DOCUMENT

Address to 1894 Convention of American Railway Union by Jennie Curtis

Debs faced his toughest crisis at the Pullman Palace Car Company in Chicago. The company maintained a model company town near Chicago—naturally, called Pullman—where management controlled all aspects of workers' lives. Late in 1893, as the depression worsened, the Pullman Company cut wages by one-third and laid off many workers, without reducing rents or prices in its stores. Forced to pay in rent what they could not earn in wages, working families struggled through the winter. Those working experienced speedups, threats, and further wage cuts. Desperate Pullman workers joined the ARU in the spring of 1894 and struck.

In late June, after Pullman refused to submit the dispute to arbitration, Debs led the ARU into a sympathy strike in support of the striking Pullman workers. Remembering the ill-fated railroad strike of 1877, Debs advised his lieutenants to "use no violence" and "stop no trains." Rather, he sought to boycott trains handling Pullman cars throughout the West. As the boycott spread, the General Managers Association, which ran the 24 railroads centered in Chicago, came to Pullman's support. Hiring 2,500 strikebreakers, the GMA appealed to the state and federal governments for military and judicial support in stopping the strike.

Governor Richard Altgeld of Illinois, sympathizing with the workers and believing that local law enforcement was sufficient, opposed using federal troops. But U.S. Attorney General Richard Olney, a former railroad lawyer, obtained a court injunction on July 2 to end the strike as a "conspiracy in restraint of trade." Two days later, President Cleveland ordered federal troops to crush the strikers. Violence escalated rapidly. Local and federal officials hired armed guards, and the railroads paid them to help the troops. Within two days, strikers and guards were fighting bitterly. As troops poured into Chicago, the violence worsened, leaving scores of workers dead.

Debs's resources would run out unless he could enlist wider labor support. "We must all stand together or go down in hopeless defeat," he warned other unions. When Gompers refused support, the strike collapsed. Debs and several other leaders were found guilty of contempt of court. Hitherto a lifelong Democrat, Debs became a staunch socialist. His arrest and the defeat of the Pullman strike killed the American Railway Union. In 1895, in *In Re Debs*, the Supreme Court upheld the legality of using an injunction to stop a strike, giving management a powerful weapon against unions. Most unions survived the difficult days of the 1890s, but the labor movement emerged as a distinct underdog in its conflicts with organized capital.

Although in smaller communities strikes against outside owners might win local middle-class support, most labor conflicts encountered the widespread middle- and upper-class conviction that unions were un-American. Many people claimed to accept the idea of worker organizations, but would not concede that unions should participate in making economic or work decisions. Most employers violently resisted union demands as infringements of their right to manage their business. The sharp competition of the late nineteenth century, combined with a pattern of falling prices, stiffened employers' resistance to workers' demands. State and local governments and the courts frequently supported them.

The severe depressions of the 1870s and 1890s further undermined working-class activism. Workers could not focus on union issues when survival itself was in question. Many unions collapsed during hard times.

A fundamental problem was the reluctance of most workers to organize even in favorable times. In 1870, less than one-tenth of the industrial workforce belonged to unions, about the same as on the eve of the Civil War. Thirty years later, despite the expansion of the workforce, only 8.4 percent (mostly skilled workers) were union members. Why were workers so slow to join unions? Certainly, diverse work settings and ethnic differences made it difficult for workers to recognize common bonds. Many unskilled workers sensed that labor "aristocrats" did not have their interests at heart. Moreover, many native-born American workers still clung to the tradition of individualism or dreamed of entering the middle class.

An Irish woman highlighted another important point. "There should be a law ... to give a job to every decent man that's out of work," she declared, "and another law to keep all them I-talians from comin' in and takin' the bread out of the mouths of honest people." Ethnic and religious diversity complicated forging a common front. Many foreigners, planning to return to their homeland, had limited interest in changing conditions in the United States—and because their goal was to work, they took jobs as scabs. Much of the violence that accompanied working-class actions erupted when owners brought in strikebreakers. Some Americans blamed immigrants for both low wages and failed worker actions.

Tension within laboring ranks appeared most dramatically in the anti-Chinese campaign of the 1870s and 1880s as white workers in the West began to blame the Chinese for economic hardships. A meeting of San Francisco workers in 1877 in favor of the eight-hour day exploded into a rampage against the Chinese.

DOCUMENT

Chinese Exclusion Act (1882)

In following years, angry mobs killed Chinese workers in Tacoma, Seattle, Denver, and Rock Springs, Wyoming. Local hostility was expressed at the national level when, in 1882, Congress passed the Chinese Exclusion Act with the support of the Knights of Labor, prohibiting the immigration of Chinese workers for a 10-year period. It was extended in 1892 and made permanent in 1902.

Yet many immigrants, especially skilled ones, supported unions and cooperated with native-born Americans. Often ethnic bonds tied members to one another and to the community. For example, in the 1860s and 1870s, as the Molders' Union in Troy, New York, battled with manufacturers, its Irish membership won sympathy and support from the Irish-dominated police force, the Roman Catholic Church, fraternal orders, and public officials.

The importance of workers' organizations lay not so much in their successful struggles and protests as in the implicit criticism they offered of American society. Using the language of republicanism, many workers lashed out at an economic order that robbed them of their dignity and humanity. As producers of wealth, they protested that so little of it was theirs. As members of the working class, they rejected the middle-class belief in individualism and social mobility.

The Balance Sheet

Except for skilled workers, most laboring people found it impossible to earn much of a share in the material bounty industrialization created. Newly arrived immigrants suffered especially. Long hours on the job and walking to and from work left workers little free time. Family budgets included, at best, only small amounts for recreation.

Yet this harsh view of working-class life partly reflects standards of what is acceptable today. Because so few working-class men or women recorded their thoughts, it is hard to know how they viewed their experiences. But culture and background influenced perspectives. The family tenement, one Polish immigrant said, "seemed quite advanced when compared with our home" in Poland. Jews found American poverty preferable to Russian pogroms.

Studies of several cities show that nineteenth-century workers achieved some occupational mobility. One worker in five in Los Angeles and Atlanta during the 1890s, for example, managed to climb into the middle class. Most immigrant workers were stuck in ill-paid, insecure jobs, but their children did better.

TIMELINE

1843–1884	"Old immigration"	**1873–1879**	Depression
1870s–1880s	Consolidation of continental railroad network	**1885–1914**	"New immigration"
		1886	American Federation of Labor founded
1873	Bethlehem Steel begins using Bessemer process		Haymarket Riot in Chicago
		1893–1897	Depression

Mobility, like occupation, was related to background. Native-born whites, Jews, and Germans rose more swiftly and fell less often than Irish, Italians, or Poles. Cultural attitudes, family size, education, and group leadership all produced different ethnic mobility patterns. Jews, for example, valued education and sacrificed to keep children in school. With an education, they moved upward. Slavs, however, who valued a steady income over mobility and education, took their children out of school and sent them to work young. This not only helped the family, they thought, but also gave the child a head start toward reliable, stable employment. A southern Italian proverb, "Do not make your child better than you are," suggests valuing family success over individual success. Different attitudes led to different aspirations and career patterns.

Two groups found little mobility. African Americans were largely excluded from the industrial occupational structure and were restricted to unskilled jobs. Unlike immigrant industrial workers, they could not move to better jobs as new unskilled workers took the positions at the bottom. Hispanic residents in Los Angeles made minimal gains there and probably elsewhere.

Although occupational mobility was limited for immigrants, other rewards often compensated for the lack of workplace success. Home ownership—all but impossible in their homeland—loomed important for the Irish. Owning a home also meant extra income from boarders and some protection against uncertainties and old age. The Irish proved adept politicians and came to dominate big-city government in the late nineteenth century. They succeeded in the construction industry and dominated the hierarchy of the Catholic Church in the United States. Even Irish who did not share this upward mobility could benefit from ethnic connections and take pride in their group's achievements.

Likewise, social clubs and fraternal orders compensated in part for lack of advancement at work. Ethnic associations, parades, and holidays provided a sense of identity and security that offset the limitations of the job world.

A few rags-to-riches stories always encouraged the struggling masses. The family of John Kearney in Poughkeepsie, New York, for example, achieved modest success. After 20 years as a laborer, he started his own business as a junk dealer and even bought a simple house. His sons started off in better jobs than their father had. One became a grocery store clerk, later a baker, a policeman, and, finally, at the age of 40, an inspector at the waterworks. Another was an iron molder, and the third son was a post office worker and eventually the superintendent of city streets. If this success paled next to that of industrial giants such as Andrew Carnegie and John D. Rockefeller, it was still enough to keep the American dream alive.

Conclusion

The Complexity of Industrial Capitalism

The rapid growth of the late nineteenth century made the United States one of the world's industrial giants. Many factors contributed to the "wonderful accomplishments" of the age. They ranged from sympathetic government policies to the rise of big business and the emergence of a cheap industrial workforce. But it was also a turbulent period. Many Americans benefited only marginally from the new wealth. Some of them protested by joining unions, by walking out on strike, or by initiating on-the-job actions. Most lived their lives more quietly without Thomas O'Donnell's opportunity to tell their story. But middle-class Americans began to wonder about the O'Donnells of the country. It is to their concerns, worries, and aspirations that we now turn.

Questions for Review and Reflection

1. What explains the United States' rise to industrial and economic prominence in the late nineteenth century?

2. In what ways did American cities change in this period?

3. Explain which groups were able to realize the American dream of success and which were not and why.

4. Compare and contrast the experiences of middle-class and working-class women.

5. What factors undermined the working-class efforts at collective action and which promoted them? In your opinion, which were the most important factors underlying the failures of the working class? Why?

Discovering U.S. History Online

The Rockefellers www.pbs.org/wgbh/amex/rockefellers/index.html
Companion to the PBS film of the same title, the site presents audio clips from historians, illustrated essays, maps, and images about this famous industrialist.

Angel Island: The Pacific Gateway www.internationalchannel.com/education/angelisland
Angel Island was the principal gateway for Chinese immigrants. This site documents and illustrates the experiences of these immigrants as they entered the United States.

Lower East Side Tenement Museum www.thirteen.org/tenement/index.html
This site presents digital exhibits from the museum, whose goal is "to preserve and interpret the history of the immigrant experience on the Lower East Side."

Ellis Island www.ellisisland.com/indexHistory.html
This official museum site presents a timeline and an overview of the Ellis Island immigration experience.

American Labor History www.geocities.com/CollegePark/Quad/6460/AmLabHist/
This site provides a general chronological survey of the history of labor in America. The author also has included with each section an extensive list of Internet references on labor history.

Fiction and Film

Theodore Dreiser tells the story of a young rural woman who comes to Chicago and violates its social norms to acquire some of the city's offerings in *Sister Carrie* (1900). Stephen Crane's novel *Maggie: A Girl of the Streets* (1893) gives a grim picture of life in urban slums. Thomas Bell follows several generations of the same immigrant family whose American life is entwined with steel in *Out of This Furnace* (1976 ed.). *The Richest Man in the World: Andrew Carnegie,* a 1997 film made for PBS, analyzes the personal and professional life of Carnegie, making good use of interviews with business and labor historians. It offers extended treatment of the Homestead strike, for which the film holds Carnegie largely responsible. *The Age of Innocence* (1993), which takes place in 1870s New York, offers a splendid picture of the sumptuous lives of the rich and their norms and values. This Martin Scorsese film is based on the novel by the same name by Edith Wharton.

Recommended Reading

www.ablongman.com/nash
The Companion Website has a list of recommended readings about industrialization, urbanization, the middle and laboring classes, and capital versus labor.

CHAPTER 19

Politics and Reform

CHAPTER OUTLINE

- Politics in the Gilded Age
- Middle-Class Reform
- Politics in the Pivotal 1890s
- Conclusion: Looking Forward

American Stories

A Utopian Novelist Warns of Two Americas

At the start of his best-seller *Looking Backward* (1888), Edward Bellamy likened the American society of his day to a huge stagecoach. Dragging the coach along sandy roads and over steep hills were the "masses of humanity." While they strained desperately "under the pitiless lashing of hunger," at the top sat the favored few—who, however, constantly feared that they might fall from their seats and have to pull the coach themselves.

Bellamy's famous coach allegory began a utopian novel in which the class divisions and pitiless competition of the nineteenth century were replaced by a classless, caring, cooperative new society. Economic anxieties and hardships were supplanted by satisfying labor and leisure. In place of the coach, all citizens in the year 2000 walked together and shopped in equal comfort and security under a huge umbrella (not unlike modern malls) over the sidewalks of the city.

The novel opens in 1887. The hero, a wealthy Bostonian, falls asleep worrying about the effect local labor struggles might have on his upcoming wedding. When he wakes up, it is the year 2000. Utopia has been achieved peacefully through the development of one gigantic trust, owned and operated by the national government. Every citizen between the ages of 21 and 45 works in an industrial army with equal pay and work difficulty. Retirement after 45 is devoted to hobbies, reading, culture, and the minimal leadership necessary in a society without crime, corruption, poverty, or war.

Bellamy's book was popular with educated middle-class Americans, who were attracted by his vision of a society in which humans were both morally good and materially well off—and in which core values of the 1880s survived intact, including individual incentive, private property, and rags-to-riches presidents. Women married for love and were relieved of housework by labor-saving gadgets. Although they worked in the industrial army in "lighter occupations," their primary role was still to supervise domestic affairs, nurture the young, and beautify culture.

Like most middle-class Americans of his day, Bellamy disapproved of European socialism. Although some features of his utopia were socialistic, he and his admirers called his system "nationalism." This appealed to a new generation of Americans who had put aside Civil War antagonisms to embrace the greatness of a growing, if now economically divided, nation. In the early 1890s, with Americans buying nearly 10,000 copies of *Looking Backward* every week, over 160 Nationalist clubs were formed to crusade for the adoption of Bellamy's ideas.

The inequalities of wealth described in Bellamy's coach scene reflected a political life in which many participated, but only a few benefited. The wealthiest 10 percent, who rode high on the coach, dominated national politics, while untutored bosses held sway in governing cities. Except for token expressions of support, national political leaders ignored the cries of factory workers, immigrants, farmers, African Americans, Native Americans, and other victims of the vast transformation of American industrial, urban, and agrarian life in the late nineteenth century. But as the century closed, middle-class Americans like Bellamy, as well as labor, agrarian, and ethnic leaders themselves, proposed various reforms. Their concern was never more appropriate than during the depression of the mid-1890s, a real-life social upheaval that mirrored the worst features and fears of Bellamy's fictional coach.

In this chapter, we will examine American politics at the national and local level from the end of Reconstruction to the 1890s, a period that for the most part bolstered the rich and neglected the corrosive human problems of urban industrial life. Then we will look at the growing social and political involvement of educated middle-class reformers who, despite their distaste for mass politics, were inspired by a religious and social gospel to work for social change both locally and nationally. We will conclude with an account of the pivotal importance of the 1890s, highlighted by the Populist revolt, the depression of 1893 to 1897, and the election of 1896. In an age of strong national identity and pride, the events of the 1890s shook many comfortable citizens out of their apathy and began the reshaping of American politics.

POLITICS IN THE GILDED AGE

Co-authoring a satirical book in 1873, Mark Twain coined the expression "Gilded Age" to describe Grant's corrupt presidency. The phrase has come to characterize social and political life in the last quarter of the nineteenth century. Although politics was marred by corruption, and politicians avoided fundamental issues in favor of a politics of mass entertainment, voter participation in national elections between 1876 and 1896 hovered at an all-time high of 73 to 82 percent of all registered voters.

DOCUMENT

Mark Twain, from *The Gilded Age* (1873)

Behind the glitter, two gradual changes occurred that would greatly affect twentieth-century politics. First was the development of a professional bureaucracy. In congressional committees and executive branch offices, elite specialists and experts emerged as a counterfoil to the perceived dangers of majority rule represented by high voter participation, especially by the millions of immigrant "newcomers alien to our traditions," as a New England poet put it. Second, after a period of close elections and party stalemate, new issues and concerns fostered a party realignment in the 1890s.

Gilded Age Politics   Although this 1892 painting by John Klir shows the outcome of a "Lost Bet" in the election that year, note the ethnic, racial, and class diversity of the street crowds, momentarily united in enjoyment of the humiliated loser pulling his victorious opponent (and a wagon full of American flags). What kinds of diversity do you see in the painting? Will a more diverse America hold together? *(Library of Congress)*

Politics, Parties, Patronage, and Presidents

DOCUMENT

Edward Bellamy, from *Looking Backward* (1888)

American government in the 1870s and 1880s clearly supported the interests of riders atop Bellamy's coach. Few nineteenth-century Americans would have agreed that the national government should tackle problems of poverty, unemployment, and trusts. They mistrusted organized power and believed that all would benefit from an economic life free of government interference. Political leaders favored governmental passivity that would allow industrial expansion and wealth creation.

"One might search the whole list of Congress, Judiciary, and Executive during the twenty-five years 1870–95," wrote Henry Adams, "and find little but damaged reputation." Few eras of American government were so corrupt, and Adams was especially sensitive to the low quality of politics compared to the exalted morality of his grandfather John Quincy Adams and great-grandfather John Adams.

During the weak Johnson and Grant presidencies, Congress emerged as the dominant branch of government with power in the committee system. Senators James G. Blaine (Maine) and Roscoe Conkling (New York) typified the moral quality of congressional leadership. Despite lying about having been paid off by railroads, Blaine was probably the most popular Republican politician of the era. Charming, intelligent, witty, and able, he served twice as secretary of state and was a serious contender for the presidency in every election from 1876 to 1892.

His foe, Conkling, dispensed lucrative jobs at the New York customhouse and spent most of his career bickering over patronage. In more than two decades in Congress, he never drafted a bill.

In 1879, a disgusted student of legislative politics, Woodrow Wilson, wrote: "No leaders, no principles; no principles, no parties." The two big parties diverged mostly over patronage rather than principles. A British observer, Lord Bryce, concluded that the two parties, like two bottles, bore different labels, yet "each was empty."

Yet these characterizations were not entirely accurate. There were differences, as party professionals solidified their popular base to achieve political ends. Republican votes came from northeastern Yankee industrial interests, New England migrants, and Scandinavian Lutherans across the Upper Midwest. Democrats depended on southern whites, northern workers, and urban immigrants. Affiliation reflected interest in important cultural, religious, and ethnic questions. Because the Republican party was willing to mobilize the power of the state to reshape society, people who wanted to regulate moral and economic life were attracted to it. Catholics and various immigrant groups preferred the Democratic party because it opposed government efforts to regulate morals. Said one Chicago Democrat, "A Republican is a man who wants you t' go t' church every Sunday. A Democrat says if a man wants t' have a glass of beer on Sunday he can have it."

For a few years, Civil War and Reconstruction issues generated party differences. But after 1876, the two parties were evenly matched, and they avoided controversial stands on national issues. In three of the five presidential elections between 1876 and 1892, a mere 1 percent of the vote separated the two major candidates. In 1880, James Garfield won by only 7,018 votes; in 1884, Grover Cleveland squeaked by Blaine by a popular vote margin of 48.5 to 48.2 percent. In two elections (1876 and 1888), the electoral vote winner had fewer popular votes. Only twice, each time for only two years, did one party control the White House and both houses of Congress. Although all the presidents in the era except Cleveland

A Political Cartoon Grover Cleveland's hypocrisy as "Grover the Good" is lampooned by this cartoon from the election of 1884 showing a tearful mother with Cleveland's "illegitimate" child. The people elected him anyway. Why do you think they did so? *(The Granger Collection, New York)*

were Republicans, Democrats controlled the House of Representatives in eight of ten sessions of Congress between 1875 and 1895.

Gilded Age presidents were undistinguished and played a minor role in national life. None of them—Hayes (1877–1881), Garfield (1881), Chester A. Arthur (1881–1885), Cleveland (1885–1889 and 1893–1897), and Benjamin Harrison (1889–1893)—served two consecutive terms. The only Democrat in the group, Cleveland, differed little from the Republicans. When Cleveland violated the expectation that presidents should not initiate ideas by devoting his entire annual message in 1887 to a call for a lower tariff, Congress did nothing. Voters turned him out of office a year later.

National Issues

Four issues were important at the national level in the Gilded Age: the tariff, currency, civil service, and government regulation of railroads (see Chapter 18). In confronting these issues, legislators tried to serve both their own self-interest and the national interest of an efficient, productive, growing economy.

The tariff was one issue where party, as well as regional attitudes toward the use of government power, made some difference. Republicans wanted government to support business interests and stood for a high tariff to protect businessmen, wage earners, and farmers from foreign competition. Democrats demanded a low tariff because "the government is best which governs least." But politicians accommodated local interests when it came to tariffs. Democratic senator Daniel Vorhees of Indiana explained: "I am a protectionist for every interest which I am sent here by my constituents to protect."

Tariff revisions were bewilderingly complex as legislators catered to these many special interests. Most tariffs included a jumble of higher and lower rates. The federal government depended on tariffs and excise taxes (primarily on tobacco and liquor) for most of its revenue, so there was little chance that the tariff would be abolished or substantially lowered. Surpluses produced by the tariff during the Gilded Age helped the parties finance patronage jobs and government programs.

The money question was even more complicated. During the Civil War, the federal government had circulated paper money (greenbacks) that could not be exchanged for gold or silver (specie). In the late 1860s and 1870s, politicians debated whether the United States should return to a metallic standard, which would allow paper money to be exchanged for specie. "Hard-money" advocates supported either withdrawing all paper money from circulation or making it convertible to specie. They opposed increasing the volume of money, fearing inflation. "Soft-money" Greenbackers argued that there was not enough currency in circulation for an expanding economy and urged increasing the supply of paper money in order to raise farm prices and cut interest rates.

Hard-money interests had more clout. In 1873, Congress demonetized silver. In 1875, it passed the Specie Resumption Act, gradually retiring greenbacks from circulation and putting the nation firmly on the gold standard. But as large supplies of silver were mined in the West, pressure resumed for increasing the money supply by coining silver. Soft-money advocates pushed for the unlimited coinage of silver in addition to gold. In an 1878 compromise, the Treasury was required to buy between $2 million and $4 million of silver each month and coin it as silver dollars. Despite this increase in the money supply, the period was not inflationary. Prices fell, disappointing supporters of soft money. They pushed for more silver, continuing the controversy into the 1890s.

The issue of civil service reform was, Henry Adams said, a "subject almost as dangerous in political conversation in Washington as slavery itself in the old days before the war." The worst feature of the spoils system was that parties financed themselves by assessing holders of patronage jobs, often as much as 1 percent of their annual salaries. Reformers, mostly genteel native white Protestants, demanded competitive examinations to create an honest and professional civil service—but also one that would bar immigrants and their urban political machine bosses from the spoils of office.

Most Americans expected their presidents to reward the faithful with government jobs, but Garfield's assassination by a crazed office seeker created a public backlash. "My God! Chet Arthur in the White House!" someone exclaimed, knowing that the new president was closely identified with Conkling's corrupt machine. Arthur surprised doubters by being a capable and dignified president, responsive to growing demands for civil service reform. Congress found itself forced into passing the Pendleton Act of 1883, mandating merit examinations for about one-tenth of federal offices. Gradually, more bureaucrats fell under its coverage, but parties became no more honest. As campaign contributions from government employees dried up, parties turned to huge corporate contributions, which in 1888 helped elect Benjamin Harrison.

DOCUMENT

Pendleton Civil
Service Act
(1883)

The Lure of Local Politics

The fact that the major parties did not disagree substantially on issues such as money and civil service does not mean that nineteenth-century Americans found politics dull. Far more eligible voters turned out in the late nineteenth century than at any time since. The 78.5 percent average turnout to vote for president in the 1880s contrasts sharply with the near 50 percent of eligible Americans who voted in 2000 and 2004.

American men were drawn to the polls in part by the hoopla, but also by local issues. Iowa farmers turned out to vote for state representatives who favored curbing the power of the railroads. But emotional issues of race, religion, nationality, and alcohol often overrode economic self-interest. Voters expressed strong interest in temperance, anti-Catholicism, compulsory school attendance and Sunday laws, aid to parochial schools, racial issues, immigration restriction, and "bloody shirt" reminders of the Civil War.

The new urban immigrants played a large role in stimulating political participation. As traditional native-born elites left local government for more lucrative and higher-status business careers, city bosses stepped in. Their control rested on their ability to deliver the immigrant vote, which they secured by operating informal welfare systems. Bosses handed out jobs and money for rent, fuel, and bail, and they provided a personal touch in a strange environment. As New York City's boss, George Washington Plunkitt, said, "There's got to be in every ward somebody that any bloke can come to—no matter what he's done—and get help."

Party leaders also won votes by making politics exciting. The parades, rallies, and oratory of nineteenth-century campaigns generated excitement as party leaders used hoopla subtly to win voters for substantive issues. In the election of 1884, for example, emotions ran high over the moral lapses of the opposing candidates—Blaine's corruption and Cleveland's illegitimate child. Cleveland won in part because an unwise Republican clergyman called the Democrats the party of "rum, Romanism, and rebellion," ensuring Cleveland an outpouring of Catholic support in crucial New York. But beneath the emotional issues were rational concerns over tariffs, money, and civil service.

Party leaders used local and ethnic issues to solidify party affiliation and mobilize voters for their national agendas. Spirited local contests occurred, particularly over prohibition. Many Americans considered drinking a serious social problem. Annual consumption of brewery beer had risen from 2.7 gallons per capita in 1850 to 17.9 in 1880. In one city, saloons outnumbered churches 31 to 1. Such statistics shocked those who believed that drinking would destroy character, corrupt politics, and cause poverty, crime, and unrestrained sexuality. Because they were often the targets of violent drunken men, women especially supported temperance. Rather than try to persuade individuals to give up drink, as the pre–Civil War temperance movement had done, many now sought to ban drinking by putting the question of prohibition on the ballot.

IMAGE

"The Drunkard's Progress"— Cartoon, 1846

Emotional conflicts boiled in the 1880s at the state level over issues such as education. In Iowa, Illinois, and Wisconsin, Republicans sponsored laws mandating that children attend "some public or private day school" where instruction was in English. These laws aimed to undermine parochial schools, which taught in the language of the immigrants. Irish Catholics in New York sought political support for their parochial schools. In Iowa, where a state prohibition law also passed, the Republican slogan was "A schoolhouse on every hill, and no saloon in the valley." Local Republicans bragged that "Iowa will go Democratic when hell goes Methodist," and indeed they won. But in Wisconsin, a law for compulsory school attendance was so strongly anti-Catholic that it backfired. Many voters, disillusioned with Republican moralism, shifted to the Democratic party.

MIDDLE-CLASS REFORM

Most middle-class Americans avoided reformist politics. But urban corruption and labor violence of the 1880s frightened many out of their aversion to politics.

Frances Willard and the Women's Christian Temperance Union (WCTU) is an example. As president of the WCTU from 1879 until 1898, Willard headed the largest women's organization in the country. Most WCTU members were church-going, white Protestant women who believed drunkenness caused poverty and family violence. But after 1886 the WCTU reversed its position, attributing drunkenness to poverty, unemployment, and bad labor conditions. Willard joined the Knights of Labor in 1887 and by the 1890s influenced the WCTU to extend its programs to alleviate the problems of workers, particularly women and children.

The Gospel of Wealth

Willard called herself a Christian socialist because she believed in applying the ethical principles of Jesus to economic life. For her and many other educated middle-class reformers, Christianity called for a cooperative social order that would reduce inequalities of wealth. But for most Gilded Age Americans, Christianity supported the competitive individualistic ethic. Philadelphia Baptist preacher Russell Conwell's famous sermon "Acres of Diamonds," delivered 6,000 times to an estimated 13 million listeners, praised riches as a sure sign of "godliness" and stressed the power of money to "do good."

Andrew Carnegie expressed the ethic most clearly. In an article, "The Gospel of Wealth" (1889), Carnegie celebrated competition for producing better goods at lower prices. The concentration of wealth in a few hands, he concluded, was "not only beneficial but essential to the future of the race." The fittest would bring order and efficiency out of the chaos of rapid industrialization. Carnegie's defense of the new economic order found as many supporters as Bellamy's *Looking Backward*. Partly this was because Carnegie insisted that the rich must spend some of their wealth to benefit their "poorer brethren." Carnegie built hundreds of libraries and promoted world peace.

Carnegie's ideas reflected an ideology known as social Darwinism, based on the work of naturalist Charles Darwin. In his *Origin of Species*, published in 1859, Darwin concluded that plant and animal species evolved through natural selection. Some managed to adapt to their environment and survived; others failed to adapt and perished. Herbert Spencer, an English social philosopher, applied this "survival of the fittest" notion to human society. Progress, Spencer said, resulted from relentless competition in which the weak were eliminated and the strong climbed to the top, as in Bellamy's coach. Spencer warned against any interference in the economic world by tampering with the natural laws of selection: "The whole effort of nature is to get rid of such as are unfit, to clear the world of them, and make room for better."

DOCUMENT

Herbert Spencer, Social Darwinism (1857)

Spencer's leading American followers, Carnegie and Yale economist William Graham Sumner, insisted that poverty resulted from the struggle for existence. It was "absurd," Sumner wrote, to pass laws permitting society's "worst members" to survive, or to "sit down with a slate and pencil to plan out a new social world."

The scientific vocabulary of social Darwinism injected scientific rationality into what often seemed a baffling economic order. Sumner and Spencer argued that underlying social laws, like those of the natural world, dictated economic affairs. Social Darwinists also believed in the superiority of the Anglo-Saxon race, which they maintained had reached the highest stage of evolution. Their theories were used to justify race supremacy and imperialism, as well as the monopolistic efforts of American businessmen. "The growth of a large business," John D. Rockefeller, Jr., told a YMCA class, "is merely the survival of the fittest."

Reform Darwinism and Pragmatism

Others questioned social Darwinism. Brooks Adams wrote that social philosophers like Spencer and Sumner were "hired by the comfortable classes to prove that everything was all right." Intellectual reformers directly challenged the gloomy social Darwinian notion that nothing could be done to alleviate poverty and injustice. With roots in antebellum abolitionism, women's rights, and other crusades for social justice, men such as Franklin Sanborn and Henry George and women such as Elizabeth Cady Stanton and Susan B. Anthony transferred their reform fervor to post-bellum issues. Sanborn, for example, an inspector of charities in Massachusetts, founded the American Social Science Association in 1865 to "treat wisely the great social problems of the day." Sanborn was known as the "leading social worker of his day."

Henry George, an amateur social scientist, observed that wherever the highest degree of "material progress" had been realized, "we find the deepest poverty." George's book, *Progress and Poverty* (1879), was an early statement of the contradictions of American life. With Bellamy's *Looking Backward*, it was the most influential book of the age, selling 2 million copies by 1905. George admitted that economic growth had produced wonders, but pointed out the social costs and the loss of Christian values. His remedy was to break up land-holding monopolists who profited from the increasing value of their land, which they rented to those who actually did the work. He proposed a "single tax" on the unearned increases in land value.

George's solution may seem simplistic, but his religious tone and optimistic faith in the capacity of humans to effect change appealed to many middle-class intellectuals. Some went further. Sociologist Lester Frank Ward and economist Richard T. Ely both found examples of cooperation in nature and demonstrated that competition and laissez-faire had proved both wasteful and inhumane. Reform Darwinists urged an economic order marked by cooperation and regulation.

Two pragmatists, John Dewey and William James, established a philosophical basis for reform. James, a professor at Harvard, argued that while environment was important, so was human will. "What is the 'cash value' of a thought, idea, or belief?" James asked. What was its result? "The ultimate test for us of what a truth means," he suggested, was in the consequences of a particular idea and what kind of moral "conduct it dictates."

James and young social scientists including Ward and Ely gathered statistics documenting social wrongs and rejected social determinism. They argued that the application of intelligence and human will could change the "survival of the fittest" into the "fitting of as many as possible to survive." Their position encouraged educators, economists, and reformers of every stripe, giving them an intellectual justification to struggle against misery and inequalities of wealth.

Settlements and Social Gospel

DOCUMENT

Jane Addams, from *Twenty Years at Hull House* (1910)

Jane Addams saw the gap between progress and poverty in the winter of 1893. She had long been aware that life in big cities for working-class families was bitter and hard. Born in rural Illinois, Addams founded Hull House in Chicago in 1889 "to aid in the solution of the social and industrial problems which are engendered by the modern conditions of life in a great city." Also in 1889, Wellesley literature professor Vida Scudder and six other Smith graduates formed an organization of college women to work in settlement houses.

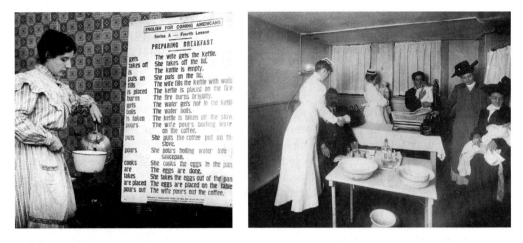

Settlement House Service (left) What is being taught to immigrant women in this typical settlement house poster? The health clinic (right) is in Vida Scudder's Denison House in Boston. Settlement house work, Scudder wrote, fulfilled "a biting curiosity about the way the Other Half lived, and a strange hunger for fellowship with them." What evidence do you see of cross-cultural, cross-class bonding? Do you have opportunities to engage in this kind of service learning today? *(Left: U.S. Government Education Bureau/National Geographic Image Collection; right, Schlesinger Library, Radcliffe Institute, Harvard University)*

Middle-class activists like Addams and Scudder worried in particular about the degradation of life and labor in America's cities, factories, and farms. Most of them drew upon the ethical teachings of Jesus for inspiration in solving social problems. They preferred a society marked by cooperation rather than competition—where, as they liked to say, people were guided by the "golden rule rather than the rule of gold." Some preferred to put their goals in more secular terms, speaking of radically transforming American society. Most, however, worked within existing institutions. As middle-class intellectuals and professionals, they tended to stress an educational approach to problems. But they were also practical, seeking tangible improvements by running for public office, crusading for legislation, mediating labor disputes, and living among the poor.

The settlement house movement typified 1890s middle-class reformers' blend of idealism and practicality. The primary purpose of settlement houses was to help immigrant families, especially women, adapt Old World rural styles of child-rearing and housekeeping to American urban life. They launched day nurseries, kindergartens, and boarding rooms for working women; they offered classes in sewing, cooking, nutrition, health care, and English; and they tried to keep young people out of saloons by organizing sports clubs and coffeehouses.

A second purpose of the settlement house movement was to give college-educated women meaningful work at a time when they faced professional barriers and to allow them to preserve the strong feelings of sisterhood they had experienced at college. A third goal was to gather data exposing social misery in order to spur legislative action—developing city building codes for tenements, abolishing child labor, and improving factory safety. Hull House, Addams said, was intended in part "to investigate

IMAGE

Tenement Families—Jacob Riis Photo

and improve the conditions in the industrial districts of Chicago." The settlement house movement, with its dual emphasis on the scientific gathering of facts and spiritual commitment, thus blending academic study and Christian beliefs, nourished the new discipline of sociology, first taught in divinity schools.

By contrast, Dwight Moody preached a traditional evangelical Christianity in cities, leading hundreds of urban revivals in the 1870s. The revivals appealed to lower-class rural folk who were both drawn to the city by their hopes and pushed there by economic ruin. Supported by businessmen who believed that religion would make workers and immigrants more docile, revivalists battled sin through individual conversion. The revivals helped to nearly double Protestant church membership in the last two decades of the century. Although some urban workers drifted into socialism, most remained conventionally religious.

Other Protestant ministers embraced the Social Gospel movement of the 1890s, which tied salvation to social betterment. Like the settlement house workers, these religious leaders sought to make Christianity relevant to urban problems. Congregational minister Washington Gladden advocated collective bargaining and corporate profit sharing. A young Baptist minister in the notorious Hell's Kitchen area of New York City, Walter Rauschenbusch, raised an even louder voice. Often called on to conduct funeral services for children killed by the airless, diseased tenements and sweatshops, Rauschenbusch scathingly attacked capitalism and church ignorance of socioeconomic issues. His progressive ideas for social justice and a welfare state were later published in two landmark books, *Christianity and the Social Crisis* (1907) and *Christianizing the Social Order* (1912).

Perhaps the most influential book promoting social Christianity was a bestselling novel *In His Steps*, published in 1897 by Charles Sheldon. The novel portrayed the dramatic changes made possible by a few community leaders who resolved to base all their actions on a single question: "What would Jesus do?" For a minister, this meant seeking to "bridge the chasm between the church and labor." For the idle rich, it meant settlement house work and reforming prostitutes. For landlords and factory owners, it meant improving the living and working conditions of tenants and laborers. Although filled with naive sentimentality characteristic of much of the Social Gospel, Sheldon's novel prepared thousands of influential middle-class Americans for progressive civic leadership after 1900.

Reforming the City

DOCUMENT

Tammany Hall
(1835)

No late-nineteenth-century institution needed reforming more than urban government, called by the president of Cornell "the worst in Christendom—the most expensive, the most inefficient, and the most corrupt." A Philadelphia committee pointed to years of "inefficiency, waste, badly paved and filthy streets, unwholesome and offensive water, and slovenly and costly management." New York and Chicago were even worse.

Creating a "city beautiful" through environmental remedies was one approach. Urban planners put in water mains and sewers and landscape architects built parks and planted trees along broadened boulevards lined by elegant homes and public buildings—libraries, theaters, music halls. But these transformations

Favors from a Party Boss Reformers wanted to eliminate the rule of urban party bosses. What in this *Puck* magazine cartoon would they criticize and want to change? What good did bosses do? Did the good outweigh the bad? What is local politics like in *your* city? *(Courtesy of the Newberry Library, Chicago)*

of urban space rarely reached the squalid sections of the city inhabited by recent immigrants and rural transplants.

Rapid urban growth swamped city leaders with new demands for service. As city governments struggled, they raised taxes and incurred vast debts, which bred graft and the rise of the boss. Urban bosses awarded utility franchises and construction contracts to local businesses in return for kickbacks, while new immigrant voters received jobs and welfare in return for their votes. Bosses tipped off friendly real estate men about projected city improvements and received favors from the owners of saloons, brothels, and gambling clubs in return for help with police protection, bail, and influence with judges. These institutions were vital to the urban economy and played an important role in easing the immigrants' way into American life. For many young women, prostitution meant economic survival. For men, the saloon offered friendship, cheap meals, and job leads.

Bossism deeply offended these ethnocentric, well-intentioned middle-class urban reformers. "Goo-goos" (as bosses called advocates of "good government") opposed not only graft and vice, but also the perversion of democracy by the exploitation of ignorant immigrants. The immigrants, said one, "follow blindly leaders of their own race, are not moved by discussion, and exercise no judgment of their own"—and so were "not fit for the suffrage."

Urban reformers' programs were similar in most cities. They not only worked for the "Americanization" of immigrants in public schools (and opposed parochial schooling), but also formed voters' leagues to discuss the failings of municipal government. They delighted in exposing electoral irregularities and large-scale graft. These discoveries led to strident calls for replacing the mayor, especially an Irish Catholic, with an Anglo-Saxon Protestant reformer.

Politics colored every reform issue. Anglo-Saxon men favored prohibition partly to remove ethnic saloon owner influence from politics and supported woman suffrage partly to gain a middle-class political advantage against male immigrant voters. Most urban reformers disdained the "city proletariat mob." They proposed to replace bosses with expert city managers, who would bring honest professionalism to city government. They hoped to make government cheaper and thereby lower taxes. One effect of their emphasis on cost efficiency was to cut services to the poor. Another was to disfranchise working-class and ethnic groups, whose political participation depended on the boss system.

Not all urban reformers were elitist. Samuel Jones, for example, both opposed bossism and passionately advocated political participation by urban immigrants. He himself had begun as a poor immigrant in the Pennsylvania oil fields but worked his way up to the ownership of several oil fields and a factory in Toledo, Ohio. In 1894, he decided to "apply the Golden Rule as a rule of conduct" in his factory, with an eight-hour day, a $2 minimum daily wage (50 to 75 cents higher than the local average for 10 hours), cooperative insurance, and a Christmas dividend. He hired social outcasts, offered employees cheap lunches and recreational facilities, and established Golden Rule Hall, where social visionaries could speak. In 1897, he was elected to the first of an unprecedented four terms as mayor. A maverick Republican who antagonized prominent citizens, Jones advocated municipal ownership of utilities, public works jobs and housing for the unemployed, more civic parks and playgrounds, and free vocational education and kindergartens. A pacifist, he took away policemen's weapons. In police court, Jones regularly dismissed most cases of petty theft and drunkenness on grounds that the accused were victims of social injustice, and he often released prostitutes after fining every man in the room 10 cents—and himself a dollar—for condoning prostitution. Crime in notoriously sinful Toledo fell. When "Golden Rule" Jones died in 1904, nearly 55,000 tearful people filed past his coffin.

The Struggle for Woman Suffrage

Women served, in Jane Addams's phrase, as "urban housekeepers" in the settlement house and good government movements, which reflected the tension many women felt between their public and private lives, their obligations to self, family, and society. This tension was seldom expressed openly. A few women writers, however, began to vent the frustrations of middle-class domestic life. In her novel *The Awakening* (1899), Kate Chopin told the story of a young woman who, in discovering her own sexuality and life's possibilities beyond being a "mother-woman," defied conventional expectations of a woman's role. Her sexual affair and eventual suicide prompted a St. Louis newspaper to label the novel "poison."

Some middle-class women, Addams and Scudder, for example, avoided marriage, preferring the nurturing relationships found in the female settlement house community. A few women boldly advocated free love or, less openly, formed lesbian relationships. Although most preferred traditional marriages and chose not to work outside the home, the generation of women that came of age in the 1890s married less—and later—than any other in American history until the present time.

Many women reconciled the conflicting pressures between their private and public lives—and deflected male criticism—by seeing their work as maternal. Addams called Hull House the "great mother breast of our common humanity." Frances Willard told Susan B. Anthony in 1898 that "government is only housekeeping on the broadest scale," a job men had botched, requiring women's saving participation. One of the leading labor organizers was "Mother" Jones, and the fiery feminist anarchist Emma Goldman titled her monthly journal *Mother Earth*. By using nurturant language to describe their work, women furthered the very arguments used against them. Many remained economically dependent on men, and all women still lacked the essential rights of citizenship. How could they be municipal housekeepers if they could not even vote?

After the Seneca Falls Convention in 1848, women's civil and political rights advanced very slowly. Although several western states gave women the vote in municipal and school board elections, before 1890 only the territory of Wyoming (1869) granted full political equality. Colorado, Utah, and Idaho enfranchised women in the 1890s, but no other states granted suffrage until 1910. This slow pace resulted in part from male opposition led by an odd combination of ministers, saloon interests, and men threatened in various ways by women's voting rights. "Equal suffrage," a Texas senator said, "is a repudiation of manhood."

In the 1890s, leading suffragists reexamined their situation. The two wings of the women's rights movement, split since 1869, combined in 1890 as the National American Woman Suffrage Association (NAWSA). Although Elizabeth Cady Stanton and Susan B. Anthony continued to head the association, both were in their seventies, and leadership passed to younger, more moderate women who concentrated on the single issue of the vote.

Suffragist Speaking

Changing leadership meant a shift in the arguments for the suffrage. Since 1848, suffragists had argued primarily from the principle of "our republican idea, individual citizenship." But the younger generation shifted to three expedient arguments. The first was that women needed the vote to pass self-protection laws to guard against rapists and unsafe industrial work. The second argument, Addams's notion of urban housekeeping, pointed out that political enfranchisement would further women's role in cleaning up immoral cities and corrupt politics.

The third expedient argument reflected urban middle-class reformers' prejudice against non-Protestant immigrants who voted. Suffragists argued that educated, native-born American women should get the vote to counteract the undesirable influence of male immigrants. In a speech in Iowa in 1894, Carrie Chapman Catt, who would succeed Anthony as president of NAWSA in 1900, argued that the "Government is menaced with great danger ... in the votes possessed by the males in the slums of the cities," a danger that could be averted only by cutting off that vote and giving it instead to women. In the new century, under the leadership of women like Catt, suffrage would finally be secured, and anti-immigrant attitudes would continue.

POLITICS IN THE PIVOTAL 1890S

Americans mistakenly think of the last decade of the nineteenth century as the "gay nineties," symbolized by mustached ball players and sporty Gibson girls riding bicycles. The 1890s was indeed an era of baseball and bicycles, but it was also a decade of disturbing gaps between rich and poor. The nineties featured enormous wealth but also dark tenements, grinding work, and desperate unemployment. The early 1890s saw Populism and protesting farmers; Wounded Knee and the "second great removal" of Native Americans; disfranchisement, segregation, and lynchings for blacks; and a changing workplace and devastating labor defeats at Coeur d'Alene, Homestead, and Pullman.

Anticipated by Bellamy, the 1890s was a decade of contrasts and crises. Supreme Court Justice John Harlan saw a "deep feeling of unrest" everywhere among people worrying that the nation was in "real danger from ... the slavery that would result from aggregations of capital in the hands of a few." Populist "Sockless" Jerry Simpson simply saw a struggle between "the robbers and the robbed."

Although Simpson was wrong about the absence of a middle ground, the gap was indeed huge between Kansas orator Mary E. Lease, who in 1890 said, "What you farmers need to do is to raise less corn, and more Hell," and the wealthy Indianapolis woman who told her husband, "I'm going to Europe and spend my money before these crazy people take it." The pivotal nature of the 1890s hinged

Gap Between Rich and Poor The threat of social upheaval is dramatically illustrated in this turn-of-the-century work, called "From the Depths." What do you think will happen next in this photo? *(Courtesy of The Newberry Library, Chicago)*

Major Legislative Activity of the Gilded Age

In the table, note the kinds of issues dealt with at the different levels: mostly money, tariff, immigration, and civil service legislation at the national level and "hot button" emotional, social, and value issues in the states and localities. Which three or four issues would you have been most concerned with? Which still exist today?

National

1871	National Civil Service Commission created
1873	Coinage Act demonetizes silver
	"Salary Grab" Act (increased salaries of Congress and top federal officials) partly repealed
1875	Specie Resumption Act retires greenback dollars
1878	Bland-Allison Act permits partial coining of silver
1882	Chinese Exclusion Act
	Federal Immigration Law restricts certain categories of immigrants and requires head tax of all immigrants
1883	Standard time (four time zones) established for the entire country
	Pendleton Civil Service Act
1887	Interstate Commerce Act sets up Interstate Commerce Commission
	Dawes Act divides Indian tribal lands into individual allotments
1890	Dependent Pension Act grants pensions to Union army veterans
	Sherman Anti-Trust Act
	Sherman Silver Purchase Act has government buy more silver
	McKinley Tariff sets high protective tariff
	Federal elections bill to protect black voting rights in South fails in Senate
	Blair bill to provide support for education defeated
1891	Immigration law gives federal government control of overseas immigration
1893	Sherman Silver Purchase Act repealed
1894	Wilson-Gorman Tariff lowers duties slightly
1900	Currency Act puts United States on gold standard

State and Local

1850s–1880s	State and local laws intended to restrict or prohibit consumption of alcoholic beverages
1871	Illinois Railroad Act sets up railroad commission to fix rates and prohibit discrimination
1874	Railroad regulatory laws in Wisconsin and Iowa
1881	Kansas adopts statewide prohibition
1882	Iowa passes state prohibition amendment
1880s	Massachusetts, Connecticut, Rhode Island, Montana, Michigan, Ohio, and Missouri all pass local laws prohibiting consumption of alcohol
	Santa Fe ring dominates New Mexico politics and land grabbing
1889	New Jersey repeals a county-option prohibition law of 1888
	Laws in Wisconsin and Illinois mandate compulsory attendance of children at schools in which instruction is in English
	Kansas, Maine, Michigan, and Tennessee pass antitrust laws
1889–1890	Massachusetts debates bill on compulsory schooling in English
1899–1902	Eleven former Confederate states amend state constitutions and pass statutes restricting the voting rights of blacks
1890–1910	Eleven former Confederate states pass segregation laws
1891	Nebraska passes eight-hour workday law
1893	Colorado adopts woman suffrage
1894–1896	Woman suffrage referenda defeated in Kansas and California

on this feeling of polarizing unrest and upheaval as the nation underwent the traumas of change from a rural to an urban society. The new immigration from Europe and the internal migrations of African Americans and farmers added to the "great danger" against which Catt warned. The depression of 1893 widened the economic gap and accelerated demands for reform. The bureaucracy slowly began to adapt to the needs of governing a complex specialized society, and Congress purposefully moved to confront national economic problems.

Republican Legislation in the Early 1890s

Harrison's election in 1888 was accompanied by Republican control of both houses of Congress. The Republicans moved forward in the first six months of 1890 with legislation in five areas: pensions for Civil War veterans and their dependents, trusts, the tariff, the money question, and rights for blacks. A bill providing generous support of $160 million a year for Union veterans and their dependents sailed through Congress.

The Sherman Anti-Trust Act passed with only one nay vote. It declared illegal "every contract, combination ... or conspiracy in restraint of trade or commerce." Although the Sherman Act was vague and not really intended to break up big corporations, it was an initial attempt to restrain large business combinations. But in *United States* v. *E. C. Knight* (1895), the Supreme Court ruled that the American Sugar Refining Company, which controlled more than 90 percent of the nation's sugar-refining capacity, was not in violation of the Sherman Act.

A tariff bill introduced in 1890 by Ohio Republican William McKinley stirred more controversy. McKinley's bill raised tariffs higher than ever. Despite heated opposition from agrarian interests, whose products were generally not protected, the bill passed the House and, after nearly 500 amendments, also the Senate.

Silver was trickier. Recognizing the appeal of free silver to agrarian debtors and the new Populist party, Republican leaders feared their party might be destroyed by the issue. Senator Sherman proposed a compromise that momentarily satisfied almost everyone. The Sherman Silver Purchase Act ordered the Treasury to buy 4.5 million ounces of silver monthly and to issue treasury notes for it. Silverites were pleased by the proposed increase in the money supply. Opponents felt they had averted the worst—free coinage of silver. The gold standard still stood.

Republicans were also prepared to confront violations of the voting rights of southern blacks in 1890. Political considerations paralleled moral ones. Since 1877, the South had become a Democratic stronghold, where party victories could be traced to fraud and intimidation of black Republican voters. "To be a Republican ... in the South," said one Georgian, "is to be a foolish martyr." Republican legislation, then, was intended to honor old commitments to the freedmen and improve party fortunes in the South. An elections bill, proposed by Massachusetts Senator Henry Cabot Lodge, sought to ensure African American voter registration and fair elections. A storm of Democratic disapproval arose. Ex-president Cleveland called it a "dark blow at the freedom of the ballot," and the Mobile *Daily Register* claimed that it "would deluge the South in blood." Senate Democrats delayed action with a filibuster.

To pass the McKinley Tariff, Republican leaders bargained away the elections bill, ending major-party efforts to protect African American voting rights in the South until the 1960s. In a second setback for black southerners, the Senate, fearful of giving the federal government a role in education, defeated a bill to provide federal aid to black schools in the South that received a disproportionately small share of local and state funds. "The plain truth is," said the New York *Herald*, "the North has got tired of the negro," foreshadowing a similar abandonment of civil rights legislation 100 years later.

The legislative efforts of the summer of 1890, impressive by nineteenth-century standards, fell far short of solving the nation's problems. Trusts grew more rapidly after the Sherman Act than before. Union veterans were pleased by their pensions, but southerners were incensed that Confederate veterans were left out. Others, seeing the pension measure as extravagant, labeled the 51st Congress the "billion-dollar Congress." Despite efforts to please farmers, many still viewed tariff protection as a benefit primarily for eastern manufacturers. Farm prices continued to slide, and gold and silver advocates were only momentarily silenced. African American rights were put off to another time. Polarizing inequalities of wealth remained. Voters abandoned the GOP in droves in the 1890 congressional elections, dropping House Republicans from 168 to 88.

Two years later, Cleveland won a presidential rematch with Harrison. "The lessons of paternalism ought to be unlearned," he said in his inaugural address, "and the better lesson taught that while the people should ... support their government, its functions do not include the support of the people."

Formation of the People's Party, 1892

Farmers knew all too well that government did not support them. In February 1892, the People's, or Populist, party was established with Leonidas Polk, president of the National Farmers Alliance, as its presidential candidate. "The time has arrived," he thundered, "for the great West, the great South, and the great Northwest, to link their hands and hearts together and march to the ballot box and take possession of the government ... and run it in the interest of the people." But by July, at the party convention in Omaha, Polk had died and the party nominated James B. Weaver, Union army veteran from Iowa, for president and a former Confederate soldier for vice president.

DOCUMENT

N. A. Dunning, ed., Alliance's Vision of Community (1891)

The platform preamble, written by Ignatius Donnelly, a Minnesota farmer-politician, blazed with the urgent spirit of the agrarian protest movement, proclaiming that in the midst of political and corporate corruption "the people are demoralized. ... The fruits of the toil of millions are boldly stolen to build up colossal fortunes ... we breed two great classes—paupers and millionaires." To heal that divide, Donnelly advocated ending "the controlling influences dominating the old political parties."

The Omaha demands expanded the Ocala platform of 1890. They included more direct democracy (popular election of senators, direct primaries, the initiative and referendum, and the secret ballot) and several pro-labor planks (the eight-hour day, immigration restriction, and condemnation of the use of Pinkerton agents).

DOCUMENT

The People's
Party Platform
(1892)

The Populists also endorsed a graduated income tax, the free and unlimited coinage of silver at a ratio of 16 to 1, and government ownership of railroads, telephone, and telegraph. "The time has come," the platform said, "when the railroad corporations will either own the people or the people must own the railroads."

Although attempting to widen political debate by promoting a new vision of government activism to resolve farmers' problems, the Populists faced monumental obstacles: weaning the South from Democrats, encouraging southern whites to work with blacks, and persuading voters of both parties to abandon familiar political ties. But the new party pressed ahead. Weaver campaigned actively in the South, where he faced egg- and rock-throwing Democrats, who fanned racial fears in opposing his efforts to include blacks in the People's party. Despite hostile opposition, Weaver won over 1 million popular votes (the first third-party candidate to do so), and he carried four states (Kansas, Colorado, Idaho, and Nevada) and parts of Oregon and North Dakota, for a total of 22 electoral votes.

The Populists' support was substantial but regional, coming from western miners and mine owners who favored the demand for silver coinage and from rural Americans from the Great Plains. But the People's party failed to break the Democratic stranglehold on the South, and it did not appeal to city workers of the Northeast, who were suspicious of the party's anti-urban tone and its desire for higher agricultural prices (which meant higher food prices). Perhaps most damaging, the Populists made little inroads among Midwestern farmers, who were relatively better off than farmers elsewhere and saw little value in the Omaha platform. Although the Populists were not yet finished, most discontented farmers in 1892 voted for Cleveland and the Democrats, not for the Populists.

The Depression of 1893

Though winning the election, Cleveland soon faced a difficult test. No sooner had he taken office than began one of the worst depressions ever to grip the American economy, lasting from 1893 to 1897. Its severity was heightened by the growth of a national economy and economic interdependence. The depression started in Europe and spread to the United States as overseas buyers cut back on purchases of American products. Shrinking markets abroad soon crippled American manufacturing. Foreign investors, worried about the stability of American currency, dumped some $300 million of their securities in the United States. As gold left the country to pay for these securities, the nation's money supply declined. At the same time, falling prices hurt farmers, who discovered that it cost more to raise their crops and livestock than they could make in the market. Workers fared no better: wages fell faster than the price of food and rent.

The collapse in 1893 was also caused by an overextension of the domestic economy, especially in railroad construction. Farmers, troubled by falling prices, planted more, hoping that the market would pick up. As the realization of overextension spread, confidence faltered, and then gave way to financial panic. When Wall Street crashed early in 1893, investors frantically sold their shares, companies plunged into bankruptcy, and disaster spread. People rushed to exchange

A City of Contrasts in 1893 These two scenes from Chicago, boating on the lagoon by the Palace of Electricity at the World's Columbian Exposition and children playing on a street near Hull House, are less than a mile away from each other. What do these scenes say about the American people and their politics? *(top: Library of Congress; bottom: Library of Congress)*

paper notes for gold, reducing gold reserves and confidence in the economy even further. Banks called in loans, which by the end of the year led to 16,000 business bankruptcies and 500 bank failures.

The capital crunch and the diminished buying power of rural and small-town Americans (still half the population) forced massive factory closings. Within a year, an estimated 3 million Americans—20 percent of the workforce—lost jobs. People fearfully watched tramps going from city to city, looking for work.

As in Bellamy's coach image, the misery of the many was not shared by the few, which only increased discontent. While unemployed men foraged in garbage dumps, the wealthy gave lavish parties sometimes costing $100,000. While poor families shivered in poorly heated tenements, the very rich built million-dollar summer resorts at Newport, Rhode Island, or grand mansions on New York's

Fifth Avenue. While Lithuanian immigrants walked or rode streetcars, wealthy men luxuriated on huge pleasure yachts.

Nowhere were these inequalities more apparent than in Chicago during the World's Columbian Exposition, which opened on May 1, 1893, five days before a plummeting stock market began the depression. The Chicago World's Fair showcased, as President Cleveland said in an opening-day speech, the "stupendous results of American enterprise." When he pressed an ivory telegraph key, he started electric current that unfurled flags, spouted water through gigantic fountains, lit 10,000 electric lights, and powered huge steam engines. For six months, some 27 million visitors strolled around the White City, admiring its wide lagoons, its neoclassical buildings, and its exhibit halls filled with inventions. Built at a cost of $31 million, the fair celebrated the marvelous accomplishments of American enterprise and of a "City Beautiful" movement to make cities more livable.

But as fairgoers sipped champagne, in immigrant wards less than a mile away people drank contaminated water, crowded into packed tenements, and looked in vain for jobs. "If Christ came to Chicago," British journalist W. T. Stead wrote in 1894, this would be "one of the last precincts into which we should care to take Him." Stead's book showed readers the "ugly sight" of corruption, poverty, and wasted lives in a city with 200 millionaires and 200,000 unemployed men.

Despite the magnitude of despair during the depression, national politicians and leaders were reluctant to respond. Only mass demonstrations forced city authorities to provide soup kitchens and places for the homeless to sleep. When an army of unemployed led by Jacob Coxey marched on Washington in the spring of 1894 to press for public work relief, its leaders were arrested for walking on the Capitol grass. Cleveland's reputation for callousness worsened later that summer when he sent federal troops to Chicago to crush the Pullman strike.

The president focused on tariff reform and repeal of the Silver Purchase Act, which he blamed for the depression. Although repeal was ultimately necessary to establish business confidence, in the short run Cleveland only worsened the financial crisis, highlighted the silver panacea, and hurt conservative Democrats. With workers, farmers, and wealthy silver miners alienated, in the midterm elections of 1894 voters abandoned the Democrats in droves, giving both Populists and Republicans high hopes for 1896.

The Crucial Election of 1896

The campaign of 1896, waged during the depression and featuring a climactic battle over the currency, was one of the most critical in American history. Although Cleveland was in disgrace for ignoring depression woes, few leaders in either major party thought the federal government was responsible for alleviating the suffering of the people. But the disadvantaged, unskilled, and unemployed everywhere wondered where relief might be found. Would either major party respond to the pressing human needs of the depression? Would the People's party set a new national agenda for politics? These questions were raised and largely resolved in the election of 1896.

As the election approached, Populist leaders emphasized the silver issue and debated whether to fuse with one of the major parties by agreeing on a joint ticket,

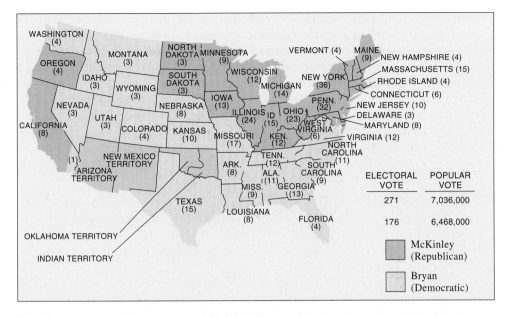

THE PRESIDENTIAL ELECTION OF 1896 In his sweep of the densely populated urban Northeast and Midwest, McKinley beat Bryan by the largest popular vote margin since 1872. In his cabled congratulations, Bryan wrote, "We have submitted the issues to the American people and their will is law." How does the country divide politically today? Was there a "red states" and "blue states" similarity in 1896?

which meant abandoning much of the Populist platform. Influenced by silver mine owners, many Populists became convinced that they must make a single-issue commitment to the free and unlimited coinage of silver at the ratio of 16 to 1.

In the throes of the depression in the mid-1890s, silver took on enormous importance as the symbol of the many grievances of downtrodden Americans. Popular literature captured the rural, moral dimensions of the silver movement. L. Frank Baum's *The Wonderful Wizard of Oz* (1900) was a free-silver allegory of rural values (Kansas, Auntie Em, the uneducated but wise scarecrow, and the good-hearted tin woodsman) and Populist attitudes and policies (the wicked witch of the East and the magical silver shoes in harmony with the yellow brick road in "Oz"—ounces).

The Republicans nominated William McKinley. As a congressman and governor of Ohio, McKinley was identified with the high protective tariff that bore his name. Citing the familiar argument that prosperity depended on the gold standard and protection, Republicans blamed the depression on Cleveland's attempt to lower the tariff.

The excitement of the Democratic convention in July contrasted with the staid, smoothly organized Republican gathering. With Cleveland already repudiated by his party, state after state elected convention delegates pledged to silver. Gold Democrats, however, had enough power to wage a close battle for the platform plank on money. The Democrats' surprise nominee was an ardent young silverite, William Jennings Bryan, a

DOCUMENT

William Jennings Bryan, "Cross of Gold" Speech (1896)

36-year-old congressman from Nebraska. Few saw him as presidential material, but Bryan arranged to give the closing argument for a silver plank himself. His dramatic speech swept the convention for silver and ensured his nomination. Concluding one of the most famous political speeches in American history, Bryan attacked the "goldbugs":

> Having behind us the producing masses of this nation ... and toilers everywhere, we will answer their demand for a gold standard by saying to them: "You shall not press down upon the brow of labor this crown of thorns, you shall not crucify mankind upon a cross of gold."

Bryan stretched out his arms as if on a cross, and the convention exploded in applause.

Populist strategy lay in shambles when the Democrats named a silver candidate. Some party leaders favored fusion with the Democratic ticket, but anti-fusionists were outraged. Unwisely, the Populists nominated Bryan, with Georgia Populist Tom Watson for vice president. Running on competing silver slates damaged Bryan's chances.

During the campaign, McKinley stayed home in Canton, Ohio, where 750,000 admirers came to visit him, brought by low excursion rates offered by the railroads. The Republicans made an unprecedented effort to reach voters through a highly sophisticated media campaign, heavily financed by major corporations. Party leaders hired thousands of speakers and distributed more than 200 million pamphlets in 14 languages to a voting population of 15 million, all advertising McKinley as the "advance agent of prosperity."

McKinley appealed not only to the business classes but also to unemployed workers, to whom he promised a "full dinner pail." Free silver, he warned, would cause inflation and more economic disaster. Recovery depended not on money, but on tariff reform to stimulate industry and provide jobs.

Bryan took his case to the people. Three million people in 27 states heard him speak as he traveled over 18,000 miles, giving as many as 30 speeches a day. Bryan's message was simple: prosperity required free coinage of silver, and government should attend to the needs of the producing classes rather than the vested interests. But his rhetoric favored rural toilers. "The great cities rest upon our broad and fertile prairies," he had said in the "Cross of Gold" speech. Urban workers were not inspired by this rhetoric, nor were immigrants by Bryan's prairie moralizing. To influential easterners, the brash young Nebraskan represented a threat. Theodore Roosevelt wrote, "this silver craze surpasses belief. Bryan's election would be a great calamity."

Voters turned out in record numbers. In key states such as Illinois, Indiana, and Ohio, 95 percent of those eligible to vote went to the polls. McKinley won 271 electoral votes to Bryan's 176, the largest margin of victory since Grant trounced Greeley in 1872. Millionaire Mark Hanna jubilantly wired McKinley: "God's in his heaven, all's right with the world."

Although Bryan won over 6 million votes (47 percent of the total), more than any previous Democratic winner, he failed to carry the Midwest or the urban industrial masses, who had little confidence that the Democrats could stimulate economic growth or cope with industrialism. McKinley's promise of a "full dinner pail" was more convincing. Northern laborers feared that inflation would leave them even poorer—that prices and rents would rise faster than their wages. Catholic immigrants distrusted Populist Protestantism. Chance also played a part in Bryan's defeat. Bad wheat harvests in India, Australia, and Argentina drove up world grain prices, and many of the complaints of American farmers evaporated.

The New Shape of American Politics

The landslide Republican victory broke the stalemate in post–Civil War American politics. Republicans dropped their identification with the politics of piety and strengthened their image as the party of prosperity and national greatness, which gave them a party dominance that lasted until the 1930s. The Democrats, under Bryan's leadership until 1912, put on the mantle of Populist moralism, but were largely reduced to a sectional party, reflecting narrow southern views on money, race, and national power. The 1896 election demonstrated that the Northeast and Great Lakes states had acquired so many immigrants that they now controlled the nation's political destiny. The demoralized Populists disappeared, yet within the next 20 years many Populist issues were adopted by the two major parties.

Another result of the election of 1896 was a change in political participation. Because the Republicans were so dominant outside of the South and Democrats so powerful in the South, few states had vigorous two-party political battles and therefore mobilized large numbers of voters. With results so predictable, voters had little motivation to cast a ballot. Many black voters in the South, moreover, were disfranchised, and middle-class good government reformers were not as effective as party bosses in turning out urban voters. The tremendous rate of political participation that had characterized the nineteenth century since the Jackson era gradually declined. In the twentieth century, political involvement among poorer Americans diminished considerably, a phenomenon unique among western industrial countries.

McKinley had promised that Republican rule meant prosperity, and as soon as he took office, the economy recovered. Discoveries of gold in the Yukon and the Alaskan Klondike increased the money supply, ending the silver mania. Industrial production returned to full capacity. Touring the Midwest in 1898, McKinley spoke to cheering crowds about the shift from "industrial depression to industrial activity."

McKinley's election marked not only the return of economic health, but also the emergence of the executive as the dominant focus of the American political system. Just as McKinley's campaign set the pattern for the extravagant efforts to win office that have dominated modern times, his conduct as president foreshadowed the presidency to this day. McKinley rejected traditional views of the president as the passive executor of laws, instead playing an active role in dealing with Congress and the press. His frequent trips away from Washington showed an increasing regard for public opinion. As we shall see in Chapter 20, McKinley began the transformation of the presidency into a potent force, not only in domestic life, but in world affairs as well.

TIMELINE

1873	Congress demonetizes silver		1890	Flurry of Congressional Acts
1883	Pendleton Civil Service Act		1893	World's Columbian Exposition, Chicago
1888	Edward Bellamy, *Looking Backward*		1893–1897	Financial panic and depression
1889	Jane Addams establishes Hull House		1896	Populist party fuses with Democrats
	Andrew Carnegie's "The Gospel of Wealth"			William McKinley elected president

Conclusion

Looking Forward

This chapter began with Edward Bellamy's imaginary look backward from the year 2000 at the grim economic realities and unresponsive politics of American life in the late nineteenth century. McKinley's triumph in 1896 indicated that in a decade marked by depression, Populist revolt, and cries for action to close the inequalities of wealth—represented by Bellamy's coach—the established order remained intact and politics remained as unresponsive as ever. Calls for change did not necessarily lead to change. But in the areas of personal action and the philosophical bases for social change, intellectual middle-class reformers such as Edward Bellamy, Henry George, Jane Addams, "Golden Rule" Jones, and many others foreshadowed the progressive reforms in the new century. More Americans were able to look forward to the kind of cooperative, caring, and cleaner world envisioned in Bellamy's utopian novel.

As 1900 approached, people took a predictably intense interest in what the new century would be like. Henry Adams envisioned an ominous future, predicting the explosive and ultimately destructive energy of unrestrained industrial development, symbolized by the "dynamo" and other engines of American power. Such forces, he warned, would overwhelm the gentler, moral forces represented by art, woman, and religious symbols. Others were more optimistic, preferring to place their confidence in America's historic role as an exemplary nation, demonstrating to the world the moral superiority of its economic system, democratic institutions, and middle-class Protestant values. Surely the new century, most thought, would see not only the continued perfection of these values and institutions, but also the spread of American influence throughout the world. Such confidence resulted in foreign expansion by the American people even before the old century had ended. We turn to that next.

Questions for Review and Reflection

1. How would you characterize the politics of the Gilded Age? How does it compare to present-day politics?

2. What political issues concerned the American people in the late nineteenth century, and do you think they were the appropriate ones? How are they similar to today's issues?

3. What role did middle-class reformers, especially women, play in dealing with social and political problems in the Gilded Age? How did religion influence reform?

4. Why was the election of 1896 such a crucial and pivotal one in the development of American political parties? How were the policies and areas of support of the two major parties similar to and different from those of the present?

5. To what extent was the American democratic system responsive to the needs of the American people? Was it even "democratic"? How well did politics reflect national ideals and values?

Discovering U.S. History Online

Gilded Age Presidents www.potus.com/rbhayes.html www.potus.com/jagarfield.html www.potus.com/caarthur.html www.potus.com/gcleveland.html www.potus.com/bharrison.html
These sites contain basic factual data about Gilded Age presidents Hayes, Garfield, Arthur, Cleveland, and Harrison, including speeches and online biographies.

Late Nineteenth-Century Articles www.boondocksnet.com
This site includes several exhibitions with links to contemporary articles, art, and cartoons about the late nineteenth century and early twentieth century, including "World's Fairs and Expositions: Defining America and the World, 1876–1916" and "Mark Twain on War and Imperialism."

The Election of 1896 www.iath.virginia.edu/seminar/unit8/home.htm
This fine University of Virginia site contains biographical information, images, great cartoons, and related links about the pivotal election of 1896.

1896: The Presidential Campaign: Cartoons and Commentary www.iberia.vassar.edu/1896/
The site contains several sections: "Cartoons," "Parties and Platforms," "Leaders," "Campaign Themes," and "Special Features," as well as background on the depression of 1893.

World's Columbian Exhibition http://www.boondocksnet.com/expos/columbian.html
Part of a larger site, "World's Fairs and Expositions: Defining America and the World, 1876–1916," superbly edited by Jim Zwick, this site is full of links to contemporary articles, art, and cartoons about the Columbian Exhibition in Chicago in 1893, with attention to architecture, art and literature, race relations, religion, social issues, and technology. A virtual visit to the fair.

Fiction and Film

Mark Twain and Charles D. Warner's *The Gilded Age* (1873) spares no one in its satirical critique of the social, political, and economic life of late nineteenth-century America. Henry Adams's *Democracy: An American Novel* (1880) uses an ironic title to capture the elitist nature of politics and life in Washington in the Gilded Age. Two novels by William Dean Howells, *A Hazard of New Fortunes* (1889) and *The Rise of Silas Lapham* (1885), portray the social life of the new rich in the 1880s. Edward Bellamy's *Looking Backward* (1888) is the utopian novel that began this chapter and that stimulated much late nineteenth-century reform. Kate Chopin's *The Awakening* (1899), set in New Orleans in the 1890s, tells the story of a woman's discovery of self. Theodore Dreiser's *Sister Carrie* (1900), influenced by social Darwinian determinism and set in Chicago and New York, shows the life of a young farm girl who rises to fame and fortune in the city. Frank Norris's immense novel *The Octopus* (1901), set in the San Joaquin Valley of California, shows struggles not only between ranchers and railroads but also between rich and poor, city and country, commercial wheat farmers and sheepherders, and native-born and immigrant Americans.

Anzia Yezierska's *Bread Givers* (1925) reveals the struggles between an Old World Jewish father and his Americanized daughter. *Hester Street* (1975), like the *Bread Givers*, is a wonderfully teachable video about Jewish immigrants in New York City and the process of Americanization. Edgar L. Doctorow's *Ragtime* (1975) is an innovative novel that plays fast and loose with the history and historical figures of turn-of-the-century America; it was also made into a recent Broadway play. Upper-class life in the late nineteenth-century is portrayed in the Hollywood film *The Bostonians* (1998), based on a novel by Henry James. Gore Vidal's *1876: A Novel* (1976) takes a playful, imaginative look at America in its centennial year.

Recommended Reading

www.ablongman.com/nash

The Companion Website has a list of recommended readings on late nineteenth-century politics and urban reform.

Becoming a World Power

CHAPTER OUTLINE

- Steps Toward Empire
- Expansionism in the 1890s
- War in Cuba and the Philippines
- Theodore Roosevelt's Energetic Diplomacy
- Conclusion: The Responsibilities of Power

American Stories

Private Grayson Kills a Soldier in the Philippines

In January 1899, the United States Senate was locked in a dramatic debate over whether to ratify the Treaty of Paris concluding the recent war with Spain over Cuban independence. At the same time, American soldiers uneasily faced Filipino rebels across a neutral zone around the outskirts of Manila, capital of the Philippines. Until recent weeks, the Americans and Filipinos had been allies, together defeating the Spanish to liberate the Philippines. The American fleet under Admiral George Dewey had destroyed the Spanish naval squadron in Manila Bay on May 1, 1898. Three weeks later, an American ship brought from exile the native Filipino insurrectionary leader, Emilio Aguinaldo, to lead rebel forces on land while U.S. gunboats patrolled the seas.

At first, the Filipinos looked on the Americans as liberators. Although the intentions of the United States were never clear, Aguinaldo believed that, as in Cuba, the Americans had no territorial ambitions. They would simply drive the Spanish out and then leave. In June, therefore, Aguinaldo declared the independence of the Philippines and began setting up a constitutional government. American officials pointedly ignored the independence ceremonies. When an armistice ended the war in August, American troops denied Aguinaldo's Filipino soldiers an opportunity to liberate their own capital city and shunted them off to the suburbs. The armistice agreement recognized American rights to the "harbor, city, and bay of Manila," while the proposed Treaty of Paris gave the United States the entire Philippine Islands archipelago.

As a result, tension mounted in the streets of Manila and along 14 miles of trenches separating American and Filipino soldiers. Taunts, obscenities, and racial epithets were shouted across the neutral zone. Barroom skirmishes and knifings filled the nights; American soldiers searched houses without warrants and looted stores. Their behavior was not unlike that of the English soldiers in Boston in the 1770s.

On the night of February 4, 1899, Privates William Grayson and David Miller of Company B, 1st Nebraska Volunteers, were on patrol in Santa Mesa, a Manila suburb surrounded on three sides by insurgent trenches. The Americans had orders to shoot any Filipino soldiers in the neutral area. As the two Americans cautiously worked their way to a bridge over the San Juan River, they heard a Filipino signal whistle, answered by another. Then a red lantern flashed from a nearby blockhouse. The two froze as four Filipinos emerged from the darkness on the road ahead. "Halt!" Grayson shouted. The native lieutenant in charge answered, "Halto!," either mockingly or because he had similar orders. Standing less than 15 feet apart, the two men repeated their commands. After a moment's hesitation, Grayson fired, killing his opponent with one bullet. The other Filipinos jumped out at them and Grayson and Miller shot two more. Then they turned and ran back to their own lines shouting warnings of attack. A full-scale battle followed.

The next day, Commodore Dewey cabled Washington that the "insurgents have inaugurated general engagement" and promised a hasty suppression of the insurrection. The outbreak of hostilities ended the Senate debates. On February 6, the Senate ratified the Treaty of Paris, thus formally annexing the Philippines and sparking a war between the United States and Filipino nationalists.

In a guerrilla war similar to those fought later in Vietnam, Afghanistan, and Iraq, Aguinaldo's Filipino nationalists tried to undermine the American will by hit-and-run attacks. American soldiers remained in heavily garrisoned cities and undertook search-and-destroy missions to root out rebels and pacify the countryside. The Filipino-American War lasted until July 1902, three years longer than the Spanish-American War that caused it, and involved far more troops, casualties, and monetary and moral costs.

How did all this happen? What brought Private Grayson to "shoot my first nigger," as he put it, halfway around the world? For the first time in history, regular American soldiers found themselves fighting outside North America. The "champion of oppressed nations," as Aguinaldo said, had turned into an oppressor nation itself, imposing the American way of life and American institutions on faraway peoples against their will. It would not be the last time.

The war in the Philippines marked a critical transformation of America's role in the world. As the United States sought to exert its influence on the world, so also did global events influence America. Within a few years at the turn of the century, the United States acquired an empire, however small by European standards, and established itself as a world power. In this chapter, we will review the historical dilemmas of America's role in the world, especially those of the expansionist nineteenth century. Then we will examine the motivations for intensified expansionism in the 1890s and how they were manifested in Cuba, the Philippines, and elsewhere. Finally, we will look at how the fundamental patterns of modern American foreign policy were established for Latin America, Asia, and Europe in the early twentieth century. Throughout, we will see that the tension between idealism and self-interest that has permeated America's domestic history has also guided its foreign policy.

STEPS TOWARD EMPIRE

The circumstances that brought Privates Grayson and Miller from Nebraska to the Philippines originated deep in American history. As early as the seventeenth-century Puritan migration, Americans worried about how to do good in a world that does wrong. John Winthrop sought to set up a "city on a hill" in the New World, a model community of righteous living for the rest of the world to imitate. "Let the eyes of the world be upon us," Winthrop had said. That wish, reaffirmed during the American Revolution, became a permanent goal of American policy toward the outside world.

America as a Model Society

Nineteenth-century Americans continued to believe in the nation's special mission. The Monroe Doctrine in 1823 warned Europe's monarchies to keep out of the republican New World. In succeeding decades, distinguished European visitors came to observe the "great social revolution." They found widespread democracy, representative and responsive political and legal institutions, a Protestant religious commitment to human perfectibility, unlimited energy, and an ability to apply unregulated economic activity and inventive genius to produce more things for more people.

"Uncle Sam Teaching the World"—*Puck* Cartoon

In an evil world, Americans then, as now, believed that they stood as a transforming force for good. But how could a nation in the western hemisphere do the transforming? One way was to encourage other nations to observe and imitate the good example set by the United States. Often, however, other nations and peoples were attracted to competing models of modernization, like socialism, or preferred their own religious traditions, like Muslim nations. Such differences often led to a more aggressive foreign policy, as seen in the aftermath of the September 11, 2001, terrorist attack on New York City and the Pentagon.

Americans have rarely just focused on perfecting the good example at home and waiting for others to copy it, which requires patience and passivity, two traits not characteristic of Americans. Rather, throughout history, the American people have actively and sometimes forcefully imposed their ideas and institutions on others. The international crusades of the United States, usually well intentioned if not always well received, have been motivated by a mixture of noble idealism and crass self-interest. Hence, the effort to spread the American model to an imperfect world has been both a blessing and a burden—for others as well as for the American people.

Early Expansionism

Persistent expansionism marked the first century of American independence. Jefferson's purchase of Louisiana in 1803, the removal of Native Americans westward, and the midcentury pursuit of "Manifest Destiny" into Mexico spread the United States across North America. In the 1850s, Americans began to look beyond their own continent as Commodore Perry in 1853 "opened" Japan and southerners sought more cotton lands in the Caribbean. After the Civil War, Secretary of State William Seward spoke of an America that would hold a "commanding sway in the world," destined to exert commercial domination "on the Pacific ocean, and its islands and continents." He purchased Alaska from Russia in 1867 for $7.2 million and acquired a coaling station in the Midway Islands near Hawaii, where missionaries and merchants were already active. He advocated annexing

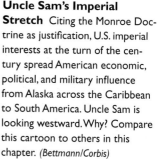

Uncle Sam's Imperial Stretch Citing the Monroe Doctrine as justification, U.S. imperial interests at the turn of the century spread American economic, political, and military influence from Alaska across the Caribbean to South America. Uncle Sam is looking westward. Why? Compare this cartoon to others in this chapter. *(Bettmann/Corbis)*

Cuba and other West Indian islands, tried to negotiate a treaty for an American-built canal through Panama, and dreamed of "possession" of the entire North and Central American continent and ultimately "control of the world."

In 1870, foreshadowing the Philippine debates 30 years later, supporters of President Grant tried to persuade the Senate to annex Santo Domingo (the Dominican Republic) on the island of Hispaniola. They cited the strategic importance of the Caribbean and argued forcefully for the economic value that Santo Domingo would bring. Opponents responded that expansionism violated American principles of self-determination and government by the consent of the governed. They claimed that the Caribbean peoples were unassimilable. Expansionism might also involve foreign entanglements, a large and expensive navy, bigger government, and higher taxes; the Senate rejected the annexation treaty.

Although reluctant to add territory outright, Americans eagerly sought commercial dominance in Latin America and Asia. But American talk of building a canal across Nicaragua produced only Nicaraguan suspicions. In 1881, Secretary of State James G. Blaine sought to convene a conference of American nations to promote hemispheric peace and trade. Latin Americans may have wondered what Blaine intended, for in 1881 he intervened in three separate border disputes in Central and South America, in each case at the cost of goodwill. After an incident and threat of war with Chile in 1889, Blaine's efforts resulted in the first Pan-American Conference to improve economic ties among the nations of the Americas.

American economic influence spread to the Pacific. In the mid-1870s, American sugar-growing interests in the Hawaiian Islands were strong enough to put whites in positions of influence over the monarchy. In 1875, they obtained a treaty admitting Hawaiian sugar duty-free to the United States, and in 1887 the United States also won exclusive rights to build a naval base at Pearl Harbor. Native Hawaiians resented the influence of American sugar interests, especially as they brought in Japanese to replace native people—many of whom died from white diseases—in the sugarcane fields. In 1891, the nationalistic queen Liliuokalani assumed the throne and pursued a policy of "Hawaii for the Hawaiians." In 1893, white planters staged a coup with the help of U.S. gunboats and marines and imprisoned the queen. An annexation treaty was presented to the Senate by the Harrison administration. But when Grover Cleveland, who opposed imperial expansion, returned to the presidency for his second term, he stopped the move. The white sugar growers waited patiently for a more desirable time for annexation, which came during the war in 1898.

American Expansionism in Global Context

American forays into the Pacific and Latin America brought the United States increasingly into contact and conflict with European nations. The nineteenth century was marked by European imperial expansionism throughout much of the world. In southern and southeastern Asia, the British were in India, Burma, and Malaya; the French in Cambodia, Vietnam, and Laos; the Dutch in Singapore and the East Indies; and the Spanish in the Philippines. These and other colonial powers divided China, its Manchu dynasty weakened by the opium trade, internal conflicts, and European pressure, into spheres of economic influence. A China newspaper editorial complained that other nations "all want to satisfy their ambitions to nibble at China and swallow it." The Russians wrested away Manchuria, and Japan took Korea after intervention in a Korean peasant rebellion in 1894. In addition, China was forced to cede Taiwan and southern Manchuria to Japanese influence and control.

World Colonial Empires, 1900

In Africa, Europeans scrambled to gain control of both coastal and interior areas, with England, France, Germany, Portugal, and Belgium grabbing the most land and exploiting African peoples. Only two independent African nations existed in the late nineteenth century: Liberia, founded in 1822 by Americans to resettle free blacks, and the fragmented kingdom of Ethiopia, which thrashed the Italians when they invaded in 1896. With nearly all of Africa divided, the only way imperial powers could acquire more land was to fight each other. Thus, in 1899, war broke out in southern Africa between the British and the Boers, descendants of Dutch settlers—a war waged with a savagery Europeans usually reserved for indigenous peoples. The English destroyed Boer farms and property and drove civilians into camps where an estimated 20,000 women and children perished from starvation and malnutrition. The British won, but at a horrific cost.

Rudyard Kipling, "The White Man's Burden" (1899)

Africa was not then of interest to the United States, but in the Pacific and Caribbean, it was inevitable that the United States, a late arrival to imperialism, would bump into European rivals. Moving outward from Hawaii closer to the markets of eastern Asia, the United States acquired a naval and coaling station in the Samoan Islands in 1878. American and German naval forces almost fought each other there in 1889—before a typhoon ended the crisis by wiping out both navies. Troubles in the Pacific also occurred in the late 1880s over the American seizure of several Canadian ships in fur seal and fishing disputes in the Bering Sea, settled only by the threat of British naval action and an international arbitration commission ruling, which ordered the United States to pay damages.

Closer to home, the United States sought to replace Great Britain as the most influential nation in Central America and northern South America. In 1895, a boundary dispute between Venezuela and British Guiana threatened to bring British intervention against the Venezuelans. President Cleveland, needing a popular political issue during the depression, asked Secretary of State Richard Olney to send a message to Great Britain. Invoking the Monroe Doctrine, Olney's note (stronger than Cleveland intended) called the United States "practically sovereign on this continent" and demanded international arbitration to settle the dispute. The British ignored the note, and war loomed. Both sides realized that war would be an "absurdity," and the boundary dispute was settled.

Despite these expansionist efforts, the United States in 1895 had neither the means nor a consistent policy for enlarging its role in the world. The diplomatic service was small and unprofessional. No U.S. embassy official in Beijing spoke Chinese. The U.S. Army, with about 28,000 men, was smaller than Bulgaria's. The navy, dismantled after the Civil War and partly rebuilt under President Arthur, ranked no higher than tenth in the world and included dangerously obsolete ships. By 1898, things would change.

EXPANSIONISM IN THE 1890S

In 1893, historian Frederick Jackson Turner wrote that for three centuries "the dominant fact in American life has been expansion." The "extension of American influence to outlying islands and adjoining countries," he thought, indicated still more expansionism. Turner struck a responsive chord in a country that had always been restless and optimistic. With the western frontier closed, Americans would surely look for new frontiers, for mobility and markets as well as for morality and missionary activity. The motivations for the expansionist impulse of the late 1890s resembled those that had prompted Europeans to settle the New World in the first place: greed, glory, and God. We will examine expansionism as a reflection of profits, patriotism, piety, and politics.

Profits: Searching for Overseas Markets

Senator Albert Beveridge of Indiana bragged in 1898 that "American factories are making more than the American people can use; American soil is producing more than they can consume. Fate has written our policy for us; the trade of the world must and shall be ours." Americans like Beveridge revived older dreams of an American commercial empire in the Caribbean Sea and the Pacific Ocean. American businessmen saw huge profits beckoning in heavily populated Latin America

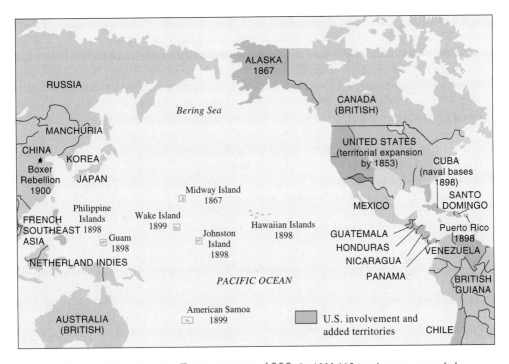

UNITED STATES TERRITORIAL EXPANSION TO 1900 By 1900, U.S. involvement expanded beyond North America to include (in green) islands in the Pacific and the Caribbean as well as parts of South America. How did this happen? What patterns and problems do you see?

and Asia and wanted to get their share of these markets, as well as access to the sugar, coffee, fruits, oil, rubber, and minerals that were abundant in these lands.

Understanding that commercial expansion required a stronger navy and coaling stations and colonies, business interests began to shape diplomatic and military strategy. But not all businessmen in the 1890s liked commercial expansion or a vigorous foreign policy. Some preferred traditional trade with Canada and Europe rather than risky new ventures in Asia and Latin America. Some thought it more important to recover from the depression than annex islands.

But the drop in domestic consumption during the depression also encouraged businessmen to expand into new markets. The tremendous growth of American production in the post–Civil War years made expansionism more attractive than drowning in overproduction, cutting prices, or laying off workers, which would increase social unrest.

Despite the 1890s depression, products spewed from American factories at a staggering rate. The United States moved from fourth place in the world in manufacturing in 1870 to first place in 1900, doubling the number of factories and tripling the value of farm output. Manufactured goods grew nearly fivefold between 1895 and 1914. The total value of American exports tripled, from $434 million in 1866 to nearly $1.5 billion in 1900. By 1914, exports had risen to $2.5 billion, a 67 percent increase over 1900. The increased trade continued to go mainly to Europe rather than Asia. In 1900, for example, only 3 to 4 percent of U.S. exports went to China and Japan. Nevertheless, interest in Asian markets grew, especially as agricultural output continued to increase and prices stayed low.

Investments followed a similar pattern. American direct investments abroad increased from about $634 million to $2.6 billion between 1897 and 1914. Although investments were largest in Britain, Canada, and Mexico, most attention focused on actual and potential investment in Latin America and eastern Asia. Central American investment increased from $21 million in 1897 to $93 million by 1914, mainly in mines, railroads, and banana and coffee plantations. At the turn of the century came the formation and growth of America's biggest multinational corporations, including du Pont, Alcoa, and the United Fruit Company. Although slow to respond to investment and market opportunities abroad, these companies soon supported an aggressive foreign policy.

Patriotism: Asserting National Power

In 1898, a State Department memorandum stated that "we can no longer afford to disregard international rivalries now that we ourselves have become a competitor in the world-wide struggle for trade." The national state, then, should support commercial interests.

More Americans, however, saw expansion in terms of national glory and greatness. In the late 1890s, a group centered around Assistant Secretary of the Navy Theodore Roosevelt and Massachusetts Senator Henry Cabot Lodge emerged as highly influential leaders of a changing American foreign policy. These intensely nationalistic young men shifted official policy to what Lodge called the "large policy." Roosevelt agreed that economic interests should take second place to questions of what he called "national honor."

Naval strategist Alfred Thayer Mahan greatly influenced the new foreign policy elite. Mahan's books argued that in a world of Darwinian struggle for survival, national power depended on naval supremacy, control of sea lanes, and vigorous development of domestic resources and foreign markets. He advocated colonies in both the Caribbean and the Pacific, linked by a canal built and controlled by the United States. In a world of constant "strife," he said, it was imperative that Americans begin "to look outward."

Piety: The Missionary Impulse

As Mahan's and Roosevelt's statements suggest, a strong sense of duty and the missionary ideal of doing good for others also motivated expansionism—and sometimes rationalized the exploitation and oppression of weaker peoples. As a missionary put it in 1885, "The Christian nations are subduing the world in order to make mankind free." Richard Olney agreed, saying in 1898, "the mission of this country is ... to forego no fitting opportunity to further the progress of civilization" as defined by American values and political interests.

Josiah Strong, a Congregationalist minister, was another ardent advocate of American missionary expansionism. He argued that in the struggle for survival among nations, the United States had emerged as the center of Anglo-Saxonism and was "divinely commissioned" to spread political liberty, Protestant Christianity, and civilized values over the earth. "This powerful race," he wrote, "will move down upon Mexico, down upon Central and South America, out upon the islands of the sea, over upon Africa and beyond." In a cruder statement of the same idea, Senator Albert Beveridge of Indiana said in 1899 that God had prepared English-speaking Anglo-Saxons to become "the master organizers of the world to establish and administer governments among savages and senile peoples."

DOCUMENT

Theodore
Roosevelt, "Our
Poorer Brother"
(1897)

Missionaries carried Western values to non-Christian lands around the world, especially China. The number of American Protestant missionaries in China increased from 436 in 1874 to 5,462 in 1914, and the estimated number of Christian converts in China jumped from 5,000 in 1870 to nearly 100,000 by 1900. Although this was much less than missionaries hoped, this tiny fraction of the Chinese population included young reformist intellectuals who, absorbing Western ideas, in 1912 helped overthrow the Manchu dynasty. Economic relations between China and the United States increased at approximately the same rate as missionary activity.

Politics: Manipulating Public Opinion

Although less significant than the other factors, politics also played a role. As in the past, public opinion on international issues helped shape presidential politics. The psychological tensions and economic hardships of the 1890s depression jarred national self-confidence. Foreign adventures provided an emotional release from domestic turmoil and promised to restore patriotic pride—and maybe even win votes.

This process was helped by the growth of a highly competitive popular press, which brought international issues before a mass readership. When New York City newspapers, notably William Randolph Hearst's *Journal* and Joseph Pulitzer's *World*, competed in stirring up public support for the Cuban rebels against Spain, politicians dared not ignore the outcry. Daily reports of Spanish atrocities in 1896 and 1897 kept public moral outrage constantly a part of political discourse.

Politics, then, joined profits, patriotism, and piety in motivating the expansionism of the 1890s. These four impulses interacted to produce the Spanish-American War, the annexation of the Philippine Islands and subsequent war, and the energetic foreign policy of President Theodore Roosevelt.

WAR IN CUBA AND THE PHILIPPINES

Lying 90 miles off Florida, Cuba had been the object of intense American interest for a half century. Spain could not halt the continuing struggle of the Cuban people for a measure of autonomy and relief from exploitive labor in the sugar plantations, even after slavery itself ended. The most recent uprising, which lasted from 1868 to 1878, raised tensions between Spain and the United States, just as it whetted the Cuban appetite for complete independence.

The Road to War

When the Cuban revolt flared up anew in 1895, the Madrid government again failed to implement reforms. Instead, it sent General Weyler, dubbed the "butcher" by the American press, with 50,000 troops to quell the disturbance.

When Weyler began herding rural Cubans into "reconcentration" camps, Americans were outraged. An outpouring of sympathy swept the nation, especially as sensationalist reports of horrible suffering and the deaths of thousands in the camps filled American newspapers.

The Cuban struggle appealed to a country convinced of its role as protector of the weak and defender of the right of self-determination. Motivated in part by genuine humanitarian concern and a sense of admiration for the heroic Cuban freedom fighters, many Americans held rallies to raise money and food for famine relief and called for land reform and even armed intervention. But neither Cleveland nor McKinley wanted war.

Self-interest also played a role. For many years, Americans had noted the profitable resources and strategic location of the island. American companies had invested extensively in Cuban sugar plantations. Appeals for reform had much to do with ensuring a stable environment for further investments and trade ($27 million in 1897), as well as for protecting the sugar fields.

The election of 1896 only temporarily diverted attention from Cuba. A new government in Madrid made halfhearted concessions. Conditions worsened in the reconcentration camps, and the American press kept harping on the plight of the Cuban people. McKinley, eager not to upset recovery from the depression, skillfully resisted war pressures. But he could not control Spanish misrule or Cuban aspirations for freedom.

Events early in 1898 sparked the outbreak of hostilities. Rioting in Havana intensified both Spanish repression and American outrage. A letter from the Spanish minister to the United States, Depuy de Lôme, calling McKinley a "weak," hypocritical politician, was intercepted and made public. Americans fumed.

A second event was more serious. When the rioting broke out, the U.S. battleship *Maine* was sent to Havana harbor to protect American citizens. On February 15, a tremendous explosion blew up the *Maine*, killing 262 men. Newspapers trumpeted slogans such as "Remember the *Maine!* To hell with Spain!"

Assistant Secretary of the Navy Theodore Roosevelt had been preparing for war for many years. He said that he believed the *Maine* had been sunk "by an act of dirty treachery on the part of the Spaniards" and would "give anything if President McKinley would order the fleet to Havana tomorrow." When the president did not, Roosevelt privately declared that McKinley had "no more backbone than a chocolate éclair" and continued readying the navy for action. Although a board of inquiry at the time concluded that an external submarine mine caused the disaster, it is probable that a faulty boiler or some other internal problem set off the explosion. Even Roosevelt later conceded this possibility.

After the sinking of the *Maine*, Roosevelt took advantage of Secretary of the Navy John Long's absence from the office one day to cable Commodore George Dewey, commander of the United States' Pacific fleet at Hong Kong. Roosevelt ordered Dewey to fill his ships with coal and, "in the event" of a declaration of war with Spain, to sail to the Philippines and make sure "the Spanish squadron does not leave the Asiatic coast." "The Secretary is away and I am having immense fun running the Navy," Roosevelt wrote in his diary that night.

Roosevelt's act was consistent with policies he had been urging on his more cautious superior for more than a year. As early as 1895, the navy had contingency

Waging War in the Philippines Describe what is happening in these two visuals. How did it happen that the United States went to war against Spain to free Cuba from colonial domination yet ended up committing many similar atrocities in the Philippines? *(Above, Courtesy of The Newberry Library, Chicago; Left, Keystone-Mast Collection, UCR/California Museum of Photography, University of California, Riverside)*

plans for attacking the Philippines. Influenced by Mahan and Lodge, Roosevelt wanted to enlarge the navy. He also believed that the United States should construct an interoceanic canal, acquire the Danish West Indies (the Virgin Islands), annex Hawaii, and oust Spain from Cuba. As Roosevelt told McKinley late in 1897, he was putting the navy in "the best possible shape" for the day "when war began."

The public outcry over the *Maine* drowned out McKinley's efforts to avoid war. With the issues politicized, McKinley pressured the Madrid government to make concessions. Spain did, though refusing to grant full independence to the Cubans, and the president finally acted. On April 11, 1898, he sent an ambiguous message to Congress that seemed to call for war. Two weeks later, Congress authorized using troops against Spain and recognized Cuban independence, actions amounting to a declaration of war. In a significant additional resolution, the Teller Amendment, Congress stated that the United States had no intention of annexing Cuba. A Cuban revolutionary general was more cautious, saying, "I expect nothing from the Americans. We should trust everything to our efforts. It is better to rise or fall without help than to contract debts of gratitude with such a powerful neighbor."

"A Splendid Little War": Various Views

The outbreak of war between Spain and the United States did not go unnoticed in Europe. German Kaiser Wilhelm II sarcastically offered to join with other European monarchs to help Spain resist the efforts of "the American-British Society for International Theft and Warmongering ... to snatch Cuba from Spain." But Spain was left to face the United States alone, fully expecting a defeat. When war broke out, a Spanish rear admiral said that the ruptured relations with the United States "would surely be fatal."

Indeed, the war was short and relatively easy for the Americans and "fatal" for the Spanish, who at the war's conclusion were left with "only two major combat vessels." The Americans won naval battles almost without return fire. At both major engagements, Manila Bay and Santiago Bay in Cuba, only two Americans died, one of them from heat prostration while stoking coal. Guam and Puerto Rico were taken virtually without a shot. Only 385 men died from Spanish bullets, but more than 5,000 succumbed to tropical diseases. As the four-month war neared its end in August, Secretary of State John Hay wrote Roosevelt that "it has been a splendid little war; begun with the highest motives, carried on with magnificent intelligence and spirit."

The Spanish-American War seemed splendid in other ways, as letters from American soldiers suggest. One young man wrote that his comrades were all "in good spirits" because oranges and coconuts were plentiful and "every trooper has his canteen full of lemonade all the time." Another wrote his brother that he was having "a lot of fun chasing Spaniards."

But the war was not much fun for other soldiers. One said, "Words are inadequate to express the feeling of pain and sickness when one has the fever. For about a week every bone in my body ached and I did not care much whether I lived or not." Another described a fellow soldier shot in the head as "a mass of blood." Nor was the war splendid for African American soldiers, who fought in segregated units and noted stark differences between receiving rude treatment in the American South yet warm greetings in Cuba and Puerto Rico.

For Colonel Roosevelt, who resigned from the Navy Department to lead a cavalry unit as soon as war was declared, the war was excitement and political opportunity. After a close brush with death in Cuba, Roosevelt declared with delight that he felt "the wolf rise in the heart" during "the power of joy in battle."

But ironically, he needed help from African American soldiers to achieve his goals. His celebrated charge up Kettle Hill near Santiago was made possible by black troops first clearing the hill and then protecting his flank. The "charge" made three-inch headlines and propelled him toward the New York governor's mansion. "I would rather have led that charge," he said later, "than served three terms in the U.S. Senate." More than anyone, Roosevelt used the war to advance not only his political career but also the glory of national expansionism.

VIDEO

Roosevelt's Rough Riders

The Philippines Debates and War

Roosevelt's ordering Admiral Dewey to Manila initiated a chain of events that led to the annexation of the Philippines. The most crucial battle of the Spanish-American War occurred on May 1, 1898, when Dewey destroyed the Spanish fleet in Manila Bay and cabled McKinley for additional troops. He sent twice as many troops as Dewey had asked for and began shaping American public opinion to accept the "political, commercial [and] humanitarian" reasons for annexing the Philippines. The Treaty of Paris gave the United States the islands in exchange for a $20 million payment to Spain.

The treaty went to the Senate for ratification during the winter of 1898–1899. Senators hurled arguments across the floor of the Senate as American soldiers hurled oaths and taunts across the neutral zone at Aguinaldo's insurgents near Manila. Private Grayson's encounter, as we have seen, led to the passage of the treaty in a close Senate vote—and began the Filipino-American War and the debates over what to do with the Philippines.

The entire nation joined the argument. At stake were two very different views of foreign policy and of America's vision of itself. After several months of quietly seeking advice and listening to public opinion, McKinley finally recommended annexation. Many Democrats supported the president out of fear of being labeled disloyal. At a time when openly racist thought flourished in the United States, fellow Republicans confirmed McKinley's arguments for annexation, adding even more insulting ones. Filipinos were described as childlike, dirty, and backward. "The country won't be pacified," a Kansas veteran of the Sioux wars told a reporter, until the Filipinos are "killed off like the Indians."

A small but prominent and vocal Anti-Imperialist League vigorously opposed war and annexation. These dignitaries included ex-presidents Harrison and Cleveland, Andrew Carnegie, Jane Addams, and Mark Twain. In arguments heard again recently about Iraq, anti-imperialists argued that taking over other countries contradicted American ideals. First, the annexation of territory without postwar planning or steps toward statehood was unprecedented and unconstitutional. Second, to occupy and govern a foreign people without their consent violated American ideals. Third, social reforms needed at home demanded American energies and money: "Before we attempt to teach house-keeping to the world," one writer said, we needed "to set our own house in order."

DOCUMENT

Mark Twain, "Incident in the Philippines" (1924)

Not all anti-imperialist arguments were so noble. A racist position alleged that Filipinos were nonwhite, Catholic, inferior in size and intelligence, and therefore unassimilable. A practical argument suggested that once in possession of the Philippines, the United States would have to occupy and defend them, necessitating the acquisition of more territories—in turn leading to higher taxes and bigger government, and perhaps requiring that American troops fight distant Asian wars.

The last argument became fact when Private Grayson's encounter started the Filipino-American War. Before it ended in 1902, some 126,500 American troops served in the Philippines, 4,234 died there, and 2,800 more were wounded. The cost was $400 million. Filipino casualties were much worse. In addition to 18,000 killed in combat, perhaps 200,000 Filipinos died of famine and disease as American soldiers burned villages and destroyed crops and livestock. General Jacob H. Smith told his troops that "the more you kill and burn, the better you will please me." Insurgent ineptness, Aguinaldo's inability to extend the fight across ethnic boundaries, and atrocities on both sides increased the frustrations of a lengthening war. The American "water cure" and other tortures were especially brutal.

DOCUMENT

Ernest Howard Crosby, "The Real 'White Man's Burden'" (1899)

As U.S. treatment of the Filipinos became more like Spanish treatment of the Cubans, the hypocrisy of American behavior became even more evident. This was especially true for black American soldiers who fought in the Philippines. They identified with the dark-skinned insurgents, whom they saw as tied to the land, burdened by debt, and pressed by poverty like themselves. "I feel sorry for these people," a sergeant in the 24th Infantry wrote. "You have no idea the way these people are treated by the Americans here."

The war starkly exposed the hypocrisies of shouldering the white man's burden. On reading a report that 8,000 Filipinos had been killed in the first year of the war, Carnegie wrote a letter, dripping with sarcasm, congratulating McKinley for "civilizing the Filipinos. ... About 8,000 of them have been completely civilized and sent to Heaven. I hope you like it." Another writer penned a devastating one-liner: "Dewey took Manila with the loss of one man—and all our institutions."

The anti-imperialists failed either to prevent annexation or to interfere with the war effort. However prestigious and principled, they had little political power and were out of tune with the period of exuberant expansionist national pride, prosperity, and promise.

Expansionism Triumphant

By 1900, Americans had ample reason to be patriotic. Within a year, the United States had acquired several island territories in the Pacific and Caribbean. But several questions arose over what to do with the new territories. Were they colonies? Would they be granted statehood or would they develop gradually from colonies to constitutional parts of the United States? Did Hawaiians, Puerto Ricans, and Filipinos have the same rights as American citizens on the mainland? Were they protected by the Constitution?

Although slightly different governing systems were worked out for each new territory, the solution in each case was to define its status somewhere between a colony and a candidate for statehood. The indigenous people were usually allowed to elect their own legislature, but had governors and other judicial and administrative officials appointed by the president. The first full governor of the

Philippines, McKinley appointee William Howard Taft, effectively moved the Filipinos toward self-government, which came finally in 1946.

The question of constitutional rights was resolved by deciding that Hawaiians and Puerto Ricans, for example, would be treated differently from Texans and Oregonians. In the "insular cases" of 1901, the Supreme Court ruled that these people would achieve citizenship and constitutional rights only when Congress said they were ready.

In the election of 1900, Bryan was again the Democratic nominee and tried to make imperialism the "paramount issue" of the campaign. He failed, in part because the country strongly favored annexing the Philippines. In the closing weeks of the campaign, Bryan shied away from imperialism and focused on domestic issues.

That did Bryan no good either. Prosperity returned with the discovery of gold in Alaska, and cries for reform fell on deaf ears. The McKinley forces rightly claimed that four years of Republican rule had brought more money, jobs, thriving factories, and manufactured goods, as well as the tremendous growth in American prestige abroad. As Tom Watson put it, noting the end of the Populist

Republican Campaign Poster Analyze this 1900 campaign poster for McKinley showing Republican claims for what had changed in four years. Why would voters want to vote again for McKinley and why not for the Democrats? What several arguments are made in this poster, including the rationale for expansion? Note McKinley's vice presidential nominee to his right. What role does the flag play in this poster? *(From the David J. and Janice L. Frent Collection/Corbis)*

revolt with the war fervor over Cuba, "The blare of the bugle drowned out the voice of the reformer."

He was more right than he knew. Within one year, expansionist Theodore Roosevelt went from assistant secretary of the navy to colonel of the Rough Riders to governor of New York. For some Republican politicos, who thought he was too vigorous and independent, this quick rise as McKinley's potential rival came too fast. One way to eliminate Roosevelt politically, or at least slow him down, was to make him vice president, which they did in 1900. But six months into McKinley's second term, an anarchist killed him, the third presidential assassination in less than 40 years. "Now look," exclaimed party boss Mark Hanna, who had opposed putting Roosevelt on the ticket, "that damned cowboy is President of the United States!"

THEODORE ROOSEVELT'S ENERGETIC DIPLOMACY

At a White House dinner party in 1905, a guest told a story about visiting the Roosevelt home when "Teedie" was a baby. "You were in your bassinet, making a good deal of fuss and noise," the guest reported, "and your father lifted you out and asked me to hold you." Secretary of State Elihu Root looked up and asked, "Was he hard to hold?" Whether true or not, the story reveals much about President Roosevelt's principles and policies on foreign affairs. As president from 1901 to 1909, and as the most dominating American personality for the 15 years between 1897 and 1912, Roosevelt made a lot of noise about the activist role the United States should play in the world, and he often seemed "hard to hold." Roosevelt's energetic foreign policy in Latin America, Eastern Asia, and Europe paved the way for a century and more of the United States as a world power.

Foreign Policy as Darwinian Struggle

Roosevelt advocated both individual physical fitness and collective national strength. An undersized boy, he had pursued a rigorous body-building program, and as a young man on his North Dakota ranch he learned to value the "strenuous life." Reading Darwin taught him that life was a constant struggle for survival. As president, his ideal was a "nation of men, not weaklings." Although he believed in Anglo-Saxon superiority, he admired—and feared—Japanese military prowess. Powerful nations, like individuals, Roosevelt believed, had a duty to cultivate vigor, strength, courage, and moral commitment to civilized values. In practical terms, this meant developing natural resources, building large navies, and being ever prepared to fight.

Although famous for saying "Speak softly and carry a big stick," Roosevelt often not only wielded a large stick but spoke loudly as well. In a speech in 1897, he used the word *war* 62 times, saying, "no triumph of peace is quite so great as the supreme triumphs of war." But despite his bluster, Roosevelt was usually restrained in exercising force. He won the Nobel Peace Prize in 1906 for helping end the Russo-Japanese War. The big stick and the loud talk were meant to preserve order and peace.

TR as Caribbean Policeman Compare this cartoon with others in the chapter. What images are conveyed in the cartoon? What symbols and stereotypes are portrayed? *(Puck, 1901)*

Roosevelt divided the world into "civilized" and "uncivilized" nations. The civilized ones had a responsibility to "police" the uncivilized, not only maintaining order but also spreading "superior" values and institutions. Taking on the "white man's burden," civilized nations sometimes had to wage war on the uncivilized—justly so, he argued, because the victors bestowed the blessings of culture and racial superiority on the vanquished. A war between two civilized nations (for example, Germany and Great Britain) would be foolish. Above all, Roosevelt believed in the balance of power. Strong, advanced nations had a duty to use their power to preserve order and peace. With a booming economy and population, Americans could no longer "avoid responsibilities" to exercise a greater role in world affairs.

Roosevelt developed a highly personal style of diplomacy. Bypassing the State Department, he preferred face-to-face contact and personal exchanges of letters with foreign diplomats and heads of state. A British emissary observed that Roosevelt had a "powerful personality" and a commanding knowledge of the world. Ministries from London to Tokyo respected both the president and the growing power of the United States.

When threats failed to accomplish his goals, Roosevelt used direct personal intervention. When he wanted Panama, Roosevelt bragged later, "I took the Canal Zone" rather than submitting a long "dignified State Paper" for congressional debate. And while Congress debated, he pointed out, the building of the canal began. Roosevelt's executive activism in foreign affairs, for better or worse, influenced presidents from Woodrow Wilson to George W. Bush.

Recovering the Past

One of the most enjoyable ways of recovering the values and attitudes of the past is through political cartoons. Ralph Waldo Emerson once said, "Caricatures are often the truest history of the times." A deft drawing of a popular or unpopular politician can freeze ideas and events in time, conveying more effectively than columns of print the central issues—and especially the hypocrisies and misbehaviors—of an era. Cartoonists are often at their best when they are critical, exaggerating a physical feature of a political figure or capturing public sentiment against the government.

The history of political cartoons in the United States goes back to Benjamin Franklin's "Join or Die" cartoon calling for colonial cooperation against the French in 1754. But political cartoons were rare until Andrew Jackson's presidency. Even after such cartoons as "King Andrew the First" in the 1830s, they did not gain notoriety until the advent of Thomas Nast's cartoons in *Harper's Weekly* in the 1870s. Nast drew scathing cartoons exposing the corruption of William "Boss" Tweed's Tammany Hall, depicting Tweed and his men as vultures and smiling deceivers. "Stop them damn pictures," Tweed ordered. "I don't care so much what the papers write about me. My constituents can't read. But, damn it, they can see pictures." Tweed sent some of his men to Nast with an offer of $100,000 to "study art" in Europe. The $5,000-a-year artist negotiated up to a half million dollars before refusing Tweed's offer. "I made up my mind not long ago to put some of those fellows behind bars," Nast said, "and I'm going to put them there." His cartoons helped to drive Tweed out of office.

The emergence of the United States as a world power and the rise of Theodore Roosevelt gave cartoonists plenty to draw about. At the same time, the rise of cheap newspapers such as William Randolph Hearst's *Journal* and Joseph Pulitzer's *World* provided a rich opportunity for cartoonists, whose clever images attracted more readers. When the Spanish-American War broke out, newspapers whipped up public sentiment by having artists draw fake pictures of fierce Spaniards

"The Spanish Brute Adds Mutilation to Murder," by Grant Hamilton, in *Judge,* July 9, 1898. *(Culver Pictures)*

"Liberty Halts American Butchery in the Philippines," from *Life*, 1899. (Life Magazine, *1899*)

stripping American women at sea and killing helpless Cubans. Hearst used these tactics to increase his paper's daily circulation to 1 million copies.

By the time of the debates over Philippine annexation, many cartoonists took an anti-imperialist stance, pointing out American hypocrisy. Within a year, cartoonists shifted from depicting "The Spanish Brute Adds Mutilation to Murder" (1898) to "Liberty Halts American Butchery in the Philippines" (1899), both included here. Note the similarities in that both cartoons condemn the "butchery" of native peoples. But the villain has changed. Although Uncle Sam as a killer is not nearly as menacing as the figure of Spain as an ugly gorilla, both cartoons share similarities of an aggressive stance, blood-covered swords, and a trail of bodies behind.

REFLECTING ON THE PAST   Describe each cartoon. What is the apparent message of each cartoonist? What symbols and images do you see in these two cartoons? Who is the woman figure and what does she represent? How would you explain the change of bloodied sword bearer within one year? In addition to these two cartoons, look at cartoons in this and other chapters. How do the images and symbols used in these reflect the cartoonist's point of view? How are various nationalities depicted in the Theodore Roosevelt cartoon? Check some recent newspapers: Who is criticized today and how do cartoonists reveal their attitudes and political positions? Is American imperialism still an issue?

Taking the Panama Canal

To justify the intervention of 2,600 American troops in Honduras and Nicaragua in 1906, Philander Knox, later a secretary of state, said, "because of the Monroe Doctrine" the United States is "held responsible for the order of Central America." The closeness of the canal, he said, "makes the preservation of peace in that neighborhood particularly necessary." The Panama Canal was not yet finished when Knox spoke, but it had already become a cornerstone of U.S. policy.

Three problems had to be surmounted in order to dig an interoceanic connection. First, an 1850 treaty bound the United States to build a canal jointly with Great Britain, a problem resolved in 1901 when the British canceled the treaty in exchange for an American guarantee that the canal would be open to all nations. A second problem was where to dig it. American engineers rejected a long route through Nicaragua in favor of a shorter, more rugged path across Panama, where a French firm had already begun work. This raised the third problem: Panama was a province of Colombia, which rejected the terms the United States offered. Roosevelt called the Colombians "Dagoes" who tried to "hold us up" like highway robbers.

Teddy Roosevelt at Panama Canal, 1906

Aware of Roosevelt's fury, encouraged by hints of American support, and eager for the economic benefits that a canal would bring, Panamanian nationalists in 1903 staged a revolution led by several rich families and Philippe Bunau-Varilla of the French canal company. An American warship deterred Colombian intervention, and local troops were separated from their officers, who were bought off. A bloodless revolution occurred on November 3; on November 4, Panama declared its independence; and on November 6 the United States recognized it. Two weeks later, a treaty established the American right to build and operate a canal through Panama and to exercise "titular sovereignty" over the 10-mile-wide Canal Zone. The Panamanian government protested, calling it a "treaty that no Panamanian signed." Roosevelt later claimed that the diplomatic and engineering achievement, completed in 1914, would "rank ... with the Louisiana Purchase and the acquisition of Texas."

Policing the Caribbean

Activities of the United States in the Caribbean, 1898–1930s

As late as 1901, the Monroe Doctrine was still regarded, according to Roosevelt, as the "equivalent to an open door in South America." To the United States, this meant that although no nation had a right "to get territorial possessions," all nations had equal commercial rights in the Western Hemisphere south of the Rio Grande. But as American investments poured into Central America and the Caribbean, the policy changed to one of asserting U.S. dominance in the Caribbean basin.

This change was demonstrated in 1902 when Germany and Great Britain blockaded Venezuela's ports to force the government to pay defaulted debts. Roosevelt was especially worried that German influence would replace the British. He insisted that the European powers accept arbitration and threatened to "move Dewey's ships" to the Venezuelan coast. The crisis passed, largely for other reasons, but Roosevelt's threat of force made very clear the paramount presence and self-interest of the United States in the Caribbean.

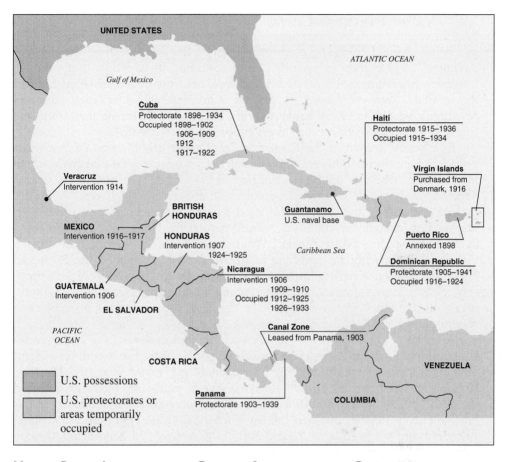

UNITED STATES INVOLVEMENT IN CENTRAL AMERICA AND THE CARIBBEAN, 1898–1939 Can you update the location of further interventions in Central America and the Caribbean since the 1950s? What do Latin Americans think of *Norte Americanos* today?

The United States kept liberated Cuba under a military governor until 1902, when the Cubans elected a congress and president. The United States honored Cuban independence, as it had promised to do, but through the Platt Amendment, which Cubans reluctantly added to their constitution in 1901, the United States obtained many economic rights in Cuba, a naval base at Guantanamo Bay (recently a government prison), and the right to intervene if Cuban sovereignty were ever threatened.

American policy intended to make Cuba a model of how a newly independent nation could achieve orderly self-government with only minimal guidance. Cuban self-government, however, was shaky. When, in 1906, a political crisis threatened to spiral into civil war, Roosevelt expressed his fury with "that infernal little Cuban republic." He sent warships to patrol the coastline and special commissioners and troops "to restore order and peace and public confidence." Along with economic development, which mostly benefited American companies, American political and even military involvement in Cuban affairs would continue for over a century.

The pattern was repeated throughout the Caribbean. The Dominican Republic, for example, suffered from unstable governments and great poverty. In 1904, as a revolt erupted, European creditors pressured the Dominican government for payment of $40 million in defaulted bonds. Sending its warships to discourage European intervention, the United States took over the collection of customs in the republic. Two years later, the United States intervened in Guatemala and Nicaragua, where American bankers controlled nearly 50 percent of all trade, the first of several twentieth-century interventions in those countries.

In a policy known as the Roosevelt Corollary to the Monroe Doctrine, the president announced in his annual message to Congress in 1904 that civilized nations should "insist on the proper policing of the world." The goal of the United States, he said, was to have "stable, orderly and prosperous neighbors." A country that paid its debts and kept order "need fear no interference from the United States." But "chronic wrong-doing" would require the United States to intervene as an "international police power." Whereas the Monroe Doctrine had warned European nations not to intervene in the Western Hemisphere, the Roosevelt Corollary justified American intervention. Starting with a desire to protect property, loans, and investments, the United States wound up supporting the tyrannical regimes of elites who owned most of the land, suppressed the poor, blocked reforms, and acted as American surrogates.

After 1904, the Roosevelt Corollary was invoked in several Caribbean countries. Intervention usually required the landing of U.S. Marines to counter a threat to American property. Occupying the capital and major seaports, Marines, bankers, and customs officials remained for several years until they were satisfied that stability had been reestablished. Roosevelt's successors, William Howard Taft and Woodrow Wilson, pursued the same interventionist policy. So would late-twentieth-century presidents Ronald Reagan (Grenada and Nicaragua), George Bush (Panama), and Bill Clinton and George W. Bush (Haiti).

Opening Doors to China and Closing Doors to America

Throughout the nineteenth century, American relations with China were restricted to a small but profitable trade. The British, in competition with France, Germany, and Russia, took advantage of the crumbling Manchu dynasty to force treaties on China creating "treaty ports" and granting exclusive trading privileges in various parts of the country. After 1898, Americans with dreams of exploiting the seemingly unlimited markets of China wanted to join the competition and enlarge their share. Those with moral interests, however, including many missionaries, reminded Americans of their revolutionary tradition against European imperialism. They made clear their opposition to U.S. commercial exploitation of a weak nation and supported China's political integrity as the other imperial powers moved toward partitioning the country.

Although a few Americans admired China's ancient culture, the dominant American attitude viewed the Chinese as heathen, exotic, backward, and immoral. The Exclusion Act of 1882 barring further immigration and riots against Chinese workers in the 1870s and 1880s reflected this negative stereotype. The Chinese, in turn, regarded the United States with a mixture of admiration, curiosity, resentment, suspicion, and disdain.

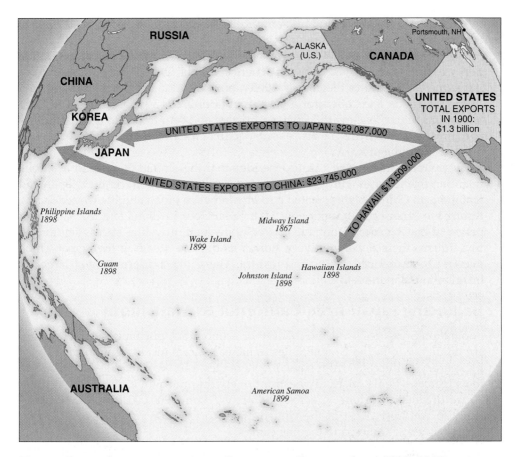

UNITED STATES INVOLVEMENT IN THE PACIFIC AND EASTERN ASIA, 1898–1909 By 1898, the United States expanded far into eastern Asia and the Pacific. Which motivation do you think was most important in this expansion: profits, patriotism, piety, or politics? What major events in the past 100 years have followed American expansion into the Pacific and East Asia? Where else has the United States been involved? Hint: get a world map.

The annexation of Hawaii and the Philippines in 1898 and 1899 convinced Secretary of State Hay that the United States should announce a China policy. He did so in the Open Door notes of 1899–1900, which became the cornerstone of U.S. policy in eastern Asia for half a century. The first note demanded an open door for American trade by declaring the principle of equal access to commercial rights in China by all nations. The second note, addressing Russian movement into Manchuria, called on all countries to respect the "territorial and administrative integrity" of China. This second principle announced a larger American role in Asia, offering China protection and preserving the East Asian balance of power.

An early test of this new role came during the Boxer Rebellion in 1900. The Boxers were a society of young traditionalist Chinese in revolt against both the Manchu dynasty and the growing Western presence in China. During the summer of 1900, Boxers killed some 242 missionaries and other foreigners and besieged the western quarter of Peking (Beijing). Eventually an international military force of 19,000 troops, including some 3,000 Americans, marched on Beijing to end the siege.

The relationship with China was plagued by the exclusionist immigration policy of the United States. Despite barriers and riots, Chinese workers kept coming to the United States illegally. In 1905, Chinese nationalists at home boycotted American goods and called for a change in immigration policy. Roosevelt, contemptuous of the "backward" Chinese, bristled and sent troops to the Philippines as a threat. Halfheartedly, he also asked Congress for a modified immigration bill, but nothing came of it.

Despite exclusion and insults, the idea that the United States had a unique guardian relationship with China persisted into the twentieth century. Japan had ambitions in China, so this created a rivalry between Japan and the United States, testing the American commitment to the Open Door in China and the balance of power in eastern Asia. Economic motives, however, proved to be less significant. Investments there developed very slowly, as did the dream of the "great China market" for American grains and textiles. The China trade remained larger in imagination than in reality.

Balancing Japan from California to Manchuria

Population pressures, war, and a quest for economic opportunities caused Japanese immigration to the United States to increase dramatically around the turn of the century. Some came from Hawaii, where they had "worked like machines" in the sugarcane fields, many dying from overwork and white diseases. Pursuing "huge dreams of fortune ... across the ocean," some 200,000 Japanese went directly to the West Coast of the United States to work on railroads and in West Coast canneries, mines, and logging camps.

Others worked on farms in the valleys of Oregon and California, many successfully rising to own their own lands and turning marginal farmlands into productive agricultural businesses. Japanese-owned farms increased from 4,698 acres in 1900 to 194,742 by 1910, when they produced 70 percent of the California strawberry crop. Kinji Ushijima, for example, developed 10,000 acres of potato lands worth $500,000 in the fertile deltas between Stockton and Sacramento. By 1912, known then as Shima the "Potato King," he was praised by the *San Francisco Chronicle*. But when Shima moved to a well-to-do neighborhood in Berkeley, local newspapers and protesting professors complained of the "Yellow Peril in College Town." Shima refused to move.

Threatened by this competitive success, native white Californians sought ways to exclude Japanese immigrants, discriminate against them, and limit their ability to own or lease land. Japanese workers were barred from factory jobs. In 1906, the San Francisco school board, claiming that Japanese children were "crowding the whites out of the schools," segregated them into separate schools. Californians passed an anti-Japanese resolution and asked Roosevelt to persuade Japan to stop the emigration. Denouncing anti-Japanese rioting in San Francisco, Roosevelt favored restriction rather than exclusion. In the "Gentlemen's Agreement" notes of 1907–1908, the Japanese agreed to limit the migration of unskilled workers to the United States. In return, Californians repealed some of their anti-Japanese laws. Tensions continued.

It was one thing to check Japanese power in California but quite another to stop it in eastern Asia, where Roosevelt was determined to maintain the balance of power. The Boxer Rebellion of 1900 left Russia with 50,000 troops in Manchuria, making it the strongest regional power. Roosevelt's admiration for the Japanese as a "fighting" people and valuable factor in the "civilization of the future" contrasted with his low respect for the Russians. As Japan moved into Korea and Russia into Manchuria, Roosevelt hoped that each would check the other.

Roosevelt welcomed news in 1904 that Japan had successfully mounted a surprise attack, beginning the Russo-Japanese War. But as Japanese victories continued, Americans worried that Japan might play the game too well, shutting the United States out of Asian markets. Roosevelt tilted toward Russia. When the Japanese expressed an interest in ending the war, the American president was pleased to exert his influence.

Roosevelt's goal was to achieve peace and leave a balanced situation. Nothing better symbolized the new American presence in the world than the 1905 negotiation and signing of a peace treaty in Portsmouth, New Hampshire, ending a war between Russia and Japan halfway around the globe in Manchuria. The Treaty of Portsmouth left Japan dominant in Manchuria (as well as in Korea) and established the United States as the major balance to Japan's power. In the Root-Takahira Agreement of 1908, in return for recognizing these developments, Roosevelt got Japan's promise to honor U.S. control in the Philippines and to make no further encroachments into China.

The agreement barely papered over Japanese-American tensions. Some Japanese blamed Roosevelt for the fact that the Treaty of Portsmouth had not given them indemnities from Russia. American insensitivity on the immigration issue left bad feelings. In Manchuria, the U.S. consul general aggressively pushed an anti-Japanese program of financing capital investment projects in banking and railroads. This policy, known as "dollar diplomacy" under Roosevelt's successor, William Howard Taft, like the pursuit of markets, was larger in prospect than results. Nevertheless, the United States was in Japan's way, and rumors of war circulated.

It was clearly a moment for Roosevelt's "big stick." In 1907, he told Secretary of State Root that he was "more concerned over the Japanese situation than almost any other. Thank Heaven we have the navy in good shape." Although the naval buildup had begun over a decade earlier, under Roosevelt the U.S. Navy developed into a formidable force. In 1907, to make it clear that "the Pacific was as much our home waters as the Atlantic," Roosevelt sent his "Great White Fleet" on a goodwill world tour. The first stop was Yokohama. Although American sailors were greeted warmly, the act may have stimulated navalism in Japan, which came back to haunt the United States in 1941. But for the time being, the balance of power in eastern Asia was preserved.

Preventing War in Europe

The United States had stretched the Monroe Doctrine to justify sending Marines and engineers to Latin America and the navy and dollars to eastern Asia. Treaties, agreements, and the protection of territories and interests entangled the United States with foreign nations from Panama and Nicaragua to the

Philippines and China. Toward European nations, however, traditional neutrality continued.

Roosevelt believed that the most serious threats to world peace and civilized order lay in the relationships among Germany, Great Britain, and France. He established two fundamental policies toward Europe that would define the U.S. role throughout the century. The first was to make friendship with Great Britain the cornerstone of U.S. policy. The second was to prevent a general war in Europe among strong nations. Toward this end, Roosevelt depended on his personal negotiating skills with the leaders of major European nations.

The Venezuelan crisis of 1895 shocked the United States and Britain into an awareness of their mutual interests. Both nations appreciated the neutrality of the other in their respective colonial wars in the Philippines and South Africa. Roosevelt supported British imperialism because he favored the dominance of the "English-speaking race" and believed that Britain was "fighting the battle of civilization." Furthermore, both nations worried about growing German power around the world. As German naval power increased, Britain had to bring its fleet closer to home. Friendly allies were needed to police parts of the world formerly patrolled by the British navy. The United Kingdom therefore concluded a mutual-protection treaty with Japan in 1902 and willingly let the Americans police Central America and the Caribbean Sea.

Language, cultural traditions, and strategic self-interest drew the two countries together. Roosevelt, moreover, was unashamedly pro-British. He knew, as he wrote to Lodge in 1901, that the United States had "not the least particle of danger to fear" from Britain and that German ambitions and militarism represented the major threat to peace in Europe. As Roosevelt left the presidency in 1909, one of his final acts was to proclaim the special American friendship with Great Britain.

German Kaiser Wilhelm II thought that Roosevelt was really pro-German. Roosevelt cultivated the Kaiser's illusion, flattering him while cleverly rejecting his overtures for diplomatic advantages. During the Moroccan crisis in 1905 and 1906, when Germany and France threatened to go to war over the control of Morocco, Roosevelt arranged a conference in Algeciras, Spain, to head off conflict. The treaty signed in 1906 peacefully settled the Moroccan issue favorably for the French. When the German emperor tried to promote a German-Chinese-American entente to balance the Anglo-Japanese Treaty in Asia, Roosevelt rebuffed him. Touring Europe in 1910, the retired American president was warmly entertained by Wilhelm, who continued to misunderstand him. Roosevelt kept urging his English friends to counter the German naval buildup in order to maintain peace in Europe. In 1911, he wrote that there would be nothing worse than that "Germany should ever overthrow England and establish the supremacy in Europe she aims at."

Roosevelt's European policy included cementing friendship with England and, while maintaining official neutrality, using diplomacy to prevent European hostilities. The relationship between Great Britain and Germany continued to deteriorate, however, and by 1914, a new American president, Woodrow Wilson, faced the terrible reality that Roosevelt had skillfully sought to prevent. When World War I finally broke out, no American was more eager to fight on the British side against the Germans than Colonel Roosevelt of the Rough Riders.

TIMELINE

1875–1877	United States acquires Hawaiian Islands			Platt Amendment
1898	Spanish-American War	**1903**		Panamanian revolt and independence
	Annexation of Hawaiian Islands	**1904**		Roosevelt Corollary to the Monroe Doctrine
	Treaty of Paris; annexation of the Philippines	**1904–1906**		United States intervenes in Nicaragua, Guatemala, and Cuba
1899–1902	Filipino-American War			
1899–1900	Open Door notes and Boxer Rebellion in China	**1907**		"Gentleman's Agreement" with Japan
1902	U.S. military occupation of Cuba ends	**1914**		Opening of the Panama Canal
				World War I begins

Conclusion

The Responsibilities of Power

The realities of power in the 1890s brought increasing international responsibilities. Roosevelt said in 1910 that because of "strength and geographical situation," the United States had itself become "more and more, the balance of power of the whole world." This ominous responsibility was also an opportunity to extend American economic, political, and moral influence around the globe.

As president in the first decade of the twentieth century, Roosevelt established aggressive American policies toward the rest of the world that President Bush would emulate in the first decade of the twenty-first century. The United States dominated and policed Central America and the Caribbean Sea to maintain order and protect its investments and other economic interests. In eastern Asia, Americans marched through Hay's Open Door with treaties, troops, navies, and dollars to protect the newly annexed Philippine Islands, to develop markets and investments, and to preserve the balance of power in Asia. In Europe, the United States sought to remain neutral and uninvolved in European affairs and at the same time to cement Anglo-American friendship and prevent "civilized" nations from going to war.

How well these policies worked would unfold in the next century. Making both friends and enemies, the fundamental ambivalence of America's sense of itself as an example to others remained. As questionable actions around the world—Private Grayson's in the Filipino-American War, for example—painfully demonstrated, it was increasingly difficult for the United States to be both responsible and good, both powerful and loved. The American people experienced, therefore, the satisfactions and burdens, the profits and costs, of their growing international responsibilities.

Questions for Review and Reflection

1. What is the fundamental dilemma of American foreign policy inherited from the Puritans, and to what extent do you think it applies today in America's relations with the rest of the world?

2. What are the four P's (or the three G's) that explain the motivations for American expansionism in the 1890s—and perhaps still today?

3. What are the major differences and similarities in the causes and consequences of the Spanish-American and Filipino-American wars?

4. Give three or four justifications for annexing the Philippine Islands and three or four reasons opposing annexation. Which set of arguments do you think is most compelling? Can the United States be both powerful and good?

5. Outline the major principles, with examples, of President Roosevelt's foreign policy in the Caribbean, eastern Asia, and Europe. How well have these policies worked in the 100 years since Roosevelt's time?

6. Do you think American foreign policy has made America primarily an interventionist savior of other nations or an interfering expansionist into the affairs of other nations? Or some of both? Give examples.

Discovering U.S. History Online

Imperialism in the Making of America www.boondocksnet.com/moa/
This site by Jim Zwick is a rich source of nineteenth-century articles and visual materials about imperialism from archival sites at the University of Michigan and Cornell University.

Anti-Imperialism in the United States, 1898–1935 www.boondocksnet.com/ai
Jim Zwick edits this extensive collection of primary written and visual documents about anti-imperialism in America.

The Age of Imperialism www.smplanet.com/imperialism/toc.html
An online history of U.S. imperialism with teaching resources and links.

Images from the Philippine-United States War www.historicaltextarchive.com/USA/twenty/filipino.html
An archive of historical photos from the war.

William McKinley www.history.ohio-state.edu/projects/McKinley/SpanAmWar.htm
The Ohio State University site contains a collection of essays, photos, and cartoons about McKinley and the Spanish-American War.

America, 1900 www.pbs.org/wgbh/amex/1900
A companion to the documentary video, this site contains information on more than 20 key figures from the period and many key events from the early 1990s.

Fiction and Film

William Schroder's *Cousins of Color* (2004) is a compelling novel of a black soldier in the Philippines who realizes that he has more in common with the Filipino rebels he is fighting than with his fellow Americans. Ernest Howard Crosby's *Captain Jinks, Hero* (1902), a delight if you can find it, is an anti-imperialist novel set in the Philippines. James Michener's *Hawaii* (1959) is an immense saga of the multicultural history of the islands annexed by the United States in 1898. *The Woman Warrior* by Maxine Hong Kingston (1975) faithfully reflects Chinese culture in the coming-of-age story of a young Chinese-American woman in California. Frank Chinn's *Donald Duk* (1911) is a fanciful story of San Francisco's Chinatown, with flashbacks to the history of Chinese railroad workers in the late nineteenth-century.

The PBS video *Crucible of Empire: The Spanish-American War* (1999) uses rare archival materials, photos, motion pictures, newspapers, and popular songs to recreate the war. Two PBS videos from *The American Experience* series depict the history of the era: "Hawaii's Last Queen" (1997) describes the clash between native Hawaiians and U.S. business interests and Marines, and "America, 1900" (1998) focuses on the year 1900, including the second presidential race between McKinley and Bryan. *In Our Image: America's Empire in the Philippines* (1989), a history of America in the Philippines from 1898 to 1946, is a video produced to accompany Stanley Karnow's book of the same name.

Recommended Reading

www.ablongman.com/nash

The Companion Website has a list of recommended readings about expansionism, the war in Cuba and the Philippines, and Theodore Roosevelt.

CHAPTER 21

The Progressives Confront Industrial Capitalism

CHAPTER OUTLINE

- The Social Justice Movement
- The Worker in the Progressive Era
- Reform in the Cities and States
- Theodore Roosevelt and the Square Deal
- Woodrow Wilson and the New Freedom
- Conclusion: The Limits of Progressivism

American Stories

A Professional Woman Joins the Progressive Crusade

Frances Kellor, a young woman who grew up in Ohio and Michigan, received her law degree in 1897 from Cornell University and became one of the small but growing group of professionally trained women. Deciding that she was more interested in solving the nation's social problems than in practicing law, she moved to Chicago, studied sociology, and trained herself as a social reformer. Kellor believed passionately that poverty and inequality could be eliminated in America. She also had the progressive faith that if Americans could only hear the truth about the millions of people living in urban slums, they would rise up and make changes. She was one of the experts who provided the evidence to document what was wrong in industrial America.

Like many progressives, Kellor believed that environment was more important than heredity in determining ability, prosperity, and happiness. Better schools and better housing, she thought, would produce better citizens. Even criminals, she argued, were simply victims of environment. Kellor demonstrated that poor health and deprived childhoods explained the only differences between criminals and college students. If it were impossible to define a criminal type, then it must be possible to reduce crime by improving the environment.

Kellor was an efficient professional. Like the majority of the professional women of her generation, she never married but devoted her life to social research and social reform. She lived for a time at Hull House in Chicago and at the College Settlement in New York, centers not only of social research and reform but also of lively community. For many young people the settlement, with its sense of commitment and its exciting conversation around the dinner table, provided an alternative to the nuclear family or the single apartment.

While staying at the College Settlement, Kellor researched and wrote a muckraking study of employment agencies, published in 1904 as *Out of Work*. She revealed how employment agencies exploited immigrants, blacks, and other recent arrivals in the city. Kellor's book, like the writing of most progressives, sizzled with moral outrage. But Kellor went beyond moralism to suggest corrective legislation at the state and national levels. Kellor became one of the leaders of the movement to Americanize the immigrants pouring into the country in unprecedented numbers. Between 1899 and 1920, over 8 million people came to the United States, most from southern and eastern Europe. Many feared that this flood of immigrants threatened the very basis of American democracy. Kellor and her coworkers represented the side of progressivism that sought state and federal laws to protect the new arrivals from exploitation and to establish agencies and facilities to educate and Americanize them. Another group of progressives, often allied with organized labor, tried to pass laws to restrict immigration. Kellor was not entirely free of her generation's ethnic prejudice, but she did maintain that all immigrants could be made into useful citizens.

Convinced of the need for a national movement to push for reform legislation, Kellor helped to found the National Committee for Immigrants in America, which tried to promote a national policy "to make all these people Americans," and a federal bureau to organize the campaign. Eventually, she helped establish the Division of Immigrant Education within the Department of Education. A political movement led by Theodore Roosevelt excited her most. More than almost any other single person, Kellor had been responsible for alerting Roosevelt to the problems the immigrants faced in American cities. When Roosevelt formed the new Progressive party in 1912, she was one of the many social workers and social researchers who joined him. She campaigned for Roosevelt and directed the Progressive Service Organization, educating voters in all areas of social justice and welfare after the election. After Roosevelt's defeat and the collapse of the Progressive party, Kellor continued to work for Americanization. She spent the rest of her life promoting justice, order, and efficiency and looking for ways of resolving industrial and international disputes.

Frances Kellor's life illustrates two important aspects of progressivism, the first nationwide reform movement of the modern era: first, a commitment to promote social justice, to ensure equal opportunity, and to preserve democracy; and second, a search for order and efficiency in a world complicated by rapid industrialization, immigration, and spectacular urban growth. Like many progressives, she was part of a global movement to confront these problems, and she was influenced by writers and reformers in England and Germany as well as by those in the United States. But no one person can represent all facets of so complex a movement. Borrowing from populism and influenced by a number of reformers from the 1890s as well as by social welfare legislation passed in several European countries, progressivism reached a climax in the years from 1900 to 1914. The progressive movement did not plot to overthrow the government; rather, it sought to reform the system in order to ensure the survival of the American way of life.

This chapter traces the important aspects of progressivism. It examines the social justice movement, which sought to promote reform among the poor and to improve life for those who had fallen victim to an urban and industrial civilization. It surveys life among workers, a group the reformers sometimes helped but often misunderstood. Then it describes the reform movements in the cities and states, where countless officials and experts tried to reduce chaos and promote order and democracy. It traces the gradual movement from dependence on voluntary action to solve social problems to the passage of state and federal laws to promote social reform. Finally, it examines progressivism at the national level during the administrations of Theodore Roosevelt and Woodrow Wilson, the first thoroughly modern presidents.

THE SOCIAL JUSTICE MOVEMENT

Historians write of a "progressive movement." Actually there were a number of movements, some of them contradictory, but all focusing on the problems created by a rapidly expanding urban and industrial world. Some reformers, often from the middle class, sought to humanize the modern city—improving housing and schools and providing a better life for immigrants. Others focused on working conditions and the rights of labor. Still others sought to make politics responsive to popular interests, including those of women. Progressivism had roots in the 1890s, when many reformers were shocked by the devastation caused by the depression of 1893, and the progressives were influenced by George's *Progress and Poverty* (1879); Bellamy's *Looking Backward* (1888); a British pamphlet, *The Bitter Cry of Outcast London*; and the Social Gospel movement (see Chapter 19).

The Progressive Movement in a Global Context

Most progressives lived in an international world. Many had studied in European universities. They attended international conferences on urban problems, belonged to organizations like the International Association for Labor Legislation, and read the latest sociological literature from Great Britain, France, Sweden, and Germany. Many were inspired by visiting Toynbee Hall, the pioneer social settlement in the slums of London, and they observed municipal housing experiments in Glasgow and Dresden.

The United States lagged behind much of the industrialized world in passing social legislation, perhaps because it lacked Europe's strong labor and socialist movements. Germany had sickness, accident, and disability insurance by the 1880s. Great Britain passed workmen's compensation laws in the 1890s. But American cities were filled with immigrants with cultural adjustments and language barriers to overcome. Reform battles had to be fought first on the local and state levels, slowing the reform process in the United States.

Intellectually, the progressives were influenced by Darwinism. Believing that the world was in flux, they rebelled against the fixed and the formal. Progressive philosopher John Dewey wrote that ideas could become instruments for change. William James, in his philosophy of pragmatism, explained ideas in terms of their consequences. Most progressives were convinced that social environment was much more important than heredity in forming character. Building better schools and houses would make better people and a more perfect society. Yet even the more advanced reformers thought in racial and ethnic categories, convinced that some groups could be molded more easily than others. Progressivism did not usually mean progress for blacks.

In many ways, progressivism was the first modern reform movement. It sought to bring order and efficiency to a world that had been transformed by rapid growth and new technology. Yet elements of nostalgia infected the movement as reformers tried to preserve preindustrial handicrafts and to promote small-town and rural values in urban settings. Progressive leaders were almost always middle class, and they quite consciously tried to teach middle-class values to immigrants and working people. Often progressives seemed more interested in control than in reform; frequently, they displayed paternalism toward those they tried to help.

The progressives were part of a statistics-minded, realistic generation. They conducted surveys, gathered facts, wrote reports, and usually had faith that all this would lead to change. Their urge to document and to record came out in haunting photographs of young workers taken by Lewis Hine, in the stark and beautiful city paintings by John Sloan, and in the realist novels of Theodore Dreiser and William Dean Howells.

Optimistic about human nature, progressives believed that change was possible. They may seem naive or bigoted today, but they wrestled with many social questions, some of them old but fraught with new urgency in an industrialized society. What is the proper relation of government to society? In a world of large corporations and huge cities, how much should the government regulate and control? How much responsibility does society have for its poor and needy? Progressives could not agree on the answers, but for the first time in American history, they struggled with the questions.

The Muckrakers

Writers who exposed corruption and other social evils were labeled "muckrakers" by Theodore Roosevelt. Not all muckrakers were reformers—some just wrote for the money—but reformers learned from their techniques of exposé.

In part, the muckrakers were a product of the journalistic revolution of the 1890s. Nineteenth-century magazines had elite audiences. The new magazines had slick formats, more advertising, and wider sales. Competing for readers, editors eagerly published articles telling the public what was wrong in American society.

Lincoln Steffens, a young California journalist, wrote articles exposing the connections between respectable businessmen and corrupt politicians. When published as a book in 1904, *The Shame of the Cities* became a battle cry for people determined to clean up city government. Ida Tarbell, a teacher turned journalist, revealed the ruthlessness of John D. Rockefeller's Standard Oil Company. David Graham Phillips uncovered the alliance of politics and business in *The Treason of the Senate* (1906). Robert Hunter, a young settlement worker, shocked Americans in 1904 with his book *Poverty*. Upton Sinclair's novel *The Jungle* (1906) described the horrors of the Chicago meatpacking industry, and Frank Norris dramatized the railroads' stranglehold on farmers in *The Octopus* (1901).

Women and Children

Nothing disturbed the social justice progressives more than the sight of children as young as 8 or 10 working long hours in dangerous and depressing factories. Florence Kelley was one of the most important leaders in the crusade against child labor. Kelley had grown up in an upper-class Philadelphia family and was a member of the first generation of college women. Refused admission to an American graduate school because of her gender, she went to the University of Zurich in Switzerland and became a socialist. After her marriage failed, Kelley moved into Hull House and poured her energies into the campaign against child labor. When no Chicago attorney would argue child labor cases against prominent corporations, she went to law school, passed the bar exam, and argued the cases herself.

Kelley and other child labor reformers quickly recognized the need for state laws. Marshaling their evidence about the tragic effects on growing children of

Newsboys Nothing disturbed the reformers more than the sight of little children, sullen and stunted, working long hours in factory, farm, and mine. But of all child laborers perhaps the newsboys caused the most concern. They often had to pick up their papers late at night or very early in the morning. They sometimes were homeless and slept wherever they could find a place. But even more troubling, they associated with unsavory characters and fell prey to bad habits. In this photo Lewis Hine captures three young newsboys in St. Louis in 1910. Why were reformers upset by photos like this? If you had to work, would you prefer the mine or the factory or would you become a newsboy? *(The Metropolitan Museum of Art, Gift of Phyllis D. Massar, 1970. [1970.727.1] All Rights Reserved, The Metropolitan Museum of Art/Art Resource, NY.)*

long working hours in dark and damp factories, they pressured the Illinois legislature into passing a child labor law. A few years later, however, the state supreme court ruled it unconstitutional, convincing reformers that action at the national level was essential. Kelley led the charge.

The National Child Labor Committee was the brainchild of Edgar Gardner Murphy, a Social Gospel clergyman from Alabama. Headquartered in New York, it drew up a model state child labor law, encouraged state and city campaigns, and coordinated the movement around the country. Although two-thirds of the states passed some form of child labor law between 1905 and 1907, many had loopholes, and a national bill was defeated in 1906. But reformers convinced Congress in 1912 to establish a Children's Bureau in the Department of Labor. Compulsory school attendance laws, however, did more to reduce the number of children who worked than federal and state laws, which proved difficult to pass and even more difficult to enforce.

DOCUMENT

Mother Jones, "The March of the Mill Children" (1903)

The crusade against child labor was a typical social justice reform effort. Its origins lay in the moral indignation of middle-class reformers. But reformers went beyond moral outrage; they gathered statistics, took photographs, and used their evidence to push for legislation, first on the local level, then in the states, and eventually in Washington.

Like other progressive reform efforts, the battle against child labor was only partly successful. Too many businessmen profitably employed children. Too many politicians and judges were reluctant to regulate the work of children or adults. And some parents, desperately needing their child's wages, opposed the reformers and broke the law.

Reformers worried over the young people who got into trouble with the law, often for pranks that in rural areas would have seemed harmless. By setting up juvenile courts, the progressives hoped to separate young people from the criminal justice system while preventing them from being turned into hardened criminals by adult prisons. Yet juvenile courts frequently deprived young offenders of all rights of due process, as the Supreme Court finally recognized in 1967.

Closely connected with the anti-child labor movement was the effort to limit the hours of women's work. Florence Kelley and the National Consumers League led the campaign. It was foolish and unpatriotic, they argued, to allow the "mothers of future generations" to work long hours in dangerous industries. The most important court case on women's work came before the U.S. Supreme Court in 1908. Josephine Goldmark, Kelley's friend, wrote the brief for *Muller v. Oregon* that her brother-in-law, Louis Brandeis, used when he argued the case. The Court upheld the Oregon 10-hour law largely because Goldmark's sociological argument detailed the danger and disease that factory women faced. Brandeis opposed laissez-faire legal concepts, arguing that the government had a special interest in protecting citizens' health. Most states fell into line with the Supreme Court decision and passed protective legislation for women, though many companies managed to circumvent the laws. But even the 10 hours of work permitted by the law seemed too long for women who had to come home to child care and housekeeping.

Contending that "women are fundamentally weaker than men in all that makes for endurance," reformers won some protection for women workers. But their arguments would later be used to reinforce gender segregation at work.

RECOVERING THE PAST

Photographs are a revealing way of recovering the past visually. But when looking at a photograph, especially an old one, it is easy to assume that it is an accurate representation of the past. Photographers, however, like novelists and historians, have a point of view. They take their pictures for a reason and often to prove a point. As one photographer remarked, "Photographs don't lie, but liars take photographs."

To document the need for reform in the cities, progressives collected statistics, made surveys, described urban problems, and even wrote novels. But they discovered that the photograph was often more effective than words. Jacob Riis, the Danish-born author of *How the Other Half Lives* (1890), a devastating exposure of conditions in New York City tenement house slums, was also a pioneer in urban photography. Others had taken pictures of dank alleys and street urchins before, but Riis was the first to photograph slum conditions with the express purpose of promoting reform. At first he hired photographers, but then he bought a camera and taught himself how to use it. He even tried a new German flash powder to illuminate dark alleys and tenement rooms in order to record the horror of slum life.

Riis made many of his photographs into lantern slides and used them to illustrate his lectures on the need for housing reform. Although he was a creative and innovative photographer, his pictures were often far from objective. His equipment was awkward, his film slow. He had to set up and prepare carefully before snapping the shutter. His views of tenement ghetto streets and poor children now seem like clichés, but they were designed to make Americans angry, to arouse them to reform.

Another important progressive photographer was Lewis Hine; like Riis, he taught himself photography. Trained as a sociologist, Hine used his camera to illustrate his lectures at the Ethical Culture School in New York. In 1908, he was hired as a full-time investigator by the National Child Labor Committee. His haunting photographs of children in factories helped convince many Americans of the need to abolish child labor. Hine's children were appealing human beings. He showed them eating, running, working, and staring wistfully out factory windows. His photographs avoided the pathos that Riis was so fond of recording, but just as surely they documented the need for reform.

Another technique that the reform photographer used was the before-and-after shot. The two photographs shown here of a one-room apartment in Philadelphia early in the century illustrate how progressive reformers tried to teach immigrants to imitate middle-class manners. The "before" photograph shows a room cluttered with washtubs, laundry, cooking utensils, clothes, tools, even an old Christmas decoration. In the "after" picture, much of the clutter has been cleaned up. A window has been installed to let in light and fresh air. The wallpaper, presumably a haven for hidden bugs and germs, has been torn off. The cooking utensils and laundry have been put away. The woodwork has been stained, and some ceremonial objects have been gathered on a shelf.

What else can you find that has been changed? How well do you think the message of the photographic combinations like this one worked? Would the immigrant family be happy with the new look and condition of their room? Could anyone live in one room and keep it so neat?

REFLECTING ON THE PAST   As you look at these, or any photographs, ask yourself: What is the photographer's purpose and point of view? Why was this particular angle chosen for the picture? And why center on these particular people or objects? What does the photographer reveal about his or her purpose? What does the photographer reveal unintentionally? How have fast film and new camera styles changed photography? On what subjects do reform-minded photographers train their cameras today?

The reality of one-room tenement apartments (top) contrasted with the tidiness that reformers saw as the ideal (bottom). *(Temple University Urban Archives)*

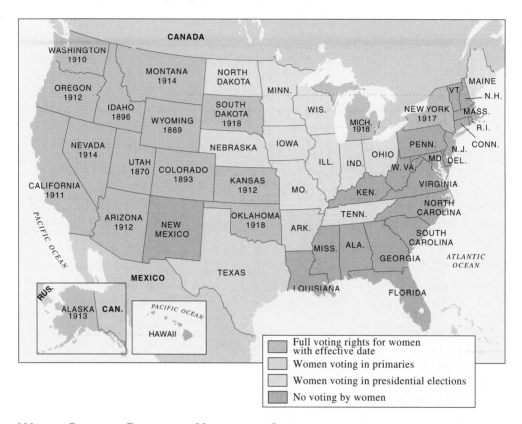

CANADA

WASHINGTON
1910

OREGON
1912

MONTANA
1914

NORTH
DAKOTA

MINN.

IDAHO
1896

WYOMING
1869

SOUTH
DAKOTA
1918

WIS.

MICH.
1918

NEW YORK
1917

MAINE

VT
N.H.

MASS.

R.I.

NEVADA
1914

UTAH
1870

NEBRASKA

IOWA

OHIO

PENN.

N.J. CONN.

COLORADO
1893

ILL.

IND.

MD DEL.

W. VA.

CALIFORNIA
1911

KANSAS
1912

MO.

KEN.

VIRGINIA

ARIZONA
1912

NEW
MEXICO

OKLAHOMA
1918

ARK.

TENN.

NORTH
CAROLINA

SOUTH
CAROLINA

MISS. ALA.

GEORGIA

*ATLANTIC
OCEAN*

PACIFIC OCEAN

MEXICO

TEXAS

LOUISIANA

FLORIDA

RUS.

ALASKA CAN.
1913

PACIFIC OCEAN

HAWAII

- Full voting rights for women with effective date
- Women voting in primaries
- Women voting in presidential elections
- No voting by women

WOMAN SUFFRAGE BEFORE THE NINETEENTH AMENDMENT Western states led the battle for women's right to vote, but key victories in New York (1917) and Michigan (1918) and a carefully organized campaign in all parts of the country finally led to the ratification of the Nineteenth Amendment. It was a triumph of progressive reform.

Besides seeking legislation to protect working women, the social justice progressives also campaigned for woman suffrage. Like so much of progressivism, it was part of a global crusade. The women leading the American movement met their foreign counterparts at conventions of the International Suffrage Alliance. The United States lagged behind several other countries in granting female suffrage. Women in New Zealand won the vote in 1893, Australia in 1902, Finland in 1906, Norway in 1913, Denmark and Iceland in 1915, and Canada and Great Britain (for some local elections) in 1918.

Woman Suffrage
Before the
Nineteenth
Century

The political process that eventually led to woman suffrage in the United States was slowed by the difficulty of amending the Constitution and the need to fight the battle one state at a time. The earliest success came in the West where Wyoming (1869), Utah (1870), Colorado (1893), Idaho (1896), Washington (1910), California (1911), Arizona and Oregon (1912), and Montana and Nevada (1914) gave women the vote at least in some elections. Many men in the East and Midwest feared that women, if given the vote, would support prohibition, while some women argued that the votes of middle-class women would cancel the vote of immigrant men. But progressives like Jane Addams supported votes for all women because, she argued, in an urban and industrial age women needed to be municipal housekeepers to protect their families. The progressive insistence that all women needed the vote helped to push woman suffrage toward victory during World War I.

Much more controversial than either votes for women or protective legislation was the birth control movement. Even many advanced progressives could not imagine themselves teaching immigrant women how to prevent conception (which was also illegal under federal law).

Margaret Sanger, a nurse who had watched poor women suffer from too many births and even die from dangerous, illegal abortions, was one of the founders of the modern American birth control movement. Middle-class Americans had limited family size in the nineteenth century through abstinence, withdrawal, abortion, and primitive birth control devices, but much ignorance remained, even among middle-class women. Sanger obtained the latest medical and scientific European studies and in 1914 explained in her magazine, *The Woman Rebel,* and in a pamphlet, *Family Limitation,* that women could separate sex from procreation. She was indicted for violation of the postal code and fled to Europe to avoid arrest.

Birth control long remained controversial—and in most states, illegal. Yet Sanger helped to bring sexuality and contraception out into the open. When she returned to the United States in 1921, she founded the American Birth Control League, which became the Planned Parenthood Federation in 1942.

Home and School

Reformers believed that better housing and education could transform the lives of the poor and create a better world. Books such as Jacob Riis's *How the Other Half Lives* (1890) horrified them. With vivid language and haunting photographs, Riis had documented the misery of New York's slums.

In the first decade of the twentieth century, the progressives took a new approach to the housing problems. They collected statistics, conducted surveys, organized committees, and constructed exhibits to demonstrate the effect of urban overcrowding. Tenement house laws, passed in several cities, were often ineffectual. In 1910, reformers organized the National Housing Association, and some hoped for federal laws and even government-subsidized housing. But the reformers' ideas often clashed with the values of those they tried to help.

Many middle-class women reformers who tried to teach working-class families how to live in their tenements had never organized their own homes. Those who lived in settlement houses never worried about cooking or chores. Some, however, began to realize that domestic tasks kept women of all classes from taking their full place in society. Charlotte Perkins Gilman sketched an alternative to traditional notions of "the woman's sphere," suggesting that entrepreneurs build apartment houses with common dining facilities where women could combine motherhood with careers. However, most Americans of all political persuasions continued to view the home as sacred space where the mother ruled supreme.

DOCUMENT

Charlotte Perkins Gilman, "If I Were a Man" (1914)

Next to better housing, the progressives stressed better schools as a way to produce better citizens. Public school systems were often rigid and corrupt and seemed to reinforce old habits. A Chicago teacher told her students: "Don't stop to think; tell me what you know."

Progressive education, like many other aspects of progressivism, opposed the rigid in favor of flexibility. John Dewey was the key philosopher of progressive education. He tried to create in the city a sense of the small rural community of his native Vermont. He experimented with new educational methods, including seats that could be arranged in small groups rather than bolted down in rows.

Dewey insisted that the schools be child-centered, not subject-oriented. Teachers should teach children rather than teach history or mathematics. He did not mean that history and math should not be taught, but that those subjects should be related to the students' experience. Students should not just learn about democracy; the school itself should operate like a democracy.

Dewey also maintained, somewhat controversially, that the schools should become instruments for social reform. But like most progressives, Dewey was never clear whether he wanted the schools to help the students adjust to the existing world or to turn out graduates who would change the world. Although he wavered, the spirit of progressive education, like the spirit of progressivism in general, was optimistic. The reformers believed that the schools could create more flexible, better-educated adults who would eventually improve society.

Crusades Against Saloons, Brothels, and Movie Houses

Given their faith in the reforming potential of healthy and educated citizens, it was logical that most social justice progressives opposed the sale of alcohol. Some came from Protestant homes where drinking was considered a sin, but most favored prohibition for pragmatic reasons: to reform the city and conserve human resources.

Americans did drink a lot, and the amount they consumed rose rapidly after 1900, peaking between 1911 and 1915. Only three states still had prohibition laws dating from the 1850s. The modern anti-liquor movement was spearheaded in the 1880s and 1890s by the Women's Christian Temperance Union and after 1900 by the Anti-Saloon League and a coalition of religious leaders and social reformers. Seven states passed temperance laws between 1906 and 1912.

Reformers were often appalled as they watched young children enter saloons to buy a pail of beer for the family. They were horrified by tales of abuse by alcoholic fathers and mothers, and they blamed the saloon for many of the problems they saw in the cities. "Why should the community have any more sympathy for the saloon ... than ... for a typhoid-breeding pool of filthy water?" one irate reformer asked.

Although they never quite understood the role alcohol played in the social life of many ethnic groups, Jane Addams and other settlement workers appreciated the saloon's importance as a social center. Addams started a coffeehouse at Hull House to lure people away from the saloon. The progressives never found a substitute for the saloon, but they did work for local and state prohibition laws. As in many other progressive efforts, they joined with diverse groups to push for change, and won. On December 22, 1917, Congress sent to the states for ratification a constitutional amendment prohibiting the sale, manufacturing, or importing of intoxicating liquor within the United States. The spirit of wartime sacrifice facilitated its rapid ratification.

Besides the saloon, progressives saw the urban dance hall and movie theater as threats to youthful morals. The motion picture, invented in 1889, developed as an important form of entertainment only during the first decade of the twentieth century, at first appealing mainly to a lower-class and largely ethnic audience.

VIDEO

Luna Park at Coney Island

Not until World War I, when D. W. Griffith produced long feature films, did the movies begin to attract a middle-class audience. The most popular of these early films was Griffith's *The Birth of a Nation* (1915), a blatantly racist and distorted epic of black debauchery during Reconstruction. Many early films were imported from France, Italy, and Germany; because they were silent, they could be subtitled in any language. But viewers did not need to know the language, or even be able to read, to enjoy the action. That was part of early films' attraction. Many depicted premarital sex, adultery, and violence, and, unlike later films, many attacked authority and had tragic endings. *The Candidate* (1907) showed an upper-class reform candidate who gets dirt thrown at him when he tries to clean up the town. In *Down with Women* (1907), well-dressed men denounced woman suffrage and the incompetence of "the weaker sex," but throughout the film, only strong women were depicted.

Some of the films stressed slapstick humor or romance and adventure; others bordered on pornography. The reformers objected not only to the plots and content of the films, but also to the location of the theaters—near saloons and burlesque houses—and to their dark interiors, which could stimulate immoral activity. This disturbed reformers. But for young immigrant women, who made up the bulk of the audience at most urban movie theaters, the films provided rare exciting moments in their lives.

Saloons, dance halls, and movie theaters all seemed to progressives somehow connected with the worst evil of all: prostitution. Nineteenth-century anti-prostitution campaigns were nothing compared with the progressives' crusade to wipe out the "social evil." All major cities and many smaller ones appointed vice commissions, whose reports, often running to several thick volumes, were typical progressive documents, filled with elaborate statistical studies and moral outrage.

The progressive anti-vice crusade attracted many kinds of people, for often contradictory reasons. Racists and those who wanted to restrict immigration claimed that "inferior people"—blacks and recent immigrants— became prostitutes and pimps. Social hygiene progressives published vivid accounts of prostitution as part of their campaign to fight sexual ignorance. Some women reformers promoted a single moral standard for men and women. Others worried that prostitutes would spread venereal disease to unfaithful husbands, who would pass it on to wives and babies. Most progressives, however, stressed the environmental causes of vice. They believed that prostitution, like child labor and poor housing, could be eliminated through education and reform.

VIDEO

Ellis Island Immigrants (1903)

Despite all their efforts, the progressives failed to end prostitution and did virtually nothing to address its roots in poverty. "Do you suppose I am going back to earn five or six dollars a week in a factory," one prostitute asked an investigator, "when I can earn that amount any night and often much more?" Reformers wiped out a few red-light districts, closed some brothels, and managed to push a bill through Congress (the Mann Act of 1910) that prohibited the interstate transport of women for immoral purposes. Perhaps more important, in several states, they got the age of consent for women raised, and in 20 states they made the Wassermann test for syphilis mandatory for both men and women before a marriage license could be issued.

THE WORKER IN THE PROGRESSIVE ERA

Progressive reformers sympathized with industrial workers, who struggled to earn a living for themselves and their families, and they sought legislation to protect working women and children. But often they had little understanding of what it was really like to sell one's strength by the hour. For example, they supported labor's right to organize at a time when labor had few friends, yet they often opposed the strike as a weapon against management. And neither organized labor nor the reformers, individually or in shaky partnership, had much power over industry in the years before World War I.

Adjusting to Industrial Labor

Many workers, whether from eastern Europe or Michigan, found the factory bewildering. Unlike farm or craft work, the factory was ruled by the clock and the boss. Workers continued to resist the pace of factory work and subtly sabotaged employers' efforts to control them (see Chapters 10 and 18). They stayed home on holidays when they were supposed to work, took unauthorized breaks, and set their own productivity schedules. Often they were fired or quit. In New York textile shops in 1912 and 1913, the turnover rate was over 250 percent. Overall, one-third of the workers stayed at their jobs less than a year, and about 40 percent of immigrant workers returned to their native lands in the first decade of the twentieth century.

The nature of work continued to change in the early twentieth century as industrialists extended late-nineteenth-century efforts to make their factories and workers more efficient, productive, and profitable. In some industries, new machines revolutionized work and eliminated highly paid, skilled jobs. The moving assembly line, perfected by Henry Ford, transformed the nature of work and turned many laborers into unskilled machine-tenders.

The influence of the machine was uneven, having a greater impact in some industries than in others. Although some skilled weavers and glassblowers were transformed into unskilled operators, the machines themselves created the need for new skilled workers. In the auto industry, for example, the new elite workers were the mechanics and the tool and die men who kept the assembly line running. But the trend toward mechanization was unstoppable, and even the most skilled workers were eventually removed from making decisions about production.

The principles of scientific management were also important in altering industrial work. Here the key figure was Frederick Taylor, the son of a prominent Philadelphia family. Taylor had a nervous breakdown as a youth, and his physicians prescribed manual labor as a cure. Working in a Philadelphia steel plant and studying engineering at night, he became chief engineer in the 1880s. Later he used this experience to rethink the organization of industry.

Taylor was obsessed with efficiency. He emphasized centralized planning, systematic analysis, and detailed instructions. He timed workers with a stopwatch to determine the most efficient way to perform a task. Many owners enthusiastically adopted his concepts of scientific management, seeing an opportunity to increase their profits and their control of the workplace. Not surprisingly, many workers resented "Taylorism."

Union Organizing

Samuel Gompers, head of the American Federation of Labor, quickly saw that Taylorism would reduce workers to "mere machines." Under his guidance, the AFL prospered during the progressive era. By 1914, the AFL alone had over 2 million members. Gompers's "pure and simple unionism" was most successful among coal miners, railroad workers, and the building trades. As we saw in Chapter 18, Gompers ignored unskilled and immigrant workers and concentrated on raising the wages and improving the working conditions of the skilled craftsmen who were members of unions affiliated with the AFL.

For a time, Gompers's strategy seemed to work. Several industries negotiated with the AFL to avoid disruptive strikes. But cooperation was short-lived. Labor unions were defeated in a number of disastrous strikes, and the National Association of Manufacturers (NAM) launched an aggressive counterattack. The NAM and other employer associations provided strikebreakers, used industrial spies, and blacklisted union members to bar them from other jobs.

The Supreme Court came down squarely on management's side, ruling in the *Danbury Hatters* case in 1908 that trade unions were subject to the Sherman Anti-Trust Act. Thus union members could be held personally liable for money lost by a business during a strike. Courts at all levels often declared strikes illegal and were quick to issue restraining orders.

Working women and their problems aroused more sympathy among progressive reformers than the plight of working men. The number of women working outside the home increased steadily during the progressive era, from over 5 million in 1900 to nearly 8.5 million in 1920. But few belonged to unions, and the percentage had declined by 1910 before increasing a little after that date with aggressive organizing in the textile and clothing trades.

Although the AFL had hired Mary Kenney, a bookbinder by trade, as an organizer in the 1890s and accepted a few women's unions into affiliation, Gompers and other labor leaders generally opposed organizing women workers (see Chapter 18). "The demand for female labor," one leader announced, "is an insidious assault upon the home."

Of necessity, women continued to work to support themselves and their families. Many upper-class women reformers tried to help these working women. Tension and misunderstanding often developed between the reformers and the

Triangle Fire Victims The Triangle fire shocked the nation, and dramatic photographs, such as this candid shot showing bodies and bystanders waiting for more young women to jump, helped stimulate the investigation that followed. What event in your lifetime was as shocking as this photo? *(Brown Brothers)*

working women, but one organization in which there was genuine cooperation was the Women's Trade Union League. Founded in 1903, the league was organized by several progressive reformers but drew leaders from the working class, such as Mary Kenney and Rose Schneiderman, a Jewish immigrant cap maker. The league established branches in most large eastern and midwestern cities and served for more than a decade as an important force in helping to organize women into unions. It forced the AFL to pay more attention to women, helped out in time of strikes, put up bail money for those arrested, and publicized the plight of working women.

Garment Workers and the Triangle Fire

Thousands of young women, most of them Jewish and Italian, were employed in the garment industry in New York City. Most were between the ages of 16 and 25. They worked a 56-hour, 6-day week that paid about $6. New York had over 600 shirtwaist (blouse) and dress factories employing more than 30,000 workers.

Like other industries, garment manufacturing had changed. Once conducted in thousands of dark and dingy tenement rooms, all operations were now centralized in large loft buildings in lower Manhattan. Though an improvement over the tenements, many were still overcrowded and had few safety features. Scientific management made life miserable for the workers. Most of the women rented their sewing machines and even paid for their electricity. They were penalized for mistakes or for talking loudly, and were usually supervised by a male contractor who badgered and sometimes sexually harassed them.

In 1909, some of the women went out on strike to protest the working conditions. The International Ladies' Garment Workers Union (ILGWU) and the Women's Trade Union League supported them. But strikers were beaten and sometimes arrested. On November 22, after an impassioned speech in Yiddish by a young shirtwaist worker who had been injured on the picket line, a mass meeting voted for a general strike.

This "uprising of the twenty thousand" startled the nation. Jews and Italians learned a little of each other's language so they could communicate on the picket line. A young state legislator, Fiorello La Guardia, later a congressman and mayor, was one of many public officials who joined clergy and social reformers in aiding the strikers.

The shirtwaist workers won, and in part, the success of the strike made the garment union one of the most powerful in the AFL. But some companies refused to go along, and work conditions remained oppressive and unsafe. That became dramatically obvious on Saturday, March 25, 1911, when a fire broke out on the eighth floor of the 10-story loft building housing the Triangle Shirtwaist Company. Within minutes, the top three floors of the factory were ablaze. The managers had locked many exit doors. The elevators broke down. With no fire escapes, 46 women jumped to their deaths and over 100 died in the flames.

A shocked state legislature appointed a commission to investigate working conditions in the state. One investigator for the commission was a young social worker, Frances Perkins, who in the 1930s would become secretary of labor. She took politicians on a tour through the garment district to show them the miserable conditions under which young women worked. The result was state legislation limiting the work of women to 54 hours a week, prohibiting labor by children under the age of 14, and improving safety regulations in factories. One supporter of the bills was a young state senator named Franklin Delano Roosevelt.

The investigative commission was a favorite progressive tactic, and the Industrial Relations Commission, created in 1912, was one of the most important. The commission studied the causes of industrial unrest and violence and investigated a dramatic labor-management conflict in Colorado called the Ludlow Massacre. When the mine workers struck for an eight-hour day, better safety, and the removal of armed guards, the Rockefeller-dominated company refused to negotiate. The strike turned violent, and in the spring of 1914, strikebreakers and national guardsmen fired on the workers, killing 11 children and two women.

The Industrial Relations Commission forced John D. Rockefeller, Jr., to testify and implied that he was personally guilty of murder. Its report concluded that violent class conflict could be avoided only by limiting the use of armed guards and detectives, by restricting monopoly, by protecting workers' right to organize, and, most dramatically, by redistributing wealth through taxation. Not surprisingly, the report fell on deaf ears. Most progressives, like most Americans, denied its conclusion that class conflict was inevitable.

Radical Labor

Not everyone accepted the progressives' faith in investigations and protective labor legislation. Nor did everyone approve of Samuel Gompers's conservative tactics or his emphasis on getting better pay for skilled workers. About 200 radicals met in Chicago in 1905 to form a new union as an alternative to the AFL. They called it the Industrial Workers of the World (IWW). Like the Knights of Labor in the 1880s, the IWW welcomed all workers, regardless of skill, gender, or race.

DOCUMENT

Eugene V. Debs, "The Outlook for Socialism in America" (1900)

Eugene Debs attended the organizational meeting. He had become a socialist after the Pullman strike of 1894 and emerged by 1905 as one of the outstanding radical leaders in the country. Also there was "Big Bill" Haywood of the Western Federation of Miners, and the legendary "Mother" Jones, who dressed like a society matron but attacked labor leaders "who sit on velvet chairs in conferences with labor's oppressors." Now in her sixties, she had been a dressmaker, a Populist, and a member of the Knights of Labor.

The IWW remained small and troubled by internal squabbling. Haywood dominated the movement, which played an important role in organizing the militant strikes of textile workers in Lawrence, Massachusetts, in 1912 and the following year in Paterson, New Jersey, and Akron, Ohio. The IWW had its greatest success organizing lumbermen and migrant workers in the Northwest. Elsewhere, especially in times of high unemployment, the "Wobblies" helped the unskilled workers vent their anger against their employers.

But most American workers did not feel, as European workers often did, that they were involved in a class struggle. Some immigrant workers, intent on earning enough money to go home, had no time to join the conflict. Most of those who stayed dreamed the American dream—a better job or moving up into the middle class—and avoided labor militancy. They believed that even if they failed, their sons and daughters would profit from the American way. The AFL, not the IWW, became the dominant American labor organization.

REFORM IN THE CITIES AND STATES

The reform movements of the progressive era usually started at the local level, moved to the state, and finally reached the nation's capital. Progressivism in the cities and states had roots in the depression and discontent of the 1890s. The reform banners called for more democracy, more power for the people, and legislation regulating railroads and other businesses. Yet often the professional and business classes were the movement's leaders. They intended to bring order out of chaos and to modernize the city and the state during a time of rapid growth.

Municipal Reformers

American cities grew rapidly in the last part of the nineteenth and the first part of the twentieth centuries. New York, which had a population of 1.2 million in 1880, grew to 3.4 million by 1900 and 5.6 million in 1920. Chicago expanded even more dramatically. Los Angeles, a town of 11,000 in 1880, multiplied ten times by 1900 and then increased another five times, to more than a half million, by 1920.

The spectacular and continuing growth of the cities created a need for housing, transportation, and municipal services. But the kind of people who were filling the cities gave cause for worry. Fully 40 percent of New York's population and 36 percent of Chicago's were foreign-born in 1910; including immigrant children, the percentage approached 80 percent in some cities. "Beaten men from beaten races, representing the worst failures in the struggle for existence," was how the president of MIT described them.

Fear of the city and its new inhabitants motivated progressive municipal reform. Early twentieth-century reformers, mostly middle-class citizens, wanted to regulate the sprawling metropolis, restore democracy, cut corruption, and limit the power of bosses and their immigrant allies. When these reformers talked of restoring power to the people, they usually meant people like themselves.

Municipal reform movements varied from city to city. In Boston, reformers tried to strengthen the power of the mayor, break the hold of the city council, and eliminate council corruption. But in 1910 John Fitzgerald, grandfather of John F. Kennedy and a foe of reform, was elected mayor, defeating the reform candidate. Elsewhere reformers used different tactics, but they almost always conducted elaborate studies and campaigned to reduce corruption.

The most dramatic innovation was the replacement of both mayor and council with a nonpartisan commission of administrators. This innovation began quite accidentally when a hurricane devastated Galveston, Texas, in September 1900—one of the worst natural disasters in the nation's history, killing more than 6,000 people. The existing government was helpless to deal with the crisis, so the state legislature appointed five commissioners to run the city during the emergency.

The idea of government by commission spread rapidly, especially to the small and mid-sized cities in the Midwest and the Pacific Northwest. Dayton, Ohio, went one step further. After a disastrous flood in 1913, the city hired a city manager to run the city and to report to the elected council. Government by experts was the perfect symbol of what most municipal reformers had in mind.

In most large cities, however, the commission and the expert manager did not replace the mayor. One of the most flamboyant and successful of the progressive mayors was Tom Johnson of Cleveland, a wealthy man converted to reform by Henry George's *Progress and Poverty*. Elected mayor of Cleveland in 1901, he cut transit fares and built parks and municipal bathhouses throughout the city. He also broke the connection between the police and prostitution by promising "madams" and brothel owners that he would not bother them if they would not steal from customers or pay off the police. His most controversial move was to advocate city ownership of the street railroads and utilities. He was defeated in 1909, in part because he alienated many powerful business interests, but one of his lieutenants, Newton D. Baker, was elected mayor in 1911 and carried on many of his programs. Cleveland was one of many cities that began to regulate municipal utilities or to take them over from the private owners.

Tom Johnson and Newton Baker promoted the arts, music, and adult education, supervised construction of a civic center, and built a library and a museum. Such efforts were part of a "city beautiful movement." The architects of this movement constructed grand boulevards and built structures based on the architecture of Rome or the Renaissance. They tried to make the city more attractive for the middle and upper classes. Unfortunately, the museums and libraries were closed on Sundays, the only day the working class could visit them.

The social justice progressives, especially those connected with the social settlements, were more concerned with neighborhood parks and playgrounds. Hull

House established the first public playground in Chicago. Jacob Riis and Lillian Wald of the Henry Street Settlement campaigned in New York for small parks and the opening of schoolyards on weekends. Some progressives, remembering their own rural youth, tried to get urban children out of the city to summer camps. But they also tried to make the city more livable and beautiful.

Most progressives both feared and loved the city. Some saw the great urban areas filled with immigrants as a threat, but one of Tom Johnson's young assistants, Frederic C. Howe, wrote a book called *The City: The Hope of Democracy* (1905). Hope or threat, the progressives realized that the United States had become an urban nation and that the problems of the city had to be faced.

Reform in the States

The progressive movements in the states had many roots and took many forms. In some states, especially in the West, progressive attempts to regulate railroads and utilities were simply an extension of populism. In other states, progressivism bubbled up from urban reform efforts. Most states passed laws designed to extend democracy and give more authority to the people. Initiative and referendum laws allowed citizens to originate legislation and to overturn laws passed by the legislature, and recall laws gave the people a way to remove elected officials. Most of these "democratic" laws worked better in theory than in practice, but they did represent a genuine effort to remove special privilege from government.

Much progressive state legislation concerned order and efficiency, but many states passed social justice measures as well. Maryland enacted the first workers' compensation law in 1902, paying employees for days missed because of job-related injuries. Illinois approved a law aiding mothers with dependent children. Several states passed anti-child labor bills, and Oregon's law restricting women's labor to 10 hours per day became a model for other states.

States with the most successful reform movements elected strong governors: Charles Evans Hughes in New York, Hoke Smith in Georgia, Woodrow Wilson in New Jersey, and Robert La Follette in Wisconsin. After Wilson, La Follette was the most famous, and in many ways, the model progressive governor. Of small-town origin and an 1879 graduate of the University of Wisconsin, he began his career as a railroad lawyer and became a reformer only after the depression of 1893. Taking advantage of the general mood of discontent, he won the governorship in 1901. Ironically, La Follette owed his victory to his attack on the railroads. But La Follette was a shrewd politician. He used professors from the University of Wisconsin to prepare reports and do statistical studies. Then he worked with the legislature to pass a state primary law and an act regulating the railroads. "Go back to the first principles of democracy; go back to the people" was his battle cry. Journalists touted Wisconsin as the "laboratory of democracy." La Follette became a national figure and was elected to the Senate in 1906.

The progressive movement did improve government and make it more responsible to the people in states like Wisconsin. For example, the railroads were brought under the control of a railroad commission. But by 1910, the railroads no longer complained about the new taxes and restrictions. They had discovered that it was to their advantage to make their operations more efficient, and they often convinced the commission that they should raise rates or abandon unprofitable lines. Progressivism in the states, like progressivism everywhere, had mixed results. But the spirit of reform that swept the country was real, and progressive movements on the local level did eventually have an impact on Washington.

THEODORE ROOSEVELT AND THE SQUARE DEAL

An anarchist shot President McKinley in Buffalo on September 6, 1901. When McKinley died eight days later, Theodore Roosevelt, at 42, became history's youngest president. As the nation mourned its fallen leader, anarchists and other radicals were rounded up in many cities.

No one knew what to expect from Roosevelt. Some politicians thought he was too radical, but a few social justice progressives remembered his suggestion that the soldiers fire on strikers during the 1894 Pullman strike. Nonetheless, under his leadership, progressivism reshaped the national political agenda. Although early progressive reformers had attacked problems that they saw in their own communities,

TR's Bully Pulpit Theodore Roosevelt was a dynamic public speaker who used his position to influence public opinion. Despite his high-pitched voice, he could be heard at the back of the crowd in the days before microphones. Note the row of reporters decked out in their summer straw hats writing their stories as the president speaks. How have presidential speeches and the role of reporters changed since Roosevelt's time? *(Brown Brothers)*

they gradually understood that some problems could not be solved at the state or local level. The emergence of a national industrial economy had spawned conditions that demanded national solutions.

Progressives at the national level turned their attention to the economic system—the railroads and other large corporations, the state of the natural environment, and the quality of American industrial products. And as they fashioned legislation to remedy economic flaws, they vastly expanded the national government's power.

A Strong and Controversial President

IMAGE

Collage Spanning the Career of Teddy Roosevelt

Roosevelt came to the presidency with considerable experience. He had run unsuccessfully for mayor of New York and served a term in the New York state assembly. He had spent four years as a U. S. civil service commissioner and two years as New York City's police commissioner. His exploits in the Spanish-American War brought him to the public's attention, but he had also been an effective assistant secretary of the navy and a reform governor of New York. While police commissioner and governor, he had been influenced by progressives like his friend Jacob Riis and a group of New York City settlement workers.

But no one was sure how he would act as president. He came from an upper-class family, had associated with the important and the powerful all over the world. He had written books and was one of the most intellectual presidents since Thomas Jefferson. But none of this ensured that he would be a progressive in office.

Roosevelt loved being president. He called the office a "bully pulpit," and he enjoyed talking to the people and reporters. His appealing personality and sense of humor made him a good subject for the new mass-market press. The public quickly adopted him as their favorite. They called him "Teddy" and named a stuffed bear after him. Sometimes his exuberance got a little out of hand. On one occasion, he took a foreign diplomat on a nude swim in the Potomac River. You have to understand, someone remarked, that "the president is really only six years old."

Roosevelt, however, was more than an exuberant child; he was the strongest president since Lincoln. By revitalizing the executive branch, reorganizing the army command structure, and modernizing the consular service, he made many aspects of the federal government more efficient. He established the Bureau of Corporations, appointed commissions staffed with experts, and enlisted talented men to work for the government. "TR" called a White House conference on the care of dependent children, and in 1905 he even summoned college presidents and coaches to discuss ways to limit violence in football. He angered many social justice progressives by not going far enough. But he was the first president to listen to the pleas of the progressives and to invite them to the White House. Learning from experts like Frances Kellor, he became more concerned with social justice as time went on.

Dealing with the Trusts

One of Roosevelt's first actions as president was to attempt to control the large industrial corporations. He took office amid an unprecedented wave of business consolidation. Between 1897 and 1904, some 4,227 companies combined to form 257 large corporations. U.S. Steel, the first billion-dollar corporation, was formed in 1901 by joining Carnegie Steel with its eight main competitors. The new company controlled two-thirds of the market, and J. P. Morgan made $7 million on the deal.

The Sherman Anti-Trust Act of 1890 had been virtually useless in controlling the trusts, but a new outcry from muckrakers and progressives called for regulation. Some even demanded the return to the age of small business. Roosevelt opposed neither bigness nor the right of businessmen to make money. "We draw the line against misconduct, not against wealth," he said.

To the shock of much of the business community, he directed his attorney general to file suit to dissolve the Northern Securities Company, a giant railroad monopoly put together by Morgan and railroadman James J. Hill. "If we have done anything wrong," Morgan suggested, "send your man to my man and they can fix it up." A furious Roosevelt let Morgan and other businessmen know that the president of the United States was not just another tycoon. The government won its case and proceeded to prosecute some of the largest corporations, including Standard Oil of New Jersey and the American Tobacco Company.

Roosevelt's antitrust policy did not end the power of the giant corporations or even alter their methods of doing business. Nor did it force down the price of kerosene, cigars, or railroad tickets. But it breathed some life into the Sherman Anti-Trust Act and increased the role of the federal government as regulator. It also caused large firms such as U.S. Steel to diversify to avoid antitrust suits.

Roosevelt tried to strengthen the regulatory powers of the federal government in other ways. He steered the Elkins Act through Congress in 1903 and the Hepburn Act in 1906, which together increased the power of the Interstate Commerce Commission (ICC). The first act eliminated the use of rebates by railroads; the second broadened the power of the ICC and gave it the right to investigate and enforce rates, though opponents in Congress weakened both bills.

Roosevelt firmly believed in corporate capitalism, detested socialism, and was not comfortable around labor leaders. Yet he saw his role as mediator and regulator. His view of the power of the presidency was illustrated in 1902 during the anthracite coal strike. Led by the United Mine Workers, coal miners went on strike to protest low wages, long hours, and dangerous conditions. In 1901, a total of 513 coal miners had died in industrial accidents. The mine owners refused to talk to the miners, hiring strikebreakers and using private security forces to intimidate workers. In the fall of 1902, schools began closing for lack of coal, and it looked like many citizens would suffer through the winter. Over the managers' protests about talking to "outlaws," Roosevelt called owners and union leaders to the White House and appointed a commission that included both union and community representatives. Within weeks, the miners were back at work with a 10 percent raise.

Meat Inspection and Pure Food and Drugs

Roosevelt's first major legislative reform began almost accidentally in 1904 when Upton Sinclair, a 26-year-old muckraking journalist, started to research Chicago's stockyards. His novel, *The Jungle,* was published in 1906. The novel documented labor exploitation and tried to convert readers to socialism, but its description of contaminated meat turned stomachs and set off an outcry for better regulation of the meatpacking industry. Roosevelt, who read the book, reportedly could no longer enjoy his breakfast sausage. He ordered a study of the industry and used the report to pressure Congress and the meatpackers to accept a reform bill.

In the end, the Meat Inspection Act of 1906 was a compromise. It enforced some federal inspection and mandated sanitary conditions in all companies selling meat in interstate commerce. The meatpackers defeated a provision that would have required the dating of all meat. Some large companies supported the compromise bill because it gave them an advantage against smaller firms. But the bill was a beginning. It illustrates how muckrakers, social justice progressives, and public outcry eventually led to reform legislation. It also shows how Roosevelt used the public mood and manipulated the political process to get a bill through Congress. He was always willing to settle for half a loaf rather than none at all. Ironically, the Meat Inspection Act restored public confidence in the meat industry and helped it increase profits.

Publicity surrounding *The Jungle* generated legislation to regulate food and drug sales. Many packaged and canned foods contained dangerous chemicals and impurities. Americans consumed an enormous quantity of patent medicines; one popular remedy was revealed to be 44 percent alcohol, and often medicines were laced with opium. Many people unwittingly became alcoholics or drug addicts. The Pure Food and Drug Act (1906) was not perfect, but it corrected some of the worst abuses, including eliminating cocaine from Coca-Cola.

Conservation Versus Preservation

Roosevelt, an outdoorsman and amateur naturalist, considered his conservation program his most important domestic achievement. Using his executive authority, he more than tripled the land set aside for national forests, bringing the total to more than 150 million acres.

Roosevelt understood, as few easterners did, the problems created by limited water in the western states. In 1902, with his enthusiastic support, Congress passed the Newlands Act, setting aside the proceeds from the sale of public land in 16 western states to pay for the construction of irrigation projects in those states. Although it tended to help big farmers the most, the Newlands Act federalized irrigation for the first time.

More important, Roosevelt raised public consciousness about saving natural resources. He appointed a National Conservation Commission charged with making an inventory of the natural resources in the entire country, chaired by Gifford Pinchot, probably the most important conservationist in the country. An advocate of selective logging, fire control, and limited grazing on public lands, Pinchot became a friend and adviser to Roosevelt.

Pinchot's conservation policies pleased many in the timber and cattle industries and angered those who simply wanted to exploit the land. But the followers of John Muir, a passionate advocate of preserving wilderness, denounced Pinchot's philosophy and policies. Muir had founded the Sierra Club in 1862 and had led a successful campaign to create Yosemite National Park in California. He looked eccentric, but thousands agreed when he argued that to preserve the wilderness was a spiritual and psychological necessity for overcivilized city residents. Muir was one of the leaders in the turn-of-the-century "back-to-nature" movement, which also included the founding of the Boy Scouts (1910) and the Camp Fire Girls (1912).

The conflicting conservation philosophies of Pinchot and Muir were most dramatically demonstrated by the controversy over Hetch-Hetchy, a remote valley deep within Yosemite National Park. It was a pristine wilderness area, and Muir and his followers wanted to keep it that way. But in 1901, the mayor of San Francisco decided the valley would make a perfect place for a dam and reservoir to supply his growing city with water. Muir argued that wilderness soon would be scarcer than water, though more important for the nation's moral strength. Pinchot and other conservationists argued that it was immoral to sacrifice the welfare of the great majority to the aesthetic enjoyment of a tiny group. In the end, Roosevelt and Congress sided with the conservationists, and the valley became (and remains) a lake. The debate between conservationists and preservationists still goes on today.

Progressivism for Whites Only

Like most whites of his generation, Roosevelt believed that blacks, Indians, and Asians were inferior, and he feared that massive migrations from southern and eastern Europe threatened Anglo-Saxon dominance. But Roosevelt was a politician, so he made gestures of goodwill to most groups. He even invited Booker T. Washington to the White House in 1901, despite vicious southern protests, and appointed several qualified blacks to minor federal posts. But he could also be insensitive to African Americans, as he surely was in his handling of the Brownsville, Texas, riot of 1906. Members of a black army unit who were stationed there rioted, angered by discrimination against them. No one is sure exactly what happened, but one white man was killed and several were wounded. After the midterm elections of 1906, Roosevelt ordered all 167 members of three companies dishonorably discharged—an unjust punishment for an unproven crime. Sixty-six years later, the secretary of the army granted honorable discharges to the men, most of whom were dead by then.

The progressive era coincided with the years of greatest segregation in the South, but even the most advanced progressives seldom included blacks in their reform schemes. Like most settlements, Hull House was segregated, although Addams, more than most progressives, struggled to overcome the racist attitudes of her day. She helped found a settlement that served a black neighborhood in Chicago, and she spoke out repeatedly against lynching. In 1909, Addams supported the founding of the National Association for the Advancement of Colored People (NAACP), the most important organization of the progressive era aimed at promoting equality and justice for blacks.

The founding of the NAACP is the story of cooperation between a group of white social justice progressives and courageous black leaders. Even in the age of segregation and lynching, blacks in all parts of the country—through churches, clubs, and schools—sought to promote a better life for themselves.

An American History Class Tuskegee Institute followed Booker T. Washington's philosophy of black advancement through accommodation to the white status quo. Here students study white American history, but most of their time was spent on more practical subjects. This photo was taken in 1902 by Frances Benjamin Johnston, a pioneer woman photographer. How have classrooms changed in the last hundred years? How have they stayed the same? (*Library of Congress*)

DOCUMENT

Booker T. Washington, Atlanta Exposition Address (1895)

The most important black leader who argued for equality and opportunity for his people was W. E. B. Du Bois. As discussed in Chapter 17, Du Bois differed dramatically with Booker T. Washington on the proper position of blacks in American life. Whereas Washington advocated vocational education, Du Bois argued that the "talented tenth" of the black population should get the best education possible. Against Washington's talk of compromise and accommodation to the dominant white society, Du Bois increasingly urged aggressive action for equality.

Denouncing Washington in 1905, Du Bois called a meeting of young and militant blacks across from Niagara Falls in Canada. "We believe in taking what we can get but we don't believe in being satisfied with it and in permitting anybody for a moment to imagine we're satisfied," said the Niagara movement's angry manifesto. Du Bois's small band was soon augmented by white liberals concerned with violence against blacks, including Jane Addams and Oswald Garrison Villard, grandson of abolitionist William Lloyd Garrison. In 1910, the Niagara movement merged with the NAACP, and Du Bois became editor of its journal, *The Crisis*. He toned down his rhetoric but tried to promote equality for all blacks. The NAACP was a typical progressive organization, seeking to work within the American system to promote reform. But Roosevelt and many other progressives thought it dangerously radical.

William Howard Taft

After two terms as president, Roosevelt decided to step down and go big-game hunting in Africa. But he soon regretted leaving the White House. He was only 50 years old and at the peak of his popularity and power.

William Howard Taft, Roosevelt's choice for the Republican nomination in 1908 and winner over William Jennings Bryan for the election, was a distinguished lawyer and federal judge—the first civil governor of the Philippines and Roosevelt's secretary of war. In some ways, he was more progressive than Roosevelt. His administration instituted more suits against monopolies in one term than Roosevelt had in two. He supported the eight-hour workday and legislation to make mining safer. He supported the Mann-Elkins Act in 1910, which strengthened the ICC. Taft and Congress also authorized the first tax on corporate profits, and he encouraged the process that eventually led to the passage of the federal income tax, which was authorized under the Sixteenth Amendment and was ratified in 1913.

But Taft's presidency quickly ran into difficulties. His biggest problem was his style. He weighed over 300 pounds, wrote ponderously, and spoke with little inspiration. He also lacked Roosevelt's political skills and angered many of the progressives in the Republican party, especially the midwestern insurgents led by La Follette, when he signed the Payne-Aldrich Tariff of 1909. Many progressives thought it favored the eastern industrial interests and left the rates too high.

Even Roosevelt was infuriated when his successor reversed many of his conservation policies and fired Chief Forester Gifford Pinchot, who had attacked Secretary of the Interior Richard A. Ballinger for giving away rich coal lands in Alaska to mining interests. Roosevelt broke with Taft, letting it be known that he was willing to run again for president. This set up one of the most exciting and significant elections in American history.

The Election of 1912

Woodrow Wilson won the Democratic presidential nomination in 1912. The son and grandson of Presbyterian ministers, he grew up in a comfortable and intellectual southern household. He graduated from Princeton in 1879, got a Ph.D., and published *Congressional Government* (1885), which established his reputation as a shrewd political analyst. He taught history and became a Princeton professor. Less flamboyant than Roosevelt, he was a persuasive speaker. In 1902, he was elected president of Princeton University; during the next few years, he established a national reputation as an educational leader. He eagerly accepted the Democratic machine's offer to run for governor of New Jersey in 1910, but then showed courage by quickly alienating some of the conservatives who had helped elect him. Building a reform coalition, he put through a direct primary law and other progressive reforms. By 1912, Wilson had acquired the reputation of a progressive.

Roosevelt, who had been speaking out on a variety of issues since 1910, competed with Taft for the Republican nomination. As the incumbent president and party leader, Taft won it—but Roosevelt startled the nation by walking out of the convention and forming a new political party, the Progressive party. It appealed to progressives who had become frustrated with the conservative leadership in both major parties. Its platform contained provisions that reformers had been advocating for years: an eight-hour workday; a six-day workweek; abolition of child labor under age 16; federal accident, old age, and unemployment insurance; and—unlike the Democrats—woman suffrage.

Most supporters of the Progressives in 1912 hoped to organize a new political movement that would replace the Republican party, just as the Republicans had replaced the Whigs after 1856. Progressive leaders, led by Frances Kellor, had plans to apply the principles of social research by educating voters between elections.

The Progressive party convention in Chicago seemed like a religious revival or a social work conference. Delegates sang "Onward Christian Soldiers" and "The Battle Hymn of the Republic," and when Jane Addams seconded Roosevelt's nomination, a large group of women marched around the auditorium with a "Votes for Women" banner. The Progressive cause "is based on the eternal principles of righteousness," Roosevelt cried.

But behind the unified facade lurked many disagreements. Roosevelt had become more progressive on many issues since leaving the presidency. He even attacked the financiers "to whom the acquisition of untold millions is the supreme goal of life, and who are too often utterly indifferent as to how these millions are obtained." But he was less committed to social reform than some delegates. A number of social justice progressives fought hard to include a plank in the platform supporting equality for blacks and for seating a black delegation, but Roosevelt hoped to carry several southern states. In the end, no blacks were seated and the platform made no mention of black equality.

The 1912 campaign became a contest primarily between Roosevelt and Wilson, who vigorously debated the proper relationship of government to society in a modern industrial age. Advancing what he called the New Nationalism, Roosevelt argued that in a modern industrial society, large corporations were "inevitable and necessary." What was needed was a strong president and increased power in the hands of the federal government to regulate business and industry for the benefit of the people. He argued for using Hamiltonian means to ensure Jeffersonian ends, for using strong central government to guarantee the rights of the people.

Wilson responded with a program and a slogan of his own: the New Freedom. Drawing on the writings of Louis Brandeis, he emphasized the Jeffersonian tradition of limited government with open competition. He spoke of the "curse of bigness" and argued against too much federal power. "What I fear is a government of experts," Wilson declared, implying that Roosevelt's New Nationalism would mean regulated monopolies and even collectivism.

This was one of the few elections in American history in which important ideas were actually discussed. It also marked a watershed for political thought for liberals who rejected Jefferson's distrust of a strong central government. It is easy to exaggerate the differences between Roosevelt and Wilson. Both urged reform within the American system, defended corporate capitalism, and opposed socialism and radical labor organizations. Both wanted more democracy and stronger but conservative labor unions. Both were very different in style and substance from the fourth candidate, Eugene Debs, who ran on the Socialist party ticket in 1912.

Debs, at the time, was the most important socialist leader in the country. Socialism has always been a minority movement in the United States, but it stood at its pinnacle in the first decade of the twentieth century. Thirty-three cities had socialist mayors, and two socialists sat in Congress. The most important socialist periodical increased its circulation from about 30,000 in 1900 to nearly 300,000 in 1906. Its following was quite diverse. In the cities, some who called themselves socialists merely favored municipal ownership of street railways. Some reformers, such as Florence Kelley, joined out of frustration with the slow pace of reform. Many recent immigrants brought to the party a European sense of class and loyalty to socialism.

IMAGE

Socialist Cartoon (1919)

A tremendously appealing figure and a great orator, Debs had run for president in 1900, 1904, and 1908, but in 1912, he reached much wider audiences in more parts of the country. His message differed radically from that of Wilson or Roosevelt. Unlike the progressives, socialists argued for fundamental change in the American system. Debs polled almost 900,000 votes in 1912 (6 percent of the popular vote), the best showing ever for a socialist in the United States. Wilson received 6.3 million votes, Roosevelt a little more than 4 million, and Taft 3.5 million. Wilson garnered 435 electoral votes, Roosevelt 88, and Taft only 8.

WOODROW WILSON AND THE NEW FREEDOM

Wilson was elected largely because Roosevelt and the Progressive party split the Republican vote. But once elected, Wilson became a vigorous and aggressive chief executive who set out to translate his ideas about progressive government into legislation. He was the first southerner elected president since Zachary Taylor in 1848 and only the second Democrat since the Civil War. Wilson, like Roosevelt, had to work with his party, and that restricted how progressive he could be. He was also constrained by his background and inclinations. Still, like Roosevelt, Wilson became more progressive during his presidency.

DOCUMENT

Woodrow Wilson, from *The New Freedom* (1913)

Tariff and Banking Reform

Wilson had a more difficult time than Roosevelt relating to small groups, but he was an excellent public speaker who dominated through the force of his intellect. He probably had an exaggerated belief in his ability to persuade and tended to trust his own intuition too much. His accomplishment in pushing a legislative program through Congress during his first two years in office was matched only by Franklin Roosevelt during the first months of the New Deal and by Lyndon Johnson in 1965. But his early success bred overconfidence, portending trouble.

Within a month of his inauguration, Wilson went before a joint session of Congress to outline his legislative program. He recommended reducing the tariff, freeing the banking system from Wall Street control, and restoring industrial competition. By appearing in person before Congress, he broke a precedent of written presidential messages established by Thomas Jefferson.

First on Wilson's agenda was tariff reform. The Underwood Tariff, passed in 1913, was not a free-trade bill, but it did reduce the schedule for the first time in many years. Attached to the Underwood bill was a provision for a small and slightly graduated income tax, recently allowed by passage of the Sixteenth Amendment. It imposed a modest rate of 1 percent on income over $4,000 (thus exempting a large portion of the population), with a surtax rising to 6 percent on high incomes. The income tax was enacted to replace the money lost from lowering the tariff. Wilson seemed to have no interest in using it to redistribute wealth.

A financial panic in 1907 had revealed the need for a central bank, and much of the private banking system was dominated by a few firms such as J. P. Morgan & Company, but few people could agree on what should be done. Progressive Democrats argued for a banking system and currency controlled by the federal government. But talk of banking reform raised the specter among conservative Democrats and the business community of socialism, populism, and the monetary ideas of William Jennings Bryan.

The Federal Reserve System, created by compromise legislation in 1913, was the first reorganization of the banking system since the Civil War. The law gave the federal government some control over the banking system. It also created a flexible currency, based on Federal Reserve notes, that could be expanded or contracted as need required. The Federal Reserve System was not without its flaws, as later developments would show, and it did not end the power of the large eastern banks; but it was an improvement, and it appealed to the part of the progressive movement that sought order and efficiency.

Wilson was not very progressive in some of his early actions. He failed to support a plan for long-term rural credit financed by the federal government. He opposed a woman suffrage amendment and refused to back an anti-child labor bill. And he ordered the segregation of blacks in several federal departments. "I sincerely believe it to be in their [the blacks'] best interest," he said in rejecting the NAACP's protests.

Moving Closer to a New Nationalism

Wilson and Roosevelt had vigorously debated how to control the great corporations. Wilson's solution was the Clayton Act, which prohibited various unfair trading practices, outlawed the interlocking directorate, and forbade corporations to purchase stock in other corporations if this tended to reduce competition. But the law was vague and hard to enforce, and the courts interpreted it to mean that labor unions remained subject to court injunctions during strikes.

More important was the creation of the Federal Trade Commission (FTC). Powerful enough to move directly against corporations accused of restricting

TIMELINE

1901	McKinley assassinated
	Theodore Roosevelt becomes president
	Robert La Follette elected governor of Wisconsin
	Tom Johnson elected mayor of Cleveland
1903	Women's Trade Union League founded
	Elkins Act
1904	Roosevelt reelected
	Lincoln Steffens, *The Shame of the Cities*
1906	Upton Sinclair, *The Jungle*
	Hepburn Act
	Meat Inspection Act
	Pure Food and Drug Act
1908	*Muller v. Oregon*
	Danbury Hatters case
	William Howard Taft elected president
1909	Herbert Croly, *The Promise of American Life*
	NAACP founded

1911	Frederick Taylor, *The Principles of Scientific Management*
	Triangle Shirtwaist Company fire
1912	Progressive party founded by Theodore Roosevelt
	Woodrow Wilson elected president
	Children's Bureau established
	Industrial Relations Commission founded
1913	Sixteenth Amendment (income tax) ratified
	Underwood Tariff
	Federal Reserve System established
	Seventeenth Amendment (direct election of senators) passed
1914	Clayton Act
	Federal Trade Commission Act
	AFL has over 2 million members
	Ludlow Massacre in Colorado

competition, the FTC was the idea of Louis Brandeis. Wilson accepted it even though it seemed to move him more toward the philosophy of New Nationalism.

The FTC and the Clayton Act did not end monopoly. The success of Wilson's reform agenda appeared minimal in 1914, but the outbreak of war in Europe and the need to win the election of 1916 would force him into becoming more progressive.

Neither Wilson nor Roosevelt satisfied advanced progressives. Most of the efforts of the two progressive presidents were spent trying to regulate economic power rather than promoting social justice. Yet their most important legacy was their attempts to strengthen the office of president and the executive branch of the federal government. The nineteenth-century American presidents after Lincoln had been relatively weak, and much of the federal power had resided with Congress. The progressive presidents reasserted presidential authority, modernized the executive branch, and began the creation of the federal bureaucracy, which has had a major impact on the lives of Americans in the twentieth century.

Both Wilson and Roosevelt used the presidency to advertise and promote their reform agenda. TR called the office a "bully pulpit." He strengthened the Interstate Commerce Commission and Wilson created the Federal Trade Commission, forerunners of many other federal regulatory bodies. By personally delivering his annual message before Congress, Wilson symbolized the new power of the presidency.

More than the increased power of the executive branch changed the nature of politics. The new bureaus, committees, and commissions brought to Washington a new kind of expert, trained in the universities, at the state and local level, and in the voluntary organizations. Julia Lathrop, a coworker of Jane Addams at Hull House, was typical. Appointed by President Taft in 1912 to become chief of the newly created Children's Bureau, she was the first woman ever named to such a position. She used her post not only to work for better child labor laws, but also to train a new generation of women experts who would take their positions in state, federal, and private agencies in the 1920s and 1930s. Other experts emerged in Washington during the progressive era to influence policy in subtle and important ways. The expert, the commission, the statistical survey, and the increased power of the executive branch were all legacies of the progressive era.

Conclusion

The Limits of Progressivism

The progressive era was a time when many Americans set out to promote reform because they saw poverty, despair, and disorder in the country transformed by immigration, urbanism, and industrialism. However, unlike the socialists, the progressives saw nothing fundamentally wrong with the American system. Progressivism, part of a global movement to regulate and control the worst aspects of industrialism, was largely a middle-class movement that sought to help the poor, the immigrants, and the working class. Yet the poor were rarely consulted about policy, and many groups, especially African Americans, were almost entirely left out of reform plans. Progressives had an optimistic view of human nature and an exaggerated faith in statistics, commissions, and committees. They talked of the need for more democracy, but they often succeeded in promoting bureaucracy and a government run by experts. Frances Kellor was one of those experts; she represented a growing group of well-educated women who found a role during the progressive era in the new government agencies and private foundations. The progressives believed there was a need to regulate business, promote efficiency, and spread social justice, but these were often contradictory goals. In the end, their regulatory laws tended to aid business and to strengthen corporate capitalism, while social justice and equal opportunity remained difficult to achieve. By contrast, most of the industrialized nations of western Europe, especially Germany, Austria, France, and Great Britain, passed legislation during this period providing for old-age pensions and health and unemployment insurance.

Progressivism was a broad, diverse, and sometimes contradictory movement that had its roots in the 1890s and reached a climax in the early twentieth century. It began with many local movements and voluntary efforts to deal with the problems created by urban industrialism and moved to the state and finally the national level. Women played important roles in organizing reform, and many became experts at gathering statistics and writing reports. Eventually they began to fill positions in the new agencies in the state capitals and in Washington. Neither Theodore Roosevelt nor Woodrow Wilson was an advanced progressive, but during both their administrations, progressivism achieved some success. Both presidents strengthened the power of the presidency, and both promoted the idea that the federal government had the responsibility to regulate and control and to promote social justice. Progressivism would achieve a certain climax during World War I, but during the 1920s, there was a general reaction against most progressive measures. Still the spirit of progressivism survived to influence the New Deal during the 1930s.

Questions for Review and Reflection

1. What contributions did women make to the progressive movement?

2. Why did the United States lag behind several European countries in passing social legislation?

3. Was Prohibition a progressive measure?

4. How did progressivism differ from socialism?

Discovering U.S. History Online

The American Experience: America 1900 http://www.pbs.org/wgbh/pages/amex/1900/
This is the companion site to the PBS documentary *America 1900*. It includes audio clips of respected historians on the economics, politics, and culture of 1900; a primary-source database; a timeline of the year; downloadable software to compile your family tree; and other materials.

The Evolution of the Conservation Movement, 1850–1920 http://memory.loc.gov/ammem/ amrvhtml/conshome.html
This Library of Congress site brings together scores of primary sources and photographs about "the historical formation and cultural foundations of the movement to conserve and protect America's natural heritage."

Triangle Fire http://www.ilr.cornell.edu/trianglefire/
The Kheel Center for Labor-Management Documentation and Archives at Cornell University has put together this excellent site composed of oral histories, cartoons, images, and essays about the shirtwaist factory fire of March 1911.

The Trial of Bill Haywood http://www.law.umkc.edu/faculty/projects/ftrials/haywood/haywood.htm
This site contains images, chronology, and court and official documents maintained by Dr. Doug Linder at the University of Missouri–Kansas City Law School. Bill Haywood was a labor radical accused of ordering the assassination of former governor of Idaho Frank Steunenberg in 1907.

Theodore Roosevelt Association http://www.theodoreroosevelt.org/
This site contains much biographical and research information about this famous American.

IPL Potus—Woodrow Wilson http://www.ipl.org/ref/POTUS/wwilson.html
This Internet Public Library–Presidents of the United States site contains basic factual data about Wilson's election and presidency, speeches, and online biographies.

Fiction and Film

Fiction from the period includes Theodore Dreiser's novel *Sister Carrie* (1900), a classic of social realism; Upton Sinclair's *The Jungle* (1906), a novel about the meatpacking industry and the failure of the American dream; *Susan Lenox* (1917) by David Graham Phillips, an epic of slum life and political corruption; and Charlotte Perkins Gilman's *Herland* (1915), the story of a feminist utopia.

Birth of a Nation (1915) is an important film, not only because of its innovative technique, but also because it is a mirror of the worst racism of the progressive era. *Hester Street* (1975) creates a realistic picture of the urban immigrant experience during the progressive period.

Recommended Reading

www.ablongman.com/nash
The Companion Website has a list of recommended readings about the social justice movement, workers, urban and state reform, Theodore Roosevelt and the Square Deal, and Woodrow Wilson and the New Freedom.

CHAPTER OUTLINE

- The Early War Years
- The United States Enters the War
- The Military Experience
- Domestic Impact of the War
- Planning for Peace
- Conclusion: The Divided Legacy of the Great War

American Stories

A Young Man Enlists in the Great Adventure

On April 7, 1917, the day after the United States declared war on Germany, 22-year-old Edmund P. Arpin, Jr., from Grand Rapids, Wisconsin, enlisted in the army. The war seemed to provide a solution for his aimless drifting. It was not patriotism but his craving for adventure that led him to join the army. A month later, he was at Fort Sheridan, Illinois, along with hundreds of other eager young men, preparing to become an army officer. He felt pride, purpose, and especially comradeship, but the war was far away.

Arpin finally arrived with his unit in Liverpool, England, on December 23, 1917, aboard the *Leviathan*, a German luxury liner that the United States had seized and turned into a troop transport. American troops were not greeted as saviors. English hostility simmered partly because of the previous unit's drunken brawls. Despite the efforts of the U.S. government to protect soldiers from the sins of Europe, drinking seems to have been a preoccupation of Arpin's outfit. He also learned something about French wine and women, but he spent most of the endless waiting time learning to play contract bridge.

Arpin saw some of the horror of war when he went to the front with a French regiment, but his own unit did not go into combat until October 1918, when the war was almost over. He took part in the bloody Meuse-Argonne offensive, which helped end the war. But he discovered that war was not the heroic struggle of carefully planned campaigns that newspapers and books described. War was filled with misfired weapons, mix-ups, and erroneous attacks. Wounded in the leg in an assault on an unnamed hill and awarded a Distinguished Service Cross for his bravery, Arpin later learned that the order to attack had been recalled, but word had not reached him in time.

When the armistice came, Arpin was in a field hospital. He was disappointed that the war had ended so soon, but he was well enough to go to Paris to take part in the victory celebration and to explore famous restaurants and nightclubs. In many ways, the highlight of his war experiences was not a battle or his medal, but his postwar adventure. With a friend, he went AWOL and explored Germany, making it back without being arrested.

Edmund Arpin was one of 4,791,172 Americans who served in the army, navy, or marines, one of the 2 million who went overseas, and one of the 230,074 who were wounded. Some of his friends were among the 48,909 who were killed. Mustered out in March 1919, he felt confused. Being a civilian was not nearly as exciting as being in the army and visiting exotic places.

In time, Arpin settled down. He became a successful businessman, married, and reared a family. A member of the American Legion, he periodically went to conventions and reminisced with men from his division about their escapades in France. Although the war changed their lives in many ways, most would never again feel the same sense of common purpose and adventure. "I don't suppose any of us felt, before or since, so necessary to God and man," one veteran recalled.

For Edmund P. Arpin, Jr., the Great War was the most important event of a lifetime. Just as war changed his life, so, too, did it alter the lives of most Americans. The power and influence of the federal government increased. Not only did the war promote woman suffrage, prohibition, and public housing, but it also helped create an administrative bureaucracy that blurred the lines between public and private, between government and business—a trend that continued through the twentieth century.

In this chapter, we examine the complicated circumstances that led the United States into war and share the wartime experiences of American men and women at home and abroad. We will study not only military actions, but also the war's impact on domestic policies and on the lives of ordinary Americans, including the migration of African Americans into northern cities. The war left a legacy of prejudice and hate and raised a basic question: Could the tenets of American democracy, such as freedom of speech, survive participation in a major war? The chapter concludes with a look at the idealistic efforts to promote peace at the end of the war, and the disillusion that followed. The Great War was a global war in every sense, and it thrust the United States into world leadership, but many Americans were reluctant to accept that role.

THE EARLY WAR YEARS

Few Americans expected the war that erupted in Europe in the summer of 1914 to affect their lives or to alter their comfortable world. But when a Serbian terrorist shot Archduke Franz Ferdinand of Austria-Hungary in Sarajevo, a place almost no Americans had even heard of, this precipitated a series of events that led to the most destructive war the world had ever known.

The Causes of War

The Great War, as everyone called it, was ultimately caused by intense rivalry over trade, empire and military strength, yet it did not seem inevitable in 1914. There had been many wars throughout the nineteenth century, including the American Civil War, but most had been local conflicts. And there were many signs of international cooperation with agreements on telegraphs in 1865, postage in 1875, copyright in 1880, and even time zones by 1890. In addition, a World Court at The Hague in the Netherlands, set up in 1899, promised to solve international

THE GREAT WAR IN EUROPE AND THE MIDDLE EAST The Great War had an impact not only on Europe but also on North Africa and the Middle East. Even the countries that remained neutral felt the influence of global war. ■ **Reflecting on the Past** For most Americans, the war was in France on the western front. Where else were major battles fought?

disputes, while politicians and diplomats predicted that improved technology and communications would lead to permanent peace.

Yet the same technology that promised to bring nations together led to a growing sense of nationalism, a pride in being French or English, and a growing rivalry among nations. Germany, which was created in 1871 from a number of small states, began to increase its navy, causing Great Britain to build more battleships. Rivalry and jealousy led to a series of treaties: Austria-Hungry and Germany (the Central Powers) became military allies and Britain, France, and Russia (the Allied Powers) agreed to assist one another in case of attack. Despite peace conferences and international agreements, many promoted by the United States, the European balance of power rested precariously on these treaties.

b/c there were so many allies made before a incedent, they were all dragged into war

The incident in Sarajevo destroyed that balance. The leaders of Austria-Hungary wanted to punish Serbia for killing Franz Ferdinand, the heir to the throne. Russia mobilized to aid Serbia. Germany, supporting Austria-Hungary, declared war on Russia and France. When Germany invaded Belgium to attack France, Britain declared war. The slaughter began. Within a few months, the Ottoman Empire (Turkey) and Bulgaria joined the Central Powers. Italy joined the Allies after being secretly promised additional territory after the war. Japan declared war on Germany in order to acquire German rights in China and the Pacific islands. Spain, Switzerland, the Netherlands, Denmark, Norway, Sweden, and initially the United States, remained neutral.

The American sense that the nation would never succumb to the barbarism of war, combined with the knowledge that they were insulated by the Atlantic, brought relief after the first shock wore off. Wilson's official proclamation of neutrality on August 4, 1914, reinforced the belief that the United States had no major stake in the outcome and would stay uninvolved. The president urged Americans to "be neutral in fact as well as in name ... impartial in thought as well as in action." But it was difficult to stay uninvolved, at least emotionally.

American Reaction

Although many Americans worked to promote world peace and a few sought to end the war through mediation, others could hardly wait to leap into the adventure. Hundreds of young American men, mostly college students or recent graduates, joined ambulance units. Among the most famous were Ernest Hemingway, John Dos Passos, and e. e. cummings (as he spelled his name), who later turned their wartime adventures into literary masterpieces. Others volunteered for the French Foreign Legion or the Lafayette Escadrille—volunteer American pilots attached to the French army. Many of these young men were inspired by an older generation who pictured war as a romantic and manly adventure.

DOCUMENT

Eugene V. Debs, Critique of World War I (1916)

Many Americans saw war as a test of idealism and manhood because the only conflict they remembered was the "splendid little war" of 1898. Older Americans recalled the Civil War, whose horrors had faded, leaving only the memory of heroic triumphs. But Oliver Wendell Holmes, the Supreme Court justice who had been wounded in the Civil War, remarked, "War, when you are at it, is horrible and dull. It is only when time has passed that you see that its message was divine."

Early reports from the battlefields should have indicated that the message was anything but divine. This would be a modern war in which men died by the thousands, cut down by an improved and efficient technology of killing.

The New Military Technology

The Germans' plan called for a rapid strike through Belgium to attack Paris and the French army from the rear. However, the French stopped the Germans in September 1914, and the fighting bogged down. Soldiers on both sides dug miles of trenches and strung out barbed wire. Hundreds of thousands died in battles that gained only a few yards or nothing at all. Rapid-firing rifles, improved explosives, incendiary shells, and tracer bullets all added to the destruction. Most devastating of all was the improved artillery that could hit targets miles behind the lines. Machine guns neutralized frontal assaults, but generals on both sides continued to order their men to charge to almost certain death.

DOCUMENT

Adolf K. G. E. von Spiegel, U-boat 202 (1919)

The war was the last major conflict in which cavalry was used and the first to employ a new generation of military technologies. By 1918, airplanes were creating terror with their bombs. Tanks made a tentative appearance in 1916, but it was not until the last days of the war that this new offensive weapon began to neutralize the machine gun. Poison gas, first used in 1914, added special fear and horror to trench warfare.

The Great War was truly a global struggle. For most Americans, the war consisted of the western front in France and Belgium, but there was also bitter fighting in Russia and Italy, while submarines and battleships carried the fight around the world. On the western front, soldiers from New Zealand and Australia fought side by side with French-speaking black Africans. The British and the French fought in Africa, trying to capture the German colonies. The British occupied Mesopotamia (Iraq) and fought a bloody war against the Turks along the Black Sea. The Turks used the war to massacre an estimated 800,000 Armenians in one of the worst acts of genocide in history, but few protested at the time.

Neutrality in a Global Conflict

Despite Wilson's efforts to promote neutrality, most Americans favored the Allied cause. About 8 million people of German and Austro-Hungarian descent lived in the United States, and some supported the Central Powers. The anti-British feelings of some Irish Americans led them to side not so much with Germany as against England. A number of American scholars, physicians, and intellectuals fondly remembered studying in Germany, and they admired its culture and progressive social planning. For most Americans, however, the ties of language and culture tipped the balance toward the Allies. After all, did not the English-speaking people of the world have special bonds and responsibilities? Memories of Lafayette's role in the American Revolution and France's gift of the Statue of Liberty made many Americans pro-French.

Other reasons made real neutrality nearly impossible. The fact that U.S. trade with the Allies was much more important than with the Central Powers caused many American businesses to support the Allies. Wilson's advisers openly supported the French and British. Most newspaper owners and editors had close ethnic, cultural, and sometimes economic ties to the Allies. The newspapers were quick to picture the Germans as barbaric Huns and to accept atrocity stories, some of them planted by British propaganda experts. Gradually for Wilson, and probably for most Americans, the perception that England and France were fighting to preserve civilization from evil Prussians replaced the idea that all Europeans were decadent. But as for going to war to save civilization, let France and England do that.

Wilson sympathized with the Allies for practical and idealistic reasons. He wanted to keep the United States out of the war, but he did not object to using force to promote diplomatic ends. The war, he hoped, would show the futility of imperialism and would usher in a world of free trade in both products and ideas, a world in which the United States had a special role to play. Remaining neutral while maintaining trade with the belligerents became increasingly difficult. The need to trade and the desire to control the peace finally led the United States into the Great War.

World Trade and Neutrality Rights

The United States was part of an international economic community in 1914 in a way that it had not been during the nineteenth century. The outbreak of war in the summer of 1914 caused immediate economic panic in the United States. On July 31, 1914, the Wilson administration closed the stock exchange. It also discouraged loans by American banks to belligerent nations. Most difficult was the matter of neutral trade. Wilson insisted on Americans' right to trade with both sides and with other neutrals, but Great Britain instituted an illegal naval blockade, mined the North Sea, and began seizing American ships. The first crisis that Wilson faced was whether to accept the illicit British blockade. To do so would be to surrender one of the rights he supported most ardently: free trade.

Wilson eventually accepted British control of the sea. His conviction that the destinies of the United States and Great Britain were intertwined outweighed his idealistic belief in free trade and caused him to react more harshly to German than to British violations of international law. American trade with the Central Powers declined between 1914 and 1916 from $169 million to just over $1 million, whereas American trade with the Allies increased during the same period from $825 million to over $3 billion. At the same time, the U.S. government eased restrictions on private loans to belligerents. With dollars as well as sentiments, the United States gradually ceased to be neutral.

Germany retaliated against British control of the seas with submarine warfare. International law obligated a belligerent warship to warn a passenger or merchant ship before attacking, but a submarine rising to the surface to issue a warning would have been blown out of the water by an armed merchant ship. On February 4, 1915, Germany announced a submarine blockade of the British Isles. Until Britain gave up its campaign to starve the German population, the Germans would sink even neutral ships. Wilson warned Germany that it would be held to "strict accountability" for illegal destruction of American ships or lives.

In March 1915, a German submarine sank a British liner, killing 103 people, including one American. Wilson's advisers could not agree on an appropriate response. Robert Lansing, a legal counsel at the State Department, urged the president to issue a strong protest, charging a breach of international law. William Jennings Bryan, the secretary of state, argued that an American traveling on a British ship was guilty of "contributory negligence" and urged Wilson to ban Americans from belligerent ships in the war zone. Before Wilson could decide what to do, on May 7, 1915, a submarine torpedoed the British luxury liner *Lusitania* off the Irish coast. The unarmed liner, which was carrying war supplies, sank in 18 minutes with a loss of nearly 1,200 lives, including 128 Americans. Suddenly Americans realized that modern war killed civilians as easily as it killed soldiers.

Some Americans called for war. Wilson and most Americans had no intention of fighting, but the president rejected Secretary of State Bryan's advice that Americans be prohibited from traveling on ships from the countries at war. Instead, he demanded reparation for the loss of American lives and a German pledge to cease attacking ocean liners without warning. Bryan resigned as secretary of state, charging that the United States was not being truly neutral. The president replaced him with Robert Lansing, who was more eager to oppose Germany, even at the risk of war.

The tense situation eased late in 1915. After a German submarine sank the British steamer *Arabic*, which claimed two American lives, the German ambassador promised that Germany would not attack ocean liners without warning. But the *Lusitania* crisis caused an outpouring of books and articles urging the nation to prepare for war. However, a group of progressive reformers formed the American Union Against Militarism, fearing that preparedness advocates planned to destroy liberal social reform at home and promote imperialism abroad.

Wilson sympathized with the preparedness groups to the extent of asking Congress on November 4, 1915, for an enlarged and reorganized army. The bill met great opposition, especially from southern and western congressmen, but the Army Reorganization Bill that Wilson signed in June 1916 increased the regular army to just over 200,000 and integrated the National Guard into the defense structure. Few Americans expected those young men to go to war. But soon Wilson used the army and the marines in Mexico and Central America.

Intervening in Mexico and Central America

Wilson envisioned a world purged of imperialism, a world of free trade, and a world where American ideas and American products would find their way. Combining the zeal of a Christian missionary with the conviction of a college professor, he spoke of "releasing the intelligence of America for the service of mankind." Along with Secretary of State Bryan, Wilson denounced the "big stick" and "dollar diplomacy" of the Roosevelt and Taft years. Yet Wilson's administration used force more systematically than his predecessors. The rhetoric was different, yet like Roosevelt, Wilson tried to maintain stability in the countries to the south in order to promote American economic and strategic interests.

At first, Wilson's foreign policy seemed to reverse the most callous aspects of dollar diplomacy in Central America. Bryan signed a treaty with Colombia in 1913 paying $5 million for the loss of Panama and virtually apologizing for Roosevelt's treatment of Colombia. But the Senate refused to ratify the treaty.

The change in spirit proved illusory. After a disastrous civil war in the Dominican Republic, the United States offered in 1915 to take over the country's finances and police force. When Dominican leaders rejected a treaty making their country virtually an American protectorate, Wilson ordered in the marines. They took control of the government in May 1916. Although Americans built roads, schools, and hospitals, the Dominican people resented their presence. Americans also intervened in Haiti, with similar results. In Nicaragua, Wilson kept the marines (sent by Taft in 1912) to prop up a pro-American regime and acquired the right through a treaty to intervene at any time to preserve order and protect American property. Except briefly in the mid-1920s, the marines remained until 1933.

Wilson's policy of intervention ran into its greatest difficulty in Mexico, a country that had been ruled by dictator Porfirio Díaz, who had long welcomed American investors. By 1910, more than 40,000 American citizens lived in Mexico, and more than $1 billion of American money was invested there. In 1911, however, Francisco Madero, a reformer who wanted to destroy the privileges of the upper classes, overthrew Díaz. Two years later, Madero was deposed and murdered by Victoriano Huerta, the head of the army.

To the shock of many diplomats and businessmen, Wilson refused to recognize the Huerta government. Everyone admitted that Huerta was a ruthless dictator, but diplomatic recognition, the exchange of ambassadors, and the regulation of trade and communication had never meant approval. But Wilson set out to remove what he called a "government of butchers."

At first, Wilson applied diplomatic pressure. Then, using a minor incident as an excuse, he asked Congress for power to involve American troops if necessary. Few Mexicans liked Huerta, but they liked North American interference even less, and they rallied around the dictator. The United States landed troops at Veracruz, Mexico. Mobs destroyed American property wherever they could find it. Wilson's action outraged many in Europe, Latin America, and the United States.

Wilson's intervention drove Huerta from power, but a civil war between the forces of Venustiano Carranza and those under General Francisco "Pancho" Villa ensued. The United States sent arms to Carranza, who was considered less radical than Villa, and Carranza's soldiers defeated Villa's. When Villa led what was left of his army in a raid on Columbus, New Mexico, in March 1916, Wilson sent an expedition under Brigadier General John Pershing to track down Villa and his men. An American army charged 300 miles into Mexico, but it was unable to catch the elusive villain. Mexicans feared that Pershing's army was planning to occupy northern Mexico. Carranza shot off a bitter note to Wilson, but Wilson refused to withdraw. Tensions rose. An American patrol attacked a Mexican garrison. Wilson finally agreed to recall the troops and to recognize the Carranza government. But this was in January 1917, and had it not been for the growing crisis in Europe, war would likely have resulted.

THE UNITED STATES ENTERS THE WAR

A significant minority of Americans opposed going to war in 1917, and that decision would remain controversial when it was reexamined in the 1930s. But once involved, the government and the American people made the war into a patriotic crusade that influenced all aspects of American life.

The Election of 1916

American political campaigns do not stop even for international crises. In 1915 and 1916, Wilson had to think of reelection as well as of preparedness, submarines, and Mexico. His chances seemed poor. If supporters of the Progressives in 1912 returned to the Republican fold, Wilson would probably lose. Because the Progressive party had done very badly in the 1914 congressional elections, Roosevelt seemed ready to seek the Republican nomination.

Wilson knew that he had to win over voters who had favored Roosevelt in 1912. In January 1916, he nominated Louis D. Brandeis to the Supreme Court. The first Jewish justice, Brandeis was confirmed over strong opposition. His appointment pleased the social justice progressives because he had always championed reform causes. They made it clear to Wilson that the real test for them was whether or not he supported the anti-child labor and workers' compensation bills pending in Congress.

Within a few months, Wilson reversed his earlier New Freedom doctrines, which called for limited government, and aligned the federal government on the side of reform. In August 1916, he pushed through Congress the Workmen's Compensation Bill, which gave some protection to federal employees, and the Keatings-Owen Child Labor Bill, which barred from interstate commerce goods produced by children under the age of 14 and in some cases under the age of 16. This bill, later declared unconstitutional, was a far-reaching proposal that for the first time used federal control over interstate commerce to dictate the conditions under which products could be manufactured. To attract farm support, Wilson backed the Federal Farm Loan Act to extend long-term credit to farmers. Urged on by organized labor as well as by many progressives, he supported the Adamson Act, establishing an eight-hour day for all interstate railway workers.

The flurry of legislation early in 1916 provided a climax to the progressive movement. The strategy seemed to work, for progressives of all kinds enthusiastically endorsed the president.

The election of 1916, however, turned as much on foreign affairs as on domestic policy. Ignoring Roosevelt, Republicans nominated staid Charles Evans Hughes, a former governor of New York and future Supreme Court chief justice. Their platform called for "straight and honest neutrality" and "adequate preparedness." Hughes attacked Wilson for not promoting American rights in Mexico more vigorously and for giving in to what he called labor's unreasonable demands. Wilson implied that electing Hughes would guarantee war with both Mexico and Germany and that his opponents were somehow not "100 percent Americans." As the campaign progressed, the peace issue became more important, and the cry "He kept us out of war" echoed through every Democratic rally. It was a slogan that would soon seem strangely ironic.

The election was extremely close. Wilson went to bed on election night thinking he had lost, and the result was not clear until he won California by less than 4,000 votes. Wilson triumphed by carrying the West as well as the South.

Deciding for War

Wilson's victory in 1916 seemed to be a mandate for staying out of the European war. But the campaign rhetoric made the president nervous. He had tried to emphasize Americanism, not neutrality.

Those who supported Wilson as a peace candidate applauded in January 1917 when he went before the Senate to clarify the American position on a negotiated settlement of the war. The German government had indicated earlier that it might be willing to go to the conference table. Wilson outlined a plan for a negotiated settlement, without indemnities or annexations. The agreement Wilson outlined could have worked only if Germany and the Allies were willing to settle for a draw.

Early in 1917, however, German leaders thought they could win. On January 31, 1917, Berlin announced that any ship, belligerent or neutral, sailing toward Britain or France would be sunk on sight. A few days later, the United States broke diplomatic relations with Germany. An intercepted telegram from the German foreign secretary, Arthur Zimmermann, to the German minister in Mexico increased anti-German feeling. If war broke out, the German minister was to offer Mexico the territory it had lost in Texas, New Mexico, and Arizona. In return, Mexico would join Germany in a war against the United States. When this telegram was released to the press on March 1, 1917, many Americans demanded war against Germany. Wilson still hesitated.

As the country waited on the brink of war, news of revolution in Russia reached Washington. That event would prove as important as the war itself. The March 1917 revolution in Russia was a spontaneous uprising of workers, housewives, and soldiers against the tsarist government's inept conduct of the war. The army had suffered staggering losses. Civilian conditions were desperate. Food was scarce, and the railroads and industry had nearly collapsed. At first, Wilson and other Americans were enthusiastic about the new republic led by Alexander Kerensky, who promised to continue the struggle against Germany. But within months, the revolution took a more extreme turn. Vladimir Ilyich Ulyanov, known as Lenin, returned from exile in Switzerland and led the radical Bolsheviks to victory over the Kerensky regime in November 1917.

Lenin, a brilliant revolutionary tactician, was a follower of Karl Marx (1818–1883). Marx was a German radical philosopher who had described the alienation of the working class under capitalism and predicted a growing split between the proletariat (unpropertied workers) and the capitalists. Lenin extended Marx's ideas and argued that capitalist nations eventually would be forced to go to war over raw materials and markets. Believing that capitalism and imperialism went hand in hand, Lenin argued that the only way to end imperialism was to end capitalism. Communism, Lenin predicted, would eventually dominate the globe. The Russian Revolution threatened Wilson's vision of the world and his plan to bring the United States into the war "to make the world safe for democracy."

DOCUMENT

President Wilson's War Message to Congress (1917)

More disturbing than the first news of revolution in Russia, however, was the situation in the North Atlantic, where German submarines sank five American ships between March 12 and March 21, 1917. On April 2, Wilson urged Congress to declare war. "It is a fearful thing," he concluded, "to lead this great, peaceful people into war, into the most terrible and disastrous of all wars." The war resolution swept the Senate 82 to 6 and the House of Representatives 373 to 50.

Once war was declared, most Americans forgot their doubts. Young men rushed to enlist; women volunteered to become nurses or to serve in other ways.

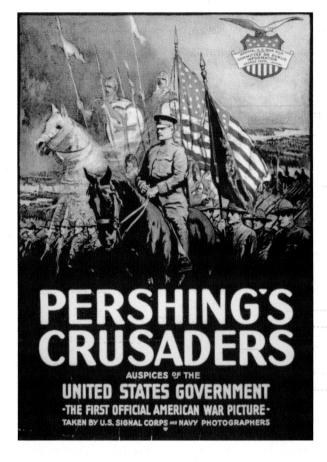

PERSHING'S CRUSADERS
AUSPICES ᴼF THE
UNITED STATES GOVERNMENT
·THE FIRST OFFICIAL AMERICAN WAR PICTURE·
TAKEN BY U.S. SIGNAL CORPS ᴬᴺᴰ NAVY PHOTOGRAPHERS

Pershing's Crusaders This official 1917 U.S. government publication compares American soldiers to medieval knights. It makes explicit the American belief that by entering World War I, they were joining not only a war but also a crusade to make the world safe for democracy. They were not just supporting the Allied cause, but they had a special mission to rescue the old world and to spread the American way of life. How do you suppose Europeans reacted to this American sense of mission and superiority? *(Library of Congress)*

A Patriotic Crusade

Not all Americans applauded. Some pacifists and socialists and a few others opposed the U.S. entry into the war. "I feel that we are about to put the dollar sign on the American flag," Senator George Norris of Nebraska announced on the Senate floor. But for most Americans in the spring of 1917, the war seemed remote. A few days after war was declared, a Senate committee listened to a member of the War Department staff list the vast quantities of materials needed to supply an American army in France. One of the senators, jolted awake, exclaimed, "Good Lord! You're not going to send soldiers over there, are you?"

To convince senators and citizens alike that the war was real and that American participation was just, Wilson appointed a Committee on Public Information, headed by journalist George Creel. His committee launched a gigantic campaign to persuade the American public that the United States had gone to war to promote democracy and prevent the "Huns" from overrunning the world.

IMAGE

Gee! I Wish I Were a Man!

The patriotic crusade soon became stridently anti-German and anti-immigrant. Most school districts forbade teaching German. Sauerkraut was renamed "liberty cabbage." Many families Americanized German surnames. Several cities banned music by German composers. South Dakota prohibited speaking German on the telephone. The most notorious incident occurred in East St. Louis, Illinois, which had a large German population. In April 1918, a mob seized Robert Prager, a young German American, stripped off his clothes, dressed him in an American flag, marched him through the streets, and lynched him. Brought to trial, the ringleaders were acquitted on the grounds that the lynching was a "patriotic murder."

The Wilson administration did not condone domestic violence and murder, but the heated patriotism fanned by the war led to irrational hatreds and fears. Suspect were not only German Americans, but also radicals, pacifists, and anyone with doubts about the American war efforts or the government's policies. The Los Angeles police ignored complaints that Mexicans were being harassed because they believed that all Mexicans were pro-German. Senator La Follette, who had voted against declaring war, was burned in effigy and censured by the University of Wisconsin. At a number of universities, professors were dismissed, sometimes for questioning the morality or necessity of America's participation in the war.

On June 15, 1917, Congress, at Wilson's behest, passed the Espionage Act, providing imprisonment of up to 20 years or a fine of up to $10,000, or both, for people who aided the enemy or who "willfully cause ... insubordination, disloyalty, mutiny or refusal of duty in the military ... forces of the United States." The act also authorized the postmaster general to bar from the mails any matter he thought advocated treason or forcible resistance to U.S. laws. The act was used to stamp out dissent, even to discipline anyone who questioned the administration's policies.

Congress later added the Trading with the Enemy Act and a Sedition Act. The latter prohibited disloyal, profane, scurrilous, or abusive remarks about the form of government, flag, or uniform of the United States. It even prohibited citizens from opposing the purchase of war bonds. In the most famous case tried under the act, Socialist Eugene Debs was sentenced to 10 years in prison for opposing the war. In 1919, the Supreme Court upheld the conviction, even though Debs had not explicitly urged violating the draft laws. While still in prison, Debs polled close to 1 million votes in the presidential election of 1920. Ultimately, the government prosecuted 2,168 people under the Espionage and Sedition Acts and convicted about half of them. These figures do not include the thousands who were persecuted informally.

One woman was sentenced to prison for writing, "I am for the people and the government is for the profiteers." Ricardo Flores Magon, a leading Mexican American labor organizer and radical in the Southwest, got 20 years in prison for criticizing Wilson's Mexican policy and violating the Neutrality Acts. The attorney general of the United States, speaking of critics, said, "May God have mercy on them for they need expect none from an outraged people and an avenging government."

The Civil Liberties Bureau, an outgrowth of the American Union Against Militarism, protested the blatant abridgment of freedom of speech during the war, but the protests fell on deaf ears at the Justice Department and in the White House. Rights and freedoms have been reduced or suspended during all wars, but the massive disregard for basic rights was greater during World War I than during the Civil War—especially ironic because Wilson had often written and spoken of the need to preserve freedom of speech and civil liberties. During the war, however, he tolerated the vigilante tactics of his own Justice Department. Wilson was so convinced his cause was just that he ignored the rights of those who opposed him.

Raising an Army

The debate over a volunteer army versus the draft had been going on for several years before the United States entered the war. People who favored some form of universal military service argued that college graduates, farmers, and young men from eastern slums could learn from one another as they trained together. Critics pointed out that those making such claims were usually the college graduates, who assumed they would command the boys from the slums. The draft, they argued, was simply the tool of an imperialist power bent on ending dissent. Some recalled the massive draft riots during the Civil War.

Wilson and his secretary of war, Newton Baker, both initially opposed the draft, but in the end concluded that it was the most efficient way to organize military manpower. Ironically, Theodore Roosevelt tipped Wilson in favor of the draft. With failing health and blind in one eye, the old Rough Rider wanted to recruit a volunteer division and lead it personally against the Germans.

The thought of Roosevelt, whom Wilson considered his enemy, blustering about Europe so frightened Wilson that he supported the Selective Service Act in part, at least, to forestall such volunteer outfits as Roosevelt planned. Yet the House finally insisted that the minimum age for draftees should be 21, not 18. On June 5, 1917, some 9.5 million men between the ages of 21 and 31 registered, with little protest. In August 1918, Congress extended the act to men between the ages of 18 and 45. In all, over 24 million men registered and over 2.8 million were inducted—over 75 percent of soldiers who served in the war. The draft worked well, but it was not quite the perfect system that Wilson claimed. Most Americans took seriously their obligation of "service" during time of war, but draft protests erupted in a few places, the largest in Oklahoma, where a group of tenant farmers planned a march on Washington to take over the government and end the "rich man's war." A local posse arrested about 900 protesters and took them off to jail.

Some men escaped the draft. Thousands were deferred because of war-related jobs, and others resisted by claiming exemption for reasons of conscience. The Selective Service Act did exempt men who belonged to pacifist religious groups, but religious motivation was often difficult to define, and nonreligious conscientious objection was even more complicated. Thousands of conscientious objectors were inducted. Some served in noncombat positions; others went to prison.

THE MILITARY EXPERIENCE

For years afterward, men and women who lived through the war (like Edmund Arpin and his friends) remembered nostalgically what it had meant to them. They sang the songs popular during the war, and they carefully preserved their

Trench Warfare World War I, especially on the western front, was a war of position and defense. Troops on both sides lived in elaborate trenches that turned into a sea of mud when it rained. The men tried to protect themselves with barbed wire and gas masks against new and terrifying technology. But there was little defense against the machine gun that mowed down the troops as they charged from their trenches. Here American soldiers from the New York National Guard, part of the 42nd Division, dig in behind their sandbag-lined trenches in the woods near the Marne River in June 1918. What attitudes toward war might be formed among these soldiers? *(U.S. Signal Corps., National Archives)*

wartime photos. For some, the war was a tragedy in which they saw the horrors of the battlefield firsthand. For others, it was liberating—the most exciting adventure in their lives.

The American Doughboy

The typical soldier stood 5 feet 7½ inches tall, weighed 141½ pounds, and was about 22 years old. He took a physical exam, an intelligence test, and a psychological test, and he probably watched a movie called *Fit to Fight*, warning about venereal disease. The majority of American soldiers had not attended high school. The median amount of education for native whites was 6.9 years, and for immigrants 4.7 years, but only 2.6 years for southern blacks. As many as 31 percent of the recruits were declared illiterate, but the tests were so primitive that they probably tested social class more than anything else. Fully 29 percent of the recruits were rejected as physically unfit for service, shocking health experts.

Most World War I soldiers were ill-educated, unsophisticated young men from farms, small towns, and urban neighborhoods. Coming from all classes and ethnic groups, most were transformed into soldiers. The military experience changed the lives and often the attitudes of many young men. Women also contributed to the war effort as telephone operators and clerk-typists in the navy and the marines, as nurses, or with organizations such as the Red Cross. Yet the military experience was predominantly male. Even going to training camp was new and often frightening. A leave in Paris or London, or even in New York or New Orleans, was an adventure to remember for a lifetime. Many soldiers saw their first movie or their first truck in the army. Men learned to shave with the new safety razor and to wear the new wristwatch. The war also popularized the cigarette, which, unlike a pipe or cigar, could be smoked during a short break.

Soldiers Taking an IQ Test During WWI

The Black Soldier

Blacks had served in all American wars, and many fought valiantly in the Civil War and the Spanish-American War. Yet black soldiers had most often performed menial work in segregated units. Black leaders hoped it would be different this time. W. E. B. Du Bois urged blacks to support the war, predicting that the war experience would cause the "walls of prejudice" to crumble gradually before the "onslaught of common sense." But the walls did not crumble.

The Selective Service Act made no mention of race, and African Americans in most cases registered without protest. Many whites, especially in the South, at first feared having too many blacks trained in the use of arms. In some areas, draft boards exempted single white men, but drafted black fathers. Still, most southern whites found it difficult to imagine a black man in the uniform of the U.S. Army.

White attitudes toward African Americans sometimes led to conflict. In August 1917, violence erupted in Houston, Texas, involving soldiers from the regular army's all-black 24th Infantry Division. Harassed by the Jim Crow laws, which had been tightened for their benefit, a group of soldiers went on a rampage, killing 17 white civilians. Over 100 soldiers were court-martialed; 13 were condemned to death and hanged three days later before appeals could be filed.

This violence, coming only a month after a race riot in East St. Louis, Illinois, brought on in part by the migration of southern blacks to the area, caused great concern about the handling of African American soldiers. Secretary of War Baker made it clear that the army had no intention of upsetting the segregated status quo.

Some African Americans were trained as junior officers and were assigned to the all-black 92nd Division, where the high-ranking officers were white. But blacks were officially considered unfit to fight. Most of the black soldiers, including about 80 percent of those sent to France, worked as stevedores and common laborers under white noncommissioned officers. Other black soldiers acted as servants, drivers, and porters for the white officers. It was a demeaning and ironic policy for a government that advertised itself as standing for justice, honor, and democracy.

African American Soldiers Under French Command, WWI

RECOVERING THE PAST

All governments produce propaganda. Especially in time of war, governments try to convince their citizens that the cause is important and worthwhile even if it means sacrifice. Before the United States entered the war, both Great Britain and Germany presented their side of the conflict through stories planted in newspapers, photographs, and other devices. Some historians argue that the British propaganda depicting the Germans as barbaric Huns who killed little boys and Catholic nuns played a large role in convincing Americans of the righteousness of the Allied cause.

When the United States entered the war, a special committee under the direction of George Creel did its best to persuade Americans that the war was a crusade against evil. The committee organized a national network of "four-minute men," local citizens with the proper political views, who could be used to whip up a crowd into a patriotic frenzy. These local rallies, enlivened by bands and parades, urged people of all ages to support the war effort and buy war bonds. The Creel Committee also produced literature for the schools, much of it prepared by college professors who volunteered their services. One pamphlet, titled *Why America Fights Germany,* described in lurid detail a possible German invasion of the United States. The committee also used the new technology of motion pictures, which proved to be the most effective propaganda device of all.

There is a narrow line between education and propaganda. As early as 1910, Thomas Edison made films instructing the public about the dangers of tuberculosis, and others produced movies that demonstrated how to avoid everything from typhoid to tooth decay. However, during the war, the government quickly realized the power of the new medium and adopted it to train soldiers, instill patriotism, and help the troops avoid the temptations of alcohol and sex.

After the United States entered World War I, the Commission on Training Camp Activities made a film called *Fit to Fight* that was shown to almost all male servicemen. It was an hour-long drama following the careers of five young recruits. Four of them, by associating with the wrong people and through lack of willpower, caught venereal disease. The film interspersed a simplistic plot with grotesque shots of men with various kinds of venereal disease. The film also glorified athletics, especially football and boxing, as a substitute for sex. It emphasized the importance of patriotism and purity for America's fighting force. In one scene, Bill Hale, the only soldier in the film to remain pure, breaks up a peace rally and beats up the speaker. "It serves you right," the pacifist's sister remarks. "I'm glad Billy punched you."

Fit to Fight was so successful that the government commissioned another film, *The End of the Road,* to be shown to women who lived near military bases. The film is the story of Vera and Mary. Although still reflecting progressive attitudes, the film's message is somewhat different from that of *Fit to Fight.* Vera's strict mother tells her daughter that sex is dirty, leaving Vera to pick up "distorted and obscene" information about sex on the street. She falls victim to the first man who comes along and contracts a venereal disease. Mary, in contrast, has an enlightened mother who explains where babies come from. When Mary grows up, she rejects marriage and becomes a professional woman, a nurse. In the end, she falls in love with a doctor and gets married. *The End of the Road* has a number of subplots and many frightening shots of syphilitic sores. Several illustrations show the dangers of indiscriminate sex. Among other things, the film preached the importance of science and sex education and the need for self-control.

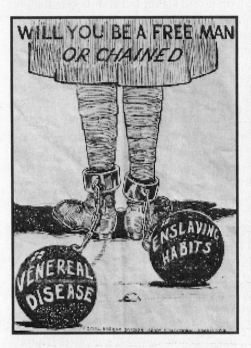

Anti-VD poster issued by the U.S. Commission on Training Camp Activities. *(Army Educational Commission/National Archives)*

Scene from *Fit to Fight*. *(War Department Commission on Training Camps)*

REFLECTING ON THE PAST   What do the anti-VD films tell us about the attitudes, ideas, and prejudices of the World War I period? What images do they project about men, women, and gender roles? Would you find the same kind of moralism, patriotism, and fear of VD today? How have attitudes toward sex changed? Were you shown sex education films in school? Were they like these? Who sponsored them? What can historians learn from such films? Does the government produce propaganda today?

Over There

AUDIO

Over There

The conflict that Wilson called the war "to make the world safe for democracy" had become a contest of stalemate and slaughter. To this ghastly war, Americans made important contributions; without their help, the Allies might have lost. But the American contribution was most significant only in the war's final months.

When the United States went to war in the spring of 1917, the fighting had dragged on for nearly three years. In one battle in 1916, a total of 60,000 British soldiers were killed or wounded in a single day, yet the battle lines did not move an inch. By the spring of 1917, the British and French armies were down to their last reserves. Italy's army had nearly collapsed. In the East, Russia plunged into a bitter internal struggle, and soon Lenin would make a separate peace, freeing German divisions in the East to join in one final assault in the West. The Allies desperately needed fresh American troops, but those troops had to be trained, equipped, and transported to the front.

Token American regiments arrived in France in the summer of 1917 under the command of "Black Jack" Pershing, who had led the Mexican expedition in 1916. When they paraded in Paris on July 4, 1917, the crowd showered them with flowers. But the American commanders worried that many of their soldiers were so inexperienced they did not know how to march, let alone fight. The first American units saw action near Verdun in October 1917. By March 1918, over 300,000 American soldiers had reached France, and by November 1918, that number had risen to more than 2 million.

One reason that the U.S. forces were slow to see actual combat was Pershing's insistence that they be kept separate from French and British divisions. An exception was made for four regiments of black soldiers who were assigned to the French army. Despite the American warning to the French not to "spoil the Negroes" by allowing them to mix with the French civilian population, these soldiers fought so well that the French later awarded three of the regiments the Croix de Guerre, their highest unit citation.

In the spring of 1918, with Russia out of the war and the British blockade becoming more and more effective, the Germans launched an all-out offensive to win the war before full American military and industrial power became a factor. By late May, the Germans pushed within 50 miles of Paris. American troops helped stem the German advance at Château-Thierry, Belleau Wood, and Cantigny, names that proud survivors would later endow with almost sacred significance. Americans also took part in the Allied offensive in the summer of 1918.

In September, over a half million American troops fought near St. Mihiel, the first battle where large numbers of Americans went into action. One enlisted man "saw a sight which I shall never forget. It was zero hour and in one instant the entire front as far as the eye could reach in either direction was a sheet of flame, while the heavy artillery made the earth quake." The Americans suffered over 7,000 casualties, but they captured more than 16,000 German soldiers. The victory, even if it came against exhausted and retreating German troops, seemed to vindicate Pershing's insistence on a separate American army. The British and French commanders were critical of what they considered the disorganized, inexperienced, and ill-equipped American forces.

In the fall of 1918, the combined British, French, and American armies drove the Germans back. Faced with low morale among the German soldiers and finally the mutiny of the German fleet and Austria-Hungary's surrender, Kaiser Wilhelm II abdicated, and the armistice was signed on November 11. More than a million American soldiers took part in the final Allied offensive. Many were inexperienced, and some "90-day wonders" had never handled a rifle before arriving in France. Edmund Arpin was wounded in an unnecessary battle. There were many other mistakes, some disastrous. The most famous blunder was the "lost battalion," which advanced beyond its support and was cut off and surrounded. It suffered 70 percent casualties.

The performance of the all-black 92nd Division was also controversial. The 92nd had been deliberately dispersed around the United States and had never trained as a unit. Its higher officers were white, and they repeatedly asked to be transferred. Many of its men were partly trained and poorly equipped, and they were continually being called away to work as common laborers. At the last minute during the Meuse-Argonne offensive, the 92nd was assigned to a particularly difficult position on the line, without maps or wire cutters. Battalion commanders lost contact with their men, and several times the troops ran in the face of enemy fire. The division was withdrawn in disgrace. For years, politicians and military leaders used this incident to claim that black soldiers would never make good fighting men, ignoring the difficulties under which the 92nd fought and the valor shown by black troops assigned to the French army.

The war produced a few American heroes. Joseph Oklahombie, a Choctaw, overran several German machine gun nests and captured more than 100 German soldiers. Sergeant Alvin York, a former conscientious objector from Tennessee, single-handedly killed or captured 160 Germans using only his rifle and pistol. But his heroics were not typical. Artillery, machine guns, and, near the end, tanks, trucks, and airplanes won the war.

With few exceptions, the Americans fought hard and well. Although the French and British criticized the Americans' inexperience and disarray, they admired their exuberance, "pep," and ability to move large numbers of men and equipment efficiently. Sometimes the Americans simply overwhelmed the enemy with their numbers. They suffered over 120,000 casualties in the Meuse-Argonne campaign alone. One officer estimated that he lost 10 soldiers for every German his men killed in the final offensive.

The United States entered the war late but still lost more than 48,000 service personnel and had many more wounded. Disease claimed 15 of every 1,000 soldiers each year (compared with 65 per 1,000 in the Civil War). But the British lost 900,000 men, the French 1.4 million, and the Russians 1.7 million. The United States contributed huge amounts of men and supplies in the last months of the war, and that finally tipped the balance. But it had entered late and sacrificed little compared with France and England. That would influence the peace settlement.

The end of the Great War brought joy to most Americans, but not to those who came down with the flu. In the fall of 1918 an influenza pandemic swept around the world, killing an estimated 50 million people. There were 675,000 deaths in the United States in a little more than a year. Unlike most epidemics, which were most deadly for children and the elderly, this one hit hardest among young adults. Over 43,000 American servicemen died from the flu, almost as many as died in battle. There were no antibiotics to treat the disease, and the surgical masks, required in some cities, did not work. The speed with which the disease spread around the world was another reminder that in the modern age all countries were interconnected and isolation impossible.

DOMESTIC IMPACT OF THE WAR

For at least 30 years before the United States entered the Great War, a debate raged over the proper role of the federal government in regulating industry and protecting people who could not protect themselves. Even within the Wilson administration, advisers disagreed on the proper role of the federal government. But the war and the problems it raised increased the power of the federal government. The wartime experience did not end the debate, but the United States emerged from the war a more modern nation, with more power residing in Washington.

Financing the War

The war, by one calculation, cost the United States over $33 billion, and interest and veterans' benefits brought the total to nearly $112 billion. Early on, when an economist suggested that the war might cost the United States $10 billion, everyone had laughed. Yet many in the Wilson administration knew the war was going to be expensive, and they set out to raise the money by borrowing and by increasing taxes.

Secretary of the Treasury William McAdoo shouldered the task of financing the war. Studying the policies that Treasury Secretary Salmon Chase had followed during the Civil War, he decided that Chase should have appealed to popular emotions. His campaign to sell liberty bonds to ordinary American citizens at a very low interest rate stirred patriotism. "Lick a Stamp and Lick the Kaiser," one poster urged. Celebrities promoted the bonds, Boy Scouts sold them, and McAdoo implied that people who did not buy them were traitors.

The public responded enthusiastically, but they discovered after the war that their bonds had dropped to about 80 percent of face value. Because the interest on the bonds was tax-exempt, well-to-do citizens profited more from buying the bonds than did ordinary people. But the wealthy were not as pleased with McAdoo's other plan to finance the war by raising taxes. The War Revenue Act of 1917 boosted the tax rate sharply, taxed excess profits, and increased estate taxes. The next year, the tax rate on the largest incomes soared to 77 percent. The wealthy protested, but a number of progressives were just as unhappy, for they wanted to confiscate all income over $100,000 a year. Despite taxes and liberty bonds, however, World War I, like the Civil War, was financed in large part by inflation. Food prices, for example, nearly doubled between 1917 and 1919.

At first, Wilson tried to work through state agencies to mobilize resources. The need for more central control soon led Wilson to create a series of emergency federal agencies. The first crisis was food. Poor grain crops for two years and an increasing demand for American food in Europe caused shortages. Wilson appointed Herbert Hoover, a young engineer who had won great prestige organizing relief for Belgium, to direct the Food Administration. He instituted "wheatless" and "meatless" days and urged housewives to cooperate. Women emerged during the war as the most important group of consumers. The government urged them to save, just as later it would urge them to buy.

The Wilson administration used the authority of the federal government to organize resources for the war effort. The War Industries Board, led by Bernard Baruch, a shrewd Wall Street broker, used government power to control scarce materials and, on occasion, to set prices and priorities. The government itself went into the shipbuilding business and ran the railroads. When a severe winter and a lack of coordination brought the rail system near collapse in December 1917, Wilson put all the nation's railroads under the control of the United Railway Administration. The government spent more than $500 million to improve the rails and equipment, and in 1918 the railroads did run more efficiently than they had under private control. Some businessmen complained of "war socialism" and regulation. But everyone agreed that the war had increased the power of the federal government.

War Workers

The Wilson administration sought to protect and extend the rights of organized labor during the war, while mobilizing workers to keep the factories running. The National War Labor Board insisted on adequate wages and reduced hours, and it tried to prevent exploitation of working women and children. If a munitions plant refused to accept the board's decision, the government seized it. When workers threatened to strike, the board often ruled that they either had to work or be drafted.

The Wilson administration favored the conservative labor movement of Samuel Gompers and his AFL, and the Justice Department put the radical Industrial Workers of the World "out of business." After September 1917, federal agents conducted massive raids on IWW offices and arrested most of the leaders. Yet the government tolerated ruthless vigilante groups. In Bisbee, Arizona, the sheriff and 2,000 deputies rounded up 1,200 striking workers and sent them by boxcar to New Mexico. They spent two days in the desert without food or water before help came.

Gompers took advantage of the crisis to strengthen the AFL's position. He lent his approval to administration policies by making it clear that he opposed the IWW, socialists, and communists. As the AFL won a voice in home-front policy, its membership increased from 2.7 million in 1916 to over 4 million in 1917. Organized labor's wartime gains, however, would prove only temporary.

The war opened up industrial opportunities for black men. With 4 million men in the armed forces and the flow of immigrants ended by the war, factories for the first time hired African Americans in large numbers. Northern labor agents and the railroads actively recruited southern blacks, but the news of jobs in northern cities spread by word of mouth as well. By 1920, more than 300,000 African Americans had joined the "great migration" north. This massive movement, which continued into the 1920s, had

there was always a push, first time there was a pull

DOCUMENT

Letters from the Great Migration (1917)

Icewomen Women proved during the war that they could do "men's work." These two young women deliver ice, a backbreaking task, but one that was necessary in the days before electric refrigerators. Despite women like these, the war did not change the American ideal that women's proper place was in the home. Has that ideal changed since 1918? *(National Archives)*

MAP

African American Population, 1910 and 1950

a permanent impact on the South as well as on the northern cities. As African Americans trekked north, thousands of Mexicans crossed into the United States. Immigration officials relaxed regulations because of the need for labor in the farms and factories of the Southwest.

The war also created new employment opportunities for women. Posters and patriotic speeches urged women to do their duty for the war effort. One poster showed a woman at her typewriter, the shadow of a soldier in the background, with the message: "STENOGRAPHERS, WASHINGTON NEEDS YOU."

Women responded to these appeals out of both patriotism and a need to increase their earnings and to make up for inflation, which cut real wages. Women went into every kind of industry. They labored in brickyards and factories, as railroad conductors, and in munitions plants. The Woman's Land Army mobilized female labor for the farms. They demonstrated that women could do any kind of job. Black women left domestic service for textile mills and even stockyards. But racial discrimination, even in the North, kept them from moving very far up the ladder.

Even though women demonstrated that they could do "male" jobs, their wartime progress proved temporary. Only about 5 percent of the women employed during the war, mostly unmarried, were new to the workforce. For most, it meant a shift of occupations or a move up to a better-paying position. Moreover, the war accelerated trends already under way. It increased the need for telephone operators, sales personnel, secretaries, and other white-collar workers, and in these occupations women soon became a majority. Telephone operator became an almost exclusively female job by 1917.

In the end, the war did provide limited opportunities for some women, but it did not change the dominant perception that a woman's place was in the home. After the war was over, the men returned, and women's gains almost disappeared. There were 8 million women in the workforce in 1910 and only 8.5 million in 1920.

The Climax of Progressivism

Many progressives, especially the social justice progressives, opposed the entry of the United States into the war until a few months before Congress declared war. But after April 1917, many began to see the "social possibilities of war." They deplored the war's death and destruction, the abridgment of freedom of speech, and the extreme patriotism, but praised the social planning that war stimulated. They approved the Wilson administration's support of collective bargaining, the eight-hour day, and protection for women and children in industry. They welcomed government-owned housing projects, woman suffrage, and prohibition. Many endorsed the government takeover of the railroads and control of business. For many social justice progressives who had fought hard, long, and frustrating battles to humanize the industrial city, it was refreshing that suddenly people in high places were listening and approving.

One of the best examples of the progressives' influence on wartime activities was the Commission on Training Camp Activities, set up early in the war to mobilize, entertain, and protect American servicemen at home and abroad. It organized community singing and baseball, established post exchanges and theaters, and even provided university extension lectures. The overriding assumption was that the military experience would produce citizens ready to vote for social reform.

The Commission on Training Camp Activities also incorporated the progressive crusades against alcohol and prostitution. Laws banned liquor sales to men in uniform and prostitution and alcohol around military bases. "Fit to fight" was the motto. It was a typical progressive effort, combining moral indignation with scientific prophylaxis. The commissioners prided themselves on eliminating all "red-light" districts near the training camps. When the boys go to France, the secretary of war remarked, "I want them to have invisible armor to take with them."

France tested that "invisible armor." Despite hundreds of letters from American mothers, the government decided that it could not stop soldiers from drinking wine, but it did forbid them to buy or accept as gifts anything but light wine and beer. If Edmund Arpin's outfit is typical, troops ignored the rules. Sex was even more difficult to regulate. The British and the French armies tried to control venereal disease by licensing and inspecting prostitutes. French premier Georges Clemenceau accused the Americans of spreading disease throughout the French population and offered to provide the Americans with licensed prostitutes. When Clemenceau's letter reached Baker, the secretary of war said, "For God's sake, ... don't show this to the President or he'll stop the war." The offer was never accepted.

Suffrage for Women

In the fall of 1918, Wilson asked the Senate's support of woman suffrage as "vital to the winning of the war." Wilson had earlier opposed the vote for women. His positive statement at this late date was not necessary, but his voice was a welcome addition to a rising chorus of support for an amendment to the Constitution that would permit the female half of the population to vote. Many still argued that voting would make women less feminine and less fit as wives and mothers. The National Association Opposed to Woman Suffrage declared that woman suffrage, socialism, and feminism were "three branches of the same Social Revolution."

Carrie Chapman Catt, an efficient administrator and tireless organizer, devised the strategy that finally secured the vote for women. In 1915, she became president of the National American Woman Suffrage Association (NAWSA), coordinating the state campaigns from the office in Washington and directing a growing army of dedicated workers. The careful planning began to produce results, but a group of more militant reformers, impatient with the slow progress, broke off from NAWSA to form the National Woman's Party (NWP) in 1916. This group was led by Alice Paul, who had participated in suffrage battles in England. Paul and her group picketed the White House, chained themselves to the fence, and blocked the streets. They carried banners that asked, "MR. PRESIDENT, HOW LONG MUST WOMEN WAIT FOR LIBERTY?" In the summer of 1917, the government arrested more than 200 women and charged them with "obstructing the sidewalk." It was just the kind of publicity the militant group sought, and it made the most of it. Wilson, fearing more embarrassment, began to cooperate with moderate reformers.

Careful organizing by the NAWSA and the NWP's more militant tactics both contributed to the final success of the woman suffrage crusade. The war did not cause the passage of the Nineteenth Amendment, but it did accelerate it. In 1917, 14 state legislatures petitioned Congress, urging enactment; an additional 26 states did the same in 1919. Early in 1919, the House of Representatives passed the amendment 304 to 90, and the Senate approved 56 to 25. Fourteen months later, the required 36 states had ratified, and women at last had the vote. But this would not prove the triumph of feminism, nor the signal for the beginning of a new reform movement that the women leaders expected.

PLANNING FOR PEACE

Wilson turned U.S. participation in the war into a crusade to make the world safe for democracy—and more. On January 8, 1918, partly to counter Bolshevik charges that the war was merely an imperialist struggle, he announced his plan. Called the Fourteen Points, it argued for "open covenants of peace openly arrived at," freedom of the seas, equality of trade, and the self-determination of all peoples. But his most important point, the fourteenth, called for a "league of nations" to preserve peace.

The Versailles Peace Conference

Late in 1918, Wilson announced that he would head the American delegation to Paris to attend the peace conference. Wilson and his entourage of college professors, technical experts, and advisers sailed for France on December 4, 1918. Secre-

To Great Britain		New states as of 1921	
To France		Border of German Empire in 1914	
To Belgium		Border of Austrian-Hungarian Empire in 1914	
To Denmark		Border of Russian Empire in 1914	
To Romania		Border of Ottoman Empire in 1914	
To Greece		New boundaries as a result of postwar treaties	
To Italy			
Became independent		Boundaries as of 1914	

EUROPE AND THE NEAR EAST AFTER WORLD WAR I Led in part by President Wilson's goal to promote the self-determination of people and in part by a desire to block the expansion of Germany and the Soviet Union, the diplomats meeting at Versailles reconfigured the map of Europe and the Near East. Redrawing the map, however, was easier than solving the problems of nationalism and ethnic conflict.

tary of State Lansing, Wilson's confidant Edward House, and a number of other advisers were there. Conspicuously missing was Henry Cabot Lodge, the most powerful man in the Senate, or any other Republican senator—a serious blunder, for the Republican-controlled Senate would have to approve the treaty. It is difficult to explain Wilson's lack of political insight, except to say that he hated Lodge and compromise with equal intensity and had supreme confidence in his ability to persuade.

Wilson's self-confidence grew during a triumphant tour through Europe before the conference. He was cheered enthusiastically by ordinary people, but he had greater difficulty convincing the political leaders at the peace conference.

Though Wilson was more naive and idealistic than his European counterparts, he won many concessions at the peace table, sometimes by threatening to go home. The Allied leaders were determined to punish Germany and enlarge their empires. Wilson believed that he could create a new kind of international relations based on his Fourteen Points. He did achieve limited endorsement of self-determination, his dream that each national group could have its own country and that people should decide in what country they wanted to live.

The peacemakers carved Austria, Hungary, and Yugoslavia out of what had been the Austro-Hungarian empire. They hoped that the new countries of Poland, Czechoslovakia, Finland, Estonia, Latvia, and Lithuania would help contain bolshevism in eastern Europe. France was to occupy Germany's industrial Saar region for 15 years, until a plebiscite determined whether its people wanted to be part of Germany or France. Italy gained the port of Trieste. Dividing up the map of Europe was difficult at best, but perhaps the biggest mistake that Wilson and other major leaders made was to give the small nations little power at the negotiating table and to exclude Soviet Russia entirely.

Wilson had to make major concessions at the peace conference. He was forced to agree that Germany should pay reparations (later set at $56 billion), lose much of its oil- and coal-rich territory, and admit war guilt. He accepted a mandate system that allowed France and Britain to take over portions of the Middle East and gave Germany's Pacific colonies as well as China's Shantung province to Japan. He acquiesced when the Allies turned Germany's African colonies into "mandate possessions" because they did not want to allow self-determination for blacks in Africa. Wilson did not envision a reordering of global race relations. He opposed a measure, introduced by Japan, that would have supported racial equality around the world. W. E. B. DuBois, who was in Paris to attend the first Pan-African Congress, supported the Japanese resolution and denounced colonialism. But Wilson and the others at Versailles ignored Du Bois.

This was not a "peace without victory," as Wilson had promised; and German feelings of betrayal would later have grave repercussions. Wilson did not achieve freedom of the seas or the abolition of trade barriers, but he did get the League of Nations, which he hoped would prevent future wars. The key to collective security was Article 10 of the league covenant, which pledged all members "to respect and preserve against external aggression the territorial integrity" of all other members.

Wilson's Failed Dream

While the statesmen met at Versailles to make peace and divide up Europe, a group of prominent and successful women (some from the Central Powers) convened in Zurich, Switzerland. The American delegation was led by Jane Addams and included Montana Congresswoman Jeannette Rankin, who had voted against war in 1917. They formed the Women's International League for Peace and Freedom with Addams as president and denounced the one-sided peace terms of the Versailles treaty that called for disarmament of only one side and exacted gigantic economic penalties from the Central Powers.

Hate and intolerance were legacies of the war. Clemenceau especially wanted to humiliate Germany. The peace conference was also haunted by the Bolshevik

TIMELINE

1914	Archduke Franz Ferdinand assassinated
	World War I begins
	United States declares neutrality
	American troops invade Mexico and occupy Veracruz
1915	Germany announces submarine blockade of Great Britain
	Lusitania sunk
	Arabic pledge
1916	Expedition into Mexico
	Wilson reelected
	Workmen's Compensation Bill
	Keatings-Owen Child Labor Bill
	Federal Farm Loan Act
	National Women's Party founded
1917	Germany resumes unrestricted submarine warfare
	United States breaks relations with Germany

	Zimmermann telegram
	Russian Revolution
	United States declares war on Germany
	War Revenue Act
	Espionage Act
	Trading with the Enemy Act
	Selective Service Act
1918	Sedition Act
	Flu epidemic sweeps nation
	Wilson's Fourteen Points
	American troops intervene in Russian Revolution
1919	Paris peace conference
	Eighteenth Amendment prohibits alcoholic beverages
	Senate rejects Treaty of Versailles
1920	Nineteenth Amendment grants woman suffrage

success in Russia. This threat seemed so great that the Allies sent American and Japanese troops to Russia in 1919 to defeat bolshevism and create a moderate republic. By 1920 the mission had failed. The troops withdrew, but the Russians never forgot, and the threat of bolshevism remained.

Probably most Americans supported the concept of the League of Nations in the summer of 1919, yet the Senate refused to accept American membership. The League of Nations treaty, one commentator has suggested, was killed by its friends and not by its enemies.

First there was Lodge, who had earlier endorsed some kind of international peacekeeping organization. He objected to Article 10, claiming that it would force Americans to fight the wars of foreigners. Chairman of the Senate Foreign Relations Committee, Lodge (like Wilson) was a lawyer and a scholar as well as a politician. He disliked all Democrats, especially Wilson, whose missionary zeal infuriated him.

Then there was Wilson, whose only hope of passage of the treaty in the Senate was a compromise to bring moderate senators to his side. But Wilson refused to compromise or to modify Article 10. Angry at his opponents, who were exploiting the disagreement for political advantage, he stumped the country to convince the American people of the rightness of his plan. They did not need to be convinced. They greeted Wilson much the way the people of France had. Traveling by train, he gave 37 speeches in 29 cities in the space of three weeks. When he described the graves of American soldiers in France and announced that American boys would never again die in a foreign war, the people responded with applause.

After one dramatic speech in Pueblo, Colorado, Wilson collapsed. His health had been failing for some months, and the strain of the trip was too much. He was rushed back to Washington, where a few days later he suffered a massive stroke. For the final year and a half of his term, the president was incapable of running the government and could not lead a fight for the league.

The Senate finally killed the league treaty in March of 1920. Had the United States joined the League of Nations, it probably would have made little difference in the international events of the 1920s and 1930s, nor would American participation have prevented World War II. The United States did not resign from the world of diplomacy or trade, nor by that single act become isolated. But the rejection of the league treaty was symbolic of the refusal of many Americans to admit that the world and America's place in it had changed dramatically since 1914.

Conclusion

The Divided Legacy of the Great War

For Edmund Arpin and many of his friends who left small towns and urban neighborhoods to join the military forces, the war was a great adventure. For the next two decades, at American Legion conventions and Armistice Day parades, they continued to celebrate their days of glory. For others who served, the war's results were more tragic. Many died. Some came home injured, disabled by poison gas, or unable to cope with the complex world that had opened up to them.

In a larger sense, the war was both a triumph and a tragedy for the American people. The war created opportunities for blacks who migrated to the North, for women who found more rewarding jobs, and for farmers who suddenly discovered a demand for their products. But much of the promise and the hope proved temporary.

The war provided a certain climax to the progressive movement. The passage of the woman suffrage and prohibition amendments, and the use of federal power in a variety of ways to promote justice and order pleased reformers, who had been working toward these ends for many decades. But the results were often disappointing. Once the war ended, much federal legislation was dismantled or reduced in effectiveness, and votes for women had little initial impact on social legislation.

The Great War marked the coming of age of the United States as a world power, but the country seemed reluctant to accept the new responsibility. The war stimulated patriotism and pride in the country, but it also increased intolerance. With this mixed legacy from the war, the country entered the new era of the 1920s.

Questions for Review and Reflection

1. Why did the United States, so determined to stay out of the Great War in 1914, join the Allied cause enthusiastically in 1917?

2. Why did the war lead to hate, prejudice, and the abridgment of civil liberties?

3. How did the war affect women and minorities in America?

4. Why did Wilson's idealistic peace plan fail?

5. What were the long-range consequences of World War I? For the United States? For the world?

Discovering U.S. History Online

World War I Document Archive http://www.lib.byu.edu/~rdh/wwi/
This archive contains sources about World War I in general, not just America's involvement.

The American Experience: Influenza http://www.pbs.org/wgbh/pages/amex/influenza
This PBS site reveals the impact of the great flu epidemic of 1918.

History of the Suffrage Movement http://www.rochester.edu/SBA/hisindx.html
This site includes a chronology, important texts relating to woman suffrage, and biographical information on Susan B. Anthony and Elizabeth Cady Stanton.

World War I: Trenches on the Web http://www.worldwar1.com/index.html
This site provides a mass of data concerning the prosecution of the world's first global war.

Chicago: Destination for the Great Migration: African American Mosaic Exhibition http://lcweb.loc.gov/exhibits/african/afam011.html
This Library of Congress site looks at the black experience of the great migration through the lens of one prominent destination.

Explorers Hall @ National Geographic http://www.nationalgeographic.com/society/ngo/explorer/titanic/movie.html
This site offers historical perspective and balanced coverage of the sinking of the *Titanic*, including a 14-minute 3-D tour of the ship's wreckage.

Fiction and Film

Erich Maria Remarque highlights the horror of the war in his classic *All Quiet on the Western Front* (1929); John Dos Passos describes the war as a bitter experience in *Three Soldiers* (1921); and Ernest Hemingway portrays its futility in *A Farewell to Arms* (1929). In *Regeneration* (1991), Pat Barker recreates the nightmare of the western front through British eyes.

All Quiet on the Western Front was made into a powerful movie (1930) that became an anti-war classic. *Reds* (1981) is a Hollywood film about socialists, feminists, and communists. It tells the story of John Reed and his radical friends in Greenwich Village before the war and their support of the Russian Revolution after 1917.

Recommended Reading

www.ablongman.com/nash

The Companion Website has a list of recommended readings about the early war, the U.S. entry into the war, the military experience, the war's domestic impact, and the peace.

CHAPTER 23

Affluence and Anxiety

CHAPTER OUTLINE

- Postwar Problems
- A Prospering Economy
- Hopes Raised, Promises Deferred
- The Business of Politics
- Conclusion: A New Era of Prosperity and Problems

American Stories

A Black Sharecropper and His Family Move North

John and Lizzie Parker were black sharecroppers living in a "stubborn, ageless hut squatted on a little hill" in central Alabama. They had two daughters, one age 6, the other already married. The whole family worked hard in the cotton fields with little to show for it. One day in 1917, Lizzie declared, "I'm through. I've picked my last sack of cotton. I've cleared my last field."

Like many southern African Americans, the Parkers sought a better life in the North. World War I cut off the flow of immigrant workers from Europe. Some companies sent trains into the South to recruit African Americans. John Parker signed up with a mining company in West Virginia. The company offered free transportation for his family. "You will be allowed to get your food at the company store and there are houses awaiting for you," the agent promised.

But it turned out that the houses in the company town in West Virginia were little better than those they left in Alabama. After deducting for rent and for supplies from the company store, almost no money was left at the end of the week. John hated the dirty and dangerous work in the mine and realized that he would never get ahead by staying there. He ran away, leaving his family in West Virginia.

John drifted to Detroit, where he got a job with the American Car and Foundry Company. It was 1918, and the pay was good, more than he had ever made before. After a few weeks, he rented an apartment and sent for his family. For the first time, Lizzie had a gas stove and an indoor toilet, and Sally, now 7, started school. It seemed as if their dream had come true.

Detroit was not quite the dream, however. It was crowded with all kinds of migrants, attracted by the wartime jobs at the Ford Motor Company and other factories. The new arrivals increased racial tensions already present in the city. Sally was beaten up by a gang of white youths at school. Even in their neighborhood, which had been solidly Jewish before their arrival, the shopkeeper and the old residents made it clear that they did not like blacks moving in. The Ku Klux Klan, which gained many new members in Detroit, also made life uncomfortable for the blacks who had moved north to seek jobs and opportunity. Suddenly the war ended, and almost immediately John lost his job. Then the landlord raised the rent, and the Parkers had to leave their apartment for housing in a section just outside the city near Eight Mile Road. The surrounding suburbs had paved streets, wide lawns, and elegant houses, but this black ghetto's dirt streets and shacks reminded the Parkers of the company town in West Virginia. Lizzie had to get along without her bathroom. There was no indoor plumbing and no electricity, only a pump in the yard and an outhouse.

The recession winter of 1921 to 1922 was particularly difficult. The auto industry and the other companies laid off most of their workers. John found only part-time employment, while Lizzie worked as a servant for white families. Because no bus route connected the black community to surrounding suburbs, she often had to trek miles through the snow. Their shack was freezing cold, and it was cramped because their married daughter and her husband had joined them in Detroit.

Lizzie did not give up her dream. With strength, determination, and a sense of humor, she kept the family together. In 1924, Sally entered high school. By the end of the decade, she had graduated from high school, and the Parkers finally had electricity and indoor plumbing, though the streets were still unpaved. Those unpaved streets symbolized their unfulfilled dream. The Parkers, like most African Americans who moved north in the decade after World War I, had improved their lot, but they still lived outside Detroit—and, in many ways, outside America.

Like most Americans in the 1920s, the Parkers pursued the American dream of success. For them, a comfortable house, a steady job, a new bathroom, and an education for their younger daughter constituted that dream. For others during the decade, the symbol of success was a new automobile, a new suburban house, or perhaps making a killing on the stock market. The 1920s, the decade between the end of World War I and the stock market crash, has often been referred to as the "jazz age," a time when the American people had one long party complete with flappers, speakeasies, illegal bathtub gin, and young people doing the Charleston long into the night. This frivolous interpretation has some basis in fact, but most Americans did not share in the party, for they were too busy struggling to make a living.

In this chapter, we will explore some of the conflicting trends of an exciting decade. First, we will examine the intolerance that influenced almost all the events and social movements of the time. We will also look at technological developments, especially the automobile, which changed life for almost everyone during the 1920s and created the illusion of prosperity for all. We will then focus on groups—women, blacks, industrial workers, and farmers—whose hopes were raised but not always fulfilled. We will close by considering how business, politics, and foreign policy intertwined in the era of Harding, Coolidge, and Hoover.

POSTWAR PROBLEMS

Enthusiasm for social progress evaporated in 1919. The year after the war ended was marked by strikes and violence and by fear that Bolsheviks, blacks, foreigners, and others were destroying the American way of life. Some of the anxiety grew out of wartime patriotism, and some reflected the postwar economic and political turmoil that forced Americans to deal with new and immensely troubling situations.

Red Scare

Radicals and dissidents have often been feared as threats to the American way of life. In the early twentieth century, anarchists seemed the worst danger, but the Russian Revolution of 1917 suddenly made the Bolshevik the most dangerous radical, somehow mixed with that other villain, the German. In the spring of 1919, with the Bolsheviks advocating worldwide revolution, many Americans feared that the Communists planned to take over the United States.

Immediately after the war, there were perhaps 25,000 to 40,000 American Communists, but they never threatened the United States. Some were idealists such as John Reed, the son of a wealthy businessman, who had been converted to socialism in New York's Greenwich Village. Appalled by the carnage of the capitalistic war, Reed went to Russia as a journalist in 1917. His eyewitness account of the Bolshevik takeover, *Ten Days That Shook the World*, optimistically predicted a worldwide revolution. Seeing little hope for that revolution in postwar America, he returned to Moscow, where he died in 1920, disillusioned by the new regime's authoritarianism.

Though small in number, the Communists seemed to be a threat in 1919, especially as a series of devastating strikes erupted across the country. American workers had suffered from wartime inflation, which had almost doubled prices between 1914 and 1919, while most wages remained the same. In 1919, more than 4 million workers staged 4,000 strikes. Few wanted to overthrow the government; they demanded higher wages, shorter hours, and sometimes more control over the workplace.

On January 21, 1919, some 35,000 shipyard workers struck in Seattle. Within a few days, a general strike paralyzed the city. The mayor called for federal troops. Within five days, using strong-arm tactics, he put down the strike and was hailed as a "red-blooded patriot."

Yet other strikes erupted. In September 1919, all 343,000 employees of U.S. Steel walked out in an attempt to win an eight-hour day and an "American living wage." Within days, the strike spread to Bethlehem Steel. Owners blamed the steel strikes on Bolsheviks. They imported strikebreakers, provoked riots, broke up union meetings, and used police and soldiers to end the strike. Eighteen strikers were killed. Because most people believed the Communists had inspired the strike, the issue of long hours and poor pay got lost, and eventually the union surrendered.

From the beginning, corporate owners blamed the strikes on Bolsheviks, and the "bomb-throwing radical" became almost a cliché. On April 28, 1919, a bomb was discovered in a small package delivered to the home of the mayor of Seattle. The next day, the maid of a former senator opened a package and had her hands blown off. Other bombings occurred in June; one shattered the front of Attorney General A. Mitchell Palmer's home. The bombings seem to have been the work of a few misguided radicals who thought they might spark a revolution. But their effect was to convince many that revolution was a real and immediate threat.

No one was more convinced than Palmer. In the summer of 1919, he decided to destroy the Red network. He organized a special antiradical division within the Justice Department and put young J. Edgar Hoover in charge of coordinating information on domestic radical activities. Obsessed by the "Red Menace," Palmer instituted a series of raids to round up radical foreign workers. In December, 249 aliens, including the famous anarchist Emma Goldman, were deported, although few had any desire to overthrow the government of the United States.

The Palmer raids, probably the most massive violation of civil liberties in America up to that time, found few dangerous radicals but did increase fear and intolerance. Palmer briefly became a national hero, though in the end only about 600 aliens were deported out of more than 5,000 arrested. The worst of the "Red Scare" was over by the end of 1920, but fear of radicalism influenced almost every aspect of life during the 1920s.

The Red Scare promoted many patriotic organizations and societies determined to purge Communists. These organizations made little distinction between Communists, Socialists, progressives, and liberals, and they saw Bolsheviks everywhere. The best-known of the superpatriot organizations was the American Legion, but all provided a sense of purpose and belonging by attacking radicals and preaching patriotism.

Ku Klux Klan

Among the superpatriotic organizations claiming to protect the American way of life, the Ku Klux Klan was the most extreme. The Klan was revived in Georgia by

IMAGE

Ku Klux Klan on Parade (1928)

William J. Simmons, a lay preacher, salesman, and member of many fraternal organizations. He adopted the name and white-sheet garb of the old anti-black Reconstruction organization that was glorified in 1915 in the immensely popular but racist film *Birth of a Nation*. Simmons appointed himself head ("Imperial Wizard") of the new Klan, which was thoroughly Protestant and antiforeign, anti-Semitic, and anti-Catholic. It opposed the teaching of evolution; glorified old-time religion; supported immigration restriction; denounced short skirts, petting, and "demon rum"; and upheld patriotism and the purity of women. The Klan was also militantly antiblack; its members took as their special mission the task of keeping blacks in their "proper place." They often used peaceful measures to accomplish their aim, but if those failed, they resorted to violence, kidnapping, and lynching. The Klan grew slowly until after the war, but added over 100,000 new members in 1920 alone. Postwar fear and confusion, along with aggressive recruiting, explained its explosive growth.

DOCUMENT

"Creed of Klanswomen" (1924)

The Klan flourished in the small-town and rural South, but soon it spread throughout the country. The Klan was especially strong in the working-class neighborhoods of Chicago, Detroit, Indianapolis, and Atlanta, where African Americans and other ethnic minorities were settling. At the peak of its power, it had several million members, many of them women who campaigned for more rights for white, Protestant women. The Klan also influenced politics, especially in Indiana, Oregon, Oklahoma, Louisiana, and Texas. The Klan declined after 1924, but widespread fear of everything "un-American" remained.

Ethnic and Religious Intolerance

One result of the Red Scare and fear of foreign radicals was the conviction and sentencing of two Italian anarchists, Nicola Sacco and Bartolomeo Vanzetti. Ar-

Women of the Ku Klux Klan The Ku Klux Klan, with its elaborate rituals and uniforms, exploited the fear of blacks, Jews, liberals, and Catholics while preaching "traditional" values. The appeal of the Klan was not limited to the South, and many women joined. This is a photo of women Klan members marching in an America First Parade in Binghamton, New York. Why did so many women join the Klan? Is there anything like it today? *(Bettmann/Corbis)*

rested in 1920 for allegedly murdering a guard during a robbery in Massachusetts, the two were sentenced to die in 1921 on what many liberals considered flimsy evidence. Indeed, it seemed to many that the two Italians, who spoke in broken English and were admitted anarchists, were punished because of their radicalism and foreign appearance.

The case took on symbolic significance as many intellectuals in Europe and America rallied to their defense. Appeal after appeal failed, and the two were electrocuted on August 23, 1927, despite massive protests and midnight vigils around the country. Recent evidence, including ballistic tests, suggests that they may have been guilty, but the trial and its aftermath pointed to the ethnic prejudice and divisions in American society.

The Ku Klux Klan and well-publicized cases like Sacco–Vanzetti touched relatively few people, but intolerance affected millions of lives. Henry Ford published anti-Semitic diatribes. Barred from fashionable resorts, Jews built their own hotels in the Catskills in New York State and elsewhere. Many colleges, private academies, and medical schools had Jewish quotas, and many suburbs explicitly limited residents to "Christians." Catholics, too, were prohibited from many organizations, and few even tried to enroll in the elite colleges. Although prejudice and intolerance had always existed, during the 1920s much of that intolerance was made more formal; in some cases, it was translated into law.

A PROSPERING ECONOMY

The decade after World War I was also a time of industrial expansion. After recovering from a postwar depression in 1921 and 1922, the economy took off. Fueled by new technology and more efficient management, industrial production almost doubled during the decade, but the benefits of prosperity were not equally distributed. A construction boom created new suburbs around American cities, and new skyscrapers transformed the cities themselves. While the American economy boomed, much of the rest of the world suffered in the aftermath of the war. As part of a global economy, the United States would eventually be affected by the economic stagnation in other parts of the world.

The Rising Standard of Living

Signs of the new prosperity abounded. Millions of homes and apartments were built and equipped with the latest conveniences. Perhaps the most tangible sign of the new prosperity was the modern American bathroom. In the early 1920s, the enameled tub, toilet, and washbasin became standard. The bathroom, with unlimited hot water, privacy, and clean white fixtures, symbolized American affluence, but a great many in rural America still used outdoor privies.

Many Americans now had more leisure time. Persistent efforts by labor unions had gradually reduced the 60-hour workweek of the late nineteenth century to a 45-hour week. Paid vacations, unknown in the nineteenth century, became prevalent. The American diet also improved. The consumption of cornmeal and potatoes declined, but the sale of fresh vegetables increased by 45 percent. Health improved and life expectancy lengthened. But not all Americans enjoyed better health and more leisure. A white male born in 1900 had a life expectancy of 48 years and a white female of 51 years. By 1930, these figures had increased to 59 and 63 years. For a black male born in 1900, however, the life expectancy was only 33 years, and for the black female, 35 years. These figures increased to 48 and 47 by 1930, but the discrepancy remained.

Yet almost all Americans benefited to some extent from the new prosperity. Some took advantage of expanding educational opportunities. In 1900, only one in ten young people of high school age was in school. By 1930, that number had increased to six in ten, and much of the improvement came in the 1920s. College enrollment also grew, but only a small percentage went beyond high school during the decade.

The Rise of the Modern Corporation

The structure and practice of American business were transformed in the 1920s. After the economic downturn of 1920 to 1922, business boomed until the crash of 1929. Mergers increased during the decade at a rate greater than at any time since the end of the 1890s. What emerged were not monopolies but oligopolies (industry domination spread among a few large firms). By 1930, the 200 largest corporations—which were becoming more diversified—controlled almost half the corporate wealth.

How Others See Us

Perhaps the most important business trend of the decade was the emergence of a new kind of manager. The prototype was Alfred P. Sloan, Jr., an engineer who reorganized General Motors and made marketing and advertising as important as production. Continuing the trends started by Frederick Taylor (see Chapter 21), the new managers tried to keep employees working efficiently, but they also introduced pensions, recreation facilities, cafeterias, and even paid vacations and profit-sharing plans. This "welfare capitalism" was designed to reduce worker discontent and discourage labor unions. Planning was the key to the new corporate structure, and planning often meant a continuation of the business-government cooperation that had developed during World War I. Even though all the planning failed to prevent the economic collapse in 1929, the modern corporation survived the depression to exert a growing influence on American life in the 1930s and after.

Electrification

The 1920s also marked the climax of the "second Industrial Revolution," powered by electricity and producing a growing array of consumer goods. By 1929, electrical generators provided 80 percent of the power used in industry. Less than one of every ten American homes had electricity in 1907; by 1929, more than two-thirds did, and workers were turning out twice as many goods as a similarly sized workforce had 10 years earlier.

Electricity brought dozens of gadgets and labor-saving devices into the home. But the new machines did not reduce the time the average housewife spent doing housework. In many ways, the success of the electric revolution increased the contrast in American life. Urban "Great White Ways" symbolized progress, but they also made slums and rural hamlets seem even darker. For poor women, especially in rural America, the traditional female tasks of carrying water, pushing, pulling, and lifting continued.

A Global Automobile Culture

Automobile manufacturing, like electrification, grew spectacularly in the 1920s. The automobile was a major factor in the postwar boom. It stimulated and transformed the petroleum, steel, and rubber industries; it forced the construction and upgrading of streets and highways at the cost of millions of dollars for labor and concrete. From the beginning, the United States loved autos. There were nearly 1 million autos in 1912, and in the 1920s, autos came within the reach of the middle class. In 1929, Americans purchased 4.5 million cars, and by the end of that year, nearly 27 million were registered. The roads, mostly maintained by state and local governments, were often poor and sometimes impassable. European roads, maintained by national governments, were better, but there were not as many cars in Europe in the 1920s.

Downtown Scene with Cars (1911)

The auto created new suburbs and allowed families to live miles from work. Gasoline stations, diners, and tourist courts (forerunners of motels) became familiar landmarks on the American scene. But there was an environmental downside as oil and gasoline contaminated streams, piles of old tires and rusting hulks of discarded cars began to line the highways, and emissions from thousands and then millions of internal combustion engines fouled the air.

The auto transformed American life in other ways. Small crossroads stores and many small churches disappeared as rural families drove into town. Trucks and tractors changed farming. Buses began to eliminate the one-room school, and the tiny rural church began to disappear. Autos also changed courting habits by allowing young people to escape the watchful eyes of their parents.

Over the decade, the automobile became a sign of status. Advertising made it the symbol of the good life, sex, freedom, and speed. The auto transformed advertising and altered the way products were purchased. By 1926, three-fourths of the cars sold were bought on some kind of deferred-payment plan, and "buy now, pay later" was soon used to sell other consumer products. The auto industry, like most American businesses, consolidated. In 1908, more than 250 companies were making automobiles in the United States. By 1929, only 44 remained. But one name became synonymous with the automobile itself—Henry Ford.

Ford had a reputation as a progressive industrial leader and champion of ordinary people. As with all men and women who become symbols, the truth is less dramatic. For example, his famous assembly line was invented by a team of engineers. Introduced in 1913, it cut production time for a car from 14 hours to an hour and a half. The product of this carefully planned system was the Model T, the prototype of the inexpensive family car. By contrast, most European cars were custom made.

In 1914, Ford startled the country by increasing the minimum pay of the Ford assembly-line worker to $5 a day (almost twice the national average pay for factory workers). Ford was not a humanitarian. He wanted a dependable workforce and knew that skilled workers were less likely to quit if they were well paid. Ford was one of the first to appreciate that workers were also consumers who might buy Model Ts. But despite the high wages, work on the assembly line was numbing, and when the line closed down, workers were released without compensation.

The Model T, which cost $600 in 1912, was reduced gradually in price until it sold for only $290 in 1924. Except for adding a self-starter, offering a closed model, and making a few minor face-lifts, Ford kept the Model T in 1927 as he had introduced it in 1909. By that time, its popularity had declined as many people traded up to sleeker, more colorful, and, they thought, more prestigious autos put out by Ford's competitors; as a result, wages at Ford dipped below the industry average.

The Exploding Metropolis

The automobile both pushed urban areas out into the countryside and brought industry to the suburbs. The great expansion of suburban population came in the 1920s. Shaker Heights, outside Cleveland, was typical. Two businessmen planned and built the new suburb on the site of a former Shaker community. No blacks were allowed. Curving roads and landscape design created a parklike atmosphere. Between 1919 and 1929, the population grew from 1,700 to over 15,000, and the price of lots multiplied by 10. Other suburbs grew just as rapidly—none more than Beverly Hills, California, whose population soared by 2,485 percent. The biggest land boom of all occurred in Florida, where Miami mushroomed from 30,000 people in 1920 to 75,000 in 1925. A plot in West Palm Beach sold for $800,000 in 1923, and two years later it was worth $4 million.

The automobile transformed every city, but the growth was most spectacular in two cities that the car virtually created. Detroit grew from 300,000 in 1900 to 1,837,000 in 1930. Los Angeles, held together by a network of roads, expanded from 114,000 in 1900 to 1,778,000 in 1930. In 1900 there were 52 metropolitan areas of over 100,000 people; by 1930 there were 115.

Cities expanded horizontally in the 1920s, sprawling into the countryside, but city centers grew vertically. A building boom that peaked near the end of the decade created new skylines for most urban centers. The most famous skyscraper of all, the 102-story Empire State Building in New York, was finished in 1931 but was not completely occupied until after World War II.

A Communications Revolution

Changing communications altered the way Americans lived as well as the way they conducted business. The telephone was first demonstrated in 1876, and by 1899, more than a million phones were in operation. During the 1920s, the number of homes with phones increased from 9 million to 13 million. Still, by the end of the decade, more than half of American homes lacked telephones.

Even more than the telephone, the radio symbolized the changes of the 1920s. The first station began commercial broadcasting in the summer of 1920,

AUDIO

Hungarian Rag

and that fall, election returns were broadcast for the first time. The next year a Newark station transmitted the World Series, beginning a process that would transform American sports. In 1922, a radio station in New York broadcast the first commercial.

Much early broadcasting consisted of classical music, but soon there was news analysis and coverage of important events. Serials and situation comedies made radio a national medium, with millions tuning in to the same program. The record industry grew just as rapidly. By the end of the decade, people everywhere were humming the same popular songs, while actors and announcers became celebrities.

Even more dramatic was the phenomenon of the movies. Forty million viewers a week went to the movies in 1922, and by 1929 that total exceeded 100 million. To countless Americans, the stars were more famous and important than most government officials. Motion pictures before the war had attracted mostly the working class, but now they seemed to appeal to everyone. Many parents feared that they would dictate ideas about sex and life. One young college woman admitted that movies taught her how to smoke, and in some movies "there were some lovely scenes which just got me all hot 'n' bothered."

Sports heroes like Babe Ruth and Jack Dempsey were as famous as the movie stars. The great spectator sports of the decade owed much to the increase of leisure time and to the automobile, the radio, and the mass-circulation newspaper. Thousands drove to college towns to watch football; millions listened for scores or read about the results the next day. The popularity of sports, like the movies and radio, was a product of technology.

IMAGE

Charles Lindbergh and *Spirit of St Louis*

The year 1927 seemed to mark the beginning of the new age of mechanization and progress. Henry Ford produced his 15 millionth car and introduced the Model A. Radio-telephone service linked San Francisco and Manila. The first radio network was organized (CBS), and the first sound movie was released (*The Jazz Singer*). The Holland Tunnel, the first underwater vehicular roadway, connected New York and New Jersey, and Charles Lindbergh flew his single-engine plane from New York to Paris and captured the world's imagination. When Americans cheered Lindbergh, they were reaffirming their belief in the American dream and their faith in individual initiative as well as in technology.

HOPES RAISED, PROMISES DEFERRED

The 1920s was a time when all kinds of hopes seemed realizable. "Don't envy successful salesmen—be one!" one ad screamed. Buy a car. Build a house. Start a career. Invest in land or in stocks. Make a fortune.

Not all Americans, of course, dreamed of making a killing on Wall Street; some merely wished to retain traditional values in a society that seemed to question them. Others wanted a steady job and a little respect. Still others hungered for the new appliances described so alluringly in magazine ads and on the radio. Many discovered, however, that even the most modest hopes lay tantalizingly out of reach.

Clash of Values

During the 1920s, radio, movies, advertising, and mass-circulation magazines promoted a national, secular culture. But this new culture of consumption, pleasure, upward mobility, and sex clashed with traditional values: hard work, thrift, church, family, home. This was not simply an urban-rural conflict, for many people clinging to old ways had moved into the cities. Still, many Americans feared that familiar ways of life were threatened by new values, scientific breakthroughs, bolshevism, relativism, Freudianism, and biblical criticism. A trial over the teaching of evolutionary ideas in a high school in the little town of Dayton, Tennessee, symbolized (even as it exaggerated) the clash of traditional versus modern, city versus country.

The scientific community and most educated people had long accepted Darwinian evolution. But many evangelical Protestants saw the Bible as literal truth and the dramatic changes of the 1920s as a major spiritual crisis. The theory of evolution epitomized the challenge to traditional faith, and in some states its teaching was outlawed. John Scopes, a young biology teacher, broke the law, and Tennessee put him on trial. The famous lawyer Clarence Darrow defended Scopes, while the World Christian Fundamentalist Association hired former presidential candidate and Secretary of State William Jennings Bryan to assist the prosecution. Bryan was old and tired (he died only a few days after the trial), but he was deeply religious and still eloquent. In cross-examination, Darrow reduced Bryan's statements to intellectual rubble. Nevertheless, the jury declared Scopes guilty.

The national press covered the trial and upheld science and academic freedom. The journalist H. L. Mencken had a field day poking fun at Bryan and the fundamentalists. "Heave an egg out a Pullman window," Mencken wrote, "and you will hit a Fundamentalist almost anywhere in the United States today. ... They are everywhere where learning is too heavy a burden for mortal minds to carry."

Religious Fundamentalism

Some, including Mencken, thought that the Scopes trial ended "the fundamentalist menace." Yet fundamentalism continued to survive in an urbanizing, modernizing, and sophisticated world. All fundamentalists believed in the literal interpretation and infallibility of the Bible. They rejected secularism, liberal theology, pluralism, the Social Gospel, and any sense that earthly reform could lead to perfection. They also had an unshakable belief in what they believed was the truth.

Throughout the 1920s and the 1930s, attendance at Christian colleges and the circulation of fundamentalist publications increased dramatically. Evangelical preachers reached large audiences, sometimes using flamboyant performances. One of the most popular of the ministers was Billy Sunday, a former baseball player who jumped about the stage as he pitched his brand of Christianity. Another popular preacher was Aimee Semple McPherson, a glamorous faith healer who became famous for chasing the devil out of her auditorium with a pitchfork.

Radio extended the reach of the fundamentalist preachers even more dramatically. McPherson was the first woman to hold a radio license, and she had the

John Steuart Curry, *Baptism in Kansas* John Steuart Curry was one of the regionalist painters in the 1920s who found inspiration in the American heartland. In *Baptism in Kansas*, he depicts a religious ritual that underscores the conflict between rural and urban values. Is there still a religious split today between urban and rural America? Or is the cultural divide defined differently today? *(Whitney Museum of American Art, New York; Gift of Gertrude Vanderbilt Whitney)*

second most popular radio show in Los Angeles in the late 1920s. For many, the period between the wars was an age of secular humanism, technological marvels, and modernism in all fields, but for many others, it was a time when fundamentalist religion and old-fashioned values prospered.

Immigration and Migration

Immigrants and anyone else "un-American" seemed to threaten old ways. The fear and intolerance of the war years and the period right after the war resulted in major restrictive legislation.

The first strongly restrictive immigration law passed in 1917 over Wilson's veto. It required a literacy test for the first time and barred radicals. This did not stop the more than 1 million immigrants who poured into the country in 1920 and 1921.

In 1921 and again in 1924, Congress imposed quotas on European immigration. The tighter 1924 quota allowed only 2 percent of those from each country who were in the United States in 1890—before the great flood of newcomers had begun arriving from southern and eastern Europe. All immigrants from Asia were banned. In 1927, a ceiling of 150,000 European immigrants a year was set; more than 60 percent could come from Great Britain and Germany, but fewer than 4 percent were allowed from Italy.

Ethnicity increasingly became a factor in political alignments. Republican-sponsored immigration laws drove Jews, Italians, and Poles to the Democrats. By 1924, the Democratic party was so evenly divided between northern urban Catholics and southern rural Protestants that its convention voted—by a very small margin—to condemn the Klan.

The immigration acts of 1921, 1924, and 1927 cut off the streams of cheap labor that had provided muscle for industrialization since the early nineteenth century. At the same time, by exempting Western Hemisphere immigrants, the new laws opened the country to Mexicans eager to work in the fields and farms of California and the Southwest. Mexicans soon became the country's largest first-generation immigrant group. Mexican farmworkers often lived in primitive camps, where conditions were unsanitary and health care nonexistent. "When they have finished harvesting my crops I will kick them out on the country road," one employer announced.

Mexicans also migrated to industrial cities, recruited by northern companies that paid for their transportation. During the 1920s, El Paso became more than half Mexican. The Mexican population in California reached 368,000 in 1929, and Los Angeles was about 20 percent Mexican. Like African Americans, the Mexicans found opportunity by migrating, but they did not escape prejudice or hardship.

African Americans migrated north in great numbers from 1915 to 1920. The black population of Chicago increased from 44,000 in 1910 to 234,000 by 1930. Reduced European immigration and continuing industrial growth caused many northern companies to recruit southern blacks. Trains in small southern depots sometimes picked up hundreds of blacks in a single day. "I don't care where so long as I go where a man is a man," wrote one. It was the young and mostly unskilled who tended to move.

African Americans unquestionably improved their lives by moving north. But for most, like the Parkers, dreams were only partly fulfilled. Most crowded into segregated housing and faced hatred. "Black men stay South," the *Chicago Tribune* advised, and offered to pay the transportation for any who would return.

Often the young black men moved first, and only later brought their wives and children, putting great pressure on many black families. Some young men, like John Parker, restrained their anger, but others, like Richard Wright's fictional Bigger Thomas, portrayed movingly in *Native Son* (1940), struck out violently against white society. The concentration of African Americans in northern industrial cities created black ghettos and increased the racial tension that sometimes flared into violence.

One of the worst race riots took place in Chicago in 1919. The riot began on a hot July day when a black youth drowned in a white swimming area—hit by stones, blacks said, but the police refused to arrest any white men. When African

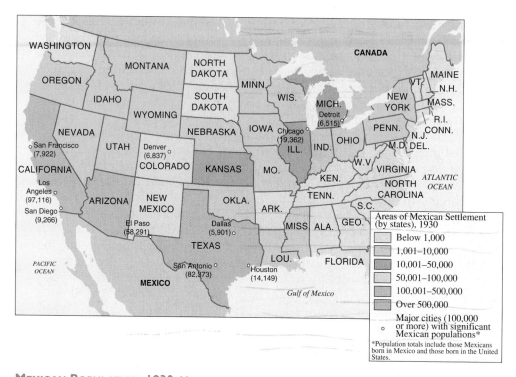

MEXICAN POPULATION, 1930 Mexicans migrated across the border in great numbers in the 1920s; by 1930, they constituted a significant Spanish-speaking minority, especially in Texas, California, and Arizona.

Americans attacked the police, a four-day riot was on. Several dozen were killed, and hundreds were wounded. The tension between the races did not die when the riot was over. Nor were other cities exempt.

The wave of violence and racism angered and disillusioned W. E. B. Du Bois, who had urged African Americans to support the American cause during the war. In an angry editorial for *The Crisis,* he called on blacks to "fight a sterner, longer, more unbending battle against the forces of hell in our own land. We return. We return from fighting. We return fighting. Make way for Democracy; we saved it in France, and by the Great Jehovah, we will save it in the United States of America, or know the reason why."

Marcus Garvey: Black Messiah

Du Bois was not the only postwar militant black leader. Marcus Garvey, a flamboyant Jamaican who arrived in New York at the age of 29, fed black pride. Although he never abandoned Booker T. Washington's self-help philosophy, Garvey thoroughly transformed it. Washington focused on economic betterment; Garvey saw self-help as political empowerment by which African peoples would reclaim their homelands.

In Jamaica, Garvey had founded the Universal Negro Improvement Association. By 1919, he had established 30 branches in the United States and the

Black Messiah Marcus Garvey (second from the right), shown dressed in his favorite uniform, became a hero for many black Americans. How did his appeal differ from that of other African American leaders? *(Hulton Archive/Getty Images)*

Caribbean. He also set up a newspaper, the Black Cross Nurses, and chains of stores and restaurants. His biggest project was the Black Star Line, a steamship company that was to be owned and operated by African Americans. Advocating blacks' return to Africa, he declared himself the "provisional president of Africa."

He won converts through the force of his oratory and powerful personality, but especially through his message of black pride. "Up you mighty race, you can accomplish what you will," Garvey thundered. Thousands of blacks cheered his Universal African Legions, marching in blue and red uniforms and waving a red-black-green flag. Thousands invested in the Black Star Line—which soon collapsed, in part because white entrepreneurs sold Garvey inferior ships. Garvey was arrested for using the mails to defraud shareholders and sentenced to five years in prison. Coolidge commuted the sentence. Ordered deported as an undesirable alien, Garvey left America in 1927. Despite his failures, he convinced thousands of black Americans, especially the poor and discouraged, and those who had recently migrated from the South, that they could unite and feel pride in their heritage.

The Harlem Renaissance and the Lost Generation

After the war, a group of black writers, artists, and intellectuals who settled in Harlem, an uptown neighborhood in New York City, led a movement related in some ways to Garvey's black nationalism crusade, and in the end, more important. They studied anthropology, art, history, and music, and in their novels, poetry, dance, and music explored the ambivalent role of blacks in America. Like Garvey, they expressed black pride and sought African and folk roots. Unlike

Garvey, they wanted to be both black and American and had no desire to go back to Africa.

Alain Locke, the first black Rhodes scholar, was the father of the renaissance. His *The New Negro* (1925) announced the movement to the outside world and outlined black contributions to American culture and civilization. Langston Hughes, a poet and novelist, wrote bitter but humorous poems, using black vernacular to describe the pathos and pride of African Americans. In *Weary Blues*, he adapted the rhythms of jazz and the blues.

Jazz was an important force in Harlem in the 1920s, and prosperous whites came to listen to Louis Armstrong, Duke Ellington, and other black musicians. Many brought up in Victorian white America were intrigued by what they saw as Harlem's primitive emotions and erotic atmosphere. American jazz was also exported to Europe. In Paris jazz singer Josephine Baker, star of *Revue Négre*, was the toast of the town. Many Europeans criticized the United States for its materialism. They were not impressed with American literature or art, but they loved American jazz. It was the beginning of the export of American popular culture that would impress most of the rest of the world in the decades after World War II.

Jamaican Claude McKay wrote about the underside of life in Harlem in *Home to Harlem* (1925), one of the most popular "new Negro" novels. McKay portrayed two black men—one, Jake, who finds a life of simple and erotic pleasure in Harlem's cabarets, the other an intellectual unable to make such an easy choice and conscious that "My damned white education has robbed me of ... primitive vitality." Many Harlem writers agonized about how to be both black and intellectual. They worried about white patrons who pressured them to conform to the white elite's idea of black authenticity, but they knew that patronage was their only hope to be recognized.

Many African American writers felt alienated from American society. They tried living in Paris or Greenwich Village, but most felt drawn to Harlem, which in the 1920s was rapidly becoming the center of New York's black population. Over 117,000 whites left during the decade, while over 87,000 blacks moved in. Countee Cullen remarked, "In spite of myself I find that I am activated by a strong sense of race consciousness." So was Zora Neale Hurston, who came to New York to study at Barnard College, earned an advanced degree in anthropology from Columbia University, and used her interest in folklore to write stories of robust and passionate rural blacks. The Harlem writers were read by only a few people, but another generation of young black intellectuals in the 1960s would rediscover them.

DOCUMENT

T. S. Eliot, Excerpt from "The Love Song of J. Alfred Prufrock" (1917)

Many white intellectuals, writers, and artists also felt estranged from what they saw as the narrow materialism of American life. Some, like F. Scott Fitzgerald, Ernest Hemingway, e. e. cummings, and T. S. Eliot, moved to Europe—where they wrote novels, plays, and poems about America. Like so many American intellectuals in all periods, they had a love-hate relationship with their country.

For many writers, disillusionment began with the war. Hemingway eagerly volunteered to go to Europe as an ambulance driver. But when he was wounded on the Italian front, he reevaluated the meaning of all the slaughter. His novel *The Sun Also Rises* (1926) is the story of the purposeless European wanderings of a group of Americans, as well as the story of Jake Barnes, who was made impotent by a war injury. His "unreasonable wound" symbolized the futility of postwar life. Fitzgerald, who loved the cafés and parties in Paris, became a celebrity during the 1920s. He epitomized some of the despair of his generation, which had "grown up to find all Gods dead, all wars fought, all faiths in man shaken." His best novel, *The Great Gatsby* (1925), was a critique of the American success myth.

It was not necessary to live in France to criticize American society. Sherwood Anderson created a fictional midwestern town in *Winesburg, Ohio* (1919), describing the dull, narrow, warped lives that seemed to provide a metaphor for American culture. Sinclair Lewis, another midwesterner, wrote scathing parodies of middle-class, small-town life in *Main Street* (1920) and *Babbitt* (1922). But no one had more fun laughing at the American middle class than Baltimore's H. L. Mencken, whose magazine *The American Mercury* overflowed with his assaults on "the booboisie." Harding's speeches reminded him of "a string of wet sponges, ... of stale bean soup, of college yells, of dogs barking idiotically through endless nights."

DOCUMENT

John F. Carter, "'These Wild Young People' by One of Them" (1920)

Ironically, while intellectuals despaired over American society and complained that art could not survive in a business-dominated civilization, literature flourished. The 1920s were one of the most creative decades in American literature.

Women Struggle for Equality

An indelible image of the 1920s is the flapper—a young woman with a short skirt, bobbed hair, and a boyish figure doing the Charleston, smoking, drinking, and being very casual about sex. Fitzgerald's heroines in novels like *This Side of Paradise* (1920) and *The Great Gatsby* (1925) provided role models for young people, and movie stars such as Clara Bow and Gloria Swanson, aggressively seductive on the screen, supplied even more vivid examples of provocative behavior.

Working Women of the 1920s Although the flapper look of short skirts and bobbed hair appeared in the workplace in the 1920s, for most working women of the era, employed in low-paying jobs as file clerks, typists, and telephone operators, the flapper lifestyle of freedom and equality was more illusion than reality. Does this workplace seem to empower or inhibit individual freedom? (*Corbis*)

DOCUMENT

Eleanor Rowland
Wembridge,
"Petting and the
Campus" (1925)

Without question, women acquired more sexual freedom in the 1920s. "None of the Victorian mothers had any idea how casually their daughters were accustomed to being kissed," Fitzgerald wrote. However, it is difficult, if not impossible, to know how accustomed those daughters (and their mothers) were to kissing and enjoying other sexual activity. Contraceptives became more readily available, and Margaret Sanger (who had been indicted for sending birth control information through the mail in 1914) organized the first American birth control conference in 1921. Birth control devices and literature, however, were still often illegal.

DOCUMENT

Margaret Sanger,
"Happiness in
Marriage" (1926)

Family size declined during the decade (from 3.6 children in 1900 to 2.5 in 1930), and young people were apparently more inclined to marry for love than for security. More women expected sexual satisfaction in marriage (nearly 60 percent in one poll) and felt that divorce was the best solution for an unhappy marriage. Nearly 85 percent in another poll approved of sexual intercourse as an expression of love and affection, rather than simply for procreation. But these polls tended to be biased toward urban middle-class attitudes. Despite more freedom for women, the double standard persisted.

Middle-class women's lives were shaped by innovations like electricity, running water, and labor-saving devices. But as standards of cleanliness rose, they spent more time on housework while being bombarded with advertising urging them to make themselves better housekeepers yet still be beautiful. The young adopted new styles quickly, and they also learned to swim, play tennis, and ride bicycles.

More women worked outside the home—22 percent in 1933, compared to 17 percent in 1890. But their share of manufacturing jobs fell from 19 to 16 percent between 1900 and 1930. The greatest expansion of jobs was in white-collar occupations that were being feminized—secretary, bookkeeper, clerk, telephone operator. Although more married women had jobs (an increase of 25 percent during the decade), most held low-paying jobs, and most single women assumed that marriage would end their employment.

For some working women—secretaries and teachers, for example—marriage indeed often led to dismissal. Yet an office was a good place to meet eligible men, and a secretary learned endurance, self-effacement, and obedience—traits that many thought would make her a good wife. Considering these attitudes, it is not surprising that the male-female pay disparity widened. By 1930, women earned only 57 percent of what men were paid.

The image of the flapper in the 1920s promised more freedom and equality for women than they actually achieved. The flapper was young, white, slender, and upper class, and most women did not fit those categories. Although the proportion of women lawyers and bankers increased slightly, the rate of growth declined. The number of women doctors and scientists dropped.

The promise of prewar feminists and suffrage advocates remained unfulfilled. In some states, women needed their husband's consent in order to hold office, own a business, or sign a contract. Women were usually held responsible for an illegitimate birth, and divorce laws almost always favored men.

Alice Paul, who had led the militant National Woman's Party in 1916, chained herself to the White House fence once again to promote an equal rights amendment to the Constitution. The amendment got support in several states, but many women opposed it, fearing that it would cancel the special legislation to protect women in industry. Feminists disagreed in the 1920s on the proper way to promote equality and rights for women, but the political and social climate was not conducive to feminism.

Rural America in the 1920s

Most farmers did not share in the decade's prosperity. During the war, farmers had responded to worldwide demand and rising commodity prices by investing in land and equipment. Then prices and farm income tumbled. Many farmers could not make payments on their mortgages, and they lost their farms.

The changing nature of farming was part of the problem. Chemical fertilizers and new hybrid seeds increased yields. Farming became more mechanized and efficient. Production swelled just as worldwide demand for American farm products tumbled.

Few farmers could afford the products of the new technology. Although many middle-class urban families were more prosperous than ever before, only one farm family in ten had electricity in the 1920s. The lot of the farm wife had not changed for centuries.

Farmers tried to act collectively to solve their problems. Most of their effort went into passing the McNary-Haugen Farm Relief Bill, which provided for government support for key agricultural products. The government would buy crops at a "fair exchange value" and then market the excess on the world market at a lower price. The bill passed Congress twice, in 1927 and 1928, and twice was vetoed by President Coolidge. But farm organizations across the country learned how to cooperate and influence Congress, with important future ramifications.

Farmers were particularly vulnerable to the power of nature, and that became apparent in the spring of 1927, when the worst flood in the nation's history devastated the Mississippi River valley. Despite efforts to improve the levies, over 27,000 square miles of land were flooded. Nearly a million people were made homeless. There was over a billion dollars in property damage, and 246 people died. The black sharecroppers, who often lived near the river, bore the brunt of the disaster. President Coolidge appointed Secretary of Commerce Herbert Hoover to coordinate flood relief. Hoover, who believed in voluntary efforts, enlisted the help of the Red Cross, the American Legion, and other groups, but the total relief efforts remained inadequate. The next year, Coolidge signed a flood control bill that for the first time committed the federal government to build levies to control the Mississippi River. But the debate continued about the best way to control nature and how to solve the farmers' problems.

The Workers' Share of Prosperity

Hundreds of thousands of workers improved their standard of living in the 1920s, yet inequality grew. Between 1923 and 1929, real wages increased 21 percent, but corporate dividends went up by nearly two-thirds. The richest 5 percent of the population increased their share of the wealth from a quarter to a third, and the wealthiest 1 percent controlled a whopping 19 percent of all income. Workers did not profit from the increased production they helped generate.

Even among workers, there was great disparity. For example, those employed on auto assembly lines saw their wages go up and their hours go down. Yet the majority of American working-class families could not move much beyond subsistence. One study suggested that a family needed between $2,000 and $2,400 in 1924 to maintain an "American standard of living." That year, 16 million families earned under $2,000.

Although some workers prospered in the 1920s, organized labor did not. Union membership dropped from about 5 million in 1921 to under 3.5 million in 1929. The National Manufacturing Association carried on a vigorous campaign to restore the open shop, while many businesses added pensions and company unions to lure employees away from unions.

The conservative American Federation of Labor suffered during the 1920s, but so did the more aggressive unions like the United Mine Workers, led by the bombastic John L. Lewis. Internal strife weakened the union, and Lewis had to accept wage reductions in 1927. Organized labor, like so many other groups, struggled desperately to share in the prosperity of the 1920s. But affluence and a share of the American dream were beyond the reach of most workers.

THE BUSINESS OF POLITICS

"Among the nations of the earth today America stands for one idea: *Business*," a popular writer announced in 1921. Bruce Barton, the head of the largest advertising firm in the country, published one of the most popular nonfiction books of the decade. In *The Man Nobody Knows (1925)*, he depicted Christ as "the founder of modern business." He took 12 men from the bottom of society and forged them into a successful organization.

Business, especially big business, prospered in the 1920s. The government reduced regulation, lowered taxes, and helped aid business expansion at home and abroad. Business and politics, always intertwined, became especially close during the decade. Wealthy financiers played important roles in formulating government policy. Even more significant, a new kind of businessman was elected president in 1928. Herbert Hoover, international engineer and efficiency expert, was the very symbol of modern business techniques and practices.

Harding and Coolidge

The Republicans, almost assured of victory in 1920 because of bitter reaction against Woodrow Wilson, might have preferred nominating their old standard-bearer, Theodore Roosevelt, but he had died the year before. Warren G. Harding, a former Ohio newspaper editor, captured the nomination after meeting late at night with some of the party's most powerful men in a Chicago hotel room. To balance the ticket, the Republicans chose as their vice presidential candidate Calvin Coolidge. Meanwhile, after 44 roll calls, the Democrats nominated Governor James Cox of Ohio and picked Franklin D. Roosevelt, the assistant secretary of the navy, for vice president.

Harding won in a landslide. His 60.4 percent of the vote was the widest margin yet recorded in a presidential election. More significant, fewer than 50 percent of the eligible voters went to the polls. Newly enfranchised women, especially in working-class neighborhoods, avoided the voting booths. So did large numbers of men. Many people did not care who was president.

In contrast to the reform-minded presidents Roosevelt and Wilson, Harding reflected the conservatism of the 1920s. A visitor to the White House found Harding and his cohorts discussing the problems of the day, with "the air heavy with tobacco smoke, trays with bottles containing every imaginable brand of whiskey." A few blocks away, Harry Daugherty, Harding's attorney general and longtime associate, did a brisk business in selling favors, taking bribes, and organizing illegal schemes.

Harding was not personally corrupt, and the nation's leading businessmen approved of his high-tariff, low-tax policies. Nor did Harding spend all his time drinking with his pals. He called a conference on disarmament and another on unemployment. Harding once remarked that he could never be considered a great president, but he thought perhaps he might be "one of the best loved." When he died suddenly in August 1923, the American people genuinely mourned.

Only after Coolidge became president did the full extent of the Harding scandals come out. A Senate committee discovered that Secretary of the Interior Albert Fall had illegally leased government-owned oil reserves in the Teapot Dome section of Wyoming to businessmen for over $300,000 in bribes. Illegal activities were turned up in the Veterans Administration and elsewhere. Harding's attorney general resigned in disgrace, the secretary of the navy barely avoided prison, two of Harding's advisers committed suicide, and Fall went to jail.

Coolidge was dour, taciturn—and honest. Born in a little town in Vermont, he was sworn in as president by his father, a justice of the peace, whom he was visiting when news of Harding's death came. To many, Coolidge represented old-fashioned values, simple religious faith, and personal integrity. But Coolidge felt ill at ease posing for photographers holding a pitchfork, and he was much more comfortable around corporate executives.

Coolidge ran for reelection in 1924 with the financier Charles Dawes as his running mate. There was little question that he would win. The Democrats were so equally divided between northern urban Catholics and southern rural Protestants that it took 103 ballots to nominate John W. Davis, an affable corporate lawyer.

Dissidents, mostly representing the farmers and laborers dissatisfied with both nominees, formed a new Progressive party. They adopted the name, but little else, from Theodore Roosevelt's party of 1912. Nominating Robert La Follette for president, their platform called for government ownership of railroads and ratification of an anti-child labor amendment. La Follette attacked the "control of government and industry by private monopoly." He received nearly 5 million votes, only 3.5 million short of Davis's total. But Coolidge and prosperity won easily.

Like Harding, Coolidge was immensely popular. Symbolizing his administration was his wealthy secretary of the treasury, Andrew Mellon. In 1922, Congress, with Mellon's endorsement, repealed the wartime excess profits tax. The federal income tax exempted most families by giving everyone a $2,500 exemption, plus

$400 for each dependent. In 1928, Congress slashed taxes further, removed most excise taxes, and lowered the corporate tax rate. The 200 largest corporations increased their assets during the decade from $43 billion to $81 billion. "The chief business of the American people is business," Coolidge said. His idea of the proper role of the federal government was to have as little as possible to do with the functioning of business and the lives of the people. "No other president in my time slept so much," a White House usher remembered. But most Americans approved of their president.

Herbert Hoover

One bright light in the lackluster Harding and Coolidge administrations was Secretary of Commerce Herbert Hoover. He had made a fortune as a mining engineer before 1914 and earned the reputation of a great humanitarian during the war. Many Progressives supported him as a presidential candidate in 1920.

Hoover was a dynamo. He expanded his department to regulate the airlines, radio, and other new industries. Through the Bureau of Standards, Hoover standardized the size of almost everything manufactured in the United States, from light bulbs to mattresses. He supported zoning codes, the eight-hour day in major industries, better nutrition for children, and conservation. He pushed through the Pollution Act of 1924, the first attempt to control coastal oil pollution.

While secretary of commerce, Hoover used the authority of the federal government to regulate, stimulate, and promote, but he believed first of all in American free enterprise and local volunteer action. In 1921, he convinced Harding of the need to do something about unemployment during the postwar recession. The president's conference on unemployment, convened in September 1921, marked the first time the national government had admitted any responsibility for the unemployed. The conference (the first of many that Hoover was to organize) unleashed a flood of publicity and expert advice. The conference report urged state and local governments and businesses to cooperate voluntarily to solve the problem. The primary responsibility of the federal government, Hoover believed, was to educate and promote, but not to initiate reform.

Global Expansion

The 1920s are often called a time of isolation. But the United States remained involved—indeed, increased its involvement—in international affairs. Although the United States never joined the League of Nations, and a few staunch isolationists blocked membership in the World Court, the United States cooperated with many league agencies. And it took the lead in trying to reduce naval armaments and to solve the problems of international finance caused in part by the war.

There were ominous clouds on the horizon. Germany was mired in economic and political chaos. Japan and Italy were unhappy with the peace settlement. Colonial powers still dominated Africa. Fascism was establishing a foothold in Italy and Spain, while Soviet communism was becoming more firmly entrenched in Russia. The Middle East was fragmented both economically and politically and presented problems that would persist for the rest of the twentieth century and beyond.

The sevenfold expansion of American corporate investments overseas turned the United States from a debtor to a creditor nation. Business, trade, and finance marked the decade as one of international expansion, and the United States increased its leadership in cable communications, wireless telegraphy, and film. Ninety-five percent of the movies shown in Great Britain and Canada and 70 percent of those shown in France in 1926 were American made. Yet the United States took up its role of international power reluctantly and with a number of contradictory and disastrous results.

"We seek no part in directing the destiny of the world," Harding announced in his inaugural address, but he discovered that international problems would not go away. One that required immediate attention was the naval arms race, for which purpose the United States convened the Washington Conference on Naval Disarmament, the first international disarmament conference, in November 1921.

Secretary of State Charles Evans Hughes startled the conference by proposing a 10-year "holiday" on warship construction and offering to sink or scrap 845,000 tons of American ships, including 30 battleships. He urged Britain and Japan to do the same. The delegates cheered Hughes's speech, and they sank more ships than all their admirals had managed to do in a century. The conference ultimately fixed the tonnage of capital ships at a ratio of the United States and Great Britain, 5; Japan, 3; and France and Italy, 1.67. Japan agreed only reluctantly, after the United States promised not to fortify its Pacific islands.

The Washington Conference has often been criticized in the light of Pearl Harbor, but in 1921 it was appropriately hailed as the first time in history that the major nations of the world had agreed to disarm. The conference neither caused nor averted World War II. But it was a creative beginning to reducing tensions and to meeting the challenges of the modern arms race.

American foreign policy in the 1920s tried to reduce the risk of international conflict, resist revolution, and make the world safe for trade and investment. Nobody in the Republican administrations even suggested that the United States remain isolated from Latin America. American diplomats supported an open door to trade in China, but in Latin America, the United States had always assumed a special and distinct role. Throughout the decade, American investment increased in the Western Hemisphere. The United States bought nearly 60 percent of Latin America's exports and sold the region nearly 50 percent of its imports.

By the end of the decade, the United States controlled the financial affairs of 10 Latin American nations. The Dominican Republic remained a virtual protectorate of the United States until 1941. First the marines—and later the Nicaraguan troops they trained—had a difficult time containing a guerrilla band led by charismatic Augusto Sandino. In 1934, he was murdered by the followers of General Anastasio Somoza, a ruthless leader supported by the United States. For more than 40 years, Somoza and his two sons would rule Nicaragua.

Mexico frightened American businessmen in the mid-1920s by beginning to nationalize foreign holdings in oil and mineral rights. Fearing that further military activity would "injure American interests," businessmen and bankers urged

Coolidge to negotiate. Coolidge did, and his ambassador's conciliatory attitude led to agreements protecting American investments.

The U.S. policy of promoting peace and trade was not always consistent, especially in Europe. The United States was owed more than $10 billion in war loans, three-fourths of it by Britain and France. Both countries, mired in economic problems, suggested that the United States forgive the debts, arguing that they had paid for the war in lives and property destroyed. But the United States, although adjusting the interest and the payment schedule, refused. "They hired the money, didn't they?" Coolidge supposedly asked.

The only way European nations could repay the United States was by exports, but Congress supported high tariffs. In 1930, the Hawley-Smoot Tariff raised rates even further, despite the protests of many economists. The American policy of high tariffs (a counterproductive policy for a creditor nation) caused retaliation and restrictions on American trade, which American corporations were trying to increase.

Europeans' inability to export to the United States and repay their loans was intertwined with the reparation agreement made with Germany. The postwar German economy was beset by inflation and its industrial plant throttled by the peace treaty. By 1921, Germany was defaulting on reparations payments. Hoping to maintain international stability, the United States introduced the Dawes Plan, under which the German debt would be spread over a longer period while American bankers and the American government lent Germany hundreds of millions of dollars. This enabled Germany to pay reparations to Britain and France so that they could continue debt repayments to the United States.

Although the United States had displaced Great Britain as the dominant force in international finance, it was a reluctant and inconsistent world leader. The United States stayed out of the League of Nations and hesitated to join multinational agreements. But the Kellogg–Briand pact seemed irresistible. French foreign minister Aristide Briand suggested a Franco-American pact, to commemorate long years of friendship between the two countries, but Secretary of State Frank B. Kellogg in 1928 expanded the idea to a multinational treaty outlawing war. Fourteen nations initially signed the treaty and 62 eventually did, but the only power behind it was moral force, and moral force would not prevent World War II.

The Survival of Progressivism

The decade of the 1920s saw a reaction against reform, but progressivism did not simply die. Progressives interested in efficiency and order were perhaps happier during the 1920s than those who tried to promote social justice, but the fights against poverty and for better housing persisted, as did campaigns to protect children.

The greatest success of the social justice movement was the 1921 Sheppard-Towner Maternity Act, one of the first pieces of federal social welfare legislation and the product of long progressive agitation. The bill, controversial from the beginning, called for a million dollars a year to assist states in providing medical aid, and visiting nurses to teach expectant mothers how to care for themselves and their babies. The American Medical Association attacked it as socialism, and the opponents of woman suffrage argued that it was supported by extreme feminists and Communists.

But the bill passed Congress and was signed by President Harding in 1921. The appropriation for the bill was only for six years, and the opposition, still trembling at a feminist-Socialist-Communist plot, got it repealed in 1929. Yet the Sheppard–Towner Act, promoted and fought for by a group of progressive women, indicated that concern for social justice was not dead in the age of Harding and Coolidge.

Temperance Triumphant

By 1918, over three-fourths of Americans lived in dry states or counties, but the war allowed antisaloon advocates to link Prohibition and patriotism. At first, beer manufacturers supported limited Prohibition, but in the end, patriotic fervor prohibited the sale of all alcoholic beverages. "We have German enemies across the water," one prohibitionist announced. "We have German enemies in this country too. And the worst of all our German enemies, the most treacherous, the most menacing are Pabst, Schlitz, Blatz and Miller."

The Volstead Act, passed in 1919, banned the brewing and selling of beverages containing more than 0.5 percent alcohol. The Eighteenth Amendment was ratified in June 1919, but the country had been effectively dry since 1917. A social worker predicted that the Eighteenth Amendment would reduce poverty, nearly wipe out prostitution and crime, improve labor, and "substantially increase our national resources by setting free vast suppressed human potentialities."

The Prohibition experiment probably did reduce the total consumption of alcohol in the country, especially in rural areas and urban working-class neighborhoods. Fewer arrests for drunkenness were made, and deaths from alcoholism declined. But Prohibition showed the difficulty of using law to promote moral reform. Most people who wanted to drink during the "noble experiment" found a way. Speakeasies replaced saloons, and people consumed many strange and dangerous homemade concoctions. Bartenders invented the cocktail to disguise the poor quality of liquor, and middle- and upper-class women began to drink in public for the first time.

Prohibition also created great bootlegging rings, tied in many cities to organized crime. Chicago's Al Capone was the most famous underworld figure whose power and wealth were based on the sale of illegal alcohol. His organization grossed an estimated $60 million in 1927. Many Prohibition supporters slowly came to favor repeal, because Prohibition stimulated too much illegal activity and it did not seem worth the costs.

AUDIO

Prohibition Is a Failure

The Election of 1928

On August 2, 1927, President Coolidge announced, "I do not choose to run for President in 1928." Hoover immediately became the logical Republican candidate, and he easily got the nomination. Few doubted that the prospering country would elect him. The Democrats nominated Alfred Smith, the colorful, "wet," and Catholic governor of New York who seemed to contrast sharply with Hoover.

Anti-Catholicism became a major component of the campaign. But the two candidates differed little. Both were self-made men, and both were progressives. Both sought women voters, favored organized labor, defended capitalism, and were advised by millionaires and corporate executives.

Hoover won in a landslide, receiving 444 electoral votes to Smith's 76. But the campaign revitalized the Democratic party. Smith polled nearly twice as many votes as Davis had in 1924, and for the first time Democrats carried the 12 largest cities.

Stock Market Crash

Hoover had only six months to apply his progressive, efficient methods to running the country. In the fall of 1929, the seemingly endless prosperity suddenly fizzled. In 1928 and 1929, rampant speculation made the stock market boom. Money could be made everywhere: in real estate, business ventures, and especially the stock market. "Everybody ought to be Rich," Al Smith's campaign manager proclaimed in an article in the *Ladies' Home Journal* early in 1929. A large number got into the game in the late 1920s because it seemed a safe and sure way to make money. The *New York Times* index of 25 industrial stocks reached 100 in 1924, moved up to 181 in 1925, dropped a bit in 1926, and rose again to 245 by the end of 1927.

VIDEO

Prosperity of the 1920s and the Great Depression

Then the orgy started. During 1928, the market zoomed to 331. Many investors and speculators began to buy on margin (borrowing to invest). Money went into the market that would ordinarily have gone into houses, cars, and other goods. Yet even at the peak, probably only about 1.5 million Americans owned stock.

In early September 1929, the *New York Times* index peaked at 452 and then began to drift downward. On October 23, the market lost 31 points. The next day ("Black Thursday"), it first seemed that everyone was trying to sell, but at the end of the day, the panic appeared over. It was not. By mid-November, the market had plummeted to 224, about half what it had been two months before—a loss on paper of over $26 billion. Still, a month later, some businessmen got back into the market, thinking that it had reached its low point. But it continued to go down. Tens of thousands of investors lost everything. There was panic and despair, but the legendary stories of executives jumping out of windows were grossly exaggerated.

Conclusion

A New Era of Prosperity and Problems

The stock market crash ended the decade of prosperity. The crash did not cause the Great Depression, but the stock market debacle revealed the weakness of the economy. The Depression was related to the global economy and to problems created by the war and the peace settlement. The fruits of economic expansion had been unevenly distributed. African American families like the Parkers (the family we met at the beginning of this chapter) did not share much of the affluence created during the decade. Many other Americans, including many workers and

TIMELINE

1919 Treaty of Versailles	Teapot Dome scandal
Strikes in Seattle, Boston, and elsewhere	**1925** Scopes trial in Dayton, Tennessee
Red Scare and Palmer raids	F. Scott Fitzgerald, *The Great Gatsby*
Race riots in Chicago and other cities	Bruce Barton, *The Man Nobody Knows*
Marcus Garvey's Universal Negro Improvement Association spreads	Alain Locke, *The New Negro*
	Claude McKay, *Home to Harlem*
1920 Warren Harding elected president	Five million enameled bathroom fixtures produced
Women vote in national elections	**1927** McNary–Haugen Farm Relief Bill
First commercial radio broadcast	Sacco and Vanzetti executed
Sacco and Vanzetti arrested	Lindbergh flies solo, New York to Paris
Sinclair Lewis, *Main Street*	First talking movie, *The Jazz Singer*
1921 Immigration Quota Law	Henry Ford produces 15 millionth car
Disarmament Conference	**1928** Herbert Hoover elected president
First birth control conference	Kellogg–Briand Treaty
Sheppard–Towner Maternity Act	Stock market soars
1922 Fordney–McCumber Tariff	**1929** 27 million registered cars in country
Sinclair Lewis, *Babbitt*	10 million households own radios
1923 Harding dies; Calvin Coolidge becomes president	Stock market crash

farmers, could not afford to buy the autos, refrigerators, and other products pouring from American factories. Prosperity had been built on a shaky foundation. When that foundation crumbled in 1929, the nation slid into a major depression.

Looking back from the vantage point of the 1930s or later, the 1920s seemed a golden era—an age of flappers, bootleg gin, constant parties, literary masterpieces, sports heroes, and easy wealth. The truth is much more complicated. More than most decades, the 1920s was a time of paradox and contradictions.

The 1920s was a time of prosperity, yet a great many people, including farmers, blacks, and other ordinary Americans, did not prosper. It was a time of modernization, but only about 10 percent of rural families had electricity. It was a time when women achieved more sexual freedom, but the feminist movement declined. It was a time of Prohibition, but many Americans increased their consumption of alcohol. It was a time of reaction against reform, yet progressivism survived. It was a time when intellectuals felt disillusioned with America, yet it was one of the most creative and innovative periods for American writers. It was a time of flamboyant heroes, yet the American people elected the lackluster Harding and Coolidge as their presidents. It was a time of progress, when almost every year saw a new technological breakthrough, but it was also a decade of hate and intolerance. The complex and contradictory legacy of the 1920s continued to fascinate and to influence Americans in the 1930s and after.

Questions for Review and Reflection

1. What was the Harlem Renaissance?
2. Did the Prohibition experiment succeed or fail?
3. In foreign policy during the 1920s, why did the United States try to isolate itself from the rest of the world?
4. What groups did not share in the prosperity of the decade?
5. Why are Harding and Coolidge often considered among our worst presidents?

Discovering U.S. History Online

Automotive History http://mel.lib.mi.us/business/autos-history.html
This site, from the Michigan Electronic Library, has several links to sites about automotive history in America.

National Arts & Crafts Archives http://arts-crafts.com/archive/archive.shtml
This site serves as a guide to materials on the Arts & Crafts movement, which lasted roughly from 1890 to 1929.

Harlem 1900–1940: An African American Community http://www.si.umich.edu./CHICO/Harlem
The New York Public Library's Schomburg Center for Research in Black Culture hosts this site, which includes a database, a timeline, and an exhibit.

Photographs from the Golden Age of Jazz http://memory.loc/gov/ammem/wghtml/wghome.html
The Music Division of the Library of Congress offers numerous images, audio elements, and scanned articles from the 1940s.

Negro League Baseball http://www.negroleaguebaseball.com/
Essays about desegregation, baseball, and Jim Crow, as well as images of teams and players, constitute much of this site.

American Temperance and Prohibition http://www.cohms.ohio-state.edu/history/projects/prohibition/
This site looks at the temperance movement over time and contains many informative links.

Flapper Culture & Style http://www.geocities.com/flapper_culture/
This site contains many links to information about the popular culture of the 1920s, with special reference to the flapper.

Fiction and Film

Ernest Hemingway's novel *The Sun Also Rises* (1926) is a classic tale of disillusionment and despair in the 1920s; F. Scott Fitzgerald gives a picture of the life of the rich in *The Great Gatsby* (1925); and Claude McKay's novel *Home to Harlem* (1928) is one of the best to come out of the Harlem Renaissance.

Front Page (1931) is a movie that depicts the world of corrupt politicians and cynical newspapermen in Chicago during the Roaring Twenties. The 1974 film version of *The Great Gatsby,* starring Robert Redford, is not entirely faithful to the novel, but it still captures some of the opulence and pathos of the very rich in the 1920s.

Recommended Reading

www.ablongman.com/nash
The Companion Website has a list of recommended readings about industrialization, urbanization, the middle and laboring classes, and capital versus labor.

The Great Depression and the New Deal

CHAPTER OUTLINE

- The Great Depression
- Roosevelt and the First New Deal
- One Hundred Days
- The Second New Deal
- The Last Years of the New Deal
- The Other Side of the 1930s
- Conclusion: The Mixed Legacy of the Great Depression and the New Deal

American Stories

Coming of Age and Riding the Rails During the Depression

Flickering in a Seattle movie theater in the depths of the Great Depression, the Hollywood production *Wild Boys of the Road* captivated 13-year-old Robert Symmonds. The film, released in 1933, told the story of boys hitching rides on trains and tramping around the country. It was supposed to warn teenagers of the dangers of rail-riding, but for some it had the opposite effect. Robert, a boy from a middle-class home, already had a fascination with hobos. He had watched his mother give sandwiches to the transient men who sometimes knocked on the back door. He had taken to hanging around the "Hooverville" shantytown south of the King Street railroad station, where he would sit next to the fires and listen to the rail-riders' stories. Stoked for adventure, when school let out in 1934, Robert and a school friend hopped onto a moving boxcar on a train headed out of town. Hands reached out to pull them aboard the car, which already held 20 men. The two boys journeyed as far as Vancouver, Washington, and home to Seattle again. It was frightening, and exhilarating.

In 1938, under the weight of the Depression, the Symmonds family's security business failed. Years later, Robert recalled the effects on his father: "It hurt him bad when he went broke and all his friends deserted him. He did the best he could but never recovered his self-esteem and his pride." The loss of income forced Robert's family to accept a relative's offer of shelter in a three-room mountain cabin without electricity. Because of the move, Robert could no longer attend high school in Seattle. Once again, this time out of necessity, he turned to the rails, leaving his parents and three sisters behind.

Robert faced a personal challenge of surviving difficult times, but he also was part of a looming problem which troubled the administration of Franklin D. Roosevelt. Thousands of young people were graduating from high school, or leaving school earlier, with very few jobs open to them. An estimated 250,000 young people were among the drifters who resorted to the often-dangerous practice of hitching rides on trains around the country. Robert rode the rails during summers to find work harvesting fruit up and down the West Coast. In 1939, his travels took him to Montana, where he encountered the Roosevelt administration's solution for the "youth problem": the Civilian Conservation Corps. When he enlisted in the CCC, Robert became one of nearly 3 million young men aged 17 and older who found work in government-sponsored conservation projects between 1933 and 1942. In exchange for their work, CCC workers earned $25 a month for their families back home plus $5 a month spending money for themselves.

The CCC was known as Roosevelt's "tree army" because the Corps planted trees covering more than 2 million acres, improved more than 4 million acres of existing forest, and fought forest fires. In addition, the CCC worked on a wide variety of conservation-related projects in a nation suffering from deforestation, erosion, drought, dust storms, and other environmental problems. CCC workers improved parks and recreation areas and even historic sites from the Civil War, including the notorious Andersonville prison camp in Georgia. In many ways, the CCC operated like a military organization, with workers wearing surplus World War I uniforms and following a fixed regimen of work and recreation that began with a bugler's call at 6 A.M. Many of its veterans credited the Corps with transforming them from boys into men, although others chafed under the discipline of the camps.

One historian has called the CCC the greatest peacetime mobilization in U.S. history, and it set the stage for the wartime mobilization that followed. By the time Robert Symmonds joined the CCC in 1939, war loomed in Europe. Like many CCC veterans, Robert's next stop in life was military service. He joined the navy and after the war became a merchant seaman. In later years, like many Americans of his generation, Robert remembered his experiences of the Great Depression grimly, but with some nostalgia. He even returned to hopping rides on railroad cars again during his retirement years, out of a sense of adventure rather than necessity. "It's something that got into my blood years ago," he explained. "I guess it's a freedom thing."

The Great Depression changed the lives of all Americans and separated that generation from the one that followed. An exaggerated need for security, the fear of failure, a nagging sense of guilt, and a real sense that it might happen again divided the Depression generation from everyone born after 1940. Like Robert Symmonds, most Americans never forgot those bleak years.

This chapter explores the causes and consequences of the Great Depression. We will look at Herbert Hoover's efforts to combat it and then turn to Franklin Roosevelt, the dominant personality of the 1930s. We will examine the New Deal and Roosevelt's program of relief, recovery, and reform. But we will not ignore the other side of the 1930s, for the decade did not just mean unemployment and New Deal agencies. It was also a time of great strides in technology, when innovations in radio, movies, and the automobile affected the lives of most Americans.

THE GREAT DEPRESSION

There had been recessions and depressions in American history, notably in the 1830s, 1870s, and 1890s, but nothing compared to the devastating economic collapse of the 1930s. The Great Depression was all the more shocking because it came after a decade of unprecedented prosperity, when most experts assumed that the United States was immune to a business-cycle downturn. The Great Depression affected all areas of American life; perhaps most important, it destroyed American confidence in the future.

The Depression Begins

Few people anticipated the stock market crash in the fall of 1929. But even after the collapse of the stock market, no one expected the entire economy to go into a tailspin. General Electric stock, selling for $396 in 1929, fell to $34 in 1932. By 1932, the median income had plunged to half what it had been in 1929. Construction spending fell to one-sixth of the 1929 level. By 1932, at least one of every four American breadwinners was out of work, and industrial production ground almost to a halt.

Why did the country sink deeper and deeper into depression? The prosperity of the 1920s was superficial. Farmers and coal and textile workers had suffered all through the 1920s from low prices, and the farmers were the first group in the 1930s to plunge into depression. But other economic sectors also lurched out of balance. Two percent of the population received about 28 percent of the national income, but the lower 60 percent got only 24 percent. Businesses increased profits while holding down wages and the prices of raw materials. This pattern depressed consumer purchasing power. Workers, like farmers, did not have the money to buy the goods they helped to produce. There was a relative decline in purchasing power in the late 1920s, unemployment was high in some industries, and the housing and automobile industries were already slackening before the crash.

Well-to-do Americans were investing a significant portion of their money in stock market speculation. Their illusion of permanent prosperity helped fire the

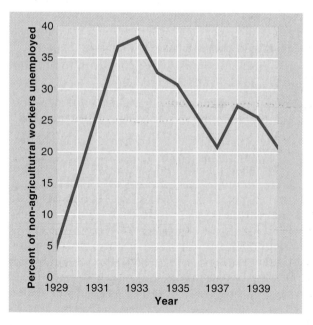

UNEMPLOYMENT RATE, 1929–1940 Although the unemployment rate declined during the New Deal years, the number still unemployed remained tragically high until World War II brought full employment. (*Source: U.S. Bureau of the Census*)

boom of the 1920s, just as their pessimism and lack of confidence helped exaggerate the Depression in 1931 and 1932.

But there were other factors. The stock market crash revealed serious structural weaknesses in the financial and banking systems. The Federal Reserve Board, fearing inflation, tightened credit—the opposite of what it should have done. But the Depression was also caused by global economic problems. High American tariffs during the 1920s had reduced trade, and when American investment in Europe slackened in 1928 and 1929, European economies declined. As the European financial situation worsened, the American economy spiraled downward.

The federal government might have prevented the Wall Street crash and the Depression by more careful regulation of business and the stock market. Central planning might have ensured a more equitable distribution of income. But that kind of policy would have taken more foresight than most people had in the 1920s. It certainly would have required different people in power, and it is unlikely that the Democrats, had they been in control, would have altered the government's policies in fundamental ways.

Hoover and the Great Depression

Initial business and government reactions to the stock market crash were optimistic. "All the evidence indicates that the worst effects of the crash upon unemployment will have been passed during the next sixty days," Herbert Hoover predicted, but he did not sit idly by and watch the country drift toward disorder.

He acted aggressively. More than any president before him, he used the power of the federal government and the office of the president to deal with a crisis that seemed much like earlier cyclic recessions. Hoover called conferences of businessmen and labor leaders. He encouraged mayors and governors to speed up public works projects. He created agencies and boards, such as the National Credit Corporation and the Emergency Committee for Employment, to obtain voluntary action to solve the problem. Hoover even supported a tax cut, which Congress enacted in December 1929, but it did little to stimulate spending.

A Global Depression

Voluntary action and psychological campaigns could not stop the Depression. The stock market, after appearing to bottom out in the winter of 1930 and 1931, continued its decline, responding in part to the European economic collapse that threatened international finance and trade. Of course, not everyone lost money. Joseph Kennedy, film magnate, entrepreneur, and father of a future president, and a few others made millions by selling short as the market went down.

More than a collapsing market afflicted the economy. Over 1,300 banks failed in 1930. Despite Hoover's pleas, many factories cut production, and some simply closed. More than 4 million Americans were out of work in 1930, and that number increased to at least 12 million by 1932. Foreclosures and evictions created thousands of personal tragedies. While the middle class watched in horror as life savings and dreams disappeared, the rich worried increasingly as the price of government bonds (the symbol of safety and security) dropped. They began to hoard gold and fear revolution.

Out of Work The worst result of the Great Depression was hopelessness and despair. Those emotions are captured in this painting of an unemployment office by Isaac Soyer. When did the unemployment crisis finally end? *(Whitney Museum of American Art, New York; Purchase)*

IMAGE

Depression Era
Breadlines

There was never any real danger of revolution. Some farmers organized to dump their milk to protest low prices, and when a neighbor's farm was sold, they gathered to hold a penny auction, bidding only a few cents for equipment and returning it to their dispossessed neighbor. But everywhere people despaired as the Depression deepened in 1931 and 1932. For unemployed blacks and many tenant farmers, the Depression had little immediate effect because their lives were already so depressed. The 98 percent of Americans who did not own stock hardly noticed the crash; for them, the Depression meant a lost job or a foreclosure. Not everyone went hungry, stood in breadlines, or lost jobs, but almost everyone suffered, and many tended to blame themselves.

The Depression probably disrupted women's lives less than men's. When men lost their jobs, their identity and sense of purpose as the family breadwinner generally collapsed. Some men helped out with family chores, usually with bitterness. For women, however, even when money was short, there were still chores, and they were still in command of their households. Yet many women had to do extra work: taking in laundry, renting a room to a boarder, and making clothes they formerly would have bought. They also bore the psychological burden of unemployed husbands, hungry children, and unpaid bills. Many families moved in with relatives. The marriage rate, the divorce rate, and the birthrate all dropped during the decade, creating tensions that statistics cannot capture.

Hoover kept urging more voluntary action. He insisted on maintaining the gold standard and a balanced budget, but so did almost everyone else. Hoover increasingly blamed the Depression on international economic problems, and he was partly right. The legacy of the war and the global economic policies of the 1920s were among the causes of the economic downturn in the United States. As the United States sank into Depression, the world followed. In May 1931, the leading Austrian bank collapsed; by June, the German financial system was in chaos; and in September, England abandoned the gold standard. Soon most of the industrialized world, including Argentina, Brazil, and Japan, was caught in the Depression. Despite the global nature of the crisis, Americans began to blame Hoover. The president became isolated and bitter. The shanties that grew near all the large cities were called "Hoovervilles." Unable to admit mistakes and take a new tack, he could not communicate personal empathy for the poor and the unemployed.

Dorothea Lange Photo—"Migrant Mother"

Hoover did try innovative schemes. More public works projects were built during his administration than in the previous 30 years. In the summer of 1931, he organized a pool of private money to rescue banks and businesses that were near failure. When that private effort failed, he turned reluctantly to Congress, which in 1932 authorized the Reconstruction Finance Corporation (RFC). It lent to banks, insurance companies, farm mortgage companies, and railroads. Some critics charged that it was simply a trickle-down measure while the unemployed were ignored. Hoover, however, understood the immense costs to individuals and communities when a bank or mortgage company failed. The RFC helped shore up shaky financial institutions and remained the major government finance agency until World War II.

Hoover also asked Congress for a Home Financing Corporation to make mortgages more readily available. The Federal Home Loan Bank Act of 1932 became the basis for the Federal Housing Administration of the New Deal years. He also pushed the passage of the Glass–Steagall Banking Act of 1932, which expanded credit in order to make more loans available to businesses and individuals.

But Hoover rejected calls for the federal government to restrict production in hopes of raising farm prices—that, he believed, was too much federal intervention. He firmly believed in loans, not direct subsidies, and he thought it was the responsibility of state and local governments, as well as private charity, to provide direct relief to the unemployed and the needy.

The Bonus Army

Many World War I veterans lost their jobs during the Great Depression; beginning in 1930, they lobbied for immediate payment of their veterans' bonuses that were due in 1945. In May 1932, about 17,000 veterans marched on Washington. Some took up residence in a shantytown, called Bonus City, outside town.

In mid-June, the Senate defeated the bonus bill, and most of the disappointed veterans accepted a free railroad ticket home. Several thousand remained, however, along with some wives and children, in the unsanitary shacks during the steaming summer heat. Among them were a few Communists and other radicals. Hoover, who exaggerated the subversive elements among those still camped out in Bonus City, refused to talk to the leaders, and finally called out the U.S. Army.

General Douglas MacArthur, the army chief of staff, ordered troops to disperse the veterans, "a mob," he said, "... animated by the essence of revolution." With tanks, guns, and tear gas, troops routed men who 15 years before had worn the same uniform. Two Bonus marchers died. Far from attacking revolutionaries in the streets of Washington, the army was routing bewildered, confused, unemployed men whose American dream had collapsed.

The Bonus army fiasco, breadlines, and shantytowns called Hoovervilles became the symbols of Hoover's presidency. He deserved better because he tried to use the power of the federal government to solve growing and increasingly complex economic problems. But his personality and background limited him. He could not understand why veterans marched on Washington to ask for a handout when they should be back home working hard, practicing self-reliance, and cooperating. He believed that the greatest problem besetting Americans was a lack of confidence. He could not communicate with these people or inspire their confidence. Willing to give federal support to business, he could not accept giving federal aid to the unemployed. He feared an unbalanced budget and a large federal bureaucracy that would interfere with the "American way." Ironically, his actions and inactions soon led to a massive increase in federal power and in federal bureaucracy.

ROOSEVELT AND THE FIRST NEW DEAL

DOCUMENT

Franklin D. Roosevelt, First Inaugural Address (1933)

The first New Deal, from 1933 to early 1935, focused mainly on recovery and relief for the poor and unemployed. Some of its programs were borrowed from the Hoover administration or from the progressive period. Others were inspired by the nation's experiences in mobilizing for World War I. No single ideological position united all the programs, for Roosevelt was a pragmatist who was willing to try different programs. More than Hoover, however, he believed in economic planning and in government spending to help the poor.

Roosevelt's caution and conservatism shaped the first New Deal. He did not promote socialism. The basic assumption of the New Deal was that a just society could be created by superimposing a welfare state on the capitalist system, leaving the profit motive in place. Roosevelt believed he could achieve this through cooperation with the business community. Later he would move toward reform, but at first his concern was primarily relief and recovery.

The Election of 1932

In the summer of 1932, the Republicans nominated Hoover for a second term, but the Depression and Hoover's unpopularity opened the way for the Democrats. Franklin D. Roosevelt won the nomination. Distantly related to Theodore Roosevelt, he had served as assistant secretary of the navy during World War I and was the Democratic vice presidential candidate in 1920. Crippled by polio not long after, he had recovered enough to serve as governor of New York for two terms. Despite his considerable experience, he was not especially well-known by the general public in 1932.

As governor, Roosevelt had promoted cheaper electric power, conservation, and old-age pensions, and he became the first governor to support state aid for the unemployed. But it was difficult to tell during the campaign exactly what he stood for. Ambiguity was probably the best strategy in 1932, but Roosevelt had no master plan to save the country. Yet he won overwhelmingly, carrying more than 57 percent of the popular vote.

During the campaign, Roosevelt had promised a "new deal for the American people." But the New Deal had to wait for four months, because the Constitution provided for presidents to be inaugurated on March 4. (This was changed to January 20 by the Twentieth Amendment, ratified in 1933.) During the long interregnum, the state of the nation deteriorated badly. The banking system was near collapse, and hardship increased. Despite his bitter defeat, Hoover tried to cooperate with the president-elect and a hostile Congress. But he could accomplish little. Everyone waited for the new president to take office.

In his inaugural address, Roosevelt announced confidently, "The only thing we have to fear is fear itself." This, of course, was not true: The country faced the worst crisis since the Civil War. But Roosevelt's confidence and ability to communicate with ordinary Americans were obvious early in his presidency. He had clever speechwriters, a sense of pace and rhythm in his speeches, and an ability, in his "fireside chats" on the radio, to convince listeners that he was speaking directly to them. When he said "my friends," millions believed that he meant it.

VIDEO

FDR's
Inauguration

Roosevelt's Advisers

During the interregnum, Roosevelt surrounded himself with intelligent and innovative advisers. His cabinet consisted of a mixture of people from different backgrounds who often did not agree with one another. Harold Ickes, the secretary of the interior, was a Republican lawyer from Chicago and onetime supporter of Theodore Roosevelt. Another Republican, Henry Wallace of Iowa, a plant geneticist and agricultural statistician, became the secretary of agriculture. Frances Perkins, the first woman ever appointed to a cabinet post, became the secretary of labor. A disciple of Jane Addams and Florence Kelley, she had been a settlement resident, the secretary of the New York Consumers League, and an adviser to Al Smith.

Besides the formal cabinet, Roosevelt had an informal "Brain Trust," including Adolph Berle, Jr., a young expert on corporation law, and Rexford Tugwell, a Columbia University authority on agricultural economics and a committed national planner. Roosevelt also listened to Raymond Moley, another Columbia professor who later became one of the president's severest critics, and to Harry Hopkins, a nervous, energetic man who loved to bet on horse races and was passionately concerned for the poor and unemployed.

Eleanor Roosevelt was a controversial first lady. She wrote a newspaper column, made radio broadcasts, traveled widely, and was constantly giving speeches and listening to the concerns of women, minorities, and ordinary Americans. Attacked by critics who thought she had too much power, she took courageous stands for social justice and civil rights, pushing the president toward social reform. Roosevelt was an adept politician. He was not well read, especially on economic matters, but he demonstrated that he could learn from his advisers and yet not be dominated by them. He took ideas, plans, and suggestions from conflicting sources and combined them. An improviser who once likened himself to a quarterback who called one play and, if it did not work, called a different one, Roosevelt was an optimist by nature. And he believed in action.

ONE HUNDRED DAYS

Congress was ready to pass almost any legislation that Roosevelt put before it. In three months, a bewildering number of bills were rushed through. Some were not well thought out, and some contradicted other bills. But many of these laws would have far-reaching implications for the relationship of government to society. Roosevelt was an opportunist, but unlike Hoover, he was willing to use direct government action against depression and unemployment. None of the bills passed during the first 100 days cured the Depression, but taken together, the "Hundred Days" were one of the most innovative periods in American political history.

The Banking Crisis

The most immediate problem Roosevelt faced was the banking crisis. Many banks had closed, and citizens were hoarding money and gold. Roosevelt immediately declared a four-day bank holiday. Three days later, an emergency session of Congress approved his action and within hours gave the president broad powers over financial transactions, prohibited the hoarding of gold, and allowed for the reopening of sound banks, sometimes with RFC loans.

Over the next few years, Congress gave the federal government more regulatory power over the stock market and over the process by which corporations issued stock. The Banking Act of 1933 strengthened the Federal Reserve System, established the Federal Deposit Insurance Corporation (FDIC), and insured individual deposits up to $5,000. Although the American Bankers Association opposed the plan, banks were soon attracting depositors by advertising that they were protected by government insurance.

The Democratic platform in 1932 called for reduced government spending and an end to Prohibition. Roosevelt moved quickly on both. The Economy Act, which passed easily, called for a 15 percent reduction in government salaries and a reorganization of federal agencies to save money. The bill also cut veterans' pensions, despite the protests of veterans' organizations. But other bills called for additional spending. The Beer-Wine Revenue Act legalized 3.2-percent-alcohol beer and light wines and levied a tax on both. The Twenty-First Amendment, ratified on December 5, 1933, repealed the Eighteenth Amendment and officially ended Prohibition.

Despite some opposition, Congress gave the president broad power to devalue the dollar and induce inflation. Bankers and businessmen feared inflation, but farmers and debtors favored some inflation to put more dollars in their pockets. Roosevelt rejected the more extreme inflationary plans of many congressmen from agricultural states, but he did take the country off the gold standard. No longer would paper currency be redeemable in gold. The action terrified some conservative businessmen, and even Roosevelt's director of the budget announced solemnly that it "meant the end of Western Civilization."

Devaluation neither ended Western civilization nor produced instant recovery. Roosevelt and his advisers fixed the price at $35 an ounce in January 1934 (against the old price of $20.63), inflating the dollar by about 40 percent. Soon the country settled down to a slightly inflated currency and a dollar based on both gold and silver.

Relief Measures

Roosevelt believed in economy in government and in a balanced budget, but he also wanted to help the unemployed and the homeless. One survey estimated that in 1933 1.5 million Americans were homeless. A man with a wife and six children who was being evicted wrote, "I have 10 days to get another house, no job, no means of paying rent, can you advise me as to which would be the most humane way to dispose of myself and family, as this is about the only thing that I see left to do."

Roosevelt's answer was the Federal Emergency Relief Administration (FERA), which Congress authorized with an appropriation of $500 million in direct grants to cities and states. A few months later, Roosevelt created a Civil Works Administration (CWA) to put more than 4 million people to work on various state, municipal, and federal projects. Hopkins, who ran both agencies, believed it was much better to pay people to work than to give them charity. So did most people in need. An accountant working on a road project said, "I'd rather stay out here in that ditch the rest of my life than take one cent of direct relief."

The CWA was not always effective, but in just over a year, it built or restored a half-million miles of roads and constructed 40,000 schools and 1,000 airports. It hired 50,000 teachers to keep rural schools open and others to teach adult education courses in the cities. The CWA helped millions of people get through the bitterly cold winter of 1933 to 1934. It also put over a billion dollars of purchasing power into the economy. Roosevelt, who later would be accused of deficit spending, feared that the program was costing too much and might create a permanent class of relief recipients. In the spring of 1934, he ordered the CWA closed down.

The Public Works Administration (PWA), directed by Harold Ickes, lasted longer. Between 1933 and 1939, the PWA built hospitals, courthouses, and school buildings. Its projects included the port of Brownsville, Texas, two aircraft carriers, and low-cost slum housing. One purpose of the PWA was economic pump priming—to stimulate the economy through government spending. Afraid of scandals, Ickes spent money slowly and carefully. And the PWA projects, worthwhile as most of them were, provided little economic stimulus.

The American Dream Margaret Bourke-White, one of the outstanding documentary photographers of the 1930s, captured the disjunction between the ideal and the real in the Depression era. This photograph, depicting African American flood victims lining up for food in Louisville, Kentucky, underneath a propaganda billboard erected by the National Association of Manufacturers, contrasts the American Dream with the reality of racism and poverty. Does this famous photograph depict the contrast in American life unfairly? *(Margaret Bourke-White/Time Life Picture Collection/Getty Images)*

Agricultural Adjustment Act

By 1933, most farmers were desperate, caught between mounting surpluses and falling prices. Some in the Midwest even talked of revolution. But most observers saw only despair in farmers who had worked hard but were still losing their farms.

Congress passed a number of bills in 1933 and 1934 to deal with the agricultural crisis, including foreclosures and evictions. But the New Deal's principal solution was the Agricultural Adjustment Act (AAA), which sought to control the overproduction of basic commodities so that farmers might regain their pre–World War I purchasing power. To guarantee these "parity prices" (the average prices in the years 1909 to 1914), the production of major agricultural staples—wheat, cotton, corn, hogs, rice, tobacco, and milk—would be controlled by paying the farmers to reduce their acreage under cultivation. The AAA levied a tax at the processing stage to pay for the program.

The act caused great disagreement among farm leaders and economists, but the controversy was nothing compared with the public outcry in the summer of 1933, when, to boost prices, the AAA ordered 10 million acres of cotton plowed up and 6 million young pigs slaughtered. It seemed immoral to kill pigs and plow up cotton when millions of people were hungry and ill-clothed.

The Agricultural Adjustment Act did raise the prices of some agricultural products. But it helped the larger farmers more than the small operators, and it was often disastrous for the tenant farmers and sharecroppers. When they reduced their acreage, landowners often discharged tenant families. Many were simply cast out on the road with nowhere to go. Large farmers cultivated their fewer acres more intensely, so that the total crop was little reduced. In the end, the prolonged drought that hit the Southwest in 1934 did more than the AAA to limit production and raise agricultural prices. But the long-range significance of the AAA, which was later declared unconstitutional, was to entrench the idea that the government should subsidize farmers for limiting production.

Industrial Recovery

The legislation during the first days of the Roosevelt administration contained something for almost every group. The National Industrial Recovery Act (NIRA) was designed to help business, raise prices, control production, and put people back to work. Its goal was to restrict competition, restrain profits, and produce labor-management harmony. The act established the National Recovery Administration (NRA), with the power to set fair competition codes in all industries. For a time, everyone forgot about antitrust laws and talked of cooperation. There were parades and rallies, a postage stamp, and "We Do Our Part" posters for cooperating industries. But the results were somewhat less than the promise.

Section 7a of the NIRA, included at labor unions' insistence, guaranteed labor's right to organize and to bargain collectively and established the National Labor Board to see that unions' rights were respected. But the board, usually dominated by businessmen, often interpreted the labor provisions of the contracts loosely. In addition, small businessmen complained that the NIRA was unfair to their interests. Any attempt to set prices led to controversy.

Many consumers suspected that the codes and contracts were raising prices, while others feared the return of monopoly. When the Supreme Court declared the NIRA unconstitutional in 1935, few complained. Still, the NIRA was an ambitious attempt to bring some order into a confused business situation, and its labor provisions were picked up later by the National Labor Relations Act.

Civilian Conservation Corps

One of the most popular and successful New Deal programs, the Civilian Conservation Corps (CCC), combined work relief with the preservation of natural resources. It put young, unemployed men between the ages of 17 and 25—2.5 million of them—to work on reforestation, road and park construction, flood control, and other projects. The men lived in work camps and earned $30 a month, $25 of which had to be sent home to their families.

The CCC ran separate camps for young black men, and eventually a few camps were organized for unemployed young women, but the program was designed to help unemployed young men. Some complained that the camps were

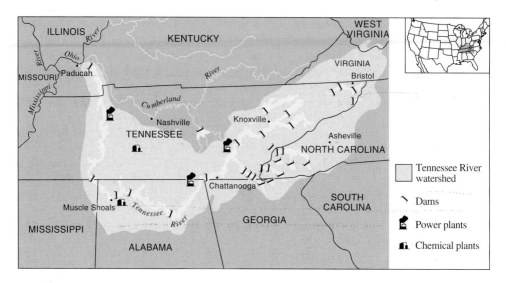

THE TENNESSEE VALLEY AUTHORITY The TVA transformed the way the Tennessee valley looked; it replaced a wild river with a series of flood-control and hydroelectric dams and created a series of lakes behind the dams. It stopped short of the coordinated regional planning that some people wanted, but it was one of the most important New Deal projects, as it had an impact on portions of seven states.

too military in their organization. Despite complaints, the CCC was one of the most successful and least controversial of all the New Deal programs.

Tennessee Valley Authority

DOCUMENT

Tennessee Valley Authority Act

FDR, like TR, believed in conservation. He promoted flood-control projects and added millions of acres to the country's national forests, wildlife refuges, and fish and game sanctuaries. But the most important New Deal conservation project, the Tennessee Valley Authority (TVA), owed more to Republican George Norris, a progressive senator from Nebraska, than to Roosevelt.

During World War I, the federal government had built a hydroelectric plant and two munitions factories at Muscle Shoals, on the Tennessee River in Alabama.

MAP

The Tennessee Valley Authority

The government tried unsuccessfully to sell these facilities to private industry, but all through the 1920s, Norris campaigned to have the federal government operate them for the benefit of the valley's residents. Twice Republican presidents vetoed bills providing for federal operation, but Roosevelt endorsed Norris's idea and expanded it into a regional development plan.

Congress authorized the TVA as an independent public corporation to sell electricity and fertilizer and to promote flood control and land reclamation. The TVA built nine major dams and many minor ones between 1933 and 1944, affecting parts of Virginia, North Carolina, Georgia, Alabama, Mississippi, Tennessee, and Kentucky. Some private utility companies claimed that the TVA unfairly competed with private industry, but it was an imaginative experiment in regional planning. For residents of the valley, it meant cheaper electricity and changed lifestyles. The largest federal construction project ever launched, it also created jobs for many thousands who helped build the dams. But government officials and businessmen who feared that the experiment would lead to socialism curbed the regional planning possibilities of the TVA.

Critics of the New Deal

The furious legislative activity during the first 100 days of the New Deal helped alleviate the country's pessimism and despair. The stock market rose slightly, and industrial production was up 11 percent at the end of 1933. Still, the country remained locked in depression, and nearly 12 million Americans lacked jobs.

Roosevelt captured the imagination of ordinary Americans everywhere, but conservatives became increasingly angry. Many businessmen, after being impressed with Roosevelt's early economy measures and approving programs such as the NIRA, began to fear that the president was leading the country toward socialism.

The conservative revolt against Roosevelt surfaced in the summer of 1934 as the congressional elections approached. A group of disgruntled politicians and businessmen formed the Liberty League. Led by Alfred E. Smith and John W. Davis, the league supported conservative or at least anti–New Deal candidates for Congress, but it had little influence. In the election of 1934, the Democrats increased their majority from 310 to 319 in the House and from 60 to 69 in the Senate (only the second time in the twentieth century that the party in power had increased its control of Congress in the midterm election). A few people were learning to hate "that man in the White House," but most Americans approved of what he was doing.

But what Roosevelt and his advisers found much more disturbing in 1934 and 1935 than people who thought the New Deal too radical were those on the left who maintained that the government had not done enough to help the poor. The Communist party increased its membership from 7,500 in 1930 to 75,000 in 1938. Communists organized protest marches and tried to reach out to the oppressed and unemployed. While a majority who joined the party came from the working class, communism had a special appeal to writers, intellectuals, and some college students during a decade when the American dream had turned into a nightmare.

More Americans, however, were influenced by other movements promising easy solutions. In Minnesota, Governor Floyd Olson accused capitalism of causing the Depression and thundered, "I hope the present system of government goes right to hell." In California, Upton Sinclair, the muckraking socialist and author of *The Jungle,* ran for governor on the EPIC platform ("End Poverty in California"). He promised to pay everyone over 60 years of age a pension of $50 a month, financed by higher income and inheritance taxes. He won the primary but lost the election, and his movement collapsed.

California also produced Dr. Francis E. Townsend, who claimed a national following of over 5 million. His supporters backed a scheme that promised $200 a month to all unemployed citizens over age 60 on the condition that they spend it in the same month they received it. Economists laughed, but followers organized thousands of Townsend Pension Clubs.

DOCUMENT

Father Charles E. Coughlin, "A Third Party" (1936)

More threatening to Roosevelt and the New Deal were the protest movements led by Father Charles E. Coughlin and Senator Huey P. Long. Father Coughlin, a Roman Catholic priest from a Detroit suburb, attracted an audience of 30 million to 45 million to his national radio show. At first he supported Roosevelt's policies, but later he savagely attacked the New Deal as excessively pro-business. Mixing religious commentary with visions of a society without bankers and big businessmen, he roused his audience with blatantly anti-Semitic tirades.

DOCUMENT

Huey Long, "Share Our Wealth" (1935)

Like Coughlin, Huey Long had a charisma that won support from the millions still trying to survive in a country where the continuing Depression made day-to-day existence a struggle. Elected governor of Louisiana in 1928, Long called his program "Share Our Wealth." He taxed the oil refineries and built hospitals, schools, and thousands of miles of new highways. By 1934, he was the virtual dictator of his state, personally controlling the police and the courts. Long talked about a guaranteed $2,000 to $3,000 income for all American families (18.3 million families earned less than $1,000 per year in 1936) and promised pensions for the elderly and college educations for the young, all to be paid for by soaking the rich. Had an assassin not killed Long in September 1935, he might have mounted a third-party challenge to Roosevelt.

THE SECOND NEW DEAL

Responding in part to lower-middle-class discontent but also to head off utopian schemes, Roosevelt moved his programs in 1935 toward the goals of social reform and social justice. At the same time, he ceased trying to cooperate with the business community. "In spite of our efforts and in spite of our talk, we have not weeded out the overprivileged and we have not effectively lifted up the underprivileged," Roosevelt announced in his annual message to Congress in January 1935.

Work Relief and Social Security

IMAGE

WPA's Federal Art Project

The Works Progress Administration (WPA), authorized by Congress in April 1935, was the first massive attempt to deal with unemployment and its demoralizing effect on millions of Americans. The WPA employed about 3 million people a year (at wages below what private industry paid) on projects ranging from bridges to libraries. It built nearly 6,000 schools, more than 2,500 hospitals, and 13,000 playgrounds. Nearly 85 percent of its funds went directly to workers. A minor but important part of its funding supported writers, artists, actors, and musicians.

Only one member of a family could get a WPA job—always a man unless a woman headed the household. But eventually more than 13 percent of the people who worked for the WPA were women, usually making over old clothes. "For unskilled men we have the shovel. For unskilled women we have only the needle," one official explained.

The WPA was controversial from the beginning. Its initials, critics said, stood for "We Putter Around." Yet the WPA not only did useful work but also gave millions of unemployed Americans a sense that they were working and supporting their families.

The National Youth Administration (NYA) supplemented the work of the WPA and assisted young men and women between the ages of 16 and 25 (including Richard Nixon, a young law student at Duke University). Lyndon Johnson began his political career as director of the Texas NYA.

DOCUMENT

Frances Perkins and the Social Security Act (1935, 1960)

By far the most enduring reform was the passage of the Social Security Act of 1935. Since the progressive period, reformers had argued for national health and unemployment insurance and old-age pensions. By the 1930s, the United States was the only major industrial country without them. Secretary of Labor Perkins argued most strongly for social insurance, but Roosevelt also wanted to head off popular schemes like the Townsend Plan.

The Social Security Act of 1935 was a compromise. To appease the medical profession, Congress quickly dropped a plan for federal health insurance. The act's central provision was old-age and survivor insurance, paid for by a tax of 1 percent on both employers and employees. The act also established a cooperative federal-state system of unemployment compensation, gave federal grants to the states for the disabled and the blind, and provided aid to dependent children—the provision that years later expanded to become the largest federal welfare program.

Conservatives denounced Social Security for regimenting people and destroying self-reliance. But in no other country was social insurance paid for in part by a regressive tax on the workers' wages. "With those taxes in there, no damn politician can ever scrap my Social Security program," Roosevelt later explained, insisting that by paying the taxes wage earners won a moral claim on their benefits. But farm laborers and domestic servants were not covered. The system discriminated against married women wage earners and failed to protect against sickness. Still, it was one of the most important New Deal measures, and it marked the beginning of the welfare state that would expand greatly after World War II.

Aiding the Farmers

The Social Security Act and the Works Progress Administration were only two signs of Roosevelt's greater concern for social reform. The flurry of legislation in 1935 and early 1936, often called the "second New Deal," also included an effort to help American farmers. The Resettlement Administration (RA), motivated in part by a Jeffersonian ideal of yeoman farmers working their own land, tried to relocate tenant farmers to land purchased by the government. But it failed to accomplish much, a victim of underfunding and of scare talk about Soviet-style collective farms.

Much more important in improving the lives of farm families was the Rural Electrification Administration (REA), which was authorized in 1935 to lend money to cooperatives to generate and distribute electricity in isolated rural areas not served by private utilities. Only 10 percent of the nation's farms had electricity in 1936. When the REA's lines were finally attached, they dramatically changed the lives of millions of farm families who had only been able to dream about the radios, washing machines, and farm equipment advertised in magazines.

The Dust Bowl: An Ecological Disaster

Those who tried to farm on the Great Plains fell victim to years of drought and dust storms, as record heat waves and below-average rainfall in the 1930s turned the Oklahoma panhandle and western Kansas into a giant dust bowl. Thousands died of "dust pneumonia." By the end of the decade, 10,000 farm homes were abandoned, 9 million acres of farmland were reduced to wasteland, and 3.5 million people had joined a massive migration to find a better life. Many tenant farmers and hired hands were evicted, their plight immortalized by John Steinbeck in his novel *The Grapes of Wrath* (1939).

The dust bowl was a natural disaster, aided and exaggerated by human actions. The semiarid plains west of the 98th meridian were not suitable for intensive agriculture, and 60 years of improper land use had exposed the thin soil to the elements. When the winds came, much of the land simply blew away. In the end, it was a matter of too little government planning and regulation and too many farmers using new technology to exploit nature. The Roosevelt administration did try to deal with the problem. The Taylor Grazing Act of 1934 restricted the use of the public range and established the principle that the remaining public domain was not for sale. The CCC planted trees and promoted soil conservation, but in the end it was too little and too late.

Even worse, according to some authorities, government measures applied after the disaster of the 1930s encouraged farmers to return to raising wheat and other inappropriate crops, leading to more dust bowl crises in the 1950s and 1970s.

The New Deal and the West

The New Deal probably aided the West more than any other region. The CCC, the AAA, drought relief measures, and various federal agencies helped the region out of proportion to the number of people who lived there. Most important were the large-scale water projects, such as Boulder Dam (later renamed Hoover Dam) on the Colorado River and (the largest of all) Grand Coulee Dam on the Columbia River. These dams produced massive amounts of hydroelectric power, poured millions of dollars into the economy, and provided enormous amounts of water for cities and irrigation.

Despite all the federal aid to the region, many westerners bitterly criticized the regulation and the bureaucracy that came with the grants. The cattlemen in Wyoming, Colorado, and Montana desperately needed the help of the federal government, but even as they accepted the aid, they denounced the New Deal.

Controlling Corporate Power and Taxing the Wealthy

In the summer of 1935, Roosevelt set out to control the large corporations, and he even toyed with radical plans to tax the well-to-do heavily and redistribute wealth in the United States. The Public Utility Holding Company Act, passed in 1935, attempted to restrict the power of the giant utility companies, the 12 largest of which

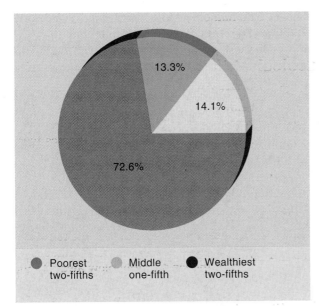

13.3%

14.1%

72.6%

● Poorest two-fifths ● Middle one-fifth ● Wealthiest two-fifths

DISTRIBUTION OF INCOME, 1935–1936 Roosevelt and the New Deal never sought consistently to redistribute wealth in America, and a great disparity in income and assets remained. *(Source: U.S. Bureau of the Census)*

controlled more than half the country's power. It gave each company five years to demonstrate that its services were efficient or face being dissolved. This was one of the most radical attempts to control corporate power in American history.

In the same year, Roosevelt urged higher taxes on the rich and a heavy inheritance tax. When Congress dropped the inheritance tax provision, however, Roosevelt did not fight for it. Even the weakened bill angered many in the business community who thought that FDR had sold out to Huey Long's "Share the Wealth" scheme.

The New Deal for Labor

Like many progressive reformers, Roosevelt was more interested in helping working people by social legislation than by strengthening unions. Yet he saw labor as an important balance to the power of industry, and he listened to his advisers, especially to Frances Perkins and to Senator Robert Wagner of New York, who persistently brought up the needs of organized labor.

Roosevelt supported the 1935 Wagner Act (officially the National Labor Relations Act), which outlawed blacklisting and a number of other practices and reasserted labor's right to organize and to bargain collectively. The act also established a Labor Relations Board with the power to certify a properly elected bargaining unit. The act did not require workers to join unions, but it made the federal government a regulator in management-labor relations. That alone made the National Labor Relations Act one of the most important New Deal reform measures.

The Roosevelt administration's friendly attitude helped increase union membership from under 3 million in 1933 to 4.5 million by 1935. Many groups, however, were left out, including farm laborers, unskilled workers, and women. Only about 3 percent of working women belonged to unions, and they earned only about 60 percent of wages paid to men for equivalent work. Still, many resented the women being employed at all. One writer had a perfect solution for unemployment: "Simply fire the women, who shouldn't be working anyway, and hire the men."

The AFL had never organized unskilled workers, but a new group of committed and militant labor leaders emerged in the 1930s to take up that task: John L. Lewis of the United Mine Workers, David Dubinsky of the International Ladies' Garment Workers, and Sidney Hillman of the Amalgamated Clothing Workers. The latter two were socialists who believed in economic planning and had worked closely with social justice progressives. These new progressive labor leaders formed the Committee of Industrial Organization (CIO) within the AFL and set out to organize workers in the steel, auto, and rubber industries. Rather than separating workers by skill or craft as the AFL preferred, they organized industrywide unions.

In 1936, the workers at three rubber plants in Akron, Ohio, went on unauthorized strikes. Instead of picketing, they took over the buildings. The "sit-down strike" became a new protest technique, disorderly but largely nonviolent (as would be civil rights demonstrations in the 1960s). After several such strikes, General Motors finally accepted the United Auto Workers (UAW) as their employees' bargaining agent. The GM strike was the most important event in a critical period of labor upheaval. Labor's voice now began to be heard in the decision-making process in major industries where labor had long been denied any role, raising the status of organized labor in the eyes of many Americans.

Violence spread along with the sit-down strikes. Chrysler capitulated, but Ford fought back with armed guards, and it took a bloody struggle before the UAW was accepted as the bargaining agent. Militantly anti-union U.S. Steel agreed to a 40-hour week and an eight-hour day, but other steel companies refused to go along. In the "Memorial Day Massacre" in 1937, police fired into a crowd of workers and their families peacefully picketing the Republic Steel plant in Chicago. All 10 who died were shot in the back.

The CIO's aggressive tactics gained many members, to the horror of AFL leaders. They expelled the CIO leaders, only to see them form a separate Congress of Industrial Organization (the initials stayed the same). Accepting unskilled workers, African Americans, and others who had never belonged to a union before, the CIO created a new spirit of optimism in the labor movement.

America's Minorities in the 1930s

A half-million African Americans joined unions through the CIO, and New Deal agencies aided many blacks. Yet familiar patterns of poverty, discrimination, and violence persisted. Lynchings in the South also increased in the New Deal years.

Throughout the decade, the nation was gripped by the "Scottsboro Boys" case in Alabama, which began in 1931 when two young white women accused nine black youths of rape. Convicted and condemned to death by an all-white jury, the blacks were given a new trial in 1933 by order of the Supreme Court on the grounds that they had not received proper legal counsel. Liberals and radicals (including the Communist party) mobilized in defense of the youths' civil rights, while many from the South saw the honor of white women at stake. Evidence supporting the alleged rapes was never presented, and eventually one of the women recanted. Yet in new trials, five of the young men were convicted and given long prison terms. Charges against the other four were dropped in 1937. Four of the remaining five were paroled in 1944, and the fifth escaped to Michigan.

The migration of blacks to northern cities, which had accelerated during World War I, continued during the 1930s. The collapse of cotton prices forced black farmers and farm laborers to flee north for survival. But since most were poorly educated, they soon became trapped in northern ghettos, where they got only the most menial jobs. The black unemployment rate was triple that of whites, and blacks often received less per person in welfare payments.

Black leaders attacked the Roosevelt administration for supporting or allowing segregation in government-sponsored facilities. Roosevelt, dependent on the vote of the South and afraid to antagonize powerful southern congressmen, refused to support the two major civil rights bills of the era: an anti-lynching bill and a bill to abolish the poll tax. Yet Ickes and Hopkins worked to ensure that blacks were given opportunities in New Deal agencies. By 1941, black federal employees totaled 150,000, more than three times the number during the Hoover administration. Most worked in the lower ranks, but some were lawyers, architects, office managers, and engineers.

VIDEO

Jesse Owens and the 1936 Olympics

Partly responsible for the presence of more black employees was the "black cabinet," a group of more than 50 young blacks working in various New Deal agencies and led by Mary McLeod Bethune, the daughter of a sharecropper and organizer of the National Council of Negro Women. She had a large impact on New Deal policy—speaking out forcefully, picketing and protesting, and intervening shrewdly to obtain civil rights and more jobs for African Americans.

Although FDR appointed some blacks to government positions, he was never particularly committed to civil rights. That was not true of Eleanor Roosevelt, who was educated in part by Bethune. In 1939, when the Daughters of the American Revolution denied black concert singer Marian Anderson their stage, the First Lady protested by resigning her DAR membership and arranged for Anderson to sing from the steps of the Lincoln Memorial before an audience of 75,000.

Hundreds of thousands of Mexicans, brought to the United States for work in the 1920s, lost their jobs in the Depression. Drifting to the Southwest or settling in urban *barrios*, they met signs like "No Niggers, Mexicans, or Dogs Allowed." Some New Deal agencies helped destitute Mexicans, but as aliens and migrants, most could not qualify for relief. The preferred solution was to ship them back to Mexico, often after illegal roundups. One estimate placed the number sent back in 1932 at 200,000, which included some American citizens. But some who remained adopted militant tactics to obtain fair treatment.

Asians (Chinese, Japanese, and a smaller number of Koreans and Asian Indians) also suffered during the Depression. Most lived in ethnic enclaves and were treated like foreigners—not quite black, but not white either. The second generation were troubled by their "twoness." They were American citizens because they had been born in the United States, but their parents wanted them to retain their ties to the old country. One young Japanese woman wrote: "I became equally adept with knife and fork and with chopsticks. I said grace at mealtime in Japanese, and recited the Lord's Prayer in English." But to most Americans, who had difficulty distinguishing Japanese from Chinese from Korean, they were all foreigners.

By the 1930s, Native American hunger, disease, and despair had been compounded by years of exploitation. Native Americans had lost over 60 percent of the 138 million acres allocated to them under the Dawes Act in 1887 (see Chapter 17), and many who remained on the reservations were not even citizens. In 1924, Congress granted citizenship to all Indians born in the United States, but that did not end their suffering.

FDR brought a new spirit to Indian policy by appointing John Collier as commissioner of Indian affairs. Collier was primarily responsible for passage of the Indian Reorganization Act of 1934, which sought to restore tribes' political independence, to end the Dawes Act's allotment policy, and to promote the "study of Indian civilization." Not all Indians agreed with the new policies. Some Americans charged that the act was inspired by communism or would increase government bureaucracy, while missionaries claimed that the government was promoting paganism.

The paradox of U.S. policy toward the Indians can be illustrated by Collier's attempt to solve the Navajo problem. The Navajo lands, like most of the West, were overgrazed, and soil erosion threatened to fill the new lake behind Hoover Dam with silt. By supporting a policy of reducing the herds of sheep and goats on Indian land and by promoting soil conservation, Collier contributed to the change in the Navajo lifestyle and to the end of their self-sufficiency, something his other policies supported.

Women and the New Deal

Women made some gains during the 1930s, and more women occupied high government positions than in any previous administration. Some of these women had collaborated as social workers and now joined government bureaus to continue the fight for social justice. But they were usually in offices where they did not threaten male prerogatives. Despite some gains, the early New Deal programs did nothing for an estimated 140,000 homeless women. Married women were often fired from their jobs on the grounds that they should be home caring for their families rather than depriving men of employment.

Despite the number of women working for the government, feminism declined in the 1930s. The older feminists died or retired, and younger women did not replace them. Despite some dramatic exceptions, the image of a woman's proper role in the 1930s continued to be that of a housewife and mother.

THE LAST YEARS OF THE NEW DEAL

The New Deal was not a consistent or well-organized effort to end the Depression and restructure society. A pragmatic politician, Roosevelt was unconcerned about ideological or programmatic consistency. The first New Deal in 1933 and 1934 had concentrated on relief and recovery; the legislation of 1935 and 1936 stressed social reform. In many ways, the election of 1936 marked the high point of Roosevelt's power and influence. After 1937, in part because of the growing threat of war but also because of increasing opposition in Congress, the pace of social legislation slowed. Yet several measures passed in 1937 and 1938 had such far-reaching significance that some historians refer to a third New Deal.

The Election of 1936

The Republicans in 1936 nominated a moderate, Governor Alfred Landon of Kansas. Although he attacked the New Deal, charging it with waste and too much bureaucracy, Landon promised to do the same thing more efficiently. The *Literary Digest* magazine predicted his victory on the basis of its "scientific" telephone poll.

Roosevelt, helped by signs of economic recovery and supported by a coalition of the Democratic South, organized labor, farmers, and urban voters, won easily. For the first time, a majority of African Americans deserted the GOP—"the party of Lincoln"—out of appreciation for New Deal relief programs. No viable candidate to the left of the New Deal materialized. Winning by over 10 million votes and carrying every state except Maine and Vermont, Roosevelt now had a mandate to continue his New Deal reforms.

The Battle of the Supreme Court

"I see one-third of a nation ill-housed, ill-clad, ill-nourished," Roosevelt declared in his second inaugural address, and he vowed to alter it. But the president's first action in 1937 was a plan to reform the federal judiciary and the Supreme Court, whose "nine old men" had struck down various important New Deal measures.

To create a more sympathetic Court, FDR asked for power to appoint an extra justice for each of the six justices over 70 years of age. He also called for modernizing the court system at all levels, but that plan got lost in the public outcry over "court-packing."

Roosevelt's plan foundered. Republicans accused him of subverting the Constitution. Many congressmen from his own party refused to support him. Led by Vice President John Nance Garner of Texas, a number of southern Democrats broke with the president and formed a coalition with conservative Republicans that lasted for more than 30 years. Finally Roosevelt admitted defeat. He had perhaps misunderstood his mandate, and he certainly underestimated the respect, even reverence, that most Americans felt for the Supreme Court. Even amid economic catastrophe, Americans proved themselves fundamentally conservative toward their institutions.

Ironically, though he lost the battle of the Supreme Court, Roosevelt won the war. By the spring of 1937, the Court began to reverse its position and in a 5–4 decision upheld the National Labor Relations Act. When a conservative justice retired, Roosevelt made his first Supreme Court appointment, thus ensuring at least a shaky liberal majority on the Court. But Roosevelt triumphed at great cost. His attempt to reorganize the Court slowed the momentum of his legislative program. The most unpopular action he took as president, it made him vulnerable to criticism from New Deal opponents, and even some of his supporters were dismayed by what they regarded as an attack on the separation of powers.

In late 1936 and early 1937, recovery from the Depression seemed real: employment was up, and even the stock market had recovered some of its losses. But in August, the fragile prosperity collapsed. Unemployment increased nearly to the peak levels of 1934, industrial production fell, and Wall Street plummeted. A believer in balanced budgets, Roosevelt had cut federal spending and reduced outlays for relief. Now, facing an embarrassing economic slump and charges that the New Deal had failed, he gave in to those of his advisers who were followers of British economist John Maynard Keynes.

Keynes argued that to get out of a depression, the government must spend massively on goods and services. This would spur demand and revive production. By increasing appropriations for the WPA and other agencies, the Roosevelt administration consciously incurred a deficit for the first time in order to stimulate consumption and production. But the economy responded slowly, never fully recovering until wartime expenditures, beginning in 1940, eliminated unemployment and ended the Depression.

The Third New Deal

Despite increasing hostility, Congress passed a number of important bills in 1937 and 1938 that completed the New Deal reform legislation. The Bankhead-Jones Farm Tenancy Act of 1937 created the Farm Security Administration (FSA) to aid tenant farmers, sharecroppers, and owners who had lost their farms. The FSA, which provided loans to grain collectives, also set up camps for migratory workers. But the FSA never had enough money to make a real difference.

Congress passed a new Agricultural Adjustment Act in 1938 that tried to solve the problem of farm surpluses by controlling production. Under the new act, the federal treasury made direct payments to farmers. It introduced a soil conservation program and tried to market surplus crops. But only the outbreak of World War II would end the problem of farm surplus—temporarily.

A shortage of urban housing continued to be a problem. Reformers who had worked in the first experiment with federal housing during World War I convinced FDR that federal low-cost housing should be part of New Deal reform. The National Housing Act of 1937 provided federal funds for slum clearance projects and the construction of low-cost housing. By 1939, however, only 117,000 units had been built—mostly bleak, boxlike structures that soon became a problem rather than a solution.

New Deal housing legislation had a greater impact on middle-class housing policies and patterns. During the first 100 days of the New Deal, Congress created the Home Owners Loan Corporation (HOLC) at Roosevelt's urging, which over the next two years made more than $3 billion in low-interest loans and helped over a million people save their homes from foreclosure. The HOLC also had a strong impact on housing policy by introducing the first long-term fixed-rate mortgages. (Formerly, mortgages ran no longer than five years and were subject to frequent renegotiation.) The HOLC also introduced a uniform system of real estate appraisal that tended to undervalue urban property, especially in old, crowded, and ethnically mixed neighborhoods. The system gave the highest ratings to suburban developments in which the HOLC determined there had been no "infiltration of Jews"—the beginning of the practice later called "redlining" that made it nearly impossible for certain prospective homeowners to obtain a mortgage.

The Federal Housing Administration (FHA), created in 1934 by the National Housing Act, expanded and extended many HOLC policies. The FHA-insured mortgages, many of them for 25 or 30 years, reduced the minimum down payment from 30 percent to under 10 percent and allowed over 11 million families to buy homes between 1934 and 1972. It also tended to favor purchasing new suburban homes rather than repairing older urban residences.

An equally important reform measure was the Fair Labor Standards Act, passed in June 1938. Roosevelt's bill proposed for all industries engaged in interstate commerce a minimum wage of 25 cents an hour and a maximum workweek of 44 hours. Despite congressional watering down, when the act went into effect, 750,000 workers immediately got raises, and by 1940, some 12 million had them. The law also barred child labor in interstate commerce, making it the first permanent federal law to prohibit youngsters under 16 from working. And the law made no distinction between men and women, thus diminishing the need for special legislation for women.

The New Deal had many weaknesses, but it did dramatically increase government support for the needy. In 1913, local, state, and federal government spent $21 million on public assistance. By 1932, that had risen to $218 million; by 1939, it was $4.9 billion.

THE OTHER SIDE OF THE 1930S

The Great Depression and the New Deal so dominate the history of the 1930s that it is easy to conclude that there were only breadlines and relief agencies. But there is another side of the decade. A communications revolution changed the lives of middle-class Americans. The sale of radios and attendance at movies increased during the 1930s, and literature flourished. Americans were fascinated by technology, especially automobiles. Many people traveled and looked ahead to a brighter future of streamlined appliances and gadgets that would mean a better life.

Taking to the Road

"People give up everything in the world but their car," a banker in Muncie, Indiana, remarked during the Depression, and that seems to have been true all over the country. Although automobile production dropped off after 1929 and did not recover until the end of the 1930s, the number of motor vehicles registered, which declined from 26.7 million in 1930 to just over 24 million in 1933, increased to over 32 million by 1940. Even the "Okies" fled the dust bowl of the Southwest in cars—secondhand, run-down ones, to be sure, but Europeans were shocked that in America even the poor owned cars.

A Streamlined Age The age of the Great Depression was also a time of modern, streamlined design. There were streamlined trains, cars, and planes. There were even streamlined refrigerators, radios, and pencil sharpeners. The 1939 New York World's Fair was marked by modern design and exhibits that depicted a streamlined future based on technology. Even during the nation's greatest economic crisis, some Americans planned for a better future. How do you explain the irony of looking ahead to a streamlined future during a decade of despair? *(Underwood & Underwood/Corbis)*

The American middle class traveled at an increasing rate after the low point of 1932 and 1933. In 1938, the tourist industry was the third largest in the United States, behind only steel and automobile production.

The Electric Home

If the 1920s was the age of the bathroom, the 1930s was the era of the modern kitchen. In 1930, the number of electric refrigerators that were produced exceeded the number of iceboxes for the first time, and refrigerator production peaked at 2.3 million in 1937. At first, the refrigerator looked like an icebox with a motor on top. In 1935, however, the refrigerator, like most other appliances, became streamlined. The Sears Coldspot, which quickly influenced the look of all other models, was designed by Raymond Loewy. He was one of a group of industrial designers who emphasized sweeping horizontal lines and rounded corners.

Streamlining became the symbol of modern civilization in the 1930s. At the end of the decade, in 1939, the World's Fair in New York glorified the streamlined technology of the future. This reverence for progress contrasted with the economic despair in the 1930s, but people adapted to it selectively. The electric washing machine and electric iron revolutionized washday—but Monday continued to be washday and Tuesday ironing day.

HOW OTHERS SEE US

Georges Duhamel, A French Writer Visits the United States and Finds Nothing to Admire

Georges Duhamel, a French novelist, traveled in the United States at the beginning of the Great Depression. He used Chicago to symbolize all that he disliked about America. As much as he hated everything he saw, he feared that American culture was going to spread around the world.

O painters, my friends and brothers, you can never make anything of Chicago! You will never paint this world, for it is beyond the human grasp. Chicago is no more paintable than the desert. It is prodigious and untamed; it is not a living thing....

America is devoted to its ephemeral works. It erects, not monuments, but merely buildings. Should it fall into ruins tomorrow, we should seek in its ashes in vain for the bronze statuette that is enough to immortalize a little Greek village. Ruins of Chicago!—prodigious heap of iron-work, concrete, and old plaster, the sole beauty of which will be gay plants and moss—I evoke you with horror and weariness of spirit....

In that ridiculous moral atmosphere in which swarms not a great nation, but a confusion of races, how can one possibly find that sublime serenity which art must have if it is to quicken and flower ...? North America, which has not inspired painters—which has not raised up any sculptors, which has prompted the song of no musicians, unless it be that of the monotonous Negro, and whose barbarously industrial architecture seems to care not at all for the judgment of future times, has yet produced poets and writers. Almost all of them—oh mockery!—have turned from their native soil, in bitterness of spirit....

But to paint Chicago? How can one do it with mere words or colors? Music alone, it seems to me, could accomplish the task. And rather than any imitative rhythm, soon lost in this tumult, it should be bitter chords, a heavy prelude to chaos.

- *Is Duhamel's criticism fair?*
- *Is it perhaps influenced by the time he visited?*
- *Is this kind of attack (that the United States has no culture, no tradition) still common among European visitors?*

Ironically, despite these new conveniences, a great many middle-class families maintained their standard of living during the 1930s only because the women in the family learned to stretch and save and make do, and most wives spent as much time on housework as before. Some also took jobs outside the home to maintain their level of consumption. The number of married women who worked increased substantially during the decade.

The Age of Leisure

During the Depression, many middle-class people found themselves with time on their hands. The 1920s had been a time of spectator sports watched by huge crowds. Those sports continued during the Depression decade, although attendance suffered. Cheap forms of entertainment like softball and miniature golf also

RECOVERING THE PAST

Just as some historians have used fiction to help define the cultural history of a decade, others in the twentieth century have turned to film to describe the "spirit of an age." On an elementary level, the movies help us appreciate changing styles in dress, furniture, and automobiles. We can even get some sense of how a particular time defined a beautiful woman or a handsome man, and we can learn about ethnic and racial stereotypes and assumptions about gender and class.

The decade of the 1930s is sometimes called the "golden age of the movies." Careful selection among the 500 or so feature films Hollywood produced each year during the decade—ranging from gangster and cowboy movies to Marx Brothers comedies, from historical romances to Busby Berkeley musical extravaganzas—could support a number of interpretations about the special myths and assumptions of the Depression era. But one historian has argued that especially after 1934, "Not only did the movies amuse and entertain the nation through its most severe economic and social disorder, holding it together by their capacity to create unifying myths and dreams, but movie culture in the 1930s became a dominant culture for many Americans, providing new values and social ideas to replace shattered old traditions."

The year 1934 was a dividing line for two reasons. The motion picture industry, like all other industries, had suffered during the Depression; 1933 marked the low point in attendance, with more than a third of the theaters in the country shut down. The next year, however, attendance picked up, heralding a revival that lasted until 1946. Also in 1934, the movie industry adopted a code for which the Catholic Legion of Decency and other religious groups had lobbied. The new code prohibited the depiction of "sex perversion, interracial sex, abortion, incest, drugs and profanity." Even married couples could not be shown together in a double bed. Although a movie could depict immoral behavior, sin always had to be punished. "Evil and good should never be confused," the code announced.

Before the code, Hollywood had indeed produced graphic films, such as *The Public Enemy* (1931) and *Scarface* (1932), with a considerable amount of violence; musicals, such as *Gold Diggers of 1933* (1933), filled with scantily clad young women; films featuring prostitutes, such as Jean Harlow in *Red Dust* (1932) and Marlene Dietrich in *Blond Venus* (1930); and other films that confronted the problems of real life. But after 1934, Hollywood concentrated on movies that created a mythical world where evil was always punished, family moral values won out in the end, and patriotism and American democracy were never questioned. Although the code was modified from time to time, it was not abandoned until 1966, when it was replaced by a rating system.

It Happened One Night (1934) and *Drums Along the Mohawk* (1939), two films out of thousands, illustrate some of the myths the movies created and sustained. Frank Capra, one of Hollywood's masters at entertaining without disturbing, directed *It Happened One Night*, a comedy-romance. A rich girl, played by Claudette Colbert, dives from her father's yacht off the coast of Florida and takes a bus for New York. She meets a newspaper reporter, played by Clark Gable, and they have a series of madcap adventures and fall in love. But mix-ups and misunderstandings make it appear that she will marry her old boyfriend. In the end, however, they are reunited and marry in an elaborate outdoor ceremony. Afterward, they presumably live happily ever after. The movie is funny and entertaining and presents a variation on the poor-boy-marries-rich-girl theme. Like so many movies of the time, this one suggests that life is fulfilled for a woman only if she can find the right man to marry.

Claudette Colbert also stars in *Drums Along the Mohawk*, this time with Henry Fonda. Based on a 1936 novel by Walter Edmonds, *Drums* is a sentimental story about a man who builds a house in

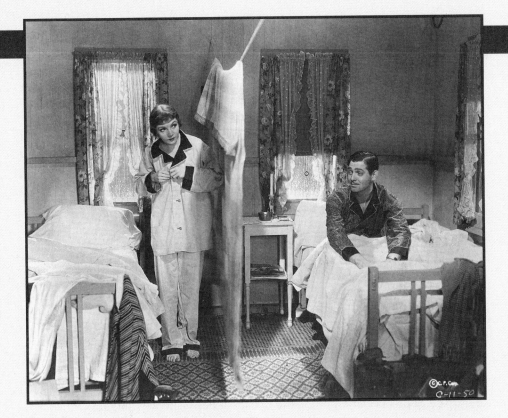

A scene from *It Happened One Night*, 1934. *(The Kobal Collection)*

the wilderness, marries a pretty girl, fights off the Indians, and works with the simple country folk to create a satisfying life in the very year the American colonies rebel against Great Britain. *Drums* was one of a number of films based on historical themes that Hollywood released just before World War II. *The Howards of Virginia* (1940), *Northwest Passage* (1939), and most popular of all, *Gone with the Wind* (1939) were others in the same genre. Historical themes had been popular before, but with the world on the brink of war, the story of men and women in the wilderness struggling for family and country against the Indians (stereotyped as savages) proved comforting as well as entertaining.

REFLECTING ON THE PAST   Can a historian use movies to describe the values and myths of a particular time, or are the complexities and exaggerations too great? Are the most popular or most critically acclaimed films more useful than others in getting at the "spirit of an age"? What films popular today tell us most about our time and culture? Is there too much sex and violence in movies today? Should the government control the language, themes, and values depicted in movies? Are movies as important today as they were in the 1930s in defining and influencing the country's myths and values?

became popular. But leisure in the 1930s fascinated professionals, who published 450 new books on the subject.

Many popular games of the period had elaborate rules. Contract bridge swept the country. Monopoly was the most popular game of all, as Americans became fascinated by a game of building real estate and utility monopolies and bankrupting their opponents.

Literary Reflections of the 1930s

Though much of the literature of the 1930s reflected the decade's troubled currents, reading continued to be a popular and cheap entertainment. John Steinbeck described the plight of Mexican migrant workers in *Tortilla Flat* (1935) and in his 1939 novel *The Grapes of Wrath* followed the deteriorating fortunes of an Okie family. His novels expressed his belief that there was in American life a "crime ... that goes beyond denunciation"—the crime being the toleration of suffering and injustice.

Other writers also questioned the American dream. John Dos Passos's trilogy *U.S.A.* (1930–1936) conveyed a deep pessimism about American capitalism that many intellectuals shared. Less political were the novels of Thomas Wolfe and William Faulkner, who more sympathetically portrayed Americans caught up in the web of local life and facing modern complexities. Faulkner's fictional Yoknapatawpha County, brought to life in *The Sound and the Fury, As I Lay Dying, Sanctuary,* and *Light in August* (1929–1932), documented the South's racial problems, poverty, and stubborn pride. But a far more optimistic and far less complex book about the South became one of the decade's best-sellers—Margaret Mitchell's Civil War novel *Gone with the Wind* (1936). Its success showed that most Americans read to escape, not to explore their problems.

Radio's Finest Hour

The number of radios purchased increased steadily during the 1930s. In 1929, slightly more than 10 million households owned a radio; by 1939, the number had increased to 27.5 million. In Chicago's working-class neighborhoods in 1930, there was one radio for every two or three households, but often families and friends gathered to listen to the radio. The radio became a focal point of the living room. Families gathered around it at night to laugh at Jack Benny and during the day to listen to soap operas. "Between thick slices of advertising," wrote James Thurber, "spread twelve minutes of dialogue, add predicament, villainy, and female suffering in equal measure, throw in a dash of nobility, sprinkle with tears, season with organ music, cover with a rich announcer sauce and serve five times a week."

Radio allowed many people to feel connected to distant places and to believe they knew the performers personally. Radio was also responsible for one of the most widespread episodes of mass hysteria of all time. Orson Welles's Halloween 1938 broadcast of "The War of the Worlds" was so realistic that thousands actually believed that Martians had just landed in New Jersey. If anyone needed proof, that single program demonstrated the power of the radio.

TIMELINE

1929 Stock market crashes

Agricultural Marketing Act

1932 Reconstruction Finance Corporation established

Federal Home Loan Bank Act

Glass-Steagall Banking Act

Federal Emergency Relief Act

Bonus march on Washington

Franklin D. Roosevelt elected president

1933 Emergency Banking Relief Act

Twenty-First Amendment repeals Eighteenth Amendment, ending Prohibition

Agricultural Adjustment Act

National Industrial Recovery Act

Civilian Conservation Corps

Tennessee Valley Authority established

Public Works Administration established

1934 Federal Housing Administration established

Indian Reorganization Act

1935 Works Progress Administration established

Social Security Act

Rural Electrification Act

National Labor Relations Act

Public Utility Holding Company Act

Committee for Industrial Organization (CIO) formed

1936 United Auto Workers hold sit-down strikes against General Motors

Roosevelt reelected president

Economy begins to rebound

1937 Attempt to expand the Supreme Court

Economic collapse

Farm Security Administration established

National Housing Act

1938 Fair Labor Standards Act

Agricultural Adjustment Act

1939 John Steinbeck, *The Grapes of Wrath*

The Silver Screen

The 1930s were the golden decade of the movies. Between 60 million and 90 million Americans went to the movies every week. Even in the depth of the Depression, movie money was almost as important as food money for many families. City residents could go to an elaborate movie palace and live in a fantasy world far removed from the reality of Depression America. In small towns across the country, for a quarter (a dime for those under age 12), people could see at least four movies during the week. There was a Sunday–Monday feature film (except in communities where the churches forbade Sunday movies), a different feature of somewhat lesser prominence on Tuesday–Wednesday, and another on Thursday–Friday. On Saturday there was a cowboy or detective movie. Sometimes a double feature played, and always there were short subjects, a cartoon, and a newsreel. The Saturday serial would leave the heroine or hero in such a dire predicament that patrons just had to come back the next week. The animated cartoons of Walt Disney, one of the true geniuses of the movie industry, were so popular that Mickey Mouse was more famous and familiar than most politicians.

Conclusion

The Mixed Legacy of the Great Depression and the New Deal

The New Deal, despite its great variety of legislation, did not end the Depression, nor did it solve the problem of unemployment. For many Americans, like Robert Symmonds's father, the most vivid memory was the shame and guilt of being unemployed, the despair and fear that came from losing a business or being evicted from a home or an apartment. Parents who lived through the decade urged their children to find a secure job, get married, and settle down. "Every time I've encountered the Depression it has been used as a barrier and a club," one daughter of Depression parents remembered; "older people use it to explain to me that I can't understand anything: I didn't live through the Depression."

New Deal legislation did not solve the country's problems, but it did strengthen the federal government, especially the executive branch. Federal agencies like the Federal Deposit Insurance Corporation and programs like Social Security influenced the daily lives of most Americans, and rural electrification, the WPA, and the CCC changed the lives of millions. The New Deal also established the principle of federal responsibility for the health of the economy, initiated the concept of the welfare state, and dramatically increased government spending to help the poor. Federally subsidized housing, minimum-wage laws, and a policy for paying farmers to limit production—all aspects of these principles had far-reaching implications.

The New Deal was as important for what it did not do as for what it did. It did not promote socialism and it did not redistribute income. It promoted social justice and social reform, but it provided little for people at the bottom of American society. In the long run, it probably strengthened corporate capitalism.

With his colorful personality and dramatic response to the nation's crisis, FDR dominated his times in a way few presidents have done. And his legacy has remained controversial. For all of the twentieth century, and even into the twenty-first, much of American politics has centered on preserving and extending or trying to abolish or revise legislation passed during the Depression decade. But the Depression was global in its impact and its consequences. The worldwide economic disaster in the 1930s would be one of the causes of World War II.

Questions for Review and Reflection

1. Explain the origins of the Great Depression. How was the Depression in the United States related to global economic factors?

2. Explain the major phases of the New Deal. What programs were enacted in each phase, and what did they seek to accomplish?

3. Who criticized the New Deal and why?

4. How did communication technologies and popular culture change during the 1930s?

5. Why are the Depression and the New Deal considered to have a mixed legacy?

Discovering U.S. History Online

Voices from the Dust Bowl http://memory.loc.gov/ammem/afctshtml/tshome.html
Farm Security Administration (FSA) studies of migrant work camps in central California in 1940 and 1941 compose the bulk of this site. The collection includes audio recordings, photographs, manuscript materials, and publications.

New Deal Network http://newdeal.feri.org/
This database includes photographs, political cartoons, and texts—including speeches, letters, and other historic documents—from the New Deal period.

IPL Potus—Franklin Delano Roosevelt http://www.ipl.org/ref/POTUS/fdroosevelt.html
This Internet Public Library—Presidents of the United States site provides information about FDR, the only president to serve more than two terms.

A New Deal for the Arts http://www.nara.gov/exhall/newdeal/newdeal.html
Artwork, documents, and photographs recount the federal government's efforts to fund artists in the 1930s in this National Archives site.

The Price of Civilization http://www.taxhistory.org/civilization
This site is part of the Tax History Project at Tax Analysts, an online tax information resource. It includes thousands of searchable pages of documents and analysis on tax issues during the Depression and WWII and is part of a larger site that contains a cartoon gallery and WWII–era posters.

Fiction and Film

James Farrell describes growing up in Depression Chicago in *Studs Lonigan* (1932–1935); John Steinbeck shows Okies trying to escape the dust bowl in his novel *The Grapes of Wrath* (1939); Richard Wright details the trials of a young black man in *Native Son* (1940).

Modern Times (1936) is a classic film that features Charlie Chaplin at his best as he depicts the impersonality of industrial civilization, where machines dominate people. *Grapes of Wrath* (1940) is another classic film. Although it doesn't exhibit the despair and anger of the book on which it is based, it is still a powerful film that explores the human cost of the dust bowl and the Depression.

Recommended Reading

www.ablongman.com/nash

The Companion Website has a list of recommended readings about the Great Depression, Roosevelt, the First New Deal, the Second New Deal, and cultural aspects of the 1930s.

World War II

CHAPTER OUTLINE

- The Twisting Road to War
- The Home Front
- The Social Impact of the War
- A War of Diplomats and Generals
- Conclusion: Peace, Prosperity, and International Responsibilities

American Stories

A Native American Boy Plays at War

N. Scott Momaday, a Kiowa Indian born in Lawton, Oklahoma, in 1934, grew up on reservations. He was only 11 years old when World War II ended, yet the war changed his life. Shortly after the United States entered the war, Momaday's parents moved to New Mexico, where his father got a job with an oil company and his mother worked in the civilian personnel office at an army air force base. Like many couples, they had struggled through the hard times of the Depression. The war meant jobs.

Momaday's best friend was Billy Don Johnson. Together they played war, digging trenches and dragging themselves through imaginary minefields. They hurled grenades and fired endless rounds from their imaginary machine guns, pausing only to drink Kool-Aid from their canteens. At school, they were taught how to hate the enemy and be proud of America. They recited the Pledge of Allegiance to the flag and sang "God Bless America," "The Star-Spangled Banner," and "Remember Pearl Harbor." Like most Americans, they believed that World War II was a good war fought against evil empires. The United States was always right, the enemy always wrong. It was an attitude that would influence Momaday and his generation for the rest of their lives.

Momaday's only difficulty was that his Native American face was often mistaken for that of an Asian. Almost every day on the playground, someone would yell, "Hi ya, Jap," and a fight was on. Billy Don always came to his friend's defense, but it was disconcerting to be taken for the enemy. His father read old Kiowa tales to Momaday, who was proud to be an Indian but prouder still to be an American. On Saturday, he and his friends would cheer at the movies as they watched a Japanese Zero or a German ME-109 go down in flames.

Near the end of the war, Momaday's family moved again, as so many families did, so that his father might get a better job. This time they lived right next door to an air force base, and Momaday fell in love with the B-17 "Flying Fortress," the bomber that military strategists thought would win the war in the Pacific and in Europe.

Looking back, Momaday reflected on the importance of the war in his growing up. "I see now that one experiences easily the ordinary things of life," he decided, "the things which cast familiar shadows upon the sheer, transparent panels of time, and he perceives his experience in the only way he can, according to his age." Though Momaday's life during the war differed from the lives of boys old enough to join the armed forces, the war was no less real for him.

The Momadays fared better than most Native Americans. Although they had been made U.S. citizens by an act of Congress in 1924, the Momadays, like all Native Americans living in Arizona and New Mexico, were denied the right to vote by state law. Jobs, even in wartime, were hard to find. Native American servicemen returning from the war discovered that as "Indians" they still faced blatant discrimination in many states. Still, Momaday thought of himself not so much as an Indian but as an American, and that too was a product of his generation. But as he grew to maturity, he became a successful writer and spokesman for his people. In 1969, he won the Pulitzer Prize for his novel *House Made of Dawn*. In his writing, he stresses the Indian's close identification with the land. Writing about his grandmother, he says: "The immense landscape of the continental interior lay like memory in her blood."

No American cities were bombed and the country was never invaded, but World War II still influenced almost every aspect of American life. The war ended the Depression. Industrial jobs were plentiful, and even though prejudice and discrimination did not disappear, blacks, Hispanics, women, and other minorities had new opportunities. Like World War I, this second global war expanded cooperation between government and industry and increased the influence of government in all areas of American life. The war also ended the last remnants of American isolationism. The United States emerged from the war in 1945 as the most powerful and most prosperous nation in the world.

This chapter traces the gradual involvement of the United States in the international events during the 1930s that finally led to participation in the most devastating war the world had seen. It traces the diplomatic and military struggles of the war and the search for a secure peace. It also explores the war's impact on ordinary people and on American attitudes about the world, on patriotism and the American way of life. Even those, like Momaday, who grew up during the war and were too young to fight, were influenced by the war—and the sense of moral certainty that the war inspired—for the rest of their lives. The war brought prosperity to some, death to others. It left Americans the world's richest people and the United States its most powerful nation.

THE TWISTING ROAD TO WAR

Looking back on the events between 1933 and 1941 that eventually led America into World War II, it is easy to criticize decisions made or actions not taken, or else to see everything as inevitable. But historical events are never inevitable, and leaders who must make decisions never have the advantage of hindsight. They must deal with situations as they find them, and they never have all the facts.

Foreign Policy in a Global Age

In March 1933, Roosevelt faced not only overwhelming domestic difficulties but also an international crisis. The worldwide depression had caused near financial disaster in Europe. Germany had defaulted on its reparation payments, and most European countries were unable to pay their debts to the United States.

Roosevelt had no master plan in foreign policy, just as he had none in the domestic sphere. In the first days of his administration, he gave conflicting signals about the international situation. First it seemed that FDR would cooperate in some kind of international economic agreement on tariffs and currency, which was to be negotiated in London. But then he refused to go along with any such agreement. In 1933, Roosevelt believed it was more important to solve the domestic economic crisis than to achieve international economic cooperation. His actions signaled a decision to "go it alone" in foreign policy.

Roosevelt did, however, alter some of the foreign policy decisions of previous administrations. He recognized the Soviet government. In reversing the 1920s nonrecognition policy (which rested largely on anti-Communist sentiments), Roosevelt hoped to gain a market for surplus American grain—a trade bonanza that never materialized. But diplomatic recognition opened communications between two emerging world powers.

The United States continued to support dictators, especially in Central America, because they promised to promote stability and preserve U.S. economic interests. But Roosevelt, extending the Good Neighbor policy Hoover had initiated, completed the removal of American military forces from Haiti and Nicaragua in 1934. In a series of pan-American conferences, he joined in pledging that no country in the hemisphere would intervene in the "internal or external affairs" of any other.

The new policy's first test came in Cuba, where a revolution threatened American investments of more than a billion dollars. But the United States did not send troops. Instead, Roosevelt dispatched envoys to work out a conciliatory agreement. A short time later, when a coup led by Fulgencio Batista overthrew the revolutionary government, the United States not only recognized the Batista government but also offered a large loan. The United States agreed to abrogate the Platt Amendment (which made Cuba a virtual protectorate of the United States) in return for continued rights to the Guantanamo naval base.

The Trade Agreements Act of 1934 empowered the president to lower tariff rates by as much as 50 percent. Secretary of State Cordell Hull negotiated a series of pacts that improved trade. By 1935, half of American cotton exports and a large proportion of other products were going to Latin America. So the Good Neighbor policy was also good business for the United States. But increased trade did not solve the economic problems for either the United States or Latin America.

Another test for Latin American policy came in 1938 when Mexico nationalized the property of American oil companies. Instead of intervening, as many businessmen urged, the State Department patiently worked out an agreement that included some compensation for the companies. Washington might have acted differently had not the threat of war in Europe in 1938 created a sense that all the Western Hemisphere nations should cooperate. At a pan-American conference held that year, the United States and most Latin American countries agreed to resist all foreign intervention in the hemisphere.

Neutrality in Europe

On January 30, 1933, about two months before Roosevelt's inauguration, Nazi leader Adolf Hitler became German chancellor. Born in Austria in 1889, he served in the army during World War I. Like so many other Germans, he was angered by the harsh terms of the Treaty of Versailles. But Hitler blamed the German defeat in the war on Jews and Communists. He had a charismatic style and a plan that attracted many followers. Shortly after he became chancellor, he suspended the constitution and made himself Fuehrer (leader) and dictator and set out to conquer Europe. As the first step, in 1934 he announced German rearmament, violating the Versailles Treaty. That same year, Italy's Fascist dictator Benito Mussolini (who had come to power a decade earlier) threatened to invade the East African country of Ethiopia. These ominous rumblings frightened Americans at the very time they were reexamining the history of American entry into the Great War and vowing that it would never happen again.

Senator Gerald P. Nye of North Dakota launched an investigation into the connection between corporate profits and American participation in World War I. His committee's public hearings revealed that many American businessmen had close relationships with the War Department. Although no conspiracy was proved, it was easy to conclude that the United States had been tricked into going to war by the people who profited heavily from it.

On many campuses, students demonstrated against war. They joined organizations like the Veterans of Future Wars and protested Reserve Officer Training Corps programs on their campuses. They were determined never again to support a foreign war. But in Europe, Asia, and Africa, there were already rumblings of another great international conflict.

Ethiopia and Spain

In May 1935, Italy invaded Ethiopia after rejecting the League of Nations' offer to mediate disputes between the two countries. The remote Ethiopian war frightened Congress into passing the Neutrality Act, which authorized the president to prohibit all arms shipments to nations at war and to advise all U.S. citizens not to travel on belligerents' ships except at their own risk. Congress was determined to prevent America from entering another world war.

Although he would have preferred a more flexible bill, Roosevelt used the authority of the Neutrality Act of 1935 to impose an arms embargo. The League of Nations condemned Italy as the aggressor. But neither Britain nor the United States wanted to stop oil shipments to Italy or join the fight. The embargo had little impact on Italy but was disastrous for the poor African nation. After defeating Ethiopia, Mussolini made an alliance with Germany, creating the Rome–Berlin Axis, in 1936.

"We shun political commitments which might entangle us in foreign war," Roosevelt announced in 1936. But isolation became more difficult when General Francisco Franco, supported by the Catholic church, large landowners, and reactionary politicians, revolted against the republican government of Spain. Germany and Italy aided Franco, sending planes and other weapons, while the Soviet Union supplied the Spanish republican Loyalists.

The Spanish Civil War polarized the United States. Most Catholics and many anti-Communists sided with Franco. But many American liberals and radicals—even those who said they opposed all war—found the republican cause worth fighting for. Over 3,000 Americans joined the Abraham Lincoln Brigade, and hundreds died fighting fascism. "If this were a Spanish matter, I'd let it alone," wrote Sam Levenger, an Ohio State student. "But the rebellion would not last a week if it weren't for the Germans and the Italians." Levenger was killed in Spain in 1937 at the age of 20.

The U.S. government took neutrality seriously. The Neutrality Act, extended in 1936, did not apply to civil wars. However, when an American businessman tried to send 400 used airplane engines to the Loyalists, Roosevelt asked Congress to extend the arms embargo to Spain. While the United States, Britain, and France stayed neutral, Franco consolidated his dictatorship with German and Italian help. Meanwhile, Congress in 1937 passed another Neutrality Act, this time forbidding American citizens to travel on belligerents' ships. The embargo on arms was tightened, and belligerents could buy nonmilitary items only on a cash-and-carry basis.

So the United States tried to avoid repeating the mistakes that had led it into World War I. Unfortunately, World War II, which moved closer each day, would be a different kind of war, and the lessons of the first war would be of little use.

War in Europe

Roosevelt had no careful strategy to deal with the rising tide of troubles in Europe in the late 1930s. He was no isolationist, but he wanted to keep the United States out of any European conflict. When he publicly announced, "I hate war," he meant it. Unlike his distant cousin Theodore Roosevelt, he did not view war as a test of manhood. In foreign policy, as in domestic affairs, he responded to events, but he moved reluctantly toward greater American involvement.

In March 1938, Hitler annexed Austria, and in September he occupied the Sudetenland, a part of Czechoslovakia. Within six months, Hitler seized the rest of that country. Little protest came from the United States. Most Americans sympathized with the victims of Hitler's aggression, and eventually some were horrified by rumors of the murder of hundreds of thousands of Jews. But because newspapers avoided intensive coverage of these well-documented but unpleasant stories, many Americans did not learn of the Holocaust until near the end of the war.

At first, almost everyone hoped that Europeans could work out compromises. But that notion was destroyed on August 23, 1939, by the news of a Nazi–Soviet pact. Many Americans had hoped that Nazi Germany and Soviet Russia would destroy each other. Now these ideological enemies had signed a nonaggression pact. A week later, Hitler's army attacked Poland, marking the onset of World War II. Britain and France came to Poland's defense. "This nation will remain a neutral nation," Roosevelt said, "but I cannot ask that every American remain neutral in thought as well."

Roosevelt asked for repeal of the embargo section of the Neutrality Act and for approval of cash-and-carry arms sales to France and Britain. And he took some risks. In August 1939, physicist Albert Einstein, a Jewish refugee from Nazi Germany, warned him that German scientists were working on an atomic bomb. The president feared the consequences of Hitler being the first to possess such a weapon, and authorized secret research. The top-secret Manhattan Project—known only to a few advisers and key members of Congress—was officially launched in 1941. Ultimately it would change the course of human history.

There was a lull in the war after Germany and the Soviet Union crushed Poland in September 1939. Great Britain sent several divisions to aid the French against the expected German attack, but for months nothing happened. The "phony war" dramatically ended on April 9, 1940, when Germany attacked Norway and Denmark. At the beginning of May, the German *Blitzkrieg* ("lightning war") swept into the Low Countries. A week later, mechanized German forces stormed into France, sweeping around fortifications known as the Maginot line. France surrendered in June as the British army fled across the English Channel.

DOCUMENT

Charles
Lindbergh, Radio
Address (1941)

How should the United States respond to this desperate situation? Some concerned citizens organized the Committee to Defend America by Aiding the Allies, but others, including Charles Lindbergh, supported a group called America First. They argued that the United States should forget England and concentrate on defending America. Roosevelt steered a cautious course. He sent Britain 50 old American destroyers. In return, the United States received the right to establish naval and air bases from Newfoundland to Bermuda and British Guiana. British Prime Minister Winston Churchill asked for much more.

But Roosevelt hesitated. In July 1940, he authorized $4 billion for more American warships. In September, Congress passed the Selective Service Act, providing for America's first peacetime draft. Over 1 million men were to serve for one year, but only in the Western Hemisphere.

The Election of 1940

Part of Roosevelt's reluctance to aid Great Britain more aggressively came from his genuine desire to keep the United States out of the war, but it also reflected the presidential campaign of 1940. Roosevelt broke tradition by seeking a third term. The increasing support he was drawing from the liberal wing of the Democratic party led him to select liberal farm economist Henry Wallace from Iowa as his running mate.

The Republicans nominated energetic Wendell Willkie of Indiana. Despite his big-business ties, Willkie approved of most New Deal legislation and supported aid to Great Britain. Willkie was the most exciting Republican candidate since Theodore Roosevelt. Yet amid the international crisis, the voters stayed with FDR—27 million to 22 million. Roosevelt carried 38 of the 48 states.

Lend-Lease

After the election, Roosevelt invented a "lend-lease" scheme for sending aid to Britain without demanding payment. He compared this to lending a garden hose to a neighbor whose house was on fire. Republican Senator Robert Taft thought it was more like lending chewing gum: "Once it had been used you did not want it back."

The Lend-Lease Act, which Congress passed in March 1941, destroyed the fiction of neutrality. By then, U-boats were sinking a half-million tons of Atlantic shipping each month. In June, Roosevelt proclaimed a national emergency. Then, on June 22, Germany attacked Russia.

When Roosevelt extended lend-lease aid to Russia, the former Communist enemy, in November 1941, many Americans were shocked. But most quickly shifted from viewing the Soviet Union as an enemy to treating it like a friend.

By the autumn of 1941, the United States was virtually at war with Germany in the Atlantic. On September 11, Roosevelt issued a "shoot on sight" order for all American ships operating in the Atlantic, and on October 30, a German submarine sank an American destroyer. The war in the Atlantic was undeclared, and many Americans opposed it. However, it was not Germany but Japan that dragged the United States into World War II.

The Path to Pearl Harbor

Japan, controlled by ambitious military leaders, was the aggressor in the Far East as Hitler's Germany was in Europe. Intent on becoming a major world power and desperate for natural resources, especially oil, Japan was willing to risk war to get them. It invaded Manchuria in 1931 and launched an all-out assault on China in 1937. But Japanese leaders wanted to put off attacking the Philippines. For its part, the United States feared a two-front war and was willing to delay a confrontation with Japan until it had dealt with the German threat. Thus between 1938 and 1941, the United States and Japan engaged in diplomatic shadow boxing.

America exerted economic pressure on Japan in July 1939, giving the required six months' notice for cancellation of the 1911 commercial agreement between the two countries. In September 1940, the administration forbade shipping aircraft fuel and scrap metal to Japan. Other items were added to the embargo until by the spring of 1941 only oil could be shipped to Japan; the administration hoped that the threat of cutting off that important resource would force negotiations and avert a crisis. Japan opened negotiations with the United States, but there was little to discuss. Japan would not withdraw from China and occupied French Indochina. In July 1941, Roosevelt froze all Japanese assets in the United States, effectively embargoing trade with Japan.

Roosevelt had an advantage in negotiating with Japan, for Americans had broken the Japanese secret diplomatic code. But Japanese intentions were hard to decipher from the intercepted messages. American leaders knew that Japan planned to attack, but they didn't know where. In September 1941, the Japanese decided to strike sometime after November unless the United States offered real concessions.

On the morning of December 7, 1941, Japanese airplanes launched from aircraft carriers attacked the U.S. fleet at Pearl Harbor, in Hawaii. The surprise attack destroyed or disabled 19 ships (including five battleships) and 150 planes and killed 2,335 soldiers and sailors and 68 civilians. On the same day, Japan invaded

Pearl Harbor This photo shows an exploding American destroyer at Pearl Harbor on December 7, 1941. The attack on Pearl Harbor united the country and came to symbolize Japanese treachery and American lack of preparedness. Photographs such as this were published throughout the war to inspire Americans to work harder. Does Pearl Harbor still have meaning in our society today? *(Official U.S. Navy Photo, The National Archives)*

the Philippines, Guam, Midway, and British Hong Kong and Malaya. The next day, Congress declared war on Japan.

December 7, 1941, was a day that "would live in infamy," Franklin Roosevelt told Congress and the nation as he asked for the declaration of war. It was also a day that would have far-reaching implications for American foreign policy and for American attitudes toward the world. The surprise attack united the country—even isolationists and "America Firsters"—as nothing else could have.

After the shock and anger subsided, Americans searched for a villain. The myth still persists that the villain was Roosevelt, who supposedly knew of the Japanese attack but failed to warn the military so that the American people might unite behind the war against Germany. But Roosevelt did not know. There was no warning that the attack was coming against Pearl Harbor, and the American ability to read Japanese coded messages was no help because the fleet kept radio silence.

The Americans underestimated the Japanese, partly because of racial prejudice. They ignored many warning signals because they simply did not believe the Japanese capable of attacking a target as far away as Hawaii. Roosevelt and most experts expected the Japanese to attack the Philippines or Thailand. Many people blundered, but there was no conspiracy.

Even more important in the long run was the Japanese attack's effect on a generation of military and political leaders. Pearl Harbor became the symbol of unpreparedness. For a generation that had been stunned by an unscrupulous enemy attack, the lesson was to be ready to stop an aggressor before it struck. That lesson would influence American policy in Korea, Vietnam, and beyond.

THE HOME FRONT

Too often wars are described in terms of leaders, grand strategy, and elaborate campaigns. But wars affect all people—the soldiers who fight and the women and children and men who stay home. World War II especially had an impact on all aspects of society: the economy, entertainment, even attitudes toward women and blacks. For many people, the war represented opportunity and the end of the Depression. On others, it left lasting scars.

Mobilizing for War

Converting American industry to war production was a complex task. Shortly after Pearl Harbor, Roosevelt created the War Production Board (WPB) and appointed Donald Nelson, executive vice president of Sears, Roebuck, to mobilize resources for an all-out war effort. The Roosevelt administration tried hard to gain the cooperation of businessmen, many of them alienated by New Deal policies. The president appointed many business executives to key positions and abandoned antitrust actions in any industry that was remotely war related.

The policy worked. Industrial production and net corporate profits nearly doubled during the war. Large commercial farmers also profited. The war years accelerated the mechanization of the farm and dramatically increased the use of fertilizer, but between 1940 and 1945, the farm population declined by 17 percent.

Many government agencies besides the War Production Board helped run the war effort efficiently. The Office of Price Administration (OPA) set prices to control inflation and rationed products—and because it affected so many lives so disagreeably, many Americans regarded it as oppressive. The National War Labor Board (NWLB) had the authority to set wages and hours and to monitor working conditions, and it could seize plants whose owners refused to cooperate.

Union membership grew rapidly, aided by government policy. In return for a "no-strike pledge," the NWLB allowed agreements that required workers to retain their union membership through the life of a contract. Responding to labor leaders' protests, the NWLB finally allowed a 15 percent cost-of-living increase on some contracts, but that did not apply to overtime pay, which helped drive up wages in some industries during the war by about 70 percent.

Besides imposing wage and price controls and rationing, the government fought inflation by selling war bonds and increasing taxes. The Revenue Act of 1942 raised tax rates, broadened the tax base, boosted corporate taxes to 40 percent, and set the excess-profits tax at 90 percent. In addition, the government initiated payroll deductions, making the income tax a reality for most Americans for the first time.

Despite some unfairness and much confusion, the American economy turned out the equipment and supplies that eventually won the war. American industries built 300,000 airplanes, 88,140 tanks, and 3,000 merchant ships. In 1944 alone, American factories produced 800,000 tons of synthetic rubber to replace natural rubber, cut off by the Japanese. By the war's end, the American economy was turning out an astonishing 50 percent of all the world's goods.

Although the national debt grew from about $143 billion in 1943 to $260 billion in 1945, taxes paid for about 40 percent of the war's cost. At the same time, full employment and the increase in two-income families, together with forced savings, helped amass capital for postwar expansion. In a limited way, the tax policy also tended to redistribute wealth, which the New Deal had failed to do. The top 5 percent income bracket, which controlled 23 percent of the disposable income in 1939, accounted for only 17 percent in 1945.

The war stimulated the growth of the federal bureaucracy and accelerated the trend, begun during World War I and extended in the 1920s and 1930s, toward a federal government role in the economy. The war also increased the cooperation between industry and government, creating what would later be called a military-industrial complex. But for most Americans, despite their anger at the OPA and the income tax, the war meant the end of the Depression.

Patriotic Fervor

The war, so horrible elsewhere, was remote in the United States—except for the thousands of families that received the official telegram telling of a loved one killed in action. The government tried to keep the conflict alive in Americans' minds, and the country united behind the war effort. The Office of War Information promoted patriotism and controlled the news that the public received about the war. The government also sold war bonds, not only to help pay for the war and reduce inflation but also to sell the war to the American people. As during World War I, celebrities appeared at bond rallies. Schoolchildren purchased war stamps and pasted them in an album until they had accumulated stamps worth $18.75, enough to buy a $25 bond (redeemable 10 years later). Their bonds, they were told, would purchase bullets or an airplane part to kill "Japs" and Germans. Working men and women purchased bonds through payroll deduction plans and looked forward to spending the money on consumer goods after the war. In the end, the government sold over $135 billion in war bonds. While the bond drives did help control inflation, they were most important in making millions of Americans feel that they were contributing to the war effort.

Those too old or too young to join the armed forces served as air raid wardens or civilian defense and Red Cross volunteers. They raised victory gardens, contributed to scrap drives, and did without. "Hoarders are the same as spies," one ad announced.

Internment of Japanese Americans

Cooperating with the war effort fostered pride and a feeling of community—but also hate for the enemy. The Nazis, especially Hitler and his Gestapo, were synonymous with evil before 1941. Later, most Americans ceased making distinctions between Germans and Nazis, although the anti-German hysteria that had swept the country during World War I never returned.

The Japanese were easier to hate. The attack on Pearl Harbor created a special animosity toward them, but depicting them as warlike and subhuman owed something to an old American distrust of all Asians. Two weeks after Pearl Harbor, *Time* magazine told Americans how to distinguish the friendly Chinese from "the Japs." "Chinese ... have an easy gait. The Chinese expression is likely to be more kindly, placid, open; the Japanese more positive, dogmatic, arrogant."

SAVE FREEDOM OF SPEECH

BUY WAR BONDS

Fighting for Freedom
Norman Rockwell, a popular illustrator, created four paintings to illustrate the Four Freedoms that President Roosevelt mentioned in his 1941 address to spell out what the United States was fighting for: Freedom of Worship, Freedom of Speech, Freedom from Fear, and Freedom from Want. Commissioned by the *Saturday Evening Post,* these paintings were turned into posters and used to support the sale of war bonds. What does this poster reveal about American freedom? *(The National Archives)*

Racial stereotypes played a role in the treatment of Japanese Americans during the war. They were the only group confined in concentration camps, in the greatest mass abridgment of civil liberties in American history.

At the time of Pearl Harbor, about 127,000 Japanese Americans lived in the United States, most on the West Coast. About 80,000 were *nisei* (Japanese born in the United States and holding American citizenship) and *sansei* (the sons and daughters of *nisei*); the rest were *issei* (aliens born in Japan who were ineligible for U.S. citizenship). They had long suffered from prejudice—barred, for example, from intermarriage with other groups and excluded from many clubs, restaurants, and recreation facilities. Many worked as tenant farmers, fishermen, or small businessmen, or were landowning farmers, but some belonged to a small professional class of lawyers, teachers, and doctors.

Although many retained cultural ties to Japan and spoke Japanese, these people posed no more threat to the country than did the much larger groups of Italian Americans and German Americans. But their appearance made them stand out.

The Enemy During the war American magazines and newspapers often depicted the Japanese as monkeys, insects, or rodents. Germans were rarely pictured this way. This December 12, 1942, issue of *Collier's* magazine pictures Japanese prime minister Hideki Tojo as a vampire bat carrying a bomb to drop on the United States. The Japanese, on the other hand, often pictured Americans and British as bloated capitalists and imperialists. What effect, do you suppose, did these caricatures have on attitudes and actions during the war? *(akg-images)*

After Pearl Harbor, an anti-Japanese panic seized the West Coast. Rumors suggested that Japanese fishermen were preparing to mine harbors, blow up tunnels, and poison water supplies.

West Coast politicians and citizens urged the War Department to remove the Japanese. The president capitulated and issued Executive Order 9066, authorizing the evacuation in February 1942. "The continued pressure of a largely unassimilated, tightly knit racial group, bound to an enemy nation by strong ties of race, culture, custom and religion, constituted a menace which had to be dealt with," General John De Witt argued, justifying the removal on military grounds. But racial fear and hatred, not military necessity, explained the order.

"The Japs live like rats, breed like rats, and act like rats. We don't want them," the governor of Idaho announced. So it was in remote, often arid, sections of the West that eventually the government built the primitive "relocation centers." "When I first entered our room, I became sick to my stomach," a Japanese American woman remembered.

The government evacuated about 110,000 Japanese, who lost almost all of their property. Farmers left their crops to be harvested by their American neighbors. Store owners sold out for a small percentage of what their goods were worth. Japanese Americans lost all of their personal possessions, and something more—their pride and respect.

The evacuation was unjustified. In Hawaii, with its much larger Japanese American population, there was no evacuation, and no sabotage and little disloyalty occurred. Late in the war, the government allowed Japanese American men to volunteer for military service, and many served bravely in the European theater. The 442nd Infantry Combat Team, made up entirely of *nisei*, became the most decorated unit in all the military service—another indication of the loyalty and patriotism of the Japanese Americans. In 1988, Congress belatedly apologized and voted limited compensation for Japanese Americans relocated during World War II.

American Minorities in Time of War

The Pacific War made China an ally of the United States, but Congress did not repeal the Chinese Exclusion Act until 1943, and then only 105 Chinese a year were allowed to enter the United States. Despite this, over 13,000 Chinese Americans joined the U.S. Army, while others took jobs in war industries. The Korean, Filipino, and Asian Indian population also contributed to the war effort, even though they constantly faced prejudice and were often denied service in restaurants.

Even in the North the United States remained a segregated society during the war. Black Americans profited little from the wartime revival of prosperity and the expansion of jobs early in the war. Those who joined the military were usually assigned to menial jobs, always in segregated units with whites as the high-ranking officers. The myth persisted that black soldiers had failed to perform well in World War I.

DOCUMENT

Sterling A. Brown, "Out of Their Mouths" (1942)

Some black leaders found it especially ironic that as the country prepared to fight Hitler and his racist policies, the United States kept its own brand of racism. A black labor leader, A. Philip Randolph, decided to act. Randolph had worked with the first wave of African Americans migrating from the South to the northern cities during and just after World War I. Afterwards he organized and led the Brotherhood of Sleeping Car Porters and in 1937 finally won grudging recognition of the union from the Pullman Company.

Admired by black leaders of all political persuasions, Randolph convinced many of them in 1941 to join him in a march on Washington to demand equal rights. Roosevelt was alarmed. He talked to Randolph and finally struck a bargain. The president refused to desegregate the armed forces, but in return for Randolph's calling off the march, he issued Executive Order 8802, which stated that it was government policy that "there shall be no discrimination in the employment of workers in defense industries or government because of race, creed, color or national origin." To enforce the order, he established the Fair Employment Practices Commission (FEPC).

By threatening militant action, the black leaders wrested a major concession from the president. But the executive order did not end prejudice, and the FEPC (which its chairman described as the "most hated agency in Washington") had limited success in erasing the color line. Many black soldiers were angered and humiliated throughout the war by being made to sit in the back of buses and being barred from hotels and restaurants. A former black soldier recalled being refused service in a restaurant in Salina, Kansas, while the same restaurant served German prisoners from a camp nearby. "We continued to stare," he recalled. "This was really happening. ... The people of Salina would serve these enemy soldiers and turn away black American GI's."

Jobs in war industries helped many African Americans improve their economic conditions. Continuing the migration that had begun during World War I,

about 2 million southern blacks moved to northern and western cities. Some became skilled workers, and a few became professionals. The new arrivals increased pressure on overcrowded housing and other facilities, accentuating tension among all hard-pressed groups. In Detroit, a major race riot broke out in the summer of 1943 after Polish Americans protested a public housing development that promised to bring blacks into their neighborhood. A series of incidents led to fights between black and white young people and then to looting in the black community. Before federal and state troops restored order, 25 blacks and 9 whites had been killed and more than $2 million worth of property destroyed. Groups of whites roamed the city attacking blacks, overturning cars, setting fires, and sometimes killing wantonly. Other riots broke out in Mobile, Los Angeles, New York, and Beaumont, Texas. In all these cities, and in many others where the tension did not lead to open violence, the legacy of hate lasted long after the war.

Mexican Americans, like most minority groups, benefited from wartime job opportunities, but they, too, faced prejudice. In California and in many parts of the Southwest, Mexicans could not use public swimming pools and certain restaurants. Usually they were limited to menial jobs and were constantly harassed by the police. In Los Angeles, anti-Mexican prejudice got violent. Most of the anger focused on Mexican gang members wearing zoot suits—long, loose coats with padded shoulders, ballooned pants, and wide-brimmed hats.

Zoot-suiters especially angered soldiers and sailors in Los Angeles. After many provocative incidents, the violence peaked on June 7, 1943, when gangs of servicemen attacked all the young zoot-suiters they could find or anyone who looked Mexican. The servicemen, joined by others, beat up the Mexicans, stripped off their offensive clothes, and cut the long, duck-tailed hair that was part of the look. The police usually looked the other way or arrested the victims. The local press and the chamber of commerce hotly denied that race was a factor, but *Time* magazine was probably closer to the truth when it called the riots the "ugliest brand of mob action since the coolie race riots of the 1870s."

THE SOCIAL IMPACT OF THE WAR

Modern wars have been incredibly destructive of lives and property, but they have had social consequences as well. World War II altered patterns of work, leisure, education, and family life; caused a massive migration of people; created jobs; and changed lifestyles. It is difficult to overemphasize the war's social impact.

Wartime Opportunities

More than 15 million American civilians moved during the war. Like the Momadays, many left home seeking better jobs. For Native Americans, wartime opportunities caused a migration into the cities—as it did for countless other Americans who left farms and small towns for urban defense jobs. California alone gained more than 2 million people during the war. But Americans also moved from the rural South into northern cities, and a smaller number moved from the North to the South. Two hundred thousand came to the Detroit area, nearly a half-million to Los Angeles, and about 100,000 to Mobile, Alabama.

Nowhere was the change more dramatic than in the West, which the wartime boom transformed more dramatically than any development since the nineteenth-century economic revolution created by the railroads and mining. The federal government spent over $70 billion in California (one-tenth of the total for the entire country) on army bases, shipyards, supply depots, and testing sites. Private industry built so many facilities that the region became the center of a growing military-industrial complex. San Diego was transformed from a sleepy port into a sprawling metropolis, while Vallezo, a small city near Oakland, grew from 20,000 to over 100,000 in just two years. This spectacular growth created housing shortages and overwhelmed schools, hospitals, and municipal services. Crime, prostitution, and racial tension all increased.

For the first time in years, many families had money to spend, but they had nothing to spend it on. The last new car rolled off the assembly line in February 1942. There were no washing machines, refrigerators, or radios in the stores, little gasoline, and few tires. Even when people had time off, they tended to stay home, go to the movies, or listen to the radio.

The war required major adjustments in American family life. With several million men in the service or working at faraway defense jobs, the number of households headed by a woman increased dramatically. The number of marriages also rose sharply. Early in the war, a young man could be deferred if he had a dependent, including a wife. Later, many servicemen got married, often to women they barely knew, because they wanted a little excitement and perhaps someone to come home to. Reversing a decline that extended back to the colonial period, the birthrate also began to rise in 1940, as young couples started families as fast as they could. Since birthrates had been especially low during the Depression, the shift marked a significant change. Some children—"good-bye babies"—were conceived just before the husband joined the military or went overseas. Illegitimacy and divorce rates also went up sharply. Yet most wartime marriages survived, and many of the women left behind looked ahead to a normal life after the war.

Women Work for Victory

IMAGE

Women in an
Airplane Factory

Thousands of women took jobs in heavy industry that once would have been considered unladylike. They built tanks, airplanes, and ships, but they still earned less than men. At first, women were rarely taken on because, as the war in Europe pulled American industry out of its long slump, unemployed men snapped up the newly available positions.

But by 1943, with many men drafted and male unemployment virtually nonexistent, the government was quick to suggest that it was women's patriotic duty to join the assembly line. A popular song was "Rosie the Riveter," who helped her marine boyfriend by "working overtime on the riveting machine."

At the end of the war, the labor force included 19.5 million women, but three-fourths of them had been working before the conflict, and some of the new ones

VIDEO

Rosie the Riveter

might have sought work in normal times. The new women war workers tended to be older, and they were more often married than single. Some worked for patriotic reasons. "Every time I test a batch of rubber, I know it's going to help bring my three sons home quicker," said a female worker in a rubber plant. But others worked for the money or to have something useful to do. Yet in 1944, women's weekly wages averaged $31.21, compared with $54.65 for men, reflecting women's menial tasks and low seniority as well as outright discrimination. Married women with young children found it difficult to obtain jobs. There were few day-care facilities, and women were often told that they should be home with their children. Women workers often had to endure overt sexual harassment. Still, most persisted, and they tried to look feminine despite work clothes.

Black women faced the most difficult situation. Often, when they applied for work, they were told something like "We have not yet installed separate toilet facilities." Not until 1944 did the telephone company in New York City hire a black operator. Still, some black women moved during the war from domestic jobs to higher-paying factory work.

Many women war workers quickly left their jobs after the war ended. Some left by choice, but dismissals ran twice as high for women as for men. Some women who learned what an extra paycheck meant for the family's standard of living would have preferred to keep working. But most women, and even more men, agreed at the war's end that women did not deserve an "equal chance with men" for jobs.

Entertaining the People

According to one survey, Americans listened to the radio an average of four and a half hours a day during the war. The major networks increased their news programs from less than 4 percent of broadcasting time to nearly 30 percent. Americans heard Edward R. Murrow broadcasting from London during the German air blitz with air-raid sirens in the background. Often static made listening difficult, but the live broadcasts had an authenticity never before possible. Commentators became celebrities on whom millions depended for war news.

The war intruded on almost all programming. Serials, the standard fare of daytime radio, adopted wartime themes. Popular music, which occupied a large share of radio programming, mirrored the war. There was "Goodbye, Mama (I'm Off to Yokohama)," but more numerous were songs of romance, love, separation, and hope for a better time after the war. The danceable tunes of Glenn Miller and Tommy Dorsey became just as much a part of wartime memories as ration books and far-off battlefields.

For many Americans, the motion picture became the most important leisure activity. Movie attendance averaged about 100 million viewers a week. There might not be gasoline for Sunday drives, but the whole family could go to the movies. Even those in the military could watch American movies on-board ship or at a remote outpost. "Pinups" of Hollywood stars decorated barracks, tanks, and planes wherever American troops went.

The war engulfed Hollywood. Newsreels offering a visual synopsis of war news, always with an upbeat message and a touch of human interest, preceded most movies. Their theme was that the Americans were winning, even if early on there was little evidence of it. Many feature films also had a wartime theme, picturing the Pacific war complete with grinning Japanese villains (usually played by Chinese or Korean actors). Movies set in Europe differed somewhat from those depicting the Pacific war. British and American heroes behind enemy lines outwitted Nazis at every turn, sabotaged installations, and made daring escapes from prison camps. Many wartime movies featured a multicultural platoon led by a veteran sergeant with a Protestant, a Catholic, a Jew, an African American, a farmer, and a city resident. The message was that we could all get along and cooperate to defeat the enemy. But in the real army blacks served in segregated platoons.

A number of Hollywood actors went into the service, and some even became heroes. Most, like Ronald Reagan, were employed to produce, narrate, or act in government films. The Office of War Information produced short subjects and documentaries, some of them distinguished, like John Huston's *Battle of San Pietro,* a realistic depiction of war on the Italian front. More typical were propaganda films aimed at American civilians. *Letter from Bataan* (1942) portrayed a wounded GI who wrote home asking his brother-in-law to save his razor blades because "it takes twelve thousand razor blades to make a one-thousand-pound bomb."

Religion in Time of War

"Freedom of worship," according to President Roosevelt, was one of the freedoms threatened by the war. According to one poll, 30 percent of Americans said the war had strengthened their religious faith. Most thought of the United States as a "Christian nation," and by that they usually meant Protestant. The war increased religious tolerance, but anti-Semitism and anti-Catholicism remained. Those who joined the armed forces were asked to check Protestant, Catholic, or Jew. There was no room for

DOCUMENT

Franklin D. Roosevelt, "The Four Freedoms" (1941)

Hindu, Buddhist, Muslim, or atheist. Over 70,000 men claimed exemption from service on religious grounds. The government honored about half those claims, and most were assigned to noncombat military service.

Many clergymen of all faiths volunteered to serve as chaplains. A few remained pacifist, but far fewer than in World War I. One influential minister and theologian who argued for force to combat evil was Reinhold Niebuhr. In books like *Children of Light and Children of Darkness* (1944), he opposed what he saw as a naïve faith in the goodness of man, a faith that permeated the Social Gospel movement, progressivism, and the New Deal. In a world gone mad, he saw all men as sinful and he argued for the use of force against evil. His Christian realism influenced the continuing debate in the 1930s, 1940s, and 1950s over the proper American response to evil around the world.

The GIs' War

GI, short for *government issue,* became the affectionate designation for the ordinary soldier in World War II. The GIs came from every background and ethnic group. Some served reluctantly, some eagerly. A few became genuine heroes, and all were turned into heroes by the press and the public, who seemed to believe that one American could easily defeat at least 20 Japanese or Germans. Ernie Pyle, a war correspondent who chronicled the authentic story of the ordinary GI, wrote of soldiers "just toiling from day to day in a world full of insecurity, discomfort, homesickness, and a dulled sense of danger."

In the midst of battle, the war was no fun, but only one soldier in eight ever saw combat, and even for many of them the war was a great adventure (as World War I had been). "When World War II broke out I was delighted," Mario Puzo, author of *The Godfather,* remembered. "My country called."

Mexican Americans were drafted and volunteered in great numbers. A third of a million served in all branches of the military, a larger percentage than for many other ethnic groups. Although they encountered prejudice, they probably found less in the armed forces than at home, and many returned to civilian life with new ambitions and self-esteem.

Many Native Americans also served, often recruited for special service in the Marine Signal Corps. One group of Navajo completely befuddled the Japanese with a code based on their native language. But the Navajo code talkers and all other Indians who chose to return to reservations after the war were ineligible for benefits like veterans' loans and hospitalization. (They lived on federal land, and that, by law, canceled the advantages that other veterans enjoyed.)

For African Americans, who served throughout the war in segregated units and faced prejudice everywhere, the military experience also had much to teach. Fewer blacks were sent overseas (about 79,000 out of 504,000 blacks in the service in 1943), and fewer were in combat outfits, so the percentage of black soldiers killed and wounded was low. Many illiterate blacks, especially from the South, learned to read and write. Blacks who went overseas began to realize that not everyone viewed them as inferior. Most realized the paradox of fighting for freedom when they themselves had little freedom; they hoped things would improve after the war.

Because the war lasted longer than World War I, its impact was greater. In all, over 16 million men and women served in the military. About 322,000 were killed, and more than 800,000 were wounded. The 12,000 listed as missing just disappeared. The war claimed many more lives than World War I and was the nation's costliest after the Civil War. But penicillin, blood plasma, sulfa drugs, and rapid battlefield evacuation made it twice as likely for the wounded in World War II to survive as in World War I. Penicillin also minimized the threat of venereal disease, but all men who served still saw an anti-VD film.

Women in Uniform

Women have served in all American wars as nurses and cooks and in other support capacities, and during World War II many continued in these roles. A few nurses landed in France just days after the Normandy invasion. Nurses with the army and the marines in the Pacific dug their own foxholes and treated men under fire. Sixty-six nurses spent the entire war in the Philippines as prisoners of the Japanese. Most nurses, however, were far behind the lines.

Although nobody objected to women nurses, not until April 1943 did women physicians win the right to join the Army and Navy Medical Corps. Despite some objections, Congress authorized full military participation (except combat duty) for women because they would free men for combat. World War II thus became the first U.S. war in which women received regular military status. About 350,000 women joined up, most in the Women's Army Corps (WACS) and the women's branch of the Navy (WAVES), but there were others in the coast guard, marines, and the air force.

Still, men and women were not treated equally. Women were explicitly kept out of combat situations and were often underused by male officers who found it difficult to view women in nontraditional roles. Army nurses with officer rank were forbidden to date enlisted men. Men were informed about contraceptives and encouraged to use them, but information about birth control was explicitly prohibited for women. Rumors charged many service women with promiscuity, spread apparently by men uncomfortable with women's invasion of the male military domain. Pregnancy brought instant dismissal; yet the pregnancy rate for both married and unmarried women remained low.

Despite difficulties, women played important roles during the war, and when they left the service, they had the same rights as male veterans. The women in the service did not permanently alter the military or the public's perception of women's proper role, but they did change a few minds, and many of these women had their lives altered and their horizons broadened.

A WAR OF DIPLOMATS AND GENERALS

Pearl Harbor thrust the country into war with Japan. On December 11, 1941, Hitler declared war on the United States. The reason why has never been fully explained. He was not required by his treaty with Japan to go to war with the

United States, and without his action, the United States might have concentrated on fighting Japan. Hitler forced the United States into war against the Axis powers in both Europe and Asia.

War Aims

Why were we fighting the war? In a speech before Congress in January 1941, Roosevelt had mentioned the four freedoms: freedom of speech and expression, freedom of worship, freedom from want, and freedom from fear. For many Americans, this was what they were fighting for. Roosevelt spoke vaguely of extending democracy and establishing a peacekeeping organization, but in direct contrast to Woodrow Wilson, he never spelled out in any detail the political purposes for fighting. But others were more explicit. Henry Luce, the editor of *Life* magazine, published an essay before Pearl Harbor called "The American Century," where he argued that the United States had the responsibility to spread the American way of life around the world. That is what we were fighting for.

Roosevelt and his advisers decided on a holding action in the Pacific while concentrating efforts against Hitler in Europe. But the United States was not fighting alone. It joined the Soviet Union and Great Britain in a difficult, but ultimately effective, anti-Nazi alliance. Churchill and Roosevelt got along well, although they often disagreed on strategy. Roosevelt's relationship with Stalin was much more strained, but often he agreed with the Soviet leader about the way to fight the war. Stalin, who had murdered hundreds of thousands of potential or actual opponents, distrusted both the British and the Americans, but he needed them, just as they depended on him. Without the tremendous Russian sacrifices in 1941 and 1942, Germany would have won the war before the vast American military and industrial might could be mobilized.

Year of Disaster, 1942

The first half of 1942 was disastrous for the Allies. The Japanese captured the resource-rich Dutch East Indies, swept into Burma, took Wake and Guam, and invaded Alaska's Aleutian Islands. They pushed American forces in the Philippines onto the Bataan peninsula and finally onto the tiny island of Corregidor, where General Jonathan Wainwright surrendered more than 11,000 men to the Japanese. American reporters tried to play down the disasters, concentrating on tales of American heroism against overwhelming odds.

In Europe, the Germans pushed deep into Russia, threatening to take all the industrial centers, the valuable oil fields, and even Moscow. In North Africa, General Erwin Rommel's mechanized Afrika Korps neared the Suez Canal. U-boats sank British and American ships faster than they could be replaced. For a few dark months in 1942, it seemed that the Axis would win before the United States got prepared for war.

The Allies could not agree on a military strategy in Europe. Churchill advocated tightening the ring around Germany, using bombing raids to weaken the enemy and encouraging resistance among the occupied countries. He wanted to avoid any direct assault on the continent until success was ensured. Stalin, on the other hand, demanded a second front, an invasion of Europe in 1942 to relieve the

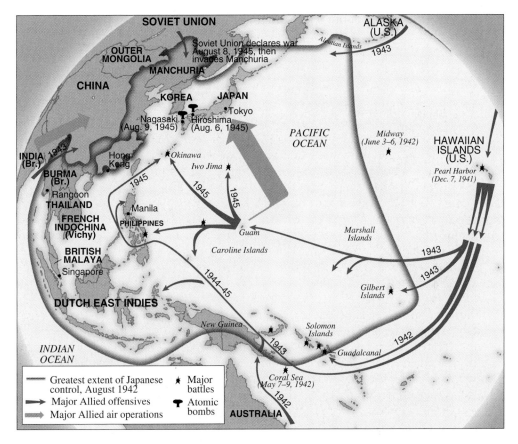

WORLD WAR II: PACIFIC THEATER After the surprise attack on Pearl Harbor, the Japanese extended their control in the Pacific from Burma to the Aleutian Islands and almost to Australia. But after American naval and air victories at Coral Sea and Midway in 1942, the Japanese were increasingly on the defensive. ■ **Reflecting on the Past** How did the great distances in the Pacific influence military plans for both sides? Why was the aircraft carrier more important than the battleship in the Pacific War? Was there any alternative to the American strategy of moving slowly from one Japanese-occupied island to another? Why did China play such a crucial role in the war against Japan?

pressure on the Red Army, which faced 200 German divisions along a 2,000-mile front. Roosevelt agreed to an offensive in 1942. But the invasion in 1942 was not in France but in North Africa. The decision was probably right from a military point of view, but it taught Russia to distrust Britain and the United States.

MAP

World War II in Europe

Landing in North Africa in November 1942, American and British troops tried to link up with a beleaguered British army fighting westward from Egypt. The American army, enthusiastic but inexperienced, met little resistance until, at Kasserine Pass in Tunisia, the Germans counterattacked and destroyed a large American force, inflicting 5,000 casualties. Roosevelt, who launched the invasion in part to give the American people a victory to relieve dreary news from the Far East, learned that victories often came with long casualty lists.

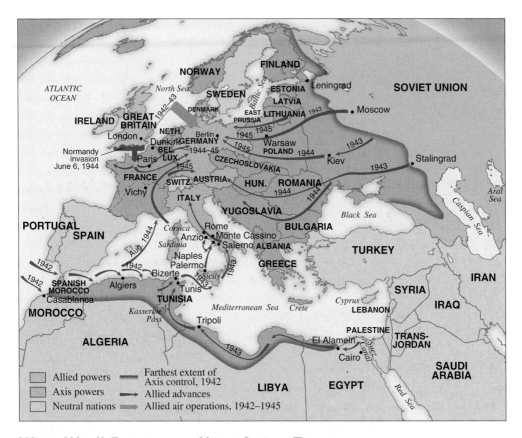

WORLD WAR II: EUROPEAN AND NORTH AFRICAN THEATERS The German war machine swept across Europe and North Africa and almost captured Cairo and Moscow, but after major defeats at Stalingrad and El Alamein in 1943, the Axis powers were in retreat. Many lives were lost on both sides before the Allied victory in 1945. ■ **Reflecting on the Past** How was the African campaign important to the Allies' strategy to defeat Germany and Italy? Why was the invasion of France necessary even after the capture of North Africa and a portion of Italy? Why was the Soviet Union crucial to the war in Europe? Why was the war in Europe very different from the war in the Pacific?

Conquering French North Africa drew Roosevelt into unpleasant political compromises. To gain a cease-fire, the United States recognized a provisional government under Admiral Jean Darlan, a former Nazi collaborator. Did this mean that the United States would negotiate with Mussolini? Or with Hitler? The Darlan deal reinforced Soviet distrust of the Americans and angered many Americans.

Roosevelt never made a deal with Hitler, but he did aid Fascist Spain in return for safe passage of American shipping into the Mediterranean. But the United States did not aid only right-wing dictators like Franco. It also supplied arms to the left-wing resistance in France, to the Communist guerrilla Tito in Yugoslavia, and to Ho Chi Minh, the anti-French resistance leader in Indochina. Roosevelt also authorized large-scale, lend-lease aid to the Soviet Union. Although liberals criticized his support of dictators, Roosevelt was willing to do almost anything to win the war. Military expediency often dictated his political decisions.

Even on the issue of the plight of the Jews in Nazi-occupied Europe, Roosevelt's solution was to win the war as quickly as possible. By November 1942, confirmed information reached the United States that the Nazis were systematically exterminating Jews. Yet the administration did nothing for more than a year, and even then it did scandalously little. Only 21,000 refugees were allowed to enter the United States over a period of three and a half years, just 10 percent of those who could have been admitted under immigration quotas. The War Department refused to bomb the Auschwitz gas chambers, and officials turned down many rescue schemes. Widespread anti-Semitism in the United States in the 1940s and fears of massive Jewish immigration partly explain the administration's policy. The failure of the media, Christian leaders, and even American Jews to bring effective pressure on the government does not excuse the president for his shameful indifference to the systematic murder of millions of people. Roosevelt could not have prevented the Holocaust, but vigorous action by him could have saved many thousands of lives.

VIDEO

Nazi Murder Mills

Buchenwald Only at the end of the war did most Americans learn about the horrors of Nazi concentration camps and gas chambers. Senator Alben Barkley of Kentucky looks in disbelief at dead Jews stacked like wood at Buchenwald, April 24, 1945. Why didn't Americans learn about the Holocaust sooner? *(The National Archives)*

A Strategy for Ending the War

The commanding general of the Allied armies in the North African campaign emerged as a genuine leader. Born in Texas, Dwight D. Eisenhower spent his boyhood in Abilene, Kansas. His small-town background made it easy for the media to make him an American hero. Eisenhower, however, had not come to hero status easily. In World War I, he trained soldiers in Texas. He was only a lieutenant colonel when World War II erupted. But George Marshall, who became the army's top general in September 1939, had discovered Eisenhower's talents even before the war began. He was quickly promoted to general and achieved a reputation as an expert planner and organizer. Gregarious and outgoing, "Ike" had a broad smile that made most people like him instantly. He was not a brilliant field commander and made many mistakes in the African campaign, but he could get diverse people working together, which was crucial because British and American units had to cooperate.

The American army moved slowly across North Africa, linked up with the British, invaded Sicily in July 1943, and finally stormed ashore in Italy in September. The Italian campaign proved long and bitter. After the overthrow of Mussolini and Italy's surrender in September 1943, the Germans occupied the country and the American army bogged down. The Allies did not reach Rome until June 1944, and they never controlled all of Italy.

Despite the decision to make the war in Europe the first priority, American ships and planes halted the Japanese advance in the spring of 1942. In the Battle of Coral Sea in May 1942, American carrier-based planes inflicted heavy damage on the Japanese fleet and probably prevented the invasion of Australia. It was the first naval battle in history in which surface ships did not fire on each other; airplanes did all the damage. In World War II, aircraft carriers were more important than battleships. A month later, at the Battle of Midway, American planes sank four Japanese carriers and destroyed nearly 300 planes. This first major Japanese defeat restored some balance of power in the Pacific and ended the threat to Hawaii.

World War II in the Pacific

In 1943, the American sea and land forces leapfrogged from island to island, retaking territory and building bases to attack the Philippines and eventually Japan. Progress often had terrible costs. In November 1943, about 5,000 marines landed on the coral beaches of the tiny island of Tarawa. Despite heavy naval bombardment and the support of hundreds of planes, they met massive resistance. The four-day battle killed more than 1,000 Americans and wounded over 3,000. The Pacific war was often brutal and dehumanizing. American soldiers collected Japanese skulls and ears, something never done in the European war. Correspondent Ernie Pyle decided that the Japanese were looked upon as something subhuman, like "cockroaches and mice."

The Invasion of France

Operation Overlord, the code name for the largest amphibious invasion in history, the invasion Stalin had wanted in 1942, finally began on June 6, 1944. It was, according to Churchill, "the most difficult and complicated operation that has ever taken place." The initial assault along a 60-mile stretch of the Normandy coast was conducted with 175,000 men supported by 600 warships and 11,000 planes. Within a month, over 1 million troops and more than 170,000 vehicles had landed. During the first hours of the invasion, there seemed to be too many supplies. It cost 2,245 killed and 1,670 wounded to secure the beachhead. "It was much lighter than anybody expected," one observer remarked. "But if you saw faces instead of numbers on the casualty list, it wasn't light at all."

The Allies dropped more than 1.5 million tons of bombs on Europe. Evidence gathered after the war suggests that this bombardment disrupted German war production less than Allied strategists expected. Often a plant or a rail center would be back in operation days or hours after an attack, and the bombing of the cities may have strengthened the German people's resolve to fight to the bitter end. Nor did the destruction of German cities come cheaply. German fighter planes and antiaircraft guns shot down thousands of American and British planes.

The most destructive bombing raid of the war, against Dresden on the night of February 13–14, 1945, had no strategic purpose. The British and Americans launched the raid to help demonstrate to Stalin that they were aiding the Russian offensive. Dresden, a city of 630,000, was a communications center. Three waves of planes dropped 650,000 incendiary bombs, causing a firestorm that swept over eight square miles, destroying everything in its path, and killing an estimated 100,000 civilians.

With eccentric General George Patton leading the charge and staid General Omar Bradley in command, the American army broke out of the Normandy beachhead in July 1944 and swept across France. American productive capacity and the ability to supply a mobile and motorized army eventually brought victory. But not all American equipment was superior. The American fighter plane, the P-40, could not compete early in the war with the German ME-109. The United States was far behind Germany in the development of rockets, but that was not as important as the American inability, until the end of the war, to develop a tank that could compete in armament or firepower with the German tanks. The American army partly made up for the deficiency of its tanks by having superior artillery. Perhaps even more important, most American soldiers had grown up tinkering with cars and radios. Children of the machine age, they managed to keep tanks, trucks, and guns functioning under difficult circumstances, which gave the American army superior mobility.

By late 1944, the American and British armies had driven across France, while the Russians had pushed far into eastern Europe. The war seemed nearly over. However, just before Christmas in 1944, the Germans launched a massive counterattack on the western front against thinly dispersed and inexperienced American troops. The Germans drove 50 miles inside the American lines before they were checked. During this "Battle of the Bulge," Eisenhower was so desperate for additional troops that he offered to pardon any military prisoners in Europe who would go into battle. Most declined. Eisenhower also promised any black soldiers in the service and supply outfits an opportunity to become infantrymen in the white units, though usually with a lower rank. However, his chief of staff pointed out that this was the "most dangerous thing I have seen in regard to race relations." Eisenhower recanted, not wishing to start a social revolution.

The Politics of Victory

As American and British armies assaulted Germany in the winter and spring of 1945, the political and diplomatic aspects of the war began to overshadow military concerns. Relations between the Soviet Union and the other Allies had been badly strained at times during the war; with victory in sight, the tension grew worse. Although the American press idealized Stalin and the Russian people, a number of high-level American diplomats and presidential advisers distrusted the Russians and anticipated a postwar confrontation. They urged Roosevelt to make military decisions with the postwar political situation in mind.

The main issue in the spring of 1945 was who would capture Berlin. The British wanted to beat the Russians to the capital city. Eisenhower, however, fearing that the Germans might hold out indefinitely in the Alps, ordered the armies south rather than toward Berlin. He also wanted to avoid unnecessary American casualties, and he planned to meet the Russian army at an easily marked spot to avoid any unfortunate incidents. British and American forces could probably not have arrived in Berlin before the Russians, but Eisenhower's decision generated controversy after the war. Russian and American troops met on April 25, 1945, at the Elbe River. On May 2, the Russians took Berlin. Hitler committed suicide. The long war in Europe finally ended on May 8, 1945.

Meanwhile, throughout 1944, the United States had tightened the noose on Japan. Long-range B-29 bombers began sustained strikes on the Japanese mainland in June 1944, and by November, they were firebombing Tokyo. In a series of naval and air engagements, especially at the Battle of Leyte Gulf, American planes destroyed most of the remaining Japanese navy. By the end of 1944, an American victory in the Pacific was all but ensured. American forces recaptured the Philippines early the next year. Yet it might take years to conquer the Japanese home islands.

While the military campaigns reached a critical stage, Roosevelt ran for a fourth term. He dropped Vice President Henry Wallace from the ticket because some thought him too radical and impetuous. To replace him, the Democratic convention selected a relatively unknown senator from Missouri. Harry S Truman's only fame had come from leading a Senate investigation of war contracts.

The Republicans nominated Thomas Dewey, the colorless and moderate governor of New York, who had a difficult time criticizing Roosevelt without appearing unpatriotic. Roosevelt seemed haggard and ill during much of the campaign, but he won easily. He would need all his strength to deal with the difficult problems of ending the war and constructing a peace settlement.

The Big Three at Yalta

Roosevelt, Churchill, and Stalin met at the Soviet resort city of Yalta in February 1945 to discuss the peace settlements. Most of the Yalta agreements were secret, and during the subsequent Cold War they would become controversial. Roosevelt wanted Soviet help in ending the Pacific war, to avoid the slaughter of American men in an invasion of Japan. In return for a promise to enter the war within three months after the war in Europe was over, the Soviet Union was granted the Kurile

Islands, the southern half of Sakhalin Island, and railroads and port facilities in Korea, Manchuria, and Mongolia. That later seemed like a heavy price to pay, but realistically the Soviet Union controlled most of this territory and could not have been dislodged without going to war.

When the provisions of the secret treaties were revealed much later, many people would accuse Roosevelt of trusting Stalin too much. But Roosevelt wanted to retain a working relationship with Moscow to preserve the peace, and he hoped to get Soviet agreement to cooperate with the new international organization, the United Nations.

The European section of the Yalta agreement proved even more controversial. The diplomats decided to partition Germany and to divide Berlin. The Polish agreements were even more difficult to swallow. The Polish government-in-exile in London was militantly anti-Communist and looked forward to returning home after the war. Stalin demanded that eastern Poland be given to the Soviet Union. Churchill and Roosevelt finally agreed to the Russian demands with the proviso that Poland be compensated with German territory on its western border. Stalin agreed to include some London Poles in the pro-Soviet Polish government and to "free and unfettered elections as soon as possible."

The Polish settlement would prove divisive after the war, for it quickly became clear that what the British and Americans wanted in eastern Europe contrasted with what the Soviet Union intended. Yet at the time it seemed imperative that Russia enter the war in the Pacific, and the reality was that in 1945 the Soviet army occupied most of eastern Europe.

The most potentially valuable accomplishment at Yalta was Stalin's agreement to join Roosevelt and Churchill in calling a conference in San Francisco in April 1945 to draft a United Nations charter. The charter gave primary responsibility for keeping global peace to the Security Council, composed of five permanent members (the United States, the Soviet Union, Great Britain, France, and China) and six other nations elected for two-year terms. Just as important was the Bretton Woods Conference held in the summer of 1944 in New Hampshire. It established the World Bank and the International Monetary Fund and fixed the rate for international exchange using dollars as the standard, in the process recognizing that it would be the United States, not Great Britain, that would be the economic power in the postwar world.

The Atomic Age Begins

Two months after Yalta, on April 12, 1945, Roosevelt died suddenly. Hated and loved to the end, he was replaced by Harry Truman, who was more difficult to hate and harder to love. In the beginning, Truman seemed tentative and unsure. Yet it fell to him to make some of history's most difficult decisions.

The Manhattan Project, organized in 1941, was one of the best-kept secrets of the war. A distinguished group of scientists at Los Alamos, New Mexico, had orders to build an atomic bomb before Germany did. But by the time the bomb was successfully tested in the New Mexico desert on July 16, 1945, the war in Europe had ended.

HOW OTHERS SEE US

Yamaoka Michiko, On the Ground at Hiroshima

Yamaoka Michiko, a young Japanese high school student, was 15 on August 6, 1945, when the Enola Gay dropped the first atomic bomb. She survived, but she was horribly burned and disfigured. After the war she was one of 25 victims brought to the United States to receive treatment and plastic surgery.

That morning I left the house at about seven forty-five. I heard that the B-29s had already gone home. Mom told me, "Watch out, the B-29s might come again." My house was one point three kilometers from hypocenter. ... I heard the faint sound of planes as I approached the river. The planes were tricky. Sometimes they only pretended to leave. I could still hear the very faint sound of planes. Today, I have no hearing in my left ear because of the blast. I thought, how strange, so I put my right hand above my eyes and looked up to see if I could spot them. The sun was dazzling. That was the moment. ...

They say temperatures of seven thousand degrees centigrade hit me. You can't really say it washed over me. It is hard to describe. I simply fainted. I remember my body floating in the air. That was probably the blast, but I don't know how far I was blown. When I came to my senses, my surroundings were silent. ...

The only medicine was tempura oil, I put it on my body myself. I lay on the concrete for hours. My skin was now flat, not puffed up anymore. A scorching sky was overhead. The flies swarmed over me and covered my wounds, which were already festering. People were simply left lying around. When their faint breathing became silent, they'd say, "This one's dead," and put the body in a pile of corpses. Some called for water, and if they got it, they died immediately. ...

When I went to America I had a deep hatred toward America. I asked myself why they ended the war by means which destroyed human beings. When I talked about how I suffered, I was told, "Well, you attacked Pearl Harbor!" I didn't understand much English then, and it's probably just as well. From the American point of view, they dropped that bomb in order to end the war faster, in order to create more damage faster. But it's inexcusable to harm human beings in this way. I wonder what kind of education there is now in America about atomic bombs. They're still making them, aren't they?

- *Can you answer Yamaoka Michiko's question?*
- *Does the plastic surgery she received in America make up for her pain and suffering?*

The scientists working on the bomb assumed they were perfecting a military weapon. Yet when they first saw its ghastly power, remembered J. Robert Oppenheimer, a leading scientist on the project, "some wept, a few cheered. Most stood silently." Some opposed using the bomb. They realized its revolutionary power and worried about the future reputation of the United States if it unleashed this new force. But a presidential committee made up of scientists, military leaders, and politicians recommended that it be dropped on a military target in Japan as soon as possible.

"The final decision of where and when to use the atomic bomb was up to me," Truman later remembered. "Let there be no doubt about it. I regarded the bomb as a military weapon and never had any doubt that it should be used." But the deci-

TIMELINE

1933	Hitler becomes German chancellor		Germany attacks Russia
	United States recognizes the Soviet Union		Japanese attack Pearl Harbor
	Roosevelt extends Good Neighbor policy		Germany declares war on United States
		1942	Internment of Japanese Americans
1935	Italy invades Ethiopia		Second Allied front in Africa launched
	First Neutrality Act		
1936	Spanish civil war begins	**1943**	Invasion of Sicily
			Italy surrenders
	Second Neutrality Act		United Mine Workers strike
	Roosevelt reelected		
1938	Hitler annexes Austria, occupies Sudetenland		Race riots in Detroit and other cities
	German persecution of Jews intensifies	**1944**	Normandy invasion (Operation Overlord)
1939	Nazi–Soviet Pact		Roosevelt elected for a fourth term
	German invasion of Poland	**1945**	Yalta Conference
	World War II begins		Roosevelt dies
1941	FDR's "Four Freedoms" speech		Harry Truman becomes president
	Executive order outlaws discrimination in defense industries		Germany surrenders
			Hiroshima and Nagasaki bombed
	Lend-Lease Act		Japan surrenders

sion had military and political ramifications. Even though Japan had lost most of its empire by the summer of 1945, it still had several million troops and thousands of kamikaze planes, whose pilots gave their lives by crashing planes, heavily laden with bombs, into American ships. There was little defense against them.

Even with the Russian promise to enter the war, it appeared that an amphibious landing on the Japanese mainland would be necessary. The monthlong battle for Iwo Jima, 750 miles from Tokyo, had killed over 4,000 Americans and wounded 15,000, and the battle for Okinawa was even more costly. Invading the Japanese mainland would presumably be far worse. The bomb, many thought, could end the war without an invasion. Some people involved in the decision wanted to avenge Pearl Harbor, and still others felt they needed to justify spending over $2 billion on the project in the first place. To some historians, the timing of the first bomb indicates that the decision was intended to impress the Russians and ensure that they had little to do with the peace settlement in the Far East.

Historians debate whether the use of the atomic bomb on Japanese cities was necessary to end the war, but for the hundreds of thousands of American troops waiting to invade Japan, there was no question about the rightness of the decision. They believed that it saved their lives. On August 6, 1945, two days before the Soviet Union had promised to enter the war against Japan, a B-29 bomber, the *Enola Gay*, dropped a single atomic bomb over Hiroshima. It killed or severely wounded 140,000 civilians and destroyed four square miles of the city. One of the men on the plane thought that they had missed the target: "I didn't see any sign of the city." The Soviet Union entered the war on August 8. When Japan refused to surrender, a second bomb destroyed Nagasaki on August 9. The Japanese surrendered five days later. The war was over, but the problems of the atomic age and the postwar world were only beginning.

Conclusion

Peace, Prosperity, and International Responsibilities

The United States emerged from World War II with an enhanced reputation as the world's most powerful industrial and military nation. The demands of the war had finally ended the Great Depression and brought prosperity to most Americans. Even N. Scott Momaday's family found better jobs because of the war, but like many Americans, they had to relocate in order to take those jobs. The war had also increased the power of the federal government. The payroll deduction of federal income taxes, begun during the war, symbolized the growth of a federal bureaucracy that affected the lives of all Americans. Ironically, the war to preserve freedom was fought with a segregated army. Yet the war had also ended American isolationism and made the United States into the dominant international power. Of all the nations that fought in the war, the United States had suffered the least. No bombs were dropped on American factories, and no cities were destroyed. Although more than 300,000 Americans lost their lives, even this carnage seemed minimal when compared with the more than 20 million Russian soldiers and civilians who died or the 6 million Jews and millions of others systematically exterminated by Hitler.

Americans greeted the end of the war with joy and relief. They looked forward to the peace and prosperity for which they had fought. Yet within two years, the peace would be jeopardized by the Cold War, and the United States would be rearming its former enemies, Japan and Germany, to oppose its former friend, the Soviet Union. The irony of that situation reduced the joy of the hard-won peace and made the American people more suspicious of their government and its foreign policy. Yet the memory of World War II and the perception that the country was united against evil enemies, indeed, that World War II was a "good war," would have an impact on American foreign policy, and even on Americans' perception of themselves, for decades to come.

Questions for Review and Reflection

1. Trace the series of international events that led to the U.S. entry into World War II. Could the United States have stayed neutral?

2. Explain why and how the United States interned Japanese Americans in the aftermath of the attack on Pearl Harbor. Was the internment justified?

3. How did the war change the lives of women, African Americans, and Hispanic Americans?

4. What were the war aims of the United States, and how were they achieved?

5. What led the United States to develop the atomic bomb? What were the consequences of this new weapon for the Japanese, for Americans, and for the outcome of World War II?

Discovering U.S. History Online

World War II Exhibit: A People at War http://www.nara.gov/exhall/people/people.html
This National Archives exhibit takes a close look at the contributions millions of Americans made to the war effort.

Powers of Persuasion—Poster Art of World War II http://www.nara.gov/education/teaching/posters/poster.html
These powerful posters at the National Archives were part of the battle for the hearts and minds of the American people during WWII.

A-Bomb WWW Museum http://www.csi.ad.jp/ABOMB/
This site offers information about the impact of the first atomic bomb as well as the background and context of weapons of total destruction.

United States Holocaust Memorial Museum http://www.ushmm.org
This is the official Web site of the Holocaust Museum in Washington, D.C.

Tuskegee Airmen http://www.wpafb.af.mil/museum/history/prewwii/ta.htm
The Air Force Museum at Wright-Patterson Air Force Base maintains this site about the African American pilots of Word War II.

Resource Listing for WWII http://www.sunsite.unc.edu/pha/index.html
This site has a large number of searchable primary texts from all aspects of World War II.

Japanese Internment http://www.lib.washington.edu/exhibits/harmony
The Japanese American Exhibit and Access Project at the University of Washington deals with all aspects of the Japanese wartime internment, relocation centers, and the human stories behind the massive removal of Japanese Americans from the West Coast.

Fiction and Film

In *The Dollmaker* (1954), Harriette Arnow tells the story of a young woman from Kentucky who finds herself in wartime Detroit. Two powerful novels that tell the story of the battlefield experience are Norman Mailer, *The Naked and the Dead* (1948), and Irwin Shaw, *The Young Lions* (1948).

Pearl Harbor (2001) is a blockbuster film worth seeing for the special effects, but more interesting is *Tora! Tora! Tora!* (1970), a film that tells the story of the attack on Pearl Harbor from both the American and Japanese point of view. It is compelling even as it oversimplifies history. *Saving Private Ryan* (1998), a film about one platoon's adventures on D-Day and after, is sentimental and romantic in spots but contains some graphic scenes from the invasion of Normandy.

Recommended Reading

www.ablongman.com/nash

The Companion Website has a list of recommended readings about events leading to the war, the home front, the social impact of the war, and the role of diplomats and generals.

Postwar America at Home, 1945–1960

CHAPTER OUTLINE

- Economic Boom
- Demographic and Technological Shifts
- Consensus and Conformity
- Origins of the Welfare State
- The Other America
- Conclusion: Qualms amid Affluence

American Stories

An Entrepreneur Franchises the American Dream

Ray Kroc, an ambitious salesman, headed toward San Bernardino, California, on a business trip in 1954. For more than a decade he had been selling "multimixers"—stainless steel machines that could make six milkshakes at once—to restaurants and soda shops around the United States. On this trip, he was particularly interested in checking out a hamburger stand run by Richard and Maurice McDonald, who had bought eight of his "contraptions" and could therefore make 48 shakes at the same time.

Always eager to increase sales, Kroc wanted to see the McDonalds' operation for himself. The 52-year-old son of Bohemian parents had sold everything from real estate to radio time to paper cups before peddling the multimixers but had enjoyed no stunning success. Yet he was still on the alert for the key to the fortune that was part of the American dream. As he watched the lines of people at the San Bernardino McDonald's, the answer seemed at hand.

The McDonald brothers sold only standard hamburgers, french fries, and milkshakes, but they had developed a system that was fast, efficient, and clean. It drew on the automobile traffic that moved along Route 66. And it was profitable indeed. Sensing the possibilities, Kroc proposed that the two owners open other establishments as well. When they balked, he negotiated a 99-year contract that allowed him to sell the fast-food idea and the name—and their golden arches design—wherever he could.

On April 15, 1955, Kroc opened his first McDonald's in Des Plaines, a suburb of Chicago. Three months later, he sold his first franchise in Fresno, California. Others soon followed. Kroc scouted out new locations, almost always on highway "strips," persuaded people to put up the capital, and provided them with specifications guaranteed to ensure future success. For his efforts, he received a percentage of the gross take.

From the start, Kroc insisted on standardization. Every McDonald's was the same—from the two functional arches supporting the glass enclosure that housed the kitchen and take-out window to the single arch near the road bearing a sign indicating how many 15-cent hamburgers had already been sold. All menus and prices were exactly the same, and Kroc demanded that everything from hamburger size to cooking time be constant. He insisted, too, that the establishments be clean. No pinball games or cigarette machines were permitted; the premium was on a good, inexpensive hamburger, quickly served, at a nice place.

McDonald's Golden Arches McDonald's provided a model for other franchisers in the 1950s and the years that followed. The golden arches, shown here in an early version, were virtually the same wherever they appeared. Initially found along highways around the country, they were later built within cities and towns as well. How did the golden arches contribute to McDonald's popularity? *(Used with permission from McDonald's Corporation)*

McDonald's, of course, was an enormous success. In 1962, total sales exceeded $76 million. In 1964, before the company had been in operation for 10 years, it had sold over 400 million hamburgers and 120 million pounds of french fries. By the end of the next year, there were 710 McDonald's stands in 44 states. In 1974, only 20 years after Kroc's vision of the hamburger's future, McDonald's did $2 billion worth of business. When Kroc died in 1984, a total of 45 billion burgers had been sold at 7,500 outlets in 32 countries. Ronald McDonald, the clown who came to represent the company, became known to children around the globe after his Washington, D.C., debut in November 1963. When McDonald's began to advertise, it became the country's first restaurant to buy television time. Musical slogans like "You deserve a break today" and "We do it all for you" became better known than some popular songs.

The success of McDonald's provides an example of the development of new economic and technological trends in the United States in the post–World War II years. Ray Kroc capitalized on the changes of the automobile age. He understood that a restaurant had a better chance of success not in the city but along the highways, where it could draw on heavier traffic. Kroc understood, too, that the franchise notion provided the key to rapid economic growth. Finally, he sensed the importance of standardization and uniformity. He understood the mood of the time—the quiet conformity of people searching for the key to the American dream of prosperity and stability. The McDonald's image may have been monotonous, but that was part of its appeal. Customers always knew what they would get wherever they found the golden arches. If the atmosphere was "bland," that too was deliberate. As Kroc said, "Our theme is kind of synonymous with Sunday school, the Girl Scouts and the YMCA. McDonald's is clean and wholesome." It was a symbol of the age.

This chapter describes the structural and political changes in American society in the 25 years following World War II. Even as the nation became involved in the global confrontations of the Cold War with the Soviet Union (a story taken up in Chapter 27), Americans were preoccupied with the shifts in social and economic patterns that were taking place. This chapter examines how economic growth, spurred by technological advances, transformed the patterns of work and daily life in the United States. Self-interest triumphed over idealism, as most people gained a level of material comfort previously unknown. Comforted by a renewed commitment to organized religion that involved people of all persuasions, they felt confident in the patterns of their lives. The political world reflected the prosperity and affluence that followed years of depression and war. Building on the impact of the New Deal and the American role as the "arsenal of democracy" in World War II, government was larger and more involved in people's lives than ever before, despite Republican resistance in the 1950s. Political commitments in the decade and a half after the war laid the groundwork for the welfare state that emerged in the 1960s.

But even as the nation prospered, it experienced serious social and economic divisions among its diverse peoples. This chapter also shows the enormous gaps that existed between rich and poor, even in the best of times. It shows the continuing presence of what one critic eloquently called "the other America" and documents the considerable income disparity and persistent prejudice that African Americans (like members of other minority groups) encountered in their efforts to share in the postwar prosperity. The frustrations they experienced highlighted the limits of the postwar American dream and led to the reform movements that changed American society.

ECONOMIC BOOM

Most Americans were optimistic after 1945. As servicemen returned home from fighting in World War II, their very presence caused a change in family patterns. A baby boom brought unprecedented population growth. The simultaneous and unexpected economic boom had an even greater impact. Large corporations increasingly dominated the business world, but unions grew as well, and most workers improved their lives. Technology appeared triumphant, with new products flooding the market and finding their way into most American homes. Prosperity convinced the growing middle class that all was well in the United States.

The Thriving Peacetime Economy

The wartime return of prosperity after the Great Depression continued in the postwar years, and the United States solidified its position as the richest nation in the world with a sustained economic expansion. Other nations struggled with the aftereffects of World War II (see next section). Yet in the United States, which produced half the world's goods, prosperity was the norm.

The statistical evidence of economic success was impressive. The gross national product (GNP) jumped dramatically between 1945 and 1960, while per capita personal income likewise rose—from $1,087 in 1945 to $2,026 in 1960. Almost 60 percent of all families in the country were now part of the middle class, a dramatic change from the class structure in the nineteenth and early twentieth centuries.

Personal resources fueled economic growth. During World War II, American consumers had been unable to spend all they earned because factories were producing for war. With accumulated savings of $140 billion at the end of the struggle, consumers were ready to buy whatever they could. Equally important was the 22 percent rise in real purchasing power between 1946 and 1960. Families now had far more discretionary income—money to satisfy wants as well as needs—than before. At the end of the Great Depression, fewer than one-quarter of all households had any discretionary income; in 1960, three of every five did.

This new consumer power, in contrast to the underconsumption of the 1920s and 1930s, spurred the economy. Most homes now had an automobile, a television set, a washing machine, and a vacuum cleaner. But consumers could also indulge themselves with electric can openers and automatic transmissions for their cars.

The automobile industry played a key part in the boom. Just as cars and roads transformed America in the 1920s when mass production came of age, so they contributed to the equally great transformation three decades later. Limited to the production of military vehicles during World War II, the auto industry expanded dramatically in the postwar period. Seventy thousand cars were made in 1945; 8 million were manufactured in 1955; and not quite 7 million were produced in 1960. Customers now chose from a wide variety of engines, colors, fancy styles, and optional accessories.

The development of a massive interstate highway system also stimulated auto production and so contributed to prosperity. Through the Interstate Highway Act of 1956, the Eisenhower administration poured $26 billion, the largest public works expenditure in American history, into building over 40,000 miles of federal highways, linking all parts of the United States. Federal officials claimed the system would make evacuation quicker in the event of nuclear attack. President Dwight D. Eisenhower boasted that "the amount of concrete poured to form these roadways would build ... six sidewalks to the moon. ... More than any single action by the government since the end of the war, this one would change the face of America." Significantly, this massive effort helped create a nation dependent on oil.

A housing boom also fed economic growth as home-ownership rates rose from 53 percent in 1945 to 62 percent in 1960. Much of the stimulus came from the GI Bill of 1944. In addition to giving returning servicemen priority for many jobs

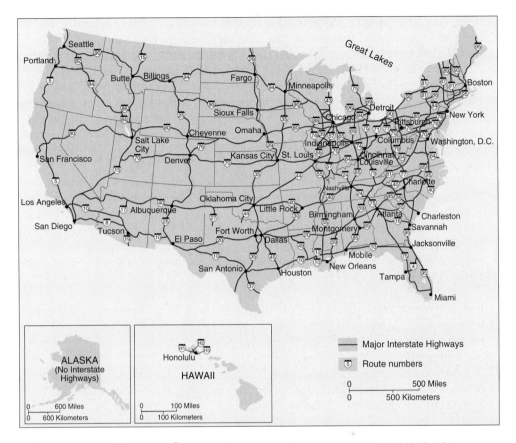

U.S. INTERSTATE HIGHWAY SYSTEM The interstate highway system, established by legislative action in 1956, created an extensive network of roads that changed the landscape and living patterns of people throughout the United States. ■ **Reflecting on the Past** How fully did the interstate highway network cover the entire country? Which areas were most extensively built? Why were there more roads in some parts of the country than in others?

and providing educational benefits, it offered low-interest home mortgages. Millions of former servicemen from all social classes eagerly purchased their share of the American dream.

The government's increasingly active economic role both stimulated and sustained the expansion. Businesses were allowed to buy almost 80 percent of the factories built by the government during the war for much less than they cost. Even more important was the dramatic rise in defense spending as the Cold War escalated. In 1947, Congress passed the National Security Act creating the Department of Defense and authorized an initial budget of $13 billion. With the onset of the Korean War, the defense budget rose to $22 billion in 1951 and to about $47 billion in 1953. Approximately half of the total federal budget went to the armed forces. This spending, in turn, helped stimulate the aircraft and electronic industries. The government underwrote 90 percent of aviation and space research,

65 percent of electricity and electronics work, and 42 percent of scientific instrument development. Meanwhile, the close business–government ties of World War II grew stronger.

Most citizens welcomed the huge expenditures, not only because they supported the American stance in the struggle against communism (see Chapter 27) but also because they understood the economic impact of military spending. Columnist David Lawrence noted in 1950, "Government planners figure they have found the magic formula for almost endless good times. Cold war is an automatic pump primer. Turn a spigot, and the public clamors for more arms spending."

Postwar American growth avoided some of the major problems that often bedevil periods of economic expansion—inflation and the enrichment of a few at the expense of the many. Inflation, a problem in the immediate postwar period, slowed from an average of 7 percent per year in the 1940s to a gentle 2 to 3 percent per year in the 1950s. And though the concentration of income remained the same—the bottom half of the population still earned less than the top tenth—the ranks of middle-class Americans grew.

American products were sold around the world. People in other countries had developed a taste for Coca-Cola during the war. Now numerous other goods became available overseas. American books, magazines, movies, and records promoted the spread of American culture and provided still more profits for American entrepreneurs.

A major economic transformation had occurred in the United States. Peaceful, prosperous, and productive, the nation had became what economist John Kenneth Galbraith called the "affluent society."

Postwar Growth Around the World

Elsewhere in the world, postwar reconstruction began but affluence took longer to arrive. Both European and Asian countries had suffered greater casualties than the United States, and some nations, even those on the winning side, had to deal with enormous devastation.

Great Britain was ravaged by the war, and rationing—necessary to provide the equitable distribution of scarce resources—lasted until the early 1950s. British factories, which had been the first to industrialize, were now inefficient and outdated. Meanwhile, Britain lagged behind other European nations in developing a modern superhighway system that could spur industrial development.

In the general election of 1945, British voters ousted Winston Churchill and the Conservative party in favor of the Labour party, which was committed to social change. It took over the coal and railroad industries and began to nationalize the steel industry. While owners were compensated, some critics argued that the government's actions stifled industrial progress. Nevertheless, Great Britain began an economic and social recovery. It even provided a system of socialized medicine far in advance of anything in the United States.

While France was on the winning side of the war, it had suffered the indignity of occupation. It, too, experienced recovery, thanks in part to a rising birthrate, which was also occurring in the United States. At the same time, France, like

Britain, was struggling with the demands of its colonial empire to be free. Brutal struggles in Indochina and Algeria caused financial instability and helped undermine economic development until France pulled out of both areas in the 1950s.

Defeated nations showed the most dramatic development of all. As the United States decided that a strong West Germany was necessary as a buffer against the Soviet Union, it helped cause what came to be known as "the German miracle." Because much of German industrial capacity had been destroyed by the war, new factories could be built with modern technological equipment. In the early 1950s, the West German rate of growth reached 10 percent a year, while the gross national product rose from $23 billion in 1950 to $103 billion in 1964.

Japan likewise revived quickly. Like Germany, it suffered tremendous wartime destruction, due to both conventional bombing and to the new atomic bombs that devastated Hiroshima and Nagasaki in 1945. Under the direction of General Douglas MacArthur, the United States spearheaded the reconstruction effort and created a democratic framework. As political change occurred, the economy grew rapidly, and Japan overtook France and West Germany, soon ranking third in the world behind the United States and the Soviet Union.

So too did the Soviet Union rebuild. Reparations from West Germany and industrial extractions from Eastern Europe helped promote the reconstruction effort. The totalitarian structure of the Soviet state eliminated public debate about the allocation of resources, and the nation embarked upon a series of initiatives that led to the development of a Soviet atomic bomb and an increase in the size of collective farms.

The Corporate Impact on American Life

After 1945, the major corporations in the United States tightened their hold on the American economy. Government policy in World War II had produced tremendous industrial concentration. The government suspended antitrust actions that might impede the war effort, while government contracts spurred expansion of the big corporations at the expense of smaller firms.

Industrial concentration continued after the war, making oligopoly—domination of a given industry by a few firms—a feature of American capitalism. Several waves of mergers had taken place in the past, including one in the 1890s and another in the 1920s. Still another occurred in the 1950s. At the same time, the booming economy encouraged the development of conglomerates—firms with holdings in a variety of industries in order to protect themselves against instability in one particular area.

Expansion took other forms as well. Even as the major corporations grew, so did smaller franchise operations like McDonald's, Kentucky Fried Chicken, and Burger King. Ray Kroc, introduced at the start of this chapter, provided a widely imitated pattern.

While expanding at home, large corporations also moved increasingly into foreign markets, as they had in the 1890s. But at the same time, they began to build plants overseas, where labor costs were cheaper. In the decade after 1957, General Electric built 61 plants abroad, and numerous other firms did the same. Corporate planning, meanwhile, developed rapidly, as firms sought managers

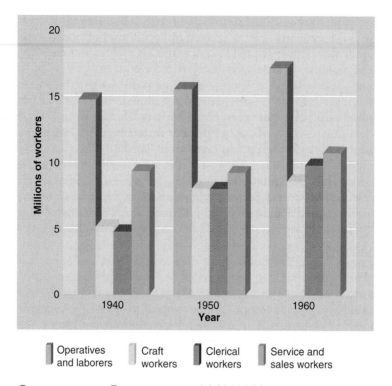

Operatives and laborers   **Craft workers**   **Clerical workers**   **Service and sales workers**

OCCUPATIONAL DISTRIBUTION, 1940–1960 In the postwar years, the size of the workforce increased considerably. In this graph, observe how all categories grew, and indicate which expanded most extensively. How was the workforce different in 1960 than it had been in 1940? How did shifting patterns affect the attitudes of working men and women? *(Sources: U.S. Department of Labor and Historical Statistics of the United States.)*

who could assess information, weigh marketing trends, and make rational decisions to maximize profit.

Changing Work Patterns

As corporations changed, so did the world of work. Reversing a 150-year trend after World War II, the United States became less a goods producer and more a service provider. Between 1947 and 1957, the number of factory workers fell by 4 percent, while the number of clerical workers increased 23 percent and the number of salaried, middle-class employees rose 61 percent. By 1956, a majority of American workers held white-collar jobs, and these new workers served as corporate managers, office workers, salespeople, and teachers.

Yet white-collar jobs came at a price. Work in the huge corporations became ever more impersonal and bureaucratic, and white-collar employees seemed to dress, think, and act the same (as depicted in a popular novel and film of the 1950s, *The Man in the Gray Flannel Suit*). Corporations, preaching that teamwork was all-important, indoctrinated employees with the appropriate standards of conduct. RCA issued company neckties. IBM had training programs to teach employees the company line. Social critic C. Wright Mills observed, "When white-collar people get jobs, they sell not only their time and energy but their personalities as well."

But not all Americans held white-collar jobs. Many were still blue-collar assembly line workers, who made the goods others enjoyed. They too dreamed of owning a suburban home and several cars and providing more for their children than they had enjoyed while growing up. Their lives were now more comfortable than ever before, as the union movement brought substantial gains (see the next section). These were the more fortunate members of the working class. Millions of others, perhaps totaling 40 percent of the workforce, held less appealing and less well-paying positions as taxi drivers, farm laborers, or dime-store sales clerks. For them, jobs were less stable, less secure, and less interesting.

The Union Movement at High Tide

The union movement had come of age during the New Deal (see Chapter 24), and the end of World War II found it even stronger. There were more union members—14.5 million—than ever before. Ten million belonged to the American Federation of Labor (AFL); the other 4.5 million belonged to the Congress of Industrial Organizations (CIO). Having taken a wartime no-strike pledge and given their full support to the war effort, they now looked forward to better pay and a greater voice in workplace management.

The immediate postwar period was difficult. Cancellation of defense orders laid off war workers and prompted fears of a depression like the one that had followed World War I. Even workers who held their jobs lost the overtime pay they had enjoyed during the war. Many responded by striking. In 1946 alone, 4.6 million workers went out on strike—more than ever before in U.S. history. These disruptions alienated middle-class Americans and outraged conservative Republicans who felt that unionization had gone too far.

In the late 1940s, a new equilibrium emerged. In many industries, big business at last recognized the basic rights of industrial workers, and union leaders and members in turn acknowledged the prerogatives of management and accepted the principle of fair profit. Corporations in the same industry agreed to cooperate rather than compete with one another over labor costs. This meant that once a leading firm reached agreement with the union, the other firms in that area adopted similar terms.

At the same time, companies made material concessions to workers—for example, adjusting their pay to protect them against inflation. In 1948, General Motors offered the United Automobile Workers a contract that included a cost-of-living adjustment (COLA) and a 2 percent "annual improvement factor" wage increase intended to share GM's productivity gains with workers. In 1955, automobile workers won a guaranteed annual wage. The merger of the AFL and CIO that same year ratified the changes that had occurred in the labor movement, as the new organization, led by building trade unionist George Meany, represented more than 90 percent of the country's now larger group of 17.5 million union members. By the end of the 1950s, the COLA principle was built into most union contracts.

Union gains, like middle-class affluence, came at a price. Co-opted by the materialistic benefits big business provided, workers fell increasingly under the control of middle-level managers and watched anxiously as companies automated at home or expanded abroad, where labor was cheaper. The anti-Communist crusade, described in the next chapter, also undermined union radicalism. And throughout the period, in unions, as in other institutions, women and blacks faced continued discrimination.

Agricultural Workers in Trouble

The agricultural world changed even more than the industrial world in the postwar United States. On the eve of World War II, agriculture had supported one of every five Americans. Now, in one generation, mechanization and consolidation forced that figure down to one of every twenty. Altogether, some 15 million rural jobs disappeared.

New technology revolutionized farming. Improved planting and harvesting machines and better fertilizers and pesticides brought massive gains in productivity. Increasing profitability led to agricultural consolidation. In the 25 years after 1945, average farm size almost doubled and farming became a big business—often called "agribusiness." Family farms found it difficult to compete, and small farmers watched their share of the market fall.

In response, farmers left the land in increasing numbers. Some were midwestern whites who generally found jobs in offices and factories. In the South, many of the uprooted agricultural workers were African Americans, who became part of the huge migration north that had been going on since World War I. Millions of them gravitated to cities, where they faced difficulties described later in this chapter. The agricultural life, as it had been known for decades, even centuries, was over.

DEMOGRAPHIC AND TECHNOLOGICAL SHIFTS

The postwar economic boom was intertwined with a series of demographic changes. The population grew dramatically and continued to move west, while at the same time, millions of white Americans left the cities for the suburbs that began to grow exponentially in the postwar years. New patterns, revolving around television, air conditioning, and other gadgets provided by the advances of technology, came to characterize the consumer culture that dominated suburban life.

Population Growth

In post–World War II America, a growing population testified to prosperity's return. The birthrate soared as millions of Americans began families. The "baby boom" peaked in 1957, with a rate of more than 25 births per 1,000. In that year,

4.3 million babies were born—one every seven seconds—while in that entire decade, population growth increased by 29 million.

The rising birthrate was the dominant factor affecting population growth, but the death rate was also declining. Miracle drugs such as penicillin and streptomycin helped cure bacterial infections and more serious illnesses such as tuberculosis. A polio vaccine introduced a decade after the war virtually eliminated that dreaded disease. Life expectancy rose: midway through the 1950s, the average was 70 years for whites and 64 for blacks, compared with 55 for whites and 45 for blacks in 1920.

Movement West

Wartime mobility encouraged the development of the West. Although the scarcity of water in the western states required massive water projects to support population growth, war workers and their families streamed to western cities where shipyards, airplane factories, and other industrial plants were located. After the war, this migration pattern persisted. The Sun Belt—the region stretching along the southern tier of the United States from Florida to California—attracted millions from the working class and middle class alike. Cities like Houston, Albuquerque, Tucson, and Phoenix expanded phenomenally, and Los Angeles pulled ahead of Philadelphia as the third-largest city in the United States. By 1963, in a dramatic illustration of the importance of the West, California passed New York as the nation's most populous state.

The migration west resulted from a number of reasons. Servicemen who had been stationed in the West liked the scenery, climate, and pace of life. Many returned with their families after the war. Also, much of the Cold War military expansion occurred in the West. By 1962, the Pacific Coast as a whole held almost half of all Defense Department research and development contracts.

MAP

Population Shifts, 1940–1950

The West also benefited from the boom in the service economy. The percentage of workers in service jobs was higher in virtually all western states than in eastern counterparts. Denver became a major regional center of the federal bureaucracy in the postwar years. Albuquerque likewise gained numerous federal offices and became known as "little Washington." The old West of cowboys, farmers, and miners was turning into a new West of bureaucrats, lawyers, and clerks.

The New Suburbs

As the population shifted westward after World War II, another form of movement was taking place. Millions of white Americans fled the inner city, intensifying a movement that had begun before the war. Fourteen of the nation's largest cities, including New York and Chicago, actually lost population in the 1950s.

As the cities declined, new suburbs blossomed. If the decade after World War I had witnessed a rural-to-urban shift, the decades after World War II saw a reverse shift to the regions outside the central cities, usually accessible only by car. By the end of the 1950s, one-third of all Americans resided in suburbs that promised the American dream of a home of one's own and seemed insulated from the troubles of the world outside.

AUDIO

Little Boxes

Levittown Step-by-step mass production, with units completed in assembly-line fashion, was the key to William Levitt's approach to housing. But the suburban developments he and others created were marked by street after street of houses that all looked the same. The Levittown in this picture was built on 1,200 acres of potato fields on Long Island in New York. How did the pattern you see here reflect the overall culture of the 1950s? *(Cornell Capa/Magnum Photos, Inc.)*

The pioneer of the postwar suburbanization movement was William J. Levitt, a builder eager to gamble and reap the rewards of a growing demand. Levitt had recognized the advantages of mass production during World War II, when his firm constructed housing for war workers. Aware that the GI Bill made mortgage money readily available, he saw the possibilities of suburban development. But to cash in, Levitt had to use new construction methods.

Individually designed houses were a thing of the past, he believed. "The reason we have it so good in this country," he said, "is that we can produce lots of things at low prices through mass production." Houses were among them. Working on a careful schedule, Levitt's team brought precut and preassembled materials to each site, put them together, and then moved on to the next location.

Levitt proved that his system worked. Construction costs at Levittown, New York, a new community of 17,000 homes built in the late 1940s, were only $10 per square foot, compared with the $12 to $15 common elsewhere. Other Levittowns appeared in Pennsylvania and New Jersey. Levitt's success provided a model for other developers.

Levitt argued that his homes helped underscore American values. "No man who owns his own house and lot can be a Communist," he once said. "He has too much to do." Levitt also helped perpetuate segregation by refusing to sell homes to blacks. "We can solve a housing problem, or we can try to solve a racial problem but we cannot combine the two," he declared in the early 1950s.

Suburbanization transformed the American landscape. Huge tracts of former fields, pastures, and forests were now divided into tiny standardized squares, each bearing a small house with a two-car garage and a manicured lawn. Stands of trees disappeared, for it was cheaper to cut them down than to work around them.

As suburbs flourished, businesses followed their customers out of the cities. Shopping centers led the way. In a single three-month period in 1957, 17 new centers opened; by 1960, there were 3,840 in the United States. Shopping centers catered to the suburban clientele and transformed consumer patterns. They allowed shoppers to avoid the cities entirely and further eroded urban health.

The Environmental Impact

Suburbanization had environmental consequences. Rapid expansion often took place without extensive planning and encroached on some of the nation's most attractive rural areas. Before long, virtually every American city was ringed by an ugly highway sporting garish neon signs. Billboard advertisements filled whatever space was not yet developed.

Despite occasional protests, there was little real consciousness of environmental issues in the early post–World War II years. The term *environment* itself was hardly used prior to the war. Yet the very prosperity that created the dismal highway strips in the late 1940s and 1950s was leading more and more Americans to appreciate natural environments as treasured parts of their rising standard of living. The shorter workweek provided more free time, and many Americans now had the means for longer vacations. They began to explore mountains and rivers and ocean shores and to ponder how to protect them. In 1958, Congress established the National Outdoor Recreation Review Commission, a first step toward consideration of environmental issues that became far more common in the next decade. Americans also began to recognize the need for open space in their communities in order to compensate for urban overdevelopment.

Technology Supreme

A technological revolution transformed postwar America. Some developments— the use of atomic energy, for example—flowed directly from war research. Federal support for scientific activity increased dramatically, as the pattern of wartime collaboration continued. The government established the National Institutes of Health in 1948 to coordinate medical research and the National Science Foundation in 1950 to fund basic scientific research.

The advent of the Cold War led to ever-greater government involvement. The Atomic Energy Commission, created in 1946, and the Department of Defense, established in 1949, provided rapidly increasing funding for research and development. Scientists engaged in both basic and applied research and helped design nuclear weapons, jet planes, satellites, and consumer goods that were often the side products of military research.

Computers both reflected and assisted the process of technological development. Prior to World War II, Vannevar Bush, an electrical engineer at the Massachusetts Institute of Technology, had built a machine filled with gears and shafts, along with electronic tubes in place of some mechanical parts, to solve differential equations. Even more complicated was the Electronic Numerical Integrator and Calculator, called ENIAC, built in 1946 at the University of Pennsylvania. It was large, containing 18,000 electronic tubes and requiring tremendous amounts of electricity and special cooling procedures. It also needed to be "debugged" to remove insects attracted to the heat and light, giving rise to the term still used today by computer scientists for fixing software glitches. ENIAC performed impressively for the time but at a snail's pace by modern standards.

A key breakthrough in making computers faster and more reliable was the development of the transistor in 1948. Computers transformed American society as surely as industrialization had changed it a century before, and computer programmers and operators were in increasing demand as computers contributed dramatically to the centralization and interdependence of American life.

Computers were essential for space exploration, which in the postwar years became increasingly sophisticated. Rocketry had developed during World War II but came of age after the war. Rockets could deliver nuclear weapons but could also launch satellites and provide the means to venture millions of miles into outer space.

An ominous technological trend related to computerization was the advent of automation. Mechanization was not new, but now it became far more widespread, threatening both skilled and unskilled workers. The implications of falling purchasing power as machines replaced workers were serious for an economy dependent on consumer demand.

The Consumer Culture

Cover Illustration for "The Desi-Lucy Love Story" (1956)

Americans were excited by everything they could buy. Television, developed in the 1930s, became a major influence on American life after World War II. In 1946, there were fewer than 17,000 television sets, but by 1960, three-quarters of all American families owned at least one set, and in 1955, the average American family tuned in four to five hours each day. Young Americans grew up to the melodies of "The Mickey Mouse Club," while older viewers watched situation comedies like *I Love Lucy* and *Father Knows Best* and live dramas such as *Playhouse 90*.

Americans maintained an ardent love affair with the appliances and gadgets produced by modern technology. By the end of the 1950s, most families had at least one automobile, as well as the staple appliances they had begun to purchase earlier—refrigerator, washing machine, television, and vacuum cleaner. Dozens of less essential items such as electric pencil sharpeners and electric toothbrushes also became popular.

Such consumption, increasingly a pillar of the American economy, required a vast expansion of consumer credit. Installment plans facilitated buying a new car, while credit cards encouraged the purchase of smaller items such as television sets and household appliances. The first of the consumer credit cards—the Diner's Club card—appeared in 1950, followed at the end of the decade by the American Express card and the BankAmericard (later renamed VISA). By the end of the 1960s, there were about 50 million credit cards of all kinds in use in the

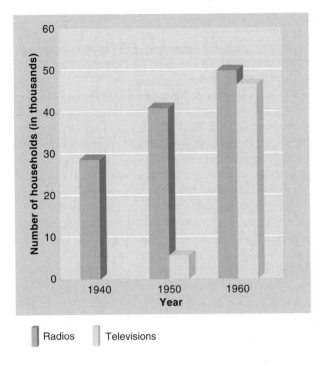

HOUSEHOLDS OWNING RADIOS AND TELEVISIONS, 1940–1960 Radio became increasingly popular in the postwar years, but observe the astronomical increase in the number of households owning television sets in the decade after 1950. Why do you think there were still more radios than televisions in 1960? How did the increasing number of television sets affect American culture? *(Source: U.S. Bureau of the Census.)*

United States. Consumer credit—total private indebtedness—increased from $8.4 billion in 1946 to nearly $45 billion in 1958.

For consumers momentarily unsure about new purchases, a revitalized advertising industry was ready to convince them to go ahead and buy. Advertising had come of age in the 1920s, as businesses persuaded customers that buying new products brought status and satisfaction. It had faltered when the economy collapsed in the 1930s but began to revive during the war, as firms kept the public aware of consumer goods, even those in short supply. With the postwar boom, advertisers again began to hawk their wares, this time even more aggressively than before.

Having weathered the poverty and unemployment of the 1930s and made sacrifices during a long war, Americans now regarded abundance and leisure as their due, sometimes neglecting to look beyond the immediate objects of their desire. As journalist William Shannon wrote, the decade was one of "self-satisfaction and gross materialism. ... The loudest sound in the land has been the oink and grunt of private hoggishness. ... It has been the age of the slob."

CONSENSUS AND CONFORMITY

As the economy expanded, an increasing sense of sameness pervaded American society. Third- and fourth-generation ethnic Americans became much more alike. As immigration slowed to a trickle after 1924, ties to Europe weakened, assimilation sped up, and interethnic marriage skyrocketed. Television gave young and old a shared, visually seductive experience. Escaping the homogenizing tendencies was difficult.

Contours of Religious Life

Postwar Americans discovered a shared religious sense and returned to their churches in record numbers. By the end of the 1950s, fully 95 percent of all Americans identified with some religious denomination.

Ecumenical activities—worldwide efforts on the part of different Christian churches—promoted greater religious involvement. Within the United States, evangelical revivalism, led by Southern Baptist Billy Graham and others, became increasingly popular. Catholicism also sought to broaden its appeal when Pope John XXIII convened the Vatican Ecumenical Council in 1962 to make the Catholic church's traditions and practices more accessible. Judaism likewise assimilated into the mainstream. Jews relied on the GI Bill to move to the suburbs, where they bought new homes and built new synagogues, most of which followed the more casual patterns of Reform or Conservative, rather than Orthodox, Judaism. Across all faiths, religious revivals reinforced the importance of family life, for, according to one slogan, "The family that prays together stays together."

President Dwight D. Eisenhower reflected the national mood when he observed that "our government makes no sense unless it is founded in a deeply felt religious faith—and I don't care what it is." In 1954, Congress added the words "under God" to the pledge to the flag and the next year voted to require the phrase "In God We Trust" on all U.S. currency. Yet the revival sometimes seemed to rest on a shallow base of religious knowledge. In one public opinion poll, 80 percent of the respondents indicated that the Bible was God's revealed word, but only 35 percent were able to name the four Gospels, and over half were unable to name even one.

Traditional Roles for Men and Women

World War II had interrupted traditional patterns of behavior for both men and women. As servicemen went overseas, women left their homes to work. After 1945, women faced tremendous pressure to leave their jobs and conform to accepted prewar gender patterns, even though, paradoxically, more women entered the workforce than ever before.

DOCUMENT

Ladies Home
Journal, "Young
Mother" (1956)

Men and women had different postwar expectations. Most men expected to go to school and then find jobs to support their families as the primary breadwinners. For women, the situation was more complex. While they wanted to resume patterns of family life that had been disrupted by the war, many had enjoyed working in the military plants and were reluctant to retreat to the home, despite pressure to do so.

By the 1950s, middle-class doubts and questions had largely receded. The baby boom increased average family size and made the decision to remain home easier. The flight to the suburbs gave women more to do, and they settled into the routines of redecorating their homes and gardens and transporting children to and from activities and schools.

Marriage and home became the most important priorities. Many women went to college to find husbands—and dropped out if they succeeded. Almost two-thirds of the women in college, but less than half the men, left before completing a degree. Women were expected to marry young, have children early, and encourage their husbands' careers. An article in *Esquire* magazine in 1954 called working wives a "menace."

In 1946 pediatrician Benjamin Spock published *Baby and Child Care*, the book most responsible for the child-rearing patterns of the postwar generation. In it, he advised mothers to stay at home if they wanted to raise stable and secure youngsters. Working outside the home might jeopardize their children's mental and emotional health.

Popular culture highlighted the stereotype of the woman concerned only about marriage and family. Author Betty Friedan described these patterns in her explosive 1963 critique *The Feminine Mystique*. "It was unquestioned gospel," she wrote, "that women could identify with *nothing* beyond the home—not politics, not art, not science, not events large or small, war or peace, in the United States or the world, unless it could be approached through female experience as a wife or mother or translated into domestic detail."

Movies reinforced these expectations. Doris Day, charming and wholesome, was a favorite heroine. In film after film, she showed how an attractive woman who played her cards right could land her man.

The family was all-important in this scenario. Fewer than 10 percent of all Americans felt that an unmarried person could be happy. In a pattern endlessly reiterated by popular television programs, the family was meant to provide all satisfaction and contentment. The single-story ranch house that became so popular in this period reflected the focus on the family as the source of recreation and fun. Now houses, with far more shared and open space, stressed livability and family comfort.

Sexuality was a troublesome if compelling postwar concern. In 1948, zoologist Alfred C. Kinsey published *Sexual Behavior in the Human Male*, based on his research on the sexual lives of 5,300 white males. He shocked the country with his statistics on premarital, extramarital, and otherwise illicit sexual acts. Among males who went to college, he concluded, 67 percent had engaged in sexual intercourse before marriage as had 84 percent of those who went to high school but not beyond. Thirty-seven percent of the total male population had experienced some kind of overt homosexual activity. Five years later, Kinsey published a companion volume, *Sexual Behavior in the Human Female*, which detailed many of the same sexual patterns. Although critics denounced Kinsey for what they considered his unscientific methodology and challenged his results, both books sold widely, for they opened the door to a subject previously considered taboo.

Interest in sexuality was reflected in the fascination with sex goddesses like Marilyn Monroe. The images of such film stars corresponded to male fantasies of women, visible in *Playboy* magazine, which first appeared in 1953 and soon achieved a huge readership. As for men's wives, they were expected to manage their suburban homes and to be cheerful and willing objects of their husbands' desire.

Despite reaffirming the old ideology that a woman's place was in the home, the 1950s were years of unnoticed but important change. Because the supply of

Sex Symbol Marilyn Monroe Sex goddess Marilyn Monroe—shown here in a widely distributed promotional photo for *The Seven Year Itch*—stirred the fantasies of American males in the 1950s. Despite the family orientation of suburban America, millions were captivated by her seductive appeal. What messages were conveyed by this picture? *(AP/World Wide Photos)*

single women workers fell as a result of the low birthrate of the Depression years and increased schooling and early marriage, older married women continued the pattern begun during the war and entered the labor force in larger numbers than before. In 1940, only 15 percent of American wives had jobs. By 1950, 21 percent were employed, and 10 years later, the figure had risen to 30 percent. Still, the conviction that women's main role was homemaking justified low wages and the denial of promotions. Comparatively few women entered professions where they would have challenged traditional notions of a woman's place.

African American women worked as always but often lost the jobs they had held during the war. In the 1950s, however, the employment picture improved somewhat. African American women succeeded both in moving into white-collar positions and in increasing their income. By 1960, more than one-third of all black women held clerical, sales, service, or professional jobs. The income gap between white women and black women holding similar jobs dropped from about 50 percent in 1940 to about 30 percent in 1960.

Cultural Rebels

Not all Americans fit the 1950s stereotypes. Some were alienated from the culture and rebelled against its values. Many were intrigued by Holden Caulfield, the main figure in J. D. Salinger's popular novel *The Catcher in the Rye* (1951), who rebelled against the "phonies" around him threatening his individuality and independence.

Writers of the "Beat Generation" espoused unconventional values in their stories and poems as they challenged the apathy and conformity of the period. The "Beats" deliberately outraged respectability by sneering at materialism, flaunting unconventional sex lives, and smoking marijuana.

Their literary work reflected their approach to life. Jack Kerouac dispensed with conventional punctuation and paragraphing as he typed his best-selling novel *On the Road* (1957) on a 250-foot roll of paper. Poet Allen Ginsberg, who, like Kerouac, was a Columbia University dropout, became equally well known for his poem "Howl," a scathing critique of modern, mechanized culture that began with the line "I saw the best minds of my generation destroyed by madness, starving hysterical naked." He and the other "Beats" furnished a model for rebellion in the 1960s.

The signs of cultural rebellion also appeared in popular music. Parents recoiled as their children flocked to hear a young Tennessee singer named Elvis Presley, whose sexy voice, gyrating hips, and other techniques borrowed from black singers made him the undisputed "king of rock and roll." His black leather jacket and ducktail haircut became standard dress for rebellious male teenagers.

American painters, shucking off European influences that had shaped American artists for two centuries, also became a part of the cultural rebellion. Led by Jackson Pollock and the "New York school," some artists discarded the easel, laid gigantic canvases on the floor, and then used trowels, putty knives, and sticks to apply paint, glass shards, sand, and other materials in wild explosions of color. Such abstract expressionism reflected the artist's alienation from a world filled with nuclear threats, computerization, and materialism.

ORIGINS OF THE WELFARE STATE

The modern American welfare state originated in the New Deal. Franklin D. Roosevelt's efforts to deal with the ravages of the Great Depression and protect Americans from the problems stemming from industrial capitalism (see Chapter 24) provided the basis for subsequent efforts to commit the government to help those who could not help themselves, even in prosperous times. Harry Truman's Fair Deal built squarely on Roosevelt's New Deal. His Republican successor, Dwight Eisenhower, sought to scale down spending but made no effort to roll back the most important initiatives of the welfare state.

Harry S Truman

Harry S Truman, America's first postwar president, was an unpretentious man who took a straightforward approach to public affairs. He was, however, ill prepared for the office he assumed in the final months of World War II. His three months as vice president had done little to school him in the complexity of postwar issues.

Yet Truman matured rapidly. A sign on the president's White House desk read "The Buck Stops Here," and he was willing to make quick decisions on issues, even if associates sometimes wondered if he understood all the implications.

Truman took the same feisty approach to public policy that characterized his conduct of foreign affairs (see Chapter 27). Believing in plain speaking, he seldom hesitated to let others know exactly where he stood. He attacked his political enemies vigorously when they resisted his initiatives and often took his case to the American people. He was, in many ways, an old-style Democratic politician, who hoped to use his authority to benefit the middle-class and working-class Americans who made up his political base.

Truman's Struggles with a Conservative Congress

Like Roosevelt, Harry Truman believed that the federal government had the responsibility for ensuring the social welfare of all Americans. Truman wanted his administration to embrace and act upon a series of carefully defined social and economic goals to extend New Deal initiatives even further.

Less than a week after the end of World War II, Truman called on Congress to pass a 21-point program providing for housing assistance, a higher minimum wage, more unemployment compensation, and a national commitment to maintaining full employment. Truman also sent blueprints of further proposals to Congress, including health insurance and atomic energy legislation. But this liberal program soon ran into fierce political opposition.

The debate surrounding the Employment Act of 1946 hinted at the fate of Truman's proposals. This measure was a deliberate effort to apply the theory of English economist John Maynard Keynes, who argued that aggressive spending could head off another depression and maintain economic equilibrium (see Chapter 24). While liberals and labor leaders hailed the measure, business groups claimed that government intervention would undermine free enterprise and promote socialism. Congress cut the proposal to bits. As finally passed, the act created a Council of Economic Advisers to make recommendations to the president, but it stopped short of committing the government to using fiscal tools to maintain full employment when economic indicators turned downward.

As the midterm elections of 1946 approached, Truman knew he was vulnerable. As more and more people questioned his competence as president, his support dropped from 87 percent of those polled after he assumed the office to 32 percent in November 1946. Gleeful Republicans asked the voters, "Had enough?" They had. Republicans won majorities in both houses of Congress for the first time since the 1928 elections and gained a majority of the governorships as well.

After the 1946 elections, Truman faced an unsympathetic 80th Congress, which planned to reverse the liberal policies of the Roosevelt years and reestablish congressional authority. When the new Congress met, it slashed federal spending and taxes. In 1947, Congress twice passed tax-cut measures, which Truman vetoed. In 1948, another election year, Congress overrode the veto.

Angry at the gains won by labor in the 1930s and 1940s, Republicans counterattacked. They wanted to check unions and to circumscribe their right to engage in the kind of disruptive strikes that had occurred immediately after the war. In 1947 the Republicans passed the Taft-Hartley Act, which sought to limit the power of unions by restricting the weapons they could employ. It spelled out unfair labor practices (such as preventing nonunion workers from working if they wished) and outlawed the closed shop, whereby an employee had to join a union before getting a job. The law likewise allowed states to prohibit the union shop, which forced workers to join the union after they had been hired. It gave the president the right to call for an 80-day cooling-off period in strikes affecting national security and required union officials to sign non-Communist oaths.

Union leaders and members were furious. Vetoing the measure, Truman claimed that it was unworkable and unfair and went on nationwide radio to seek public approval. This regained him some of the support he had lost earlier when he had sought to force strikers to go back to work immediately after the war. Congress, however, passed the Taft-Hartley measure over Truman's veto.

The Fair Deal and Its Fate

In 1948, Truman wanted a chance to consolidate a liberal program and decided to seek the presidency in his own right. Aware that he was an accidental occupant of the White House, he won what most people thought was a worthless nomination. Not only was his own popularity waning, but the Democratic party itself seemed to be falling apart.

The civil rights issue (see the last section of this chapter) split the Democrats. When liberals defeated a moderate platform proposal and pressed for a stronger commitment to African American rights, angry delegates from Mississippi and Alabama stormed out of the convention. They later formed the States' Rights, or Dixiecrat, party. At their own convention, delegates from 13 states nominated Governor J. Strom Thurmond of South Carolina and affirmed their support for continued racial segregation. Meanwhile, Henry A. Wallace, a longtime member of the government until Truman fired him for advocating a more moderate approach to the Soviet Union, mounted his own challenge, becoming the presidential candidate of the Progressive party.

In that fragmented state, the Democrats took on the Republicans, who coveted the White House after 16 years out of power. Once again, the GOP nominated New York Governor Thomas E. Dewey, the unsuccessful candidate in 1944. Even though he was stiff and egocentric, the polls uniformly picked the Republicans to win. Truman, meanwhile, conducted a two-fisted campaign. He appealed to ordinary Americans as an unpretentious man engaged in an uphill fight. Believing that everyone was against him but the people, he called the Republicans a "bunch of old mossbacks" out to destroy the New Deal as he attacked the "do nothing" eightieth Congress. Speaking informally in his choppy, aggressive style, he appealed to crowds who yelled, "Give 'em hell, Harry!" He did.

The pollsters predicting a Republican victory were wrong. On election day, disproving the bold headline "Dewey Defeats Truman" in the *Chicago Daily Tribune*, the incumbent president scored one of the most unexpected political upsets in American history, winning 303–189 in the Electoral College. Democrats also swept both houses of Congress.

Truman won primarily because he was able to hold on to the labor, farm, and black votes that Franklin Roosevelt had won more than a decade before. Working men and women who were worried about Wallace backed Truman.

Harry Truman Celebrating His Unexpected Victory In one of the nation's extraordinary political upsets, Harry Truman beat Thomas E. Dewey in 1948. Here an exuberant Truman holds a newspaper headline printed while he slept, before the vote turned his way. Why is Truman so gleeful? *(Bettmann/Corbis)*

With the election behind him, Truman pursued his liberal program. In his 1949 State of the Union message, he declared, "Every segment of our population and every individual has a right to expect from our Government a fair deal." While parts of Truman's Fair Deal worked, others did not. Lawmakers raised the minimum wage and expanded social security programs. A housing program brought modest gains but did not really meet housing needs. A farm program, aimed at providing income support to farmers if prices fell, never made it through Congress. Although he desegregated the military, other parts of his civil rights program failed to win congressional support (see the last section of this chapter). The American Medical Association undermined the effort to provide national health insurance, and Congress rejected a measure to provide federal aid to education.

The mixed record was not entirely Truman's fault. Conservative legislators were largely responsible for sabotaging his efforts. At the same time, critics charged correctly that Truman was often unpragmatic and shrill in his struggles with an unsympathetic Congress. They argued that he sometimes seemed to provoke the confrontations that became a hallmark of his presidency. They also claimed that he was most concerned with foreign policy as he strove to secure bipartisan support for Cold War initiatives (see Chapter 27) and allowed his domestic program to suffer.

A Popular and Personable President Dwight Eisenhower provided a reassuring presence in the White House in the 1950s. His very presence conveyed the impression that everything was going to be all right. How did his wide smile, pictured here, make Americans feel good about themselves and their country? *(Hulton Archive/Getty Images)*

Still, Truman kept the liberal vision alive. The Fair Deal ratified many of the initiatives begun during the New Deal and led Americans to take programs like social security for granted. Truman had not achieved everything he wanted—he had not even come close—but the nation had taken another step toward endorsing liberal goals.

The Election of Ike

VIDEO

Ike for President: Eisenhower Campaign Ad (1952)

Acceptance of the liberal state continued in the 1950s, even as the Republicans took control. By 1952, Truman's approval rating had plummeted to 23 percent of the American people, and all indicators pointed to a political shift. The Democrats nominated Adlai Stevenson, governor of Illinois. The Republicans turned to Dwight Eisenhower, the World War II hero known as Ike.

While Stevenson approached political issues in intellectual terms, the Republicans focused on communism, corruption, and Korea as major priorities. They called the Democrats "soft on communism," condemned scandals in the administration, and promised to end the unpopular Korean War (see Chapter 27).

Eisenhower proved to be a highly effective campaigner. He had a natural talent for taking his case to the American people, speaking in simple, reassuring terms they could understand. He struck a grandfatherly pose, unified the various wings of his party, and went on to victory at the polls. He received 55 percent of the vote and carried 41 states. The new president took office with a Republican Congress as well and had little difficulty gaining a second term.

Dwight D. Eisenhower

Eisenhower stood in stark contrast to Truman. His easy manner and warm smile made him widely popular. Furthermore, he had not taken the typical route to the

Dwight D. Eisenhower

presidency. After World War II, he served successively as army chief of staff, president of Columbia University, and head of the North Atlantic Treaty Organization (NATO). Despite his lack of formal political background, he had a real ability to get people to compromise and work together.

Ike's limited experience with everyday politics conditioned his sense of the presidential role. Whereas Truman loved political infighting and wanted to take charge, Eisenhower was more restrained. The presidency for him was no "bully pulpit," as it had been for Theodore Roosevelt and even FDR. "I am not one of those desk-pounding types that likes to stick out his jaw and look like he is bossing the show," he declared.

"Modern Republicanism"

Eisenhower wanted to limit the presidential role. He was uncomfortable with the growth of the executive office over the past 20 years. Like the Republicans in Congress with whom Truman had tangled, he wanted to restore the balance between the branches of government and to reduce the authority of the national government. He recognized, however, that it was impossible to scale back federal power to the limited levels of the 1920s, and he wanted to preserve social gains that even Republicans now accepted. Eisenhower sometimes termed his approach "dynamic conservatism" or "modern Republicanism," which, he explained, meant "conservative when it comes to money, liberal when it comes to human beings."

Economic concerns dominated the Eisenhower years. The president and his chief aides wanted desperately to preserve the value of the dollar, pare down levels of funding, cut taxes, and balance the budget after years of deficit spending. Eisenhower's administration also supported business interests. This orientation became obvious when Defense Secretary Charles E. Wilson, former president of General Motors, declared at his confirmation hearing, "What is good for our country is good for General Motors, and vice versa."

Eisenhower fulfilled his promise to reduce government's economic role. The administration sought to circumscribe federal activity in the electric power field. Eisenhower opposed a TVA proposal for expansion to provide power to the Atomic Energy Commission and instead authorized a private group to build a plant for that purpose. Later, when charges of scandal arose, the administration canceled the agreement, but the basic preference for private development remained.

The administration sometimes saw its program backfire. As a result of its reluctance to stimulate the economy too much, the annual rate of economic growth declined from 4.3 percent between 1947 and 1952 to 2.5 percent between 1953 and 1960. The economy was still growing, but more slowly than before. The country also suffered three recessions—in 1953–1954, 1957–1958, and 1960–1961—in Eisenhower's eight years. During the slumps, tax revenues fell and the deficits that Eisenhower so wanted to avoid increased.

Eisenhower's understated approach led to a legislative stalemate, particularly when the Democrats regained control of Congress in 1954. Opponents gibed at Ike's restrained stance and joked about what they called nonexistent White House leadership. Yet Eisenhower understood just what he was doing and had a better grasp of public policy than his critics realized.

Even more important was his role in ratifying the welfare state. By 1960, the government had become a major factor in ordinary people's lives. It had grown enormously, employing close to 2.5 million people throughout the 1950s. Federal expenditures, which had stood at $3.5 billion in 1927, rose to $97 billion in 1960. The White House now took the lead in initiating legislation and in steering bills through Congress. Individuals had come to expect old-age pensions, unemployment payments, and a minimum wage. By accepting the fundamental features of the national state that the Democrats had created, Eisenhower ensured its survival.

DOCUMENT

Dwight D. Eisenhower, Farewell to the Nation (January 17, 1961)

Eisenhower accomplished most of his goals, and he was one of the few presidents to leave office as highly regarded by the people as when he entered it. He was the kind of leader Americans wanted in prosperous times.

THE OTHER AMERICA

Not all Americans shared postwar middle-class affluence. African Americans, uprooted from rural roots and transplanted into urban slums, were among the hardest hit. But members of other minority groups, as well as less fortunate whites, suffered similar dislocations, unknown to the middle class.

Poverty amid Affluence

Many people in the "affluent society" lived in poverty. Although the popular "trickle-down" theory argued that economic expansion benefited all classes, little wealth, in fact, reached the citizens at the bottom. In 1960, the Federal Bureau of Labor Statistics reported that 40 million people (almost one-quarter of the population) lived below what it defined as the poverty level, with nearly the same number only marginally above the line.

Michael Harrington, socialist author and critic, shocked the country with his 1962 study *The Other America*. The poor, Harrington showed, were everywhere. He described New York City's "economic underworld," where "Puerto Ricans and Negroes, alcoholics, drifters, and disturbed people" haunted employment agencies for temporary positions as "dishwashers and day workers, the fly-by-night jobs." Despite the prosperity that surrounded them, the mountain folk of Appalachia, the tenant farmers of Mississippi, and the migrant farmers of Florida, Texas, and California were all caught in poverty's relentless cycle.

Hard Times for African Americans

African Americans were among the postwar nation's least prosperous citizens. In the South, agricultural workers continued to fall victim to foreign competition, mechanization, and eviction as white farmers turned to less labor-intensive crops like soybeans and peanuts. The southern agricultural population declined dramatically, as millions of blacks moved to southern cities, where they found better jobs, better schooling, and freedom from landlords. Some achieved middle-class status; many more did not. They remained poor, with even less of a support system than they had known before.

Millions of African Americans also headed for northern cities after 1940. In the 1950s, Detroit's black population increased from 16 percent to 29 percent, and at one point in this decade, Chicago's black population rose by more than 2,200 people each week. The new arrivals congregated in urban slums, where the growth of social services failed to keep pace with population growth.

The experiences of African Americans in the cities often proved different from what they had expected. As author Claude Brown recalled, blacks were told that in the North, "Negroes lived in houses with bathrooms, electricity, running water, and indoor toilets. To them, this was the 'promised land' that Mammy had been

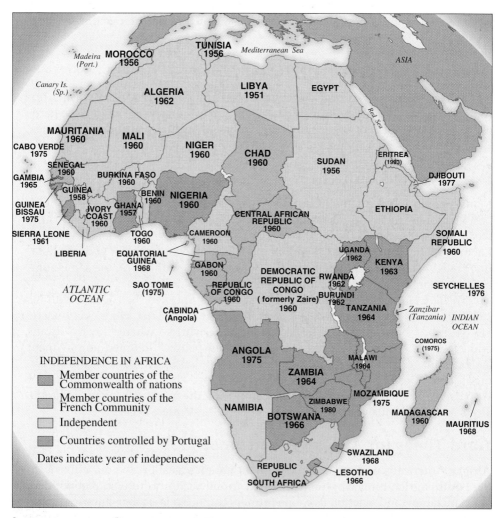

INDEPENDENCE IN AFRICA In the 1950s and 1960s, most African nations threw off their colonial rulers and achieved independence. ■ **Reflecting on the Past** During which decade did more nations become free? How did attaining independence change social and economic patterns in the African nations? What effect did it have on the patterns of the Cold War? What effect did it have on the civil rights struggle in the United States?

singing about in the cotton fields for many years." But no one had told them "about one of the most important aspects of the promised land: it was a slum ghetto." Poor conditions, and the constant slights that accompanied segregation in both the North and the South, took a heavy toll.

Still, the black community remained intact. The black church played an especially important role in sustaining African American life. Blacks moving into the cities retained churchgoing habits and a commitment to religious institutions from their rural days. The churches also offered more than religious sustenance alone. Many provided day-care facilities, ran Boy Scout and Girl Scout troops, and sponsored a variety of other social services.

The growth of the black urban population fostered the increased growth of businesses catering to the African American community. Black newspapers now provided a more regional, rather than a national, focus, but magazines such as *Jet,* a pocket-size weekly with a large, countrywide circulation, filled the void. Black-owned and black-operated banks and other financial institutions increased in number.

Yet most African Americans remained second-class citizens. Escape from the slums was difficult for many and impossible for most. Persistent poverty remained a dismal fact of life.

African American Gains

In the postwar years, African struggles for independence, such as the Kenyan Mau Mau revolt against the British, inspired African American leaders who now saw the quest for black equality in a broader context. They took enormous pride in the achievement of independence by a number of African nations and demanded comparable change at home. As Adam Clayton Powell, a Harlem preacher (and later congressman), warned, the black man "is ready to throw himself into the struggle to make the dream of America become flesh and blood, bread and butter, freedom and equality. He walks conscious of the fact that he is no longer alone—no longer a minority."

The racial question was dramatized in 1947 when Jackie Robinson broke the color line and began playing major league baseball with the Brooklyn Dodgers. Sometimes teammates were hostile, sometimes opponents crashed into him with spikes high, but Robinson kept his frustrations to himself. A splendid first season helped ease the way and resulted in his selection as Rookie of the Year. After Robinson's trailblazing effort, other blacks, formerly confined to the old Negro leagues, moved into the major leagues in baseball and then into other sports.

Somewhat reluctantly, Truman supported the civil rights movement. In 1946, he appointed a Committee on Civil Rights to investigate the problem of lynching and other brutalities against blacks and recommend remedies. The committee's report, released in October 1947, showed that black Americans remained second-class citizens in every area of American life and called for change. In February 1948, he sent a 10-point civil rights program to Congress, the first presidential civil rights plan since Reconstruction. Then he moved forward even more aggressively, first issuing an executive order barring discrimination in the federal establishment. Finally, he ordered equality of treatment in the military services.

Baseball Superstar Jackie Robinson Jackie Robinson's electrifying play as the first African American in the major leagues led to acceptance of the integration of baseball. A spectacular rookie season in 1947 opened the way for other African Americans who had earlier been limited to the Negro leagues. In this photo, taken at Ebbets Field in Brooklyn during the 1957 World Series, Robinson is about to steal home. What impression do you have of Robinson here? *(Ralph Morse/Time Life Picture Collection/Getty Images)*

Manpower needs in the Korean War broke down the last restrictions, particularly when the army found that integrated units performed well.

As the civil rights struggle gained momentum during the 1950s, the judicial system played a crucial role. The National Association for the Advancement of Colored People (NAACP) was determined to overturn the 1896 Supreme Court decision *Plessy* v. *Ferguson,* in which the Court had declared that segregation of the black and white races was constitutional if the facilities used by each were "separate but equal." The decree had been used for generations to sanction rigid segregation, primarily in the South, even though separate facilities were seldom, if ever, equal.

DOCUMENT

Brown v. Board of Education of Topeka, Kansas (1954)

A direct challenge came in 1951. Oliver Brown, the father of eight-year-old Linda Brown, sued the school board of Topeka, Kansas, to allow his daughter to attend a school for white children that she passed as she walked to the bus that carried her to a black school farther away. The case reached the Supreme Court, which grouped several school segregation cases together.

On May 17, 1954, the Supreme Court released its bombshell ruling in *Brown* v. *Board of Education.* For more than a decade, Supreme Court decisions had gradually expanded black civil rights. Now the Court unanimously decreed that "separate facilities are inherently unequal" and concluded that the "separate but equal" doctrine had no place in public education. A year later, the Court turned to the question of implementation and declared that local school boards, acting with the guidance of lower courts, should move "with all deliberate speed" to desegregate their facilities.

DOCUMENT

The Southern
Manifesto (1956)

President Eisenhower had the ultimate responsibility for executing the law. While he thought privately that the *Brown* ruling was wrong, he knew that it was his constitutional duty to see that the decision was carried out. He acted immediately to desegregate the Washington, D.C., schools as a model for the rest of the country. He also ordered desegregation in navy yards and veterans' hospitals.

The South resisted. The crucial confrontation came in Little Rock, Arkansas, in 1957. Just before the school year began, Governor Orval Faubus declared on television that it would not be possible to maintain order if integration took place. In the face of hostile mobs, National Guardsmen mobilized by the governor turned away nine black students as they tried to enter Central High School

With the lines drawn, Ike knew that such resistance could not be tolerated, and he finally took the one action he had earlier called unthinkable. For the first time since the end of Reconstruction, an American president called out federal troops to protect the rights of black citizens. Eisenhower ordered paratroopers to Little Rock and placed National Guardsmen under federal command. The black children entered the school and attended classes with the military protecting their rights. Thus desegregation began.

DOCUMENT

Cooper v. Aaron
(1958)

Meanwhile, African Americans, encouraged by their churches, began organizing themselves to take direct action, and their efforts significantly advanced the civil rights movement. The crucial event occurred in Montgomery, Alabama, in December 1955. Rosa Parks, a 42-year-old black seamstress who was also secretary of her local NAACP, sat down in the front of a bus in a section reserved by custom for whites. When ordered to move back, the longtime activist refused to budge. The bus driver called the police at the next stop, and Parks was arrested. The state NAACP president told Parks, "This is the case we've been looking for. We can break this situation on the bus with your case."

Martin Luther King, Jr., the 27-year-old minister of the Baptist church where a meeting to consider a boycott was held, soon emerged as the preeminent spokesman of the protest. King was an impressive figure and an inspiring speaker. "There comes a time when people get tired ... of being kicked about by the brutal feet of oppression," he declared. It was time to be more assertive, to cease being "patient with anything less than freedom and justice."

For almost a year, 50,000 African Americans avoided the transit system, and their actions cut gross revenue on city buses by 65 percent. Ultimately, the Supreme Court ruled that bus segregation, like school segregation, violated the Constitution, and the boycott ended. But the mood it fostered continued, as ordinary black men and women challenged the racial status quo and forced both white and black leaders to respond.

Meanwhile, a concerted effort developed to guarantee black voting rights. Largely because of the legislative genius of Senate majority leader Lyndon B. Johnson of Texas, the Civil Rights Act of 1957 created a Civil Rights Commission and empowered the Justice Department to go to court in cases where blacks were denied the right to vote. The bill was a compromise measure, yet it was the first effort to protect civil rights in 82 years. Again led by Johnson, Congress passed the Civil Rights Act of 1960. This measure set stiffer penalties for people who interfered with the right to vote but once more stopped short of authorizing federal registrars to register blacks to vote and so, like its predecessor, was generally ineffective.

Latinos on the Fringe

Latinos, like other groups, had similar difficulties in the postwar United States. Latino immigrants from Cuba, Puerto Rico, Mexico, and Central America, often unskilled and illiterate, followed other less fortunate Americans to the cities. The conditions they encountered there were similar to those faced by blacks.

Chicanos, or Mexican Americans, were the most numerous of the newcomers and faced peculiar difficulties. During World War II, as the country experienced a labor shortage at home, American farmers sought Mexican *braceros* (helping hands) to harvest their crops, and seasonal immigration continued after the war when the government signed a Migratory Labor Agreement with Mexico. Between 1948 and 1964, some 4.5 million Mexicans were brought to the United States for temporary work. *Braceros* were expected to return to Mexico at the end of their labor contract, but often they stayed. Joining them were millions more who entered the country illegally.

Conditions were harsh for the *braceros* in the best of times, but in periods of economic difficulty, troubles worsened. During a serious recession in 1953–1954, the government mounted Operation Wetback to deport illegal entrants and *braceros* who had remained in the country illegally and expelled 1.1 million. As immigration officials searched out illegal workers, all Chicanos found themselves vulnerable. Still, the demand for cheap labor attracted hundreds of thousands of newcomers.

Puerto Ricans were numerous in other parts of the country. As the island's sugarcane economy became more mechanized, nearly 40 percent of the inhabitants left their homes. By the end of the 1960s, New York City had more Puerto Ricans than San Juan, the island's capital. El Barrio, in East Harlem, became the center of Puerto Rican activity, the home of *salsa* music and small *bodegas,* grocery stores that served the neighborhood. Puerto Ricans, like many other immigrants, hoped to earn money in America and then return home. Some did; others stayed. Most failed to enjoy the promise of the American dream.

Like African Americans, Latinos fought for their own rights. The Community Service Organization mobilized Chicanos against discrimination, as did the more radical Associación Nacional México-Americana. And the League of United Latin American Citizens continued reform efforts. Chicano activism in the 1950s, however, was fragmented. Some Mexican Americans considered their situation hopeless. More effective mobilization had to await another day.

The Native American Struggle

Native Americans likewise remained outsiders in the postwar years. As power lines reached their reservations and they partook of the consumer culture, old patterns inevitably changed. Reservation life lost its cohesiveness, and alcohol be-

TIMELINE

1947	Jackie Robinson breaks the color line in major league baseball	**1955**	Montgomery, Alabama, bus boycott begins
1948	Truman defeats Dewey	**1956**	Eisenhower reelected
		1957	Little Rock, Arkansas, school integration crisis
1952	Dwight D. Eisenhower elected president		
			Civil Rights Act
1954	*Brown v. Board of Education*	**1960**	Civil Rights Act
		1963	Betty Friedan, *The Feminine Mystique*

came a major problem. With good jobs unavailable on the reservations, more and more Indians gravitated to the cities. But they often had difficulty adjusting to urban life and frequently faced hostility from white Americans.

Native Americans, like Latinos, began their own struggle for equality. They achieved an important victory just after the end of World War II when Congress established the Indian Claims Commission, but in the 1950s, federal Indian policy shifted course. As part of its effort to limit the role of the national government, the Eisenhower administration turned away from the New Deal policy of government support for tribal autonomy. In 1953, instead of trying to encourage Native American self-government, the administration adopted a new approach, known as "termination." The government proposed settling all outstanding claims and eliminating reservations as legitimate political entities. To encourage their assimilation into mainstream society, families who would leave the reservations and move to cities were offered small subsidies by the government.

The new policy infuriated American Indians. Earl Old Person, a Blackfoot elder, declared: "It is important to note that in our Indian language the only translation for termination is to 'wipe out' or 'kill off' ... How can we plan our future when the Indian Bureau threatens to wipe us out as a race?" Though promising more freedom, the new policy caused great disruption as the government terminated tribes like the Klamath in Oregon and bands of Paiute in Utah.

The policy increased Indian activism. It also sparked a dawning awareness among whites of the Indians' right to maintain their heritage. In 1958, the Eisenhower administration changed the policy of termination so that it required a tribe's consent. The policy continued to have the force of law, but implementation ceased.

Asian American Advances

For Asian Americans, conditions improved somewhat in the aftermath of World War II. The war against Nazism eroded the racism that proclaimed a commitment to white superiority. In 1952, the Immigration and Nationality Act, also known as the McCarran-Walter Act, eased immigration quotas. Although the basic frame-work of the National Origins Act of 1924 remained intact, it removed the long-standing ban on Japanese immigration and made first-generation Japanese immi-grants eligible for citizenship. It also established a quota of 100 immigrants a year from each Asian country. While that number was tiny compared to those admit-ted annually from northern and western Europe, the measure was a first step in ending the discriminatory exclusion of the past.

By the 1950s, many second- and third-generation Chinese, Japanese, and Koreans had moved into white-collar work. Promoting education for their chil-dren, they became part of the growing middle class, hoping like others to enjoy the benefits of the American dream.

Conclusion

Qualms amid Affluence

In general, the United States during the decade and a half after World War II was stable and prosperous. Recessions occurred periodically, but the economy righted itself after short downturns. For the most part, business boomed. The standard of living for many of the nation's citizens reached new heights, especially compared with standards in other parts of the world. Millions of middle-class Americans joined the ranks of suburban property owners, enjoying the benefits of shopping centers, fast-food establishments, and other material manifestations of what they considered the good life. Workers found themselves savoring the materialistic ad-vantages of the era.

Some Americans did not share in the prosperity, but they were not visible in the affluent suburbs. Many African Americans and members of other minority groups were seriously disadvantaged, although they still believed they could share in the American dream and remained confident that deeply rooted patterns of discrimination could be changed peacefully.

Beneath the calm surface, though, there were signs of discontent. The seeds for the protest movements of the 1960s had already been sown. Disquieting signs were likewise evident on other fronts. The divorce rate increased, as one-third of all marriages in the 1950s broke apart. Americans increasingly used newly devel-oped tranquilizers in an effort to cope with problems in their lives. Some Ameri-cans began to criticize the materialism that seemed to undermine American ef-forts in the Cold War. Such criticisms in turn legitimized challenges by other groups, in the continuing struggle to make the realities of American life match the nation's ideals.

Criticisms and anxieties notwithstanding, the United States—for most whites and some people of color—continued to develop according to Ray Kroc's dreams as he first envisioned McDonald's establishments across the land. Healthy and comfortable, upper- and middle-class Americans expected prosperity and growth to continue in the years ahead.

Questions for Review and Reflection

1. What were the sources of American prosperity?

2. Who prospered most in postwar America?

3. Who was left out?

4. Why did conformity become the norm in the postwar United States?

5. How would you characterize the broad social and economic changes that took place in America in the years after World War II?

Discovering U.S. History Online

The Postwar United States http://lcweb2.loc.gov/ammem/ndlpedu/features/timeline/postwar/postwar.html
In primary documents, interviews, and artifacts, the Arts and Entertainment: 1945–1968 section of this Library of Congress site gives a good overview of the culture of the postwar years.

Levittown: Documents of an Ideal American Suburb www.uic.edu/~pbhales/Levittown/
The postwar boom in housing made suburban living the cultural norm in America and shaped a generation. The story of the classic suburb, Levittown, is told on this site in pictures and text.

Creating the Interstate System www.tfhrc.gov/pubrds/summer96/p96su10.htm
An illustrated article from the U.S. Department of Transportation, Federal Highway Administration's "Public Roads Website."

Harry S Truman www.ipl.org/ref/POTUS/hstruman.html
This site contains basic factual data about Truman's election and presidency, speeches, and online biographies.

Dwight David Eisenhower www.ipl.org/ref/POTUS/ddeisenhower.html
This site contains basic factual data about Eisenhower's election and presidency, including speeches and other materials.

The Central High Crisis, Little Rock 1957 www.ardemgaz.com/prev/central/
Using articles and photographs from Arkansas newspapers, the site explores the 1957 Little Rock events.

Fiction and Film

Guillermo Cotto-Thorner's *Trópico en Manhattan* (1967) is an autobiographical novel about the Puerto Rican community in New York City; Ralph Ellison's *Invisible Man* (1952) is a powerful fictional account of an African American's journey through the 1950s; Allen Ginsberg's *Howl and Other Poems* (1956) is a collection of iconoclastic poetry challenging the materialism of contemporary life; Jack Kerouac's *On the Road* (1957) is a stream-of-consciousness novel that questions the values of the 1950s; Arthur Miller's *Death of a Salesman* (1949) is the Pulitzer Prize–winning play about the shallow values of postwar American culture; J. D. Salinger's *Catcher in the Rye* (1951) is the story of Holden Caulfield, a troubled adolescent who is overwhelmed by the phoniness of contemporary life; Sloan Wilson's *The Man in the Gray Flannel Suit* (1955) is a novel challenging the conformity of corporate America in the 1950s.

The Best Years of Our Lives (1946), the Academy Award–winning story of three servicemen returning home after World War II, captures the values of the immediate postwar era; *The Seven Year Itch* (1955) features Marilyn Monroe as the beautiful and enticing girl next door; *To Kill a Mockingbird* (1962) is a film based on Harper Lee's novel by the same title about children learning about racism—and about how to deal with it—in the South. *Kinsey* (2004) describes the life and work of Alfred Kinsey, the controversial sex researcher; *The Man in the Gray Flannel Suit* (1956), the film made from the novel of the same name, critiques the lifestyle of corporate America in the 1950s; *The Murder of Emmett Till* (2003) is a powerful documentary film about the episode that helped mobilize African Americans; *The Untold Story of the Murder of Emmett Till* (2004) is another vivid documentary that led the Justice Department to reopen the case; *No Down Payment* (1957) deals with life in the suburbs, as does the much more recent *Pleasantville* (1998), as it looks back at an earlier era.

Recommended Reading

www.ablongman.com/nash

The Companion Website has a list of recommended readings about postwar America, including the economic boom, demographic and technological shifts, consensus and conformity, the welfare state, and poverty.

Chills and Fever During the Cold War, 1945–1960

CHAPTER OUTLINE

- Origins of the Cold War
- Containing the Soviet Union
- Containment in Asia, the Middle East, and Latin America
- Atomic Weapons and the Cold War
- The Cold War at Home
- Conclusion: The Cold War in Perspective

American Stories

A Government Employee Confronts the Anti-Communist Crusade

Val Lorwin was in France in November 1950 when he learned of the charges against him. A State Department employee on leave of absence after 16 years of government service, he was in Paris working on a book. Now he had to return to the United States to defend himself against the accusation that he was a member of the Communist party and thus a loyalty and security risk. Suspicions of the Soviet Union had escalated after 1945, and a wave of paranoia swept through the United States.

Lorwin was an unlikely candidate to be caught up in the fallout of the Cold War. He had begun to work for the government in 1935, serving in a number of New Deal agencies, then in the Labor Department and on the War Production Board before he was drafted during World War II. While in the army, he was assigned to the Office of Strategic Services, an early intelligence agency, and he was frequently granted security clearances.

Lorwin, however, did have a left-wing past as an active socialist in the 1930s. He had supported Socialist party causes, particularly the unionization of southern tenant farmers and the provision of aid to the unemployed. He and his wife, Madge, drafted statements and stuffed envelopes to support their goals. But that activity was wholly open and legal, and Lorwin had from the start been aggressively anti-Communist in political affairs.

Suddenly, Lorwin, like others in the period, faced a nightmare. Despite his spotless record, Lorwin was told that an unnamed accuser had identified him as a Communist. The burden of proving his innocence was entirely on him. He was entitled to a hearing if he chose, or he could resign.

Lorwin requested a hearing that was held late in 1950. Still struck by the absurdity of the situation, he refuted all accusations but neglected to cite his own positive achievements. At the conclusion, he was informed that the government no longer doubted his loyalty but considered him a security risk, likewise grounds for dismissal from his job.

When he appealed the judgment, Lorwin was again denied access to the identity of his accuser. This time, however, he thoroughly prepared his defense. At the hearing, a total of 97 witnesses either spoke under oath on Lorwin's behalf or left sworn written depositions testifying to his good character and meritorious service.

The issues in the hearings might have been considered comic in view of Lorwin's record, had not a man's reputation been at stake. The accuser had once lived with the Lorwins in Washington, D.C. Fifteen years later, he claimed that in 1935 Lorwin had revealed that he was holding a Communist party meeting in his home and had even shown him a party card.

Lorwin proved all the charges groundless. He also showed that in 1935 the Socialist party card was red, the color the accuser reported seeing, while the Communist party card was black. In March 1952, Lorwin was finally cleared for both loyalty and security.

Lorwin's troubles were not yet over. His name appeared on one of the lists produced by Senator Joseph McCarthy of Wisconsin and he was indicted for making false statements to the State Department Loyalty-Security Board. The charges this time proved as specious as before. Finally, in May 1954, admitting that its special prosecutor had deliberately lied to the grand jury and had no legitimate case, the Justice Department asked for dismissal of the indictment. Cleared at last, Lorwin went on to become a distinguished labor historian.

Val Lorwin was more fortunate than some victims of the anti-Communist crusade. Caught up in a global conflict that engulfed most of the world, he managed to weather a catastrophe that threatened to shatter his life. People rallied around him and gave him valuable support. Despite considerable emotional cost, he survived the witch hunt of the early 1950s, but his case still reflected vividly the ugly domestic consequences of the breakdown in relations between the Soviet Union and the United States.

The Cold War, which unfolded soon after the end of World War II and lasted for nearly 50 years, powerfully affected all aspects of American life. Rejecting for good the isolationist impulse that had governed foreign policy in the 1920s and 1930s, the United States began to play a major role in the world in the postwar years. Doubts about intervention in other lands faded as the nation acknowledged its dominant international position and resolved to do whatever was necessary to maintain it. The same sense of mission that had infused the United States in the Spanish-American War, World War I, and World War II now appeared in a revived evangelical faith and committed most Americans to the struggle against communism at home and abroad.

This chapter explores that continuing sense of mission and its consequences. It examines the roots of the Cold War both in the idealistic aim to keep the world safe for democracy and in the pursuit of economic self-interest that had long fueled American capitalism. It records how the determination to prevent the spread of communism led American policymakers to consider vast parts of the world as pivotal to American security and to act accordingly, particularly in Korea and Vietnam. It notes the impact on economic development, particularly in the West, where the mighty defense industry flourished. And it considers the tragic consequences of the effort to promote ideological unity in a rigid and doctrinaire version of the American dream that led to excesses threatening the principles of democracy itself.

ORIGINS OF THE COLD WAR

The Cold War developed by degrees. It stemmed from divergent views about the shape of the post–World War II world as the colonial empires in Asia, Africa, and the Middle East began to crumble. The United States, strong and secure, was intent on spreading its vision of freedom and free trade around the world to maintain its economic hegemony. The Soviet Union, concerned about security after a devastating war, demanded politically sympathetic neighbors on its borders to preserve its own autonomy. Suppressed during World War II, these differences now surfaced in a virulent Soviet–American confrontation.

The American Stance

The United States emerged from World War II more powerful than any nation ever before, and it sought to use that might to achieve a world order that could sustain American aims. American policymakers hoped to spread the values— liberty, equality, and democracy—underpinning the American dream. They did not always recognize that what they considered universal truths were rooted in specific historical circumstances in their own country and might not flourish elsewhere.

At the same time, American leaders sought a world where economic enterprise could thrive. With the American economy operating at full speed as a result of the war, world markets were needed once the fighting stopped. Government officials wanted to eliminate trade barriers—imposed by the Soviet Union and other nations—to provide outlets for industrial products and for surplus farm commodities such as wheat, cotton, and tobacco. As the largest source of goods for world markets, with exports totaling $14 billion in 1947, the United States required open channels for growth to continue. Americans assumed that their prosperity would benefit the rest of the world, even when other nations disagreed.

Soviet Aims

The Soviet Union formulated its own goals after World War II. Russia had usually been governed in the past by a strongly centralized government, and that tradition, as well as Communist ideology, guided Soviet policy.

During the war, the Russians had played down talk of world revolution, which they knew their allies found threatening, and had mobilized domestic support with nationalistic appeals. As the struggle drew to a close, the Soviets still said little about world conquest, emphasizing socialism within the nation itself.

Rebuilding was the first priority. Devastated by the war, Soviet agriculture and industry lay in shambles. But revival required internal security. At the same time, the Russians felt vulnerable along their western flank. Twice in the twentieth century, invasions had come from the west, most recently when Hitler had attacked in 1941. Haunted by fears of a quick German recovery, the Soviets demanded defensible borders and neighboring regimes sympathetic to Russian aims. They insisted on military and political stability in the regions nearby.

Early Cold War Leadership

Both the United States and the Soviet Union had strong leadership in the early years of the Cold War. On the American side, presidents Harry Truman and Dwight Eisenhower accepted the centralization of authority Franklin Roosevelt had begun, as the executive branch became increasingly powerful in guiding foreign policy. In the Soviet Union, first Joseph Stalin, then Nikita Khrushchev provided equally forceful direction.

Truman and Eisenhower, both introduced in Chapter 26, subscribed to traditional American attitudes about self-determination and the superiority of American political institutions and values. Both were determined to stand firm in the face of the Soviet threat.

As World War II drew to an end, Truman grew increasingly hostile to Soviet actions. Viewing collaboration as a wartime necessity, he was uncomfortable with what he believed were Soviet designs in Eastern Europe and Asia as the struggle wound down. Like Truman, Eisenhower saw communism as a monolithic force struggling for world supremacy and agreed that the Kremlin in Moscow was orchestrating subversive activity around the globe. Yet Eisenhower was more willing than Truman to practice accommodation when it served his ends.

Joseph Stalin, the Soviet leader at the war's end, possessed almost absolute powers. He had presided over ruthless purges against his opponents in the 1930s. Now he was determined to rebuild Soviet society and to keep Eastern Europe within the Russian sphere of influence.

Stalin's death in March 1953 left a power vacuum in Soviet political affairs that was eventually filled by Nikita Khrushchev, who by 1958 held the offices of both prime minister and party secretary. A crude man, Khrushchev once used his shoe to pound a table at the United Nations. During his regime, the Cold War continued, but for brief periods of time Soviet–American relations became less hostile.

Disillusionment with the USSR

American support for the Soviet Union faded quickly after the war. As Americans soured on Russia, they began to equate the Nazi and Soviet systems. Just as they had in the 1930s, authors, journalists, and public officials pointed to similarities, some of them legitimate, between the regimes. Both states, they contended, maintained total control over communications and eliminated political opposition. Both states used terror to silence dissidents, and Stalin's labor camps in Siberia could be compared with Hitler's concentration camps. After the U.S. publication in 1949 of George Orwell's frightening novel *1984*, *Life* magazine noted in an editorial that the ominous figure Big Brother was but a "mating" of Hitler and Stalin. Truman spoke for many Americans when he said in 1950 that "there isn't any difference between the totalitarian Russian government and the Hitler government. ... They are all alike."

The lingering sense that the nation had not been quick enough to resist totalitarian aggression in the 1930s heightened American fears. Many people believed that the free world had not responded promptly when the Germans, Italians, and Japanese first caused international trouble, and the United States was determined never to repeat the same mistake.

The Troublesome Polish Question

The first clash between East and West came, even before the war ended, over Poland. Soviet demands for a government willing to accept Russian influence clashed with American hopes for a more representative structure patterned after the Western model. The Yalta Conference of February 1945 provided a loosely worded and correspondingly imprecise agreement (see Chapter 25), and when Truman assumed office, the Polish situation remained unresolved.

Truman's unbending stance on Poland was clear in an April 1945 meeting with Soviet foreign minister Vyacheslav Molotov. Concerned that the Russians were breaking the Yalta agreements, vague as they were, the American leader demanded a new democratic government there. Truman later recalled that when Molotov protested, "I have never been talked to like that in my life," he himself retorted bluntly, "Carry out your agreements and you won't get talked to like that." Such bluntness contributed to the deterioration of Soviet–American relations.

Truman and Stalin met face-to-face for the first (and last) time at the Potsdam Conference in July 1945, the final wartime Big Three meeting of the United States, the Soviet Union, and Great Britain. There, outside devastated Berlin, the two leaders sized each other up as they considered the Russian–Polish boundary, the fate of Germany, and the American desire to obtain an unconditional surrender from Japan. It was Truman's first exposure to international diplomacy at the highest level, and it left him confident of his abilities. When he learned during the meeting of the first successful atomic bomb test in New Mexico, he became even more determined to insist that the Soviets behave in the ways he wanted.

Economic Pressure on the USSR

One major source of controversy in the last stages of World War II was the question of U.S. aid to its allies. Responding to congressional pressure to limit foreign assistance as hostilities ended, Truman acted impulsively. Six days after the end of the European war in May 1945, he issued an executive order cutting off lend-lease supplies to the Allies. Though the policy affected all nations receiving aid, it hurt the Soviet Union most of all.

The United States used economic pressure in other ways as well. The USSR desperately needed financial assistance to rebuild after the war and, in January 1945, had requested a $6 billion loan. Roosevelt hedged, hoping to win concessions in return. In August, the Russians renewed their application, but this time for only $1 billion. Truman dragged his heels, seeking to use the loan as a lever to gain access to markets in areas traditionally dominated by the Soviet Union. Stalin refused a loan under such conditions and launched his own five-year plan instead.

Declaring the Cold War

DOCUMENT

Churchill's "Iron Curtain" Speech (March 5, 1946)

As Soviet–American relations deteriorated, both sides stepped up their rhetorical attacks. In 1946, Stalin spoke out first, arguing that capitalism and communism were on a collision course, that a series of cataclysmic disturbances would tear the capitalist world apart, and that the Soviet system would inevitably triumph. Supreme Court Justice William O. Douglas called Stalin's speech the "declaration of World War III."

The West's response to Stalin's speech came from England's former prime minister, Winston Churchill. Speaking in Fulton, Missouri, in 1946, Churchill declared that "from Stettin in the Baltic to Trieste in the Adriatic, an iron curtain has descended across the Continent." A vigilant association of English-speaking peoples was necessary to contain Soviet designs.

CONTAINING THE SOVIET UNION

Containment formed the basis of postwar American policy. While the fledgling United Nations, established in 1945, might have provided a forum to ease tensions, both the United States and the Soviet Union acted unilaterally, and with the aid of allies, in pursuit of their own ends.

Containment Defined

George F. Kennan, chargé d'affaires at the American embassy in the Soviet Union, was primarily responsible for defining the new policy of containment. After Stalin's speech in February 1946, Kennan sent an 8,000-word telegram to the State Department. In it he argued that Soviet hostility stemmed from the "Kremlin's neurotic

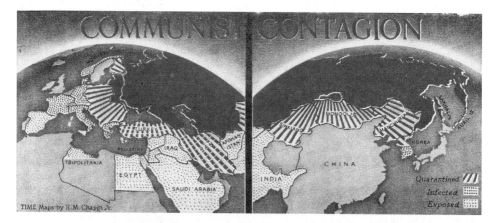

The Contagion of Communism Americans in the early postwar years were afraid that communism was a contagious disease spreading around the globe. In this picture from the spring of 1946, *Time* magazine pictured the relentless spread of an infection that would need to be contained. Why would such a map seem frightening to people who looked at it? *(Time, Inc.)*

view of world affairs," which in turn came from the "traditional and instinctive Russian sense of insecurity." The stiff Soviet stance was not so much a response to American actions as a reflection of the Russian leaders' own efforts to maintain their autocratic rule. Russian fanaticism would not soften, regardless of how accommodating American policy became. Therefore, it had to be opposed at every turn.

Kennan's "long telegram" struck a resonant chord in Washington. Soon he published an extended analysis, under the pseudonym "Mr. X," in the prominent journal *Foreign Affairs*. Soviet pressure, he suggested, had to "be contained by the adroit and vigilant application of counter-force at a series of constantly shifting geographical and political points." The concept of containment provided the philosophical justification for the hard-line stance that the United States adopted.

The First Step: The Truman Doctrine

The Truman Doctrine represented the first major application of containment policy. The Soviet Union was pressuring Turkey for joint control of the Dardanelles, the passage between the Black Sea and the Mediterranean. Meanwhile, a civil war in Greece pitted Communist elements against the ruling English-aided right-wing monarchy. Revolutionary pressures threatened to topple the government.

In February 1947, Britain—still reeling from the war—informed the State Department that it could no longer give Greece and Turkey economic and military aid. Administration officials willing to move into the void knew they needed bipartisan support to accomplish such a major policy shift. Senator Arthur Vandenberg of Michigan, a key Republican, aware of the need for bipartisanship, told top policymakers that they had to begin "scaring hell out of the country" if they wanted support for a bold new containment policy.

Truman complied. On March 12, 1947, he told Congress, in a statement that came to be known as the Truman Doctrine, "I believe that it must be the policy of the United States to support free peoples who are resisting subjugation by armed minorities or by outside pressures." Unless the United States acted, the free world might not survive. To avert that calamity, he urged Congress to appropriate $400 million for military and economic aid to Turkey and Greece.

DOCUMENT

Truman Doctrine (1947)

Not everyone approved of Truman's request. Autocratic regimes controlled Greece and Turkey, some observers pointed out. And where was the proof that Stalin had a hand in the Greek conflict? Others warned that the United States could not by itself stop encroachment in all parts of the world. Nonetheless, Congress passed Truman's foreign aid bill. In assuming that Americans could police the globe, the Truman Doctrine was a major step in the advent of the Cold War.

The Next Steps: The Marshall Plan, NATO, and NSC-68

The next step for American policymakers involved sending extensive economic aid for postwar recovery in Western Europe. At the war's end, most of Europe was economically and politically unstable, and administration officials believed that the Soviet Union might easily intervene. Another motive for decisive action was to bolster the European economy to provide markets for American goods.

HOW OTHERS SEE US

A West German Poster on the Marshall Plan

European nations welcomed the assistance provided by the Marshall Plan that could help them maintain their independence and avoid communism. This poster from West Germany hails freedom, which it calls the "free way" (freie bahn), in a play on the German word for "highway"—autobahn.

(The Art Archive)

- Why was communism a threat in postwar Europe?
- How could the Marshall Plan help European nations remain free?
- How effectively does this poster underscore the idea of freedom?

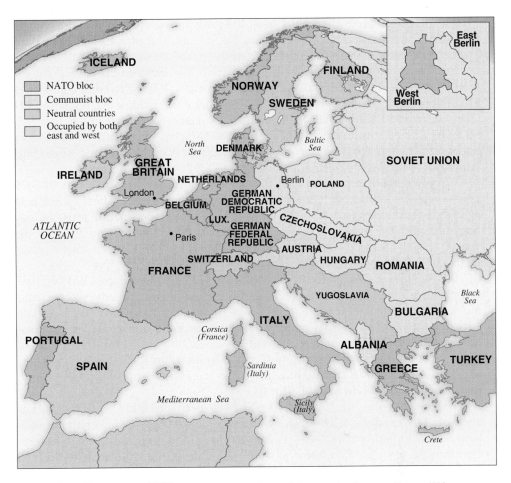

COLD WAR EUROPE IN 1950 This map shows the rigid demarcation between East and West during the Cold War. Although there were a number of neutral countries in Europe, the other nations found themselves in a standoff, as each side tried to contain the possible advances of the other. The small inset map in the upper-right-hand corner shows the division of Berlin that paralleled the division of Germany itself after World War II. ■ **Reflecting on the Past** How widespread was the policy of neutrality in Cold War Europe? How powerful was the NATO bloc? How easily could one side move against the other in divided Europe?

Excellent customers earlier, Western Europeans in the aftermath of the war were able to purchase less at a time when the United States was producing more.

George Marshall, the new secretary of state, revealed the administration's willingness to assist European recovery in a Harvard University commencement address in June 1947. He asked all troubled European nations to draw up an aid program that the United States could support, a program "directed not against any country or doctrine but against hunger, poverty, desperation, and chaos." Soviet-bloc countries were welcome to participate, Marshall announced, aware that their involvement was unlikely since they would have to set aside secrecy and disclose economic records to join.

The proposed program would assist the ravaged nations, provide the United States with needed markets, and contain the Soviets. The Marshall Plan and the Truman Doctrine, Truman noted, were "two halves of the same walnut."

Responding quickly to Marshall's invitation, the Western European nations worked out the details of massive requests. In early 1948, Congress committed $13 billion over a period of four years to 16 cooperating nations. But not all Americans supported the Marshall Plan. Henry A. Wallace, former vice president and secretary of agriculture, called the scheme the "Martial Plan" and argued that it was another step toward war. Some members of Congress feared spreading American resources too thin.

Closely related to the Marshall Plan was a concerted Western effort to integrate a rebuilt Germany into a reviving Europe. At war's end, Allied leaders had agreed to divide the defeated Nazi nation and its capital, Berlin, into four occupation zones (Soviet, American, British, and French). Allied leaders intended the division of both Germany and Berlin to be temporary, until a permanent peace treaty could be signed.

But the lines of demarcation became rigid. With the onset of the Cold War and the growing Soviet domination of Eastern Europe, the West became worried and moved to fill the vacuum in Central Europe to counter the Russian threat. In late 1946, the Americans and British merged their zones and began assigning administrative duties to German citizens. By mid-1947, despite French fears of a resurgent Germany, the process of rebuilding German industry in the combined Western sector was under way. Meanwhile, the same increasingly rigid separation into two separate cities occurred in Berlin.

The Soviet Union was furious. In mid-1948, a crisis erupted when the Soviets attempted to force the Western powers out of Berlin by refusing to allow them land access to their part of the city and banning all shipments through eastern Germany. In what became known as the Berlin airlift, the United States and the British Royal Air Force flew supplies to the beleaguered Berliners. Over the next year, more than 200,000 flights provided 13,000 tons daily of food, fuel, and other necessary materials. The airlift proved to be a public relations disaster for the Soviet Union and a triumph for the West. The Soviets finally ended the blockade, but Berlin remained a focal point of conflict, and there were now two separate German states: the Federal Republic of Germany, or West Germany, and the German Democratic Republic, or East Germany.

The next major link in the containment strategy was the creation of a military alliance in Europe in 1949 to complement the economic program. After the Soviets tightened their control over Hungary and Czechoslovakia, the United States took the lead in establishing the North Atlantic Treaty Organization (NATO). Twelve nations formed the alliance, vowing that an attack against any one member would be considered an attack against all, to be met by appropriate armed force. Despite George Washington's warning in 1796 against "entangling alliances," the United States established its first military treaty ties with Europe since the American Revolution. Congress also voted military aid for its NATO allies.

Two dramatic events in 1949—the Communist victory in the Chinese civil war and the Russian detonation of an atomic device—shocked the United States.

While the fall of China (described in the next section) was frightening, the erosion of the American atomic monopoly was horrifying. Although American scientists had understood that the Soviets could create a bomb of their own, many people believed it would take the Russians at least a decade and a half. President Truman thought they might never be able to accomplish such a feat at all. In September 1949, an air force reconnaissance plane detected radioactivity, indicating that the Soviets had tested their own bomb, just four years after the United States had ushered in the atomic age. Now a nuclear arms race beckoned.

Truman asked for a full-fledged review of U.S. foreign and defense policy. Responding to his request, the National Security Council, organized in 1947 to provide policy coordination, produced a document called NSC-68, which shaped U.S. policy for the next 20 years.

NSC-68 built on the Cold War rhetoric of the Truman Doctrine, describing challenges facing the United States in cataclysmic terms. "The issues that face us are momentous," the paper said, "involving the fulfillment or destruction not only of this Republic but of civilization itself." Conflict between East and West, the document assumed, was unavoidable. Negotiation was useless, for the Soviets could never be trusted to bargain in good faith. NSC-68 then argued that, to meet the Russian challenge, the United States must increase defense spending dramatically from the $13 billion set for 1950 to as much as $50 billion per year.

Containment in the 1950s

Because containment required detailed information about Communist moves, the government relied increasingly on the Central Intelligence Agency (CIA). Established by the National Security Act of 1947, which had also created the National Security Council, the CIA conducted espionage in foreign lands, some of it visible, more of it secret. With President Eisenhower's approval, by 1957, 80 percent of the CIA's budget went toward covert activities. More and more, Eisenhower relied on clandestine CIA actions to undermine foreign governments and assist those who supported the American stance in the Cold War.

The civil rights movement that was gaining momentum in the 1950s had an effect on Cold War policy. American policymakers were aware of the impact of stories about racial discrimination in other nations, particularly nations moving toward independence in sub-Saharan Africa. Leaders sought to portray the struggle in the best possible light in propaganda aimed abroad.

At the same time, the administration reassessed the impact of the containment policy itself. For most of Eisenhower's two terms, John Foster Dulles was secretary of state. A devout Presbyterian, he sought to move beyond containment and counter the "Godless terrorism" of communism with a holy crusade to promote democracy and to free the countries under Soviet domination. Dulles also advocated immediate retaliation in the face of hostile Soviet ventures: "There is one solution and only one: that is for the free world to develop the will and organize the means to retaliate instantly against open aggression by Red armies, so that, if it occurred anywhere, we could and would strike back where it hurts, by means of our own choosing."

Eisenhower's own rhetoric was equally strong, yet he was more conciliatory than Dulles and recognized the impossibility of changing the governments of the USSR's satellites. In mid-1953, when East Germans mounted anti-Soviet demonstrations in a challenge that foreshadowed the revolt against communism three and a half decades later, the United States maintained its distance. In 1956, when Hungarian "freedom fighters" rose up against Russian domination, the United States again stood back as Soviet forces smashed the rebels. Because Western action could have precipitated a more general conflict, Eisenhower refused to translate rhetoric into action. The policy of containment remained in effect.

CONTAINMENT IN ASIA, THE MIDDLE EAST, AND LATIN AMERICA

In a dramatic departure from its history of noninvolvement, the United States extended the policy of containment to meet challenges around the globe. Colonial empires were disintegrating, and countries seeking and attaining their independence now found themselves caught in the middle of the superpower struggle. In Asia, the Middle East, and Latin America, the United States discovered the tremendous appeal of communism and found that ever greater efforts were required to advance American aims.

A New Chinese Leader Mao Zedong, chairman of the Chinese Communist party, was a powerful and popular leader who drove Jiang Jieshi from power in 1949 and established a stronghold over the People's Republic of China. How was Mao able to defeat his opponents and win the revolutionary war? (Corbis)

The Shock of the Chinese Revolution

IMAGE

Chairman Mao
Casts His Vote
(1953)

The U.S. commitment to global containment became stronger with the
Communist victory in the Chinese civil war in 1949. An ally during World
War II, China had struggled against the Japanese, while simultaneously
fighting a bitter civil war. Mao Zedong (Mao Tse-tung),* founder of a
branch of the Communist party, gathered followers who wanted to reshape
China in a distinctive Marxist mold. Opposing the Communists were the Nationalists, led by Jiang Jieshi (Chiang Kai-shek), who wanted to preserve their power
and governmental leadership. By the early 1940s, Jiang's inefficient and corrupt
regime was exhausted.. Mao's movement, meanwhile, grew stronger as he opposed the Japanese invaders and won the loyalty of the peasantry. Mao finally
prevailed, as Jiang fled in 1949 to the island of Taiwan (Formosa). Mao's proclamation of the People's Republic of China on October 1, 1949, fanned fears of Russian domination, for he had already announced his regime's support for the Soviet
Union against the "imperialist" United States.

Events in China caused near hysteria in America. Staunch anti-Communists
argued that Truman and the United States were to blame for Jiang's defeat because they failed to provide him with sufficient support. Secretary of State Dean
Acheson briefly considered granting diplomatic recognition to the new government but backed off after the Communists seized American property, harassed
American citizens, and openly allied China with the USSR.

Stalemate in the Korean War

The Korean War highlighted growing U.S. concern about Asia. The conflict in Korea stemmed from tensions lingering after World War II. Korea, long under Japanese control, hoped for independence after Japan's defeat. But the Allies temporarily divided Korea along the 38th parallel to expedite the transition to peace after
the rapid end to the Pacific struggle when the atomic bombs were dropped on
Japan. The Soviet–American line, initially intended as a matter of military convenience, hardened after 1945, just as a similar division became rigid in Germany.
In time, the Soviets set up one Korean government in the north and the Americans
another government in the south. Each Korean government hoped to reunify the
country on its own terms.

North Korea moved first. On June 25, 1950, North Korean forces crossed the
38th parallel and invaded South Korea. While the North Koreans used Soviet-
built tanks, they operated on their own initiative. Kim Il Sung, the North Korean
leader, had visited Moscow earlier and gained Soviet acquiescence in the idea of
an attack, but both the planning and the implementation occurred in Korea.

Taken by surprise and certain that Russia had masterminded the North Korean offensive and was testing the American policy of containment, Truman responded by telling the public that "if this was allowed to go unchallenged it

---

*Chinese names are rendered in their modern *pinyin* spelling. At first occurrence, the older but
perhaps more familiar spelling (usually Wade-Giles) is given in parentheses.

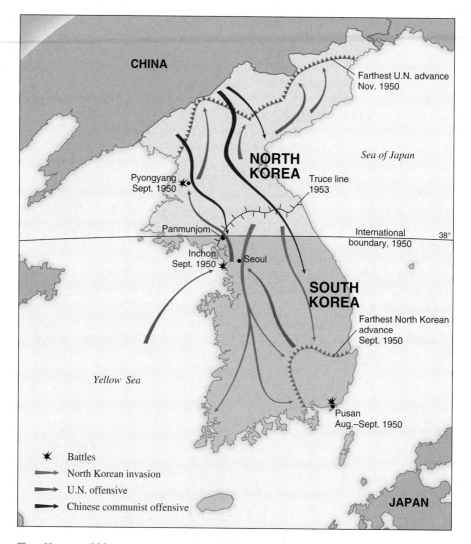

CHINA

Farthest U.N. advance
Nov. 1950

**NORTH
KOREA**

Sea of Japan

Pyongyang
Sept. 1950

Truce line
1953

Panmunjom

International
boundary, 1950   38°

Inchon
Sept. 1950   Seoul

**SOUTH
KOREA**

Farthest North Korean
advance
Sept. 1950

Yellow Sea

Pusan
Aug.–Sept. 1950

⁕ Battles
➤ North Korean invasion
➤ U.N. offensive
➤ Chinese communist offensive

JAPAN

THE KOREAN WAR This map shows the ebb and flow of the Korean War. North Korea crossed the 38th parallel first, then the UN offensive drove the North Koreans close to the Chinese border, and finally the Chinese Communists entered the war and drove the UN forces back below the 38th parallel. The armistice signed at Panmunjom in 1953 provided a dividing line very close to the prewar line. ■ **Reflecting on the Past** How far did both North Korea and South Korea penetrate into the territory of the other nation? What role did China play in the Korean War?

would mean a third world war, just as similar incidents had brought on the second world war."

Truman directed General Douglas MacArthur, head of the American occupation in Japan, to supply South Korea. The United States also went to the United Nations Security Council and secured a unanimous resolution branding North Korea an aggressor, then another resolution calling on members of the organization to assist South Korea in repelling aggression and restoring peace. This was the largest UN operation to date, and MacArthur became leader of all UN forces. While the United States and South Korea provided over 90 percent of the manpower, 15 other nations were involved in the UN effort.

Air and naval forces, then ground forces, went into battle south of the 38th parallel. Following a daring amphibious invasion that pushed the North Koreans back to the former boundary line, UN troops crossed the 38th parallel, hoping to reunify Korea under an American-backed government. Despite Chinese signals that this movement toward their border threatened their security, the UN troops pressed on. In October, Chinese troops appeared briefly in battle, then disappeared. The next month, the Chinese mounted a full-fledged counterattack, which pushed the UN forces back below the dividing line.

The resulting stalemate provoked a bitter struggle between the brilliant but arrogant General MacArthur, who called for retaliatory air strikes against China, and President Truman, who remained committed to conducting a limited war. MacArthur's statements, issued from the field, finally went too far. In April 1951, he argued that the American approach in Korea was wrong and asserted publicly that "there is no substitute for victory." Truman had no choice but to relieve the general for insubordination. The decision outraged many Americans. After the stunning victories of World War II, limited war was frustrating and difficult to understand.

The Korean War dragged on into Eisenhower's presidency. Campaigning in 1952, Ike promised to go to Korea, and three weeks after his election, he did so. When UN truce talks bogged down in May 1953, the new administration privately threatened the Chinese with the use of atomic weapons. This brought about renewed UN negotiations, and on July 27, 1953, an armistice was signed. After three long years, the unpopular war had ended.

American involvement carried a heavy price: over 33,000 Americans killed in action and more than 142,000 American casualties in all. The other 15 UN nations involved in the struggle accounted for another 17,000 casualties. But those figures paled beside as many as 2 million Koreans dead and countless others wounded and maimed.

The war significantly changed American attitudes and institutions. For the first time, American forces fought in racially integrated units. As commander in chief, Truman had ordered the integration of the armed forces in 1948, over the opposition of many generals, and African Americans became part of all military units. Their successful performance led to acceptance of military integration.

The Korean War years also saw military expenditures soar from $13 billion in 1950 to about $47 billion three years later, as defense spending followed the guidelines proposed in NSC-68. Whereas the military absorbed less than one-third of the federal budget in 1950, a decade later, it took half. More than a million military personnel were stationed around the world.

The Korean War had important political effects as well. It led the United States to sign a peace treaty with Japan in September 1951 and to rely on that nation to maintain the balance of power in the Pacific. At the same time, the struggle poisoned relations with the People's Republic of China, which remained unrecognized by the United States, and ensured a diplomatic standoff that lasted more than 20 years.

The Korean War,
1950–1953

Vietnam: The Roots of Conflict

The commitment to stopping the spread of communism led to the massive U.S. involvement in Vietnam. That struggle tore the United States apart, wrought enormous damage in Southeast Asia, and finally forced a reevaluation of America's Cold War policies.

The roots of the war extended far back in the past. Indochina—the part of Southeast Asia that included Vietnam, Laos, and Cambodia—had been a French colony since the mid-nineteenth century. During World War II, Japan occupied the region, but an independence movement, led by the Communist organizer and revolutionary Ho Chi Minh, sought to expel the Japanese conquerors from Vietnam. In 1945, the Allied powers had to decide how to deal with Ho and his nationalist movement.

France was determined to regain its colony as a way of preserving its status as a great power. Meanwhile, Ho established the Democratic Republic of Vietnam in 1945. The new government's Declaration of Independence harkened back to its American counterpart. It declared: "All men are created equal. They are endowed by their Creator with certain inalienable rights, among these are Life, Liberty and the pursuit of Happiness." Despite widespread popular support, the United States refused to recognize the new government.

A long, bitter struggle broke out between French and Vietnamese forces, which became entangled with the larger Cold War. Truman needed France to check the Soviets in Europe and that meant cooperating with France in Vietnam.

DOCUMENT

Policy Statement about U.S. Objectives in Southeast Asia (1954)

Although Ho did not have close ties to the Soviet Union and was committed to his independent nationalist crusade, Truman and his advisers assumed wrongly that Ho took orders from Moscow. Hence, in 1950, the United States formally recognized the French puppet government in Vietnam, and by 1954, the United States was paying over three-quarters of the cost of France's Indochina war.

After Eisenhower took office, France's position in Southeast Asia deteriorated, but the president refused to intervene directly. He understood the lack of American support for intervention in that far-off land. As a French fortress at Dien Bien Phu in the north of Vietnam finally fell to Ho's forces, an international conference in Geneva sought to prevent Ho Chi Minh from gaining control of the entire country. The final declaration of the conference divided Vietnam along the 17th parallel, with elections promised in 1956 to unify the country and determine its political fate.

Two separate Vietnamese states emerged. Ho Chi Minh held power in the north, while in the south, Ngo Dinh Diem, a fierce anti-Communist who had been in exile in the United States, returned to form a government. Diem enjoyed the full support of the United States, which saw him as a way of securing stability in Southeast Asia and avoiding further Communist incursions. When he decided not to hold the elections mandated in the Geneva accord, the United States backed him in that decision. In the next few years, American aid increased and military advisers—675 by the time Eisenhower left office—began to assist the South Vietnamese. The United States had taken its first steps toward direct involvement in a ruinous war halfway around the world that would escalate out of control.

Father Ho Ho Chi Minh waged a long struggle first against France, then Japan, and finally the United States for the independence of Vietnam. The Vietnamese people viewed him as the father of the country. How does this picture of him with children contribute to that impression? *(Library of Congress)*

The Creation of Israel and Its Impact on the Middle East

The creation of the state of Israel became intertwined with larger Cold War issues. Jews had longed for a homeland for years, and the Zionist movement had sought a place in Palestine, in the Middle East, since the latter part of the nineteenth century. Jewish settlers who began to gravitate to Palestine were not welcomed by the Turks, who dominated the region, or by the British, who exercised control after World War I.

Then the Holocaust—and the slaughter of 6 million Jews—during World War II created new pressure for a Jewish state. The unwillingness—and inability—of the Western powers to intervene in time to stop the Nazi genocide created a groundswell of support, particularly among American Jews, for a Jewish homeland in the Arab-dominated Middle East.

In 1948, the fledgling United Nations attempted to partition Palestine into an Arab state and a Jewish state. Truman officially recognized the new state of Israel 15 minutes after it was proclaimed. But American recognition could not end bitter animosities between Arabs, who believed they had been robbed of their territory,

DOCUMENT

Press Release
Announcing
U.S. Recognition of
Israel

and Jews, who felt they had finally regained a homeland after the horrors of the Holocaust. As Americans looked on, Arab forces invaded Israel in the first of a continuing series of conflicts that dominated the Middle East in the second half of the twentieth century. The Israelis, fighting for the survival of the new nation, won the war and added territory to what the UN had given them, but the struggle continued.

While sympathetic to Israel, the United States tried at the same time to maintain stability in the rest of the region, which had tremendous strategic importance as the supplier of oil for industrialized nations. In 1953, the CIA helped the Iranian army overthrow the government of Mohammed Mossadegh, which had nationalized oil wells formerly under British control, and placed the shah of Iran securely on the throne. After the coup, British and American companies regained command of the wells.

As it cultivated close ties with Israel, the United States also tried to maintain the friendship of oil-rich Arab states or, at the very least, to prevent them from falling into the Soviet orbit. In Egypt, the policy ran into trouble when Arab nationalist General Gamal Abdel Nasser planned a huge dam on the Nile River to produce electric power and proclaimed his country's neutrality in the Cold War. Although Dulles offered U.S. financial support for the Aswan Dam project, Nasser also began discussions with the Soviet Union. Furious, the secretary of state withdrew the American offer. Left without funds for the dam, in July 1956, Nasser seized and nationalized the British-controlled Suez Canal and closed it to Israeli ships. Now Great Britain was enraged and Europe worried about a continuing supply of oil.

In the fall, Israeli, British, and French military forces invaded Egypt. Eisenhower, who had not been consulted, was irate. Realizing that the strike might push Nasser into Moscow's arms, the United States sponsored a UN resolution condemning the attack and persuaded other nations not to send petroleum to England and France. These actions convinced the invaders to withdraw.

Before long, the United States again intervened in the Middle East. Concerned about the region's stability, the president declared in 1957, in what came to be called the Eisenhower Doctrine, that "the existing vacuum in the Middle East must be filled by the United States before it is filled by Russia." A year later he authorized the landing of 14,000 soldiers in Lebanon to prop up a right-wing government challenged from within.

Restricting Revolt in Latin America

IMAGE

A Case History of
Communist
Penetration in
Guatemala
(1957)

The Cold War also led to intervention in Latin America, the United States' traditional sphere of influence. In 1954, Eisenhower ordered CIA support for a right-wing coup aimed at ousting the elected government of reform-minded Colonel Jacobo Arbenz Guzmán in Guatemala. The takeover succeeded and established a military dictatorship that responded to U.S. wishes. These actions demonstrated again the shortsighted American commitment to stability and private investment, whatever the internal effect or ultimate cost. The interference in Guatemala fed anti-American feeling throughout Latin America.

In 1959, when Fidel Castro overthrew the dictatorship of Fulgencio Batista in Cuba, the shortsightedness of American policy became even clearer. Nationalism and the thrust for social reform were powerful forces in Latin America, as in the rest of the Third World formerly dominated by European powers. But when Castro confiscated American property in Cuba, the Eisenhower administration cut off exports and severed diplomatic ties. In response, Cuba turned to the Soviet Union for support.

ATOMIC WEAPONS AND THE COLD WAR

Throughout the Cold War, the atomic bomb was a crucial factor that hung over all diplomatic discussions and military initiatives. Atomic weapons were destructive enough, but when the United States and the Soviet Union both developed hydrogen bombs, an age of overkill began.

Sharing the Secret of the Bomb

The United States, with British aid, had built the first atomic bomb and attempted to conceal the project from its wartime ally, the Soviet Union. Soviet spies, however, learned about the effort and, even before the war was over, the Soviets had initiated a program to create their own bomb.

The United States briefly considered sharing the atomic secret. Just before he retired, Secretary of War Henry L. Stimson pushed for cooperating with the Soviet Union. Recognizing the futility of trying to cajole the Russians while "having this weapon ostentatiously on our hip," he warned that "their suspicions and their distrust of our purposes and motives will increase." Only mutual accommodation could bring international cooperation.

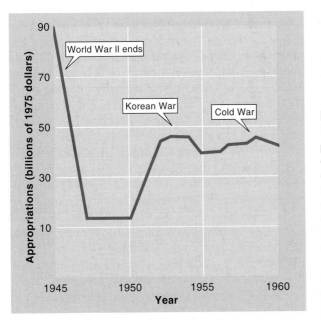

DEFENSE EXPENDITURES, 1945–1960 Defense spending plummeted after World War II, only to quadruple with the onset of the Korean War. After that increase, spending levels never dropped dramatically, even after the end of the war. Why was the United States willing to spend so much more for defense after 1950? Why did levels of spending remain relatively constant after that? *(Source: U.S. Bureau of the Census.)*

Yet as negotiations to develop a system of international arms control broke down, the United States gave up on the idea of sharing atomic secrets. Intent on retaining the technological advantage until the creation of a "foolproof method of control," Truman endorsed the Atomic Energy Act, passed by Congress in 1946. It established the Atomic Energy Commission (AEC) to supervise all atomic energy development in the United States and, under the tightest security, to authorize all nuclear activity in the nation at large. It also opened the way to a nuclear arms race once Russia developed its own bomb.

Nuclear Proliferation

As the atomic bomb found its way into popular culture, Americans at first showed more excitement than fear. In Los Angeles, the "Atombomb Dancers" wiggled at the Burbank Burlesque Theater. In 1946, the Buchanan Brothers released a record called "Atomic Power," noting the brimstone fire from heaven that was "given by the mighty hand of God."

Nevertheless, anxiety lurked beneath the exuberance, though it did not surface dramatically as long as the United States held a nuclear monopoly. Then, in September 1949, when the Soviet Union tested its own bomb, the security of being the world's only atomic power vanished. People wondered whether the Soviet test foreshadowed a nuclear attack and speculated when it might come. The editors of the *Bulletin of the Atomic Scientists,* the nation's foremost publication dealing with nuclear affairs, moved the minute hand of the "doomsday clock" on the cover of the journal from seven minutes before midnight to three minutes before midnight to reflect their fear of proliferation.

IMAGE

U.S. Hydrogen Bomb Test over Uninhabited Pacific Island (1952)

In early 1950, Truman authorized the development of a new hydrogen superbomb, potentially far more devastating than the atomic bomb, and by 1953 both the United States and the Soviet Union had unlocked the secret of fusion—joining atoms together in a reaction like that on the surface of the sun. A far more powerful reaction could do far more damage. As kilotons gave way to megatons, the stakes rose higher and higher. After the 1954 BRAVO test of a hydrogen device, Lewis Strauss, Atomic Energy Commission chairman, admitted that "an H-bomb can be made ... large enough to take out a city," even New York. Then, in 1957, shortly after the news that the Soviets had successfully tested their first intercontinental ballistic missile (ICBM), Americans learned that the Soviets had lifted the first satellite, *Sputnik,* into outer space—with a rocket that could also deliver a hydrogen bomb.

VIDEO

Duck and Cover

The discovery of radioactive fallout made matters worse. Fallout became publicly known after the BRAVO blast showered Japanese fishermen on a ship called the *Lucky Dragon* 85 miles away with radioactive dust. They became ill with radiation sickness, and several months later, one of the seamen died. Everywhere people began to realize the terrible consequences of the new weapons. Fallout had become a serious international problem—in the words of physicist Ralph Lapp, "a peril to humanity."

Authors in both the scientific and the popular press focused attention on radioactive fallout. Radiation, Lapp observed, "cannot be felt and possesses all the terror of the unknown. It is something which evokes revulsion and helplessness—

An Awesome Atomic Blast The spectacular mushroom cloud resulting from an atomic blast became a familiar sight as it accompanied hundreds of nuclear tests in the postwar years. This picture shows the hydrogen blast at Eniwetok in the Pacific in 1952. While the cloud was beautiful, it also filled the atmosphere with fallout that contaminated people, plants, and animals below. What makes this image so imposing? Why might it appear terrifying at the same time? *(National Archives)*

like a bubonic plague." Nevil Shute's best-selling 1957 novel *On the Beach,* and the film that followed, also sparked public awareness and fear. The story described a war that released so much radioactive waste that all life in the Northern Hemisphere disappeared, while the Southern Hemisphere awaited the same deadly fate. In 1959, when *Consumer Reports,* the popular magazine that tested and compared various products, warned of the contamination of milk with the radioactive isotope strontium-90, the public grew even more alarmed.

The discovery of fallout provoked a shelter craze. *Good Housekeeping* magazine carried a full-page editorial in November 1958 urging the construction of family shelters. More and more companies advertised ready-made shelters. *Life* magazine in 1955 featured an "H-Bomb Hideaway" for $3,000. By late 1960, the Office of Civil and Defense Mobilization estimated that a million family shelters had been built.

The Nuclear West

The bomb stimulated more than just shelter building. It sparked an enormous increase in defense spending and created a huge nuclear industry, particularly in the West. Contractors liked the region because of its antiunion attitudes; labor stability, they argued, would make it easier to meet government deadlines.

During World War II, a number of the Manhattan Project's major centers were located in the West. The plant at Hanford, Washington, was one of the most important producers of fissionable material, and the first atomic weapon had been produced at Los Alamos, New Mexico. Development in this area expanded after the war: Hanford continued to produce plutonium, a facility outside Denver made plutonium triggers for thermonuclear bombs, the new Sandia National Laboratory in Albuquerque provided the production engineering of nuclear bombs, and the Los Alamos laboratory remained a major atomic research center. In 1951, the United States opened the Nevada Test Site, 65 miles north of Las Vegas, and the facility had a major impact on the city. The Chamber of Commerce offered schedules of test shots, and the mushroom cloud became the logo for the Southern Nevada telephone directory.

Defense spending promoted other development as well. Naval commands had headquarters in Seattle, San Francisco, San Diego, and Honolulu. Radar sites, aimed at tracking incoming missiles, stretched all the way up to Alaska. The Boeing Company, located in Seattle, stimulated tremendous development in that city as it produced B-47 and B-52 airplanes that were the U.S. Air Force's main delivery vehicles for nuclear bombs.

"Massive Retaliation"

As Americans grappled with the implications of nuclear weapons, government policy came to depend increasingly on an atomic shield. Truman authorized the development of a nuclear arsenal but also stressed conventional forms of defense. Eisenhower, concerned with controlling the budget and cutting taxes, decided to rely on atomic weapons rather than combat forces as the key to American defense.

Secretary of State Dulles developed the policy of threatening "massive retaliation." The United States, he declared, was willing and ready to use nuclear weapons against Communist aggression on whatever targets it chose. The policy allowed troop cutbacks and promised to be cost effective by giving "more bang for the buck."

Massive retaliation provided for an all-or-nothing response, leaving no middle course, no alternatives between nuclear war and retreat. Critics called the policy "brinkmanship" and wondered what would happen if the line was crossed in the new atomic age. Eisenhower himself was horrified when he saw reports indicating that a coordinated atomic attack could leave a nation "a smoking, radiating ruin at the end of two hours." With characteristic caution, he did his best to ensure that the rhetoric of massive retaliation did not lead to war.

Atomic Protest

As the arms race spiraled, critics demanded that it end. In 1956, Democratic presidential candidate Adlai Stevenson pointed to "the danger of poisoning the atmosphere" and called for a halt to nuclear tests. Eisenhower did not respond, but

Vice President Richard Nixon called Stevenson's suggestion "catastrophic nonsense," while Dulles minimized the hazards of radiation by arguing, "From a health standpoint, there is greater danger from wearing a wrist watch with a luminous dial."

In 1957, activists organized SANE, the National Committee for a Sane Nuclear Policy. Several years later, women who had worked with SANE took the protest movement a step further. To challenge continued testing, which dropped lethal radiation on all inhabitants of the globe, the protesters called on women throughout the country to suspend normal activities for a day and strike for peace. An estimated 50,000 women marched in 60 communities around the nation. Their slogans included "Let the Children Grow" and "End the Arms Race—Not the Human Race."

Pressure from many groups produced a political breakthrough and sustained it for a time. The superpowers began a voluntary moratorium on testing in the fall of 1958. It lasted until the Soviet Union resumed testing in September 1961 and the United States began again the following March.

THE COLD WAR AT HOME

The Cold War also affected domestic affairs and led to the creation of an internal loyalty program that seriously violated civil liberties. Americans had feared radical subversion before and after the Russian Revolution (see Chapters 16, 21, and 22). Now the Soviet Union appeared ever more ominous in confrontations around the globe. As Americans began to suspect Communist infiltration at home, some determined to root out all traces of communism inside the United States.

Truman's Loyalty Program

When the Truman administration mobilized support for its containment program in the immediate postwar years, its rhetoric became increasingly shrill. For Truman, the issue confronting the world was one of "tyranny or freedom." Attorney General J. Howard McGrath spoke of "many Communists in America," each bearing the "germ of death for society." Meanwhile, Truman appointed a Temporary Commission on Employee Loyalty to head off Republican charges that Democrats were "soft on communism."

On the basis of its report, Truman established a new Federal Employee Loyalty Program in 1947. In the same week that he announced his containment policy, he ordered the FBI to check its files for evidence of subversive activity and to bring suspects before a new Civil Service Commission Loyalty Review Board. Initially, the program included safeguards and assumed that a challenged employee was innocent until proven guilty. But as the Loyalty Review Board assumed more power, it ignored individual rights, and suspects had little chance to fight back. Val Lorwin, whose story was told at the start of the chapter, was just one of many victims.

The Truman loyalty program examined several million employees and found grounds for dismissing only several hundred. Nonetheless, it bred the unwarranted fear of subversion, led to the assumption that absolute loyalty could be achieved, and legitimated investigatory tactics that were used irresponsibly to harm innocent individuals.

The Congressional Loyalty Program

At the same time, Congress launched its own program. In the early years of the Cold War, the law became increasingly explicit about what was illegal in the United States. The requirement that members of Communist organizations had to register with the attorney general led to the decline of the American Communist party. Membership, numbering about 80,000 in 1947, fell to 55,000 in 1950 and to 25,000 in 1954.

DOCUMENT

Ronald Reagan, Testimony before HUAC (1947)

The investigations of the House Un-American Activities Committee (HUAC) contributed to that decline. Intent on rooting out subversion, HUAC probed the motion picture industry in 1947, claiming that left-wing sympathizers were corrupting the American public. A frequent refrain in congressional hearings was "Are you now or have you ever been a member of the Communist party?" Altogether, HUAC called 19 Hollywood figures to testify. When 10 of them refused to answer accusatory questions by invoking their constitutional right to remain silent, Congress issued contempt citations, and they went to prison and served sentences ranging from six months to one year. At that point, Hollywood knuckled under and blacklisted anyone with even a marginally questionable past. No one on the blacklist could find a job at the studios although some managed to work secretly under other names.

Congress made a greater splash with the Hiss–Chambers case. Whittaker Chambers, a former Communist who had broken with the party in 1938, charged that Alger Hiss had been a Communist in the 1930s. Hiss was a distinguished New Dealer who had served in the Agriculture Department before becoming assistant secretary of state. Now out of the government, he denied Chambers's charge, and the matter might have died there had not freshman congressman Richard Nixon taken up the case. Nixon finally extracted from Hiss an admission that he had once known Chambers. Hiss sued Chambers for libel, whereupon Chambers changed his story and charged that Hiss was a Soviet spy.

Hiss was indicted for perjury for lying under oath about his former relationship with Chambers, for the statute of limitations prevented prosecution for espionage. The sensational case made front-page news around the nation. Chambers appeared unstable and changed his story several times. Yet Hiss, too, seemed contradictory in his testimony and never adequately explained how he had such close ties with members of the Communist party or how some copies of stolen State Department documents had been typed on his typewriter. The first trial ended in a hung jury; the second trial, in January 1950, sent Hiss to prison for almost four years. He continued to assert his innocence for the remainder of his life, although later evidence makes his involvement clear. For many Americans, the Hiss case proved that a Communist threat indeed existed in the United States and helped justify the even worse witch hunts that followed.

Congress also charged that homosexuals posed a security risk. The issue surfaced in February 1950, when Undersecretary of State John Peurifoy mentioned in testimony before the Senate Appropriations Committee that most of the 91 employees the State Department had dismissed for reasons of "moral turpitude" were homosexuals. Then, in December, the Senate released a report that painted a threatening picture of the problems of homosexuals in the civil service. They lacked moral and emotional stability, the report suggested, and were therefore likely candidates for blackmail, which threatened national security.

Senator Joe McCarthy

The key anti-Communist warrior in the 1950s was Joseph R. McCarthy. He capitalized on the fear sparked by congressional and executive investigations and made the entire country cognizant of the Communist threat.

McCarthy came to the Communist issue almost accidentally. Elected to the Senate as a Republican from Wisconsin in 1946, McCarthy had an undistinguished career for much of his first term. He first gained national attention with a speech before a Republican women's club in Wheeling, West Virginia, in February 1950, not long after the conviction of Alger Hiss. In that address, McCarthy brandished in his hand what he said was a list of 205 known Communists in the State Department. Pressed for details, McCarthy first said that he would release his list only to the president, then reduced the number of names to 57.

McCarthy's Anti-Communist Campaign Senator Joseph McCarthy's spurious charges inflamed anti-Communist sentiment in the 1950s. Here he uses a chart of Communist party organization in the United States to suggest that the nation would be at risk unless subversives were rooted out. How does the chart contribute to the impression McCarthy wanted to convey? *(Corbis)*

RECOVERING THE PAST

In recent years, historians have used a new source of evidence: the public opinion poll. People have always been concerned with what others think, and leaders have often sought to frame their behavior according to the preferences of the populace. As techniques of assessing the mind of the public have become more sophisticated, the poll has emerged as an integral part of the analysis of social and political life. Polls now measure opinion on many questions—social, cultural, intellectual, political, and diplomatic. Because of polls' increasing importance, it is useful to know how to use them in an effort to understand and recover the past.

The principle of polling is not new. In 1824, the *Harrisburg Pennsylvanian* sought to predict the winner of that year's presidential race, and in the 1880s, the *Boston Globe* sent reporters to selected precincts on election night to forecast final returns. In 1916, *Literary Digest* began conducting postcard polls to predict political results. By the 1930s, Elmo Roper and George Gallup had further developed the field of market research and public opinion polling. Notwithstanding an embarrassing mistake by *Literary Digest* in predicting a Landon victory over FDR in 1936, polling had become a scientific enterprise by World War II.

According to Gallup, a poll is not magic but "merely an instrument for gauging public opinion," especially the views of those often unheard. As Elmo Roper said, the poll is "one of the few ways through which the so-called common man can be articulate." Polling, therefore, is a valuable way to recover the attitudes, beliefs, and voices of ordinary people.

Yet certain cautions should be observed. Like all instruments of human activity, polls are imperfect and may even be dangerous. Historians using information from polls need to be aware of how large the samples were, when the interviewing was done, and how opinions might have been molded by the form of the poll itself. Questions can be poorly phrased. Some hint at the desirable answer or plant ideas in the minds of those interviewed. Polls sometimes provide ambiguous responses that can be interpreted many ways. More seriously, some critics worry that human freedom itself is threatened by the pollsters' manipulative and increasingly accurate predictive techniques.

Despite these limitations, polls have become an ever-present part of American life. In the late 1940s and early 1950s, Americans were polled frequently about topics ranging from foreign aid, the United Nations, and the occupation of Germany and Japan to labor legislation, child punishment, and whether women should wear slacks in public (39 percent of men said no, as did 49 percent of women). Such topics as the first use of nuclear arms, presidential popularity, national defense, and U.S. troop intervention in a troubled area of the world remain as pertinent today as they were then.

REFLECTING ON THE PAST   A number of the polls included here deal with foreign policy during the Cold War in the early 1950s. How did people respond to Soviet nuclear capability? How did they regard Russian intentions, and what did they feel was the appropriate American response? How do you analyze the results of these polls? What do you think is the significance of rating responses by levels of education? In what ways are the questions "loaded"? How might the results of these polls influence American foreign policy? These polls show the challenge-and-response nature of the Cold War. How do you think Americans would respond today to these questions? Polls also shed light on domestic issues. Consider the poll on professions for young men and women taken in 1950. What does it tell us about the attitudes of the pollster on appropriate careers for men and women? Why do you think both men and women had nearly identical views on this subject? How do you think people today would answer these questions? Would they be presented in the same way? Also observe the poll on women in politics. To what extent have attitudes on this issue changed in the intervening years?

Foreign Policy Polls

December 2, 1949—Atom Bomb

Now that Russia has the atom bomb, do you think another war is more likely or less likely?

More likely	45%
Less likely	28%
Will make no difference	17%
No opinion	10%

By Education
College

More likely	36%
Will make no difference	23%
Less likely	35%
No opinion	6%

High School

More likely	44%
Will make no difference	19%
Less likely	28%
No opinion	9%

Grade School

More likely	50%
Will make no difference	12%
Less likely	26%
No opinion	12%

January 11, 1950—Russia

As you hear and read about Russia these days, do you believe Russia is trying to build herself up to be the ruling power of the world—or is Russia just building up protection against being attacked in another war?

Rule the world	70%
Protect herself	18%
No opinion	12%

By Education
College

Rule the world	73%
Protect herself	21%
No opinion	6%

High School

Rule the world	72%
Protect herself	18%
No opinion	10%

Grade School

Rule the world	67%
Protect herself	17%
No opinion	16%

February 12, 1951— Atomic Warfare

If the United States gets into an all-out war with Russia, do you think we should drop atom bombs on Russia first—or do you think we should use the atom bomb only if it is used on us?

Drop A-bomb first	66%
Only if used on us	19%
No opinion	15%

The greatest difference was between men and women—72% of the men questioned favored our dropping the bomb first, compared to 61% of the women.

Source: George H. Gallup, *The Gallup Poll: Public Opinion, 1935–1971*, vol. 2 (New York: Random House, 1972). © American Institute of Public Opinion.

Domestic Policy Polls

October 29, 1949— Women in Politics

If the party whose candidate you most often support nominated a woman for President of the United States, would you vote for her if she seemed qualified for the job?

Yes 48%		No 48%
No opinion		4%

By Sex
Men

Yes 45%		No 50%
No opinion		5%

Women

Yes 51%		No 46%
No opinion		3%

By Political Affiliation
Democrats

Yes 50%		No 48%
No opinion		2%

Republicans

Yes 46%		No 50%
No opinion		4%

Would you vote for a woman for Vice President of the United States if she seemed qualified for the job?

Yes 53%		No 43%
No opinion		4%

July 12, 1950—Professions

Suppose a young man came to you and asked your advice about taking up a profession. Assuming that he was qualified to enter any of these professions, which one of them would you first recommend to him?

Doctor of medicine	29%
Government worker	6%
Engineer, builder	16%
Professor, teacher	5%
Business executive	8%
Banker	4%
Clergyman	8%
Dentist	4%
Lawyer	8%
Veterinarian	3%
None, don't know	9%

Source: George H. Gallup, *The Gallup Poll: Public Opinion, 1935–1971*, vol. 2 (New York: Random House, 1972). © American Institute of Public Opinion.

July 15, 1950—Professions

Suppose a young girl came to you and asked your advice about taking up a profession. Assuming that she was qualified to enter any of these professions, which one of them would you first recommend?

Choice of Women

Nurse	33%
Teacher	15%
Secretary	8%
Social service worker	8%
Dietitian	7%
Dressmaker	4%
Beautician	4%
Airline stewardess	3%
Actress	3%
Journalist	2%
Musician	2%
Model	2%
Librarian	2%
Medical, dental technician	1%
Others	2%
Don't know	4%

The views of men on this subject were nearly identical with those of women.

Early reactions to McCarthy were mixed. A subcommittee of the Senate Foreign Relations Committee, after investigating, called his charge a "fraud and a hoax." As his support grew, however, Republicans realized his partisan value and egged him on. Senator John Bricker of Ohio allegedly told him, "Joe, you're a dirty s.o.b., but there are times when you've got to have an s.o.b. around, and this is one of them."

McCarthy selected assorted targets in his crusade to wipe out communism. He called Dean Acheson the "Red Dean of the State Department" and slandered George C. Marshall, the architect of victory in World War II and a powerful figure in formulating both Far Eastern policy and the Marshall Plan for European recovery, as a "man steeped in falsehood ... who has recourse to the lie whenever it suits his convenience."

AUDIO

Joseph P. McCarthy Speech

A demagogue throughout his career, McCarthy gained visibility through extensive press and television coverage. He knew how to issue press releases just before newspaper deadlines and to provide reporters with leaks that became the basis for stories. Playing on his tough reputation, he did not mind appearing disheveled, and he used obscenity freely as part of his effort to appear as an ordinary man of the people.

McCarthy's tactics worked because of public alarm about the Communist threat. The arrest in 1950 of Julius and Ethel Rosenberg fed fears of internal subversion. The Rosenbergs, a seemingly ordinary American couple with two small children, were charged with stealing and transmitting atomic secrets to the Russians. To many Americans, it was inconceivable that the Soviets could have developed the bomb on their own. Treachery helped explain the Soviet explosion of an atomic device.

The next year, the Rosenbergs were found guilty of espionage. Their execution in the electric chair after numerous appeals reflected a national commitment to respond to the Communist threat. For years, supporters of the Rosenbergs claimed that they were innocent victims of the anti-Communist crusade. More recent evidence indicates that Julius was guilty. Ethel, cognizant of his activities but not involved herself, was arrested, convicted, and executed in a futile government attempt to make Julius talk.

When the Republicans won control of the Senate in 1952, McCarthy's power grew. He became chairman of the Government Operations Committee and head of its Permanent Investigations Subcommittee. He now had a stronger base and two dedicated assistants, Roy Cohn and G. David Schine, to help him.

McCarthy finally went too far. In 1953, after the army drafted Schine and then refused to allow him preferential treatment, McCarthy began to investigate army security and even top-level army leaders. When the army complained, the Senate investigated the complaint.

The Army–McCarthy hearings began in April 1954 and lasted 36 days. Beamed to a fascinated nationwide audience, they demonstrated the power of television to shape people's opinions. Americans saw McCarthy's savage tactics on screen. He came across as irresponsible and destructive, particularly in contrast to Boston lawyer Joseph Welch, who argued the army's case and showed McCarthy as the demagogue he was. At a climactic point in the hearings, Welch asked

TIMELINE

1946	Churchill's "Iron Curtain" speech	1950	Joseph McCarthy's Wheeling (West Virginia) speech on subversion
1947	Truman Doctrine		
	Federal Employee Loyalty Program		NSC-68
1948	Marshall Plan launched	1950–1953	Korean War
		1954	Fall of Dien Bien Phu ends French control of Indochina
1949	North Atlantic Treaty Organization (NATO) established		
		1959	Castro deposes Batista in Cuba
	Mao Zedong's forces win Chinese civil war		

McCarthy dramatically: "Have you no sense of decency, sir, at long last? Have you left no sense of decency?"

The hearings shattered McCarthy's mystical appeal. In broad daylight, before a national television audience, his ruthless tactics offended millions. The Senate, which had earlier backed off confronting McCarthy, finally summoned the courage to condemn him for his conduct. Although McCarthy remained in office, his influence disappeared. Three years later, at the age of 48, he died a broken man.

Yet for a time he had exerted a powerful hold in the United States. "To many Americans," radio commentator Fulton Lewis, Jr., said, "McCarthyism is Americanism." As his appeal grew, he put together a following that included both lower-class ethnic groups, whose members responded to the charges against established elites, and conservative midwestern Republicans. But his real power base was the Senate, where conservative Republicans saw McCarthy as a means of reasserting their own authority.

The Casualties of Fear

The anti-Communist campaign kindled pervasive suspicion in American society. In the late 1940s and early 1950s, dissent no longer seemed safe. Civil servants, government workers, academics, and actors all came under attack and found that the right of due process often evaporated amid the Cold War Red Scare.

This paranoia affected American life in countless ways. In New York, subway workers were fired when they refused to answer questions about their own political actions and beliefs. Navajos in Arizona and New Mexico, facing starvation in the bitter winter of 1947–1948, were denied government relief because of charges that their communal way of life was communistic and therefore un-American. Racism became intertwined with the anti-Communist crusade when African

American actor Paul Robeson was accused of Communist leanings for criticizing American foreign policy. Black author W. E. B. Du Bois, who joined the Communist party, encountered even more virulent attacks. Latino laborers faced deportation for membership in unions with left-wing sympathies. In 1949, the Congress of Industrial Organizations (CIO) expelled 11 unions with a total membership of more than 1 million for alleged domination by Communists. Val Lorwin weathered the storm of malicious accusations and was finally vindicated, but others were less lucky. They were the unfortunate victims as the United States became consumed by the passions of the Cold War.

Conclusion

The Cold War in Perspective

The Cold War dominated international relations in the post–World War II years. Tensions grew after 1945 as the United States and the Soviet Union found themselves engaged in a bitter standoff that affected all diplomatic discourse, encouraged an expensive arms race, and limited the resources available for reform at home. For the United States, it was a first experience with the fiercely competitive international relations that had long plagued the nations of Europe. And while there was seldom actual shooting, the struggle required warlike measures and imposed costs on all countries involved.

What caused the Cold War? Historians have long argued over the question of where responsibility should be placed. In the early years after the Second World War, policymakers and commentators who supported their actions justified the American stance as a bold and courageous effort to meet the Communist threat. Later, particularly in the 1960s, as the war in Vietnam eroded confidence in American foreign policy, revisionist historians began to argue that American actions were misguided, insensitive to Soviet needs, and at least partially responsible for escalating friction. As with most historical questions, there are no easy answers, but both sides must be weighed.

The Cold War stemmed from a competition for international influence between the two great world powers. After World War II, the U.S. goal was to exercise economic and political leadership in the world and thus to establish capitalist economies and democratic political institutions throughout Europe and in nations emerging from colonial rule. But these goals put the United States on a collision course with the Soviet Union, which had a different vision of what the postwar world should be like, and with anticolonial movements in emerging countries around the globe. Perceiving threats from the Soviet Union, China, and other Communist countries, the United States clung to its deep-rooted sense of mission and embarked on an increasingly aggressive effort at containment, based on its reading of the lessons of the past. American efforts culminated in the ill-fated war in Vietnam (discussed in Chapter 29) as the Communist nations of the world defended their own interests with equal force. The Cold War, with its profound effects at home and abroad, was the unfortunate result.

Questions for Review and Reflection

1. What were the roots of the conflict that turned into the Cold War?

2. Why did the United States and Soviet Union find it so difficult to get along in the years after World War II?

3. How did Cold War policy change in the 1950s from what it had been in the late 1940s?

4. What impact did the Cold War have on American society at home?

5. Could the Cold War have been avoided?

Discovering U.S. History Online

The Truman Doctrine www.trumanlibrary.org/whistlestop/study_collections/doctrine/large/doctrine.htm
Part of the Truman presidential library Web site, this site offers images of primary sources dealing with what came to be known as the "Truman Doctrine."

The Marshall Plan www.lcweb.loc.gov/exhibits/marshall
This site examines the Marshall Plan speech, reactions to the speech, and implementation of the European Recovery Program during the following 50 years. The site includes a photo exhibit of reconstruction projects at midpoint.

Korean War www.trumanlibrary.org/korea/index.html
A joint project of two presidential libraries, this site presents many of the archival resources (documents and photographs) from the two administrations involved in the Korean War.

Vietnam War www.pbs.org/wgbh/amex/vietnam/
This site contains a detailed, interactive timeline and profiles of participants in the early years of the war.

Atomic Weapons www.atomicarchive.com/index.shtml
A companion to a CD-ROM of the same name, this site offers biographies, documents, photographs, treaties, and more.

Joseph McCarthy http://www.spartacus.schoolnet.co.uk/USAmccarthy.htm
This British site amplifies the key episodes of McCarthy's career and provides links to related sites.

Fiction and Film

Fail-Safe by Eugene Burdick and Harvey Wheeler (1962) is a novel about an accidental nuclear war. *The Bridges at Toko-ri* (1953) by James A. Michener is a novel about the frustrations of fighting the Korean War when people at home do not seem to care. Walter M. Miller, Jr.'s *A Canticle for Leibowitz* (1959) is about the devastation following a nuclear war that reduces civilization to a primitive state. Nevil Shute's *On the Beach* (1957) is a novel about a nuclear war that wiped out most life and created a radioactive cloud that is killing the rest.

   Dr. Strangelove or: How I Learned to Stop Worrying and Love the Bomb (1964) is a movie made by Stanley Kubrick about the absurdity of nuclear war. *Fail-Safe* (1964) is the film from the novel of the same name about an accidental nuclear war that destroyed both Moscow and New York. *High Noon* (1952) is a Western dramatizing the need to stand up to outlaws and reflecting the need to resist the excesses of the anti-Communist crusade. *On the Beach* (1959) is the film from the novel of the same name about a nuclear war that ended all life on earth. *Good Night and Good Luck* (2005) is about Edward R. Morrow's television confrontation with Senator Joseph R. McCarthy.

Recommended Reading

www.ablongman.com/nash
The Companion Website has a list of recommended readings about the Cold War.

Reform and Rebellion in the Turbulent Sixties, 1960–1969

CHAPTER OUTLINE

- John F. Kennedy: The Camelot Years
- Lyndon B. Johnson and the Great Society
- Continuing Confrontations with Communists
- War in Vietnam and Turmoil at Home
- Conclusion: Political and Social Upheaval

American Stories

A Young Liberal Questions the Welfare State

Paul Cowan was an idealist in the 1960s. Like many students who came of age in these years, he believed in the possibility of social change and plunged into the struggle for liberal reform. He shared the hopes and dreams of other members of his generation, who felt that their government could make a difference in people's lives.

Cowan's commitment had developed slowly. He was a child of the 1950s, when most Americans were caught up in the consumer culture and paid little attention to the problems of people less fortunate than themselves. His grandfather had sold used cement bags in Chicago, but his father had become an executive at CBS television, and Cowan grew up in comfortable surroundings. He graduated from the Choate School (where John Kennedy had gone) in 1958, and then from Harvard University (where Kennedy had also been a student) in 1963.

When he entered college, Cowan was interested in politically conscious writers such as John Dos Passos, John Steinbeck, and James Agee and folk singers such as Pete Seeger and Woody Guthrie. They offered him entrance, he later recalled, into a "nation that seemed to be filled with energy and decency," one that lurked "beneath the dull, conformist facade of the Eisenhower years." While at Harvard, he was excited by antinuclear campaigns in New England and civil rights demonstrations in the South.

After college, he made good on his commitment to civil rights by going to Mississippi to work in the Freedom Summer Project of 1964. He was inspired by the example of John Kennedy, the liberal president whose administration promised "a new kind of politics" that could make the nation, and the world, a better place. During that summer, he wrote, "it was possible to believe that by changing ourselves we could change, and redeem, our America."

The Peace Corps came next. Cowan and his wife, Rachel, were convinced that this organization, the idea of the young president, "really was a unique government agency, permanently protected by the lingering magic of John F. Kennedy's name." They were assigned to the city of Guayaquil, in Ecuador, in South America. Their task was to serve as mediators between administrators of the city hall and residents of the slums. They wanted to try to raise the standard of living by encouraging local governments to provide basic services such as garbage disposal and clean water.

But the work proved more frustrating than they had imagined. They bristled at the restrictions imposed by the Peace Corps bureaucracy. They despaired at the inadequate resources local government officials had to accomplish their aims. They wondered if they were simply new imperialists, trying to impose their values on others who had priorities of their own. "From the day we moved into the *barrio*," Cowan later recalled, "the question we were most frequently asked by the people we were supposed to be organizing was whether we would leave them our clothes when we returned to the States."

Cowan came home disillusioned. "I saw that even the liberals I had wanted to emulate, men who seemed to be devoting their lives to fighting injustice, were unable to accept people from alien cultures on any terms but their own." He called his account of his own odyssey *The Making of an Un-American.*

Paul Cowan's passage through the 1960s mirrored the passage of American society as a whole. Millions of Americans shared his views of the possibilities of democracy as the period began. Mostly comfortable and confident, they supported the liberal agenda advanced by the Democratic party of John Kennedy and Lyndon Johnson. They endorsed the proposition that the government had responsibility for the welfare of all its citizens and accepted the need for a more active government role to help those who were unable to help themselves. That commitment lay behind the legislative achievements of the "Great Society," the last wave of twentieth-century reform that built upon the gains of the Progressive era and the New Deal years before.

Then political reaction set in as the nation was torn apart by the ravages of the Vietnam War. The escalation of the war, which led to charges that the United States was engaging in an imperialistic crusade like those of other nations in the past, sent more than half a million American soldiers to fight in a far-off land and provoked a protest movement that ripped society apart. Young Americans, espousing different values and a different version of the American dream, challenged the priorities of their parents. At the same time, they paraded their sexuality more openly, experimented with different forms of mystical religious faith, and enjoyed readily available drugs. In the end, their challenges helped reverse the course of the war. But in the process, liberal assumptions eroded as conservatives argued that an activist approach was responsible for the social and political chaos that consumed the country.

This chapter describes both the climax of twentieth-century liberalism and the turbulence that led to its decline. It focuses on the effort of the government, begun in the New Deal of Franklin Roosevelt, to help those caught short by the advances of industrial capitalism. It first examines the democratic commitment in the 1960s to provide necessary assistance to the less fortunate members of American society and then describes the turmoil that undermined the possibility of such aid. In pondering the possibilities of reform, this chapter outlines the various attempts to devise an effective political response to the major structural changes in the post–World War II economy described in Chapter 26. And then it shows how the Cold War assumptions outlined in Chapter 27 led to the rifts that ripped the nation apart.

JOHN F. KENNEDY: THE CAMELOT YEARS

The commitment to an American welfare state reached its high-water point in the 1960s. As the left-wing Labour Party in Great Britain played a more and more influential role and occasionally assumed power, and social democratic coalitions were equally active in other European nations, Americans took note. Democrats wanted to follow their example and broaden the role of government even further than Franklin D. Roosevelt and Harry S Truman had done in the 1930s and 1940s, in an effort to address the problems of poverty, unemployment, and racism. John F. Kennedy, a senator from Massachusetts, demanded that the United States move in the direction of what he called a "New Frontier."

An Energetic Young Leader John Kennedy's energy and enthusiasm captured the imagination of Americans and people around the world, though few were aware of the physical ailments that affected him. He was fond of using this rocking chair in the White House, which he found comfortable for his ailing back. How did Kennedy's appearance contribute to his popularity and appeal? *(Bettmann/Corbis)*

The Election of 1960

In the 1960 presidential campaign, Kennedy ran against Vice President Richard Nixon, who clearly had more executive experience. Kennedy argued that the government in general, and the president in particular, had to play an even more active role than they had in the Eisenhower years. He charged that the country had become lazy as it reveled in the prosperity of the 1950s. There were, in fact, serious problems that needed to be solved.

VIDEO

Kennedy–Nixon Debate

Seventy million Americans tuned in to watch the two candidates square off against one another in the first televised presidential debate. Kennedy appeared tanned and rested. Nixon, who had recently been hospitalized with an infection, looked tired and gaunt. Even worse, the makeup he applied to hide his heavy beard growth only accentuated it and gave him a swarthy complexion on screen. The debates made a major difference in the campaign. (see the "Recovering the Past" section of this chapter). Kennedy himself admitted, "It was TV more than anything else that turned the tide."

Kennedy overcame seemingly insuperable odds to become the first Catholic in the White House. Yet Kennedy's victory was razor-thin. The electoral margin of 303 to 219 concealed the close popular tally, in which he triumphed by fewer than 120,000 of 68 million votes cast. While Kennedy had Democratic majorities in Congress, many members of his party came from the South and were less sympathetic to liberal causes.

JFK

DOCUMENT

John F. Kennedy, Inaugural Address (1961)

John Kennedy served as a symbol of the early 1960s. He was far younger than his predecessor; at the age of 43, he was the youngest man ever elected to the presidency. He came from an Irish Catholic family from Massachusetts that saw politics as a means of acceptance in Protestant America. Raised in comfort, he graduated from Harvard University and went on to serve heroically in the navy during World War II. He was elected first to the House of Representatives in 1946, then to the Senate in 1952, and was reelected six years later by the largest majority in the history of the state.

The new president had a charismatic public presence. He was able to voice his aims in eloquent yet understandable language that motivated his followers. During the campaign, he pointed to challenges at home and abroad, observing that "the New Frontier is here whether we seek it or not." He made the same point even more movingly in his inaugural address when he declared that "the torch has been passed to a new generation of Americans" and inspired listeners by his ringing call to action: "And so, my fellow Americans: Ask not what your country can do for you—ask what you can do for your country."

For Kennedy, strong leadership was all-important. Viewing himself as "tough-minded" and "hard-nosed," he was determined to provide firm direction, just as Franklin Roosevelt had done. To do so, he surrounded himself with talented assistants. On his staff were 15 Rhodes scholars and several famous authors. The secretary of state was Dean Rusk, a former member of the State Department who had then served as president of the Rockefeller Foundation. The secretary of defense was Robert S. McNamara, the highly successful president of the Ford Motor Company.

Further contributing to Kennedy's attractive image were his glamorous wife, Jacqueline, and the Nobel Prize winners, musicians, and artists they invited to the White House. Energy, exuberance, and excitement filled the air. To many, the administration seemed like the Camelot of King Arthur's day, popularized in a Broadway musical in 1960.

The New Frontier in Action

In office, Kennedy sought to bolster the economy and to enlarge social welfare programs. On the economic front, he tried to end the lingering recession that began in Eisenhower's last year by working with the business community while controlling price inflation.

These two goals conflicted when, in the spring of 1962, the large steel companies decided on a major price increase after steel unions had accepted a modest wage package. The angry president termed the price increases unjustifiable and demanded action to force the steel companies to back down. The large companies capitulated, but they disliked Kennedy's heavy-handed approach and decided that this Democratic administration, like all others, was hostile to business. Six weeks after the steel crisis, the stock market plunged in the greatest drop since the Great Crash of 1929.

It now seemed doubly urgent to end the recession. Earlier a proponent of a balanced budget, Kennedy began to listen to his liberal advisers who proposed a Keynesian approach to economic growth. Budget deficits had promoted prosperity during the Second World War and might work in the same way in peacetime, too. A tax cut could put money in people's pockets, and their spending could stimulate the economy. In early 1963, the president called for a $13.5 billion cut in corporate taxes over the next three years. While that cut would cause a large deficit, it would also provide business capital to revive the economy and ultimately increase tax revenues.

Opposition mounted. Conservatives refused to accept the basic premise that deficits would stimulate economic growth and argued, in Eisenhower's words, that "no family, no business, no nation can spend itself into prosperity." Some liberals claimed that it would be better to stimulate the economy by spending money to improve society rather than by cutting taxes and letting people have the money. Congress pigeonholed the proposal in committee, and there it remained.

On other issues on the liberal agenda, Kennedy met similar resistance. Though he proposed legislation increasing the minimum wage and providing for federal aid for education, medical care for the elderly, housing subsidies, and urban renewal, the results were meager. His new minimum-wage measure passed Congress in pared-down form, but Kennedy did not have the votes in Congress to achieve most of his legislative program.

His inability to win necessary congressional support was most evident in the struggle to aid public education. Soon after taking office, Kennedy proposed a $2.3 billion program of education grants to the states. Immediately, a series of

RECOVERING THE PAST

Television

In the past 50 years, television has played an increasingly important part in American life, providing historians with another source of evidence about American culture and society in the recent past.

Television's popularity by the 1950s was the result of decades of experimentation dating back to the nineteenth century. In the 1930s, NBC installed a television station in the new Empire State Building in New York. Wearing green makeup and purple lipstick to provide better visual contrast, actors began to perform before live cameras in studios. At the end of the decade, *Amos 'n' Andy*, a popular radio show, was telecast, and as the 1940s began, Franklin D. Roosevelt became the first president to appear on television. World War II interrupted the development of television, and Americans relied on radio to bring them news. After the war, however, the commercial development of television quickly resumed. Assembly lines that had made electronic implements of war were now converted to consumer production, and thousands of new sets appeared on the market. The opening of Congress could be seen live in 1947; baseball coverage improved that same year owing to the zoom lens; children's shows including *Howdy Doody* made their debut; and *Meet the Press*, a radio interview program, made the transition to television.

Although sports programs, variety shows hosted by Ed Sullivan and Milton Berle, TV dramas, and episodic series (*I Love Lucy* and *Gunsmoke,* for example) dominated TV broadcasting in the 1950s, television soon became entwined with politics and public affairs. Americans saw Senator Joseph McCarthy for themselves in the televised Army–McCarthy hearings in 1954; his malevolent behavior on camera contributed to his downfall. The 1948 presidential nominating conventions were the first to be televised, but the use of TV to enhance the public image of politicians was most thoroughly developed by the fatherly Dwight D. Eisenhower and the charismatic John F. Kennedy.

In November 1963, people throughout the United States shared the tragedy of John Kennedy's assassination, sitting stunned before their sets trying to understand the events of his fateful Texas

The candidates squaring off in their debate. *(AP/Wide World Photos)*

John Kennedy (left) and Richard Nixon (right). *(AP/Wide World Photos)*

trip. The shock and sorrow of the American people was repeated in the spring of 1968 as they gazed in disbelief at the funerals of Martin Luther King, Jr., and Robert F. Kennedy. A year later, a quarter of the world's population watched as Neil Armstrong became the first man to set foot on the moon. In that same era, television played an important part in shaping impressions of the war in Vietnam. More and more Americans began to understand the nature and impact of the conflict from what they saw on TV.

This combination of visual entertainment and enlightenment made owning a television set virtually a necessity. By 1970, fully 95 percent of American households owned a TV set, a staggering increase from the 9 percent only 20 years earlier. In fact, fewer families owned refrigerators or indoor toilets.

REFLECTING ON THE PAST   The implications of the impact of television on American society are of obvious interest to historians. How has television affected other communications and entertainment industries, such as radio, newspapers, and movies? What does the content of TV programming tell us about the values, interests, and tastes of the American people?

Perhaps most significant, what impact has TV had on the course of historical events such as presidential campaigns, human relations, and wars? The pictures shown here are from the Kennedy–Nixon debates in the presidential campaign of 1960. The first picture shows the two candidates in the studio. The second picture shows a relaxed and energetic Kennedy staring directly into the TV camera. The third picture shows a taut and tense Nixon challenging the points made by his opponent. Which candidate seems to be speaking directly to the American people? Which candidate makes the better impression? Why? Polls of radio listeners taken after the first debate showed Nixon the winner; surveys of television viewers placed Kennedy in front. How do you account for this discrepancy?

prickly questions emerged: Was it appropriate to spend large sums of money for social goals? Would federal aid bring federal control of school policies and curriculum? Should assistance go to segregated schools? Should it go to parochial schools? In the end, compromise on these issues proved impossible and the school aid measure died in committee.

"Buzz" Aldrin on the Moon

Kennedy was more successful in securing funding for the exploration of space. The space program was caught up in the competition of the Cold War, and with the Soviet launching of *Sputnik* and then the first manned flights, the USSR clearly had the lead. In response, Kennedy proposed that the United States commit itself to landing a man on the moon and returning him to earth before the end of the decade. Congress assented and increased funding of the National Aeronautics and Space Administration (NASA).

Kennedy also established the Peace Corps, which sent young men and women overseas to assist developing countries by working with people at a grassroots level. Paul Cowan, introduced at the start of this chapter, was one of thousands of volunteers who hoped to share their liberal dreams.

If Kennedy's successes were modest, he had at least made commitments that could be broadened later. He had reaffirmed the importance of executive leadership in the effort to extend the boundaries of the welfare state. And he had committed himself to using modern economics to maintain fiscal stability. The nation was poised to achieve liberal goals.

Civil Rights and Kennedy's Response

So it was with civil rights. The pressures that had mounted after World War II had brought significant change in eliminating segregation in American society. As the effort continued, a spectrum of organizations carried the fight forward. The NAACP, founded in 1910, remained committed to overturning the legal bases for segregation in the aftermath of its victory in the *Brown* v. *Board of Education* case of 1954 (see Chapter 26). The Congress of Racial Equality (CORE), an interracial group established in 1942, promoted change through peaceful confrontation. In 1957, after their victory in the bus boycott in Montgomery, Alabama, Martin Luther King, Jr., and others formed the Southern Christian Leadership Conference (SCLC), an organization of southern black clergy. Far more militant was the Student Nonviolent Coordinating Committee (SNCC, pronounced "snick"), which began to operate in 1960 and recruited young Americans not previously involved.

Confrontations continued in the 1960s. On January 31, 1960, four black college students in Greensboro, North Carolina, frustrated that they were permitted to shop but not to eat at Woolworth's, a popular department store chain, sat down at the lunch counter and refused to leave. The next day more students showed up, and the following day still more. The sit-ins, which spread to other cities, captured media attention and eventually included as many as 70,000 participants. Those protesting often met with a brutal response.

The following year, sit-ins gave rise to freedom rides, aimed at testing southern transportation facilities that recently had been desegregated by a Supreme Court decision. Organized initially by CORE and aided by SNCC, the program sent groups of blacks and whites together on buses heading south. The riders, peaceful themselves, anticipated confrontations that would publicize their cause and generate political support, and they frequently ended up in jail.

The civil rights movement became the most powerful moral campaign since the abolitionist crusade before the Civil War. Anne Moody, who grew up in a small town in Mississippi, personified the awakening of black consciousness. As a child, she had watched the murder of friends and acquaintances who had somehow transgressed the limits set for blacks. Overcoming the hardships of growing up poor and black in the rural South, Moody became the first member of her family to go to college and later joined the NAACP and became involved in the activities of SNCC and CORE. Participating in sit-ins, where she was thrashed and jailed for her activities, she remained deeply involved in the movement.

Many whites also joined the struggle in the South. Mimi Feingold, a white student at Swarthmore College in Pennsylvania, helped picket the Woolworth's there. After her sophomore year, she headed south to join the freedom rides sponsored by CORE. Like many others, Feingold found herself in the midst of often-violent confrontations and went to jail as an act of conscience.

In 1962, the civil rights movement accelerated. James Meredith, a black air force veteran, applied to the all-white University of Mississippi, only to be rejected on racial grounds. Although the Supreme Court affirmed his right to attend, Governor Ross Barnett, an adamant racist, announced defiantly that Meredith would not be admitted and on one occasion personally blocked the way. A major riot followed; tear gas covered the university grounds; and by the riot's end, two men lay dead and hundreds were hurt.

Other governors were equally aggressive. In his 1963 inaugural address, George C. Wallace of Alabama declared boldly, "Segregation now! Segregation tomorrow! Segregation forever!" as he voiced his opposition to integration.

Alabama became a national focus that year as a violent confrontation unfolded in Birmingham. Though the demonstrations against segregation were nonviolent, the responses were not. City officials declared that protest marches violated city regulations against parading without a license, and, over a five-week period, they arrested 2,200 blacks, some of them schoolchildren. Police Commissioner Eugene "Bull" Connor used high-pressure fire hoses, electric cattle prods, and trained police dogs to force the protesters back. As the media recorded the events, Americans watching television and reading newspapers were horrified.

Kennedy claimed to be sickened by the pictures from Birmingham but insisted that he could do nothing, even though he had sought and won black support in 1960. The narrowness of his electoral victory made him reluctant to press white southerners on civil rights when he needed their votes on other issues. Events finally forced Kennedy to act more boldly. In the James Meredith confrontation, the president, like his predecessor in the Little Rock crisis, had to send federal troops to restore control and to guarantee Meredith's right to attend the university. The administration also forced the desegregation of the University of Alabama and helped arrange a compromise that eased discrimination in Birmingham's municipal facilities and hiring practices. And when white bombings aimed at eliminating black leaders in Birmingham caused thousands of blacks to abandon nonviolence and rampage through the streets, Kennedy readied federal troops to intervene.

Sitting In In violation of southern law, black college students refused to leave a lunch counter, launching a new campaign in the struggle for civil rights. Here the students wait patiently for service, or forcible eviction, as a way of dramatizing their determination to end segregation. What did the students hope to achieve by their actions? *(Bruce Roberts/Photo Researchers, Inc.)*

He also spoke out more forcefully than before. In a nationally televised address, he called the quest for equal rights a "moral issue" and asked, "Are we to say to the world, and, much more importantly, to each other, that this is a land of the free except for the Negroes?" Just hours after the president spoke, assassins killed Medgar Evers, a black NAACP official, in his own driveway in Jackson, Mississippi.

DOCUMENT

John Lewis,
Address at the
March on
Washington
(1963)

Kennedy sent Congress a new and stronger civil rights bill, outlawing segregation in public places, banning discrimination wherever federal money was involved, and advancing the process of school integration. Polls showed that 63 percent of the nation supported his stand.

To lobby for passage of this measure, civil rights leaders, pressed from below by black activists, arranged a massive march on Washington in August 1963. More than 200,000 people—black and white, common folk and celebrities—gathered from across the country.

The high point of the day was the address by Martin Luther King, Jr., who by now was the nation's preeminent spokesman for civil rights and proponent of nonviolent protest. King proclaimed his faith in the decency of his fellow citizens and in their ability to extend the promises of the Constitution and the Declaration of Independence to every American. With all the power of a southern preacher, he implored his audience to share his faith.

"I have a dream," King declared, "that one day this nation will rise up and live out the true meaning of its creed: 'We hold these truths to be self-evident, that all men are created equal.' I have a dream that one day on the red hills of Georgia, the sons of former slaves and the sons of former slave-owners will be able to sit together at the table of brotherhood." Each time King used the refrain "I have a dream," thousands of blacks and whites roared together. King concluded by quoting from an old hymn: "Free at last! Free at last! Thank God almighty, we are free at last!"

Civil Rights March on Washington (1963)

Not all were moved. Despite large Democratic majorities, strong white southern resistance to the cause of civil rights continued in Congress, and the bill was bottled up in committee.

LYNDON B. JOHNSON AND THE GREAT SOCIETY

Kennedy knew he faced a difficult reelection battle in 1964. He wanted not only to win the presidency for a second term but also to increase liberal Democratic strength in Congress. Instead, an assassin's attack took his life and brought a new leader to the helm.

Change of Command

In November 1963, Kennedy traveled to Texas, where he hoped to unite the state's Democratic party for the upcoming election. Dallas, one of the stops on the trip, was reputed to be hostile to the administration. Entering the city in an open car, the president encountered friendly crowds. Suddenly shots rang out, and Kennedy slumped forward as bullets ripped through his head and throat. Mortally wounded, he died a short time later at a Dallas hospital. Lee Harvey Oswald, the accused assassin, was shot and killed a few days later by a minor underworld figure as he was being moved within the jail.

Americans were stunned. For days, people stayed at home and watched endless television replays of the assassination and its aftermath. The images of the handsome president felled by bullets, the funeral cortege, and the president's young son saluting his father's casket as it rolled by on the way to final burial at Arlington National Cemetery were all imprinted on people's minds.

Vice President Lyndon Johnson succeeded Kennedy as president. Though less polished, Johnson was a more effective political leader than Kennedy and brought his own special skills and vision to the presidency.

LBJ

Johnson had taken a different road to the White House and came from a far more humble background than Kennedy. He had begun his public career as a legislative assistant in the House of Representatives in Washington, D.C., then served as a New Deal official in Texas. He won election first to the House in 1937 and then

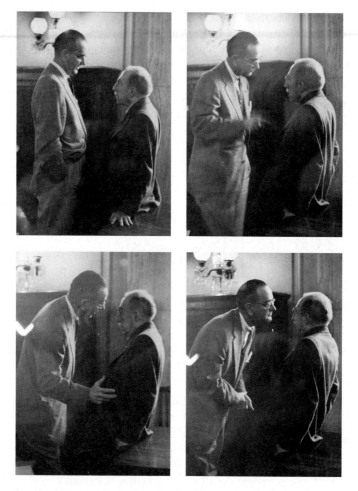

Lyndon Johnson in Action Lyndon Johnson kept tight control of the Senate in the 1950s and was known for his ability to get his way. Here he is shown giving the famous "Johnson treatment" to Senator Theodore Francis Green in 1957. Note the way Green is bending backward in an unsuccessful effort to keep his distance from LBJ. Why do you think LBJ usually got his way? *(George Tames/The New York Times)*

to the Senate in 1948. Eager to be president, he accepted the vice presidential nomination when it became clear in 1960 that Kennedy was going to win the nomination for president.

Johnson was a man of elemental force. Always manipulative, he was often difficult to like. There was a streak of vulgarity that contributed to his earthy appeal but was offensive. Those qualities notwithstanding, he was successful in the passion of his life—politics—and was the most able legislator of the postwar years. As Senate majority leader, he became famous for knowing the strengths and weaknesses of everyone he faced and for his ability to get things done. He could flatter and cajole, and became famous for what came to be called the "Johnson treatment." According to columnists Rowland Evans, Jr., and Robert Novak, he zeroed in, "his face a scant millimeter from his target, his eyes widening and narrowing, his eyebrows rising and falling." He grabbed people by the lapels, made them listen, and usually got his way.

As vice president, Johnson went into a state of eclipse. He felt useless and stifled in his new role without his power base in the Senate and felt uncomfortable with the Kennedy crowd.

Despite his own ambivalence about Kennedy, Johnson sensed the profound shock that gripped the United States after the assassination and was determined to utilize Kennedy's memory to achieve legislative success. Even more than Kennedy, he was willing to wield presidential power aggressively and to use the media to shape public opinion in pursuit of his vision of a society in which the comforts of life would be more widely shared and poverty would be eliminated.

The Great Society in Action

Lyndon Johnson had an expansive vision of the possibilities of reform. Using his considerable political skills, he succeeded in pushing through Congress the most extensive reform program in American history.

Johnson began to develop the support he needed the day he took office. In his first public address, delivered to Congress and televised nationwide, he sought to dispel the image of impostor as he embraced Kennedy's liberal program. He began, in a measured tone, with the words, "All I have, I would have given gladly not to be standing here today." He asked members of Congress to work with him, and he underscored the theme "Let us continue."

As a first step, Johnson resolved to secure the measures Kennedy had been unable to extract from Congress. Bills to reduce taxes and ensure civil rights were his first and most pressing priorities, but he was interested too in aiding public education, providing medical care for the aged, and eliminating poverty. By the spring of 1964, he began to use the phrase "Great Society" to describe his expansive reform program.

Johnson's landslide victory over conservative Republican challenger Barry Goldwater in the election of 1964 validated his approach. This was the first time in recent history that a conservative had gained the Republican nomination. Goldwater, however, frightened even members of his own party by proclaiming that "extremism in the defense of liberty is no vice," and by speaking out against such popular programs as social security. LBJ received 61 percent of the popular vote and an electoral tally of 486 to 52 and gained Democratic majorities in both the Senate and the House. Goldwater's candidacy drove moderate Republicans to vote for the Democratic party and gave Johnson a far more impressive mandate than Kennedy had ever enjoyed.

Civil rights reform was LBJ's first legislative priority and an integral part of the Great Society program (see next section), but other measures were equally important. Following Kennedy's lead, Johnson pressed for a tax cut. He accepted the Keynesian theory that deficits, properly managed, could promote prosperity. If

Roots of Selected Great Society Programs

Progressive Period	New Deal	Great Society
Settlement house activity of Jane Addams and others	Relief efforts to ease unemployment (FERA, WPA)	Poverty programs (OEO)
Efforts to clean up slums (tenement house laws)	Housing program	Rehabilitation of slums through Model Cities program
Progressive party platform calling for federal accident, old-age, and unemployment insurance	Social security system providing unemployment compensation and old-age pensions	Medical care for the aged through social security (Medicare)
Activity to break up monopolies and regulate business	Regulation of utility companies	Regulation of highway safety and transportation
Efforts to regulate working conditions and benefits	Establishment of standards for working conditions and minimum wage	Raising of minimum wage
Efforts to increase literacy and spread education at all levels	Efforts to keep college students in school through National Youth Administration	Assistance to elementary, secondary, and higher education
Theodore Roosevelt's efforts at wilderness preservation	Conservation efforts (CCC, TVA planning)	Safeguarding of wilderness lands
Establishment of federal income tax	Tax reform to close loopholes and increase taxes for the wealthy	Tax cut to stimulate business activity
Theodore Roosevelt's overtures to Booker T. Washington	Discussion (but not passage) of antilynching legislation	Civil rights measures to ban discrimination in public accommodations and to guarantee right to vote

people had more money to spend, then their purchases could stimulate the economy. Soon the tax bill passed.

With the tax cut in hand, the president pressed for the antipoverty program that Kennedy had begun to plan. Such an effort was bold and unprecedented in the United States, even though social democracy had a long history in European nations and other countries around the world. During the Progressive era and the New Deal, programs had sought to assist those Americans who could not help themselves. Now Johnson took a step that no president had taken before; in his 1964 State of the Union message, he declared an "unconditional war on poverty in America."

The centerpiece of this utopian effort to eradicate poverty was the Economic Opportunity Act of 1964. It created an Office of Economic Opportunity (OEO) to provide education and training through programs such as the Job Corps for unskilled young people trapped in the poverty cycle. VISTA (Volunteers in Service to America), patterned after the Peace Corps, offered assistance to the poor at home, while Head Start tried to give disadvantaged children a chance to succeed in school. Assorted community action programs gave the poor a voice in improving housing, health, and education. Two agencies responded to Native American pressure by allowing Indians to devise programs and budgets and administer the programs.

Aware of the escalating costs of medical care, Johnson also proposed a medical assistance plan. Both Truman and Kennedy had supported such an initiative but had failed to win congressional approval. Johnson succeeded. To head off conservative attacks, the administration limited the Medicare measure to the elderly. The complementary Medicaid program met the needs of those on welfare and certain other groups who could not afford private insurance. The Medicare–Medicaid initiative was the most important extension of federally directed social benefits since the Social Security Act of 1935.

Johnson was similarly successful in his effort to provide aid for elementary and secondary schools. His legislation allocated education money to the states based on the number of children from low-income families. Those funds would then be distributed to assist deprived children in public as well as private schools.

In LBJ's expansive vision, the federal government would ensure that everyone shared in the promise of American life. Under his prodding, Congress passed a new housing act to give rent supplements to the poor and created a Cabinet Department of Housing and Urban Development. The federal government provided new forms of aid, such as legal assistance for the poor, and provided additional funds for higher education. Congress also provided artists and scholars with assistance through the National Endowments for the Arts and Humanities, created in 1965.

At the same time, Johnson's administration provided much-needed immigration reform. The Immigration Act of 1965 replaced the restrictive policy in place since 1924 with a measure that vastly increased the ceiling on immigration and opened the door to immigrants and refugees from Asia and Latin America. By the late 1960s, some 350,000 immigrants were entering the United States annually, compared to the average of 47,000 per year between 1931 and 1945. This new stream of immigration created a population more diverse than it had been since the early decades of the twentieth century.

The Great Society also reflected the stirring of the environmental movement. In 1962, naturalist Rachel Carson alerted the public to the dangers of pesticide poisoning and environmental pollution in her book *Silent Spring*. She took aim at chemical pesticides, especially DDT, which had increased crop yields but had brought disastrous side effects.

Johnson was determined to address such problems and to provide protection for wildlife. The National Wilderness Preservation Act of 1964 set aside 9.1 million acres of wilderness, and Congress passed other measures to limit air and water pollution. In addition, Lady Bird Johnson, the president's wife, led a beautification campaign to eliminate unsightly billboards and junkyards along the nation's highways.

Achievements and Challenges in Civil Rights

Lyndon Johnson was enormously successful in advancing the cause of civil rights. Seizing the opportunity provided by Kennedy's assassination, Johnson pushed new civil rights bills through Congress as a memorial to Kennedy. The Civil

Rights Act of 1964 outlawed racial discrimination in all public accommodations and authorized the Justice Department to act with greater authority in school and voting matters. In addition, an equal-opportunity provision prohibited discriminatory hiring on grounds of race, gender, religion, or national origin in firms with more than 25 employees.

Although the law was one of the great achievements of the 1960s, widespread discrimination still existed in American society and African Americans in large areas of the South still found it difficult to vote. Freedom Summer, sponsored by SNCC and other civil rights groups in 1964, focused attention on the problem by sending black and white students to Mississippi to work for black rights. Early in the summer, two whites, Michael Schwerner and Andrew Goodman, and one black, James Chaney, were murdered. By the end of the summer, 80 workers had been beaten, 1,000 arrests had been made, and 37 churches had been bombed. In the face of such resistance, Johnson asked Congress for a voting bill that would close the loopholes of the previous two acts.

Impact of the Voting Rights Act of 1965

The Voting Rights Act of 1965, perhaps the most important law of the decade, singled out the South for its restrictive practices and authorized the U.S. attorney general to appoint federal examiners to register voters where local officials were obstructing the registration of blacks. In the year after passage of the act, 400,000 blacks registered to vote in the Deep South; by 1968, the number reached 1 million.

Despite passage of the Civil Rights Act of 1964 and the Voting Rights Act of 1965, racial discrimination remained throughout the country. Still-segregated schools, wretched housing, and inadequate job opportunities were continuing problems. As the struggle for civil rights moved north, dramatic divisions within the movement emerged.

Initially, the civil rights campaign had been integrated and nonviolent. Its acknowledged leader was Martin Luther King, Jr. But now tensions between blacks and whites flared within organizations, and younger black leaders began to challenge King's nonviolent approach. They were tired of beatings, jailings, church bombings, and the slow pace of change when dependent on white liberal support and government action.

One episode that contributed to many blacks' suspicion of white liberals occurred at the Democratic national convention of 1964 in Atlantic City. SNCC, active in the Freedom Summer project in Mississippi, had founded the Freedom Democratic party as an alternative to the all-white delegation that was to represent the state. Testifying before the credentials committee, black activist Fannie Lou Hamer reported that she had been beaten, jailed, and denied the right to vote. Yet the committee's final compromise, pressed by President Johnson, who worried about losing southern support in the coming election, was that the white delegation would still be seated, with two members of the protest organization offered seats at large. That response hardly satisfied those who had risked their lives and families to try to vote in Mississippi. SNCC, once a religious, integrated organization, began to change into an all-black cadre that could mobilize poor blacks for militant action.

Malcolm X at the Lectern "The day of nonviolence is over," Malcolm X proclaimed, as many African Americans listened enthusiastically. A compelling speaker, Malcolm made a powerful case for a more aggressive campaign for black rights. What image does Malcolm X convey in this photograph? *(Corbis)*

VIDEO

Malcolm X

Malcolm X was perhaps the leader most responsible for channeling black frustration into a new set of goals and tactics. Born Malcolm Little and reared in northern ghettos, he hustled gambling numbers and prostitutes in the big cities before becoming a convert to the Nation of Islam. Malcolm was impatient with the moderate civil rights movement. He grew tired of hearing "all of this nonviolent, begging-the-white-man kind of dying ... all of this sitting-in, sliding-in, wading-in, eating-in, diving-in, and all the rest." Espousing black separatism and black nationalism for most of his public career, he preached an international perspective embracing African peoples in diaspora, and appealed to blacks to fight racism "by any means necessary." Though Malcolm was assassinated by black antagonists in 1965, his African-centered, uncompromising perspective helped shape the struggle against racism.

One man influenced by Malcolm's message was Stokely Carmichael. Born in Trinidad, Carmichael came to the United States at the age of 11, where he grew up with an interest in political affairs and black protest. Frustrated with the strategy of civil disobedience as he became active in SNCC, he urged fieldworkers to carry weapons for self-defense. It was time for blacks to cease depending on whites, he argued, and to make SNCC into a black organization. His election as head of the student group reflected SNCC's growing radicalism.

The split in the black movement was dramatized in June 1966 when Carmichael's followers challenged those of Martin Luther King, Jr., during a march in Mississippi. King still adhered to nonviolence and interracial cooperation. Just out of jail after being arrested for his protest activities, Carmichael jumped onto a flatbed truck to address the group. "This is the twenty-seventh time I have been arrested—and I ain't going to jail no more!" he shouted. "The only way we gonna stop them white men from whippin' us is to take over. We been saying freedom for six years and we ain't got nothing. What we gonna start saying now is Black Power!" Carmichael had the audience in his hand as he repeated, and the crowd shouted back, "We ... want ... Black ... Power!"

DOCUMENT

Voting Literacy Test (1965)

Black Power was a call to build independent institutions in the African American community, and it fostered a powerful sense of black pride. The movement included a wide variety of different figures: cultural nationalists such as Maulana Ron Karenga, an activist scholar and early authority on Black Studies; advocates of black capitalism such as Nathan Wright, Jr., chairman of the 1967 and 1968 National and International Conferences on Black Power; and revolutionary nationalists such as Huey P. Newton, a proponent of aggressive liberation measures. Its most enduring legacy was political and cultural mobilization at the grassroots level, even if it only partially realized its goals.

Black Power led to demands for more drastic action. The Black Panthers, radical activists who organized first in Oakland, California, and then in other cities, formed a militant organization that vowed to eradicate not only racial discrimination but capitalism as well. H. Rap Brown, who succeeded Carmichael as head of SNCC, became known for his statement that "violence is as American as cherry pie."

Violence accompanied the more militant calls for reform and showed that racial injustice was not a southern problem but an American one. Riots erupted in New York City and several other eastern cities in 1964. In 1965, in the Watts neighborhood of Los Angeles, a massive uprising lasting five days left 34 dead, more than 1,000 injured, and hundreds of structures burned to the ground. Violence broke out again in other cities in 1966, 1967, and 1968.

A Sympathetic Supreme Court

With the addition of liberal justices appointed by Kennedy and Johnson, the Supreme Court supported the liberal agenda. Under the leadership of Chief Justice Earl Warren, the Court followed the lead it had taken in *Brown* v. *Board of Education*, outlawing school segregation by moving against Jim Crow practices in other public establishments.

The Court also supported civil liberties by beginning to protect the rights of individuals with radical political views. Similarly, the Court sought to protect accused suspects from police harassment and to provide poor defendants with free legal counsel. In *Escobedo* v. *Illinois* (1964), it ruled that a suspect had to be given access to an attorney during questioning. In *Miranda* v. *Arizona* (1966), it argued that offenders had to be warned that statements extracted by the police could be used against them and that they could remain silent.

Other decisions similarly broke new ground. *Baker* v. *Carr* (1962) opened the way to reapportionment of state legislative bodies according to the standard, defined a year later in Justice William O. Douglas's words, of "one person, one vote." This crucial ruling helped break the political control of lightly populated rural districts in many state assemblies and similarly made the U.S. House of Representatives much more responsive to urban and suburban issues. Meanwhile, the Court outraged conservatives by ruling that prayer could not be required in the public schools and that obscenity laws could no longer restrict allegedly pornographic material that might have some "redeeming social value."

The Great Society Under Attack

Supported by healthy economic growth, the Great Society worked for a few years as Johnson had hoped. The tax cut proved effective, and the consumer and business spending that it promoted led to a steady increase in gross national product. As the economy improved, the budget deficit dropped just as predicted. Unemployment fell, and inflation remained under control. Medical programs provided basic security for the old and the poor. Education flourished as schools were built, and teachers' salaries increased as a result of federal aid.

Yet Johnson's dream of the Great Society proved illusory. Some programs promised too much; others were simply ill conceived or were underfunded. Factionalism was also a problem. Lyndon Johnson had reconstituted the old Democratic coalition in his triumph in 1964, with urban Catholics and southern whites joining organized labor, the black electorate, and the middle class. But conservative white southerners and blue-collar white northerners felt threatened by the government's support of civil rights. Local urban bosses, long the backbone of the Democratic party, objected to grassroots participation of the urban poor, which threatened their own political control.

Criticisms of the Great Society and its liberal underpinnings came from across the political spectrum. Conservatives disliked the centralization of authority and the government's increased role in defining the national welfare. Even middle-class Americans, generally supportive of liberal goals, sometimes grumbled that the government was paying too much attention to the underprivileged and thereby neglecting their own needs. Radicals, meanwhile, attacked the Great Society for not going far enough. With its assumption that the American system was basically sound, they argued, the Great Society made no real effort to redistribute income and thereby transform American life.

The Vietnam War (discussed later in this chapter) dealt the Great Society a fatal blow. LBJ wanted to maintain both the war and his treasured domestic reform programs, but his effort to pursue these goals simultaneously produced serious inflation. The economy was already booming as a result of the tax cut and the spending for reform. As military expenditures increased, the productive system of the country could not keep up with demand. When Johnson refused to raise taxes, in an effort to hide the costs of the war, inflation spiraled out of control. Congress finally slashed Great Society programs, deciding it could no longer afford such extensive social reform.

CONTINUING CONFRONTATIONS WITH COMMUNISTS

The Cold War continued throughout the 1960s. Presidents John F. Kennedy and Lyndon B. Johnson were both aggressive cold warriors who subscribed to the policies of their predecessors. Their commitment to stopping the spread of communism kept the nation locked in the same bitter conflict that had dominated foreign policy in the 1950s and led to continuing global confrontations that sometimes threatened the stability of the entire world.

The Bay of Pigs Fiasco and Its Consequences

Kennedy was intensely interested in foreign affairs. In his ringing inaugural address, he eloquently described the dangers and challenges the United States faced in the Cold War. "In the long history of the world," he cried out, "only a few generations have been granted the role of defending freedom in its hour of maximum danger." The United States would "pay any price, bear any burden, meet any hardship, support any friend, oppose any foe, to assure the survival and success of liberty."

Kennedy perceived direct challenges from the Soviet Union almost from the beginning of his presidency. The first came at the Bay of Pigs in Cuba in the spring of 1961. Cuban–American relations had been strained since Fidel Castro's revolutionary army had seized power in 1959. A radical regime in Cuba, leaning toward the Soviet Union, could provide a model for upheaval elsewhere in Latin America and threaten the venerable Monroe Doctrine. One initiative to counter the Communist threat was the Alliance for Progress, which provided social and economic assistance to the less-developed nations of the hemisphere. But other, more aggressive, responses were deemed necessary as well.

Just before Kennedy assumed office, the United States broke diplomatic relations with Cuba. The CIA, meanwhile, was covertly training anti-Castro exiles to storm the Cuban coast at the Bay of Pigs. The American planners assumed the invasion would lead to an uprising of the Cuban people against Castro. While some top officials resisted the scheme, Kennedy approved the plan.

The invasion, which took place on April 17, 1961, was an unmitigated disaster. When an early air strike failed to destroy Cuban air power, Castro was able to hold off the troops coming ashore. Urged to use American planes for air cover, Kennedy refused, for by that time failure was clear. The United States stood exposed to the world, attempting to overthrow a sovereign government. It had broken agreements not to interfere in the internal affairs of hemispheric neighbors and had intervened clumsily and unsuccessfully.

Although chastened by the debacle at the Bay of Pigs, Kennedy was determined to counter the perceived Communist threat. Germany became the next battleground. For more than a decade, the nation had been divided (see Chapter 27). The Western powers had promoted the industrial development of West Germany, which was prospering and which stood in stark contrast to the drab, Soviet-controlled East Germany. Berlin, likewise divided, remained an irritant to the Russians, particularly since some 2.6 million East Germans had fled to West Germany,

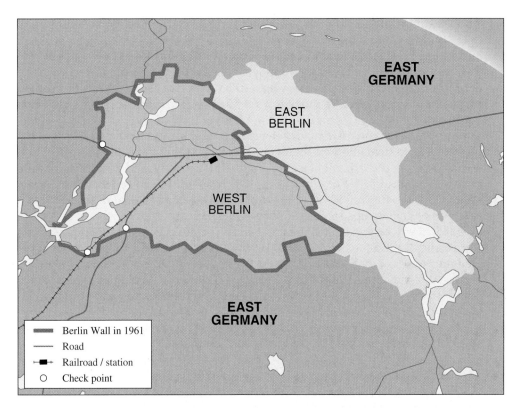

THE BERLIN WALL The Berlin Wall effectively sealed West Berlin off both from the eastern sector of the city and from East Germany itself. Now people could only enter and exit West Berlin through a number of carefully monitored checkpoints. ■ **Reflecting on the Past** Why was it so important for East Germany to prevent people from going into West Berlin? Why would people in West Berlin have wanted to go into East Berlin? How effective do you think such a wall might be in keeping people in or out?

often through the city. Following a hostile meeting with Soviet leader Nikita Khrushchev in Vienna in June 1961, Kennedy reacted aggressively. He asked Congress for $3 billion more in defense appropriations, as well as for funds for a civil defense fallout-shelter program, explicitly warning of the threat of nuclear war. The USSR responded in August by erecting a wall in Berlin to seal off its section entirely. The concrete structure, topped by barbed wire, was 96 miles long and an average of 11.8 feet high. Menacing machine-gun emplacements made escape difficult. People who were caught scaling the wall were shot. The wall became a dramatic symbol of the division between East and West.

The Cuban Missile Face-Off

The next year, a new crisis arose. American aerial photographs taken in October 1962 revealed that the USSR had begun to place what Kennedy considered offensive missiles on Cuban soil, although Cuba insisted they were defensive. This time Kennedy was determined to win a confrontation with the Soviet Union.

Top administration officials examined various alternatives. Some members of the Executive Committee of the National Security Council wanted an air strike to knock out the sites; others, including Attorney General Robert F. Kennedy, the president's brother, opposed such a move. Still, the United States moved to a state of full alert. Bombers and missiles were armed with nuclear weapons and readied to go. The fleet prepared to move toward Cuba, and troops geared up to invade the island.

Kennedy went on nationwide television to tell the American people about the missiles and to demand their removal. He declared that the United States would not shrink from the risk of nuclear war and announced he had decided to impose a naval "quarantine"—not a blockade, which would have been an act of war—around Cuba to prevent Soviet ships from bringing in additional missiles.

As the Soviet ships steamed toward Cuba and the nations stood "eyeball to eyeball," the world held its breath. Before they reached the quarantine line, Khrushchev called the Soviet ships back. He then sent a long letter by teletype, pledging to remove the missiles if the United States lifted the quarantine and promised to stay out of Cuba altogether. A second letter demanded that America remove its missiles from Turkey as well. The United States agreed to the first letter, ignored the second, and said nothing about its intention, already voiced, of removing its own missiles from Turkey. With that, the crisis ended. Secretary of State Rusk observed, "We have won a considerable victory. You and I are still alive."

The Cuban missile crisis was the most terrifying confrontation of the Cold War. Yet the president emerged from it as a hero who had stood firm. His reputation was enhanced, and his party benefited a few weeks later in the congressional elections. One consequence of the affair was the installation of a Soviet–American hotline to avoid similar episodes in the future. Another consequence was the USSR's determination to increase its nuclear arsenal so that it would never again be exposed as inferior to the United States. Despite the Limited Test Ban Treaty of 1963, which prohibited atmospheric testing, the nuclear arms race continued.

DOCUMENT

Test Ban Treaty

Confrontation and Containment Under Johnson

Johnson shared many of Kennedy's assumptions about the threat of communism. His understanding of the onset of World War II led him to believe that aggressors had to be stopped cold. Like Eisenhower and Kennedy, Johnson believed in the domino theory: if one country in a region fell, others were bound to follow. He assumed he could treat foreign adversaries just as he treated political opponents in the United States, and in 1965, he dispatched over 20,000 troops to the Dominican Republic to counter "Castro-type elements" that were actually engaged in a democratic revolution. Johnson's credibility suffered badly from the episode.

In the Middle East, the United States sought to use its influence to temper the violence that erupted in the area. In 1967, Israeli forces defeated the Egyptian army in the Six-Day War and seized the West Bank and Jerusalem, the Golan

Heights, and the Sinai Peninsula. Americans pressed for a quick end to the fighting to maintain regional equilibrium and uninterrupted supplies of oil.

WAR IN VIETNAM AND TURMOIL AT HOME

The commitment to stopping the spread of communism led to the massive U.S. involvement in Vietnam. The roots of the conflict, described in Chapter 26, extended back to the early post–World War II years, but American participation remained relatively limited until Kennedy took office. Then the United States became increasingly engaged in a major effort to resist a Communist takeover. That struggle wrought enormous damage in Southeast Asia, tore the United States apart, and finally forced a full-fledged reevaluation of America's Cold War policies.

Escalation in Vietnam

John Kennedy's commitment to Cold War victory led him to expand the American role in Vietnam. During the Kennedy administration, the number of advisers rose from 675 to more than 16,000, and American soldiers began to lose their lives.

Despite American backing, South Vietnamese leader Ngo Dinh Diem, a Catholic, was rapidly losing support in his own country. Buddhist priests burned themselves alive in the capital of Saigon to protest the corruption and arbitrariness of Diem's regime. With American approval, South Vietnamese military leaders assassinated Diem and seized the government. While Kennedy understood the importance of popular support for the South Vietnamese government, he was reluctant to withdraw and let the Vietnamese solve their own problems.

Lyndon Johnson shared the same reservations as South Vietnam became more unstable after the assassination of Diem. Guerrillas, known as Viet Cong, challenged the regime, sometimes covertly and sometimes through the National Liberation Front, their political arm. Aided by Ho Chi Minh and the North Vietnamese, the insurgent Viet Cong slowly gained ground. Johnson chose to stand firm. "I am not going to lose Vietnam," he said. "I am not going to be the president who saw Southeast Asia go the way China went." In the election campaign of 1964, he posed as a man of peace. "We don't want our American boys to do the fighting for Asian boys," he declared. But secretly he was planning to escalate the American role.

In August 1964, Johnson charged that North Vietnamese torpedo boats had made unprovoked attacks on American destroyers in the international waters of the Gulf of Tonkin, 30 miles from North Vietnam. While there had been initial conflict, in fact the attacks Johnson highlighted never occurred. But before the real nature of the engagement became clear, LBJ used the episode to obtain from Congress a resolution giving him authority to "take all necessary measures to repel any armed attack against the forces of the United States and to prevent further aggression." The Gulf of Tonkin resolution provided all the leverage he sought.

DOCUMENT

Lyndon Johnson, The Tonkin Gulf Resolution Message (1964)

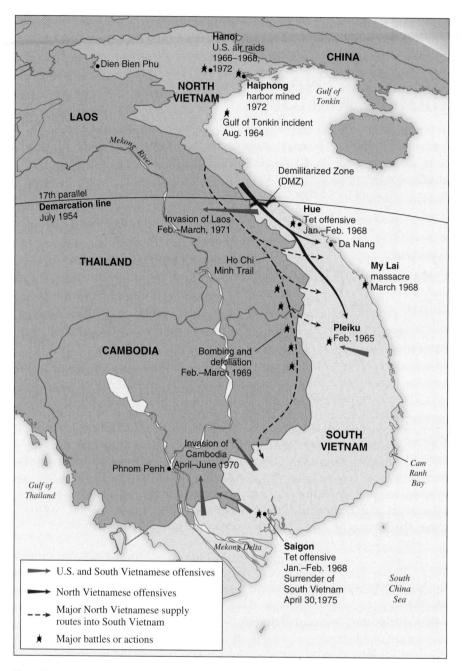

THE VIETNAM WAR This map shows the major campaigns of the Vietnam War. The North Vietnamese Tet offensive of early 1968, pictured with red arrows, turned the tide against U.S. participation in the war and led to peace talks. The U.S. invasion of Cambodia in 1970, pictured with blue arrows, provoked serious opposition.   ■   **Reflecting on the Past** What role did North Vietnam play in the war? How far did American air power penetrate? Why did the United States and South Vietnam attack neighboring nations, such as Cambodia?

Military escalation began in earnest in February 1965, after Johnson's landslide electoral victory, when Viet Cong forces killed seven Americans in an attack on an American base. Johnson responded by authorizing retaliatory bombing of North Vietnam to cut off the flow of supplies and to ease pressure on South Vietnam. A few months later, the president sent American ground troops into action. This marked the crucial turning point in the Americanization of the Vietnam War. Only 25,000 American soldiers were in Vietnam at the start of 1965; by the end of the year, there were 184,000. The number swelled to 385,000 in 1966, to 485,000 in 1967, and to 543,000 in 1968. As escalation occurred, Johnson recognized his dilemma. He understood that the war was probably unwinnable, but he feared the loss of both American power and personal prestige if he pulled out.

And so American forces became direct participants in the fight to prop up a dictatorial regime in faraway South Vietnam. Although a somewhat more effective government headed by Nguyen Van Thieu and Nguyen Cao Ky was finally established, the level of violence increased. Saturation bombing of North Vietnam continued. Fragmentation bombs, killing and maiming countless civilians, and napalm, which seared off human flesh, were used extensively. Similar destruction wracked South Vietnam. And still, despite the repeatedly expressed contention of military commander William Westmoreland that there was "light at the end of the tunnel," the violence continued without pause.

President Lyndon B. Johnson in Vietnam (1966)

Student Activism and Antiwar Protest

Americans began to protest their involvement in the war. Members of the baby boom generation who came of age in the 1960s were in the forefront of the struggle. By the end of the 1960s, college enrollment was more than four times what it had been in the 1940s. College provided necessary training but also gave students time to experiment and grow before they had to make a living. Some students joined the struggle for civil rights. Hopeful at first, they gradually became discouraged by the gap between Kennedy's New Frontier rhetoric and the government's actual commitment.

Out of that disillusionment arose the radical spirit of the New Left. Civil rights activists were among those who in 1960 organized Students for a Democratic Society (SDS). In 1962, SDS issued a manifesto, the Port Huron Statement, written largely by Tom Hayden of the University of Michigan, which outlined both complaints and goals for a participatory democracy. "We are people of this generation, bred in at least modest comfort, housed now in universities, looking uncomfortably at the world we inherit," it began. It went on to deplore the vast social and economic distances separating people from each other and to condemn the estrangement of modern life.

The first blow of the growing student rebellion came at the University of California at Berkeley in 1964. There, civil rights activists became involved in a confrontation soon known as the Free Speech Movement. When the university refused to allow students, many of them civil rights activists, to distribute protest material outside the main campus gate, they surrounded a police car and kept it from moving all night. The university regents brought charges against the student leaders, and when the regents refused to drop the charges, the students occupied the administration building. Police stormed in and arrested the students. A strike, with faculty aid, mobilized wider support for the right to free speech.

The Free Speech Movement at Berkeley was basically a plea for traditional liberal reform. Students sought only the reaffirmation of the long-standing right to express themselves as they chose. Later, in other institutions, the attack broadened. Students sought greater involvement in university affairs, argued for curricular reform, and demanded admission of more minority students.

The mounting protest against the escalation of the Vietnam War fueled and refocused the youth movement. The first antiwar teach-in took place in March 1965 at the University of Michigan. Others soon followed. Initially, both supporters and opponents of the war appeared at the teach-ins, but quickly the sessions became more like antiwar rallies than instructional affairs. Boxer Muhammad Ali legitimated draft resistance when he declared, "I ain't got no quarrel with them Viet Cong" and refused military induction. Working through SDS and other organizations, radical activists campaigned against the draft, attacked ROTC units on campus, and sought to discredit firms that produced the destructive tools of war. "Make love, not war," students proclaimed. As the antiwar movement expanded, students became even more shrill. "Hey, hey, LBJ. How many kids did you kill today?" they chanted as they marched in protest.

Working-class and middle-class Americans began to sour on the war at the time of the Tet offensive, celebrating the lunar new year, in early 1968. The North Vietnamese mounted massive attacks across South Vietnam. In Saigon, they struck the American embassy, Tan Son Nhut air base, and the presidential palace. Though beaten back, they won a psychological victory. American audiences saw images of burning huts and wounded soldiers each evening on television as they ate dinner. Gazing at such graphic representations of death and destruction, many Americans wondered about their nation's purposes and actions.

Protest became a way of life. Between January 1 and June 15, 1968, hundreds of thousands of students staged 221 major demonstrations at more than 100 educational institutions. One of the most dramatic episodes came in April 1968 at Columbia University, where the issues of civil rights and war were tightly intertwined. A strong SDS chapter urged the university to break ties with the Institute of Defense Analysis, which specialized in military research. The Students' Afro-American Society tried to stop the building of a new gymnasium, which it claimed encroached on the Harlem community and disrupted life there. Whites occupied one building, blacks another. Finally, the president of the university called in the police. Hundreds of students were arrested; many were hurt. A student sympathy strike followed, and Columbia closed for the summer several weeks early.

The student protests in the United States were part of a worldwide wave of student activism. French students demonstrated in the streets of Paris. In Germany, young radicals were equally vocal in challenging conventional norms. In Japan, students waged armed battles with police.

Death of a Viet Cong Suspect In this picture, General Nguyen Ngoc Loan, the chief of the South Vietnamese National Police, looks at a Viet Cong prisoner, lifts his gun, and calmly blows out the captive's brains. This prizewinning photograph captured the horror of the war for many Americans. What impressions do you think this picture conveyed to people who saw it? *(AP/Wide World Photos)*

The Counterculture

Cultural change accompanied political upheaval. Many Americans—some politically active, some not—found new ways to assert their individuality and independence and, as in the political sphere, the young led the way in seeking new means of self-gratification and self-expression.

Surface appearances were most visible and, to older Americans, most troubling. The "hippies" of the 1960s carried themselves in different ways. Men let their hair grow and sprouted beards; men and women both donned jeans, muslin shirts, and other simple garments. Stressing spontaneity above all else, some rejected traditional marital customs and gravitated to communal living groups.

Sexual norms underwent a revolution as more people separated sex from its traditional ties to family life. A generation of young women came of age with access to "the pill"—an oral contraceptive that was effortless to use and freed sexual experimentation from the threat of pregnancy. In 1960, the Food and Drug Administration approved Enovid, the first oral contraceptive available on the market. Within three years of its introduction, more than 2 million women were on the pill, and as the cost dropped, millions more began to use it.

Americans of all social classes became more open to exploring, and enjoying, their sexuality. Author and editor Nora Ephron summed up the sexual changes in the 1960s as she reflected on her own experiences. Initially she had "a hangover from the whole Fifties virgin thing," she recalled. "The first man I went to bed with, I was in love with and wanted to marry. The second one I was in love with, but I didn't have to marry him. With the third one, I thought I might fall in love."

The arts reflected the sexual revolution. Federal courts ruled that books such as D. H. Lawrence's *Lady Chatterley's Lover* and other suppressed works could not be banned. Nudity became more common on stage and screen.

Paintings reflected both the mood of dissent and the urge to innovate, apparent in the larger society. "Op" artists painted sharply defined geometric figures in clear, vibrant colors, starkly different from the flowing, chaotic work of the abstract expressionists. "Pop" artists such as Andy Warhol, Roy Lichtenstein, and Jasper Johns made ironic comments on American materialism and taste with their representations of everyday objects including soup cans, comic strips, and pictures of Marilyn Monroe.

Hallucinogenic drugs also became a part of the counterculture. One prophet of the drug scene was Timothy Leary, a scientific researcher experimenting with LSD at Harvard University. He aggressively asserted that drugs were necessary to free the mind and urged followers to "Tune in, turn on, drop out." Another apostle of life with drugs was Ken Kesey, author of *One Flew Over the Cuckoo's Nest*, who established a commune of "Merry Pranksters." In 1964, the group headed east in a converted school bus painted in psychedelic Day-Glo colors and stocked with enough orange juice and "acid" (LSD) to sustain the Pranksters across the continent.

Drug use was no longer confined to urban subcultures. Soldiers brought experience with drugs back from Vietnam. Taking a "tab" of LSD became part of the coming-of-age ritual for many middle-class college students. Marijuana became phenomenally popular in the 1960s. "Joints" of "grass" were passed around at high school, neighborhood, and college parties as readily as cans of beer had been in the previous generation.

Music became intimately connected with these cultural changes. The rock and roll of the 1950s and the gentle strains of folk music gave way to a new kind of rock that swept the country—and the world.

Rock festivals became popular throughout the 1960s. On an August weekend in 1969, some 400,000 people gathered in a large pasture in upstate New York for the Woodstock rock festival, which featured around-the-clock entertainment and endlessly available marijuana and went off without a hitch. Another festival four months later at Altamont in California was less fortunate. Four people died when audience members clashed with members of Hell's Angels, a motorcycle gang hired to provide security for the Rolling Stones.

The underside of the counterculture was most visible in the Haight-Ashbury section of San Francisco, where runaway "flower children" mingled with "burned-out" drug users and radical activists. For all the spontaneity and exuberance, the counterculture had a darker side.

An Age of Assassination

In 1968, American society seemed to be tearing apart. The so-called "generation gap" caused major rifts between parents and children. Political protest grew increasingly violent. And yet there was still a basic confidence that the democratic process could bring meaningful change. John Kennedy had fallen to an assassin's bullet five years before and the nation had survived that trauma. Then two more killings of highly prominent figures undermined any sense of hope.

Martin Luther King, Jr., was the most visible spokesman for African Americans in the years after 1955. By the mid-1960s, he had broadened his crusade to attack poverty and economic injustice and had also begun to speak out against the war in Vietnam.

King knew he was a target. On April 3, 1968, he referred to threats on his life. "We've got some difficult days ahead," he said. "But it doesn't matter with me now, because I've been to the mountain top ... and I've seen the promised land." The next day, as King stood on the balcony of his motel in Memphis, Tennessee, a bullet from a high-powered rifle ripped through his jaw and killed him.

King's assassination sparked a wave of violence throughout the United States. In a spontaneous outburst of rage, African Americans in 124 cities rioted, setting fires and looting stores. For all Americans, King's death eroded faith in the possibility of nonviolent change.

Several months later, Robert Kennedy likewise lost his life. Bobby had won election to the Senate from New York after his brother's death and was running for the Democratic presidential nomination. In June, he won an important victory in the California primary. That evening, after his victory speech, he too was shot by an assassin. His death likewise shattered hopes for reconciliation or reform.

The Chaotic Election of 1968

The turbulent Democratic convention undermined any hopes the party had for victory. Chicago Mayor Richard Daley was outraged that radicals and hippies were coming to his city to protest and ordered police to clear out demonstrators. They did, in front of television cameras as the country watched. Hubert Humphrey, Johnson's vice president, running for the Democratic nomination after Johnson declined to seek reelection, won a tainted victory.

Humphrey faced former Vice President Richard Nixon. He had failed in his first bid in 1960 and later lost a race for governor of California. Written off by most politicians, he staged a comeback after the Goldwater disaster of 1964, and by 1968, he seemed to have a good shot at the presidency.

Governor George C. Wallace of Alabama, a third-party candidate, exploited social and racial tensions in his campaign. Appealing to northern working-class voters as well as southern whites, Wallace hoped to ride into office on blue-collar resentment of social disorder and liberal aims.

Nixon addressed the same constituency, calling it the "silent majority." Capitalizing on the dismay these Americans felt over campus disruptions and inner-city riots and appealing to latent racism, he promised law and order if elected. He also called the Great Society a costly mistake. Nixon received 43 percent of the popular vote, not quite 1 percent more than Humphrey, with Wallace capturing the rest. But it was enough to give the Republicans a majority in the Electoral College and Nixon the presidency at last.

Continuing Protest

Meanwhile, protests continued. The next year, in October 1969, the Weathermen, a militant fringe group of SDS that took its name from a line in a Bob Dylan

TIMELINE

1960	John F. Kennedy elected president			Kennedy assassinated; Lyndon B. Johnson becomes president
	Sit-ins begin			
1961	Freedom rides		**1964**	Civil Rights Act
1962	Cuban missile crisis		**1965**	Voting Rights Act
1963	Civil rights march on Washington		**1967–1968**	Antiwar demonstrations
			1968	Martin Luther King, Jr., and Robert F. Kennedy assassinated

song—"You don't need a weatherman to know which way the wind blows"—descended on Chicago and rampaged through the streets for four days in an armed battle with police.

Why had the Weathermen launched their attack? "The status quo meant to us war, poverty, inequality, ignorance, famine and disease in most of the world," Bo Burlingham, a participant from Ohio, reflected. "To accept it was to condone and help perpetuate it." The rationale of the Chicago "national action" may have been clear to the participants, but it infuriated citizens around the country.

Conclusion

Political and Social Upheaval

The 1960s were turbulent years. In the first part of the decade, the United States was relatively calm. Liberal Democrats went even further than Franklin Roosevelt and Harry Truman as they pressed for large-scale government intervention to meet the problems that accompanied the modern industrial age. They were inspired by John Kennedy's rhetoric and saw the triumph of their approach in Lyndon Johnson's Great Society, as the nation strengthened its commitment to a capitalist welfare state. Then the Democratic party became impaled on the Vietnam War, and opposition to the conflict created more turbulence than the nation had known since the Civil War.

American society was in a state of upheaval. Young radicals challenged basic assumptions about how the government worked. They railed against social injustice at home, and they protested a foreign policy that they regarded as wrong. Their efforts faltered at first but then succeeded when they seized on the war in Vietnam as a primary focus and began to attack the Cold War policy that led to massive American military involvement. Student leaders soon found hundreds of thousands of followers, and together they finally forced the nation to reconsider its aims. Meanwhile, members of the counterculture promoted their own more fluid values, challenged the patterns of conformity so important in the 1950s, and led millions of other Americans to dress and act differently. The two strands of political activism and countercultural action were independent but intertwined, and they left the nation at the end of the decade very different than it had been before.

Most Americans, like Paul Cowan (introduced at the start of this chapter), embraced the message of John Kennedy and the New Frontier in the early 1960s and endorsed the liberal approach. But over time, they began to question the tenets of liberalism as the economy faltered, as hard economic choices had to be made, and as the country became mired in an unwinnable war in Vietnam. Conservatives deplored the chaos, while disillusioned liberals like Paul Cowan wondered if their approach could ever succeed.

Questions for Review and Reflection

1. How did John F. Kennedy represent the hopes and ideals of Americans in the early 1960s?

2. How successful was Lyndon Johnson's Great Society?

3. What impact did the war in Vietnam have on protest at home?

4. What were the most important changes experienced by the United States in the late 1960s?

5. What was the lasting impact of the protest that rocked America in the 1960s?

Discovering U.S. History Online

John Fitzgerald Kennedy www.ipl.org/ref/POTUS/jfkennedy.html
This site contains basic factual data about Kennedy's election and presidency, speeches, and online biographies.

Lyndon Baines Johnson www.ipl.org/ref/POTUS/lbjohnson.html
This site contains basic factual data about Johnson's election and presidency, speeches, and online biographies.

Martin Luther King, Jr., Papers Project www.stanford.edu/group/king/
This site has links and selected digital documents by and about Martin Luther King, Jr.

The Cuban Missile Crisis www.gwu.edu/~nsarchiv/nsa/cuba_mis_cri/
Declassified intelligence reports, photographs, audio, and essays shed new light on the Cuban missile crisis.

Free Speech Movement: Student Protest—U.C. Berkeley, 1964–65 http://bancroft.berkeley.edu/FSM/
This site describes student protest through oral histories, documents, and a chronology.

The Sixties Project http://lists.village.virginia.edu/sixties
This site has extensive exhibits, documents, and personal narratives from the 1960s.

1969 Woodstock Festival and Concert www.woodstock69.com/index.htm
This site provides pictures and lists of songs from the famous rock festival.

Fiction and Film

Richard Fariña's *Been Down So Long It Looks Like Up to Me* (1966) is a novel about hallucinatory life in the 1960s. Barbara Garson's *MacBird* (1966), a play patterned loosely after *Macbeth*, pokes fun at the overarching ambitions of Lyndon Johnson. Vaughn Meader's two record albums about *The First Family* (1962 and 1963—reissued on CD) provide a fictional glimpse at the Kennedy family. Bao Ninh's *The Sorrow of War* (1991) is a North Vietnamese novel (English version by Frank Palmos, from the original translation by Phan Thanh Hao) about the impact of the war; Tim O'Brien's *Going after Cacciato* (1978) is a novel about Vietnam in which one soldier simply decides to lay down his gun and walk home. O'Brien's *The Things They Carried* (1990) is a collection of intersecting short stories about the war.

Born on the Fourth of July (1989) is a film that tells Ron Kovic's story about being wounded in Vietnam and then returning home; Oliver Stone's film *The Doors* (1991) deals with Jim Morrison and his rock group in the 1960s. *Eyes on the Prize* (1987) is a superb, multipart documentary about the civil rights movement. *The Graduate* (1967) became a cult film as it challenged the values of the 1950s and mocked the priorities of the world in which "plastics" were most important. *JFK* (1991) is Oliver Stone's film about the Kennedy assassination, in which he suggests a conspiracy killed the president. *Malcolm X* (1992) is Spike Lee's movie about the dramatic and outspoken black rights spokesman. *Mississippi Burning* (1988) is a film about three civil rights volunteers killed in Mississippi in 1964. Oliver Stone's movie *Platoon* (1986) deals with field soldiers during the Vietnam War. *Thirteen Days* (2001) is a feature film about the Cuban missile crisis.

Recommended Reading

www.ablongman.com/nash

The Companion Website has a list of recommended readings about Kennedy, Johnson, and the 1960s.

CHAPTER 29

Disorder and Discontent, 1969–1980

CHAPTER OUTLINE

- The Decline of Liberalism
- The Ongoing Effort in Vietnam
- Constitutional Conflict and its Consequences
- The Continuing Quest for Social Reform
- Conclusion: Sorting out the Pieces

American Stories

An Older Woman Returns to School

Ann Clarke—as she chooses to call herself now—always wanted to go to college. But girls from Italian families rarely did when she was growing up. Her mother, a Sicilian immigrant and widow, asked her brother for advice: "Should Antonina go to college?" "What's the point?" he replied. "She's just going to get married."

Life had not been easy for Antonina Rose Rumore. As a child in the 1920s, her Italian-speaking grandmother cared for her while her mother worked to support the family, first in the sweatshops, then as a seamstress. Even as she dreamed about the future, she accommodated her culture's demands for dutiful daughters. Responsive to family needs, Ann finished the high school commercial course in three years. She struggled with ethnic prejudice as a legal secretary on Wall Street but still believed in the American dream and the Puritan work ethic. She was proud of her ability to bring money home to her family.

When World War II began, Rumore wanted to join the WACS. "Better you should be a prostitute," her mother said. She went off to California instead, where she worked at a number of resorts. When she left California, she vowed to return to that land of freedom and opportunity.

After the war, Antonina Rose Rumore married Gerard Clarke, a college man with an English background. Her children would grow up accepted with Anglo-Saxon names. Over the next 15 years, she devoted herself to her family. She was a mother first and foremost, and that took all her time. But she still waited for her own chance. "I had this hunger to learn, this curiosity," she later recalled. By the early 1960s, her three children were all in school. Promising her husband to have dinner on the table every night at six, she enrolled at Pasadena City College. It was not easy, for family still came first, but Ann proved creative in finding time to study. When doing dishes or cleaning house, she memorized lists of dates, historical events, and other material for school. Holidays, however, complicated her efforts to complete assignments. Clarke occasionally felt compelled to give everything up "to make Christmas." Forgetting about a whole semester's work two weeks before finals one year, she sewed nightgowns instead of writing her art history paper.

Her conflict over her studies was intensified by her position as one of the first older women to go back to college. "Sometimes I felt like I wanted to hide in the woodwork," she admitted. Often her teachers were younger than she was. It took four years to complete the two-year program. But she was not yet done, for she really wanted a bachelor's degree. Back she went, this time to California State College at Los Angeles.

As the years passed and the credits piled up, Clarke became an honors student. Her children, now in college themselves, were proud and supportive; dinners became arguments over Faulkner and foreign policy. Even so, Ann still felt caught between her world at home and the world outside. Since she was at the top of her class, graduation should have been a special occasion. But she was only embarrassed when a letter from the school invited her parents to attend the final ceremonies. Clarke could not bring herself to go.

With a college degree in hand, Clarke returned to school for a teaching credential. Receiving her certificate at age 50, she faced the irony of social change. Once denied opportunities, Italians had assimilated into American society. Now she was just another Anglo in Los Angeles, caught in a changing immigration wave; now the city sought Latinos and other minorities to teach in the schools. Jobs in education were scarce, and she was close to retirement age, so she became a substitute teacher in Mexican American areas for the next 10 years, specializing in bilingual education.

Meanwhile, Clarke was troubled by the Vietnam War. "For every boy that died, one of us should lie down," she told fellow workers. She was not an activist, but rather one of the millions of quieter Americans who ultimately helped bring about change. The social adjustments caused by the war affected her. Her son grew long hair and a beard and attended protest rallies. She worried that he would antagonize the ladies in Pasadena. Her daughter came home from college in boots and a leather miniskirt designed to shock. Clarke accepted her children's changes as relatively superficial, confident in their fundamental values; "they were good kids," she knew. She trusted them, even as she worried about them.

Ann Clarke's experience paralleled that of millions of women in the post–World War II years. Caught up in traditional patterns of family life, these women began to recognize their need for something more against a backdrop of continuing political turbulence that sometimes seemed to undermine the nation's stability. They worried about both the global and the domestic consequences of the war in Vietnam and the constitutional issues in the Watergate scandal that threatened the American democratic system and eventually brought President Richard Nixon down. Meanwhile, American women, like blacks, Latinos and Latinas, Native Americans, and members of other groups, struggled to transform the conditions of their lives and the rights they enjoyed within American society. Building on the successes of the past several decades, these diverse groups demanded their own right to equality and equitable treatment in fulfillment of their own American dreams. In the course of their struggle, they changed the nation itself.

This chapter describes the continuing upheaval that shook American society in the 1970s. It shows the ongoing impact of global events as the Nixon administration struggled to find a way of ending the devastating struggle in Vietnam. Its effort to extricate American soldiers eased domestic protest, but then its decision to widen the war with incursions into other parts of Southeast Asia created further chaos in the United States. The chapter chronicles the most serious political scandal in American history, which led the president to resign. It records the growing agitation of environmental and consumer activists as they learned how to make their voices heard. And it describes the ongoing effort to provide liberty and equality in racial, gender, and social relations. While political challenges came from middle-class activists, social complaints came from often marginalized Americans who finally spoke out in an attempt to make the nation live up to its professed values. This chapter highlights the diverse voices that continued to echo throughout the 1970s in a heated debate about the distribution of social, political, and economic power in the United States.

THE DECLINE OF LIBERALISM

After eight years of Democratic rule, many Americans were frustrated with the liberal approach. They questioned the liberal agenda and the government's ability to solve social problems. As the war in Vietnam polarized the country, critics argued that the government was trying to do too much. Capitalizing on the alienation sparked by the war, the Republican administration of Richard Nixon resolved to scale down the commitment to social change. Like Dwight Eisenhower a decade and a half before, Nixon accepted some social programs as necessary but still wanted to trim the federal bureaucracy. Furthermore, he and his political colleagues were determined to pay more attention to the needs of white, middle-class Americans who disliked the social disorder they saw as a consequence of rapid social change and resented the government's perceived favoritism toward the poor and dispossessed.

Richard Nixon and His Team

In and out of office, Nixon was a complex, remote man, who carefully concealed his private self. Born poor, he was determined to be successful and accomplished that aim in the political sphere. Yet there was, one of his aides noted, "a mean side to his nature" that he sought to keep from public view. Physically awkward and humorless, he was most comfortable alone or with a few wealthy friends. Even at work he insulated himself, preferring written contacts to personal ones.

Nixon was keenly aware of the psychology of politics in the electronic age. He believed that "in the modern presidency, concern for image must rank with concern for substance." Thus, he posed in public as the defender of American morality, though in private he was frequently coarse and profane. Earlier in his career he had been labeled "Tricky Dick" for his apparent willingness to do anything to advance his career. In subsequent years, he had tried to create the appearance of a "new Nixon," but to many he still appeared to be a mechanical man, always calculating his next step. As author and columnist Garry Wills pointed out, "He is the least 'authentic' man alive, ... There is one Nixon only, though there seem to be new ones all the time—he will try to be what people want."

The Intense Richard Nixon Speaking to the "silent majority," Nixon promised to reinstitute traditional values and restore law and order. A private man, Nixon tried to insulate himself from the public and present a carefully crafted image through the national media. What impression does Nixon convey in this photograph? How does his body language communicate his intentions? *(Hiroji Kubota/Magnum Photos)*

Philosophically, Nixon disagreed with the liberal faith in federal planning and wanted to decentralize social policy. But he agreed with his liberal predecessors that the presidency ought to be the engine of the political system. Faced with a Congress dominated by Democrats and their allocations of money for programs he opposed, he simply impounded (refused to spend) funds authorized by Congress. Later commentators saw the Nixon years as the height of what they came to call the "imperial presidency."

Nixon's cabinet appointees were white, male Republicans. For the most part, however, the president worked around his cabinet, relying on other White House staff members. In domestic affairs, Arthur Burns, a former chairman of the Council of Economic Advisers, and Daniel Patrick Moynihan, a Harvard professor of government (and a Democrat) were the most important. In foreign affairs, the talented and ambitious Henry A. Kissinger, another Harvard government professor, directed the National Security Council staff and later became secretary of state.

Another tier of White House officials—none with public policy experience but all intensely loyal—insulated the president from the outside world and carried out his commands. Advertising executive H. R. Haldeman, a tireless Nixon campaigner, became chief of staff. Working with Haldeman was lawyer John Ehrlichman. Starting as a legal counselor, he rose to the post of chief domestic adviser. Haldeman and Ehrlichman came to be called the "Berlin Wall" for the way they guarded the president's privacy. John Mitchell was known as "El Supremo" by the staff, as the "Big Enchilada" by Ehrlichman. A tough, successful lawyer, he became a fast friend and managed Nixon's 1968 campaign. In the new administration, he became attorney general and gave the president daily advice.

The Republican Agenda at Home

Although Nixon had come to political maturity in Republican circles, he understood that it was impossible to roll back the government's expanded role altogether. He sought instead to systematize and scale back the programs of the welfare state, "to reverse the flow of power and resources" away from the federal government and channel them to state and local governments, where he believed they belonged.

Despite initial reservations, Nixon proved willing to use economic tools to maintain stability. The economy was faltering when he assumed office. As inflation rose, largely as a result of the Vietnam War, Nixon reduced government spending and pressed the Federal Reserve Board to raise interest rates. Although parts of the conservative plan worked, a mild recession occurred in 1969–1970, and inflation continued to rise. Realizing the political dangers of pursuing this policy, Nixon shifted course, imposed wage and price controls to stop inflation, and used monetary and fiscal policies to stimulate the economy. After his reelection in 1972, he lifted wage and price controls, and inflation resumed.

A number of factors besides the Vietnam War contributed to the troubling price spiral. Eager to court the farm vote, the administration made a large wheat sale to Russia in 1972. With insufficient wheat left for the American market, grain prices shot up. Between 1971 and 1974, farm prices rose 66 percent, as agricultural inflation accompanied industrial inflation.

The most critical factor in disrupting the economy, though, was the Arab oil embargo. American economic expansion had rested on cheap energy, just as American patterns of life had depended on inexpensive gasoline. Turbulence in the Middle East intruded on the economic stability of the Western world.

The Six Day War in 1967 made it clear that the Middle East was still a battleground. Anticipating an attack and launching a preemptive strike, Israeli forces defeated the Egyptian army and seized the West Bank and the Golan Heights, as well as the Arab sector of Jerusalem, which was now reunited with the Israeli part of the city for the first time since 1948.

In the aftermath of the Six Day War, the Organization of Petroleum Exporting Countries (OPEC) slowly raised oil prices in the early 1970s. Another Arab-Israeli war in 1973—the Yom Kippur War—came as Jews celebrated their holiest holiday—the Day of Atonement—and took them by surprise. The war pitted Israel against Egypt, Syria, Iraq, and Jordan. Initially Egypt, in the Sinai peninsula, and Syria, in the Golan Heights, were successful, but then the Israelis fought back. In the end, after several weeks of fighting, cease-fires went into effect, leaving Egypt and Syria with modest gains but the Israelis largely in control.

Meanwhile, in the midst of the fighting, Saudi Arabia, an economic leader of the Arab nations, imposed an embargo on oil shipped to Israel's ally, the United States. Other OPEC nations continued to supply oil but quadrupled their prices. Dependent Americans faced shortages and skyrocketing prices. When the embargo ended in 1974, prices remained high. Even though oil prices around the world increased, the United States was hardest hit because of the huge amounts of oil it used.

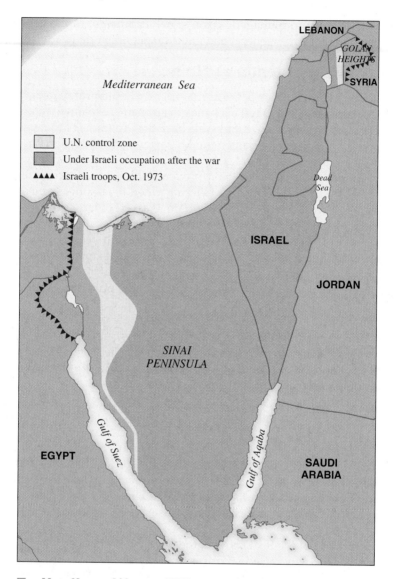

U.N. control zone
Under Israeli occupation after the war
▲▲▲▲ Israeli troops, Oct. 1973

Mediterranean Sea

LEBANON
GOLAN HEIGHTS
SYRIA

Dead Sea

ISRAEL

JORDAN

SINAI PENINSULA

Gulf of Suez

Gulf of Aqaba

EGYPT

SAUDI ARABIA

THE YOM KIPPUR WAR OF 1973 The Arab attack during the Yom Kippur holiday took Israel by surprise. Initially, Egypt and Syria regained some of their lost territory, but then the Israeli counterattack cut back many of the gains. In the end, United Nations troops were stationed on borders of the Sinai Peninsula and Golan Heights to help stabilize those regions. ■ **Reflecting on the Past** How has the map of the Middle East changed in the years after the establishment of the state of Israel in 1948? Who was the victor in the 1973 Yom Kippur War? Why could United Nations forces help maintain stability?

Manufacturers, farmers, homeowners—all were touched by high energy prices. A loaf of bread that had cost 28 cents in the early 1970s jumped to 89 cents, and automobiles cost 72 percent more in 1978 than they had in 1973. The auto industry found itself challenged by smaller Japanese imports such as Hondas and

Toyotas that were far more fuel-efficient. In 1974, inflation reached 11 percent. But then, as higher energy prices encouraged consumers to cut back on their purchases, the nation entered a recession as well. Unemployment climbed to 9 percent for several months in 1975, the highest level since the 1930s.

As economic growth and stability eluded the nation, Nixon also tried to reorganize rapidly expanding and expensive welfare programs. Critics claimed that welfare was inefficient and that benefits discouraged people from seeking work. Nixon faced a political dilemma. He recognized the conservative tide growing in the Sun Belt regions of the country, where many voters wanted cutbacks in what they viewed as excessive government programs. At the same time, he wanted to win over traditionally Democratic blue-collar workers with reassurances that the Republicans would not dismantle the parts of the welfare state on which they relied.

America's Move to the Sunbelt, 1970–1981

Nixon endorsed the Family Assistance Plan, which would have guaranteed a minimum yearly stipend of $1,600 to a family of four, with food stamps providing about $800 more. The program, aiming to cut "welfare cheaters" who took unfair advantage of the system and to encourage recipients to work, was attacked both by liberals, who believed it was too limited, and conservatives, who claimed it tried to do too much, and died in the Senate.

Nixon irritated liberals still further in his effort to restore "law and order." Political protest, rising crime rates, increased drug use, and more permissive attitudes toward sex all created a growing backlash among working-class and many middle-class Americans. Nixon decided to use government power to silence disruption and thereby strengthen his conservative political constituency.

Part of the administration's campaign involved denouncing disruptive elements. Nixon lashed out at demonstrators, but more and more he relied on his vice president to play the part of hatchet man. Spiro Agnew branded opposition elements, students in particular, as "ideological eunuchs" who made up an "effete corps of impudent snobs." At the same time, Nixon and Agnew attacked the communications industry, especially the news media, which Nixon believed voiced the views of the hostile "Eastern establishment."

The strongest part of Nixon's plan to circumscribe the liberal approach was Attorney General Mitchell's campaign against crime, sometimes waged at the expense of individuals' constitutional rights. Mitchell's plan included reshaping the Supreme Court, which had rendered increasingly liberal decisions in the past decade and a half. During his first term, Nixon had the opportunity to name four judges to the Court, and he nominated men who shared his views. His first choice was moderate Warren E. Burger as chief justice, who was confirmed quickly. Other appointments, however, were more partisan and reflected Nixon's aggressively conservative approach. Intent on appealing to white southerners, he first selected Clement Haynesworth of South Carolina, then G. Harold Carswell of Florida. Both men on examination showed such racial biases or limitations that the Senate refused to confirm them. Nixon then appointed Harry Blackmun, Lewis F. Powell, Jr., and William Rehnquist, all able and qualified, and all inclined to tilt the Court in a more conservative direction.

Not surprisingly, the Court gradually shifted to the right. It narrowed defendants' rights in an attempt to ease the burden of the prosecution in its cases and slowed the liberalizing of pornography laws. It supported Nixon's assault on the

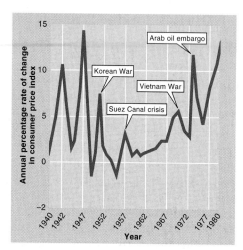

RATE OF INFLATION,
1940–1980 Inflation often accompanied military spending in the postwar years. In the early 1970s, the Arab oil embargo contributed to an even higher rate. Why have international crises often led to inflation? *(Source: U.S. Bureau of the Census.)*

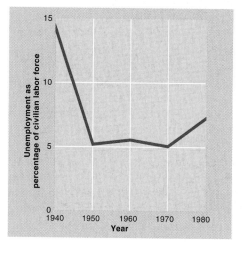

UNEMPLOYMENT RATE,
1940–1980 The unemployment rate fell dramatically during World War II, remained relatively constant from 1950 to 1969, and rose as inflation increased in the 1970s. How were unemployment and inflation related? *(Source: U.S. Bureau of Labor Statistics.)*

DOCUMENT

Roe v. Wade
(January 22,
1973)

media by ruling that journalists did not have the right to refuse to answer questions for a grand jury, even if they had promised sources confidentiality. On other questions, however, the Court did not always act as the president had hoped. In the controversial 1973 *Roe v. Wade* decision, the Court legalized abortion, stating that women's rights included the right to control their own bodies.

Continuing Confrontations in Civil Rights

Nixon was less sympathetic to the cause of civil rights than his predecessors. In 1968, the Republicans won only 12 percent of the black vote, leading Nixon to employ the "southern strategy," which concluded that any effort to woo the black electorate would endanger his attempt to obtain white southern support.

From the start, the Nixon administration sought to scale back the federal commitment to civil rights. It first moved to reduce appropriations for fair-housing

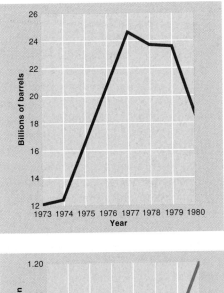

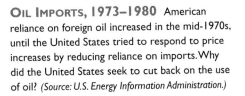

OIL IMPORTS, 1973–1980 American reliance on foreign oil increased in the mid-1970s, until the United States tried to respond to price increases by reducing reliance on imports. Why did the United States seek to cut back on the use of oil? *(Source: U.S. Energy Information Administration.)*

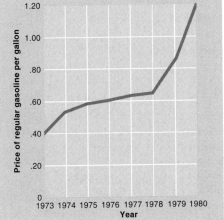

GASOLINE PRICES, 1973–1980 Gasoline prices rose steadily in the years following the Arab oil embargo and affected the entire American economy. Why did gasoline prices rise? *(Source: U.S. Energy Information Administration.)*

enforcement, then tried to block an extension of the Voting Rights Act of 1965. Although Congress approved the extension, the administration's position on racial issues was clear. When South Carolina Senator Strom Thurmond and others tried to suspend federal school desegregation guidelines, the Justice Department lent support by urging a delay in meeting desegregation deadlines in 33 of Mississippi's school districts. While a unanimous Supreme Court rebuffed the effort, the president disagreed publicly with the decision.

Nixon also faced the growing controversy over busing as a means of desegregation, a highly charged issue in the 1970s. Transporting students from one area to another to attend school was nothing new. By 1970, over 18 million students, almost 40 percent of those in the United States, rode buses to school. Yet when busing became tangled with the question of integration, it inflamed passions.

In the South, before the Supreme Court endorsed integration, busing had long been used to maintain segregated schools. Now, however, busing was a means of breaking down racial barriers. In 1971, the Supreme Court ruled that district courts had broad authority to order the desegregation of school systems—by busing, if necessary.

Nixon proposed a moratorium or even a restriction on busing and went on television to denounce it. Although Congress did not accede to his request, southerners knew where the president stood. So did northerners, for the issue became a national one. Many of the nation's largest northern cities had school segregation as rigid as in the South, largely because of residential patterns. This segregation was called *de facto* to differentiate it from the *de jure*, or legal, segregation that had existed in the South. Court decisions now ordered many northern cities to end such *de facto* segregation and to desegregate their schools.

For many younger students, attendance at different elementary schools went smoothly. Reassigned high school students were less fortunate. A white boycott at South Boston High in Massachusetts cut attendance from the anticipated 1,500 to fewer than 100 on the first day. Buses bringing in black students were stoned, and some children were injured. White, working-class South Bostonians felt that they were being asked to carry the burden of middle-class liberals' racial views. Some white families either enrolled their children in private schools or fled the city.

The Republicans managed to slow down the school desegregation movement. Nixon openly catered to his conservative constituents and demonstrated he was on their side. His successor, Gerald Ford, never came out squarely against civil rights, but his lukewarm approach to desegregation demonstrated a further weakening of the federal commitment.

Integration at the postsecondary level came easier. Federal affirmative action guidelines seeking to provide opportunities for groups discriminated against in the past brought more blacks into colleges and universities. Black enrollment in colleges reached 9.3 percent of the college population in 1976. As blacks struggled on the educational and occupational fronts, however, some whites protested that gains came at their expense and amounted to "reverse discrimination." In 1973 and 1974, for example, Allan Bakke, a white, applied to the medical school at the University of California at Davis. Twice rejected, he sued on the grounds that a racial quota reserving 16 of 100 places for minority-group applicants was a form of reverse discrimination that violated the Civil Rights Act of 1964. In 1978, the Supreme Court ordered Bakke's admission to the medical school, while allowing "consideration" of race in admissions policies, though not quotas.

The civil rights movement underscored the democratic values on which the nation was based, but the gap between rhetoric and reality remained. In an era when industrial and farming employment shrank and rents rose at a highly inflationary rate, most black families remained poor. After early optimism in the years when the movement made its greatest strides, black Americans and sympathetic whites were troubled by the wavering national commitment to reform in the 1970s.

THE ONGOING EFFORT IN VIETNAM

The war in Vietnam continued into the 1970s. When Nixon assumed office in 1969, he understood the need to heal the rifts that the struggle created in American society. During the campaign, he had spoken about a plan to end involvement in the war without specifying details. Once in office, he embarked on an effort to bring American troops home as a way of defusing opposition to the struggle. Unfortunately, his decision to try to avoid losing the war led to even further chaos at home.

Vietnamization—Bringing the Soldiers Home

Nixon gave top priority to extricating the United States from Vietnam while still seeking a way to win the war. To that end, he announced the Nixon Doctrine, which asserted that the United States would aid friends and allies but would not undertake the full burden of troop defense. The policy of Vietnamization entailed removing American forces and replacing them with Vietnamese troops. Between 1968 and 1972, American troop strength dropped from 543,000 to 39,000. Yet as the transition occurred, the South Vietnamese steadily lost ground to the Viet Cong. At the same time, Americans launched ferocious air attacks on North Vietnam. Nixon used the bombing campaign to portray himself to the North Vietnamese as a madman with his hand on the nuclear trigger, thinking that fear of annihilation would bring the enemy to the peace table.

DOCUMENT
Testimony by
William Crandell
at the Winter
Soldier
Investigation
(1971)

War protests multiplied in 1969 and 1970. In November 1969, as a massive protest demonstration took place in Washington, D.C., stories surfaced about a horrifying massacre of civilians in My Lai, a small village in South Vietnam, the year before. An American infantry company was helicoptered in to clear out the Viet Cong. Instead of troops, it found women, children, and old men. Perhaps concerned with the sometimes fuzzy distinction between combatants and civilians in a guerrilla war, the American forces lost control and mowed down hundreds of civilians in cold blood. Stories of the massacre at My Lai underscored the senseless violence associated with the war and increased pressure for the United States to get out.

VIDEO
The Vietnam War

Widening the War

As much as Nixon wanted to defuse opposition to the war, he was determined not to lose the struggle either. Realizing that the Vietnamese relied on supplies funneled through Cambodia, Nixon announced in mid-1970 that American and Vietnamese troops were invading that country to clear out Communist enclaves. Renewed demonstrations on college campuses had tragic results. Two days after the president announced his move, students at Kent State University in Ohio protested by setting the ROTC building on fire and watched it burn to the ground.

Governor James Rhodes of Ohio ordered the National Guard to the university. Tension grew, and finally the situation exploded as the Guardsmen fired without provocation on the students. When the shooting stopped, four students lay dead, nine wounded. Two of the dead had been demonstrators, who were more than 250 feet away when shot. The other two were innocent bystanders, almost 400 feet from the troops.

IMAGE
Kent State
Demonstrations

Students around the country, as well as other Americans, were outraged by the attack. Many were equally disturbed about a similar attack at Jackson State

University in Mississippi, where a few students taunted police and National Guardsmen. Two people were killed, more wounded. The dead, however, were black students at a black institution, and white America paid less attention to this attack.

In 1971, the Vietnam War made major headlines once more when the *New York Times* began publishing the Pentagon Papers, a secret Department of Defense account of American involvement that gave Americans a firsthand look at the fabrications and faulty assumptions that had guided the war. Even though the study stopped with the Johnson years, the Nixon administration tried, without success, to block publication.

The End of the War and Détente

Vietnam remained a political football as Nixon ran for reelection in 1972, and the bombing continued even as peace negotiations got under way. Although a cease-fire was finally achieved in 1973, the conflict lingered on into the spring of 1975. When at last the North Vietnamese consolidated their control over the entire country, Gerald Ford, Nixon's successor as president, called for another $1 billion in aid, but Congress refused.

The long conflict had enormous consequences. Disillusionment with the war undermined assumptions about America's role in world affairs. In the longest war in its history, the United States lost almost 58,000 men, with far more wounded or maimed. Blacks and Latinos suffered more than whites, since they were disproportionately represented in combat units. In 1965, 24 percent of all soldiers killed in Vietnam were African American—a figure far higher than their percentage of the population as a whole. Financially, the nation spent over $150 billion on the unsuccessful war. Domestic reform slowed, then stopped. Cynicism about the government increased, and American society was deeply divided.

If the Republicans' Vietnam policy was a questionable success, accomplishments were impressive in other areas. Nixon, the consummate Red-baiter of the past, dealt imaginatively and successfully with the major Communist powers, reversing the direction of American policy since World War II.

Nixon's most dramatic step was establishing better relations with the People's Republic of China. In the two decades since Mao Zedong's victory in the Chinese revolution in 1949, the United States had refused to recognize the Communist government on the mainland, insisting that Jiang Jieshi's regime on Taiwan was the rightful government. In 1971, with an eye on the upcoming elections, Nixon began softening his administration's rigid stance by announcing that he intended to visit China the following year. He suspected that he could use Chinese friendship as a bargaining chip when he dealt with the Soviet Union. He acknowledged what most nations already knew: Communism was not monolithic. He also recognized that the press and television coverage of a dramatic trip could boost his image.

Nixon went to China in February 1972. He met with Chinese leaders Mao Zedong and Zhou Enlai (Chou En-lai), talked about international problems, exchanged toasts, and saw the Great Wall and other major sights. Wherever he went, American television cameras followed, helping introduce to the American public a nation about which it knew little. Though formal diplomatic relations were not yet restored, détente between the two countries had begun.

Seeking to play one Communist state against the other, Nixon also visited Russia, where he was likewise warmly welcomed. At a cordial summit meeting, the president and Soviet premier Leonid Brezhnev signed the first Strategic Arms Limitation Treaty (SALT I), which included a five-year agreement setting ceilings on intercontinental and other ballistic missiles, and an antiballistic missile treaty restricting the number of systems each nation could develop and deploy. At the same time, the two nations agreed to cooperate in space and to ease long-standing restrictions on trade. Business applauded the new approach, and most Americans approved of détente.

Nixon also recognized the need to promote peace in the Middle East. Secretary of State Henry Kissinger engaged in shuttle diplomacy—moving from one nation to another—in an effort that helped arrange a cease-fire in the Yom Kippur War. In the aftermath of the struggle, recognizing the need for oil, Nixon and Kissinger worked to establish better relations with the Arab nations, even if they intruded on American support of Israel.

When Gerald Ford assumed office, he followed the policies begun under Nixon. He continued the strategic arms limitation talks that provided hope for eventual nuclear disarmament and culminated in the even more comprehensive SALT II agreement, signed but never ratified during Jimmy Carter's presidency.

CONSTITUTIONAL CONFLICT AND ITS CONSEQUENCES

As he dealt with chaos at home and abroad, Nixon worried about maintaining his political base. In his quest for reelection, he went too far and embroiled himself in a devastating political scandal that undermined his administration.

The Watergate Affair

Faced with a solidly Democratic Congress, the Nixon administration found many of its legislative initiatives blocked. Nixon was determined to end the stalemate by winning a second term and sweeping Republican majorities into both houses of Congress in 1972.

Nixon's reelection campaign was even better organized than the effort four years earlier. His fiercely loyal aides were prepared to do anything to win. Special counsel Charles W. Colson described himself as a "flag-waving, kick-'em-in-the-nuts, anti-press, anti-liberal Nixon fanatic." White House counsel John Dean defined his task as finding a way to "use the available federal machinery to screw our political enemies." One way was by authorizing tax audits of political opponents. Active in carrying out commands were E. Howard Hunt, a former CIA agent and a specialist in "dirty tricks," and G. Gordon Liddy, a onetime member of the FBI, who prided himself on his willingness to do anything without flinching.

How Others See US

Nations around the world opposed the American intervention in Vietnam. As the war dragged on and more and more people died, posters highlighted the growing anger at American policy. The French poster below calls for "Peace in Vietnam" and demands an end to American aggression while highlighting the right of the Vietnamese people to choose their own destiny. The German poster asks for "Solidarity with Vietnam" and declares that the members of the community organization of Querfurt in Germany have donated money for the heroically fighting Vietnamese people.

- *Why did other nations oppose American involvement in Vietnam?*
- *Who was responsible for the French poster, and what does that tell you about the dynamics of the struggle?*
- *What kind of tone do you detect in the two posters you see here?*

Source: Museum of War Atrocities, Ho Chi Minh City, Vietnam.

The Committee to Re-elect the President (CREEP), headed by John Mitchell, who resigned as attorney general, launched a massive fund-raising drive, aimed at collecting as much money as it could before a new campaign-finance law took effect. That money could be used for any purpose, including payments for the performance of dirty tricks aimed at disrupting the opposition's campaign. Other funds financed an intelligence branch within CREEP.

Early in 1972, Liddy and his lieutenants proposed an elaborate scheme to wiretap the phones of various Democrats and to disrupt their nominating convention. Twice Mitchell refused to go along, arguing that the proposal was too risky and expensive. Finally, he approved a modified version of the illegal plan to tap the phones of the Democratic National Committee at its headquarters in the Watergate apartment complex in Washington, D.C.

The wiretapping attempt took place on the evening of June 16, 1972, and ended with the arrest of those involved. Nixon's aides played down the matter and used federal resources to head off any investigation. When the FBI traced the money carried by the burglars to CREEP, the president authorized the CIA to call off the FBI on the grounds that national security was at stake. Though not involved in the planning of the break-in, the president was now party to the cover-up. In the succeeding months, he authorized payment of hush money to silence the burglars. Members of the administration, including Mitchell, perjured themselves in court to shield the top officials who were involved.

Nixon trounced Democrat George McGovern in the election of 1972, receiving 61 percent of the popular vote. In a clear indication of the collapse of the Democratic coalition, 70 percent of southern voters cast their ballots for Nixon. The president, however, failed to gain the congressional majorities he sought.

The Watergate burglars pleaded guilty and were sentenced to jail, but the case refused to die. The evidence indicated that others had played a part, and the investigation of two zealous reporters, Bob Woodward and Carl Bernstein of the *Washington Post*, uncovered many of those involved.

The Senate Select Committee on Presidential Campaign Activities undertook its own investigation, and one of the convicted burglars testified that the White House had been involved in the episode. Newspaper stories generated further leads, and the Senate hearings in turn provided new material for the press. Faced with rumors that the White House was actively involved, Nixon decided to release Haldeman and Ehrlichman to save his own neck, claiming on nationwide television, "there can be no whitewash at the White House."

VIDEO

Richard Nixon, "I am not a crook"

In May 1973, the Senate committee began televised public hearings, reminiscent of the McCarthy hearings of the 1950s. As millions of Americans watched, the drama built. John Dean, seeking to save himself, testified that Nixon knew about the cover-up, and other staffers revealed a host of illegal activities undertaken at the White House: money had been paid to the burglars to silence them; State Department documents had been forged to smear a previous administration; wiretaps had been used to prevent top-level leaks. The most electrifying moment was the disclosure that the president had installed a secret taping system in his office that recorded all conversations. Tapes could verify or disprove the growing rumors that Nixon was involved in the cover-up.

To show his own honesty, Nixon appointed Harvard law professor Archibald Cox as a special prosecutor in the Department of Justice. But when Cox tried to gain access to the tapes, Nixon resisted and finally fired him. Nixon's own popularity

DOONESBURY   by Garry Trudeau

A Cartoonist Comments on Watergate Although Nixon steadfastly denied his complicity in the Watergate affair, his tape recordings of White House conversations told a different story. In this classic *Doonesbury* cartoon from September 17, 1973, Garry Trudeau notes Nixon's efforts to head off the investigation. What do you think the cartoonist is trying to say here? *(Doonesbury © 1973 G. B. Trudeau. Reprinted with permission of Universal Press Syndicate. All rights reserved.)*

plummeted, and even the appointment of another special prosecutor, Leon Jaworski, did not help. More and more Americans now believed that the president had played at least some part in the cover-up and should take responsibility for his acts. *Time* magazine ran an editorial headlined "The President Should Resign," and Congress considered impeachment.

DOCUMENT

House Judiciary Committee's Conclusion on Impeachment (1972)

The first steps, in accordance with constitutional mandate, took place in the House of Representatives. The House Judiciary Committee, made up of 21 Democrats and 17 Republicans, began to debate the impeachment case in late July 1974. By sizable tallies, it voted to impeach the president on the grounds of obstruction of justice, abuse of power, and refusal to obey a congressional subpoena to turn over his tapes. The full House of Representatives still had to vote, and the Senate would have to preside over a trial before removal could take place. But for Nixon, the handwriting was on the wall.

IMAGE

Nixon Releases Transcripts of Oval Office Tapes

After a brief delay, on August 5, Nixon obeyed a Supreme Court ruling and released the tapes. Despite a suspicious 18½-minute silence, they contained the "smoking gun"—clear evidence of his complicity in the cover-up. His ultimate resignation became but a matter of time. Four days later, on August 9, 1974, Nixon became the first American president ever to resign.

The Watergate affair seemed disturbing evidence that the appropriate balance of power in the federal government had disappeared. Many began to question the centralization of power in the American political system. Others simply lost faith in the presidency altogether. A 1974 survey showed that trust in the presidency had declined by 50 percent in a two-year period. Coming on the heels of Lyndon Johnson's lying to the American people about involvement in Vietnam, the Watergate affair contributed to the cumulative disillusionment with politics in Washington and to the steady decrease in political participation. Barely half of those eligible to vote bothered to go to the polls in the presidential elections of 1976, 1980, and 1984.

A President by Appointment Gerald Ford, a genial man, sought to re-establish confidence in the government after succeeding Nixon as president. Far different from his predecessor, he served just over two years, as his bid for election to the presidency in 1976 ended in defeat. *(Corbis)*

Gerald Ford: Caretaker President

Gerald Ford succeeded Nixon as president. An unpretentious, middle-American Republican who believed in traditional virtues, Ford had been appointed vice president in 1973 when Spiro Agnew resigned in disgrace for accepting bribes. Although he was an able congressman, there was significant doubt that Ford was qualified to be chief executive. The new president acknowledged his own limitations, declaring, "I am a Ford, not a Lincoln."

More important than his limitations were his views about public policy. In the House of Representatives, Ford had opposed federal aid to education, the poverty program, and mass transit. He had voted for civil rights measures only when weaker substitutes he had favored had gone down to defeat. Like his predecessor, he was determined to stop the liberal advances promoted by the Democrats in the 1960s.

Ford faced a daunting task. After Watergate, Americans wondered whether any politician could be trusted to guide public affairs. Ford worked quickly to restore that trust in the presidency. He emphasized conciliation and compromise, and he promised to cooperate both with Congress and with American citizens. The nation responded gratefully. *Time* magazine pointed to a "mood of good feeling and even exhilaration in Washington that the city had not experienced for many years."

The new feeling did not last long. Ford weakened his base of support by pardoning Richard Nixon barely a month after his resignation. Ford's decidedly conservative bent in domestic policy often threw him into confrontation with a

Democratic Congress. Economic problems proved most pressing in 1974, as inflation, fueled by oil price increases, hit 11 percent, unemployment reached 6.6 percent at the end of the year, and GNP declined. Nixon, preoccupied with the Watergate crisis, had been unable to curb these problems. Not since Franklin Roosevelt took office in the depths of the Great Depression had a new president faced economic difficulties so severe.

Like Herbert Hoover 45 years before, the conservative Ford hoped to restore confidence and persuade the public that conditions would improve with patience and goodwill. But his campaign to cajole Americans to "Whip Inflation Now" voluntarily failed dismally. At last convinced of the need for strong government action, the administration introduced a tight-money policy as a means of curbing inflation. It led to the most severe recession since the Great Depression, with unemployment peaking at 9 percent in early 1975. In response, Congress pushed for an antirecession spending program. Recognizing political reality, Ford endorsed a multibillion-dollar tax cut coupled with higher unemployment benefits. The economy made a modest recovery, although inflation and unemployment remained high, and federal budget deficits soared.

VIDEO

Gerald Ford
Presidential
Campaign Ad:
Feeling Good
About America

The Carter Interlude

In the election of 1976, the nation's bicentennial year, Ford faced Jimmy Carter, former governor of Georgia. Carter, appealing to voters distrustful of political leadership, portrayed himself as an outsider. Assisted by public relations experts, he effectively utilized the media, especially television, which allowed him to bypass party machines and establish a direct electronic relationship with voters.

In the election, most elements of the old Democratic coalition came together once again, as the Democrats profited from the fallout of the Watergate affair. Carter won a 50 to 48 percent majority of the popular vote and a 297 to 240 tally in the Electoral College. He did well with members of the working class, African Americans, and Catholics. He won most of the South, heartening to the Democrats after Nixon's gains there. Racial voting differences continued, however, as Carter attracted less than half of all white voters but an overwhelming majority of black voters.

Carter stood in stark contrast to his recent predecessors. Rooted in the rural South, he was a peanut farmer who shared the values of the region. He was also a graduate of the Naval Academy, trained as a manager and an engineer. A modest man, he was uncomfortable with the pomp and incessant political activity in Washington. He hoped to take a more restrained approach to the presidency and thereby defuse its imperial stamp.

Initially, voters saw Carter as a reform Democrat committed to his party's goals, but he was hardly the old-line liberal some had hoped for. Though he called himself a populist, his political philosophy and priorities were never clear. Critics charged that he had no legislative strategy. Rather, they said with some truth, he responded to problems in a haphazard way and failed to provide firm direction. His status as an outsider led him to ignore traditional political channels. He also seemed to become mired in detail and to lose sight of larger issues.

In economic affairs, Carter gave liberals some hope at first as he accepted deficit spending. But when record deficits brought inflation to about 10 percent a year, Carter slowed down the economy by reducing spending and cutting the deficit slightly. These budget cuts fell largely on social programs and distanced Carter from reform-minded Democrats who had supported him before. Yet even that effort to arrest growing deficits was not enough. When the budget released in early 1980 still showed high spending levels, the financial community reacted strongly. Bond prices fell, and interest rates rose dramatically.

Similarly, Carter disappointed liberals by failing to construct an effective energy policy. OPEC's increase of oil prices led many Americans to resent their dependence on foreign oil and to clamor for energy self-sufficiency. Carter responded in April 1977 with a comprehensive energy program, but critics ridiculed the plan. Never an effective leader in working with the legislative branch, Carter watched his proposals bog down in Congress for 26 months. Eventually, the program committed the nation to move from oil dependence to reliance on coal, possibly even on sun and wind, and established a new synthetic-fuel corporation. Nuclear power, another alternative, seemed less attractive as costs rose and accidents occurred.

Carter further upset liberals by beginning deregulation—the removal of government controls in economic life. Arguing that certain restrictions established over the past century stifled competition and increased consumer costs, he supported decontrol of oil and natural gas prices to spur production. He also deregulated the railroad, trucking, and airline industries.

One of the high points in Carter's administration came with his involvement in the ever-turbulent Middle East. In the aftermath of the Yom Kippur War, Egyptian leader Anwar al-Sadat was disappointed in the ultimate failure of the struggle and flew to Israel in a gesture of peace. At that point, Carter intervened and invited Sadat and Israeli leader Menachem Begin to come to the United States to work out an accord in September 1978 that led to a formal peace treaty the next March. Egypt recognized Israel—and the Israeli right to exist—for the first time, and the Israelis gave up part of the occupied Sinai Peninsula. The United States promised substantial military aid to both parties, which led to a closer relationship with Egypt that has continued ever since. As the United States superseded the Soviet Union as an ally of Egypt, the Russians countered by arming the radical Palestine Liberation Organization (PLO) and helped encourage leader Yasir Arafat in the ongoing guerrilla war.

Carter puzzled people overseas by his passionate commitment to human rights. It became a hallmark of his administration, especially when he ordered the United States to pull out of the Olympics in Moscow in 1980 in protest of a Soviet invasion of neighboring Afghanistan. Some Americans wondered how this commitment squared with the long-standing American approach of supporting dictators and overlooking human rights abuses in countries whose support the United States wanted in the Cold War.

Liberals were disappointed as the 1970s ended. Their hopes for a stronger commitment to a welfare state had been dashed, and conservatives had the upper hand. Despite a tenuous Democratic hold on the presidency at the end of the decade, liberalism was in trouble. And the turbulence that had marked the beginning of the decade had not disappeared.

Celebrating a Triumph at Camp David One of Jimmy Carter's greatest achievements was taking the first steps toward peace in the Middle East. Here he celebrates the Camp David Agreement of September 1978, in which Anwar al-Sadat of Egypt, on the left, and Menachem Begin, on the right, shook hands and agreed to work together. What do the faces of these three leaders convey about the moment captured in this photograph? *(Stock Photo)*

THE CONTINUING QUEST FOR SOCIAL REFORM

A struggle for social reform was one more factor contributing to the turbulence of the 1970s. The black struggle for equality in the 1950s and 1960s helped spark a women's movement that soon developed a life of its own. This struggle, like the struggles of Latinos and Native Americans, employed the confrontational approach and the insistent vocabulary of the civil rights movement to create pressure for change. In time, other groups appropriated the same strategies and kept reform efforts alive. While these movements had preexisting roots and usually began in the 1960s, they came of age in the 1970s, and in these years achieved their greatest gains.

Attacking the Feminine Mystique

Although the civil rights movement helped spark the women's movement, broad social changes provided the preconditions. During the 1950s and 1960s, increasing numbers of married women entered the labor force (see Chapter 26). Equally important, many more young women were attending college. By 1970, women earned 41 percent of all B.A. degrees awarded, in comparison with only 25 percent in 1950. These educated young women held high hopes for themselves, even

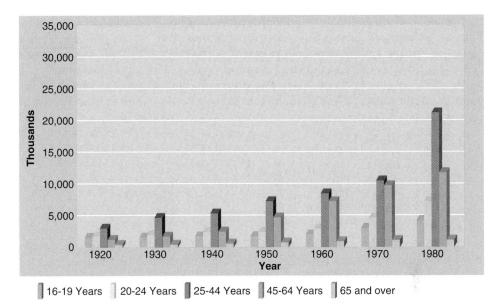

16-19 Years ▮ 20-24 Years ▮ 25-44 Years ▮ 45-64 Years ▮ 65 and over

WOMEN IN THE WORKFORCE, 1920–1980 This graph shows the dramatic increase in the number of women in the workforce over the years. Which age cohort showed the largest gain in the 1970s? Why? *(Source: U.S. Bureau of the Census.)*

if they still earned substantially less than men and were often treated as second-class citizens.

The women's movement depended on reform legislation. Title VII of the 1964 Civil Rights bill, as originally drafted, prohibited discrimination on the grounds of race. During legislative debate, conservatives opposed to black civil rights seized on an amendment to include discrimination on the basis of gender, in the hope of defeating the entire bill. The amendment passed, and then the full measure was approved, giving women a legal tool for attacking discrimination.

Women's organizations played an important role in bringing about change in the 1970s. In 1966, a group of 28 professional women, including author Betty Friedan, established the National Organization for Women (NOW) to work toward not only fair pay and equal opportunity but a new, more egalitarian form of marriage. By 1967, some 1,000 women had joined the organization, and four years later, its membership reached 15,000.

To radical feminists who had come up through the civil rights movement, NOW's agenda failed to confront adequately the problem of gender discrimination. Jo Freeman, a radical activist, observed, "Women's liberation does not mean equality with men ... [because] equality in an unjust society is meaningless." These feminists tried, through the technique of consciousness raising, to help women understand the extent of their oppression and to analyze their experience as a political phenomenon. They wanted to demonstrate, in their phrase, that the personal was political.

The radicals gained mass media attention at the Miss America pageant in Atlantic City, New Jersey, in September 1968. On the boardwalk, a hundred women

DOCUMENT

Shirley Chisholm, Equal Rights for Women (May 21, 1969)

nominated a sheep as their candidate for Miss America. They also set up a "free-dom trash can" and placed in it "instruments of torture": bras, high heels, and copies of *Playboy* and *Cosmopolitan* magazines. In the pageant hall, they chanted "Freedom for Women" and unfurled banners reading "Women's Liberation."

In 1971, singer-songwriter Helen Reddy expressed the energy of the movement in a song called "I Am Woman" that reflected a new militancy and sense of self-confidence among women:

> I am woman, hear me roar
> In numbers too big to ignore
> And I know too much to go back and pretend
> 'Cause I've heard it all before
> And I've been down there on the floor,
> No one's ever gonna keep me down again.

Real changes were under way. A 1970 survey of first-year college students showed that men interested in such fields as business, medicine, engineering, and law outnumbered women eight to one; by 1975, the ratio had dropped to three to one. Women gained access to the military academies and entered senior officer ranks, although they were still restricted from combat command ranks. According to the Census Bureau, 45 percent of mothers with preschool children held jobs outside the home in 1980. That figure was four times greater than it had been 30 years before.

Legal changes brought women more benefits and opportunities. Title IX of the Education Amendments of 1972 barred gender bias in federally assisted educational activities and programs, made easier the admission of women to colleges, and required schools to fund intercollegiate sports teams for women as well as men. By 1980, fully 30 percent of the participants in intercollegiate sports were women, compared with 15 percent before Title IX became law.

A flurry of publications spread the principles of the women's movement. In 1972, journalist Gloria Steinem and several other women founded a new magazine, *Ms.*, which attracted 200,000 subscribers by the next year. *Our Bodies, Ourselves*, a handbook published by a women's health collective, encouraged women to understand and control their bodies; it sold 850,000 copies between 1971 and 1976. Unlike older women's magazines, these publications dealt with abortion, employment, and discrimination.

Women both in and out of NOW worked for congressional passage, then ratification, of the Equal Rights Amendment (ERA) to the Constitution. Passed by Congress in 1972, with ratification seemingly assured, it stated simply, "Equality of rights under the law shall not be denied or abridged by the United States or by any State on account of sex."

Feminism was not monolithic. More radical feminists insisted that traditional gender and family roles would have to be discarded to end social exploitation. Socialist feminists claimed that capitalist society itself was responsible for women's plight. Only through revolution could women be free. Black women frequently viewed the women's movement with ambivalence. Some became feminists, but others felt that the struggle for racial equality took precedence, and they were reluctant to divert energy and attention from it. Members of NOW and similar organizations, they claimed, "suffered little more than dishpan hands" and were hardly confronting the most important issues when they burned their bras and insisted on using the title Ms. rather than Mrs. or Miss.

Not all women were feminists. Many felt the women's movement was contemptuous of women who stayed at home to perform traditional tasks. Marabel Morgan was one who still insisted that the woman had a place at home by her husband's side. In her book *The Total Woman* (1973), she counseled others to follow the 4A approach: accept, admire, adapt, appreciate. As of 1975, some 500,000 copies of the hardcover volume had been sold.

In politics, Phyllis Schlafly headed a nationwide campaign to block ratification of the ERA. The amendment, she predicted, would lead to the establishment of coed bathrooms, the elimination of alimony, and the legalization of homosexual marriage.

Schlafly and her allies had their way. Within a few years after passage of the ERA, 35 states had agreed to the measure, but then the momentum disappeared. Even with an extension in the deadline granted in 1979, the amendment could not win support of the necessary 38 states. By mid-1982, the ERA was dead.

Despite the counterattacks, the women's movement flourished in the late 1960s and 1970s. In the tenth anniversary issue of *Ms.* magazine in 1982, Gloria Steinem noted the differences a decade had made. "Ten years ago," she said, "we were trained to marry a doctor, not be one."

Latino Mobilization

Latinos, like women, profited from the example of blacks in their struggle for equality that came of age in the 1970s. Long denied equal access to the American dream, they became more vocal and confrontational as their numbers increased dramatically in the postwar years. In 1970, some 9 million residents of the United States declared they were of Spanish origin; in 1980, the figure was 14.6 million. But median household income remained less than three-fourths that of Anglos, and inferior education and political weakness reinforced social and cultural separation. Latinos included Puerto Ricans in the Northeast, Cubans in Florida, and Chicanos—Mexican Americans—in the West and Southwest. Though "Hispanic" still remained an acceptable term, "Latino" was now more commonly used. Chicanos took the lead in the protest struggle, though all groups developed a heightened sense of solidarity as they began to assert their own rights.

In the 1960s and 1970s, Mexican Americans became more active politically, winning several seats in Congress. More important than political representation was direct action, which triumphed in the 1970s. César Chávez, founder of the United Farm Workers, showed the way by organizing the migrant farmworkers of the West, among the most exploited and ignored laboring people in the country. Chávez concentrated on migrant Mexican field hands, who worked long hours for meager pay. By 1965, his organization had recruited 1,700 people and attracted volunteer help.

Recovering the Past

One way to recover the past is through music. Popular songs not only provide insight into attitudes and beliefs but also quickly convey the mood and feelings of an era. Through their lyrics, songwriters express the hopes and fears of a people and the emotional tone of an age. The decline of pop music and the rise of rock and roll in the 1950s tell historians a great deal about the mood of that period. Similarly, the popularity of both folk music and rock in the 1960s provides another way of following social change in that turbulent decade.

The music of the 1960s and 1970s moved beyond the syrupy ballads of the early 1950s and the rock and roll movement that Elvis Presley helped launch in the middle of the decade. As the United States confronted the challenges of the counterculture and the crosscurrents of political and social reform, new kinds of music began to be played.

Folk music took off at the start of the period. Building on a tradition launched by Woody Guthrie, Pete Seeger, and the Weavers, Joan Baez was one of the first folk singers to become popular. Accompanying herself on a guitar, she soon overwhelmed audiences with her crystal-clear voice. She sang ballads, laments, and spirituals such as "We Shall Overcome" and became caught up in the protest activities of the period.

Equally active was Bob Dylan, who grew up playing rock and roll in high school, then folk music in college at the University of Minnesota. Disheveled and gravelly voiced, he wrote remarkable songs including "Blowin' in the Wind" that were soon sung by other artists such as Peter, Paul, and Mary as well. His song "The Times They Are A-Changin'" (excerpted here) captured the inexorable force of the student protest movement best of all.

The Times They Are A-Changin'
BY BOB DYLAN
Come mothers and fathers
Throughout the land
And don't criticize
What you can't understand
Your sons and your daughters

Are beyond your command
Your old road is
Rapidly agin'.
Please get out of the new one
If you can't lend your hand
For the times they are a-changin'.

But these years were marked by far more than folk music alone. In the early part of the decade, an English group from Liverpool began to build a following in Great Britain. At the start of 1964, the Beatles released "I Want to Hold Your Hand" in the United States and appeared on the popular Ed Sullivan television show. Within weeks, Beatles songs held the first, second, third, fourth, and fifth positions on the *Billboard* singles chart, and *Meet the Beatles* became the best-selling LP record to date. With the release of *Sergeant Pepper's Lonely Hearts Club Band* a few years later, the Beatles branched out in new musical directions and reflected the influence of the counterculture with songs such as "Lucy in the Sky with Diamonds" (which some people said referred to the hallucinogenic drug LSD).

Mick Jagger and the Rolling Stones followed at the end of the 1960s. Another English group that changed the nature of American music, the Stones played a blues-based rock music that proclaimed a commitment to drugs, sex, and a decadent life of social upheaval. Other artists, such as Jim Morrison of the Doors and Janis Joplin, reflected the same intensity of the new rock world, and both died from drug overdoses. This music, too, continued into the 1970s.

Meanwhile, other groups were setting off in different directions. On the pop scene, Motown Records in Detroit popularized a new kind of black rhythm and blues. By 1960, the gospel-pop-soul fusion was gaining followers. By the late 1960s, Motown Records was one of the largest black-owned companies in America and one of the most successful independent recording ventures in the business.

Bob Dylan. *(AP/Wide World Photos)*

The Beatles *(Hulton Archive/Getty Images)*

The Supremes *(Brown Brothers)*

Stevie Wonder, the Temptations, and the Supremes were among the groups who became enormously popular. The Supremes, led by Diana Ross, epitomized the Motown sound with such hits as "Where Did Our Love Go."

REFLECTING ON THE PAST   What songs come to your mind when you think of the 1960s and 1970s? How is the music different from that of the 1950s? What do the lyrics tell you about the period? Look at the verse from "The Times They Are A-Changin'" that is reprinted here. What does it tell you about the turbulence of the time? What, if anything, do these lyrics imply can be done about the changes in the air? What other songs can you think of that give you a similar handle on these turbulent years?

An Advocate for Migrant Workers César Chávez organized the United Farm Workers to give migrant Mexican workers representation in their struggle for better wages and working conditions. Here he works with laborers in his tireless campaign for their support. What kind of a leader do you think Chávez was on the basis of his appearance in this picture? *(Bob Finch/Stock Photo)*

Latina women played an important part in the organizing effort. Dolores Huerta, a third-generation Mexican American who became vice president of the United Farm Workers, observed how entire families were involved:

> Excluding women, protecting them, keeping women at home, that's the middle-class way. Poor people's movements have always had whole families on the line, ready to move at a moment's notice, with more courage because that's all we had. It's a class not an ethnic thing.

Chávez first took on the grape growers of California. Calling the grape workers out on strike, the union demanded better pay and working conditions as well as recognition of the union. When the growers resisted, Chávez launched a nationwide consumer boycott of their products that was ultimately successful. Similar boycotts of lettuce and other products harvested by exploited labor also ended in success. In 1975, Chávez's long struggle for farmworkers won passage in California of a measure that required growers to bargain collectively with the elected representatives of the workers. Farmworkers now had achieved the legal basis for representation that could help bring higher wages and improved working conditions. And Chávez had become a national figure.

Meanwhile, Mexican Americans pressed for reform in other areas. In the West and Southwest, Mexican American studies programs flourished. Colleges and universities offered degrees, gave Chicanos access to their own past, and provided a network linking students together and mobilizing them for political action.

Beginning in 1968, Mexican American students began to protest conditions in secondary schools. They pointed to overcrowded and run-down institutions and to the 50 percent dropout rate that came from expulsion, transfer, or failure because students had never been taught to read. School walkouts took place in Colorado, Texas, and California and led to successful demands for Latino teachers, counselors, and courses as well as better facilities.

Other Latinos followed a more political path. In Texas, José Angel Gutiérrez formed a citizens' organization that developed into the La Raza Unida political party and successfully promoted Mexican American candidates for political offices. Throughout the 1970s, it gained strength in the West and Southwest.

Among the new Chicano leaders was the charismatic Reies López Tijerina, or "El Tigre." A preacher, he argued that the U.S. government had fraudulently deprived Chicanos of village lands. He formed an organization, La Alianza Federal de Mercedes (the Federal Alliance of Land Grants), which marched on the New Mexico state capital and occupied a number of national forests. Arrested, he stood trial and eventually served time in prison, where he became a symbol of political repression.

Rodolfo "Corky" Gonzáles was another such leader. He founded the Crusade for Justice to advance the Chicano cause through community organization. Like Tijerina, he was arrested for his part in a demonstration but was subsequently acquitted.

Latinos made a particular point of protesting the Vietnam War. Because the draft drew most heavily from the poorer segments of society, the Latino casualty rate was far higher than that of the population at large. In 1969, the National Chicano Moratorium Committee demonstrated against what it argued was a racial war, with black and brown Americans being used against their Third World compatriots.

Aware of the growing numbers and growing demands of Latinos, the Nixon administration sought to defuse their anger and win their support. Cuban American refugees, strongly opposed to communism, shifted toward the Republican party, which they assumed was more likely eventually to intervene against Fidel Castro. Meanwhile, Nixon courted Chicanos by dangling political positions, government jobs, and promises of better programs for Mexican Americans. The effort paid off, as Nixon received 31 percent of the Latino vote in 1972.

Despite occasional gains in the 1970s, Latinos from all groups faced continuing problems. Discrimination persisted in housing, education, and employment. Activists had laid the groundwork for a campaign for equal rights, but the struggle had just begun.

Native American Protest

Like Latinos, Native Americans continued to suffer second-class status in the 1960s and 1970s. But, partly inspired by the confrontational tactics of other groups, they became more aggressive in their efforts to claim their rights and improve their living and working conditions. Their soaring numbers—the census put them at 550,000 in 1960 and 1,480,000 in 1980—gave them greater visibility and political clout.

American Indians learned from the examples of protest they saw around them in the rising nationalism of the developing world and, even more important, in the civil rights revolution. They too came to understand the place of interest-group politics in a diverse society. Finally, they were chastened by the excesses of the Vietnam War. They recognized a pattern of killing people of color that connected Indian–white relations to the excesses in the Philippines at the turn of the century and to atrocities in Korea and Vietnam.

Indians in the late 1960s and 1970s successfully promoted their own values and designs. Native American fashions became more common, museums and galleries displayed Indian art, and Indian jewelry found a new market. In 1968, N. Scott Momaday won the Pulitzer Prize for his book *House Made of Dawn*. Vine Deloria, Jr.'s *Custer Died for Your Sins* (1969) had even wider readership. Meanwhile, popular films such as *Little Big Man* (1970) provided sympathetic portrayals of Indian history. Indian studies programs developed in colleges and universities. Organizations such as the American Indian Historical Society protested traditional textbook treatment of Indians and demanded more honest portrayals.

At the same time, Native Americans became more confrontational. Like other groups, they worked through the courts when they could but also challenged authority more aggressively when necessary.

Led by a new generation of leaders, American Indians tried to protect what was left of their tribal lands. For generations, federal and state governments had steadily encroached on Native American territory. That intrusion had to cease. The protest spirit was apparent on the Seneca Nation's Allegany reservation in New York State. When state authorities tried to condemn a section of Seneca land to build a superhighway through the Allegany reservation, the Indians went to court. In 1981, the state finally agreed to an exchange: state land elsewhere in addition to a cash settlement in return for an easement through the reservation. That decision encouraged tribal efforts in Montana, Wyoming, Utah, New Mexico, and Arizona to resist similar incursions on reservation lands.

Native American leaders found that lawsuits charging violations of treaty rights gave them powerful leverage. In 1967, in the first of many subsequent decisions upholding the Indian side, the U.S. Court of Claims ruled that the government in 1823 had forced the Seminole in Florida to cede their land for an unreasonably low price. The court directed the government to pay additional funds 144 years later. American Indians also vigorously and successfully protested new assaults on their long-abused water and fishing rights.

Urban Indian activism became highly visible in 1968 when George Mitchell and Dennis Banks, Chippewa living in Minneapolis, founded the activist American Indian Movement (AIM). AIM got Office of Economic Opportunity funds channeled to Indian-controlled organizations. It also established patrols to protect drunken Indians from harassment by the police. Soon chapters formed in other cities.

An incident in November 1969 dramatized Native American militancy. A landing party of 78 Indians seized Alcatraz Island in San Francisco Bay in an effort to protest symbolically the inability of the Bureau of Indian Affairs to "deal practically" with questions of Indian welfare. The Indians converted the island, with its defunct federal prison, into a cultural and educational center. In 1971, federal officials removed the Indians from Alcatraz.

Similar protests followed. In 1973, AIM took over the South Dakota village of Wounded Knee, where in 1890 the U.S. 7th Cavalry had massacred the Sioux. The

The Occupation at Wounded Knee The Native American movement's armed occupation of Wounded Knee, South Dakota, the site of a late-nineteenth-century massacre of the Sioux, resulted in bloodshed that dramatized unfair government treatment of Native Americans. What elements of this scene convey the determination behind this episode? *(AP/Wide World Photos)*

reservation surrounding the town was mired in poverty. The occupation was meant to dramatize difficult conditions and to draw attention to the 371 treaties AIM leaders claimed the government had broken. Federal officials responded by encircling the area and, when AIM tried to bring in supplies, killed one Indian and wounded another. The confrontation ended with a government agreement to reexamine the treaty rights of the Indians, although little changed.

At the same time, Native Americans devoted increasing attention to providing education and developing legal skills. Because roughly half of the Indian population continued to live on reservations, many tribal communities founded their own colleges. In 1971, the Oglala Sioux established Oglala Lakota College on the Pine Ridge Reservation in South Dakota. Nearby Sinte Gleska College was the first to offer accredited four-year and graduate programs. The number of Indians in college increased from a few hundred in the early 1960s to tens of thousands by 1980.

Indian protest brought results. The outcry against termination in the 1950s (see Chapter 26) had led the Kennedy and Johnson administrations in the 1960s to steer a middle course, neither endorsing nor disavowing the policy. Instead, they tried to bolster reservation economies and raise standards of living by persuading private industries to locate on reservations and by promoting the leasing of reservation lands to energy and development corporations. Many tribes confronted the hated policy head-on, and often gained the cancellation of such leases and the restoration of reservation status.

Legislation likewise disavowed the termination policy. In 1975, Congress passed an Indian Self-Determination Act. An Education Assistance Act that same year involved subcontracting federal services to tribal groups. Both laws reflected the government's decision to respond to Indian pressure and created a framework for federal policy.

Gay and Lesbian Rights

Closely tied to the revolution in sexual norms that affected sexual relations, marriage, and family life was a fast-growing and increasingly militant gay liberation movement. Because American society as a whole was unsympathetic, many homosexuals kept their preferences to themselves. The climate of the 1970s encouraged gays to "come out of the closet." A nightlong riot in 1969, in response to a police raid on the Stonewall Inn, a homosexual bar in Greenwich Village in New York, helped spark a new consciousness and a movement for gay rights. Throughout the 1970s, homosexuals ended the most blatant forms of discrimination against them. In 1973, the American Psychiatric Association ruled that homosexuality should no longer be classified as a mental illness, and that decision was overwhelmingly supported in a vote by the membership the next year. In 1975, the U.S. Civil Service Commission lifted its ban on employment of homosexuals.

Sign at a Gay
Pride March

In this new climate of acceptance, many gay men who had hidden or suppressed their sexuality revealed their secret. Women, too, became more open about their sexual preferences as a lesbian movement developed. But many Americans and some churches remained unsympathetic—occasionally vehemently so—to anyone who challenged traditional sexual norms.

Environmental and Consumer Agitation

Although many of the social movements of the 1960s and 1970s were defined by race, gender, and sexual preference, the environmental movement cut across all boundaries. After World War II, many Americans began to recognize that clear air, unpolluted waters, and unspoiled wilderness were indispensable to a decent existence. They worried about threats to their natural surroundings, particularly after naturalist Rachel Carson published her brilliant book *Silent Spring* in 1962 (see Chapter 28). By 1970, 53 percent of the population considered air and water pollution to be one of the major national problems.

Public concern focused on a variety of targets. In 1969, Americans learned that thermal pollution from nuclear power plants was killing fish in both eastern and western rivers. A massive oil spill off the coast of southern California turned white beaches black and wiped out much of the marine life in the immediate area. In 1978, the public became alarmed about the lethal effects of toxic chemicals dumped in the Love Canal neighborhood of Niagara Falls, New York. A few years later, attention focused on the deadly substance dioxin.

Equally frightening was the potential environmental damage from a nuclear accident. Such a calamity occurred in 1979 at Three Mile Island near Harrisburg, Pennsylvania. Human error compounded a mechanical problem and part of the nuclear core began to disintegrate. An explosion releasing radioactivity into the atmosphere appeared possible, and thousands of area residents fled. The scenario of nuclear disaster depicted in the film *The China Syndrome* (1979) seemed frighteningly real. The plant remained shut down, filled with radioactive debris, a monument to a form of energy Americans feared.

The threat of a nuclear catastrophe underscored the arguments of grassroots environmental activists. Groups such as the Clamshell Alliance in New Hampshire and the Abalone Alliance in northern California campaigned aggressively against licensing new nuclear plants at Seabrook, New Hampshire, and Diablo Canyon, California, and no new plants were authorized after 1978 in the United States, though other countries around the world continued to rely on nuclear power.

Western environmentalists were particularly worried about excessive use of water. Massive irrigation systems had boosted the nation's use of water from 40 billion gallons a day in 1900 to 393 billion gallons by 1975, though the population had only tripled. Americans used three times as much water per capita as the world's average.

California was particularly vulnerable. Because the state was naturally dry, its prosperity rested on massive irrigation projects, and in the late 1970s, it had 1,251 major reservoirs. Virtually every large river had at least one dam. Almost as much water was pumped from the ground, with little natural replenishment and even less regulation. Pointing to the destruction of the nation's rivers and streams and the severe lowering of the water table in many areas, environmentalists argued that something needed to be done. Critic Marc Reisner later noted, "Forty years ago, only a handful of heretics, howling at wilderness, challenged the notion that the West needed hundreds of new dams. Today they are almost vindicated."

Environmental agitation produced legislative results in the 1960s and 1970s. Lyndon Johnson's Great Society brought basic legislation to halt the depletion of the country's natural resources (see Chapter 28). In the next few years, environmentalists went further, pressuring legislative and administrative bodies to regulate polluters. During Richard Nixon's presidency, Congress passed the Clean Air Act, the Water Quality Improvement Act, and the Resource Recovery Act and mandated a new Environmental Protection Agency (EPA) to spearhead the effort to control abuses.

One environmental effort developed into an extraordinarily bitter economic and ecological debate. The Endangered Species Act of 1973 prohibited the federal government from supporting any projects that might jeopardize species threatened with extinction. It ran into direct conflict with commercial imperatives in the Pacific Northwest. Loggers in the Olympic Peninsula had long exploited the land by clear-cutting (cutting down all trees in a region, without leaving any standing). Environmentalists claimed that the forests they cut provided the last refuge for the spotted owl. Scientists and members of the U.S. Forest Service pushed to set aside timberland so that the owl could survive. Loggers protested that this action jeopardized their livelihood. As the issue wound its way through the courts, logging fell off drastically.

TIMELINE

1968	Richard Nixon elected president	1974	Nixon resigns; Gerald Ford becomes president
1969	La Raza Unida founded	1975	South Vietnam falls to the Communists
1970	Shootings at Kent State and Jackson State Universities	1976	Jimmy Carter elected president
1972	Nixon reelected	1978	*Bakke v. Regents of the University of California*
1973	Vietnam cease-fire agreement		
	Watergate hearings in Congress		

Related to the environmental movement was a consumer movement. As Americans bought fashionable clothes, house furnishings, and electrical and electronic gadgets, they began to worry about unscrupulous sellers, just as they had earlier in the twentieth century during the Progressive era. Over the years, Congress had established a variety of regulatory efforts as it started to safeguard citizens from marketplace abuse. In the 1970s, a stronger consumer movement developed, aimed at protecting the interests of the purchasing public and making business more responsible to consumers.

Ralph Nader, a onetime Department of Labor consultant, led the movement. His book *Unsafe at Any Speed: The Designed-in Dangers of the American Automobile* (1965) argued that many cars were coffins on wheels. Head-on collisions, even at low speeds, could easily kill, for cosmetic bumpers could not withstand modest shocks. His efforts paved the way for the National Traffic and Motor Vehicle Safety Act of 1966, which set minimum safety standards for vehicles on public highways, provided for inspection to ensure compliance, and created a National Motor Vehicle Safety Advisory Council.

The consumer movement developed into a full-fledged campaign in the 1970s. Nader's efforts attracted scores of volunteers, called "Nader's Raiders." They turned out critiques and reports and, more important, inspired consumers to become more vocal in defending their rights.

Conclusion

Sorting Out the Pieces

The late 1960s and 1970s were turbulent years. The chaos that seemed to reach a peak in 1968 continued, even as American participation in the war in Vietnam wound down. Richard Nixon recognized that he could contain the protest movement by bringing American soldiers home. He understood too the growing frustration with liberal reform and the wish of some Americans to dispense with the excesses they attributed to the young. For a time, he managed to mute protest and to promote a measure of harmony by his policy of Vietnamization, which cut back on the number of Americans dying in battle. But his desire to avoid losing the war led him to expand the conflict into neighboring parts of Indochina, and that move sparked even greater opposition than before.

Meanwhile, his own overarching ambition and need for electoral support led to the worst political scandal in American history. At just the time that the nation was trying to pick up the pieces from the unpopular war, he found himself embroiled in the Watergate affair, which threatened the United States with a real constitutional crisis that ended only when the president resigned.

During this entire time, disadvantaged groups demanded that the nation expand the meaning of equality. Building on the accomplishments of the civil rights movement in the 1950s and 1960s, women like Ann Clarke, introduced at the start of the chapter, returned to school in ever-increasing numbers and found jobs and sometimes independence after years of being told that their place was at home. Native Americans and Latinos mobilized, too, and could see the stirrings of change. Gay rights activists made their voices heard. Environmentalists created a new awareness of the global dangers the nation and the world faced. Slowly, reformers succeeded in pressuring the government to help the nation fulfill its promise and ensure the realization of the ideals of American life.

But the course of change was ragged. Reform efforts suffered from the disillusionment with liberalism. Some movements were circumscribed by the changing political climate; others simply ran out of steam. Still, the various efforts left a legacy of ferment that could help spark further change in future years.

Questions for Review and Reflection

1. What were Richard Nixon's social and political priorities in his presidency?

2. How did Nixon propose to end the war in Vietnam?

3. What impact did the Watergate crisis have on American political life?

4. What advances did the women's movement make in the 1970s?

5. How successful was the quest for social reform in the 1970s?

Discovering U.S. History Online

Richard Milhous Nixon www.ipl.org/ref/POTUS/rmnixon.html
This site contains basic factual data about Nixon's election and presidency, speeches, and online biographies.

Vietnam, A Different War www.nytimes.com/library/world/asia/vietnam-war-index.html
Drawing on its extensive coverage of the Vietnam War, this site offers both a contemporary perspective and a retrospective view of the events as a whole.

The My Lai Courts Martial, 1970 www.law.umkc.edu/faculty/projects/ftrials/mylai/mylai.htm
This site contains chronology, images, and court documents describing the massacre of Vietnamese civilians at My Lai.

Watergate www.washingtonpost.com/wp-srv/national/longterm/watergate/front.htm
From the newspaper that broke the story, this site features a chronology, images, searchable articles, and a good deal of background information about the burglary and its consequences.

Gerald Rudolph Ford www.ipl.org/ref/POTUS/grford.html
This site contains basic factual data about Ford's presidency, speeches, and online biographies.

James Earl Carter, Jr. www.ipl.org/ref/POTUS/jecarter.html
This site contains basic factual data about Carter's election and presidency, speeches, and online biographies.

César Chávez http://www.pbs.org/itvs/fightfields/
This site contains background about César Chávez and the United Farm Workers and highlights a PBS documentary film about his life and work.

Fiction and Film

Sara Davidson's *Loose Change* (1977) is a novel about the lives of three young women at the University of California at Berkeley. Marilyn French's *The Women's Room* (1977) is a novel about the impact of the women's movement on a circle of women. *House Made of Dawn* (1968) is N. Scott Momaday's Pulitzer Prize–winning novel about a young Indian living in both the white and Indian worlds. Alix Kates Shulman's *Memoirs of an Ex–Prom Queen* (1972) is the story of a young midwestern woman and her awakening during and after college.

All the President's Men* (1976) is a film (based on the book of the same name) about the effort by *Washington Post* reporters Bob Woodward and Carl Bernstein to find the truth about the Watergate scandal. *The Fight in the Fields: César Chávez and the Farmworkers' Struggle* (1997) is a documentary about the Latino leader and his impact. *Little Big Man* (1970) describes the life of a white man raised by Indians who fought General Custer. *The Times of Harvey Milk* (1984), which won the Academy Award for best documentary feature, tells the story of California's first openly gay politician, who was assassinated in 1978.

Recommended Reading

www.ablongman.com/nash
The Companion Website has a list of recommended readings about the Vietnam War, Watergate, and the decline of liberalism.

CHAPTER 30

The Revival of Conservatism, 1980–1992

CHAPTER OUTLINE

- The Conservative Transformation
- An End to Social Reform
- Economic and Demographic Change
- Foreign Policy and the End of the Cold War
- Conclusion: Conservatism in Context

American Stories

A Young Woman Embraces Republican Values

Leslie Maeby, a Republican political staffer in New York State in the 1980s, came from an immigrant family that had long been sympathetic to the Democratic party. Her great-grandfather, Aleksander Obrycki, had come to Baltimore from Poland in 1895. A common laborer who became a naturalized citizen in 1907, he worked for the Democratic party, meeting new immigrants on their arrival and introducing them to Democrats who could help them.

Leslie's grandfather Joe Obrycki became a numbers runner, collecting bets for local gamblers. More successful than his father, he survived the Great Depression of the 1930s with little difficulty. He, too, was a member of the Democratic party, a cog in the machine. As New Deal programs undermined machine rule, Joe, a ward heeler and professional gambler, ran for city council but lost. Defeat notwithstanding, he remained a loyal Democrat.

Leslie's mother, Vilma, was likewise a Democrat. Leslie's father, Jack Maeby, came from a working-class background in Baltimore and was raised as a Democrat. But as his football exploits took him to college at Bucknell University in Pennsylvania, he began to see the possibility of upward mobility. His own father, a factory worker, counseled him to "use this," pointing to his head, "instead of these," looking at his hands. Turning down an offer to go to graduate school, he entered a management training program with Montgomery Ward. The Maebys moved to Chicago first, then to the Albany, New York, area, where they settled in the suburb of Colonie. While Albany, like most big cities, voted Democratic, Colonie was Republican.

Leslie Maeby was raised in the 1950s in a home where her mother remained Democratic, though frustrated with the Albany machine, and her father was Republican. The suburb, in the midst of a housing boom, developed quickly, as whites fled the larger city—and its black population—and sought safety in the standardized tract houses that were going up everywhere. Nelson Rockefeller, the liberal Republican governor of New York, garnered the support of both of her parents and many of their neighbors. Yet besides voting, neither Jack nor Vilma was very active politically.

Leslie drifted into politics in 1968, at the age of 15, without thinking about it. A cheerleader, she was drafted into a congressional campaign by the wife of Fred Field, the Republican candidate, who wanted her to wave pom-poms for her husband and greet supporters. Like the other "Field Girls," she dressed in a blue felt skirt, a white blouse, and suspenders that were striped like the flag. Several nights a week, the group rang doorbells and passed out campaign literature to voters. Leslie often made the first overtures in a household, to be followed by the candidate himself. She found the experience intoxicating, even more so when Fred Field won.

Leslie had followed an increasingly common course into the Republican fold. In a second-grade classroom, she had supported Republican presidential candidate Richard Nixon in 1960. In a mock presidential debate in 1964, she had represented conservative Republican presidential nominee Barry Goldwater. And even though she talked about current events with her mother, a liberal Democrat, she was also influenced by her ever more conservative Republican father as well as by the Republican community in which she lived. She followed her father's political inclinations and became Republican, as she put it, "almost by default." Race riots, first in Detroit, later in Albany and other American cities, troubled her and others. The chaos in Vietnam led to the rifts in the nation that helped elect Richard Nixon—along with Fred Field—in 1968. By the time she went to the State University of New York at Albany in 1971, she was a solid Republican.

In college, she joined a sorority, where she found women of a similar personal and political bent. Her group drank beer, rather than smoking pot, and wore evening gowns to formal dances, rather than wearing tattered jeans to rock concerts. A sorority sister recommended her for a position as a page in the State Senate in Albany, and Leslie found herself immersed in the political world.

Leslie saw firsthand the underside of politics, including the ways those in power manipulated issues to their own advantage. Yet she made a decision to set aside her idealism and to work within the system. She rose quickly, serving in 1974 on the state platform committee. She worked for John Dunne, a Republican state senator, after graduating from college in 1975, and attended the Republican National Convention as a delegate-at-large in 1976. When Dunne sought the office of executive of Nassau County, Leslie ran his campaign. He lost and she left the United States and backpacked through Europe. Yet everywhere she went, she was interested in what she could find about American politics. She wanted to be part of the process as the United States—under the leadership of Ronald Reagan—moved away from the welfare state.

Returning to the United States, in 1984 Leslie took the job of salvaging the reelection campaign of a Republican state senator. She succeeded in that effort, served for four years as executive assistant to the Republican state comptroller, and in 1989, became finance director of the state Republican party.

Leslie was a rock-ribbed Republican, who, like many Americans, reacted with frustration to chaos in national life and moved right as the party moved right. "It's like if you decide to be a nurse when you're eighteen, and stay one for twenty years," she said. "It becomes who you are. How you read the paper. How you watch the news. Your whole outlook."

The experience of Leslie Maeby mirrored that of countless Americans in the 1980s who left the Democratic party and supported the Republican agenda instead. At a time when people were disturbed by continuing racial conflict, troubled by changes in the welfare state that seemed to help disadvantaged citizens at the expense of middle- and upper-class Americans, and upset at the chaos caused by the Vietnam War, they began to reassess priorities within the democratic political system. In a time of flux, the Republican party seized the initiative and consolidated its own political power. In a process that began in the 1960s (as Jack Maeby left his Democratic roots and became a Republican), a new majority emerged in the United States. Millions of Americans, including members of groups who had long considered themselves Democrats, voiced their frustration by voting Republican, some for the first time. Relying on a fervent religious faith, they succeeded in transforming their vision of the American dream into American policy, and in the 1980s and early 1990s, they watched the economy improve, though often to the benefit of the most affluent Americans. At the same time, members of a variety of minority groups continued to have difficulty finding jobs, the national debt skyrocketed, and finally, the stock market crashed. Meanwhile, harsh Cold War rhetoric led to fears that the continuing confrontation between the Soviet Union and the United States might end in nuclear war.

This chapter describes the enormous changes that occurred in the 1980s and early 1990s. It highlights the role of people like Leslie Maeby in bringing to power a new political force that altered the landscape of the United States. It describes the economic and technological shifts that affected the daily lives of millions of Americans, bringing unprecedented prosperity to people at the top of the economic pyramid but leaving millions of less fortunate Americans behind. It explores the efforts of the Republican administrations of Ronald Reagan and George H. W. Bush to redefine—and limit—the government's role in the economy, and it assesses the impact such constriction had on ordinary Americans. And, finally, it examines how foreign policy initiatives brought a successful end to the Cold War.

THE CONSERVATIVE TRANSFORMATION

In the 1980s and early 1990s, the Republican party reestablished itself as the dominant force in national politics. The Republican ascendancy that had begun in the Nixon era was now largely complete. The liberal agenda that had governed national affairs ever since the New Deal of Franklin Roosevelt gave way to a new Republican coalition determined to scale back the welfare state and prevent what it perceived as the erosion of the nation's moral values. Firmly in control of the presidency, sometimes in control of the Senate and later the whole Congress, the Republican party set the new national agenda.

The New Politics

Conservatism gained respect in the 1980s, not just in the United States but in other parts of the world as well. In Great Britain, for example, problems with both inflation and unemployment plagued the welfare state policies of the Labour party, which had gained ascendancy in the latter part of the 1960s, and by the 1980s, the

Conservative party was back in power, with Margaret Thatcher as prime minister. Elsewhere in the late 1980s, particularly as communism began to crumble in Eastern and Central Europe, moderately conservative Christian Democratic movements became increasingly popular. As socialism deteriorated, they seemed a more viable alternative.

In the United States, conservatism attracted countless new adherents after the turbulence of the 1960s and the backlash of the Vietnam War. Innovative advertising and fund-raising techniques capitalized on national disaffection with liberal solutions to continuing social problems and made the conservative movement almost unstoppable.

Conservatives seized on Thomas Jefferson's maxim: "That government is best which governs least." The dramatic economic growth of the 1960s and 1970s, they believed, left a legacy of rising inflation, falling productivity, enormous waste, and out-of-control entitlements. The liberal solution of "throwing money at social problems" no longer worked, conservatives argued. Therefore, they sought to downsize government, reduce taxes, and roll back regulations they claimed hampered business competition. They wanted to restore the focus on individual initiative and private enterprise.

The conservative philosophy had tremendous appeal. It promised profitability to those who worked long and hard hours. It attracted middle-class Americans, who were troubled that they were being forgotten in the commitment to assist minorities and the poor. It also offered hope for the revival of basic social and religious values that many citizens worried had been eaten away by rising divorce rates, legalized abortion, homosexuality, and media preoccupation with violence and sex.

The new conservative coalition covered a broad spectrum. Some followers embraced the economic doctrines of University of Chicago economist Milton Friedman, who promoted the free play of market forces and a sharp restriction of governmental control. Others applauded the social and political conservatism of North Carolina Senator Jesse Helms, a tireless foe of anything he deemed pornographic and likewise a fervent campaigner for a limited federal role. Still others flocked to the Republican fold because of their conviction that civil rights activists and "bleeding-heart liberals" practiced "reverse racism" with affirmative action, job quotas, and busing to promote equal opportunity.

The conservative coalition also drew deeply from religious fundamentalists who advocated a literal interpretation of Scripture. Millions—devout Catholics, orthodox Jews, evangelical Protestants—demanded a return to stricter standards of morality. Muslims, relying on the Qur'an, took an equally fundamentalist approach. All groups worried about sexual permissiveness, gay rights, drugs, crime, and women working outside the home, a practice they believed eroded family life. In short, fundamentalists objected to liberalizing tendencies and sought to refashion society by reaffirming scriptural morality and the centrality of religion in American life.

Many of these activists belonged to the so-called Moral Majority. The Reverend Jerry Falwell of Virginia and other television evangelists who focused on the concerns of religious fundamentalism attracted large followings in the 1980s. Emulating Father Charles E. Coughlin, the radio priest of the 1930s, they used electronic means to preach fiery sermons to enormous audiences and focused their television congregations on specific political ends. They also used their fund-raising ability to support candidates sympathetic to their cause. Moral Majority money began to fund politicians who demanded reinstituting school prayer, ending legalized abortion, and defeating the Equal Rights Amendment. Later a group calling itself the Christian Coalition became even more powerful in supporting—and electing—candidates who met its litmus test on conservative values. The Christian Coalition and similar groups believed strongly that "to proclaim Christ's lordship in politics means evaluating political candidates by their commitment to biblical principles, rather than by their pragmatism, patriotism, or personality."

Conservatives from all camps capitalized on changing political techniques more successfully than their liberal opponents. They understood the value of polling to assess and polish a candidate's image and the importance of television in providing instant access to the American public. Politicians became increasingly adept at using "sound bites," often lasting no more than 15 or 30 seconds, to state their views. They also relied on new electronic systems such as e-mail, fax machines, and the Internet to mobilize their followers.

Similarly, conservatives outdid liberals in using negative political advertising. Mudslinging has always been a part of the American political tradition, but now carefully crafted television ads concentrated not so much on conveying a positive image of a candidate's platform but on subtly attacking an opponent's character in order to create fundamental doubt in a voter's mind.

Conservatives also were most successful in raising unprecedented sums of money. Richard Viguerie, the New Right mastermind, understood how to tap the huge conservative constituency for political ends and developed direct-mail appeals that assisted conservative candidates around the country.

At the same time, conservatives understood the need to provide an intellectual grounding for their positions. Conservative scholars worked in "think tanks" and other research organizations such as the Hoover Institution at Stanford University or the American Enterprise Institute in Washington, D.C., that gave conservatism a solid institutional base. Their books, articles, and reports helped elect Ronald Reagan and other conservative politicians.

Conservative Leadership

More than any other Republican, Ronald Reagan was responsible for the success of the conservative cause. An actor turned politician, he had been a radio broadcaster in his native Midwest, then gravitated to California, where he began a movie career. Initially drawn to the Democratic party and impressed with the accomplishments of Franklin D. Roosevelt's New Deal, he was also sympathetic to union causes and served as president of the Screen Actors Guild in Hollywood. But his success on the silver screen affected his political inclinations, and he changed his affiliation from Democrat to Republican in the early 1960s. He went to work as a public spokesman for General Electric, where his visibility and ability to articulate corporate values attracted the attention of conservatives who recognized his political potential

VIDEO

Ronald Reagan Presidential Campaign Ad: A Bear in the Woods

The Rugged Ronald Reagan Ronald Reagan was fond of projecting an old-fashioned cowboy image. This picture captured the sense of rugged individualism he valued and appeared on the covers of both *Time* and *Newsweek* magazines when he died in 2004. What qualities seem to come across in this photograph? Why did this image have such a powerful appeal? *(Courtesy Ronald Reagan Library)*

and helped him win election as governor of California in 1966. He failed in his first bid for the presidency in 1976 but consolidated his strength over the next four years. By 1980, he had the firm support of the growing Right, which applauded his promise to reduce the size of the federal government but bolster military might.

Running against incumbent Jimmy Carter in 1980, Reagan scored a landslide victory, gaining a popular vote of 51 percent to 41 percent and a 489 to 49 Electoral College advantage. He also led the Republican party to control of the Senate for the first time since 1955. In 1984, he was reelected by an even larger margin. He received 59 percent of the popular vote and swamped Democratic candidate Walter Mondale in the Electoral College 525 to 13, losing only Minnesota, Mondale's home state, and the District of Columbia. The Democrats, however, netted two additional seats in the Senate and maintained superiority in the House of Representatives.

Reagan had a pleasing manner and a special skill as a media communicator. Relying on his acting experience, he used television as Franklin D. Roosevelt had used radio in the 1930s. He was a gifted storyteller who loved using anecdotes or one-liners to make his point. He was fond of invoking images of Pilgrims coming ashore in New England, American prisoners of war returning from Vietnam, and astronauts landing on the moon, and he argued that history still had a place for the nation and its ideals. In response to those who spoke of a "national malaise," he retorted, "I find nothing wrong with the American people."

DOCUMENT

Ronald Reagan, Address to the National Association of Evangelicals (1983)

Throughout his eight years in office, Reagan enjoyed enormous popularity. People talked about a "Teflon" presidency, making a comparison with nonstick frying pans, for even serious criticisms failed to stick and disagreements over policy never diminished his personal approval ratings. When he left the White House, an overwhelming 68 percent of the American public approved of his performance.

But Reagan had a number of liabilities that surfaced over time. As the oldest president the nation had ever had, his attention often drifted, and he occasionally fell asleep during meetings, including one with the pope. While he could speak eloquently with a script in front of him, he was frequently unsure about what was being asked in press conferences. Uninterested in governing, he delegated a great deal of authority, even if that left him unclear about policy decisions. Worst of all, he suffered from charges of "sleaze" in his administration, with several aides and even his attorney general forced from office for improprieties ranging from perjury to influence peddling.

In 1988, Republican George H. W. Bush, who served eight years as Reagan's vice president, ran for the presidency. Though a New Englander, he had prospered in the Texas oil industry, then served in Congress, as top envoy to China, and as head of the CIA. Termed a preppy wimp by the press, he became a pit bull who ran a mudslinging campaign against his Democratic opponent, Governor Michael Dukakis of Massachusetts. On election day, Bush swamped Dukakis, winning a 54 percent to 46 percent popular vote majority and carrying 40 states. But conservatives who admired Reagan were suspicious of Bush, and he did not have the kind of mandate Reagan had enjoyed. Even worse from the Republican point of view, Democrats controlled both houses of Congress.

Bush quickly put his own imprint on the presidency. Despite his upper-crust background, he was an unpretentious man who made a point of trying to appear down-to-earth. More than a year and a half into his term, he was still on his political honeymoon, with a personal approval rating of 67 percent. Support grew even stronger as he presided over the Persian Gulf War in 1991. Then, as the economy faltered and the results of the war seemed suspect, approval levels began to drop, and he failed in his bid for reelection in 1992 (see Chapter 31).

Republican Policies at Home

Republicans in the 1980s and early 1990s aimed to reverse the economic stagnation of the Carter years and to provide new opportunities for business to prosper. The United States, like industrialized nations around the world, had suffered from the Arab oil embargo of 1973 (see Chapter 29). As the cost of driving cars and heating homes skyrocketed, the entire economy faltered. In an increasingly globalized economy, where multinational firms had interests around the world, a downturn in one area—or one country—affected business efforts around the

George H. W. Bush on the Stump George H. W. Bush capitalized on his position as vice president under Ronald Reagan and won a resounding victory in the election of 1988. Even so, he did not have the solid conservative mandate that Reagan enjoyed. How does the flag contribute to the impression Bush hoped to convey? *(Corbis Sygma)*

world. Republicans wanted to provide American business interests with the ability to prosper at home and wherever else they operated.

To that end, Reagan proposed and implemented an economic recovery program that rested on the theory of supply-side economics. According to this much-criticized theory, reduction of taxes would encourage business expansion, which in turn would lead to a larger supply of goods to help stimulate the system as a whole. Even George Bush, during his brief run for the Republican nomination in 1980, was critical, charging that Reagan was promoting "voodoo economics." Despite such criticism, Republicans endorsed "Reaganomics."

One early initiative involved tax reductions. A 5 percent cut in the tax rate was enacted to go into effect on October 1, 1981, followed by 10 percent cuts in 1982 and 1983. Although all taxpayers received some tax relief, the rich gained far more than middle- and lower-income Americans. Poverty-level Americans did not benefit at all. Tax cuts and enormous defense expenditures increased the budget deficit. From $74 billion in 1980, it jumped to $290 billion in 1992. Such massive deficits drove the gross federal debt upward from $909 billion in 1980 to $4.4 trillion in 1992. When Reagan assumed office, the per capita national debt was $4,035; 10 years later, in 1990, it was about $12,400.

Faced with the need to raise more money and rectify an increasingly skewed tax code, in 1986 Congress passed and Reagan signed the most sweeping tax re-

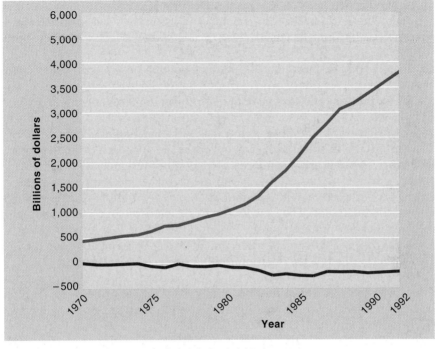

- Total yearly deficit   — Gross federal debt

FEDERAL BUDGET DEFICITS AND THE NATIONAL DEBT, 1970–1992 In the 1970s, 1980s, and early 1990s, the yearly federal budget deficit grew steadily larger, and the gross federal debt skyrocketed. In this economy, deficits and debt affected spending priorities. When did the yearly deficit begin to grow? What changes in the yearly deficit occurred in the 1980s? When did the gross federal debt grow most quickly? (*Source: Data from* Statistical Abstract *of the* United States.)

form since the federal income tax began in 1913. It lowered rates, consolidated brackets, and closed loopholes. Though it ended up neither increasing nor decreasing the government's tax take, the measure was an important step toward treating low-income Americans more equitably. Still, most of the benefits went to the richest 5 percent of Americans.

At the same time, Reagan followed Carter in a major deregulation effort that included agencies such as the Environmental Protection Agency and the Consumer Product Safety Commission. The Republican administration argued that regulations pertaining to the consumer, the workplace, and the environment were inefficient and excessively expensive, and impeded business growth.

The Federal Communications Commission (FCC), which had effectively regulated the airwaves in the public trust, now assumed a business posture. The head of the agency under Reagan scoffed at the idea that television had a public-service role. "Television is just another appliance," he declared. "It's just a toaster with pictures." The FCC increased the amount of time allotted to commercials and eliminated the rule that some programming had to be in the area of public-service broadcasts.

Meanwhile, Reagan challenged the New Deal consensus that the federal government should monitor the economy and assist the least-fortunate citizens. He had played by the rules of the system and had succeeded. Others could do the same.

Reagan needed to curtail social programs both because of sizable tax cuts and because of enormous military expenditures. Committed to a massive arms build-up, over a five-year period the administration sought an unprecedented military budget of $1.5 trillion. By 1985, the United States was spending half a million dollars a minute on defense and four times as much as at the height of the Vietnam War.

The huge cuts in social programs reversed the approach of liberals over the past 50 years. Republicans and conservative Southern Democrats eliminated public service jobs and reduced other aid to the cities, where the poor congregated. They cut back unemployment compensation and required Medicare patients to pay more for treatment. They lowered welfare benefits and food stamp allocations. Spending on human resources fell by $101 billion between 1980 and 1982. The process continued even after Reagan left office. Between 1981 and 1992, federal spending (adjusted for inflation) fell 82 percent for subsidized housing, 63 percent for job training and employment services, and 40 percent for community services. Middle-class Americans, benefiting from the tax cuts, were not hurt by the slashes in social programs. But for millions of the nation's poorest citizens, the administration's approach caused real suffering.

Ironically, despite the huge cuts, overall federal spending for social welfare rose from $313 billion in 1980 to $533 billion in 1988. The increase came about because of growth in the payments of entitlement programs, such as social security and Medicare, which provided benefits automatically to citizens in need. Even the most aggressive efforts of the Republicans could not wholly dismantle the welfare state.

Reagan wanted to place more power in the hands of state and local governments. His "New Federalism" attempted to shift responsibilities from the federal to the state level. By eliminating federal funding and instead making grants to the states, which could spend the money as they saw fit, he hoped to fortify local initiative. Critics charged that the proposal was merely a way of moving programs from one place to another while eliminating federal funding. When a prolonged recession began in 1990, the administration's policy contributed to the near-bankruptcy of a number of states and municipalities, which now bore responsibility for programs formerly funded in Washington.

Reagan took a conservative approach to social issues as well. Accepting the support of the New Right, he strongly endorsed conservative social goals. To avoid compromising his economic program, however, he provided only symbolic support at first. He spoke out for public prayer in the schools without expending political capital in Congress to support the issue. In the same way, he showed his opposition to abortion by making sure that the first nongovernmental group to receive an audience at the White House was an antiabortion March for Life contingent.

George Bush faithfully adhered to Reagan's general economic policy even after he became president. Running for president in 1988, he promised "no new taxes," although he later backed down from that pledge to join a bipartisan effort to bring the budget deficit under control.

Like Reagan, Bush wanted deep cuts in social programs. Tireless in his criticism of the Democratic majorities in the Senate and House of Representatives, he vetoed measure after measure to assist those caught in the ravages of a troubling recession that sent unemployment rates up to 8 percent and left one of every four urban children living in poverty.

Bush was more outspoken than Reagan in his support of conservative social goals. At the start of the 1980s, conservatives had questioned Bush's commitment to their social agenda, and, indeed, Bush had been sympathetic to a woman's right to choice in the abortion issue. As president, however, he firmly opposed abortion, and his Supreme Court appointments, like Reagan's, guaranteed that the effort to roll back or overturn *Roe* v. *Wade* would continue.

The Republican philosophy under Reagan and Bush dramatically reversed the nation's domestic agenda. Liberalism in the 1960s had reached a high-water mark in a time of steady growth, but in the 1980s, decisions about social programs became more difficult, and millions of Americans like Leslie Maeby—introduced at the start of the chapter—came to believe that most of the Great Society programs had failed to conquer poverty and in fact had created lifelong welfare dependency. Conservatism offered a more attractive answer, particularly to those Americans in the middle and upper classes who were already comfortable.

But the transformation was accompanied by a number of serious problems that emerged in the early 1990s. Bush faced a bankruptcy crisis in the savings and loan industry, which had used Republican deregulation policy to make unwise, high-risk investments that led to tremendous losses. Congress approved a $166 billion rescue plan (that soon reached more than $250 billion) to bail out the industry.

Republican policy also widened the gap between rich and poor. Tax breaks for the wealthy, deregulation initiatives, high interest rates for investors, permissiveness toward mergers, and enormous growth in the salaries of top business executives all contributed to the disparity. The 1980s, it became clear, produced "a decade of money fever," as author Tom Wolfe put it. The concentration of capital—an amassing of wealth at the top levels—produced dekamillionaires, centmillionaires, half-billionaires, and billionaires. According to one study, the share of national wealth of the richest 1 percent of the nation rose from about 18 percent in 1976 to 36 percent in 1989. Meanwhile, less-fortunate Americans suffered more than they had since the Great Depression. In 1987, one out of every five American children lived in poverty, up 24 percent since 1979. And millions of people, ranging from foreclosed farmers to laid-off industrial workers, struggled to make ends meet.

AN END TO SOCIAL REFORM

The Republican attack on the welfare state included an effort to limit the commitment to social reform. Enough had been done already, conservatives argued, and gains for less-fortunate Americans came at the expense of the middle class. It was time to end federal "intrusion" in this area.

Slowdown in the Struggle for Civil Rights

Republican policies slowed the civil rights movement. Reagan opposed busing to achieve racial balance, and his attorney general worked to dismantle affirmative action programs. Initially reluctant to support extension of the enormously successful Voting Rights Act of 1965, Reagan relented only under severe bipartisan criticism. He also launched an assault on the Civil Rights Commission and hampered its effectiveness by appointing members who did not support its main goals.

Yet African Americans kept the struggle for equal rights alive. The Reverend Jesse Jackson, a longtime civil rights activist, established what he called the Rainbow Coalition in 1984 and ran for the presidency. Though he lost in his bid for the Democratic nomination, he had the support of nearly 400 delegates, and in a nationally televised speech at the convention, he vowed not to forget his constituency of "the desperate, the damned, the disinherited, the disrespected, and the despised." All Americans, he went on, needed to work together for a common cause: "Our flag is red, white and blue, but our nation is a rainbow—red, yellow, brown, black and white—and we're all precious in God's sight." Four years later, in 1988, he sought the Democratic nomination again, this time with the support of 1,200 delegates at the convention, before falling short of his goal once more.

Jesse Jackson and Supporters Jesse Jackson demonstrated that an African American could attract a substantial level of support as he ran for president in 1984 and 1988. Here he is shown on the campaign trail in Chicago in 1988. Why were Jackson's campaigns so important? Who do you think his strongest supporters were? *(Photo © Marc PoKempner '88)*

Despite significant victories in mayoral elections in major cities and other electoral gains, black–white relations remained tense. A riot in Los Angeles in 1992 revealed the continuing racial polarization. The year before, Americans had watched a videotaped, savage beating of black motorist Rodney King by white police officers, the most dramatic of a long string of incidents involving police brutality. When a California jury that did not include any African Americans acquitted the policemen, many people throughout the country became convinced that people of color could not obtain equal justice under the law. In Los Angeles, thousands reacted with uncontrolled fury, targeting supermarkets, Korean businesses, restaurants, and mini-malls. Much of the chaos was orchestrated by gang members, but it also involved hundreds of ordinary citizens who acted irresponsibly, yet with a sense that the social contract had been broken by politicians and the rich who were unresponsive to their plight. After the riot had run its course, 51 people (most of them black and Latino) lay dead, 2,000 were injured, and $1 billion in damage had been done to the city. It was the worst riot in decades and served notice that racial injustice, social inequality, and poverty could no longer be ignored.

Obstacles to Women's Rights

Women had a similar experience in the 1980s and early 1990s. They, too, made significant electoral gains at the local, state, and national levels. In 1981, President Reagan named Sandra Day O'Connor as the first woman Supreme Court justice, and in 1984 Democrat Geraldine Ferraro became the first major-party female vice presidential nominee.

Yet women still faced problems that were compounded by conservative social policies. Access to new positions did not change their concentration in lower-paying jobs. In 1985, most working women were still secretaries, cashiers, bookkeepers, registered nurses, and waitresses—the same jobs most frequently held 10 years before. Even when women moved into positions traditionally held by men, their progress often stopped at the lower and middle levels and wage differentials continued to exist. In 1985, full-time working women still earned only 59 cents for every dollar earned by men.

Conservatives also waged a dedicated campaign against the right to legal abortion. Despite the 1973 Supreme Court decision legalizing abortion, the issue remained very much alive. The number of abortions increased dramatically in the decade after the decision. In response, "pro-life" forces mobilized. Opponents lobbied to cut off federal funds that allowed the poor to obtain the abortions that the better-off could pay for themselves; they insisted that abortions should be performed in hospitals and not in less expensive clinics; and they worked to reverse the original decision itself.

Though the Supreme Court underscored its judgment in 1983, the pro-life movement was not deterred. In 1989, a solidifying conservative majority on the Court ruled in *Webster* v. *Reproductive Health Services* that while women's right to abortion remained intact, state legislatures could impose limitations if they chose. In 1992, in *Planned Parenthood* v. *Casey*, the Court further declared that a 24-hour

Sandra Day O'Connor on the Court Sandra Day O'Connor became the first woman justice to sit on the U.S. Supreme Court. Her pre-Court career was similar to that of many other women, as she was denied numerous jobs when she emerged from law school. A decade later, Ruth Bader Ginsburg joined O'Connor on the nation's highest court. Here O'Connor testifies at her confirmation hearings. What impression does she convey as she answers senators' questions? *(Tom Zimberoff/ Getty Images)*

waiting period for women seeking abortions was acceptable and required teenage girls to secure the permission of a parent (or a judge) before ending a pregnancy. The ruling made an abortion harder to obtain, particularly for poor women and young women.

Women and men became more sensitive to the issue of sexual harassment. The dramatic confrontation between Supreme Court nominee Clarence Thomas and lawyer Anita Hill during confirmation hearings in 1991 dramatized both racial questions and the problem of sexual harassment. After the retirement of Thurgood Marshall, the only African American on the Supreme Court, President Bush sought to replace him with the much more conservative Clarence Thomas, putting African Americans, who wanted one of their own on the court, in a political bind. Then, during nationally televised confirmation hearings, Anita Hill accused Thomas of harassing her when she had worked for him earlier. Despite powerful opposition, the Bush administration managed to garner the necessary votes for confirmation. In the aftermath of the turbulent confirmation hearings, Americans in Congress, in the business community, and in the larger workplace all became more aware of inappropriate behavior that could no longer be tolerated.

The Limited Commitment to Latino Rights

Latinos likewise faced continuing concerns in the 1980s and early 1990s as the commitment to reform eroded. The Latino population increased substantially as a result of immigration reform during the Great Society of the 1960s (see Chapter 28). In the 1980s, 47 percent of all legal American immigration came from Mexico, the Caribbean, and Latin America. Many other immigrants arrived illegally. As the populations of Latin American nations soared and as economic conditions deteriorated, more and more people looked to the United States for relief. Many of the new arrivals were skilled workers or professionals, who still had to retool after arriving in the United States. But even more prevalent were laborers, service sector workers, and semiskilled employees, who needed the benefit of social services and counseling just as such assistance was being cut back. Spanish-speaking students often found it difficult to finish school. In 1987, 40 percent of all Latino high school students did not graduate, and only 31 percent of Latino seniors were enrolled in college-preparatory courses.

Like other groups, Latinos slowly extended their political gains. In the 1980s, Henry Cisneros became mayor of San Antonio and Federico Peña was elected mayor of Denver. In New Mexico, Governor Toney Anaya called himself the nation's highest elected Hispanic. The number of Latinos holding elective offices nationwide increased 3.5 percent between 1986 and 1987, and the number of Latina women in such offices increased 20 percent in that time. The number of Latino public officials nationwide increased 73 percent between 1985 and 1994, and Lauro Cavazos became the first Latino Cabinet official when he was appointed secretary of education in 1988.

Latino workers, however, continued to have a hard time in the employment market. Even as the nation's overall unemployment rate dropped, the rate for the 12 million Latino workers barely budged—and worsened in relation to the rate for African Americans.

Continuing Problems for Native Americans

Native Americans likewise experienced the waning commitment to reform, but they made some gains as a result of their own efforts. Some tribal communities developed business skills, although traditional Indian attitudes hardly fostered the capitalist perspective. As Dale Old Horn, an MIT graduate and department head at Little Big Horn College in Crow Agency, Montana, explained:

> The Crow Indian child is taught that he is part of a harmonious circle of kin relations, clans and nature. The white child is taught that he is the center of the circle. The Crow believe in sharing wealth, and whites believe in accumulating wealth.

Some Indian groups did adapt to the capitalist ethos. The Choctaw in Mississippi were among the most successful. Before they began a drive toward self-sufficiency in 1979, their unemployment rate was 50 percent. By the middle of the 1980s, Choctaw owned all or part of three businesses on the reservation, employed 1,000 people, generated $30 million in work annually, and cut the unemployment rate in half. After Congress approved Native American gambling in 1988, an increasing number of tribes became involved in this industry.

Despite entrepreneurial gains, Indians still remained (as the 1990 census showed) the nation's poorest group. As Ben Nighthorse Campbell, Republican senator from Colorado, noted in 1995, average Indian household income fell by 5 percent in the 1980s, while it rose for all other ethnic and racial groups. According to the 1990 census, median Indian household income was less than $20,000 a year.

Asian American Gains

Asian Americans climbed the social and economic ladder one rung at a time. The Asian American population increased dramatically with the influx of refugees at the end of the Vietnam War, with more than a half million arriving after 1975. In the 1980s, 37 percent of all immigrants to the United States came from Asia. In cities such as Los Angeles, Samoans, Taiwanese, Koreans, Vietnamese, Filipinos, and Cambodians competed for jobs and apartments with Mexicans, African Americans, and Anglos, just as newcomers had contended with one another in New York City a century earlier.

Immigrants from India, the Philippines, China, and Korea often brought skills and professional expertise, although Southeast Asian refugees were frequently less well-off when they arrived. Many of these unskilled immigrants provided the labor for the rapidly expanding West Coast electronics industry, though Indians provided impressive engineering and scientific talent. Asian immigrants, following a pattern established decades before, sought better and better opportunities for their children, and in California they became the largest group of entering students at a number of college campuses.

Sometimes the media highlighted the successes of Asian immigrants, particularly in contrast to the problems encountered by other groups. In 1986, *U.S. News & World Report* noted Asian American advances in a cover story and *Fortune* called them "America's Super Minority." Asian Americans were proud of the exposure but pointed out that many members of the working class still struggled for a foothold. In the Chinatowns of San Francisco and Los Angeles, 40 percent to 50 percent of the workers were employed in the ill-paid service sector or garment industry; in New York's Chinatown, the figure was close to 70 percent. Chinese immigrant women, in particular, often had little choice but to work as seamstresses.

Professionals from some countries had a hard time. One Vietnamese physician who resettled in Oklahoma noted, "When I come here, I am told that I must be a beginner again and serve like an apprentice for two years. I have no choice, so I will do it, but I have been wronged to be asked to do this." Professionals from other nations, with programs recognized in the United States, made the transition more easily.

Violent episodes sometimes highlighted discrimination. In 1982, in Detroit, Chinese American Vincent Chin was about to get married. At a strip club with friends the week before his wedding, he encountered two autoworkers who thought that Chin was Japanese, and they regarded Japan as responsible for the crisis in the American auto industry as Japanese cars flooded the market. They followed Chin out of the door and killed him with a baseball bat. In response to a guilty plea, both murderers received three years' probation and $3,780 in fines.

Detroit's Asian Americans were incensed but were reluctant to jeopardize what they considered their already vulnerable role in America.

Pressures on the Environmental Movement

Environmentalists, too, were discouraged by the direction of public policy in the 1980s and early 1990s. Activists found that they faced fierce opposition in the Republican years. Reagan systematically restrained the EPA in his avowed effort to promote economic growth. Under the leadership of James Watt of Colorado, the Department of the Interior opened forest lands, wilderness areas, and coastal waters to economic development, with no concern for preserving the natural environment. When asked whether he believed it was important to protect the environment for future generations, Watt, a devout Christian, responded that he did not know how many generations there were before the Second Coming. Bush initially proved more sympathetic to environmental causes and delighted environmentalists by signing new clean-air legislation. Later, as the economy faltered, he was less willing to support environmental action that he claimed might slow economic growth. In 1992, he accommodated business by easing clean-air restrictions. That same year, at a United Nations–sponsored Earth Summit in Rio de Janeiro, Brazil, with 100 other heads of state, Bush stood alone in his refusal to sign a biological diversity treaty framed to conserve plant and animal species.

ECONOMIC AND DEMOGRAPHIC CHANGE

Republicans sought to reorganize the government against the backdrop of an economy that was volatile in the 1980s and early 1990s, and left millions of workers struggling to survive the shocks. Under Republican supply-side economics, the business cycle moved from recession to boom and back to recession again. When Reagan took office in 1980, the economy was reeling under the impact of declining productivity, galloping inflation, oil shortages, and high unemployment. It revived in the early 1980s but then gave way to a deep recession that lasted from 1990 to 1992, underscoring the need for renewed productivity, full employment, and a more equitable distribution of wealth.

The Changing Nature of Work

Automation and other technological advances had a powerful impact on the American workplace. The *New York Times* reported in 1990 that "some factories look as if they have been hit by a kind of economic neutron bomb, which left assembly lines running at full speed but eliminated most of the people who worked on them." Formerly profitable jobs disappeared. One pulp mill worker voiced gloom about the future: "I think the country has a problem. The managers want everything run by computers. But if no one has a job, no one will know how to do anything anymore. Who will pay the taxes? What kind of society will it be when people have lost their knowledge and depend on computers for everything?"

In human terms, the introduction of the computer (see Chapter 26) had other consequences as well. Workers who sat for hours before their screens sometimes worried about radiation from the monitor or muscular fatigue from repetitive keyboard activity. Still others complained that they could no longer touch their work. As more Americans began to use computers, people who did not work with them complained about a growing "digital divide" that further increased the gap between rich and poor. Members of the middle and upper classes had easy access to computer technology, while less-fortunate individuals, many of whom belonged to minority groups, found themselves left behind.

Yet even as the nature of work changed, people seemed to be working more. In past decades, leisure time had seemed to expand, and there was talk of a four-day workweek in the 1950s. In subsequent years, however, the amount of time Americans worked steadily rose so that in the mid-1990s, American employees worked many more hours each year than their counterparts in Germany or France. The effort to juggle the pressures between employment and family life led to increasing stress. Problems were particularly severe for women, still trying to cope with the pressures of a double load, as they maintained responsibility for the home even when working outside. Marriages came under significant strain.

The Shift to a Service Economy

The scarcity of good jobs stemmed in part from the restructuring of the economy that occurred in the 1980s. In a trend that had been under way for more than half a century, the United States continued its shift from an industrial base, in which most workers actually produced things, to a service base, in which most provided expertise or service to others in the workforce. By the mid-1980s, three-fourths of the 113 million employees in the country worked in the service sector as fast-food workers, clerks, computer programmers, doctors, lawyers, bankers, teachers, and bureaucrats. That shift, in turn, had its roots in the decline of the country's industrial sector. The United States had been the world's industrial leader since the late nineteenth century. By the 1980s and early 1990s, however, productivity had slowed in virtually all American industries.

The causes of this decline in productivity were complex. The most important factor was a widespread failure on the part of the United States to invest sufficiently in its basic productive capacity. During the Reagan years, capital investment in real plants and equipment within the United States gave way to speculation, mergers, and spending abroad. At the end of the 1980s, domestic investment was down—5.7 percent in 1990 and 9.5 percent in 1991. The energy crisis and rising oil prices (see Chapter 29) also contributed to the industrial decline. Finally, the war in Vietnam diverted federal funds from research and development with consequences that continued even after the conflict ended.

While American industry became less productive, other industrial nations moved forward. German and Japanese industries, rebuilt after World War II with U.S. aid and aggressively modernized thereafter, reached new heights of efficiency. As a result, the United States began to lose its share of the world market for industrial goods. In 1946, the country had provided 60 percent of the world's iron and steel; in 1978, it provided a mere 16 percent. By 1980, Japanese car manufacturers had captured nearly one-quarter of the American automobile market. The auto industry, which had been a mainstay of economic growth for much of the twentieth century, suffered plant shutdowns and massive layoffs. In 1991, its worst year ever, Ford lost a staggering $2.3 billion.

Workers in Transition

In the 1980s and early 1990s, American labor struggled to hold on to the gains realized by the post–World War II generation of blue-collar workers. The shift to a service economy, while providing new jobs, was difficult for many Americans. Millions of men and women who lost positions as a result of mergers, plant closings, and permanent economic contractions now found themselves in low-paying jobs with few opportunities for advancement. Entry-level posts were seldom located in the central cities, where most of the poor lived, and even when jobs were there, minority residents often lacked the skills to get them.

Meanwhile, the trade union movement faltered as the economy moved from an industrial to a service base. Unions had been more successful in organizing the nation's industrial workers in the years since the 1930s, and the United States emerged from World War II with unions strong. In the years that followed, the percentage of workers belonging to unions dropped, from just over 25 percent in 1980 to barely over 16 percent a decade later. Between 1983 and 1993, the overall number of union members dropped from 17.7 million to 16.6 million.

Union membership declined for a number of reasons. The shift from blue-collar to white-collar work contributed to the contraction. The increase in the workforce in the numbers of women and young people (groups historically difficult to organize) was another factor, as was the more forceful opposition to unions by managers applying the provisions of the Taft-Hartley Act of 1947, which restricted labor's tactics. At the same time, union organizing efforts fell off significantly.

Union vulnerability was visible early in Reagan's first term, when the Professional Air Traffic Controllers Organization (PATCO) went on strike. Charging that the strike violated the law, the president—who had once been a union leader himself—fired the strikers, decertified the union, and ordered the training of new controllers at a cost of $1.3 billion. The message was clear: government employees could not challenge the public interest.

DOCUMENT

Ronald Reagan, on the Air Traffic Controllers Strike (1981)

Anti-union sentiments reverberated throughout the nongovernment sector as well. Many companies across the nation—confronted by falling prices and losses in revenue—sought to dissolve union agreements in hiring, wages, and benefits. Workers who kept their jobs found that their unions could not get favorable contracts. For example, in 1984 the United Auto Workers (UAW) ended a strike at General Motors by trading a pledge that GM would guarantee up to 70 percent of the production workers' lifetime jobs for a smaller wage increase than the union sought and a modification of the cost-of-living allowance that had been a part of UAW contracts since 1948.

Farmers also had to adjust as the larger workforce changed. Continuing a trend that began in the early twentieth century, the number of farms and farmers declined steadily. When Franklin Roosevelt took office in 1933, some 6.7 million farms covered the American landscape. Fifty years later, there were only 2.4 million. As family farms disappeared, farming income became more concentrated in the hands of the largest operators. In 1983, the top 1 percent of the nation's farmers produced 30 percent of all farm products, while the top 12 percent generated 90 percent of all farm income. The top 1 percent of the growers in the United States had average annual incomes of $572,000, but the small and medium-sized farmers who were being forced off the land frequently had incomes below the official government poverty line.

The extraordinary productivity of the most successful American farmers derived in part from the use of chemical fertilizers, irrigation, pesticides, and scientific management. Government price-support programs helped, too. Yet that very productivity caused unexpected setbacks. In the 1970s, food shortages abroad made the United States the "breadbasket of the world." Farmers increased their output to meet multibillion-bushel grain export orders and profited handsomely from high prices in India, China, Russia, and other countries. To increase production, farmers often borrowed heavily at high interest rates. When a worldwide economic slump began in 1980, overseas demand for American farm products declined sharply and farm prices dropped. Thousands of farmers, caught in the cycle of overproduction, heavy indebtedness, and falling prices, watched helplessly as banks and federal agencies foreclosed on their mortgages and drove them out of business.

The Roller-Coaster Economy

The economy shifted back and forth during the 1980s and early 1990s. The Reagan years began with a recession that lasted for several years. An economic boom between 1983 and 1990 gave way to a punishing recession as the new decade began. It appeared that the United States had embarked on another disturbing boom-and-bust cycle.

The recession of 1980 to 1982 began during the Carter administration, when the Federal Reserve Board tried to deal with mounting deficits by increasing the money supply. Program cuts to counter inflation brought substantial unemployment in the workforce. During Reagan's first year, the job situation deteriorated further, and by the end of 1982, the unemployment rate had climbed to 10.8 percent (and over 20 percent among African Americans). Nearly one-third of the nation's industrial capacity lay idle, and 12 million Americans were out of work.

Inflation, accompanied by heavy unemployment, continued to be a problem. The inflation rate, which reached 12.4 percent a year under Carter in 1980, fell after Reagan assumed office, to 8.9 percent in his first year and to about 5 percent during the remainder of his first term. But even the lower rate eroded the purchasing power of people already in difficulty.

The recession of 1980–1982 afflicted every region of the country. Business failures proliferated in every city and state, as large and small businesses closed their doors and fired employees. In one week in June 1982, a total of 548 businesses failed, close to the 1932 weekly record of 612. In Detroit, the nation's auto-manufacturing center, Japanese competition and high interest rates made car sales plummet. The Detroit unemployment rate rose to more than 19 percent and affected the entire city.

Even the Sun Belt—the vast southern region stretching from coast to coast—showed the effects of the recession. It had enjoyed economic growth fostered by the availability of cheap, nonunion labor, tax advantages that state governments offered corporations willing to locate plants there, and a favorable climate. Now it, too, began to suffer economic problems, and large areas began to stagnate. Overexpansion in the oil industry led to a collapse in prices that disrupted the economy in Texas, Oklahoma, Louisiana, and other oil-producing regions. World-wide gluts of some minerals, copper for example, added to unemployment elsewhere in the Southwest.

Economic conditions improved in late 1983 and early 1984, particularly for Americans in the middle- and upper-income ranges. The federal tax cut Reagan pushed through encouraged consumer spending, and huge defense expenditures had a stimulating effect. The Republican effort to reduce restrictions and cut waste sparked business confidence. A voluntary Japanese quota on car exports assisted the ailing automobile industry. The stock market climbed as it reflected the optimistic buying spree. Inflation remained low, about 3 to 4 percent annually from 1982 to 1988. Interest rates likewise fell from 16.5 percent to 10.5 percent in the same period. The unemployment rate at the end of the 1980s fell to below 6 percent nationally, and between the start of the recovery and 1988, real GNP grew at an annual rate of 4.2 percent.

But the economic upswing masked a number of problems. Millions of Americans remained poor. Many families continued to earn a middle-class income, but only by having two full-time income earners. They also went deeply into debt. To buy homes, young people accepted vastly higher mortgage interest rates than their parents had. Stiff credit card debts, often at 20 percent interest, were common. Under such circumstances, some young families struggled to remain in the middle class. Blue-collar workers had to accept lower standards of living. Single mothers were hit hardest of all.

The huge and growing budget deficits reflected the fundamental economic instability. Those deficits provoked doubts that resulted in the stock market crash of 1987. Six weeks of falling prices culminated with a 22.6 percent drop on Monday, October 19, almost double the plunge of "Black Tuesday," October 29, 1929. The deficits, negative trade balances, and exposures of Wall Street fraud all combined to puncture the bubble. The stock market revived, but the crash foreshadowed further problems.

Those problems surfaced in the early 1990s, as the country experienced another recession. A combination of massive military spending, growth of entitlement programs, and tax cuts sent budget deficits skyward. As bond traders in the 1980s speculated recklessly and pocketed huge profits, the basic productive structure of the country continued to decline. The huge increase in the national debt eroded business confidence, and this time the effects were felt not simply in the stock market but in the economy as a whole.

American firms suffered a serious decline. To cope with shrinking profits and decreased consumer demand, companies scaled back dramatically. In late 1991, General Motors announced that it would close 21 plants, lay off 9,000 white-collar employees the next year, and eliminate more than 70,000 jobs in the next several years. Hundreds of other companies did the same thing. As a result, the unemployment rate rose once again, and by mid-1991, it reached 7 percent, the highest level in nearly five years.

Around the nation, state governments found it impossible to balance their budgets without resorting to massive spending cuts. Reagan's efforts to move programs from the federal to the state level worked as long as funding lasted, but as national support dropped and state tax revenues declined, states found themselves in a budgetary gridlock. Most had constitutional prohibitions against running deficits, and so they had to slash spending for social services and education.

After a number of false starts, the economy began to recover in mid-1992. The unemployment rate dropped, the productivity index rose, and a concerted effort began to bring the federal deficit down.

Population Shifts

As the American people dealt with the swings of the economy, demographic patterns changed significantly. The nation's population increased from 228 million to approximately 250 million between 1980 and 1990—a rise of 9.6 percent (as opposed to 11.5 percent in the 1970s) that was one of the lowest rates of growth in American history. At the same time, the complexion of the country changed. In 1992, the country's nonwhite population—African Americans, Latinos, Asians, and Native Americans—stood at an all-time high of 25 percent, the result of increased immigration and of minority birthrates significantly above the white birthrate.

The population shifted geographically as well. American cities increasingly filled with members of the nation's minorities. White families continued to leave for the steadily growing suburbs, which by 1990 contained almost half the population, more than ever before. In 15 of the nation's 28 largest cities—New York, Chicago, and Houston among them—minorities made up at least half the population. Minority representation varied by urban region. In Detroit, Washington, New Orleans, and Chicago, African Americans were the largest minority; in Phoenix, El Paso, San Antonio, and Los Angeles, Latinos held that position; in San Francisco, Asians outnumbered other groups. The cities also grew steadily poorer. As had been the case since World War II, commuters from the suburbs took the better-paying jobs, while people living in the cities held lower-paying positions.

At the same time, the population was moving west. In 1900, the Mountain and Pacific states contained about 5 percent of the nation's population. By 1990, that figure stood at 21 percent. The population of the nation as a whole rose by less than 10 percent in the 1980s, but the population of the West increased by 22 percent.

That population was becoming much more urbanized. In the 50 years following 1940, the six largest metropolitan areas in the West grew by 380 percent; the six largest in the East expanded by only 64 percent. With this urban development, the West became a pacesetter for the rest of the country. If the New England village was a symbol of the eighteenth century and the midwestern town was a similar symbol of the nineteenth century, then the western metropolis had special symbolic importance in the late twentieth century. Western cities were unbounded, open-ended, and sprawling in all directions. They seemed capable of expanding indefinitely.

California was the nation's fastest-growing state, its population increasing in the 1980s by nearly 26 percent. Responding to a question about California's impact on the rest of the country, writer Wallace Stegner replied, "We *are* the national culture, at its most energetic end." Los Angeles became the most dynamic example of American vitality and creativity. The motion-picture industry exerted a worldwide impact. The city became a capital of consumption and served as a symbol of a dynamic national life.

FOREIGN POLICY AND THE END OF THE COLD WAR

In the early 1990s, the United States emerged triumphant in the Cold War that had dominated international politics since the end of World War II. In one of the most momentous turns in modern world history, communism collapsed in Eastern Europe and in the Soviet Union, and the various republics in the Soviet orbit moved toward capitalism and democracy. Other regions—the Middle East and Africa—experienced equally breathtaking change.

Reagan, Bush, and the Soviet Union

The Cold War was very much alive when Ronald Reagan assumed power in 1981. Like most of his compatriots, Reagan believed in large defense budgets and a militant approach toward the Soviet Union. He wanted to cripple the USSR economically by forcing it to spend more than it could afford on defense.

Viewing the Soviet Union as an "evil empire" in his first term, Reagan promoted a larger atomic arsenal by arguing that a nuclear war could be fought and won. The administration dropped efforts to obtain Senate ratification of SALT II, the arms reduction plan negotiated under Carter, although it observed the pact's restrictions. Then Reagan proposed the enormously expensive and bitterly criticized Strategic Defense Initiative, popularly known as "Star Wars" after a 1977 movie, to intercept Soviet missiles in outer space.

DOCUMENT

Ronald Reagan, "Evil Empire" Speech (1983)

In his second term, Reagan softened his belligerent stance. Mikhail Gorbachev, the new Soviet leader, watching his own economy collapse under the pressure of the superheated arms race, realized the need for greater accommodation with the West. He understood that the only way the Soviet Union could survive was through arms negotiations with the United States. He therefore proposed a policy of *perestroika* (restructuring the economy) and *glasnost* (political openness to encourage personal initiative). His overtures opened the way to better relations with the United States.

Concerned with his own place in history, Reagan met with Gorbachev, and the two developed a close working relationship. Summit meetings led to an Intermediate Range Nuclear Forces Treaty in 1987 that provided for the withdrawal and destruction of 2,500 Soviet and American nuclear missiles in Europe.

George Bush maintained Reagan's comfortable relationship with Gorbachev. At several summit meetings in 1989 and 1990, the two leaders signed agreements reducing the number of long-range nuclear weapons, ending the manufacture of chemical weapons, and easing trade restrictions. The Strategic Arms Reduction Treaty (START) signed in 1991 dramatically cut stockpiles of long-range weapons.

The End of the Cold War

The Cold War ended with astonishing speed. Gorbachev's efforts to restructure Soviet society and to work with the United States brought him acclaim around the world but led to trouble at home. In mid-1991, he faced an old-guard Communist coup, led by those who opposed *glasnost* and *perestroika*. He survived this right-wing challenge, but he could not resist those who wanted to go even further to establish democracy and capitalism. The forces he had unleashed finally destroyed the Soviet system and tore the USSR apart.

Boris Yeltsin, president of Russia, the strongest and largest of the Soviet republics, emerged as the dominant leader, but even he could not contain the forces of disintegration. Movements in the tiny Baltic republics of Latvia, Lithuania, and Estonia, culminating with independence in 1991, began the dismantling of the Soviet Union. The once-powerful superpower became a collection of separate states. Although the republics coalesced loosely in a Commonwealth of Independent States, led by Russia, they retained their autonomy—and independent leadership—in domestic and foreign affairs.

Meanwhile, Communist regimes throughout Europe collapsed. The most dramatic chapter in this story unfolded in Germany in November 1989. Responding to Gorbachev's softening stance toward the West, East Germany's Communist party boss announced unexpectedly that citizens of his country would be free to leave East Germany. Within hours, thousands of people gathered on both sides of the 28-mile-long Berlin Wall—the symbol of the Cold War that divided Berlin into East and West sectors. As the border guards stepped aside, East Germans flooded into West Berlin amidst dancing, shouting, and fireworks. Within days, sledgehammer-wielding Germans pulverized the Berlin Wall, and soon the Communist government itself came tumbling down. By October 1990, the two Germanys were reunited.

Reagan in Front of Berlin Wall (1987)

The fall of the Berlin Wall reverberated all over Eastern Europe. In Poland, the 10-year-old Solidarity movement led by Lech Walesa triumphed in its long struggle against Soviet domination and found itself in power in December 1990, with Walesa as president. In Czechoslovakia, two decades after Soviet tanks had rolled into the streets of Prague to suppress a policy of liberalization, the forces of freedom were likewise victorious. Like Poland, Czechoslovakia sought and received aid from the United States, but not even economic assistance could keep that nation intact, as turbulence led to the creation of separate and independent Czech and Slovak republics. The same forces that culminated in the independence of Czechoslovakia brought new regimes in Bulgaria, Hungary, Romania, and Albania.

Yugoslavia, held together by a Communist dictatorship since 1945, proved to be the extreme case of ethnic hostility resurging amid collapsing central authority.

Dismantling the Berlin Wall The destruction of the Berlin Wall in November 1989 was a symbolic blow to the entire Cold War structure that had solidified in Europe in the postwar years. People grabbed hammers and joined together in tearing down the hated wall. Joyous celebrations marked the reunification of a city that had been divided for decades. How does this dramatic picture convey the exuberant mood of the time? *(Alexandria Avakian/Woodfin Camp & Associates)*

In 1991, Yugoslavia splintered into its ethnic components. In Bosnia, the decision of the Muslim and Croatian majority to secede from Serbian-dominated Yugoslavia led Bosnian Serbs, backed by the Serbian republic, to embark upon a brutal siege of the city of Sarajevo and an even more ruthless "ethnic cleansing" campaign to liquidate opponents. The United States remained out of the conflict, unsure about what to do.

Early in 1992, Bush and Yeltsin proclaimed a new era of "friendship and partnership" and formally declared an end to the Cold War. After half a century of confrontation, the United States had won. It then extended aid to the former Soviet republics, which needed help in reorganizing their economies as free enterprise systems.

American Involvement Overseas

As the United States struggled to keep abreast of the momentous changes in Eastern Europe, it was equally involved with events in the rest of the world. Here again the nation sought to preserve stability as the Cold War drew to an end.

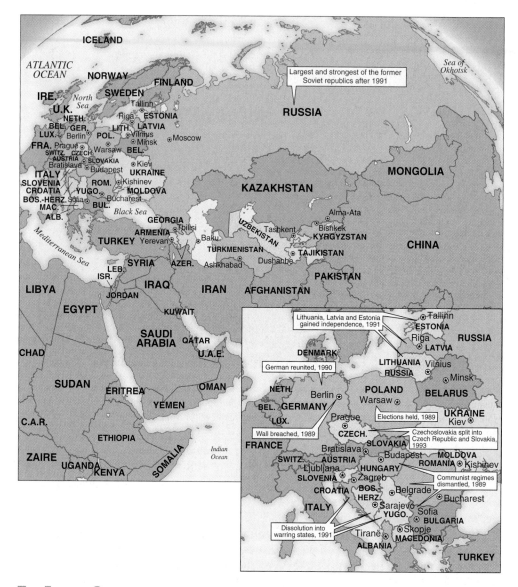

THE FALL OF COMMUNISM In the late 1980s and early 1990s, the Soviet Union fragmented and lost control of its satellites in Eastern Europe. As many countries shown here declared their independence, Czechoslovakia broke into two nations, while Yugoslavia ruptured into a group of feuding states. ■ **Reflecting on the Past** How widespread was the turbulence that led to the fall of communism? How quickly did the process take place? How did events in one country influence events in another country?

In Latin America, the United States intervened frequently as it had in the past, hoping to impose stability on the volatile region. Viewing Central America as a Cold War battlefield early in his presidency, Reagan openly opposed left-wing guerrillas in El Salvador who fought to overthrow a repressive right-wing regime.

The United States increased its assistance to the antirevolutionary Salvadoran government, heedless of a similar course followed years before in Vietnam. Efforts to destroy the radical forces failed, but in 1989, a far-right faction won the Salvadoran elections and polarized the country.

Nicaragua became an even bloodier battleground. In 1979, revolutionaries calling themselves Sandinistas (after César Sandino, who fought in the 1920s against U.S. occupation troops) overthrew the repressive Somoza family, which had ruled for three decades. During the 1980 U.S. presidential election, Republicans pledged to replace the Sandinistas with a "free and independent" government. Once in office, Reagan circumvented congressional opposition to his efforts to defeat the revolutionary reformers and signed a National Security directive in November 1981 authorizing the CIA to arm and train counterrevolutionaries known as *contras*, as Nicaragua became enmeshed in a bitter civil war. Upon discovering the secret CIA missions, Congress cut off military aid to the *contras*, and peaceful elections in early 1990 finally drove the Sandinistas out and brought the fighting to an end. Though the economy remained in desperate straits, the new regime seemed to offer the best hope of healing the wounds of the bloody conflict.

Reagan found it easier to maintain stability on the tiny Caribbean island of Grenada. The president ordered marines there in October 1983, after a coup installed a government sympathetic to Fidel Castro's Cuba. Concerned about the construction of a large airfield, 2,000 marines invaded the island, rescued a number of American medical students, and claimed triumph. Though the United Nations condemned it, Americans cheered what the administration called its "rescue mission."

Middle Eastern and Central American concerns became entangled in the Iran–*contra* affair. In 1987, Congress learned that the National Security Council had launched an effort to free American hostages in the Middle East by selling arms to Iran and then using the funds to aid the *contras*, in direct violation of both the law and congressional will. The trial of Oliver North, the National Security Council official responsible for the policy, focused on his distortions and falsifications before congressional committees and on his destruction of official documents that could have substantiated charges of wrongdoing by top officials. Convicted in 1989, North received a light sentence requiring no time in prison from a judge who recognized that North was not acting entirely on his own.

Bush, too, was involved in a variety of episodes abroad. Despite memories of past imperialism, the United States invaded Panama in 1989; the reasons it gave were to protect the canal, defend American citizens, and stop drug traffic. The campaign resulted in the capture of military leader Manuel Noriega, notorious for his involvement in the drug trade. Noriega was brought to the United States, tried, and convicted of drug-trafficking charges.

In South Africa, the United States supported the long and ultimately successful struggle against apartheid. This policy, whereby the white minority (only 15 percent of the population) segregated, suppressed, and denied basic human rights to the black majority, was part of South African law. A resistance movement, spearheaded by the African National Congress (ANC), sought to end apartheid. While the United States had long expressed its dislike of this ruthless system of segregation, economic and political ties to South Africa kept the United States

The Inspirational Nelson Mandela Nelson Mandela served as a source of inspiration to black South Africans, as the long struggle against apartheid finally brought that system of rigid segregation to an end and led to the setting up of a biracial democracy with Mandela himself as president. How did Mandela manage to convey his own sense of confidence, commitment, and reconciliation? *(AP/Wide World Photos)*

from taking steps to weaken it. Then, in 1986, bowing to increased domestic pressure, Congress imposed sanctions, including a rule prohibiting new American investments. The economic pressure damaged the South African economy and persuaded more than half of the 300 American firms doing business there to leave.

The final blow to apartheid came from the efforts of Nelson Mandela. The black ANC activist, who had become a symbol of the militant resistance movement during his 27 years in prison, steered his nation through a stunning transformation. In 1990, during Bush's presidency, Prime Minister Frederik W. de Klerk succumbed to pressure from the United States and the rest of the world and freed Mandela. Talks between the white government and the African National Congress produced a smooth shift to a biracial democracy and led to peaceful elections in 1994, in which blacks voted for the first time. The African National Congress assumed power and Mandela himself became president. American aid provided support in transitional times.

DOCUMENT

George H. W. Bush, Gulf War Address (1990)

Elsewhere in Africa, U.S. policymakers had greater difficulty in maintaining post–Cold War stability. Somalia, an impoverished East African nation, suffered from a devastating famine, compounded by struggles between warlords that led to an almost total disintegration of order. In 1992, Bush sent U.S. troops to assist a United Nations effort to stop the starvation and stabilize the country, but those efforts proved unsuccessful in a struggle that continued into the twenty-first century.

A dramatic crisis occurred in the Middle East in 1990 when Saddam Hussein, the dictator of Iraq, invaded and annexed his oil-rich neighbor Kuwait. President Bush reacted vigorously. Working through the United Nations, as Harry Truman had done in Korea, the United States persuaded the Security Council to vote unanimously to condemn the attack and impose an embargo on Iraq. After Hussein refused to relinquish Kuwait, in mid-January 1991 a 28-nation coalition struck at Iraq with an American-led multinational army of nearly half a million

TIMELINE

1980	Ronald Reagan elected president		**1988**	George H. W. Bush elected president
1981–1983	Tax cuts; deficit spending increases		**1989**	Fall of the Berlin Wall
1984	Reagan reelected		**1990**	Nelson Mandela freed in South Africa
1986	Tax reform measure passed		**1991**	Persian Gulf War
				Disintegration of the Soviet Union

troops. In Operation Desert Storm, the coalition forces' sophisticated technology swiftly overwhelmed the Iraqis. Americans were initially jubilant. Then the euphoria soured as Saddam used his remaining military power against minorities in Iraq. Bush's unwillingness to become bogged down in an Iraqi civil war and his eagerness to return U.S. troops home left the conflict unfinished. A year after his defeat, Hussein was as strongly entrenched as ever.

Meanwhile, the United States was involved in a larger, and ultimately more important, effort to bring peace to the Middle East. In the early 1990s, Secretary of State James Baker finally secured agreement from the major parties in the region to speak to one another face-to-face. A victory in the Israeli parliamentary elections in mid-1992 for Yitzhak Rabin, a soldier who recognized the need for peace and was ready to compromise, offered further hope for the talks.

VIDEO

George H. W. Bush's Early Response in the Persian Gulf War

Conclusion

Conservatism in Context

In the 1980s and early 1990s, the United States witnessed the resurgence of conservatism. The assault on the welfare state, dubbed the "Reagan Revolution," created a less regulated economy, whatever the implications for less fortunate Americans. The policies of Ronald Reagan and George Bush continued the trend begun by Richard Nixon in the 1970s. They reshaped the political agenda and reversed the liberal approach that had held sway since the New Deal of Franklin Roosevelt in the 1930s. In foreign affairs, Republican administrations likewise shifted course. Reagan first assumed a steel-ribbed posture toward the Soviet Union, then moved toward détente, and watched as his successor declared victory in the Cold War.

To be sure, there were limits to the transformation. Such fundamental programs as social security and Medicare remained securely in place, accepted by all but the most implacable splinter groups. Even the most conservative presidents of the past half century could not return to an imagined era of unbridled individualism and puny federal government. On the international front, despite the end of the Cold War, the nation's defense budget remained far higher than many Americans wished, and the nuclear arsenal continued to pose a threat to the human race.

Nor was the transformation beneficial to everyone. Periods of deep recession wrought havoc on the lives of blue-collar and white-collar workers alike. Working-class Americans were caught in the spiral of downward mobility that made them question the ability of the nation's economy to reward hard work. Liberals and conservatives both worried about the mounting national debt and the capacity of the economy to compete with Japan, South Korea, Germany, and other countries. Countless Americans fretted about the growing gaps between rich and poor. They fought with one another over what rules should govern a woman's right to an abortion. For the first time in American history, many children could not hope to do better than their parents had done. Reluctantly they tried to prepare themselves to accept a scaled-down version of the American dream.

Questions for Review and Reflection

1. How did the conservative movement become a major force in American life?

2. How successful was Reagan in implementing his conservative program?

3. What was the fate of social reform movements in the 1980s?

4. How did economic issues affect American life in the 1980s?

5. How did the Cold War finally come to an end?

Discovering U.S. History Online

Ronald Wilson Reagan http://www.ipl.org/div/POTUS/rwreagan.html
This site contains basic factual data about Reagan's election and presidency, speeches, and online biographies.

The Reagan Years http://www.cnn.com/SPECIALS/2001/reagan.years
This site includes photos and speeches from Reagan's life, especially from key moments of his presidency such as Reaganomics, the Iran-Contra affair, and his views on the Communist empire in an attempt to contribute to the "debate [on] the legacy of [his] two-term presidency."

George Herbert Walker Bush http://www.ipl.org/div/POTUS/ghwbush.html
This site contains basic factual data about George H. W. Bush's election and presidency, speeches, and online biographies.

The Forgotten Americans http://www.pbs.org/klru/forgottenamericans/
Companion site to the film, this site offers a portrait of the "Third World conditions" experienced by the mostly Latino residents of U.S. neighborhoods outside the city limits in Texas, California, Arizona, and New Mexico, called *colonias*.

Global Economy http://www.pbs.org/wgbh/commandingheights/lo
This Web site examines the "forces, values, events, and ideas that have shaped the present global economic system, including Reagan's introduction of 'supply-side' economics."

Foreign Policy http://globetrotter.berkeley.edu/clips/
This site has a three-part series, "The End of the Cold War," that includes extensive news quotes on "The Search for a U.S. Strategy," "Europe's Search for a New Identity," and "The Collapse of Communism in Eastern Europe and the Shaping of a Western Response."

Fiction and Film

Sherman Alexie's first book, *The Business of Fancydancing* (1992), is a collection of poems and short stories about American Indian life. Julia Alvarez's *How the Garcia Girls Lost Their Accents* (1992) is the fictional account of four young women from the Dominican Republic and their transition to American life. Tom Wolfe's *The Bonfire of the Vanities* (1987) is a novel about the arrogance of the upper class in New York—the masters of the universe—and the consequences when an accident occurs.

The film *Bedtime for Bonzo* (1951) shows Ronald Reagan the actor playing the part of a professor trying to teach morals to a chimpanzee. *Knute Rockne, All American* (1940) is another one of Reagan's films, in which he plays the part of George Gipp (the Gipper), a Notre Dame football player. *Wall Street* (1987) captures the sense of greed and corporate arrogance that created the tone for the 1980s. *When Harry Met Sally* (1989) is a film about the difficulties of relationships between men and women.

Recommended Reading

www.ablongman.com/nash
The Companion Website has a list of recommended readings about the rise of conservatism, economic and demographic changes during this period, and the end of the Cold War.

The Post–Cold War World, 1992–2006

CHAPTER OUTLINE

- The Changing Face of the American People
- Economic and Social Change
- Democratic Revival
- The Second Bush Presidency
- Foreign Policy in the Post–Cold War World
- Conclusion: The Recent Past in Perspective

American Stories

An Immigrant Family Struggles as the Economy Improves

In 1997, Marlene Garrett bundled up her three sleepy children—aged 4, 3, and 1—and took them to the babysitter's home every morning at 5 A.M. "Mama has to go to work so she can buy you shoes," she told them as she left for a job behind the counter at a bagel café in Fort Lauderdale, Florida, that began at 6 A.M. This was a new position and she did not want to be late.

Garrett had come to the United States from Jamaica eight years earlier. She and her husband, Rod, had high hopes for a better life in the United States, and they were fortunate enough to be employed. But both of them held entry-level jobs and had to struggle to make ends meet. Rod worked in a factory making hospital curtains and brought home about $250 a week. Marlene had just left a $5.25-an-hour job selling sneakers for her $6-an-hour job at the bagel café. It was a small improvement, but the $200 she earned weekly made it possible to pay the monthly rent of $400 and buy groceries. With luck, they could repair or replace the car, which had recently died, and perhaps begin to pay off their $5,000 debt from medical bills. They had no health insurance and could only hope that no one got sick.

Garrett was not happy about her babysitting arrangements. Her real preference was to stay at home. "Who's a better caretaker than mom?" she asked. But remaining at home was out of the question. Welfare might have been a possibility in the past, but the United States was in the process of cutting back drastically on its welfare rolls, and, in any event, Marlene was not comfortable with that alternative. "I don't want to plant that seed in my children," she said. "I want to work."

Marlene had few day-care options. She would have liked to have taken Scherrod, Angelique, and Hasia to the Holy Temple Christian Academy—her church's day-care center and preschool—but it cost $180 a week for three children and was beyond reach. Several months before, when she had been earning $8 an hour as a home health aide for the elderly, she had thought she could afford the church center and had even put money down for school uniforms for the kids. Then her car gave out and made it impossible to continue that job.

Instead of the Holy Temple Christian Academy, Garrett took the children to the home of Vivienne, a woman from the Bahamas who worked nights at the self-service laundry where she did her wash. Vivienne's apartment was simple and clean but had no toys or books anywhere in sight. Most days, the children watched television during the 10 hours that Marlene was away.

The Garretts knew how important it was to stimulate their children. Reflecting longingly on the church center and what it offered, Marlene said, "The children play games. They go on field trips. They teach them, they train them. My children are bright. You would be amazed at what they would acquire in a year." But instead of a stimulating center, the Garretts had to settle for a place that was simply safe.

At a time when the administration of Bill Clinton was trying to reconfigure the welfare system, people like the Garretts found themselves left out. Florida, like many states, budgeted most of its child-care money for families moving off of welfare to jobs. People who had never been on welfare received nothing. As the executive director of a Florida child-care referral agency observed, "Many of these parents have no choice but to leave their children in substandard arrangements that are rotting their brains, and jeopardizing their futures."

Marlene refused to give up hope. Her children were on a waiting list for help from the state that might make the Holy Temple Christian Academy accessible. Meanwhile, she took a second job working nights at the local Marriott Hotel. She had to pay Vivienne more money for the extra hours, and she worried even more about the additional time away from the children, but felt she had no choice. "It is temporary," she said. "I am doing what I have to do."

Marlene and Rod Garrett were like millions of poor Americans who found themselves left out of the prosperity that returned to the United States in the mid-1990s. Despite rosy economic indicators, more than 35 million Americans still lived below the federally defined poverty line. Life was hardly easy for the Garretts or for other families who found themselves on the bottom side of the line. Then, soon after George W. Bush succeeded Bill Clinton as president in 2001, the economy faltered. Now even more Americans found themselves in the same straits as the Garretts.

The Garretts' struggle to care for their children—and for themselves—unfolded against the backdrop of the longest period of economic growth in American history. As a deep recession in the early 1990s lifted, the economy went on a tear. American corporations, increasingly operating in a multinational context, dominated the global economy. Taking advantage of remarkable advances in communication technology, corporations found it easy to do business in a world smaller than ever before. The easy availability of money encouraged middle- and upper-class Americans to invest in the stock market and mutual funds, often enabling them to realize large gains, at least on paper. The troubling budget deficit that had soared in the Reagan administration disappeared as the government, guided by Democratic president Bill Clinton, ran a surplus for the first time in years. The unemployment level dropped, yet for Americans at the bottom of the economic ladder, some of them immigrants from abroad, conditions remained difficult. Many of the jobs now available as a result of the relentless shift toward a service economy paid little more than the minimum wage, and people like the Garretts, who dreamed of a better life, still found themselves struggling to survive.

Meanwhile, the global scene shifted abruptly. The cataclysmic events in Europe that ended nearly a half century of Cold War required the United States to redefine its international role. This led to substantial debate, as both Republicans, who controlled Congress for most of the 1990s, and Democrats, who controlled the White House for the same period, voiced reservations about playing an interventionist, and potentially expensive, role abroad. Then, as the new decade began, the United States confronted the menace of terrorism on a scale never known before. The attacks that destroyed the World Trade Center towers in New York City and left a gaping hole in the Pentagon in Washington, D.C., led to a war on terrorism and a fundamental reconfiguration of American foreign policy.

This chapter describes demographic shifts, reflected in the census of 2000, that changed the face of the American people. It highlights the revival of the economy that brought unprecedented prosperity for many but still failed to accommodate the needs of less-fortunate Americans like the Garretts, and then records the even greater suffering as the economy fell apart. It examines the political struggle between Democrats and Republicans that brought the second presidential impeachment in American history. It notes the bitterly contested national election of 2000 and its conservative aftermath. Finally, it explores the continuing effort to define the American role in the turbulent and terrorist-dominated post–Cold War world.

THE CHANGING FACE OF THE AMERICAN PEOPLE

The United States changed dramatically in the 1990s, as the continuing influx of new immigrants reshaped demographic patterns. The overall population, as reported in the census of 2000, grew more rapidly than it had in the past several decades and reflected the steady increase in the number of nonwhite Americans.

The New Pilgrims

The second great wave of immigrants in the twentieth century changed the face of America. The number of immigrants to the United States in the 20-year period from 1981 to 2000 was approximately 17.5 million, making it the most voluminous period of immigration in American history. In the decade of the 1990s, close to 10 million immigrants were counted, just less than the 10.1 million immigrants recorded in the 10 years from 1905 to 1914, which stands as the all-time record for that span of time.

Patterns of immigrant settlement changed. Whereas most immigrants around the turn of the preceding century remained near the East Coast, or in contiguous states, in 2000, 39.9 percent of the foreign-born settled in western states, with only 22.6 percent of the foreign-born living in the Northeast. The shift was a result of larger demographic shifts in the United States. As the twentieth century began, the

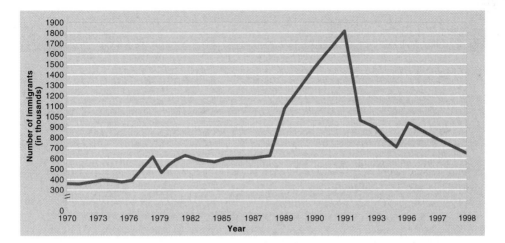

IMMIGRATION, 1970–1998 This chart shows the significant rise in immigration after 1970, as the tightly restricted quotas in force from the 1920s to 1965 were liberalized. The steady rise in the 1970s and 1980s reflected the arrival of Asian and Latin Americans, while the spike in the early 1990s occurred because of the amnesty that legalized the status of many illegal immigrants who were now officially counted. How would you describe the trend over the course of the past several decades? Why did immigration begin to decline somewhat toward the end of the twentieth century? *(Source: Data from Statistical Abstract of the United States.)*

Northeast still dominated the economic and cultural life of the nation. A hundred years later, the West was increasingly dominant. California had surpassed New York as the most populous state, and Los Angeles International Airport, known as LAX, had replaced Ellis Island as the port of entry for many immigrants.

The sources of recent immigration were similar to those of the 1970s and 1980s. In 2000, just over one-third of all immigrants—legal and illegal—came from Central America, while just over one-quarter came from Asia. Faltering economies in many countries in Latin America led people living on the fringe to look toward the United States, where a better life might be possible. Inhabitants of African nations, equally poor and faced with deteriorating living conditions, likewise saw hope for a brighter future in America.

The American influx was spurred by the Immigration Act of 1965 (see Chapter 28). Part of Lyndon Johnson's Great Society program, this act authorized the impartial acceptance of immigrants from all parts of the world and was directly responsible for the greater numbers of Asians and Latin Americans. In 1986, Congress passed the Immigration Reform and Control Act, aimed at curbing illegal immigration while offering amnesty to aliens living in the United States. The Immigration Act of 1990 opened the doors wider, raising immigration quotas while cutting back on restrictions that had limited entry in the past. It also provided for swift deportation of aliens who committed crimes. Two other measures in 1992 expanded eligibility slightly. In 2001, the United States and Mexico began to talk about how to ease the plight of Mexican immigrants and permit illegal arrivals to stay.

Recovering the Past

As we reach our own time, the historical past perhaps most worth recovering is our own. Our own story is as valid a part of the story of American history as the tale of Revolutionary War soldiers, frontier women, reform politicians, and immigrant grandparents. In this computerized age, the person we need to recover is ourself, a self that has been formed, at least in part, by the entire American experience we have been studying.

Autobiography is the form of writing in which people tell their own life's history. Although written autobiographies are at least as old as the literature of the early Christians (for example, *The Confessions of St. Augustine*), the word *autobiography* dates from the late eighteenth century, around the time of the French and American revolutions. That is no accident. These momentous events represented the triumph of individual liberty and the sovereignty of the self. *The Autobiography of Benjamin Franklin,* written between 1771 and Franklin's death in 1790 (and excerpted here), is a classic celebration of the American success story. Franklin's work set the standard for one autobiographical form, the memoir of one's public achievements and success. The other brief autobiographical memoir, from the reminiscences of Elizabeth Cady Stanton, also reflects the tone and range of this tradition.

Not all autobiographies are written late in life to celebrate one's accomplishments. The confessional autobiography, unlike most memoirs, explores the author's interior life, acknowledging flaws and failures as well as successes; it may be written at any age. The purpose of this type of autobiography is not just to reconstruct one's past to preserve it for posterity, but to find from one's past an identity in order to know better how to live one's future. The story of religious confessions and conversions is an obvious example. This form also includes secular self-examinations such as those by Maxine Hong Kingston in *The Woman Warrior* (1976), Piri Thomas in *Down These Mean Streets* (1967), or Maya Angelou in a series of five autobiographical sketches beginning with *I Know Why the Caged Bird Sings* (1969). The two confessional excerpts presented here, those of Native American Black Elk and black activist Malcolm X, are among the finest examples of confessional autobiography and suggest its variety.

These examples hardly convey the full range of the autobiographical form or how available to all people is the opportunity to tell the story of one's life. In 1909, William Dean Howells called autobiography the "most democratic province in the republic of letters." A recent critic agrees, pointing out:

> To this genre have been drawn public and private figures: poets, philosophers, prizefighters; actresses, artists, political activists; statesmen and penitentiary prisoners; financiers and football players; Quakers and Black Muslims; immigrants and Indians. The range of personality, experience, and profession reflected in the forms of American autobiography is as varied as American life itself.

Your story, too, is a legitimate part of American history. But writing an autobiography, while open to all, is deceptively difficult. Like historians, autobiographers face problems of sources, selection, interpretation, and style. As in the writing of any history, the account of one's past must be objective, not only in the verifiable accuracy of details but also in the honest selection of representative events to be described. Moreover, in fiction as well as history, the autobiographer must provide a structured form, an organizing principle, literary merit, and thematic coherence to the story. Many other challenges face the would-be autobiographer, such as finding a balance between one's public life and the private self and handling problems of memory, ego (should one, for example, use the first or third person?), and death.

REFLECTING ON THE PAST   To get an idea of the difficulties of writing an autobiography, try writing your own. Limit yourself to 1,000 words. Good luck.

Autobiographical Memoirs

Benjamin Franklin

DEAR SON,

I have ever had a pleasure in obtaining any little anecdotes of my ancestors. ... Imagining it may be equally agreeable to you to know the circumstances of my life—many of which you are yet unacquainted with—and expecting a week's uninterrupted leisure in my present country retirement, I sit down to write them for you. Besides, there are some other inducements that excite me to this undertaking. From the poverty and obscurity in which I was born and in which I passed my earliest years, I have raised myself to a state of affluence and some degree of celebrity in the world. As constant good fortune has accompanied me even to an advanced period of life, my posterity will perhaps be desirous of learning the means, which I employed, and which, thanks to Providence, so well succeeded with me. They may also deem them fit to be imitated, should any of them find themselves in similar circumstances.

Source: The Autobiography of Benjamin Franklin (1771).

Elizabeth Cady Stanton

It was 'mid such exhilarating scenes that Miss Anthony and I wrote addresses for temperance, antislavery, educational and woman's rights conventions. Here we forged resolutions, protests, appeals, petitions, agricultural reports, and constitutional arguments; for we made it a matter of conscience to accept every invitation to speak on every question, in order to maintain woman's right to do so. ...

It is often said, by those who know Miss Anthony best, that she has been my good angel, always pushing and goading me to work, and that but for her pertinacity I should never have accomplished the little I have. On the other hand it has been said that I forged the thunderbolts and she fired them. Perhaps all this is, in a measure, true. With the cares of a large family I might, in time, like too many women, have become wholly absorbed in a narrow family selfishness, had not my friend been continually exploring new fields for missionary labors.

Source: Elizabeth Cady Stanton, Eighty Years and More: Reminiscences, 1815–1897 (1898).

Confessional Autobiographies

Black Elk
And so it was all over.

I did not know then how much was ended. When I look back now from this high hill of my old age, I can still see the butchered women and children lying heaped and scattered all along the crooked gulch as plain as when I saw them with eyes still young. And I can see that something else died there in the bloody mud, and was buried in the blizzard. A people's dream died there. It was a beautiful dream.

And I, to whom so great a vision was given in my youth,—you see me now a pitiful old man who has done nothing, for the nation's hoop is broken and scattered. There is no center any longer, and the sacred tree is dead.

Source: Black Elk Speaks, as told through John G. Neihardt (1932).

Malcolm X
I want to say before I go on that I have never previously told anyone my sordid past in detail. I haven't done it now to sound as though I might be proud of how bad, how evil, I was.

But people are always speculating—why am I as I am? To understand that of any person, his whole life, from birth, must be reviewed. All of our experiences fuse into our personality. Everything that ever happened to us is an ingredient.

Today, when everything that I do has an urgency, I would not spend one hour in the preparation of a book which has the ambition to perhaps titillate some readers. But I am spending many hours because the full story is the best way that I know to have it seen, and understood, that I had sunk to the very bottom of the American white man's society when—soon now, in prison—I found Allah and the religion of Islam and it completely transformed my life.

Source: The Autobiography of Malcolm X, with the assistance of Alex Haley (1964).

The rise in the number of immigrants fueled anti-immigrant feeling in the United States that resembled similar resistance in Europe. In the 1970s and 1980s, America's efforts to help immigrants coincided with still-intact social-assistance programs of the liberal welfare state, and multiculturalism, stressing the different values that made up a larger American identity, became a dominant theme. Yet efforts to assist brought increasing opposition from Americans facing a scarcity of good jobs. There was also a cultural backlash, as opponents of immigration worried about the challenge to America's character posed by new arrivals with their own social patterns.

DOCUMENT

Illegal
Immigration
Reform and
Immigrant
Responsibility Act
(1996)

That opposition, which echoed the anti-immigrant feeling of the past, included strenuous efforts to restrict illegal immigration. Resistance came to a head in 1994 in California, where voters passed Proposition 187, denying illegal aliens access to public education and medical clinics. A federal judge issued an injunction to prevent implementation of the ballot measure, yet Proposition 187 provided a model and caught the attention of congressional members, especially Republicans, who gained control of Congress that same year. Two years later, Congress passed legislation barring legal immigrants (who were not yet citizens) from receiving food stamps and disability assistance from the federal government. Toward the end of the decade, California ended its support for bilingual education.

Economic improvement, and the move toward full employment in the latter part of the 1990s, brought a political shift in the immigration debate. In 2000, pressure mounted to admit more high-tech workers for businesses and more unskilled workers for the service sector, where there were unfilled jobs. Political considerations also played a part in the shift as both Democrats and Republicans recognized in particular the voting power of Latinos.

Immigration issues became headline news at the end of the 1990s in the highly publicized case of six-year-old Elián Gonzales. In November 1999, he was miraculously rescued near Florida when a group of Cuban boat people trying to reach the United States drowned. His father, still back in Cuba, had not given permission for the boy to leave and wanted him back. The Miami Cuban community, which hated Fidel Castro and his Communist regime, wanted the boy to stay in the United States. In the end, the Immigration and Naturalization Service (INS) seized Elián and returned him to Cuba.

The INS, already unpopular, attracted fierce criticism in the face of the terrorist attacks of September 11, 2001. It had allowed into the country immigrants from Saudi Arabia and elsewhere who had orchestrated the airplane hijackings that shocked the world. Now Americans began to look askance at Arabs or Muslims throughout the country and to condemn the INS for its laxity in screening out potential terrorists.

The Census of 2000

The 2000 census reported a 13 percent increase in the nation's population, as the United States gained 32.7 million people in the 1990s for a total of 281.4 million inhabitants. This expansion surpassed the previous 10-year record of 28 million people in the 1950s, in the midst of the baby boom after World War II. The rate of

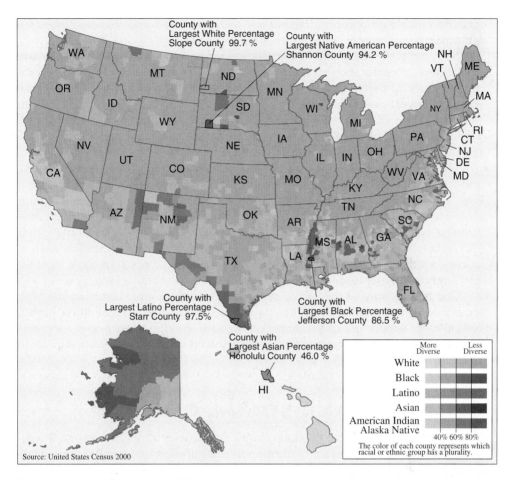

County with Largest White Percentage Slope County 99.7 %

County with Largest Native American Percentage Shannon County 94.2 %

County with Largest Latino Percentage Starr County 97.5%

County with Largest Black Percentage Jefferson County 86.5 %

County with Largest Asian Percentage Honolulu County 46.0 %

	More Diverse	Less Diverse
White		
Black		
Latino		
Asian		
American Indian Alaska Native		

40% 60% 80%

The color of each county represents which racial or ethnic group has a plurality.

Source: United States Census 2000

PORTRAIT OF A NATION The 2000 census documented changing population patterns and reported where different groups resided in the United States. Note the areas of greatest concentration of African Americans, Latinos, Asian Americans, and American Indians. ■ **Reflecting on the Past** Why was there such a concentration of African Americans in the Southeast? What does the concentration of Latinos in the Southwest tell you about the sources of Latino immigration? Why were American Indians almost entirely located in the West? (Source: "Portrait of a Nation" New York Times, April 1, 2001. Copyright © 2001 by The New York Times Co. Reprinted with permission.)

growth, which had slowed down over the past three decades, accelerated in the 1990s, reflecting increased immigration and longer life expectancy. While every state had a net increase in population, growth was greatest in the West, increasingly important in the economic and cultural life of the nation. Altogether, the West as a whole gained 10.4 million people and expanded by 19 percent.

The United States remained about 69 percent white, with a 12 percent African American and 11 percent Latino population. Latinos continued to flock to southern California, the Texas border region, and the south of Florida, and they also began to congregate in increasing numbers in places such as Chicago and Denver. Overall, their numbers increased by 38.8 percent. African Americans maintained their dominance in older northern cities such as Detroit and Washington, D.C., while continuing to move into metropolitan suburbs.

Nationally, the Asian and Pacific Islander population increased by 43 percent. In California, Asians showed the largest increase of any group. They now comprised nearly 13 percent of the state population and maintained their position as the third largest population group, after whites and Latinos. Much of the Asian population growth occurred in the suburbs, where the more affluent moved, though large pockets of poverty remained in places such as Chinatown in Los Angeles and Little Phnom Penh in Long Beach.

The 2000 census revealed that the combination of Latinos, African Americans, and Asians now outnumbered whites in California. This was the first time since 1860, when California began to provide accurate census data, that whites did not have a majority. State politics already began to reflect the shift. In 1998, Cruz Bustamante became the first Latino elected to statewide office in California since 1871, when he became lieutenant governor. The United States, founded as a white man's country, had now developed into a nation where people of color were increasingly numerous and influential.

One new feature of the 2000 census revealed the desire of large numbers of Americans to identify themselves as part of more than one racial or ethnic group. Nationwide, 2.4 percent of the American people identified themselves as multiracial. In Hawaii, 21 percent of all residents traced their heritage to two or more racial or ethnic groups.

ECONOMIC AND SOCIAL CHANGE

In the 1990s, the American economy improved dramatically. Yet despite the revival, millions of Americans remained poor, and homelessness became an increasingly visible problem. Meanwhile, groups pushing for equality made significant gains, but they still faced resistance in their long, continuing struggle for fair treatment in the United States.

Boom and Bust

American economic recovery began in mid-1992, even as other parts of the world found themselves facing industrial problems. In reunified Germany, where extraordinary economic growth had occurred in the post–World War II years, the economy—the largest in Europe—faltered. The Japanese economy, the second largest in the world after the U.S. economy, likewise encountered trouble.

Against that backdrop, the American revival was even more remarkable. The promotion of big business in the Reagan era (see Chapter 30) spurred investment and led to significant economic expansion. The lowering of interest rates by the Federal Reserve Board revived confidence and promoted consumer spending. Productivity rose steadily throughout the decade, though not quite as quickly as it had in the 1950s and 1960s. Similarly, the national economic growth rate began to rise again. Growth, like productivity, was not as dramatic as it had sometimes been in the golden years of industrial development, but it was sustained in what became the longest expansion in American history. Inflation fell to the lowest rate in more than 30 years. The unemployment rate also declined, dropping from 7.8 percent in 1992 to 4.6 percent in 1997. Taking credit for the recovery, President Bill Clinton declared that the drop in unemployment was "the latest evidence that our economy is growing, steady and strong, that the American dream is in fact alive and well."

One reflection of the return of prosperity was the soaring stock market. The decade of the 1990s was marked by a dramatic increase in the number of investors, reaching approximately 50 percent of the population in 2000. Some purchased stocks and mutual funds for themselves, often working on their own computers, without using a stockbroker. Much of the investment was in the high-tech area, where people poured billions of dollars into start-up companies not yet making a profit, in the hope that they would take off. The market soared, with the Dow Jones average topping the once-unimaginable 10,000 barrier in 1999 and quickly moving past the 11,000 mark.

An even more important sign of economic health was the dramatic reduction in the budget deficit. A Democratic effort to preempt a Republican issue and hold down spending paid off, particularly as low interest rates encouraged economic expansion. In 1998, the United States finished with a budget surplus for the first time in 29 years. With $70 billion—the largest surplus ever—left over at the end of the fiscal year, Democrats and Republicans began arguing about how the money should be used. Most Democrats favored using funds to bolster the social security system, while Republicans, who controlled Congress, preferred a politically attractive tax cut. Forgotten in the euphoria was the fact that the national debt—the total of all past deficits—remained over $5.4 trillion.

In these prosperous times, American companies embarked upon a wave of mergers like those around the turn of the century that created the great oil and steel corporations. In 1997, a record $1 trillion in mergers involving American companies took place as huge conglomerates swallowed up smaller competitors in the interests of efficiency and ever-larger profits. One consequence of the mergers, however, was layoffs of workers who duplicated tasks and seemed superfluous. The jobs available to those looking for other work were often positions like those held by Marlene and Rod Garrett, introduced earlier in the chapter, which paid far less.

Then, all too quickly, the economy faltered. Alan Greenspan, chairman of the Federal Reserve Board, warned in 1996 against "irrational exuberance" in the market, but most investors, especially those making millions of dollars, ignored his warning. In 2000, the stock market began to slide, as investors realized that many of the financial gains did not reflect commensurate gains in productivity. The year ended with the major stock indexes—the Dow Jones Industrial Average and the Nasdaq Composite—showing their worst performances in decades, and in 2001 and 2002, the market continued to fall, wiping out the paper gains of millions of large and small investors.

The nation's overall growth rate began to slow as investment declined. Lack of confidence in the market, particularly in the high-tech area that had fueled the boom, led to a corresponding lack of confidence in the economy. As a recession began in 2000, a tax cut, described later in this chapter, further undermined the stability of the economy. Promoted by Republican George W. Bush after his victory in the presidential election of 2000, the tax cut was skewed in favor of wealthy Americans and not only failed to provide a necessary stimulus but contributed to the decline.

By early 2001, it was clear that the economy was slumping. In February, manufacturing fell to its lowest point in 10 years. Unemployment rolls increased and applications for state unemployment benefits surged. Confidence in the economy was further eroded by growing reports of corporate greed and managerial fraud. Emboldened by deregulation in the 1980s, many corporations had taken advantage of lax oversight practices and made huge—and sometimes illegal—profits. Toward the end of 2001, the Enron Corporation, a company that bought and sold energy, admitted that it had filed five years of misleading reports and declared bankruptcy. As the scandal grew, it became clear that the Arthur Andersen accounting firm had participated in providing cover for financial irregularities. As the corporate empire began to tumble, the top executives cashed in their stock and made millions of dollars, while the company's workers, unaware of the looming catastrophe and prohibited from unloading stock, lost not just their jobs but their retirement savings as well.

Some people argued that the Enron case was an anomaly—a bad apple in the barrel—and contended that the rest of corporate America was in good shape. As 2002 unfolded, it became clear that many other companies, such as WorldCom, the telecommunications giant, had been falsifying their books. At the start of the twenty-first century, more and more Americans found themselves in economic trouble as boom times came to an end.

Poverty and Homelessness

Poverty was a problem even in good times. The Census Bureau reported in 1997 that 35.6 million people in the United States—the richest country in the world—still lived below what was defined as the poverty line of about $16,000 a year for a family of four. The percentage—13.3 percent—had fallen slightly in each of the previous few years, but it was still sizable, especially considering that it included one out of every three *working* Americans. Worse still was the fact that in 1998, there were 900,000 more Americans living below the poverty line than in 1990.

Poverty in the United States was different than in other parts of the world, to be sure. People in American slums had more material benefits than many of the residents of Soweto, the huge slum just outside Johannesburg in South Africa. But the poverty was still corrosive.

Urban Americans had the toughest time of all. Even as population shifts led more and more people to live in cities, government programs often failed to provide fully for urban needs. As cities lost population to the suburbs in the last half of the twentieth century, they lost their tax base at the same time and could not easily meet the demand for services.

The gap between rich and poor increased significantly in the last two decades of the twentieth century. The efforts of the Reagan and Bush administrations in the 1980s and early 1990s to cut back on government spending and eliminate social programs that had provided services for the poor contributed to the growing gap. As always, minorities fared worse than whites. The net worth of a typical white household at the beginning of the 1990s was 12 times greater than the net

Homeless in America The homeless became far more visible in the 1990s. Here a man lies sleeping under a thin sheet of plastic, serving as his blanket, right in front of the White House in Washington, D.C. What impression does the proximity to the White House convey? *(Bettmann/Corbis)*

worth of a typical black household and 8 times greater than the net worth of a typical Latino household. Minorities and women continued to lose ground faster than the rest of the population as the decade unfolded.

Just as the United States rediscovered its poor in the 1960s, so it rediscovered its homeless in the 1980s and 1990s. Even as unemployment dropped in the 1980s, the number of homeless quadrupled. Numbers were hard to ascertain, for the homeless had no fixed addresses, but one estimate in 1990 calculated that 6 million to 7 million people had been homeless at some point in the past five years. A federal report in 2000 noted that approximately 3.5 million people would become homeless at least once during the year, with 1.35 million of those being children.

People became homeless for a variety of reasons. Some started life in disturbed families. Others fell prey to alcohol and drugs. Still others had health or learning problems that eroded the possibility of a stable life. For millions of working Americans, homelessness was just a serious and unaffordable illness away.

Aging and Illness

The American population was older than ever before as the century came to an end. Between 1900 and 1994, when the population of the country tripled, the number of people over the age of 65 rose elevenfold and continued to rise in the next decade, reaching 33 million, or just about 12 percent of the population, in 2001. Underlying the rapid increase was the steady advance in medical care, which in the twentieth century had increased life expectancy in the United States from 47 to 74 years. People once considered themselves old when they reached the age of 65; now, many Americans in their 80s continued to lead productive lives—participating in activities such as writing books, teaching classes, and consulting with corporate clients.

One component of the aging revolution was Viagra, a new drug designed to help men suffering from impotence that came on the market in the 1990s. Whether sexual dysfunction was a result of prostate illness, common among older males, or emotional distress, Viagra helped ailing men enjoy normal sex lives. *Newsweek* magazine noted in 1998 that Viagra was the fastest-selling drug in history.

The elderly raised new issues in a nation suffering periodic recessions. Many wanted to continue working and opposed mandatory retirement rules that drove them from their jobs. In 1986, federal legislation amending the Age Discrimination in Employment Act prohibited mandatory retirement on the basis of age for virtually all workers and created continuing problems for younger employees in the 1990s.

Generational resentment over jobs was compounded by the knotty problems faced by the social security system, established a half century earlier. Other parts of the world—Scandinavia, for example—provided social services out of general revenues and took such expenditures for granted. However, in the United States, contributions to the system were necessary to keep it solvent, and as more and more Americans retired, the system could not generate sufficient revenue without assistance from the general governmental fund. In the early 1980s, it appeared that the entire system might collapse. A government solution involving higher taxes for those still employed and a later age for qualifying for benefits rescued the fund for a time, but many Americans in the 1990s wondered whether social security would survive. Meanwhile, millions of elderly people wondered how they could afford the rapidly increasing cost of prescription drugs.

As Americans lived longer, they suffered increasingly from Alzheimer's disease, an affliction that gradually destroys a patient's memory and ability to function mentally or physically. Diagnosis is difficult, and there is no treatment to reverse the ailment's course. The illness gained exposure in 1995 when the family of Ronald Reagan disclosed that the former president was suffering from the incurable disease.

Other illnesses affected old and young alike. The discovery of AIDS (acquired immune deficiency syndrome) in 1981 marked the start of one of the most serious diseases in the history of the United States—and the world. Some nations found themselves decimated by AIDS. In China, for example, entire villages were infected with HIV (the human immunodeficiency virus that causes AIDS) as a result of unsterile practices in blood stations. Africa was hit even harder. One estimate found that 34.3 million people in the world had AIDS, with 24.5 million of them in sub-Saharan Africa. In Zimbabwe, estimates of life expectancy were expected to fall from 61 in 2005 to 33 in 2010.

The AIDS Quilt As the AIDS epidemic caused more and more deaths, family members and friends began to create a huge quilt to celebrate the lives of those who had died. Each panel represented a different person. The quilt, shown here in Washington, D.C., was on display around the country and drew millions of viewers who came to remember those lost to the disease. How do the various portions of the quilt create a larger statement? What statement do you think the quilt is making? *(Stock Photo)*

While health conditions in the United States were better than those in many parts of the world, AIDS still had a devastating effect. The sexual revolution of the 1960s had brought a major change in sexual patterns, particularly among the young, but now sexual experimentation was threatened by this deadly new disease. Although it seemed to strike intravenous drug users and homosexuals with numerous partners more than other groups at first, it soon spread to the heterosexual population as well. AIDS became the leading cause of death in Americans between the ages of 25 and 44. The growing number of deaths—approximately 458,000 in 2001—suggested that the disease would reach epic proportions. That same year, some 800,000 to 900,000 Americans of all ages and ethnicities were living with HIV, which could burst into full-blown AIDS at any time. New drugs, taken in combination, extended the life span of those with the HIV virus and reduced the death rate in the 1990s, but AIDS remained a lethal, and ultimately fatal, disease.

Minorities and Women Face the Twenty-First Century

Americans fighting for equality made gains in the 1990s. But efforts at reform often encountered resistance.

African Americans   For African Americans, home ownership and employment figures rose. The numbers of murders and other violent crimes that involved blacks dropped. A record 40 percent of African Americans attended college in 1997, up from 32 percent in 1991. Yet incremental improvements often failed to erode racist ideas that still permeated American society. Incidents like the beating of black motorist Rodney King in Los Angeles in 1991 and the rioting that occurred the next year (see Chapter 30) made many people wonder just how much progress the civil rights movement had made.

Affirmative action was one area where blacks faced a backlash. Energized by their political victories in 1994, conservatives launched a powerful attack on the policy of giving preferential treatment to groups that had suffered discrimination in the past, pushing ballot initiatives and pressuring public agencies to bring the practice to an end. The most visible effort was Proposition 209 in California, approved by voters in the election of 1996, which prohibited the use of gender or race in awarding state government contracts or admitting students to state colleges and universities. The increasingly conservative Supreme Court waded into the controversy in 1995 by affirming a lower court ruling prohibiting colleges and universities from awarding special scholarships to African Americans or other minorities. Meanwhile, other cases moved through the legal system. In late 2003, the Supreme Court ruled in two cases involving the University of Michigan that affirmative action was acceptable, even as it rejected a point system the university used in carrying out the policy in undergraduate admissions. Before that ruling, the Texas legislature sought to craft an alternative policy guaranteeing admission to the top 10 percent of the graduating class from any Texas high school in a Texas college. That plan helped maintain diversity but aroused the ire of white parents who once again felt their children were suffering from the effort.

The booming job market in the late 1990s helped foster better race relations. It provided new opportunities for people who had been unable to find jobs. A survey in 1999 reported that young black men in particular were moving back into the economic mainstream at a faster rate than their white counterparts, and crime levels were falling in areas where joblessness was declining. The jobless rate for young black men was still twice that for young white men, but the improvement was encouraging.

Even so, tensions that had existed throughout the twentieth century persisted. Issues stemming from continuing discrimination in finding jobs and persistent antagonism by the police erupted in the spring of 2001 in Cincinnati, Ohio, when a white policeman killed an unarmed black youth. Confrontations around the city provided a bitter reminder of riots in the past.

In early 2002, African American television correspondent Ed Bradley pointed to changes he had seen in the course of his career. "When asked about progress," he said, "I'm often reminded of the old lady sitting in the church who says, 'It ain't what it ought to be, but thank God it ain't what it used to be.'" Bradley was right, but many African Americans wondered when further change would come.

Women Women likewise made steady progress in the 1990s. They were increasingly involved in academic programs and professions that had been closed to them several decades earlier. In 2001, for example, women made up 49.4 percent of all first-year law students, compared to 10 percent in 1970; that pattern was reflected in other segments of society as well. At the same time, there was still continuing resistance to inclusion at the top. Women started to become the heads of major firms as the glass ceiling, preventing women from rising to the top of the corporate ladder, began to crack in the 1990s, yet most leaders were still men.

Abortion remained a polarizing issue, particularly as antiabortion activists sought to disrupt abortion clinics. Physicians performing abortions found their lives at risk, and Barnet Slepian, a Buffalo doctor, was killed in 1998 in his own home by a sniper shooting through a window. Abortion opponents also took aim at a seldom used, late-term procedure they called "partial birth abortion." Congress passed a measure banning the procedure, but President Clinton vetoed it. In 2000, when the Food and Drug Administration finally approved a drug known as RU-486, the so-called abortion pill, abortion opponents jumped into the controversy and sought—unsuccessfully—to attach conditions that would effectively eliminate its use. Abortion remained one of the issues dividing the American people.

The abortion debate was just one measure that created a backlash against the feminist label, even as men and women both accepted the changes brought by the women's movement. Women hesitated to be associated with what they still considered a radical fringe, and that affected how they identified themselves. In 1998, only 26 percent of working women said, "To me, a career is as important as being a wife and mother," down from 36 percent in 1979. While young women took for granted the gains fought for and won by their mothers and grandmothers, fewer wanted to call themselves feminists. Yet the feminist movement persisted and brought continued improvements in the lives of women.

Latinos Latinos likewise pushed for greater equality and had demographic change on their side. The 2000 census and subsequent studies based on the data provided noted that the Latino population spread farther and faster than any previous immigrant wave, even exceeding the influx of eastern Europeans in the early twentieth century. The Latino population increase of 38 percent since 1990 dwarfed the national rise. In 2000, 46 percent of all Latinos owned their own homes, compared to 42 percent a decade before, though that figure still lagged behind the national number of 66 percent. In 2003, Latinos edged past African Americans and became the nation's largest minority group.

The emergence of a sturdy middle class gave Latinos a greater voice in social and political affairs. In 1993, Henry Cisneros became secretary of housing and urban development, and Federico Peña became secretary of transportation in Bill Clinton's administration. At the end of the decade, Latino political figures became even more numerous and visible. In California, for example, both the lieutenant governor and the speaker of the assembly were Chicano, as was the mayor of San Jose. Democrat Loretta Sanchez, who defeated eight-term congressman Robert Dornan in Orange County, served in the U.S. House of Representatives. In the George W. Bush administration, White House counsel Alberto Gonzales played a major role in advising the president during his first term and became attorney general in the second.

As the nation's overall unemployment rate dropped in the mid-1990s, the rate for the 12 million Latino workers likewise fell—from 9.8 percent in 1992 to 7.3 percent in 1997. Despite that drop, the rate remained higher than the rate for white workers. Meanwhile, median Latino household income fell, even as it rose for every other ethnic and racial group.

Latinos nevertheless had a growing impact on American culture. Merengue music could often be heard in music stores or on the radio. Argentine steakhouses could be found in many cities. Use of the Spanish language became more common around the country. President George W. Bush himself used Spanish in appealing to this important electoral bloc.

Native Americans   Native Americans found they had less influence, in part because of their smaller numbers. In the 2000 census, only 4.1 million people, or 1.5 percent of the population, identified themselves as American Indian or Alaska Native. Yet Indians still managed to keep the causes that concerned them before the public.

Indians continued their legal efforts to regain lost land. In 1999, the federal government joined the Oneida Indians in a lawsuit arguing that state and local governments in central New York had illegally acquired 270,000 acres of land from them in the late eighteenth and early nineteenth centuries and that restitution was warranted. In early 2000, the federal government returned 84,000 acres in northern Utah that it had taken from the Ute in 1916 when it sought to secure the rights to valuable reserves of oil shale. "We're trying to do the right thing, returning land to its rightful owners," Energy Secretary Bill Richardson declared.

Indians also pressed successfully for the return of their ancestors' skeletal remains, removed by white scientists and museum officials over the course of the last century. Ever since passage of the Native American Graves Protection and Repatriation Act of 1990, skeletons and sacred objects flowed back to the tribes where they belonged. In 1997, Harvard's Peabody Museum sent back the bones of nearly 2,000 Pueblo Indians in the largest single return of these remains.

Native American women became increasingly active in the reform effort. Ada Deer, who had successfully fought the government's termination policy in the 1970s (see Chapter 29), served as assistant secretary of the interior in the 1990s. Winona LaDuke, an environmental activist, directed the Honor the Earth Fund and the White Earth Land Recovery Project, fought needless hydroelectric development, and was singled out by *Time* magazine as one of the nation's 50 most promising leaders under 40 years of age. In 2000, she served as Ralph Nader's vice presidential running mate on the small Green Party ticket.

An important symbolic gesture occurred in the last months of the Clinton administration. As the Bureau of Indian Affairs celebrated its 175th anniversary, Kevin Gover, head of the agency, reversed the pattern that had been so predominant in the past when he apologized for the nation's repressive treatment of Native Americans. "In truth, this is no occasion for celebration," he said. It was, rather, a time "for sorrowful truths to be spoken, a time for contrition." He spoke of "the decimation of the mighty bison herds, the use of the poison alcohol to destroy minds and body, and the cowardly killing of women and children." The suffering inflicted on the Indians "made for tragedy on a scale so ghastly that it cannot be dismissed as merely the inevitable consequence of the clash of competing cultures."

Asian Americans   Asian Americans enjoyed real success in the 1990s. With about 11 million people—approximately 4 percent of the national population—of Asian descent in the United States in 2000, there was a now critical mass. They came from a variety of cultures, to be sure, and Filipinos often had different experiences than Chinese or Koreans or Japanese, yet together they had an increasingly important impact on American society. Many of the children enjoyed remarkable educational achievements, making up a disproportionate share of the students at the most prestigious universities. In 2000, President Clinton appointed Norman Y. Mineta as secretary of commerce, making him the first Asian American to hold a cabinet post.

Yet Asian Americans in the 1990s found themselves in an ambiguous position. While they had higher median incomes than whites, due in part to a dedicated work ethic, newcomers faced serious economic problems. Old assumptions also persisted. A report in 2000 observed that many Americans still saw Asian Americans as secretive and inscrutable. "Too many people in this country continue to see us in simple stereotypes," complained Paul M. Ong, a social policy professor at the University of California at Los Angeles.

Gays   The struggle for gay rights also continued, and slowly gays began to achieve their demands. In a major change in 2000, the Big Three automakers—General Motors, Ford, and Chrysler—announced health care benefits for partners of gay employees, a move that covered 465,000 workers. That same year, Vermont recognized same-sex relationships through civil unions, though it stopped short of permitting gay marriages. In 2002, the American Academy of Pediatricians announced its support of the right of gay men and women to adopt the children of their partners. Gay activism helped broaden the definition of family. As the gay rights movement celebrated the 30-year anniversary of the gay rights parade commemorating the 1969 riot at the Stonewall Inn in Greenwich Village that had sparked gay resistance, proponents noted that the event had changed from a protest to a party. As the *New York Times* observed, "that in itself is a sign of success."

Still, there was continuing resistance to gays playing a more visible role in American society. In 1998, 21-year-old University of Wyoming student Matthew Shepherd died after being brutally beaten and tortured by two men troubled by his lifestyle. While most American cities had thriving gay communities, in some quarters there was still deep-seated resistance to gays living openly.

Resistance became more open in the election of 2004. As Massachusetts courts ruled that gay marriage was constitutional and San Francisco permitted gay couples to marry there, a backlash helped mobilize conservatives around the country, and voters in a number of states approved constitutional bans on gay marriage.

DEMOCRATIC REVIVAL

The 1990s saw a Democratic revival. After the success of conservative Republicans in the 1980s in challenging the assumptions of the liberal welfare state and advancing a more limited conception of the role of government, Democrats regrouped, reformulated their message, and followed the lead of the Republicans in relying on new forms of media to broadcast political appeals. Nevertheless, for much of the decade, even as the Democrats regained the White House, the Republicans maintained control of Congress, and bitter partisan fighting was the result.

Democratic Victory

VIDEO

Bill Clinton Sells Himself to America: Presidential Campaign Ad (1992)

In 1992, the Democratic party mounted an aggressive challenge to Republican rule. After a fierce primary campaign, Governor Bill Clinton of Arkansas triumphed over a crowded field of candidates. Overcoming allegations of marital infidelity, marijuana use, and draft evasion, he argued that it was time for a new generation to take command. Forty-six years old, he had reached maturity in the 1960s and stood in stark contrast to President George H. W. Bush, now running for reelection, who had come of age during World War II. The third candidate in what became a three-way race was H. Ross Perot, a billionaire businessman from Texas who had made a fortune in the computer data processing field.

This campaign, more than any in the past, was fought on television. In addition to three televised presidential debates, the candidates appeared on talk shows and interview programs. Perot energized his campaign with appearances on *Larry King Live*. Bill Clinton used a post–Super Bowl appearance on *60 Minutes*

VIDEO

Bill Clinton, First Inauguration

to answer charges questioning his character and later played his saxophone on *The Arsenio Hall Show* and appeared on MTV.

On election day, Clinton won 43 percent of the popular vote to 38 percent for Bush and 19 percent for Perot. The electoral vote margin was even larger: 357 for Clinton, 168 for Bush, zero for Perot. The Democrats retained control of both houses of Congress, with more women and minority members than ever before.

The president-elect wanted to check the cynicism poisoning political life. In 1964, three-quarters of the American public trusted the government to do the right thing most of the time. Three decades later, after the deception of leaders in the Vietnam War and the Watergate affair, the number was closer to one-quarter. Clinton sought to shift the nation's course after 12 years of Republican rule with his Cabinet nominations that included four women, four African Americans, and two Latinos. In his inaugural address, Clinton declared that "a new season of American renewal has begun."

Clinton soon found his hands full at home. Although the economy finally began to improve, the public gave the president little credit for the upturn. He gained Senate ratification of the North American Free Trade Agreement (NAFTA)—aimed at promoting free trade among Canada, Mexico, and the United States—in November 1993 after a bitter battle in which opponents argued that American workers would lose their jobs to less-well-paid Mexicans. But he failed to win approval of his major legislative initiative: health care reform. The

The "Hip" Candidate Bill Clinton was an exuberant campaigner who used his musical talent to attract support when he ran for president in 1992. Here he plays his saxophone on nationwide television on *The Arsenio Hall Show* in Los Angeles. What kind of image was Clinton trying to convey in this photograph? *(AP/Wide World Photos)*

United States lagged behind most other industrialized countries in the way it provided for public health. Medicare took care of the elderly, and Medicaid provided some relief for the poor, but both were limited when compared to the coverage provided by other nations. Particularly troublesome were escalating costs and the lack of universal medical care, which left 35 million Americans with no medical insurance. Clinton's complicated remedy provoked intense opposition from the health care and insurance industries and from politicians with plans of their own. In the end, he was unable to persuade Congress either to accept his approach or adopt a workable alternative.

DOCUMENT

Clinton Health Care Reform Proposals (1993)

Republican Resurgence

Voters demonstrated their dissatisfaction in the midterm elections of 1994. Republicans argued that government regulations were hampering business and costing too much. They challenged the notion that the federal government was primarily responsible for health care and other such services. Capitalizing on the continuing appeal of the leadership of Ronald Reagan in the 1980s, they demanded a scaled-down role for the government. Republicans won control of both the Senate and the House of Representatives for the first time in over 40 years. At the state level,

Republicans picked up 12 governorships and took control in seven of the eight largest states.

The election marked the end of the commitment to the welfare state. The 104th Congress moved aggressively to make good on its promises—outlined during the campaign in the Republicans' Contract with America—to scale back the role of the federal government, eliminate environmental regulations, cut funding for educational programs such as Head Start, reduce taxes, and balance the budget. Under the leadership of Newt Gingrich, the new speaker of the House of Representatives, Congress launched a frontal attack on the budget, proposing massive cuts in virtually all social services. It demanded eliminating three Cabinet departments and gutting the National Endowment for the Humanities, the National Endowment for the Arts, and the Public Broadcasting System. When, at the end of 1995, the president and the speaker tangled with one another on the size of the cuts and refused to compromise on a budget, the government shut down and 800,000 federal employees found themselves temporarily "furloughed."

While the House of Representatives passed most of the measures proposed in the Contract with America, only a few of them became law. The Senate balked at some; the president vetoed others. After all the attention it received, voters lost interest in the Contract with America. As the election of 1996 approached, Newt Gingrich found himself out of favor as millions of Americans began to realize that they would suffer from the cuts more aggressive Republicans sought.

A Second Term for Clinton

As Bill Clinton sought a second term in 1996, the Republicans nominated Senate Minority Leader Robert Dole as their presidential candidate. The 73-year-old Dole ran a lackluster campaign. His pledge to push through a sweeping 15 percent tax reduction failed to excite voter interest. Even supporters wondered how he would balance the budget at the same time. Stung by Democratic congressional defeats two years before, Clinton reshaped his own image and co-opted Republican issues, pledging to balance the budget himself and enraging liberal supporters by signing a welfare reform bill that slashed benefits and removed millions of people from the rolls. At the same time, he posed as the protector of Medicare and other programs that were threatened by proposed Republican cuts.

Clinton's strategy worked. On election day, he won a resounding victory over Dole. He received 49 percent of the popular vote to 41 percent for Dole and 8 percent for H. Ross Perot, who ran again, though this time less successfully. In the electoral tally, Clinton received 379 votes to 159 for Dole. Yet the Republicans kept control of Congress. In the House of Representatives, they lost a number of seats but retained a majority. In the Senate, they added two seats to what they had won in 1994. Around the country, voters seemed willing to support Clinton, but not to give him the mandate he sought.

Partisan Politics and Impeachment

Democrats made small gains in the midterm elections of 1998. They worried about their prospects as election day approached, for Clinton had been accused by an independent prosecutor, appointed by the Justice Department, of having engaged in an improper sexual relationship with Monica Lewinsky, a White House intern. While Clinton denied the relationship at first, the lengthy report presented to Congress left little doubt that such a connection existed, and Clinton finally admitted to the relationship in a nationally televised address.

DOCUMENT

Articles of Impeachment Against William Jefferson Clinton (1999)

As Republicans in Congress began to consider impeachment, many Americans outside of Washington felt differently. Disturbed at what Clinton had done in his personal life, they nonetheless approved overwhelmingly of the job he was doing as president; in fact, his approval ratings were higher than those of any of his presidential predecessors in the recent past. Those sentiments were reflected in the 1998 midterm election, which saw the Republicans lose five seats in the House of Representatives and made it even more difficult for them to pursue their own agenda.

DOCUMENT

Bill Clinton, Answers to the Articles of Impeachment (1999)

Despite that clear signal from the voters, House Republicans continued their efforts to remove the president. Just weeks after the election, a majority impeached him on counts of perjury and obstruction of justice. At the start of 1999, the case moved to the Senate for a trial, where Clinton fought to retain his office, just as Andrew Johnson had done 131 years before. In the Senate, presided over by the chief justice of the Supreme Court, a two-thirds vote was necessary to find the president guilty and remove him from office. After weeks of testimony, despite universal condemnation of Clinton's personal behavior, the Senate voted for acquittal. Democrats, joined by a number of Republicans, stood by the president, and with that coalition, neither charge managed to muster even a majority: the count of perjury was decided by a 45–55 vote, while the count of obstruction of justice failed on a 50–50 vote. At long last, the ordeal was over, and the country could deal with more pressing issues again.

Clinton was an enormously successful politician. Not only had he escaped conviction in the highly visible—and embarrassing—impeachment case, but he also managed to co-opt Republican issues and seize the political center. He quietly advanced liberal goals even when he was unable to push major programs, such as his medical insurance plan, through Congress. Suits against the nation's tobacco companies using deliberately misleading advertising in the face of known health risks were popular with the public, and led in 1997 to a landmark $368 billion settlement to cover liability claims and provide reimbursement to the states for medical costs related to smoking. Throughout both terms, polls showed that Clinton remained popular (even when people disapproved of his personal conduct) to the end of his term in office.

THE SECOND BUSH PRESIDENCY

Republicans regained control of the White House in the election of 2000. Unable to oust Bill Clinton from the presidency by impeachment, they were determined to win back what they considered to be rightfully theirs in the conservative resurgence of the past 20 years. Texas Governor George W. Bush (son of former President George H. W. Bush—the first father–son combination since John Adams and John Quincy Adams), promised to return morality and respect to the White House, and appealed to those disturbed by Clinton's personal behavior.

The Election of 2000

The election of 2000 promised to be close. The strong economy gave Vice President Al Gore, the Democratic nominee, an initial advantage. Yet the Republicans, led by the younger Bush, insisted the country needed a change. The campaign revolved around what the government should do with the federal budget surplus, with Republicans arguing that much of the money should be returned to the public in the form of a tax cut and Democrats countering that the surplus should be used to bolster the ailing social security program and to pay down the national debt. In the weeks before the election, polls showed that the race was virtually tied.

On election night, neither Bush nor Gore had captured the 270 electoral votes necessary to win the presidency. The electoral vote in Florida, one of the undecided states, was large enough to give the winner a victory. A recount, required by law, began, and Florida became a battleground as lawyers for both sides swarmed to the state to monitor the counting. Democrats and Republicans argued bitterly about how the recount should proceed. Democrats also contended that in certain African American precincts, voters had been turned away from the polls. That charge was all the more significant since black voters around the country favored Gore by a 9-to-1 margin.

In December, more than five weeks after the election, after suits and countersuits by both sides, the case reached the Supreme Court. In *Bush* v. *Gore,* the justices ruled, by a 5 to 4 vote, with the most conservative justices voting in a bloc, that the recount should be curtailed, leaving Bush the winner. Although Gore won the popular vote by about 450,000 votes, Bush triumphed in the Electoral College by a 271 to 266 majority. Ill feelings persisted as a result of the partisan ruling. Supreme Court Justice John Paul Stevens wrote a scathing dissent, in which he argued: "Although we may never know with complete certainty the identity of the winner of this year's presidential election, the identity of the loser is perfectly clear. It is the nation's confidence in the judge as an impartial guardian of the law."

The voting in congressional races was equally close. The new Senate was evenly split, with each party holding 50 seats. Republicans organized the chamber and gained all committee chairs, since Vice President Dick Cheney broke the tie. Yet five months after the new session began, Senator James Jeffords of Vermont, frustrated with the approach of the Bush administration, left the Republican party, giving control to the Democrats. Republicans also lost seats in the House of Representatives, leaving them with but a nine-vote majority.

The New Leader

George W. Bush had enjoyed an eclectic career before becoming president. Born into a political family, he had shown little interest in politics himself, gravitating into the Texas oil business and then gaining part ownership of a professional baseball team before running successfully for governor of Texas.

Bush was very different from Clinton. Whereas his predecessor was interested in the details of public policy, Bush saw himself as a corporate chief executive officer (CEO) who established the broad outlines of policy but then left the details to others. Ronald Reagan had taken that approach, and while Bush lacked

Looking for a Place in History? George Bush paid close attention to the image conveyed to the American people, and photographers constantly captured him in ways that underscored his importance. Here he stands in front of Mt. Rushmore, with its famous rock sculptures of several of America's best-known presidents. What impression does the juxtaposition in this photograph convey to you? *(AP/World Wide Photos)*

Reagan's communication skills, he had a dogged tenacity that served him well. Early in his presidency, he was able to overcome the image of incompetence that many had of him and to establish close relationships with such counterparts as Vladimir Putin in Russia, Tony Blair in England, and Vicente Fox in Mexico.

Promoting the Private Sector

As president, Bush had the interests of corporate America at heart. During the campaign, he talked about a tax cut, and this became his first priority. Supply-side economists, who argued successfully in the 1980s that lower tax rates were necessary to promote economic growth (see Chapter 30), became more influential in his administration.

By mid-2001, the tax cut became law. It lowered tax rates for everyone, allowed more tax-free saving for education, and reduced estate taxes. The measure promised to save every taxpayer at least several hundred dollars a year, though it was heavily skewed in favor of the wealthy. Meanwhile, the economy continued to falter as the growth rate slowed and a full-blown recession ensued.

Like his father and Reagan, Bush wanted to reduce the size of government and squelch its intrusions into private affairs, but at the same time, he sought to bolster the military. His first budget, for example, proposed deep cuts in health programs for people without access to health insurance. But his proposals for defense called for far greater spending, even before the terrorist attacks of September 11, 2001. Military spending increased dramatically in the years that followed, providing the administration already dealing with less revenue as a result of the tax cut with an even stronger argument to cut back social programs that conservatives had never liked.

Bush infuriated environmentalists. Quietly, the new administration moved to allow road building in national forests and made it easier for mining companies to dig for gold, zinc, and copper on public lands. Under pressure from real estate interests, the administration sought to shrink legal protection of endangered species. And, catering to the interests of oil companies, it fought to promote drilling in the protected Arctic National Wildlife Refuge, even in the face of estimates that there was very little oil there to be found. When his own Environmental Protection Agency (EPA) issued a report in mid-2002 linking the use of fossil fuel (such as coal and oil) to global warming, Bush dismissed the study, making it clear that he had no confidence in the judgments of the scientists working for the EPA.

A Second Term for Bush

The election of 2004 was bitter and contentious. Running for reelection, Bush faced Massachusetts senator John Kerry, a Vietnam War hero who attacked Republican efforts in the foreign policy sphere, questioned the administration's ability to protect the nation from terrorist attacks, and charged that tax cuts had done little to revive a still-sluggish economy. Both candidates raised huge amounts of money, far more than had been solicited in the past, and both parties ended up running attack ads that questioned the integrity of the other candidate. Republican groups tore into Kerry's service record; Democratic groups called attention to Bush's successful effort to avoid the war in Vietnam by serving in the National Guard. Civility sometimes seemed to disappear. But even though Bush seemed vulnerable, Kerry failed to arouse the interest of voters. In a race that remained close to the end, Bush prevailed with 51 percent of the popular vote and a modest Electoral College majority. Republicans added to their majorities in both the Senate and the House of Representatives, as voters in the heartland of America agreed with the Republican party's conservative moral values.

At the start of his second term, Bush moved quickly to demand reform of social security. The program, which had run surpluses in the past, faced increasing pressures as the baby boom generation born just after World War II approached retirement. Experts disagreed on just when the system would run short of money, but it was clear that problems were imminent in the next few decades. Bush called for an overhaul that would allow workers to invest part of their contributions in private retirement accounts that would depend on gains in the stock market. Critics charged that the new proposal would undermine the policy of guaranteed pensions and could make millions of workers vulnerable if the market dropped, as it had just a few years before. They argued that the system could be made more secure by increasing payroll taxes, raising the amount on which such taxes were levied, or mandating that workers retire a year or two later. Even as Bush pushed ahead, members of both political parties resisted the effort.

The budget that Bush submitted to Congress in early 2005 reflected the administration's priorities. As the surplus of the Clinton years turned into an ever-larger deficit under Bush—estimated to be almost $400 billion in the year ahead—the budget still contained tax cuts of $100 billion over the next five years. Critics charged that the underlying intention was to make it impossible to support programs aimed at assisting poor people like Rod and Marlene Garrett, whom we met at the start of the chapter. They also noted the irony that this budget was the largest ever in the nation's history and pointed out that an administration that claimed to want to scale down big government was playing an ever-increasing role when it came to regulation of social issues such as faith-based initiatives and abortion.

The Midterm Elections of 2006

By the time of the 2006 midterm Congressional elections, many Americans were disturbed by the violence of the war in Iraq (see next section) and troubled by a conflict that seemed to be spiraling out of control. They were also frustrated by a series of scandals on Capitol Hill and by the tepid response of the administration to the devastation caused by Hurricane Katrina in New Orleans in September 2005. Voter discontent shifted control of Congress. Democrats won a substantial majority in the House of Representatives and a narrow margin in the Senate. In his last two years in office, Bush faced even greater challenges than before.

FOREIGN POLICY IN THE POST–COLD WAR WORLD

As the Cold War ended, the United States had to examine its own assumptions about its international role. The world was now a different place. With extraordinary communications advances, it was more closely linked than ever before. Violence and upheaval in one part of the globe now had an almost immediate impact on other areas. In this setting, new questions arose. What kind of leadership would the United States exert as the one remaining superpower on the globe? How involved would it become in peacekeeping missions in violence-wracked lands? How would it deal with the threat of terrorism? These questions, asked in different forms over the course of past centuries, helped shape foreign policy in transitional times.

The Balkan Crisis

In the Balkans, in Eastern Europe, ethnic and religious violence worsened in the mid-1990s. Yugoslavia—a collection of different ethnic constituencies held together by a Communist dictatorship—had collapsed in 1991. Muslims and Croats had fought bitterly with Serbs in the province of Bosnia (see Chapter 30). As the region became increasingly volatile, the United States remained out of the conflict, while the United Nations proved unable to bring about peace. In mid-1995, a North Atlantic Treaty Organization (NATO) bombing campaign forced the Bosnian Serbs into negotiations, and a peace conference held in Dayton, Ohio, led to the commitment of American troops, along with soldiers from other countries, to stabilize the region.

In 1999, a smoldering conflict in Kosovo, another of the provinces of the former Yugoslavia, led to war. In an effort to stop Slobodan Milosevic—the Serbian leader responsible for the devastation of Bosnia—from squelching a movement for

How Others See Us

Many Europeans opposed the U.S. invasion of Iraq in 2003. President George W. Bush lashed out equally an-grily at his European opponents as he proceeded with the war. Europeans continued to view the American government with suspicion at the start of his second term, but still hoped for a thaw in relations. This piece by Elfriede Jelinek of Austria, winner of the 2004 Nobel Prize in Literature, reflects a prevalent European view.

President Bush needs Europe. He knows it himself by now. He started a war in defiance of in-ternational law and didn't pay any attention to the Europeans, and with that he split the continent into a "new" (good) Europe and an "old" (bad) one.

Now he ought to convince Europeans that he is not planning another war (for example against Syria or Iran), while at the same time professing to think highly of the opinion of European nations and to value them. The freedom that Mr. Bush proclaimed in his inauguration speech cannot be achieved and maintained without the help of the Europeans. First and foremost he has to convince Europe that he is not planning a new war, which shouldn't be difficult.

After all, his troops can only with the greatest difficulty halfway pacify Iraq.

- *Why does Elfriede Jelinek suggest that Europeans opposed President Bush earlier?*
- *Why does Jelinek feel that Bush needs the assistance of Europe now?*
- *What does Jelinek believe Bush should do to reassure the Europeans?*

Source: New York Times, February 20, 2005. Copyright 2005 by the New York Times.

---

autonomy in Kosovo, NATO launched an American-led bombing campaign. Milo-sevic responded with an even more violent "ethnic cleansing" campaign that drove hundreds of thousands of Kosovars from their homes. Milosevic finally suc-cumbed after refusing to recognize the election victory of the opposition leader in 2000. He was arrested in 2001 and brought to the Netherlands to stand trial for crimes against humanity at the International Court of Justice in The Hague.

The Middle East in Flames

In the Middle East, Clinton tried to play the part of peacemaker, just as Jimmy Carter had done 15 years before. On September 13, 1993, in a dramatic ceremony on the White House lawn, Palestine Liberation Organization leader Yasir Arafat and Israeli prime minister Yitzhak Rabin took the first public step toward ending years of conflict as they shook hands and signed a peace agreement that led to Palestinian self-rule in the Gaza strip. In 1995, Israel and the PLO signed a further agreement, and the Israelis handed over control of the West Bank of the Jordan River to the Palestinians. A treaty between Jordan and Israel brought peace on still another border. While extremists tried to destroy the peace process by assassinat-ing Rabin, the effort to heal old animosities continued. As Clinton prepared to leave office, he sought to seal a final agreement between the Israelis and the Pales-tinians, but this time he was not successful, as the Palestinians rejected a generous

A Historic Handshake President Bill Clinton helped orchestrate this famous handshake between Israeli prime minister Yitzhak Rabin and Palestine Liberation Organization chairman Yasir Arafat in 1993. Though the two men had long been adversaries, they now began to work together to settle the bitter conflicts in the Middle East. How do Clinton's actions in the picture give a sense of his role? How do the two longtime adversaries appear to react to one another? *(AP/Wide World Photos)*

settlement offer, and the smoldering Middle Eastern tensions burst once more in flames that threatened to engulf the entire region.

The level of Mideast violence in the early twenty-first century was worse than it had ever been before. The Israeli policy of building settlements in occupied Arab land, and the Palestinian unwillingness to compromise at the negotiating table, culminated in a horrifying escalation of suicide bombings and other bloody attacks following an Israeli visit to a holy Palestinian religious site in Jerusalem, a city claimed by both sides.

Bush was at first reluctant to intervene. Eventually, as the killing cycle continued, he moved from inattention to intermittent attention, becoming increasingly sympathetic to Israel as the suicide attacks continued. He lashed out at Yasir Arafat for not speaking out against the bombings, but was unable to bring the adversaries to the negotiating table. Nor could he do anything about fences the Israelis built both in the West Bank and the Gaza Strip to protect settlements there. Meanwhile, many of the European nations, feeling that only the United States could help bring peace to the region, voiced dismay at American policy.

African Struggles

Africa also remained a source of concern to American policymakers, who struggled to deal with a series of never-ending crises. Left behind as other parts of the world industrialized and moved ahead, the continent was also ravaged by the AIDS epidemic, which infected and killed far more people than in other parts of the world. Bill Clinton made a highly publicized visit to Africa, as he sought to dramatize international responsibility for assisting the continent, and he watched with satisfaction as Nelson Mandela handed over power in South Africa to his successor in a peaceful transition. But other areas proved more problematic. Six months after Clinton became president, a firefight with one faction in war-ravaged Somalia, in East Africa, resulted in several dozen American casualties. The shooting prompted some Americans, still haunted by the memory of Vietnam, to demand withdrawal. Reluctant to back down as he groped to define his policy, Clinton first increased the number of U.S. troops, then in 1993, recalled the soldiers without having restored order.

The United States was similarly baffled by a crisis in Rwanda, in central Africa. There a fragile balance of power between two ethnic groups—the Tutsis and the Hutus—broke down, and hard-line Hutus embarked on a massive genocidal campaign that resulted in the slaughter of hundreds of thousands of innocent Tutsis and moderate Hutus. The United States, like many European nations, debated the possibility of intervention on humanitarian grounds but decided to do nothing. Eventually the killing stopped, although the friction between the rival groups remained.

George W. Bush was much less interested in Africa than his predecessor. He chose not to attend a conference on sustainable development held in South Africa in the summer of 2002, which gave a clear signal that the United States was more concerned with its own business interests than with the economic problems of the less-developed world. In 2003, he visited five African nations, but it was a whirlwind trip aimed at supporting areas sympathetic to the United States.

Relations with Russia

In the area that formerly had been the Soviet Union, the United States continued to try to promote both democracy and free-market capitalism. It worked closely with Boris Yeltsin in Russia, and then with his successor, Vladimir Putin, who assumed power on the last day of the twentieth century and was then elected president in his own right in 2001. But Russia remained unstable, still caught up in the complications of a huge political, social, and economic transformation.

Bush recognized the need to cooperate with Putin. In a series of meetings, both in Russia and in the United States, the two men developed a close working relationship that helped maintain European stability. The Soviet Union had ceased to exist, but the component parts still remained important in the larger international scene.

Terror on September 11

On September 11, 2001, three hijacked airplanes slammed into the World Trade Center towers in New York City and the Pentagon in Washington, D.C. The fire in New York from exploding jet fuel caused the towers to crumble, altering the sky-

An Indelible Image of September 11, 2001 The World Trade Center towers in New York City once dominated the skyline on the Hudson River. As two hijacked commercial airplanes crashed into the tall structures on September 11, 2001, both towers burst into flames and later collapsed, killing most of the people who were still inside. What impression does this photograph of the burning towers convey? (*Steve Ludlum/The New York Times*)

line forever. Altogether about 3,000 people died in the terrorist attacks. A fourth plane, probably headed for either the White House or the Capitol, crashed in Pennsylvania when passengers fought back against the attackers.

The hijackers were Muslim extremists, most from Saudi Arabia, trained at flight schools in the United States, who belonged to the al Qaeda network headed by Saudi exile Osama bin Laden. Bin Laden and his organization were headquartered in Afghanistan, where the extremely conservative Muslim Taliban group had literally imposed the law of the Qur'an, the Muslim holy book, on civil society. Bin Laden and his associates hated the United States for its Middle Eastern policy of support for Israel, as well as for its affluent and materialistic values that often conflicted with their religious and cultural values.

The terrorist attacks shattered America's sense of security, at least within its own borders. Irate at the unprovoked strikes, President Bush quickly launched a bombing campaign to smoke out Osama bin Laden and his network in Afghanistan. Although the bombing, followed by attacks by ground troops in

Afghanistan, defeated the Taliban and drove its members from power, the campaign failed to find Osama bin Laden, who remained at large.

DOCUMENT

George W. Bush, Address to Congress (September 20, 2001)

As Bush's approval ratings soared to over 90 percent, he vowed a lengthy campaign to root out terrorism wherever it surfaced in the world. He embarked on a massive governmental reorganization to create a new Department of Homeland Security to help prevent future attacks, and he also used terrorism as a reason to allow the government to encroach on individual liberties—in the interest of security—more extensively than in the past. Ironically, a president dedicated to smaller government now found himself in the forefront of an effort to give government an even larger role.

American Muslims were often the victims. Some faced attacks by other Americans angry about the terrorist strikes. Others were taken into custody, often without being charged with a crime, on the suspicion that they were somehow involved, as the government instituted new security measures.

DOCUMENT

George W. Bush, from "National Security Strategy of the United States of America" (September 2002)

The anti-terrorism campaign escalated. In early 2002, Bush spoke out forcefully against what he called an "axis of evil," as he referred to Iraq, Iran, and North Korea. He was particularly intent on driving Iraqi leader Saddam Hussein from power. Hussein had launched the attack on Kuwait that had led to the Gulf War during the administration of Bush's father. Now, 11 years later, Bush argued that Hussein was creating weapons of mass destruction and vowed to bring about a regime change. Within Bush's own administration, Secretary of State Colin Powell, inclined to a more restrained foreign policy, fought against Secretary of Defense Donald Rumsfeld and Vice President Dick Cheney, who enthusiastically supported an attack. Bush's argument that he could invade Iraq even without the support of Congress aroused a firestorm of protest both in the United States and around the world.

The war in Iraq, fought with British but not United Nations support, began in March 2003. American forces were successful, and just a month and a half later, Bush declared that the major phase of combat operations was over. In December, U.S. soldiers captured Saddam Hussein hiding in a hole in the ground. But even the capture of the Iraqi dictator could not quell increasing opposition to the American occupation, which led to fierce fighting in the months that followed. As the deadline for handing sovereignty over to Iraq in mid-2004 approached, Sunnis, Shiites, and Kurds fought with each other for a share of power, but were united in their opposition to the continuing American presence. Insurgent attacks against American troops and Iraqis in new official positions continued as Iraq descended into civil war. Photographs of American abuse of prisoners in the notorious Abu Ghraib prison aroused resentment in the Middle East and among people around the world. By the end of 2006, the American death toll in Iraq approached 3,000 and exceeded the number killed in the terrorist attacks of 9/11, with another 14,000 Americans wounded. As the Iraqi government demonstrated its inability to maintain order in the face of mounting sectarian conflict, more and more Americans demanded an end to involvement in what they perceived as serious, and perhaps intractable, problems.

TIMELINE

1992	Bill Clinton elected president	**1999**	Bill Clinton acquitted by the Senate
1993	Palestine Liberation Organization and Israel sign peace treaty	**2000**	George W. Bush elected president
		2001	Tax cut passed
1994	Nelson Mandela elected president of South Africa		Terrorists strike New York City and Washington, D.C.
		2003	War in Iraq begins
1996	Bill Clinton reelected	**2004**	George W. Bush reelected
1998	Bill Clinton impeached by the House of Representatives		

Conclusion

The Recent Past in Perspective

In the 1990s, the United States prospered in a period of economic growth longer than any in its history. After weathering a recession at the start of the decade, the economy began to boom, and the boom continued for the next 10 years. Most middle- and upper-class Americans prospered. The budget deficit disappeared, and the government ran a sizable surplus. Yet not all Americans shared in the prosperity. Despite the drop in the unemployment level, many of the available jobs paid little more than the minimum wage, and people like the Garretts, met at the start of the chapter, had trouble making ends meet. Members of minority groups, whose numbers grew throughout the decade, had the toughest time of all.

Meanwhile, Americans worried about their role in the outside world. As they enjoyed their newfound prosperity, some were reluctant to spend money in an activist role abroad. They debated what to do about the defense establishment, which had begun to deteriorate, and were hesitant to become deeply involved in foreign conflicts where they had trouble ascertaining American interests. Then, in 2001, the brutal terrorist attacks on New York City and Washington, D.C., mobilized the nation. Recognizing at long last that terrorism threatened the entire world, including the United States, they prepared themselves for an extended effort to try to bring it under control and to make the world a safer place. As they had in years past, in both World War I and World War II, the United States again sought to protect the democratic way of life for the American people and for people elsewhere as well.

Questions for Review and Reflection

1. What happened to the economy in the 1990s, and how did economic developments affect political action?

2. How were the Democrats able to regain power in 1992 after more than a decade of Republican rule?

3. How successful was Bill Clinton's presidency?

4. What did the closeness of the elections of 2000 and 2004 indicate about divisions in American society?

5. How did the terrorist attacks of September 11, 2001, affect the course of American foreign policy?

Discovering U.S. History Online

United States Census 2000 http://www.census.gov/main/www/cen2000.html
Includes searchable data using the "American Factfinder" and "State and Country Quick Facts."

Homelessness: Programs and the People They Serve www.huduser.org/publications/homeless/homeless_tech.html
The full text of this detailed report on the state of homelessness at the end of the twentieth century is available online in pdf format.

William Jefferson Clinton www.ipl.org/ref/POTUS/wjclinton.html
This site contains basic factual data about Clinton's election and presidency, speeches, and online biographies.

Investigating the President: The Impeachment Trial www.cnn.com/ALLPOLITICS/resources/1998/lewinsky
This site from CNN provides information and documents about the scandals surrounding President Clinton and his impeachment.

Election Collection 2000 web.archive.org/collections/e2k.html
This site contains links to 797 candidate Web sites and other sites covering the election day and its aftermath. The sites are presented in their archived state—that is, as they were at the time of the election.

George Walker Bush www.ipl.org/ref/POTUS/gwbush.html
This site contains basic factual data about Bush's election and presidency, speeches, and online biographies.

A Nation Challenged www.nytimes.com/pages/national/dayofterror
This site from the *New York Times* contains archives for six months of stories and accounts, including video images and pictures, of the September 11, 2001, terrorist attacks on the World Trade Center towers in New York City and the Pentagon in Washington, D.C.

Fiction and Film

Sherman Alexie's *The Lone Ranger and Tonto Fistfight in Heaven* (1993) is a collection of stories about contemporary Indian life; *Ten Little Indians* (2003) is an even more recent collection of Alexie's stories. Robert Olen Butler's *A Good Scent from a Strange Mountain* (1992) is a Pulitzer Prize–winning collection of short stories about Vietnamese immigrants in the United States. Joe Klein's *Primary Colors: A Novel of Politics* (1996), originally published anonymously, provides a vivid portrait of a politician very much like Bill Clinton. Alice Mattison's *Men Giving Money, Women Yelling* (1997) is a series of intersecting stories about the complexities of people's lives and relationships. Lorrie Moore's *Birds of America: Stories* (1998) is another collection of stories about modern culture and life, including one about a nuclear family involved in a meltdown.

Americanos: Latino Life in the United States (1999) is a documentary film about the impact of Hispanics around the country. *The Contender* (2000) is a movie about partisan political bickering. *Black Hawk Down* (2001) is a film about the bitter fighting in Somalia. *Philadelphia* (1993) is a movie about a lawyer who contracts the AIDS virus. *Lone Star* (1996) is a movie set in Rio County, Texas, that provides a vivid portrait of the frictions between Mexicans, Anglos, and African Americans. *Primary Colors* (1998) is the lively film made from the novel of the same name.

Recommended Reading

www.ablongman.com/nash

The Companion Website has a list of recommended readings about the recent past, including the election of 2000; demographic, social, and economic changes; and post–Cold War foreign policy.

Appendix

THE DECLARATION OF INDEPENDENCE IN CONGRESS, JULY 4, 1776

The Unanimous Declaration of the Thirteen United States of America

When, in the course of human events, it becomes necessary for one people to dissolve the political bonds which have connected them with another, and to assume, among the powers of the earth, the separate and equal station to which the laws of nature and of nature's God entitle them, a decent respect to the opinions of mankind requires that they should declare the causes which impel them to the separation.

We hold these truths to be self-evident: That all men are created equal; that they are endowed by their Creator with certain unalienable rights; that among these are life, liberty, and the pursuit of happiness; that, to secure these rights, governments are instituted among men, deriving their just powers from the consent of the governed; that whenever any form of government becomes destructive of these ends, it is the right of the people to alter or to abolish it, and to institute new government, laying its foundation on such principles, and organizing its powers in such form, as to them shall seem most likely to effect their safety and happiness. Prudence, indeed, will dictate that governments long established should not be changed for light and transient causes; and accordingly all experience hath shown that mankind are more disposed to suffer, while evils are sufferable, than to right themselves by abolishing the forms to which they are accustomed. But when a long train of abuses and usurpations, pursuing invariably the same object, evinces a design to reduce them under absolute despotism, it is their right, it is their duty, to throw off such government, and to provide new guards for their future security. Such has been the patient sufferance of these colonies; and such is now the necessity which constrains them to alter their former systems of government. The history of the present King of Great Britain is a history of repeated injuries and usurpations, all having in direct object the establishment of an absolute tyranny over these states. To prove this, let facts be submitted to a candid world.

He has refused his assent to laws, the most wholesome and necessary for the public good.

He has forbidden his governors to pass laws of immediate and pressing importance, unless suspended in their operation till his assent should be obtained; and, when so suspended, he has utterly neglected to attend to them.

He has refused to pass other laws for the accommodation of large districts of people, unless those people would relinquish the right of representation in the legislature, a right inestimable to them, and formidable to tyrants only.

He has called together legislative bodies at places unusual, uncomfortable, and distant from the depository of their public records, for the sole purpose of fatiguing them into compliance with his measures.

He has dissolved representative houses repeatedly, for opposing, with manly firmness, his invasions on the rights of the people.

He has refused for a long time, after such dissolutions, to cause others to be elected; whereby the legislative powers, incapable of annihilation, have returned to the people at large for their exercise; the state remaining, in the mean time, exposed to all the dangers of invasions from without and convulsions within.

He has endeavored to prevent the population of these states; for that purpose obstructing the laws for naturalization of foreigners; refusing to pass others to encourage their migration hither, and raising the conditions of new appropriations of lands.

He has obstructed the administration of justice, by refusing his assent to laws for establishing judiciary powers.

He has made judges dependent on his will alone, for the tenure of their offices, and the amount and payment of their salaries.

He has erected a multitude of new offices, and sent hither swarms of officers to harass our people and eat out their substance.

He has kept among us, in times of peace, standing armies, without the consent of our legislatures.

He has affected to render the military independent of, and superior to, the civil power.

He has combined with others to subject us to a jurisdiction foreign to our constitution, and unacknowledged by our laws, giving his assent to their acts of pretended legislation:

For quartering large bodies of armed troops among us;

For protecting them, by a mock trial, from punishment for any murder which they should commit on the inhabitants of these states;

For cutting off our trade with all parts of the world;

For imposing taxes on us without our consent;

For depriving us, in many cases, of the benefits of trial by jury;

For transporting us beyond seas, to be tried for pretended offenses;

For abolishing the free system of English laws in a neighboring province, establishing therein an arbitrary government, and enlarging its boundaries, so as to render it at once an example and fit instrument for introducing the same absolute rule into these colonies;

For taking away our charters, abolishing our most valuable laws, and altering fundamentally the forms of our governments;

For suspending our own legislatures, and declaring themselves invested with power to legislate for us in all cases whatsoever.

He has abdicated government here, by declaring us out of his protection and waging war against us.

He has plundered our seas, ravaged our coasts, burned our towns, and destroyed the lives of our people.

He is at this time transporting large armies of foreign mercenaries to complete the works of death, desolation, and tyranny already begun with circumstances of cruelty and perfidy scarcely paralleled in the most barbarous ages, and totally unworthy the head of a civilized nation.

He has constrained our fellow-citizens, taken captive on the high seas, to bear arms against their country, to become the executioners of their friends and brethren, or to fall themselves by their hands.

He has excited domestic insurrection among us, and has endeavored to bring on the inhabitants of our frontiers the merciless Indian savages, whose known rule of warfare is an undistinguished destruction of all ages, sexes, and conditions.

In every stage of these oppressions we have petitioned for redress in the most humble terms; our repeated petitions have been answered only by repeated injury. A prince, whose character is thus marked by every act which may define a tyrant, is unfit to be the ruler of a free people.

Nor have we been wanting in our attentions to our British brethren. We have warned them, from time to time, of attempts by their legislature to extend an unwarrantable jurisdiction over us. We have reminded them of the circumstances of our emigration and settlement here. We have appealed to their native justice and magnanimity; and we have conjured them, by the ties of our common kindred, to disavow these usurpations, which would inevitably interrupt our connections and correspondence. They, too, have been deaf to the voice of justice and of consanguinity. We must, therefore, acquiesce in the necessity which denounces our separation, and hold them, as we hold the rest of mankind, enemies in war, in peace friends.

We, therefore, the representatives of the United States of America, in General Congress assembled, appealing to the Supreme Judge of the world for the rectitude of our intentions, do, in the name and by the authority of the good people of these colonies, solemnly publish and declare, that these United Colonies are, and of right, ought to be, FREE AND INDEPENDENT STATES; that they are absolved from all allegiance to the British crown, and that all political connection between them and the state of Great Britain is, and ought to be, totally dissolved; and that, as free and independent states, they have full power to levy war, conclude peace, contract alliances, establish commerce, and do all other acts and things which independent states may of right do. And for the support of this declaration, with a firm reliance on the protection of Devine Providence, we mutually pledge to each other our lives, our fortunes, and our sacred honor.

JOHN HANCOCK

BUTTON GWENNETT	THS. NELSON, JR.	RICHD. STOCKTON
LYMAN HALL	FRANCIS LIGHTFOOT LEE	JNO. WITHERSPOON
GEO. WALTON	CARTER BRAXTON	FRAS. HOPKINSON
WM. HOOPER	ROBT. MORRIS	JOHN HART
JOSEPH HEWES	BENJAMIN RUSH	ABRA. CLARK
JOHN PENN	BENJA. FRANKLIN	JOSIAH BARTLETT
EDWARD RUTLEDGE	JOHN MORTON	WM. WHIPPLE
THOS. HEYWARD, JUNR.	GEO. CLYMER	SAML. ADAMS
THOMAS LYNCH, JUNR.	JAS. SMITH	JOHN ADAMS
ARTHUR MIDDLETON	GEO. TAYLOR	ROBT. TREAT PAINE
SAMUEL CHASE	JAMES WILSON	ELBRIDGE GERRY
WM. PACA	GEO. ROSS	STEP. HOPKINS
THOS. STONE	CAESAR RODNEY	WILLIAM ELLERY
CHARLES CARROLL	GEO. READ	ROGER SHERMAN
OF CARROLLTON	THO. MÍKEAN	SAMÍEL. HUNTINGTON
GEORGE WYTHE	WM. FLOYD	WM. WILLIAMS
RICHARD HENRY LEE	PHIL. LIVINGSTON	OLIVER WOLCOTT
TH. JEFFERSON	FRANS. LEWIS	MATHEW THORNTON
BENJA. HARRISON	LEWIS MORRIS	

THE CONSTITUTION OF THE UNITED STATES OF AMERICA

PREAMBLE
We the People of the United States, in Order to form a more perfect Union, establish Justice, insure domestic Tranquility, provide for the common defence, promote the general Welfare, and secure the Blessings of Liberty to ourselves and our Posterity, do ordain and establish this Constitution for the United States of America.

ARTICLE I.

Section 1   All legislative Powers herein granted shall be vested in a Congress of the United States, which shall consist of a Senate and House of Representatives.

Section 2   The House of Representatives shall be composed of Members chosen every second Year by the People of the several States, and the Electors in each State shall have the Qualifications requisite for Electors of the most numerous Branch of the State Legislature.

No Person shall be a Representative who shall not have attained to the Age of twenty five Years, and been seven Years a Citizen of the United States, and who shall not, when elected, be an Inhabitant of that State in which he shall be chosen.

Representatives and direct Taxes shall be apportioned among the several States which may be included within this Union, according to their respective Numbers, *which shall be determined by adding to the whole Number of free Persons, including those bound to Service for a Term of Years, and excluding Indians not taxed, three fifths of all other Persons.* The actual Enumeration shall be made within three Years after the first Meeting of the Congress of the United States, and within every subsequent Term of ten Years, in such Manner as they shall by Law direct. The Number of Representatives shall not exceed one for every thirty Thousand, but each State shall have at Least one Representative; *and until such enumeration shall be made, the State of New Hampshire shall be entitled to chuse three, Massachusetts eight, Rhode-Island and Providence Plantations one, Connecticut five, New-York six, New Jersey four, Pennsylvania eight, Delaware one, Maryland six, Virginia ten, North Carolina five, South Carolina five, and Georgia three.*

When vacancies happen in the Representation from any State, the Executive Authority thereof shall issue Writs of Election to fill such Vacancies.

The House of Representatives shall chuse their Speaker and other Officers; and shall have the sole Power of Impeachment.

Section 3   The Senate of the United States shall be composed of two Senators from each State, chosen by the Legislature thereof, for six Years; and each Senator shall have one Vote.

Immediately after they shall be assembled in Consequence of the first Election, they shall be divided as equally as may be into three Classes. The Seats of the Senators of the first Class shall be vacated at the Expiration of the second Year, of the second Class at the Expiration of the fourth Year, and of the third Class at the Expiration of the sixth Year, so that one third may be chosen every second Year; and if Vacancies happen by Resignation, or otherwise, during the Recess of the Legislature of any State, the Executive thereof may make temporary Appointments until the next Meeting of the Legislature, which shall then fill such Vacancies.

No Person shall be a Senator who shall not have attained to the Age of thirty Years, and been nine Years a Citizen of the United States, and who shall not, when elected, be an Inhabitant of that State for which he shall be chosen.

The Vice President of the United States shall be President of the Senate, but shall have no Vote, unless they be equally divided.

The Senate shall choose their other Officers, and also a President *pro tempore,* in the Absence of the Vice President, or when he shall exercise the Office of President of the United States.

The Senate shall have the sole Power to try all Impeachments. When sitting for that Purpose, they shall be on Oath or Affirmation. When the President of the United States is tried the Chief Justice shall preside: And no Person shall be convicted without the Concurrence of two thirds of the Members present.

Judgment in Cases of Impeachment shall not extend further than to removal from Office, and disqualification to hold and enjoy any Office of honor, Trust or Profit under the United States: but the Party convicted shall nevertheless be liable and subject to Indictment, Trial, Judgment and Punishment, according to Law.

Section 4   The Times, Places and Manner of holding Elections for Senators and Representatives, shall be prescribed in each State by the Legislature thereof; but the Congress may at any time by Law make or alter such Regulations, except as to the Places of chusing Senators.

The Congress shall assemble at least once in every Year, and such Meeting *shall be on the first Monday in December, unless they shall by Law appoint a different Day.*

Section 5   Each House shall be the Judge of the Elections, Returns and Qualifications of its own Members, and a Majority of each shall constitute a Quorum to do Business; but a smaller Number may adjourn from day to day, and may be authorized to compel the Attendance of absent Members, in such Manner, and under such Penalties as each House may provide.

Each House may determine the Rules of its Proceedings, punish its Members for disorderly Behaviour, and, with the Concurrence of two thirds, expel a Member.

Each House shall keep a Journal of its Proceedings, and from time to time publish the same, excepting such Parts as may in their Judgment require Secrecy; and the Yeas and Nays of the Members of either House on any question shall, at the Desire of one fifth of those Present, be entered on the Journal.

Neither House, during the Session of Congress, shall, without the Consent of the other, adjourn for more than three days, nor to any other Place than that in which the two Houses shall be sitting.

Section 6   The Senators and Representatives shall receive a Compensation for their Services, to be ascertained by Law, and paid out of the Treasury of the United States. They shall in all Cases, except Treason, Felony and Breach of the Peace, be privileged from Arrest during their Attendance at the Session of their respective Houses, and in going to and returning from the same; and for any Speech or Debate in either House, they shall not be questioned in any other Place.

No Senator or Representative shall, during the Time for which he was elected, be appointed to any civil Office under the Authority of the United States, which shall have been created, or the Emoluments whereof shall have been increased during such time; and no Person holding any Office under the United States, shall be a Member of either House during his Continuance in Office.

Section 7   All Bills for raising Revenue shall originate in the House of Representatives; but the Senate may propose or concur with Amendments as on other Bills.

Every Bill which shall have passed the House of Representatives and the Senate, shall, before it become a Law, be presented to the President of the United States; If he approve he shall sign it, but if not he shall return it, with his Objections to that House in which it shall have originated, who shall enter the Objections at large on their Journal, and proceed to reconsider it. If after such Reconsideration two thirds of that House shall agree to pass the Bill, it shall be sent, together with the Objections, to the other House, by which it shall likewise be reconsidered, and if approved by two thirds of that House, it shall become a Law. But in all such Cases the Votes of both Houses shall be determined by yeas and Nays, and the Names of the Persons voting for and against the Bill shall be entered on the Journal of each House respectively. If any Bill shall not be returned by the President within ten Days (Sundays excepted) after it shall have been presented to him, the Same shall be a Law, in like Manner as if he had signed it, unless the Congress by their Adjournment prevent its Return, in which Case it shall not be a Law.

Every Order, Resolution, or Vote to which the Concurrence of the Senate and House of Representatives may be necessary (except on a question of Adjournment) shall be presented to the President of the United States; and before the Same shall take Effect, shall be approved by him, or being disapproved by him, shall be repassed by two thirds of the Senate and House of Representatives, according to the Rules and Limitations prescribed in the Case of a Bill.

Section 8   The Congress shall have Power:

To lay and collect Taxes, Duties, Imposts and Excises, to pay the Debts and provide for the common Defence and general Welfare of the United States; but all Duties, Imposts and Excises shall be uniform throughout the United States;

To borrow Money on the credit of the United States;

To regulate Commerce with foreign Nations, and among the several States, and with the Indian Tribes;

To establish an uniform Rule of Naturalization, and uniform Laws on the subject of Bankruptcies throughout the United States;

To coin Money, regulate the Value thereof, and of foreign Coin, and fix the Standard of Weights and Measures;

To provide for the Punishment of counterfeiting the Securities and current Coin of the United States;

To establish Post Offices and post Roads;

To promote the Progress of Science and useful Arts, by securing for limited Times to Authors and Inventors the exclusive Right to their respective Writings and Discoveries;

To constitute Tribunals inferior to the supreme Court;

To define and punish Piracies and Felonies committed on the high Seas, and Offences against the Law of Nations;

To declare War, grant Letters of Marque and Reprisal, and make Rules concerning Captures on Land and Water;

To raise and support Armies, but no Appropriation of Money to that Use shall be for a longer Term than two Years;

To provide and maintain a Navy;

To make Rules for the Government and Regulation of the land and naval Forces;

To provide for calling forth the Militia to execute the Laws of the Union, suppress Insurrections and repel Invasions;

To provide for organizing, arming, and disciplining, the Militia, and for governing such Part of them as may be employed in the Service of the United States, reserving to the States respectively, the Appointment of the Officers, and the Authority of training the Militia according to the discipline prescribed by Congress;

To exercise exclusive Legislation in all Cases whatsoever, over such District (not exceeding ten Miles square) as may, by Cession of particular States, and the Acceptance of Congress, become the Seat of the Government of the United States, and to exercise like Authority over all Places purchased by the Consent of the Legislature of the State in which the Same shall be, for the Erection of Forts, Magazines, Arsenals, dock-Yards, and other needful Buildings;

To make all Laws which shall be necessary and proper for carrying into Execution the foregoing Powers, and all other Powers vested by this Constitution in the Government of the United States, or in any Department or Officer thereof.

Section 9   *The Migration or Importation of such Persons as any of the States now existing shall think proper to admit, shall not be prohibited by the Congress prior to the Year one thousand eight hundred and eight, but a Tax or duty may be imposed on such Importation, not exceeding ten dollars for each Person.*

The Privilege of the Writ of Habeas Corpus shall not be suspended, unless when in Cases of Rebellion or Invasion the public Safety may require it.

No Bill of Attainder or ex post facto Law shall be passed.

No Capitation, or other direct, Tax shall be laid, unless in Proportion to the Census or Enumeration herein before directed to be taken.

No Tax or Duty shall be laid on Articles exported from any State.

No Preference shall be given by any Regulation of Commerce or Revenue to the Ports of one State over those of another: nor shall Vessels bound to, or from, one State, be obliged to enter, clear, or pay Duties in another.

No Money shall be drawn from the Treasury, but in Consequence of Appropriations made by Law; and a regular Statement and Account of the Receipts and Expenditures of all public Money shall be published from time to time.

No Title of Nobility shall be granted by the United States: And no Person holding any Office of Profit or Trust under them, shall, without the Consent of the Congress, accept of any present, Emolument, Office, or Title, of any kind whatever, from any King, Prince, or foreign State.

Section 10   No State shall enter into any Treaty, Alliance, or Confederation; grant Letters of Marque and Reprisal; coin Money; emit Bills of Credit; make any Thing but gold and silver Coin a Tender in Payment of Debts; pass any Bill of Attainder, ex post facto Law, or Law impairing the Obligation of Contracts, or grant any Title of Nobility.

No State shall, without the Consent of the Congress, lay any Imposts or Duties on Imports or Exports, except what may be absolutely necessary for executing it's inspection Laws: and the net Produce of all Duties and Imposts, laid by any State on Imports or Exports, shall be for the Use of the Treasury of the United States; and all such Laws shall be subject to the Revision and Controul of the Congress.

No State shall, without the Consent of Congress, lay any Duty of Tonnage, keep Troops, or Ships of War in time of Peace, enter into any Agreement or Compact with another State, or with a foreign Power, or engage in War, unless actually invaded, or in such imminent Danger as will not admit of delay.

ARTICLE II.

Section 1   The executive Power shall be vested in a President of the United States of America. He shall hold his Office during the Term of four Years, and, together with the Vice President, chosen for the same Term, be elected, as follows

Each State shall appoint, in such Manner as the Legislature thereof may direct, a Number of Electors, equal to the whole Number of Senators and Representatives to which the State may be entitled in the Congress: but no Senator or Representative, or Person holding an Office of Trust or Profit under the United States, shall be appointed an Elector.

The Electors shall meet in their respective States, and vote by Ballot for two Persons, of whom one at least shall not be an Inhabitant of the same State with themselves. And they shall make a List of all the Persons voted for, and of the Number of Votes for each; which List they shall sign and certify, and transmit sealed to the Seat of Government of the United States, directed to the President of the Senate. The President of the Senate shall, in the Presence of the Senate and House of Representatives, open all the Certificates, and the Votes shall then be counted. The Person having the greatest Number of Votes shall be the President, if such Number be a Majority of the whole Number of Electors appointed; and if there be more than one who have such Majority, and have an equal Number of Votes, then the House of Representatives shall immediately chuse by Ballot one of them for President; and if no Person have a Majority, then from the five highest on the List the said House shall in like Manner chuse the President. But in chusing the President, the Votes shall be taken by States, the Representation from each State having one Vote; A quorum for this Purpose shall consist of a Member or Members from two thirds of the States, and a Majority of all the States shall be necessary to a Choice. In every Case, after the Choice of the President, the Person having the greatest Number of Votes of the Electors shall be the Vice President. But if there should remain two or more who have equal Votes, the Senate shall chuse from them by Ballot the Vice President.

The Congress may determine the Time of chusing the Electors, and the Day on which they shall give their Votes; which Day shall be the same throughout the United States.

No Person except a natural born Citizen, *or a Citizen of the United States, at the time of the Adoption of this Constitution,* shall be eligible to the Office of President; neither shall any Person be eligible to that Office who shall not have attained to the Age of thirty five Years, and been fourteen Years a Resident within the United States.

In Case of the Removal of the President from Office, or of his Death, Resignation, or Inability to discharge the Powers and Duties of the said Office, the Same shall devolve on the Vice President, and the Congress may by Law provide for the Case of Removal, Death, Resignation or Inability, both of the President and Vice President declaring what Officer shall then act as President, and such Officer shall act accordingly, until the Disability be removed, or a President shall be elected.

The President shall, at stated Times, receive for his Services, a Compensation, which shall neither be increased nor diminished during the Period for which he shall have been elected, and he shall not receive within that Period any other Emolument from the United States, or any of them.

Before he enter on the Execution of his Office, he shall take the following Oath or Affirmation: "I do solemnly swear (or affirm) that I will faithfully execute the Office of President of the United States, and will to the best of my Ability, preserve, protect and defend the Constitution of the United States."

Section 2   The President shall be Commander in Chief of the Army and Navy of the United States, and of the Militia of the several States, when called into the actual Service of the United States; he may require the Opinion, in writing, of the principal Officer in each of the executive Departments, upon any Subject relating to the Duties of their respective Offices, and he shall have Power to grant Reprieves and Pardons for Offences against the United States, except in Cases of Impeachment.

He shall have Power, by and with the Advice and Consent of the Senate, to make Treaties, provided two thirds of the Senators present concur; and he shall nominate, and by and with the Advice and Consent of the Senate, shall appoint Ambassadors, other public Ministers and Consuls, Judges of the supreme Court, and all other Officers of the United States, whose Appointments are not herein otherwise provided for, and which shall be established by Law: but the Congress may by Law vest the Appointment of such inferior Officers, as they think proper, in the President alone, in the Courts of Law, or in the Heads of Departments.

The President shall have Power to fill up all Vacancies that may happen during the Recess of the Senate, by granting Commissions which shall expire at the End of their next Session.

Section 3   He shall from time to time give to the Congress Information of the State of the Union, and recommend to their Consideration such Measures as he shall judge necessary and expedient; he may, on extraordinary Occasions, convene both Houses, or either of them, and in Case of Disagreement between them, with Respect to the Time of Adjournment, he may adjourn them to such Time as he shall think proper; he shall receive Ambassadors and other public Ministers; he shall take Care that the Laws be faithfully executed, and shall Commission all the Officers of the United States.

Section 4   The President, Vice President and all civil Officers of the United States, shall be removed from Office on Impeachment for, and Conviction of, Treason, Bribery, or other high Crimes and Misdemeanors.

ARTICLE III.

Section 1   The judicial Power of the United States, shall be vested in one supreme Court, and in such inferior Courts as the Congress may from time to time ordain and establish. The Judges, both of the supreme and inferior Courts, shall hold their Offices during good Behaviour, and shall, at stated Times, receive for their Services, a Compensation which shall not be diminished during their Continuance in Office.

Section 2   The judicial Power shall extend to all Cases, in Law and Equity, arising under this Constitution, the Laws of the United States, and Treaties made, or which shall be made, under their Authority;—to all Cases affecting Ambassadors, other public Ministers and Consuls;—to all Cases of admiralty and maritime Jurisdiction;—to Controversies to which the United States shall be a Party;—to Controversies between two or more States;—*between a State and Citizens of another State;*—between Citizens of different States;—between Citizens of the same State claiming Lands under Grants of different States, and between a State, or the Citizens thereof, and foreign States, Citizens or Subjects.

In all Cases affecting Ambassadors, other public Ministers and Consuls, and those in which a State shall be Party, the supreme Court shall have original Jurisdiction. In all the other Cases before mentioned, the supreme Court shall have appellate Jurisdiction, both as to Law and Fact, with such Exceptions, and under such Regulations as the Congress shall make.

The Trial of all Crimes, except in Cases of Impeachment, shall be by Jury; and such Trial shall be held in the State where the said Crimes shall have been committed; but when not committed within any State, the Trial shall be at such Place or Places as the Congress may by Law have directed.

Section 3 Treason against the United States, shall consist only in levying War against them, or in adhering to their Enemies, giving them Aid and Comfort. No Person shall be convicted of Treason unless on the Testimony of two Witnesses to the same overt Act, or on Confession in open Court.

The Congress shall have Power to declare the Punishment of Treason, but no Attainder of Treason shall work Corruption of Blood, or Forfeiture except during the Life of the Person attainted.

ARTICLE IV.

Section 1 Full Faith and Credit shall be given in each State to the public Acts, Records, and judicial Proceedings of every other State. And the Congress may by general Laws prescribe the Manner in which such Acts, Records and Proceedings shall be proved, and the Effect thereof.

Section 2 The Citizens of each State shall be entitled to all Privileges and Immunities of Citizens in the several States.

A Person charged in any State with Treason, Felony, or other Crime, who shall flee from Justice, and be found in another State, shall on Demand of the executive Authority of the State from which he fled, be delivered up, to be removed to the State having Jurisdiction of the Crime.

No Person held to Service or Labour in one State, under the Laws thereof, escaping into another, shall, in Consequence of any Law or Regulation therein, be discharged from such Service or Labour, but shall be delivered up on Claim of the Party to whom such Service or Labour may be due.

Section 3 New States may be admitted by the Congress into this Union; but no new State shall be formed or erected within the Jurisdiction of any other State; nor any State be formed by the Junction of two or more States, or Parts of States, without the Consent of the Legislatures of the States concerned as well as of the Congress.

The Congress shall have Power to dispose of and make all needful Rules and Regulations respecting the Territory or other Property belonging to the United States; and nothing in this Constitution shall be so construed as to Prejudice any Claims of the United States, or of any particular State.

Section 4 The United States shall guarantee to every State in this Union a Republican Form of Government, and shall protect each of them against Invasion; and on Application of the Legislature, or of the Executive (when the Legislature cannot be convened) against domestic Violence.

ARTICLE V.

The Congress, whenever two thirds of both Houses shall deem it necessary, shall propose Amendments to this Constitution, or, on the Application of the Legislatures of two thirds of the several States, shall call a Convention for proposing Amendments, which, in either Case, shall be valid to all Intents and Purposes, as Part of this Constitution, when ratified by the Legislatures of three fourths of the several States, or by Conventions in three fourths thereof, as the one or the other Mode of Ratification may be proposed by the Congress; Provided that *no Amendment which may be made prior to the Year One thousand eight hundred and eight shall in any Manner affect the first and fourth Clauses in the Ninth Section of the first Article; and* that no State, without its Consent, shall be deprived of its equal Suffrage in the Senate.

ARTICLE VI.

All Debts contracted and Engagements entered into, before the Adoption of this Constitution, shall be as valid against the United States under this Constitution, as under the Confederation.

This Constitution, and the Laws of the United States which shall be made in Pursuance thereof; and all Treaties made or which shall be made, under the Authority of the United States, shall be the supreme Law of the Land; and the Judges in every State shall be bound thereby, any Thing in the Constitution or Laws of any State to the Contrary notwithstanding.

The Senators and Representatives before mentioned, and the Members of the several State Legislatures, and all executive and judicial Officers, both of the United States and of the several States, shall be bound by Oath or Affirmation, to support this Constitution; but no religious Test shall ever be required as a Qualification to any Office or public Trust under the United States.

ARTICLE VII.

The Ratification of the Conventions of nine States, shall be sufficient for the Establishment of this Constitution between the States so ratifying the Same.

Done in Convention by the Unanimous Consent of the States present the Seventeenth Day of September in the Year of our Lord one thousand seven hundred and Eighty seven and of the Independence of the United States of America the Twelfth. IN WITNESS whereof We have hereunto subscribed our Names,

GEORGE WASHINGTON, ——————————————————————————————
President and Deputy from Virginia

North Carolina

WILLIAM BLOUNT
RICHARD DOBBS
    SPRAIGHT
HU WILLIAMSON

Pennsylvania

BENJAMIN FRANKLIN
THOMAS MIFFLIN
ROBERT MORRIS
GEORGE CLYMER
THOMAS FITZSIMONS
JARED INGERSOLL
JAMES WILSON
GOUVERNEUR MORRIS

Delaware

GEORGE READ
GUNNING BEDFORD, JR.
JOHN DICKINSON
RICHARD BASSETT
JACOB BROOM

South Carolina

J. RUTLEDGE
CHARLES C. PINCKNEY
PIERCE BUTLER

Virginia

JOHN BLAIR
JAMES MADISON, JR.

New Jersey

WILLIAM LIVINGSTON
DAVID BREARLEY
WILLIAM PATERSON
JONATHAN DAYTON

Maryland

JAMES MCHENRY
DANIEL OF ST. THOMAS
    JENIFER
DANIEL CARROLL

Massachusetts

NATHANIEL GORHAM
RUFUS KING

Connecticut

WILLIAM S. JOHNSON
ROGER SHERMAN

New York

ALEXANDER HAMILTON

New Hampshire

JOHN LANGDON
NICHOLAS GILMAN

Georgia

WILLIAM FEW
ABRAHAM BALDWIN

AMENDMENTS TO THE CONSTITUTION*

*The first ten amendments (the Bill of Rights) were adopted in 1791.

AMENDMENT I

Congress shall make no law respecting an establishment of religion, or prohibiting the free exercise thereof; or abridging the freedom of speech, or of the press; or the right of the people peaceably to assemble, and to petition the Government for a redress of grievances.

AMENDMENT II

A well regulated Militia, being necessary to the security of a free State, the right of the people to keep and bear Arms, shall not be infringed.

AMENDMENT III

No Soldier shall, in time of peace be quartered in any house, without the consent of the Owner, nor in time of war, but in a manner to be prescribed by law.

AMENDMENT IV

The right of the people to be secure in their persons, houses, papers, and effects, against unreasonable searches and seizures, shall not be violated, and no Warrants shall issue, but upon probable cause, supported by Oath or affirmation, and particularly describing the place to be searched, and the persons or things to be seized.

AMENDMENT V

No person shall be held to answer for a capital, or otherwise infamous crime, unless on a presentment or indictment of a Grand Jury, except in cases arising in the land or naval forces, or in the Militia, when in actual service in time of War or public danger; nor shall any person be subject for the same offence to be twice put in jeopardy of life or limb; nor shall be compelled in any criminal case to be a witness against himself, nor be deprived of life, liberty, or property, without due process of law; nor shall private property be taken for public use, without just compensation.

AMENDMENT VI

In all criminal prosecutions, the accused shall enjoy the right to a speedy and public trial, by an impartial jury of the State and district wherein the crime shall have been committed, which district shall have been previously ascertained by law, and to be informed of the nature and cause of the accusation; to be confronted with the witnesses against him; to have compulsory process for obtaining witnesses in his favor, and to have the Assistance of Counsel for his defence.

AMENDMENT VII

In Suits at common law, where the value in controversy shall exceed twenty dollars, the right of trial by jury shall be preserved, and no fact tried by a jury, shall be otherwise re-examined in any Court of the United States, than according to the rules of the common law.

AMENDMENT VIII

Excessive bail shall not be required, nor excessive fines imposed, nor cruel and unusual punishments inflicted.

AMENDMENT IX

The enumeration in the Constitution, of certain rights, shall not be construed to deny or disparage others retained by the people.

AMENDMENT X

The powers not delegated to the United States by the Constitution, nor prohibited by it to the States, are reserved to the States respectively, or to the people.

AMENDMENT XI [ADOPTED 1798]

The Judicial power of the United States shall not be construed to extend to any suit in law or equity, commenced or prosecuted against one of the United States by Citizens of another State, or by Citizens or Subjects of any Foreign State.

AMENDMENT XII [ADOPTED 1804]

The Electors shall meet in their respective states, and vote by ballot for President and Vice-President, one of whom, at least, shall not be an inhabitant of the same state with themselves; they shall name in their ballots the person voted for as President, and in distinct ballots the person voted for as Vice-President, and they shall make distinct lists of all persons voted for as President, and of all persons voted for as Vice-President, and of the number of votes for each, which list they shall sign and certify, and transmit sealed to the seat of the government of the United States, directed to the President of the Senate;—The President of the Senate shall, in the presence of the Senate and House of Representatives, open all the certificates and the votes shall then be counted;—The person having the greatest number of votes for President, shall be the President, if such number be a majority of the whole number of Electors appointed; and if no person have such majority, then from the persons having the highest numbers not exceeding three on the list of those voted for as President, the House of Representatives shall choose immediately, by ballot, the President. But in choosing the President, the votes shall be taken by states, the representation from each state having one vote; a quorum for this purpose shall consist of a member or members from two thirds of the states, and a majority of all the states shall be necessary to a choice. And if the House of Representatives shall not choose a President whenever the right of choice shall devolve upon them, before the *fourth day of March* next following, then the Vice-President shall act as President, as in the case of the death or other constitutional disability of the President.

The person having the greatest number of votes as Vice-President, shall be the Vice-President, if such number be a majority of the whole number of Electors appointed, and if no person have a majority, then from the two highest numbers on the list, the Senate shall choose the Vice-President; a quorum for the purpose shall consist of two thirds of the whole number of Senators, and a majority of the whole number shall be necessary to a choice. But no person constitutionally ineligible to the office of President shall be eligible to that of Vice-President of the United States.

AMENDMENT XIII [ADOPTED 1865]

Section 1   Neither slavery nor involuntary servitude, except as a punishment for crime whereof the party shall have been duly convicted, shall exist within the United States, or any place subject to their jurisdiction.

Section 2   Congress shall have power to enforce this article by appropriate legislation.

AMENDMENT XIV [ADOPTED 1868]

Section 1   All persons born or naturalized in the United States, and subject to the jurisdiction thereof, are citizens of the United States and of the State wherein they reside. No State shall make or enforce any law which shall abridge the privileges or immunities of citizens of the United States; nor shall any State deprive any person of life, liberty, or property, without due process of law; nor deny to any person within its jurisdiction the equal protection of the laws.

Section 2   Representatives shall be apportioned among the several States according to their respective numbers, counting the whole number of persons in each State, excluding Indians not taxed. But when the right to vote at any election for the choice of electors for President and Vice-President of the United States, Representatives in Congress, the Executive and Judicial officers of a State, or the members of the Legislature thereof, is denied to any of the male inhabitants of such State, being twenty-one years of age, and citizens of the United States, or in any way abridged, except for participation in rebellion, or other crime, the basis of representation therein shall be reduced in the proportion which the number of such male citizens shall bear to the whole number of male citizens twenty-one years of age in such State.

Section 3   No person shall be a Senator or Representative in Congress, or elector of President and Vice-President, or hold any office, civil or military, under the United States, or under any State, who, having previously taken an oath, as a member of Congress, or as an officer of the United States, or as a member of any State legislature, or as an executive or judicial officer of any State, to support the Constitution of the United States, shall have engaged in insurrection or rebellion against the same, or given aid or comfort to the enemies thereof. But Congress may by a vote of two thirds of each House, remove such disability.

Section 4   The validity of the public debt of the United States, authorized by law, including debts incurred for payment of pensions and bounties for services in suppressing insurrection or rebellion, shall not be questioned. But neither the United States nor any State shall assume or pay any debt or obligation incurred in aid of insurrection or rebellion against the United States, or any claim for the loss or emancipation of any slave; but all such debts, obligations and claims shall be held illegal and void.

Section 5   The Congress shall have power to enforce, by appropriate legislation, the provisions of this article.

AMENDMENT XV [ADOPTED 1870]

Section 1　The right of citizens of the United States to vote shall not be denied or abridged by the United States or by any State on account of race, color, or previous condition of servitude.

Section 2　The Congress shall have power to enforce this article by appropriate legislation.

AMENDMENT XVI [ADOPTED 1913]

The Congress shall have power to lay and collect taxes on incomes, from whatever source derived, without apportionment among the several States, and without regard to any census or enumeration.

AMENDMENT XVII [ADOPTED 1913]

The Senate of the United States shall be composed of two Senators from each State, elected by the people thereof, for six years; and each Senator shall have one vote. The electors in each State shall have the qualifications requisite for electors of the most numerous branch of the State legislatures.

When vacancies happen in the representation of any State in the Senate, the executive authority of such State shall issue writs of election to fill such vacancies: *Provided,* That the legislature of any State may empower the executive thereof to make temporary appointments until the people fill the vacancies by election as the legislature may direct.

This amendment shall not be so construed as to affect the election or term of any Senator chosen before it becomes valid as part of the Constitution.

AMENDMENT XVIII [ADOPTED 1919; REPEALED 1933]

Section 1　After one year from the ratification of this article the manufacture, sale, or transportation of intoxicating liquors within, the importation thereof into, or the exportation thereof from the United States and all territory subject to the jurisdiction thereof for beverage purposes is hereby prohibited.

Section 2　The Congress and the several States shall have concurrent power to enforce this article by appropriate legislation.

Section 3　This article shall be inoperative unless it shall have been ratified as an amendment to the Constitution by the legislatures of the several States, as provided in the Constitution, within seven years from the date of the submission hereof to the States by the Congress.

AMENDMENT XIX [ADOPTED 1920]

Section 1　The right of citizens of the United States to vote shall not be denied or abridged by the United States or by any State on account of sex.

Section 2　Congress shall have power to enforce this article by appropriate legislation.

AMENDMENT XX [ADOPTED 1933]

Section 1　The terms of the President and Vice-President shall end at noon on the 20th day of January, and the terms of Senators and Representatives at noon on the third day of January, of the years in which such terms would have ended if this article had not been ratified; and the terms of their successors shall then begin.

Section 2　The Congress shall assemble at least once in every year, and such meeting shall begin at noon on the third day of January, unless they shall by law appoint a different day.

Section 3　If, at the time fixed for the beginning of the term of the President, the President elect shall have died, the Vice-President elect shall become President. If a President shall not have been chosen before the time fixed for the beginning of his term, or if the President elect shall have failed to qualify, then the Vice-President elect shall act as President until a President shall have qualified; and the Congress may by law provide for the case wherein neither a President elect nor a Vice-President elect shall have qualified, declaring who shall then act as President, or the manner in which one who is to act shall be selected, and such person shall act accordingly until a President or Vice-President shall have qualified.

Section 4　The Congress may by law provide for the case of the death of any of the persons from whom the House of Representatives may choose a President whenever the right of choice shall have devolved upon them, and for the case of the death of any of the persons from whom the Senate may choose a Vice-President whenever the right of choice shall have devolved upon them.

Section 5 Sections 1 and 2 shall take effect on the 15th day of October following the ratification of this article.

Section 6 This article shall be inoperative unless it shall have been ratified as an amendment to the Constitution by the legislatures of three fourths of the several States within seven years from the date of its submission.

AMENDMENT XXI [ADOPTED 1933]

Section 1 The eighteenth article of amendment to the Constitution of the United States is hereby repealed.

Section 2 The transportation or importation into any State, Territory, or possession of the United States for delivery or use therein of intoxicating liquors, in violation of the laws thereof, is hereby prohibited.

Section 3 This article shall be inoperative unless it shall have been ratified as an amendment to the Constitution by conventions in the several States, as provided in the Constitution, within seven years from the date of the submission hereof to the States by the Congress.

AMENDMENT XXII [ADOPTED 1951]

Section 1 No person shall be elected to the office of the President more than twice, and no person who has held the office of President, or acted as President, for more than two years of a term to which some other person was elected President shall be elected to the office of the President more than once. But this Article shall not apply to any person holding the office of President when this Article was proposed by the Congress, and shall not prevent any person who may be holding the office of President, or acting as President, during the term within which this Article becomes operative from holding the office of President or acting as President during the remainder of such term.

Section 2 This article shall be inoperative unless it shall have been ratified as an amendment to the Constitution by the legislatures of three fourths of the several States within seven years from the date of its submission to the States by the Congress.

AMENDMENT XXIII [ADOPTED 1961]

Section 1 The District constituting the seat of Government of the United States shall appoint in such manner as the Congress may direct:

A number of electors of President and Vice-President equal to the whole number of Senators and Representatives in Congress to which the District would be entitled if it were a State, but in no event more than the least populous State; they shall be in addition to those appointed by the States, but they shall be considered, for the purposes of the election of President and Vice-President, to be electors appointed by a State; and they shall meet in the District and perform such duties as provided by the twelfth article of amendment.

Section 2 The Congress shall have power to enforce this article by appropriate legislation.

AMENDMENT XXIV [ADOPTED 1964]

Section 1 The right of citizens of the United States to vote in any primary or other election for President or Vice-President, for electors for President or Vice-President, or for Senator or Representative in Congress, shall not be denied or abridged by the United States or any State by reason of failure to pay any poll tax or other tax.

Section 2 The Congress shall have power to enforce this article by appropriate legislation.

AMENDMENT XXV [ADOPTED 1967]

Section 1 In case of the removal of the President from office or his death or resignation, the Vice-President shall become President.

Section 2 Whenever there is a vacancy in the office of the Vice-President, the President shall nominate a Vice-President who shall take the office upon confirmation by a majority vote of both houses of Congress.

Section 3 Whenever the President transmits to the President pro tempore of the Senate and the Speaker of the House of Representatives his written declaration that he is unable to discharge the powers and duties of his office, and until he transmits to them a written declaration to the contrary, such powers and duties shall be discharged by the Vice-President as Acting President.

Section 4 Whenever the Vice-President and a majority of either the principal officers of the executive departments, or of such other body as Congress may by law provide, transmit to the President pro tempore of the Senate and the Speaker of the House of Representatives their written declaration that the President is unable to discharge the powers and duties of his office, the Vice-President shall immediately assume the powers and duties of the office as Acting President.

Thereafter, when the President transmits to the President pro tempore of the Senate and the Speaker of the House of Representatives his written declaration that no inability exists, he shall resume the powers and duties of his office unless the Vice-President and a majority of either the principal officers of the executive department, or of such other body as Congress may by law provide, transmit within four days to the President pro tempore of the Senate and the Speaker of the House of Representatives their written declaration that the President is unable to discharge the powers and duties of his office. Thereupon Congress shall decide the issue, assembling within 48 hours for that purpose if not in session. If the Congress, within 21 days after receipt of the latter written declaration, or, if Congress is not in session, within 21 days after Congress is required to assemble, determines by two-thirds vote of both houses that the President is unable to discharge the powers and duties of his office, the Vice-President shall continue to discharge the same as Acting President; otherwise, the President shall resume the powers and duties of his office.

AMENDMENT XXVI [ADOPTED 1971]

Section 1 The right of citizens of the United States, who are eighteen years of age or older, to vote shall not be denied or abridged by the United States or any state on account of age.

Section 2 The Congress shall have power to enforce this article by appropriate legislation.

AMENDMENT XXVII [ADOPTED 1992]

No law, varying the compensation for the services of Senators and Representatives, shall take effect until an election of Representatives have intervened.

Presidential Elections

Year	Candidates	Parties	Popular Vote	Electoral Vote	Voter Participation
1789	GEORGE WASHINGTON		*	69	
	John Adams			34	
	Others			35	
1792	GEORGE WASHINGTON		*	132	
	John Adams			77	
	George Clinton			50	
	Others			5	
1796	JOHN ADAMS	Federalist	*	71	
	Thomas Jefferson	Democratic-Republican		68	
	Thomas Pinckney	Federalist		59	
	Aaron Burr	Dem.-Rep.		30	
	Others			48	
1800	THOMAS JEFFERSON	Dem.-Rep.	*	73	
	Aaron Burr	Dem.-Rep.		73	
	C. C. Pinckney	Federalist		64	
	John Jay	Federalist		1	
1804	THOMAS JEFFERSON	Dem.-Rep.	*	122	
	C. C. Pinckney	Federalist		14	
1808	JAMES MADISON	Dem.-Rep.	*	122	
	C. C. Pinckney	Federalist		47	
	George Clinton	Dem.-Rep.		6	
1812	JAMES MADISON	Dem.-Rep.	*	128	
	De Witt Clinton	Federalist		89	
1816	JAMES MONROE	Dem.-Rep.	*	183	
	Rufus King	Federalist		34	
1820	JAMES MONROE	Dem.-Rep.	*	231	
	John Quincy Adams	Dem.-Rep.		1	
1824	JOHN Q. ADAMS	Dem.-Rep.	108,740 (10.5%)	84	26.9%
	Andrew Jackson	Dem.-Rep.	153,544 (43.1%)	99	
	William H. Crawford	Dem.-Rep.	46,618 (13.1%)	41	
	Henry Clay	Dem.-Rep.	47,136 (13.2%)	37	
1828	ANDREW JACKSON	Democratic	647,286 (56.0%)	178	57.6%
	John Quincy Adams	National Republican	508,064 (44.0%)	83	
1832	ANDREW JACKSON	Democratic	687,502 (55.0%)	219	55.4%
	Henry Clay	National Republican	530,189 (42.4%)	49	
	John Floyd	Independent		11	
	William Wirt	Anti-Mason	33,108 (2.6%)	7	
1836	MARTIN VAN BUREN	Democratic	765,483 (50.9%)	170	57.8%
	W. H. Harrison	Whig		73	
	Hugh L. White	Whig	739,795 (49.1%)	26	
	Daniel Webster	Whig		14	
	W. P. Magnum	Independent		11	

*Electors elected by state legislators.

Presidential Elections

Year	Candidates	Parties	Popular Vote	Electoral Vote	Voter Participation
1840	WILLIAM H. HARRISON	Whig	1,274,624 (53.1%)	234	80.2%
	Martin Van Buren	Democratic	1,127,781 (46.9%)	60	
	J. G. Birney	Liberty	7,069	—	
1844	JAMES K. POLK	Democratic	1,338,464 (49.6%)	170	78.9%
	Henry Clay	Whig	1,300,097 (48.1%)	105	
	J. G. Birney	Liberty	62,300 (2.3%)	—	
1848	ZACHARY TAYLOR	Whig	1,360,967 (47.4%)	163	72.7%
	Lewis Cass	Democratic	1,222,342 (42.5%)	127	
	Martin Van Buren	Free-Soil	291,263 (10.1%)	—	
1852	FRANKLIN PIERCE	Democratic	1,601,117 (50.9%)	254	69.6%
	Winfield Scott	Whig	1,385,453 (44.1%)	42	
	John P. Hale	Free-Soil	155,825 (5.0%)	—	
1856	JAMES BUCHANAN	Democratic	1,832,955 (45.3%)	174	78.9%
	John C. Fremont	Republican	1,339,932 (33.1%)	114	
	Millard Fillmore	American	871,731 (21.6%)	8	
1860	ABRAHAM LINCOLN	Republican	1,865,593 (39.8%)	180	81.2%
	Stephen A. Douglas	Democratic	1,382,713 (29.5%)	12	
	John C. Breckinridge	Democratic	848,356 (18.1%)	72	
	John Bell	Union	592,906 (12.6%)	39	
1864	ABRAHAM LINCOLN	Republican	2,213,655 (55.0%)	212	73.8%
	George B. McClellan	Democratic	1,805,237 (45.0%)	21	
1868	ULYSSES S. GRANT	Republican	3,012,833 (52.7%)	214	78.1%
	Horatio Seymour	Democratic	2,703,249 (47.3%)	80	
1872	ULYSSES S. GRANT	Republican	3,597,132 (55.6%)	286	71.3%
	Horace Greeley	Democratic; Liberal Republican	2,834,125 (43.9%)	66	
1876	RUTHERFORD B. HAYES	Republican	4,036,298 (48.0%)	185	81.8%
	Samuel J. Tilden	Democratic	4,300,590 (51.0%)	184	
1880	JAMES A. GARFIELD	Republican	4,454,416 (48.5%)	214	79.4%
	Winfield S. Hancock	Democratic	4,444,952 (48.1%)	155	
1884	GROVER CLEVELAND	Democratic	4,874,986 (48.5%)	219	77.5%
	James G. Blaine	Republican	4,851,981 (48.2%)	182	
1888	BENJAMIN HARRISON	Republican	5,439,853 (47.9%)	233	79.3%
	Grover Cleveland	Democratic	5,540,309 (48.6%)	168	
1892	GROVER CLEVELAND	Democratic	5,556,918 (46.1%)	277	74.7%
	Benjamin Harrison	Republican	5,176,108 (43.0%)	145	
	James B. Weaver	People's	1,041,028 (8.5%)	22	
1896	WILLIAM McKINLEY	Republican	7,104,779 (51.1%)	271	79.3%
	William J. Bryan	Democratic People's	6,502,925 (47.7%)	176	
1900	WILLIAM McKINLEY	Republican	7,207,923 (51.7%)	292	73.2%
	William J. Bryan	Dem.-Populist	6,358,133 (45.5%)	155	
1904	THEODORE ROOSEVELT	Republican	7,623,486 (57.9%)	336	65.2%
	Alton B. Parker	Democratic	5,077,911 (37.6%)	140	
	Eugene V. Debs	Socialist	402,283 (3.0%)	—	

Presidential Elections

Year	Candidates	Parties	Popular Vote	Electoral Vote	Voter Participation
1908	WILLIAM H. TAFT	Republican	7,678,908 (51.6%)	321	65.4%
	William J. Bryan	Democratic	6,409,104 (43.1%)	162	
	Eugene V. Debs	Socialist	420,793 (2.8%)	—	
1912	WOODROW WILSON	Democratic	6,293,454 (41.9%)	435	58.8%
	Theodore Roosevelt	Progressive	4,119,538 (27.4%)	88	
	William H. Taft	Republican	3,484,980 (23.2%)	8	
	Eugene V. Debs	Socialist	900,672 (6.0%)	—	
1916	WOODROW WILSON	Democratic	9,129,606 (49.4%)	277	61.6%
	Charles E. Hughes	Republican	8,538,221 (46.2%)	254	
	A. L. Benson	Socialist	585,113 (3.2%)	—	
1920	WARREN G. HARDING	Republican	16,152,200 (60.4%)	404	49.2%
	James M. Cox	Democratic	9,147,353 (34.2%)	127	
	Eugene V. Debs	Socialist	919,799 (3.4%)	—	
1924	CALVIN COOLIDGE	Republican	15,725,016 (54.0%)	382	48.9%
	John W. Davis	Democratic	8,386,503 (28.8%)	136	
	Robert M. La Follette	Progressive	4,822,856 (16.6%)	13	
1928	HERBERT HOOVER	Republican	21,391,381 (58.2%)	444	56.9%
	Alfred E. Smith	Democratic	15,016,443 (40.9%)	87	
	Norman Thomas	Socialist	267,835 (0.7%)	—	
1932	FRANKLIN D. ROOSEVELT	Democratic	22,821,857 (57.4%)	472	56.9%
	Herbert Hoover	Republican	15,761,841 (39.7%)	59	
	Norman Thomas	Socialist	881,951 (2.2%)	—	
1936	FRANKLIN D. ROOSEVELT	Democratic	27,751,597 (60.8%)	523	61.0%
	Alfred M. Landon	Republican	16,679,583 (36.5%)	8	
	William Lemke	Union	882,479 (1.9%)	—	
1940	FRANKLIN D. ROOSEVELT	Democratic	27,244,160 (54.8%)	449	62.5%
	Wendell L. Willkie	Republican	22,305,198 (44.8%)	82	
1944	FRANKLIN D. ROOSEVELT	Democrat	25,602,504 (53.5%)	432	55.9%
	Thomas E. Dewey	Republican	22,006,285 (46.0%)	99	
1948	HARRY S TRUMAN	Democratic	24,105,695 (49.5%)	304	53.0%
	Thomas E. Dewey	Republican	21,969,170 (45.1%)	189	
	J. Strom Thurmond	State-Rights Democratic	1,169,021 (2.4%)	38	
	Henry A. Wallace	Progressive	1,156,103 (2.4%)	—	
1952	DWIGHT D. EISENHOWER	Republican	33,936,252 (55.1%)	442	63.3%
	Adlai E. Stevenson	Democratic	27,314,992 (44.4%)	89	
1956	DWIGHT D. EISENHOWER	Republican	35,575,420 (57.6%)	457	60.5%
	Adlai E. Stevenson	Democratic	26,033,066 (42.1%)	73	
	Other	—	—	1	
1960	JOHN F. KENNEDY	Democratic	34,227,096 (49.9%)	303	62.8%
	Richard M. Nixon	Republican	34,108,546 (49.6%)	219	
	Other	—	—	15	

Presidential Elections

Year	Candidates	Parties	Popular Vote	Electoral Vote	Voter Participation
1964	LYNDON B. JOHNSON	Democratic	43,126,506 (61.1%)	486	61.7%
	Barry M. Goldwater	Republican	27,176,799 (38.5%)	52	
1968	RICHARD M. NIXON	Republican	31,770,237 (43.4%)	301	60.6%
	Hubert H. Humphrey	Democratic	31,270,633 (42.7%)	191	
	George Wallace	American Indep.	9,906,141 (13.5%)	46	
1972	RICHARD M. NIXON	Republican	47,169,911 (60.7%)	520	55.2%
	George S. McGovern	Democratic	29,170,383 (37.5%)	17	
	Other	—	—	1	
1976	JIMMY CARTER	Democratic	40,828,587 (50.0%)	297	53.5%
	Gerald R. Ford	Republican	39,147,613 (47.9%)	241	
	Other	—	1,575,459 (2.1%)	—	
1980	RONALD REAGAN	Republican	43,901,812 (50.7%)	489	52.6%
	Jimmy Carter	Democratic	35,483,820 (41.0%)	49	
	John B. Anderson	Independent	5,719,722 (6.6%)	—	
	Ed Clark	Libertarian	921,188 (1.1%)	—	
1984	RONALD REAGAN	Republican	54,455,075 (59.0%)	525	53.3%
	Walter Mondale	Democratic	37,577,185 (41.0%)	13	
1988	GEORGE H. W. BUSH	Republican	48,886,000 (45.6%)	426	57.4%
	Michael S. Dukakis	Democratic	41,809,000 (45.6%)	111	
1992	WILLIAM J. CLINTON	Democratic	43,728,375 (43%)	370	55.0%
	George H. W. Bush	Republican	38,167,416 (38%)	168	
	Ross Perot	—	19,237,247 (19%)	—	
1996	WILLIAM J. CLINTON	Democratic	45,590,703 (50%)	379	48.8%
	Robert Dole	Republican	37,816,307 (41%)	159	
	Ross Perot	Independent	7,866,284 (9%)		
2000	GEORGE W. BUSH	Republican	50,456,062 (47%)	271	51.0%
	Albert Gore	Democratic	50,996,582 (49%)	267	
	Ralph Nader	Independent	2,858,843 (3%)	—	
2004	GEORGE W. BUSH	Republican	60,934,251 (51%)	286	
	John F. Kerry	Democrat	57,765,291 (48%)	252	
	Ralph Nader	Independent	405,933 (0%)	—	

Credits

Chapter 23

p. 697, Luigi Barzini, Jr., An Italian Student Falls in Love with the United States, From *As Others See Us: The United States Through Foreign Eyes*, Franz M. Joseph, ed. Princeton, NJ: Princeton University Press, 1959.

Chapter 24

p. 745, Georges Duhamel, A French Writer Visits the United States and Finds Nothing to Admire, From *America: The Menace: Scenes from the Life of the Future*, Georges Duhamel. London, England: George Allen & Unwin, 1931.

Chapter 25

p. 780, Yamaoka Michiko, On the Ground at Hiroshima, From Yamaoka Michiko, "Eight Hundred Meters from Hypocenter," in *Japan at War: An Oral History* by Haruko Taya Cook and Theodore F. Cook. Copyright © 1993 New Press. Reprinted by permission of The New Press.

Chapter 27

p. 845, From THE GALLUP POLL, 1935–1971 by George Gallup, copyright © 1972 by American Institute of Public Opinion. Used by permission of Random House, Inc.

Chapter 29

p. 906, Bob Dylan, lyrics to "The Times They Are A-Changin'," From "Times They Are A-Changin'" by Bob Dylan. Copyright © 1963 by Warner Bros. Inc. Copyright renewed 1991 by Special Rider Music. All rights reserved. International copyright secured. Reprinted by permission.

Chapter 31

p. 974, Elfriede Jelinek, "No New Wars," "No New Wars" by Elfriede Jelinek. New York Times, February 20, 2005. Copyright © 2005 by The New York Times Co. Reprinted with permission.

Index

Abalone Alliance, 913
Abilene, Kansas, 516
Abortion, 637, 963
  conservative fight against, 926, 929–930
  pill for, 963
  Roe v. *Wade* and, 890
Abraham Lincoln Brigade, 757
Absenteeism, 562
Abstinence from sex, 637
Abstract expressionism, 803
Acheson, Dean, 831, 846
"Acres of Diamonds" sermon (Conwell), 579
Activism. *See also* African Americans; Civil rights movement; Protest(s); Women's rights
  Chicano, 814
  consumer, 914
  environmental, 912–913
  gay and lesbian, 912
  Latino, 905–909
  Native American, 815, 909–912
  student, 756, 858, 860, 875–876, 893–894
  against Vietnam War, 875–876
  by women, 902–905
Adams, Brooks, 579–580
Adams, Henry, 506, 507, 574, 577, 596
Adamson Act (1916), 669
Addams, Jane, 554, 585, 654
  anti-imperialism and, 611
  racism and, 651, 652
  settlement house movement and, 580–581, 581–582
  temperance movement and, 638–639
  woman suffrage and, 637
  Women's International League for Peace and Freedom and, 686
  on women's roles, 584
Advertising, 698, 799, 969
  by conservatives, 921
Affirmative action, 892, 962
Affluent society, 790. *See also* Prosperity
Afghanistan, 901, 977–978
AFL. *See* American Federation of Labor (AFL)
AFL-CIO, 793–794

Africa. *See also* African Americans; Africans; North Africa; Slaves and slavery
  AIDS in, 960, 976
  black migration to, 534
  Clinton and, 976
  European imperialism in, 603
  independence in, 810 (map), 829
  in 1990s and 2000s, 976
  starvation in, 944
  World War I and, 665
African American churches, 499
African Americans. *See also* Civil rights movement; Great migration; North; Race and racism; Race riots; Slaves and slavery; South
  AFL and, 565
  Alliance and, 537
  black separatism and, 534
  in cities, 551, 938
  civil rights movement and, 866–868
  as cowboys, 516
  employment of, 533, 556–557, 569, 962
  as federal officials, 651
  in Filipino-American War, 612
  Garvey and, 704–705
  Great Depression and, 730, 738–739
  at Jackson State University, 893–894
  Jim Crow laws and, 533
  jobs of, 533
  lynchings of, 532, 533
  migration by, 534, 548, 588, 681–682, 691–692, 703–704, 739–740, 766, 810
  in New South, 530, 531–533
  in 1990s-2000s, 962–963
  in population, 955, 956
  in post-World War II society, 810–814
  poverty of, 809–810
  Proposition 209 and, 962
  during Reconstruction, 486–487, 489, 503, 504
  in Republican state governments, 502
  rights of, 489, 492
  self-help institutions of, 499–501
  in southern public schools, 502

  stereotypes of, 531–532
  unemployment among, 936
  in Vietnam War, 894
  voting and, 588–589, 928–929
  whites and, 534–535
  Wilson and, 656
  women's roles and, 802, 904–905
  in workforce, 561, 768
  World War I and, 674, 675, 679, 681–682
  World War II and, 765–766, 770, 777
"Africanization," 486
African Methodist Episcopal (AME) Church, 499, 551
African National Congress (ANC), 943–944
Africans, in World War I, 665
Afrika Korps, 772
Afro-American League, 534
Afro-American Society, 876
Age Discrimination in Employment Act, 960
Aging
  illness and, 959–961
  Medicare and, 865
  old-age pensions and, 658, 735, 809
Agnew, Spiro, 889, 899
Agricultural Adjustment Act (AAA)
  of 1933, 730–731
  of 1938, 742
Agricultural (land-grant) colleges, 513
Agriculture, 505. *See also* Farms and farming; Rural areas
  contract system of, 496
  dust bowl and, 736
  global patterns and demands, 513–515
  Great Depression and, 735–736
  innovation and productivity in, 515
  large-scale, 512, 513
  modernization of, 513–515
  Nixon and, 887
  prices in, 515
  in South, 496–498, 498–499, 530–531
  tenancy and sharecropping in, 496–498, 497 (map), 518, 531
  workers in, 794
  World War II and, 794

Aguinaldo, Emilio, 599, 600, 611
AIDS (acquired immune deficiency syndrome), 960–961, 976
AIDS quilt, 961
Airlift, Berlin, 828
Airplanes
    defense industries and, 761, 789
    Lindbergh and, 700
    for nuclear bomb delivery, 840
    in World War II, 777
Air pollution. See also Environment; Pollution
    Clean Air Act and, 913
Alabama, 859
Alaska
    gold in, 595
    purchase of, 601
Alaska Natives, 964
Albania, 940
Albuquerque, 795
Alcatraz Island, Indian seizure of, 910
Alcoa, 606
Alcohol and alcoholism. See also Temperance
    politics and, 578
    progressive reformers and, 638–639
    at work, 562
    working-class use of, 553
    World War I and, 683
Algeciras conference, 624
Alger, Horatio, 555
Algeria, 791
Alianza Federal de Mercedes, La, 909
Allegany reservation (New York State), 910
Alliance(s). See also specific alliances
    NATO as, 828
Alliance for Progress, 870
Alliance movement. See National Alliance
Allies
    in World War I, 663, 665–666, 678–680, 686
    in World War II, 772–779
Allston family
    Adele and Elizabeth, 481, 482, 505, 509
    Robert, 481
All-white primary elections, 532
Al Qaeda, 977–978
Altgeld, Richard, 567
Alzheimer's disease, 960
Amalgamated Clothing Workers, 738

America First, 695, 758, 760
American Bankers Association, 728
American Bar Association, 555
American Birth Control League, 637
"American Century, The" (Luce), 772
American Communist party, 842. See also Communism
American Enterprise Institute, 921
American Federation of Labor (AFL), 565, 641. See also AFL-CIO
    CIO and, 738
    in 1920s, 710
    in progressive era, 641
    World War I and, 681
    World War II and, 793
American Indian Historical Society, 910
American Indian Movement (AIM), 910–911
American Indians. See Native Americans
American Legion, Red Scare and, 694
American Medical Association, 555
    Sheppard-Towner Act and, 714–715
American Mercury, 707
American Missionary Association, 499
American Railway Union (ARU), 566, 567
"Americans, The" (Spencer), 555
American Social Science Association, 580
American Sugar Refining Company, 588
American Tobacco Company, 530, 649
Anarchism
    Haymarket Riot and, 564
    Red Scare and, 693–694
    Sacco-Vanzetti case and, 694–695
Anaya, Toney, 931
Ancestors, Indian, 964
Anderson, Marian, 739
Anderson, Sherwood, 707
Angelou, Maya, 952
Anglo-Japanese Treaty, 624
Anglo-Saxons
    city politics and, 584
    immigrants and, 651
Annexation
    Cuba and, 602, 609
    of Hawaii, 603, 609, 621
    of Philippines, 611–612, 617, 621

Anthony, Susan B., 493, 506, 580, 585
Anthracite, 543
Antiabortion movement, 926
Anti-Communist crusade, 841–848
    fear during, 847–848
    McCarthy and, 843–847
Anti-imperialism, 611–612, 617
Anti-Imperialist League, 611
Anti-Saloon League, 638
Anti-Semitism. See also Jews and Judaism
    Ku Klux Klan and, 694
    World War II and, 775
Antiwar protests
    against Vietnam War, 875–876, 879–880
    against World War II, 756
Appliances, 698, 744, 798
Arabic (ship), 667
Arab-Israeli wars
    Six Day War (1967), 872–873, 887
    Yom Kippur War (1973), 887, 888 (map)
Arabs. See also Islam; Muslims
    Israel and, 835–836
    Nixon and, 895
Arafat, Yasir, 901, 974–975
Arapaho Indians, 523
Arctic National Wildlife Refuge, 972
Arizona, 636
Arkansas, 813
Armaments. See also Weapons
    naval, 712, 713
Armed forces, 604. See also Military; Soldiers
    African Americans in, 610, 611
    Bonus Army and, 726
    desegregation of, 805
    religion and, 769–770
    in Spanish-American War, 610
    in World War I, 661, 667, 673
    in World War II, 770–773
Arms race. See also Atomic bomb; Nuclear weapons
    Reagan and, 926
Armstrong, Louis, 706
Army-McCarthy hearings (1954), 846–847, 856
Arpin, Edmund P., Jr., 661–662, 679, 688
Art(s). See also specific arts
    abstract expressionism in, 803
    Harlem Renaissance and, 705–706
    sexual revolution in, 878
Arthur, Chester A., 576, 577, 604

Arthur Andersen accounting firm, 958

Asia
  commerce with, 602
  containment policy in, 830–834, 835
  European imperialism in, 603
  immigration from, 549–550, 703, 739–740
  refugees from, 865

Asian Americans
  in cities, 938
  gains by, 815–816, 932–933
  during Great Depression, 739–740
  immigration restriction and, 703
  in 1990s-2000, 965
  population of, 951, 956
  World War II and, 762–765

Asian Indians, 765

As I Lay Dying (Faulkner), 748

Assembly line, 640, 699

Associación Nacional México-Americana, 814

Aswan Dam, 836

Atlanta Monthly, 532

Atomic bomb. *See also* Arms race; Nuclear weapons
  Cold War and, 829, 837–841
  Manhattan Project and, 758, 779–780
  mushroom cloud from, 839
  New Mexico test of, 779, 823
  protests against, 840–841
  Soviet Union and, 837–838

Atomic Energy Act (1946), 838

Atomic Energy Commission (AEC), 797, 838

Atomic shield, 840

Augusta, Georgia, 529

Auschwitz, 775

Australia, 665
  woman suffrage in, 636

Austria
  Great Depression and, 725
  Versailles Peace Conference and, 686
  World War II and, 757

Austria-Hungary, World War I and, 664

Autobiographies, 952–953

Autobiography of Benjamin Franklin, The, 952, 953

Automation, 798, 933

Automobiles and automobile industry, 640
  economic boom and, 788, 789 (map)

Japanese cars and, 888–889, 935, 936–937
  in 1930s, 743–744
  after World War I, 698
  World War II and, 769

Awakening, The (Chopin), 584

"Axis of evil," 978

Axis Powers, 756, 772. *See also* World War II

Babbitt (Lewis), 707

Baby and Child Care (Spock), 801

Baby boom, 794–795, 954
  Vietnam War and, 875

Back-to-nature movement, 651

Baez, Joan, 906

Baker, James, 945

Baker, Josephine, 706

Baker, Newton D., 645, 673, 675, 683

Baker v. *Carr*, 869

Bakke, Allan, 892

Balanced budgets, 938, 968

Balance of power, in 1890s, 625

Baldwin Locomotive Works, 546

Balkan crisis (1990s), 973–974

Ballinger, Richard A., 653

Bank(s) and banking, 545. *See also* Federal Reserve System
  Depression of 1893 and, 591
  in Great Depression, 723, 728–729
  national system of, 537
  reforms of, 655–656
  World Bank and, 779

Bankhead-Jones Farm Tenancy Act (1937), 742

Bank holiday, 728

Banking acts, of 1933, 728

Bankruptcy
  in savings and loan industry, 927
  of states and municipalities, 926

Banks, Dennis, 910

Baptism in Kansas (Curry), 702

Barbed wire, 519, 664

Barkley, Alben, 775

Barnett, Ross, 859

Barton, Bruce, 710

Baruch, Bernard, 681

Barzini, Luigi, Jr., 697

Baseball, 586
  Robinson and, 810, 812

Batista, Fulgencio, 755, 836–837

Battle of San Pietro (movie), 769

Battle of the Bulge, 777

Battles. *See* Wars and warfare; specific battles

Baum, L. Frank, 593

Bay of Pigs fiasco, 870–871

Beat Generation writers, 803

Beatles, 906, 907

Beautification
  of cities, 582–583, 592
  of highways, 865

Beer-Wine Revenue Act, 728

Begin, Menachem, 901, 902

Belgium, World War I and, 664

Bellamy, Edward, 572, 573, 579, 586, 596, 630

Belleau Wood, Battle of, 678

Berle, Adolph, Jr., 727

Berle, Milton, 856

Berlin airlift, 828

Berlin, Germany
  blockade of, 828
  division of, 828, 871, 871 (map), 940
  World War II and, 778

Berlin Wall, 871, 871 (map), 940, 941

Bernstein, Carl, 897

Bessemer converter, 542

Bethlehem Steel strike, 693

Bethune, Mary McLeod, 739

Beveridge, Albert, 604, 607

Beverly Hills, California, 699

B-47, 840

B-52, 840

Bias. *See also* Discrimination
  gender, 904

Bicycles, 586

Big business, 557, 588
  after Civil War, 542
  horizontal integration in, 544–545
  in 1920s, 710
  railroads as, 543
  vertical organization in, 544
  after World War II, 793

Biggerstaff, William, 532

"Big stick" policy, 667

Big Three (World War II), 778–779, 823

Bilingual education, 954

"Billion-dollar Congress," 589

Bin Laden, Osama, 977–978

Birmingham, 529
  civil rights clashes in, 859

Birth control, 555
  oral contraceptives and, 877
  World War II and, 771

Birth of a Nation (film), 490, 639, 694

Birthrate
  urban growth and, 547
  after World War II, 790, 794–795

Bitter Cry of Outcast London, The, 630

Black and tan governments, 502

Black Codes, 486–487

Black Cross Nurses, 705
Black Elk, 522, 526
  autobiography of, 952, 953
Black Hills, 506, 526
Black male suffrage, 492, 493
Blackmun, Harry, 889
Black Muslims. *See* Nation of Islam
Black Panthers, 868
Black Power movement, 868
Blacks. *See* African Americans
Black self-help institutions, 499–501
Black Star Line, 705
Black Thursday, 716
Blaine, James G., 574, 575, 578, 602
Blitzkrieg ("lightning war"), 758
Blockade
  of Berlin, 828
  in World War I, 666
"Blowin' in the Wind" (Dylan), 906
Blue-collar workers, 935
Boarding system, 561
Boeing Company, 840
Boer War, 603
Bolshevism, 670. *See also*
  Communism
  Red Scare and, 693–694
  Russian Revolution and, 670, 686,
    693
  Versailles Peace Conference and,
    686
  World War I and, 670, 686, 692
Bombs and bombings. *See also*
  Atomic bomb; Nuclear weapons
  in Birmingham, 859
  of Vietnam, 875, 893
  in World War I, 665
  in World War II, 777
Bonanza farms, 513
Bonus Army, 725–726
Bootstrap ethic, 555–556
Borders. *See* Boundaries
Bosnia, 941
  fighting in, 973
Bosnian Serbs, 973
Bosses (political), 577, 583, 584
Boston, progressive reform in, 645
Boston Labor Reform Association,
  505
Boulder Dam, 736
Boundaries, Venezuela-British
  Guiana dispute, 604
Bourke-White, Margaret, 730
Bow, Clara, 707
Boxer Rebellion, 621–622, 623
Boycotts
  by farmworkers, 908
  of Montgomery buses, 813, 858

  against segregated streetcars, 534
Boy Scouts, 651
Braceros, 814
Bradley, Ed, 962–963
Bradley, Omar, 777
Brandeis, Louis, 654, 657, 669
Bretton Woods Conference, 779
Brezhnev, Leonid, 895
Briand, Aristide, 714
Bricker, John, 846
Brinkmanship, 840
Britain. *See* England (Britain)
British Empire. *See* England
  (Britain)
British Guiana, 604
Brothels, 639–640
Brotherhood of Sleeping Car
  Porters, 765
Brown, Claude, 810
Brown, H. Rap, 868
Brown, Linda, 812
Brown, Oliver, 812
Brown v. *Board of Education,*
  812–813, 858, 868
Bryan, William Jennings
  election of 1896 and, 593–595
  election of 1900 and, 613
  election of 1908 and, 653
  Scopes trial and, 701
  World War I and, 666, 667
Buchenwald, 775
Budget. *See also* Deficit
  balancing, 938
  Clinton and, 949, 968
  for Defense Department, 789–790
  deficits in, 855, 925, 957
Buffalo (animal), 522, 527
Bulgaria, 664, 940
Bulge, Battle of the, 777
Bunau-Varilla, Philippe, 618
Bureaucracy
  development of, 573
  in 1890s, 588
Bureau of Indian Affairs
  Alcatraz seizure and, 910
  apology by, 964–965
Bureau of Standards, 712
Burger, Warren E., 889
Burma, 772
Burns, Arthur, 886
Bus boycott, 813, 858
Bush, George H. W., 620, 924
  economy and, 926
  election of 1988 and, 923
  election of 1992 and, 966
  environment and, 972
  foreign policy of, 940

  Persian Gulf War and, 923,
    944–945
Bush, George W., 620, 971–973
  Africa and, 976
  economy and, 957–958, 971
  election of 2000 and, 969, 970–971
  election of 2004 and, 972
  image and, 970
  Latino voters and, 964
  Middle East and, 975
  Russia and, 976
  taxation and, 971, 972–973
  terrorist attacks and, 971
Bush, Vannevar, 797–798
Bush v. *Gore,* 970
Business. *See also* Big business;
  Corporations
  after Civil War, 542
  federal regulation of, 588
  government and, 790
  horizontal integration of, 544–545
  international, 545–546
  and labor after World War II,
    793–794
  in recession of 1980-1982, 936–937
  suburban, 797
  trusts and, 648–649
  vertical integration of, 544
  women in, 962
  after World War I, 696–697
Business cycle, 547
Busing, 891–892

Cabinet
  Asian American in, 965
  black cabinet of Roosevelt, 739
  of Clinton, 966
  of Grant, 506
  of Hayes, 508
  Latinos in, 931, 963
  of Nixon, 886
Cable cars, 550
California
  farming in, 519–520
  growth of, 767, 939
  Indians in, 522
  irrigation in, 913
  Japanese immigrants in, 622
  Latino politicians in, 963–964
  Mexicans in, 703
  migration to, 795
  non-whites in, 956
  Proposition 187 in, 954
  Proposition 209 in, 962
  woman suffrage in, 636
California, University, Berkeley
  protests and, 875–876

California State Board of
Agriculture, 521
Cambodia, 893
Campaign(s). *See* Election(s);
Political parties
Campbell, Ben Nighthorse, 932
Camp David Agreement (1978),
902
Camp Fire Girls, 651
Canada
Bering Sea disputes with, 604
immigrants from, 518
NAFTA and, 966–967
woman suffrage in, 636
Canal Zone. *See* Panama Canal
Candidate, The (film), 639
Cantigny, Battle of, 678
Capital (financial)
for agriculture, 514
Depression of 1893 and, 591
labor and, 540–541, 561–570
Capitalism
Lenin on, 670
Native American, 931
New Deal and, 750
Stalin on, 824
welfare, 697
after World War I, 697
after World War II, 791
Capone, Al, 715
Capra, Frank, 746
Caribbean region
expansion into, 601–602, 604
Roosevelt Corollary and, 620
U.S. involvement in, 604, 612,
618–620, 619 (map)
Carmichael, Stokely, 867–868
Carnegie, Andrew, 542, 558, 612
anti-imperialism and, 611
Homestead Strike and, 566
vertical integration and, 544
Carpetbaggers, 502
Carranza, Venustiano, 668
Carson, Rachel, 865, 912
Carswell, G. Harold, 889
Carter, Jimmy, 900–901
economy and, 901, 936
election of 1976 and, 900
election of 1980 and, 922
Middle East treaty and, 901, 902
SALT II and, 895
Castro, Fidel, 836–837, 870, 943, 954
Casualties
in Civil War, 483
in Filipino-American War, 612
in Iraq War (2003–), 978
in Korean War, 833

at Pearl Harbor, 759
in Spanish-American War, 610
in World War I, 678–679
in World War II, 771, 773, 781, 782
Catcher in the Rye, The (Salinger),
802
Catholicism. *See also* Christianity;
Missions and missionaries
city politics and, 584
Democrats and, 578
of Kennedy, 854
Ku Klux Klan and, 694
parochial schools and, 578
prejudice against, 695
of Smith, Alfred, 715–716
after World War II, 800
Catholic Legion of Decency, 746
Catt, Carrie Chapman, 585, 588, 684
Cattle and cattle industry, 505,
516–517, 519
in Great Depression, 736
Cavazos, Lauro, 931
Census, of 2000, 954–956, 955 (map),
964
Central America. *See also* Latin
America
United States and, 604, 619 (map),
667–668, 755–756, 942–943
Central business districts, 550
Central Intelligence Agency (CIA),
829
covert activities of, 829
Cuba and, 870
Iran and, 836
Iran-*contra* and, 943
Latin America and, 836
Watergate affair and, 897
Central Pacific Railroad, 505
Central Powers, 663, 664, 665, 666.
See also World War I
Chambers, Whittaker, 842
Chaney, James, 866
Charter, UN, 779
Chase, Salmon P., 680
Château-Thierry, Battle of, 678
Chávez, César, 905–908
Cheney, Dick, 971, 978
Cheyenne Indians, 522–523, 524
Chicago. *See also* Hull House
(Chicago)
black population of, 810
Capone in, 715
death rate in, 547
Democratic Convention in (1968),
879
Haymarket Riot in, 564
Ku Klux Klan in, 694

meatpacking industry in, 516,
649–650
population of, 644
Pullman strike and, 566–567
race riot in (1919), 703–704
Republic Steel protests and, 738
Weathermen in, 880
World's Columbian Exposition in,
515, 591, 592
Chicago, University of, 555
Chicanos, 814, 905, 908–909. *See also*
Mexicans and Mexican
Americans
as elected officials, 963–964
Childbearing, decline in, 555
Child labor, 530, 558–559, 632–633,
643, 658
laws against, 646, 743
Children. *See also* Education;
Schools
of freedpeople, 485, 496, 499, 500
law aiding mothers with
dependent children, 646
progressive reforms and, 632–633
in southern factories, 530
after World War II, 801
*Children of Light and Children of
Darkness* (Niebuhr), 770
Children's Bureau, 633, 658
Chile, 602
Chin, Vincent, 932
China
communism in, 828–829
HIV in, 960
immigrants from, 549–550, 620
imperialism in, 603
Japan and, 603, 622, 623, 759
Korean War and, 833
missionaries in, 607
Nixon and, 894–895
Open Door policy toward,
620–622
People's Republic of, 830, 831
pinyin spelling and, 831n
trade with, 713
U.S. relations with, 833
World War I and, 664, 686
in World War II, 765
China Syndrome, The (film), 913
Chinatowns, 932
Chinese Exclusion Act (1882), 568,
620, 765
Chinese people. *See also* China
in California, 520
exclusion of, 568, 620, 622
immigration policy and, 622
labor organization by, 568

Chippewa Indians, 910
Choctaw Indians, 931
Chopin, Kate, 584
Christian Coalition, 921
Christian Democratic movements
    (Europe), 920
Christianity, 769. *See also* Missions
    and missionaries
    fundamentalist, 701–702, 920
    Gospel of Wealth and, 579
    postwar ecumenicism in, 800
    Social Gospel movement and, 582,
        630
Christianity and the Social Crisis
    (Rauschenbusch), 582
Christianizing the Social Order
    (Rauschenbusch), 582
Christian realism, 770
Chrysler, 738
Church(es). *See also* Religion(s)
    African American, 499, 551, 810
Churchill, Winston, 790
    "iron curtain" speech of, 824
    World War II and, 758, 772–773,
        776
CIA. *See* Central Intelligence
    Agency (CIA)
Cincinnati, blacks in, 962
CIO. *See* Committee of Industrial
    Organization (CIO); Congress of
    Industrial Organizations (CIO)
Cisneros, Henry, 931, 963
Cities and towns. *See also* Suburbs;
    Urban areas
    African American migration to,
        739, 794, 810
    black towns, 500, 534
    bosses in, 577
    growth of, 547–548
    immigrants in, 644–645
    Indians in slums of, 528
    industrial, 550–553
    Mexican immigrants in, 703
    migration to, 795
    in New South, 529
    populations of, 644, 699, 795, 938
    reform of, 582–584, 644
    settlement house movement and,
        580–582, 628, 637
    social geography of, 553
    social justice movement and,
        630–631
    as "walking cities," 550
Citizens and citizenship
    African Americans and, 492, 493
    Japanese Americans and, 816

    for Native Americans, 528
    people in U.S. territories and, 613
    schools and, 638
Citizens Equal Rights Association,
    534
City: The Hope of Democracy, The
    (Howe), 646
City beautiful movement, 582–583,
    592, 645–646
City upon a hill, 601
Civilian Conservation Corps (CCC),
    720–721, 731–732, 736
Civil liberties
    Palmer raids and, 693–694
    Supreme Court on, 868
Civil rights. *See also* Civil rights
    movement
    Committee on, 811
    Fourteenth Amendment and, 492
    Kennedy and, 858–861
    Nixon and, 890–892
    of Scottsboro Boys, 739
    Supreme Court and black, 531,
        533
    Truman and, 805, 806, 811–812
Civil Rights Acts
    of 1957, 813
    of 1960, 814
    of 1964, 866, 892, 903
Civil rights bills
    of 1866, 489
    of 1875, 507
    of Kennedy, 860, 861
Civil Rights Commission, 813
Civil rights movement, 813–814. *See
    also* King, Martin Luther, Jr.
    foreign policy and, 829
    Malcolm X and, 867
    in 1960s, 851, 858–861, 865–868
Civil service, 576, 577
    homosexuals in, 843
Civil Service Commission, Loyalty
    Review Board, 841
Civil war(s)
    in Iraq, 978
    in Nicaragua, 943
    in Spain, 757
Civil War (U.S.). *See also*
    Reconstruction
    casualties of, 483
    crises at end of, 482–484
    pensions for veterans, 588
Civil Works Administration
    (CWA), 729
Clamshell Alliance, 913
Clansman, The (Dixon), 490, 491

Clarke, Ann, 883–884, 915
Class conflict, 561–570, 643
Classes. *See also* Class conflict;
    specific classes
    digital divide and, 934
Clayton Act, 657
Clean Air Act, 913
Clemenceau, Georges, 683, 686
Clergy
    African American, 499
    in World War II, 770
Cleveland, Grover, 576, 588, 593
    Cuba and, 608
    Depression of 1893 and, 592
    election of 1884 and, 575, 578
    election of 1892 and, 589, 590
    expansionism and, 603
    Latin America and, 604
    Pullman strike and, 567
Cleveland, Ohio, 645
Clinton, Bill, 620
    abortion and, 963
    Africa and, 976
    economy and, 950, 957, 966
    election of 1992 and, 966
    election of 1996 and, 968
    impeachment of, 493, 968–969
    Middle East and, 974–975
    on television, 966, 967
    welfare system and, 949
Clothing, for women, 553
Coal and coal industry, 543
    strike in, 649
Coca-Cola, 790
Code talkers, Navajo Indians as, 770
Cohn, Roy, 846
COLA. *See* Cost-of-living
    adjustment
Colbert, Claudette, 746, 747
Cold War, 787, 790, 819–848. *See also*
    Nuclear weapons
    anti-Communist crusade during,
        841–848
    causes of, 848
    end of, 940–941, 942 (map)
    Europe in 1950 and, 827 (map)
    government research and
        development and, 797–798
    Latin America and, 836–837,
        942–943
    leadership in, 822
    massive retaliation policy in, 840
    McCarthyism and, 820, 843–847
    NSC-68 in, 829, 833
    origins of, 821–824
    Reagan and, 939

Truman loyalty program and, 822, 834, 841–842
world after (1992-2006), 948–981
Yalta conference and, 778–779, 823
Collective bargaining, 683
Colleges. *See* Universities and colleges
College Settlement (New York), 628
Collier, John, 740
Colombia
  Panama and, 667
  Panama Canal and, 618
Colonies and colonization. *See also* Expansion and expansionism
  expansionism and, 604–605
  imperialism and, 603–604
  World War I and, 665, 686
  after World War II, 791
Colorado, 636
Colored Farmers' Alliance, 537
Colson, Charles W., 895
Columbian Exposition (Chicago), 515, 591, 592
Columbia River, 736
Columbia University, 876
Commerce, in Western Hemisphere, 620
Commercial banks, 545
Commission form of municipal government, 645
Commission on Training Camp Activities, 683
Committee of Industrial Organization (CIO), 738. *See also* AFL-CIO
Committee on Civil Rights, 811
Committee on Public Information, 671
Committee to Re-elect the President (CREEP), 896–897
Commonwealth of Independent States, 940
Communication(s). *See also* Media
  during Great Depression, 743–744
  in 1920s, 713
  revolution in, 699–700
Communism, 790. *See also* Bolshevism
  Bay of Pigs and, 870–871
  in China, 828–829, 831
  Cold War and, 819
  collapse of, 940–941, 942 (map)
  confrontations with, 872–873
  Cuban missile crisis and, 871–872
  Eisenhower and, 822
  fears of, 824, 842–848

Hiss case and, 842, 843
Hitler and, 756
HUAC and, 842
loyalty oaths and, 841–842
McCarthy and, 843–847
in 1920s, 712
Nixon and, 895
Red Scare and, 693–694
Russian Revolution and, 670, 686, 693
in Soviet Russia, 670
Truman and, 822, 841–842
Communities. *See also* Cities and towns
  working-class, 551
Community Service Organization, 814
Competition
  in agriculture, 514–515
  Christianity and, 579
  railroads and, 544
  Rockefeller on, 545
  between U.S. and Japan, 622–623
  wastefulness of, 580
Compromise of 1877, 508
Computers, 797–798, 934
Confederate States of America. *See also* Civil War (U.S.); Reconstruction
  debt of, 488, 492
  veterans and, 589
Confessional autobiography, 953
Congregationalism, 499
Congress (U.S.)
  African Americans and, 493
  Army-McCarthy hearings and, 846–847
  corruption in, 506
  Eisenhower and, 808
  election of 2000 and, 971
  51st Congress, 589
  former Confederates in, 488, 489
  loyalty program of, 842
  in 1990s and 2000s, 967–968
  power of, 574–575
  Republican control of, 966
  Truman and, 804–805
  Wilson's appearance before, 656
  woman suffrage and, 493–494
Congressional Government (Wilson), 653
Congressional Reconstruction, 488–492
Congress of Industrial Organizations (CIO), 738, 793, 848. *See also* AFL-CIO

Congress of Racial Equality (CORE), 858, 859
Conkling, Roscoe, 574, 575, 577
Connor, Eugene "Bull," 859
Conscription. *See* Draft (military)
Conservation, 520–521
  TVA and, 732
Conservatism
  environment and, 933
  gay marriage and, 965
  of Harding, 711
  in 1980s and 1990s, 917–946
  Nixon and, 889
  of Reagan, 921–923
  of Supreme Court, 889–890
  women's rights and, 929–930
Conservative Judaism, 800
Conservative party (England), 919–920
Constitution(s), southern, 492, 501, 502, 532
Constitution (U.S.), Watergate affair and, 895–900
Constitutional crisis, at end of Civil War, 482–483
Consumer(s)
  spending by, 788, 956
  after World War II, 788
Consumer credit, 798–799
Consumer culture, 798–799
Consumer movement, 914
Consumer Product Safety Commission, 925
Consumer Reports, 839
Containment policy, 824–833. *See also* Communism
  in 1950s, 829–830
Contraception. *See* Birth control
Contract with America, 968
Conventions. *See* Democratic National Convention
Conwell, Russell, 579
Coolidge, Calvin, 709, 710–712, 715
  Mexico and, 714
CORE. *See* Congress of Racial Equality (CORE)
Corporations, 545. *See also* Business
  in Great Depression, 736–737
  lifestyle and, 791–792
  in 1920s, 712
  in 1990s and 2000s, 958
  after World War I, 696–697
  after World War II, 791–792
Corregidor, 772
Corruption, 506
  in Grant administration, 506, 573

Corruption (continued)
under Harding, 711
in Reconstruction governments, 501, 502–503
Cost-of-living adjustment, 761, 793
Cotton and cotton industry
Civil War and, 498
in South, 529, 530–531
strike by cotton pickers, 537
Cotton States and International Exposition, Booker T. Washington speech at, 534–535
Coughlin, Charles E., 734, 920
Council of Economic Advisers, 804, 886
Counterculture, 877–878
Courts. See also Supreme Court (U.S.)
southern, 489
Cowan, Paul, 851–852, 858, 881
Cowboys, 516
Cox, Archibald, 897
Cox, Jacob, 523
Cox, James, 710
Coxey, Jacob, 592
Coy, Ed, 533
Craft unions, 563
Crash. See Stock market
Credit cards, 798–799
Crédit Mobilier, 506
Creditor, United States as, 713
Creel, George, 671, 676
Creel Committee. See Committee on Public Information
Crime and criminals
Miranda case and, 868
organized crime and, 715
Prohibition and, 715
Crimes against humanity, Milosevic and, 973–974
Crisis, The, 652, 704
Crops. See also Agriculture; Farms and farming
in California, 520
"Cross of Gold" speech (Bryan), 594
Crow Indians, 931
Crusade for Justice, 909
Cuba
annexation and, 609
Batista in, 755, 836
Bay of Pigs fiasco and, 870–871
Castro in, 836–837
independence for, 610, 619
intervention in, 619
revolution in (1890s), 607–608
Spanish-American War in, 607–611

Cuban-Americans, 870, 905, 954
Cuban missile crisis, 871–872
Culture(s)
of Asian Americans, 965
automobile and, 698–699
consensus and conformity in, 799–803
consumer, 798–799
Latino impact on, 964
in 1920s, 701
of poor southern whites, 498–499
rebellion in, 802–803
spread of American, 745, 790
Currency
Depression of 1893 and, 590
in Gilded Age, 576–577
national, 800
Curry, John Steuart, 702
Custer, George, 524, 526
Czechoslovakia
breakup of, 940, 942 (map)
immigrants from, 518
Soviet control of, 828
Versailles Peace Conference and, 686
World War II and, 757
Czech republic, 940

Daley, Richard J., 879
Dallas, Kennedy assassination in, 860
Dams
Hetch-Hetchy and, 651
in New Deal, 736
TVA and, 732–733, 732 (map)
Danbury Hatters case, 641
Dance halls, 639
Danish West Indies. See Virgin Islands
Dardanelles, 826
Darlan, Jean, 774
Darrow, Clarence, 701
Darwin, Charles, 579
Darwinism
progressives and, 630–631
Scopes trial and, 701
Daugherty, Harry, 711
Daughters of the American Revolution, 749
Davis, Jefferson, 493
Davis, John W., 711, 733
Davis, Theodore R., 524
Dawes, Charles, 711
Dawes Plan, 714
Dawes Severalty Act (1887), 527–528, 740

Day care, 768, 810
Dayton peace conference (1995), 973
D-Day, Operation Overlord and, 776–777
DDT, 865
Dean, John, 895, 897
Death rate. See Mortality rate
Debates, presidential (1960), 854, 856, 857
Debs, Eugene
election of 1912 and, 655
imprisonment of, 672
IWW and, 644
Pullman strike and, 566–567
Debt. See also National debt
Confederate, 488, 492
of farmers, 515, 536
in New South, 531
of railroads, 544
in tenancy and sharecropping, 497, 498
after World War I, 714
Deer, Ada, 964
De facto segregation, 892
Defense Department, 789, 797
Defense industries, 839–840
after World War II, 793
in World War II, 761, 767, 768
Defense spending
Korean War and, 833
from 1945-1960, 837
by Reagan, 926
Deficit, 808. See also Budget
1970-1992, 925
in 1980s, 926
reduction of, 949, 957
in World War II, 855
Deflation, 515
Deforestation, 721. See also Forest(s)
De jure (legal) segregation, 892
De Klerk, Frederik W., 944
Deloria, Vine, Jr., 910
Democratic National Committee, Watergate affair and, 897
Democratic National Convention
of 1964, 866
of 1968, 879
Democratic party. See also Election(s)
election of 1948 and, 805
at end of Civil War, 484
in Gilded Age, 575
in Great Depression, 728
immigrants and, 703

in Reconstruction South, 501
(map), 503–505
revival in 1990s, 966–967
Democratic Republic of Germany.
See East Germany
Democratic Republic of Vietnam.
See North Vietnam
Demographics
population shift and, 938–939,
950–956
shift after World War II, 794–797
Demonstrations. *See* Protest(s)
Dempsey, Jack, 700
Denison House (Boston), 581
Denmark, 664
woman suffrage in, 636
Denver, 795, 931
Department stores, 553, 554
Depression (economic). *See also*
Great Depression
of 1870s, 505, 506, 546
of 1890s, 546, 554, 573, 588,
590–592, 605
workers and, 558
Depuy de Lôme, Enrique, 608
Deregulation
by Carter, 901
by Reagan, 925
savings and loan crisis and, 927
Desegregation. *See also* Integration;
Segregation
of armed forces, 766, 806,
811–812
of schools, 812–813
Detroit, 699
African Americans in, 691–692
Ku Klux Klan in, 694
migration to, 767
race riot in, 766
unemployment in, 936–937
Dewey, George, 599, 600, 608, 611
Dewey, John, 580, 630, 638
Dewey, Thomas E., 778, 805, 806
De Witt, John, 765
Diablo Canyon nuclear plant, 913
Díaz, Porfirio, 668
Dickson, Jephta, 498
Dictators, U.S. support for, 755,
774–775
Diem, Ngo Dinh, 834, 873
Diet, in 1920s, 696
Digital divide, 934
Diplomacy. *See also* Foreign policy
with China, 894–895
dollar, 623
Kissinger and, 886, 895

of Roosevelt, Theodore, 615
World War II and, 771–775
Discrimination. *See also* Civil rights
movement
banning of, 860, 866
civil rights movement and, 866
against female workers, 559, 768
Freedom Summer and, 866
gender-based, 903
in housing, 743
against Latinos, 909, 931
reverse, 892
Disease. *See also* Medicine
miracle drugs and, 795
Native Americans and, 522
in World War I, 679
Disney, Walt, 750
Distribution of wealth. *See* Income;
Wealth
Diversity. *See also* Ethnic groups
ethnic, 505, 556–557
Divorce, 502, 555, 768, 816
Dixiecrats, 805
Dixon, Thomas, Jr., 490, 491
Documentary photography, 634,
635
Dole, Robert, 968
Dollar (U.S.), 729, 779
silver, 577
Dollar diplomacy, 623, 667
Domestic policy, polls on, 845
Domestic service, 559, 560, 561
Domestic sphere, women in, 555
Dominican Republic, 602
intervention in, 620, 667, 713
Doomsday clock, 838
Dornan, Robert, 964
Dos Passos, John, 664
Douglas, William O., 824, 869
Douglass, Esther, 499
Douglass, Frederick, 494, 501, 534
on Reconstruction, 509
Dow Jones Industrial Average, 957
Down with Women (film), 639
Draft (military)
in World War I, 673
in World War II, 758, 770
Dreiser, Theodore, 631
Drinking. *See* Alcohol and
alcoholism
Drought. *See* Dust bowl
Drugs (illegal). *See also* Prescription
drugs
counterculture and, 878
Panama invasion and, 943
Drums Along the Mohawk, 746–747

Drunkenness. *See* Alcohol and
alcoholism
Dubinsky, David, 738
Du Bois, W. E. B., 495–496, 503, 534,
535, 652
anti-Communist fears and, 848
postwar racism and, 686
racial violence and, 704
World War I and, 675
Dukakis, Michael, 923
Dulles, John Foster, 829, 836, 840,
841
Dunne, John, 918
Dupont Corporation, 606
Dust bowl, 519, 736, 743
Dutch East Indies, 772
Duties. *See* Taxation
Dylan, Bob, 879–880, 906, 907

Earth Summit (Rio), 933
East, woman suffrage in, 636
East Africa, 944
East Asia, 620 (map)
Eastern Europe
collapse of communism in,
940–941, 942 (map)
immigrants from, 548
Soviet Union and, 779, 791, 828
in World War II, 777
East Germany, 828, 830. *See also*
Germany
East St. Louis, Illinois, 672, 675
Ebbesen family, 511–512
Ecology. *See* Environment
Economic Opportunity Act (1964),
864
Economics
conservative, 920
crisis at end of Civil War, 484, 485
Economy. *See also* Depression
(economic); Great Depression;
Panics; Welfare and welfare
programs
changes in, 933–938
after Civil War, 541, 545
at end of Civil War, 483, 484
family, 558–559
federal responsibility for, 750
German, 791
growth of, 956, 957
of Japan, 791
in 1980s and 1990s, 923–925, 926,
936
in 1990s-2000s, 956–958, 979
post-World War I, 696–700
post-World War II, 786–794

Economy *(continued)*
  service, 934–935
  slowdown in growth, 936–938
  in South, 529
  Soviet, 821, 823–824
  World War I and, 696–700
  World War II and, 761–762
  worldwide, 546–547
Economy Act, 728
Edison, Thomas, 543, 676
Education. *See also* Schools
  Americanization programs and, 584
  bilingual, 954
  Brown case and, 812–813, 858, 868
  compulsory attendance and, 555
  desegregation in, 812–813
  expansion of, 555
  for freedpeople, 485–486, 495, 499–500
  gender bias in, 904
  Kennedy and, 855–858
  Latino, 931
  Native Americans and, 911
  in 1920s, 696
  political conflicts over, 578
  progressive, 638
  for women, 554–555, 902–903
  of World War I soldiers, 675
Education Amendments (1972), 904
Education Assistance Act (1975), 912
Efficiency, Taylor and, 641
Egypt, 836, 901
Ehrlichman, John, 886
Eighteenth Amendment, 639, 715, 728
Eight-hour workday, 563, 653
Einstein, Albert, 758
Eisenhower, Dwight D., 807
  CIA and, 829
  Cold War and, 822, 830, 840
  Cuba and, 837
  election of 1952 and, 807
  election of 1956 and, 840–841
  highways and, 788
  Indian policy of, 815
  Korean War and, 833
  nuclear testing and, 840–841
  school desegregation and, 813
  television and, 856
  Vietnam and, 834
  in World War II, 777, 778
Eisenhower Doctrine, 836
Elbe River, 778
Elderly. *See* Aging

Election(s)
  of 1864, 484
  of 1867, 493, 506
  of 1868, 493, 503, 506
  of 1870, 503
  of 1872, 506
  of 1876, 506, 507–508
  of 1876-1892, 575
  of 1880, 575
  of 1884, 575, 578
  of 1888, 577, 588
  of 1890, 537, 589
  of 1892, 589, 590
  of 1894, 592
  of 1896, 592–595, 593 (map), 608
  of 1900, 613–614
  of 1908, 653
  of 1912, 653–654
  of 1916, 668–669
  of 1920, 710–711
  of 1924, 711
  of 1928, 715–716
  of 1932, 726–727
  of 1936, 741
  of 1940, 758–759
  of 1944, 778
  of 1946, 804
  of 1948, 805, 806
  of 1952, 807
  of 1956, 840–841
  of 1960, 854
  of 1964, 863, 866
  of 1968, 879
  of 1972, 887, 894, 897
  of 1976, 899, 900
  of 1980, 922
  of 1984, 922, 928
  of 1988, 923, 924
  of 1992, 923, 966
  of 1994, 967
  of 1996, 968
  of 2000, 507, 957, 970–971
  of 2004, 972
  of 2006, 973
  all-white primary and, 532
  to Senate, 537
Electoral College, 970–971
Electric generator, 543
Electricity, 543, 790
  Eisenhower and, 808
  in 1920s, 697–698
  Rural Electrification Administration and, 735
  TVA and, 732–733, 732 (map)
Electronics, 790
Eliot, T. S., 706

Elites and elitism, urban reformers as, 584
Elkins Act (1903), 649
Ellington, Duke, 706
Ellis Island, 950
El Paso, 703
El Salvador, 942–943
Ely, Richard T., 580
Embargo
  Arab oil, 887, 923
  on Iraq, 944
  before World War II, 756, 757, 758
Emergency Committee for Employment, 723
Emerson, Ralph Waldo, 616
Emigrants. *See* Immigrants and immigration; Migration
Empires. *See also* Imperialism
  of United States, 599, 600–604
Empire State Building, 699
Employment. *See also* Labor; Unemployment; Workforce
  of African Americans, 533, 556–557
  aging and, 960
  changes in, 934
  in cities, 548
  full, 804
  immigration and, 954
  of married women, 558
  of minorities, 962
  by U.S. government, 935
  in World War II, 766
Employment Act (1946), 804
Endangered Species Act (1973), 913
End of the Road, The (film), 676
Energy
  Arab oil embargo and, 887–888, 923
  Carter and, 901
  sources of, 543
England (Britain). *See also* Colonies and colonization; World War I; World War II
  Boer War and, 603
  Conservative Party in, 919–920
  economic leadership and, 546
  food imports of, 513
  Great Depression and, 725
  immigrants from, 518
  industrialization and, 545
  Japan and, 624
  lend-lease and, 758–759
  Panama Canal and, 618

Venezuelan crises and, 618, 624
woman suffrage in, 636
World War II and, 758, 790, 826
ENIAC computer, 798
Enola Gay, 782
Enovid, 877
Enron Corporation, 958
Entertainment. *See also* Leisure
in 1930s, 745–750
during World War II, 768–769
Entrepreneurship, 785–786, 790
Environment. *See also* Conservation
automobiles and, 698
conservation vs. preservation in,
650–651
dust bowls and, 736
Great Society and, 865
in 1920s, 712
ranching and farming impact on,
519
suburbanization and, 797
Taft and, 653
use of term, 797
of West, 517 (map)
Environmental movement, 912–913,
933
Environmental Protection Agency
(EPA), 913, 925, 972
Ephron, Nora, 877
EPIC platform ("End Poverty in
California"), 733
Epidemics. *See* Disease; specific
diseases
Equality
for Native Americans, 815
for women, 585, 902–905
Equal Rights Amendment
in 1920s, 708–709
in 1970s, 904, 905, 921
Erie Railroad, 544
Escobedo v. *Illinois,* 868
Espionage. *See* Spies and spying
Espionage Act (1917), 672
Estonia, 686, 940
Ethiopia, 603
Italy and, 756
Ethnic cleansing, in Kosovo, 974
Ethnic groups
in Balkans, 940–941
in cities, 551
in former Yugoslavia, 941
immigration of, 703
impact of, 556–557
intolerance of, 694–695
labor organization and, 567–568
mobility of, 569–570

party affiliation and, 578
progressivism and, 631, 651–653
Europe and Europeans
American agriculture and, 513
in Cold War (1950), 827 (map)
conservatism in, 919–920
imperialism of, 603–604, 620
industrialization in, 545–546
Monroe Doctrine and, 601
neutrality policy toward, 756
old and new immigration from,
548–550
after World War I, 685 (map), 686
World War II and, 757–758,
772–773, 779
Evangelicalism, 582. *See also*
Revivalism
television and, 920–921
after World War II, 800
Evers, Medgar, 860
Evolution, Darwin and, 579, 701
Excess-profits tax, 711, 712
Exchange rate, 779
Executive. *See* Presidency; President
Executive branch, 822
Executive Orders
8802, 766
9066, 764–765
Exodusters, 500
Expansion and expansionism,
601–604. *See also* Westward
movement
in 1890s, 604–607
global, 712–714
international context of, 603–604
to 1900, 605 (map)
for overseas markets, 604–606
Turner on, 604
U.S. territories and, 612–613
Exploration, space, 798, 858
Exports, 605–606
of American culture, 790
grain, 936
from Latin America, 713
of machines, 546
in 1930s, 755

Factories. *See also* Mills
children in, 530
labor in, 544, 640–644
output from, 605
women in, 530, 557, 559
workers in, 557
Fair Deal, 803, 805–807
Fair Employment Practices
Commission (FEPC), 766

Fair housing, Nixon and, 890–891
Fair Labor Standards Act (1938),
743
Fall, Albert, 711
Fallout shelters, 839
Falwell, Jerry, 920–921
Families. *See also* Divorce; Marriage
economy of, 558–559
Great Depression and, 724–725
middle-class, 555
in 1920s, 708
smaller, 555
two-income, 762
women workers and, 559, 561
after World War II, 800–802
Family Assistance Plan, 889
Family Limitation (Sanger), 637
Farms and farming. *See also*
Agriculture; Planters and
plantations
Agricultural Adjustment Acts
and, 730–731, 742
Alliance movement and, 536–538
bonanza, 513
in California, 519–520
contract system and, 496, 505
decline in, 936
Grange and, 535–536
in Great Depression, 724, 735–736
on Great Plains, 511–512, 517–519
industrial innovation and,
518–519
Interstate Commerce Act and, 536
by Japanese, 622
labor workforce and, 935–936
Mexican immigrants in, 703
in New South, 530–531
in 1920s, 709
Ocala Platform and, 537–538
one-crop, 496
southern middle class and poor
farmers, 498–499
Truman and, 805
in West, 515
World War II and, 761, 794
Farm Security Administration
(FSA), 742
Farmworkers, 520, 905–908
Far West. *See also* West
industry in, 542
Fascism, 712, 756
Faubus, Orval, 813
Faulkner, William, 748
Federal aid, 865
Federal Bureau of Labor Statistics,
809

Federal Communications
  Commission (FCC), 925
Federal Deposit Insurance
  Corporation (FDIC), 728
Federal Emergency Relief
  Administration (FERA), 729
Federal Employee Loyalty Program
  (1947), 841
Federal Farm Loan Act (1916), 669
Federal government. See
  Government (U.S.)
Federal Home Loan Bank Act
  (1932), 725
Federal Housing Administration
  (FHA), 725, 743
Federal Republic of Germany. See
  West Germany
Federal Reserve Board, 723, 887,
  956, 957
Federal Reserve System, 656, 728
Federal Trade Commission (FTC),
  656–657, 658
Feingold, Mimi, 859
Feminine Mystique, The (Friedan),
  801
Feminism
  African American, 904–905
  backlash against, 963
  in 1920s, 708–709
  in 1930s, 740
  in 1970s, 902–905
Ferraro, Geraldine, 929
Fertilizers, 709, 936
Fiction. See Literature; Novels;
  specific works
Fifteenth Amendment, 489, 493,
  494, 504, 508
51st Congress, 589
Filipino-American War, 599–600,
  609, 611–610
Filipinos, 599, 765, 965. See also
  Philippines
Films. See Movies
Finances
  Great Depression and, 723
  U.S. dominance of Latin
    American, 713
  for World War I, 680–681
  for World War II, 762
Financial panics. See Panics
Finland, 686
  woman suffrage in, 636
First New Deal, 726–734
First World War. See World War I
Fisk, Clinton, 494
Fisk University, 500

Fit to Fight (film), 676, 677
Fitzgerald, F. Scott, 706, 707
Fitzgerald, John, 643
Fixed-rate mortgages, 742
Flappers, 707, 708
Flooding
  in Mississippi River valley, 709
  TVA and, 732
Florida
  election of 2000 and, 970
  migration to, 795
  Seminole Indians in, 910
Flower children, 878
Flu pandemic, 679–680
Folk music, 906
Food. See also Crops; Diet
  production in South, 496, 531
  regulation of, 650
  shortages in, 936
  for World War I, 680–681
Food Administration, 681
Food and Drug Administration,
  877, 963
Food stamps, 926, 954
Fool's Errand, A (Tourgée), 490, 491
Force acts (1870 and 1871), 504, 505
Ford, Gerald, 892, 894, 899
Ford, Henry, 698–699
  anti-Semitism of, 695
  assembly line and, 640, 699
Ford Motor Company, 698–699, 738
Foreign aid
  Marshall Plan as, 826–829
  to Turkey and Greece, 826
Foreign-born Americans. See
  Immigrants and immigration;
  specific groups
Foreign policy
  activism in, 615
  Balkan crisis (1990s) and, 973–974
  end of Cold War and, 939–945
  in 1920s, 712–714
  in 1990s-2000s, 973–978
  polls on, 844, 845
  before World War II, 755–758
Foreign trade. See Trade
Forest(s)
  CCC and, 721
  destruction of, 521
Forest Reserve Act (1891), 521
Forest reserves, 521
Formosa. See Taiwan (Formosa)
Forrest, Nathan Bedford, 507
Forten, Charlotte, 499
Fort Laramie Treaty, 523
Fortune, T. Thomas, 534

"Forty acres and a mule," 486
Forum, 532
Four Freedoms, 763
442nd Infantry Combat Team, 765
"Four-minute men," 676
Fourteen Points, 684, 686
Fourteenth Amendment, 489, 492,
  493–494, 504, 507, 508, 533
France. See also World War I; World
  War II
  Indochina and, 834
  in 1920s, 714
  Panama Canal and, 618
  World War II and, 758, 777, 790
Franchise (voting). See Voting and
  voting rights
Franchises (retail), 785–787, 791
Franco, Francisco, 756, 774
Frank Leslie's Illustrated Newspaper,
  485, 524
Franklin, Benjamin, 616
  autobiography of, 952, 953
Franz Ferdinand (Austria-
  Hungary), 664
Freedmen's Bureau, 489, 492,
  494–496, 506. See also
  Freedpeople
Freedmen's Bureau schools, 500
Freedom(s). See also Rights
  for middle-class women, 553–555
  for slaves, 484
  in World War I, 672–673
Freedom Democratic party, 866
Freedom rides, 858–859
Freedom Summer Project (1964),
  866
Freedpeople, 482, 484–486, 506, 509
  aid for, 494–495
  Black Codes and, 486–487
  education and, 485–486, 495,
    499–500
  farming by, 496–498
  land for, 486, 494, 495, 498
  lives of, 494–498, 499–501
  presidential Reconstruction and,
    488
  self-help institutions of, 499–501
  strike by, 505
  voting rights for men, 493, 494
  westward movement of, 500
Free love, 585
Freeman, Jo, 903
Free silver
  Bryan on, 594
  McKinley on, 594
Free Speech Movement, 875–876

Free trade, 966
French Foreign Legion, World War I and, 664
French Indochina. *See* Cambodia; Vietnam
Frick, Henry Clay, 566
Friedan, Betty, 801, 903
Friedman, Milton, 920
"From the Depths" (illustration), 586
Frontier thesis (Turner), 515, 516
Fuehrer, Hitler as, 756
Full employment, 804
Fundamentalism
   Christian, 701–702, 920
   Jewish, 920
   Muslim, 920
Fusion, 838

Galbraith, John Kenneth, 790
Gallup, George, 844
Gambling, Native-American, 931
Garfield, James, 575, 576, 577
Garment workers, Triangle Fire and, 642–643
Garner, John Nance, 741
Garrett, Marlene, 948–949, 957, 973
Garrison, William Lloyd, 652
Garvey, Marcus, 704–705
Gasoline. *See also* Oil and oil industry
   prices of (1973-1980), 891
"Gay nineties," 586–588
Gays and lesbians, 585. *See also* Homosexuals
   health care for partners of, 965
   in 1990s-2000, 965
   rights of, 912
Gaza Strip, 975
Gender. *See also* Men; Sex and sexuality; Women
   Civil Rights bill (1964) and, 903
   discrimination based on, 903
   Proposition 209 and, 962
   segregation by, 633
   voting and, 494
General Electric, 921
General Managers Association, 567
General Motors (GM), 697, 738, 793, 808
   plant closings by, 937–938
   UAW and, 935
Geneva Conference (1954), 834
Genocide
   in Holocaust, 757, 775, 836
   in Rwanda, 976

George, Henry, 580, 630, 645
German Americans
   World War I and, 671–672
   after World War II, 828
German Democratic Republic. *See* East Germany
Germany. *See also* East Germany; Holocaust; Nazi Germany; West Germany; World War I; World War II
   economy in, 934, 956
   Great Depression and, 725
   immigrants from, 518, 551
   industrialization in, 545–546
   reparations and, 714
   reuniting of, 940
   student protests in, 876
   submarine warfare and (World War II), 759, 772
   Venezuela and, 618
   after World War II, 791
Gestapo, 762
Ghost Dance movement, 527 (map), 528
GI Bill (1944), 788–789, 800
Gibson girl, 553
Gilded Age
   legislation in, 587
   politics in, 573–578
Gilman, Charlotte Perkins, "woman's sphere" and, 637
Gingrich, Newt, 968
Ginsberg, Allen, 803
Ginsburg, Ruth Bader, 930
Gladden, Washington, 582
Glasnost, 939
Glass-Steagall Banking Act (1932), 725
Glidden, Joseph, 519
Global economy, world industrialization and, 546–547
Global warming, 972
GNP. *See* Gross National Product (GNP)
Godkin, Edwin Lawrence, 524
Golan Heights, 872–873, 887
Gold
   in Alaska, 595
   in Black Hills, 506, 526
   as specie, 576
   in Yukon and Klondike, 595
Goldman, Emma, 585, 694
Gold rush, in California, 520
Gold standard, 576, 588
   in Great Depression, 725, 729
Goldwater, Barry, 863, 879

Gompers, Samuel, 567, 641
   AFL and, 565, 641
   in progressive era, 641
   radical labor and, 643
   World War I and, 681
Gone with the Wind (Mitchell), 748
Gonzales, Alberto, 964
Gonzales, Elián, 954
Gonzáles, Rodolfo "Corky," 909
Goodman, Andrew, 866
Good Neighbor policy, 755
Gorbachev, Mikhail, 939
Gospel of Wealth, 579
Gould, Jay, 506, 565
Gover, Kevin, 964–965
Government(s)
   cynicism about, 894, 898
   municipal, 644–646
   reconstructed, 488, 501–503
   in U.S. territories, 612–613
   urban, 582
   women and, 659
Government (U.S.). *See also* Great Depression; Regulation
   black federal employees in, 739
   business and, 790
   economy and, 762, 789–790
   employees of, 935
   growth of, 809
   railroad land and, 543
   in World War I, 681
Governor(s)
   Republican, 968
   state reform movements and, 646
Grady, Henry, 530, 531
Graham, Billy, 800
Grain, 520
   elevators, 535, 536
   Soviet market for, 755, 936
Grand Coulee Dam, 736
Grandfather clause, 532–533
Grange, 535–536
Granger laws, 536
Grant, Ulysses S., 504, 574
   cabinet of, 506
   corruption and, 506, 573
   election of 1868 and, 493, 506
   election of 1872 and, 506
   Native Americans and, 523
   Santo Domingo and, 602
Grapes of Wrath, The (Steinbeck), 736, 748
Grayson, William, 599–600, 611, 612, 625
Great Britain. *See* England (Britain)

Great Depression, 720–751
  end of, 782
  first New Deal and, 726–734
  global nature of, 725
  legacy of, 750–751
  minorities during, 738–740
  society and lifestyle during,
    743–750
  stock market crash and, 716,
    722–723
Great Gatsby, The (Fitzgerald), 707
Great Lakes region, immigrants in,
  595
Great migration, World War I and,
  681–682
Great Plains, 511–512, 516–519. *See
  also* Plains Indians
Great Society, 863–869, 951
  attacks on, 869
  environment and, 913
  roots of programs of, 864
Great Valley (California), 521
Great War. *See* World War I
Great White Fleet, 623
Greeley, Horace, 506
Green, Theodore Francis, 862
Greenbacks, 576
Green Party, 964
Greensboro, North Carolina, 858
Greenspan, Alan, 957
Griffith, D. W., 490, 639
Gross National Product (GNP)
  in Germany, 791
  in U.S., 788
Guam
  U.S. acquisition of, 610
  World War II and, 760, 772
Guantanamo naval base, 619, 755
Guerrilla warfare. *See also* Wars and
  warfare
  in Philippines, 600
  in Vietnam, 873
Gulf of Tonkin resolution, 873
Gulf War. *See* Persian Gulf War
Guthrie, Woody, 906
Gutiérrez, José Angel, 909

Haggerty, Rose, 560
Hague, The, World Court at,
  662–663, 974
Haiti, 755
  Wilson and, 667
Haldeman, H. R., 886, 897
Hale, Bill, 676
Hamer, Fannie Lou, 866
Hanford, Washington, 840

Hanna, Mark, 594, 614
Harding, Warren G., 710–711, 713,
  715
Hard-money advocates, 576
Harlan, John, 586
Harlem Renaissance, 705–706
Harper's Weekly, 524, 525
Harrington, Michael, 809
Harrison, Benjamin, 521, 537, 576,
  588, 611
  election of 1888 and, 577
Havana harbor, 608
Hawaii, 601, 613, 622
  annexation of, 603, 621
  Japanese Americans in, 765
  Pearl Harbor attack and, 759–760
Hawley-Smoot Tariff (1930), 714
Hay, John, 610, 621
Hayden, Tom, 875
Hayes, Rutherford B., 507–508, 576
Haymarket Riot (1886), 564
Haynesworth, Clement, 889
Haywood, "Big Bill," 644
Head Start, 864, 968
Health and health care. *See also*
  Medicine
  for elderly, 959–961
  for gays, 965
  in 1920s, 696
  reform of, 966–967
  Sheppard-Towner Maternity Act
    and, 714–715
  women's health collective and,
    904
Health insurance, 658, 735
Hearst, William Randolph, 607, 616,
  617
Helms, Jesse, 920
Hemingway, Ernest, 664, 706–707
Henry Street Settlement, 646
Hepburn Act (1906), 649
Hetch-Hetchy controversy, 651
High schools, 555
Highways. *See* Roads and highways
Hill, Anita, 930
Hill, James J., 649
Hillman, Sidney, 738
Hine, Lewis, 631, 632, 634
Hippies, 877
Hiroshima, Japan, 780, 782
Hispanics. *See* Latinos
Hispaniola, 602
Hiss, Alger, 842, 843
Hitler, Adolf, 756, 757, 771, 774, 778.
  See also Nazi Germany; World
  War II

HIV (human immunodeficiency
  virus), 960, 961
Ho Chi Minh, 774, 834, 835, 873
Hollywood. *See* Movies
Holocaust, 757, 775, 836
Homeland Security, Department of,
  978
Homelessness
  Freedmen's Bureau and, 494
  in 1990s-2000s, 958–959
Home Owners Loan Corporation
  (HOLC), 742
Homestead Act (1862), 518
Homesteading, 518–519. *See also*
  Farms and farming;
  Settlement(s)
Homestead Steel Works, 543
Homestead Strike (1892), 566, 586
Home to Harlem (McKay), 706
Homosexuals. *See also* Gays and
  lesbians
  gay and lesbian rights and, 912
  as security risk, 842
Honduras, 618
Hong Kong, World War II and, 760
Hoover, Herbert
  Bonus Army and, 725–726
  business and, 710
  election of 1928 and, 715–716
  flood relief and, 709
  as Food Administration director,
    681
  Great Depression and, 723–725
  as secretary of commerce, 712
Hoover, J. Edgar, 693–694
Hoover Dam, 736, 740
Hoover Institution (Stanford), 921
Hoovervilles, 720, 726
Hopkins, Harry, 727, 729, 739
Horizontal integration, 544–545
Horse-drawn omnibus, 550
Hospitals, 494
House, Edward, 685
House Made of Dawn (Momaday),
  754, 910
House of Representatives, 506
  Nixon impeachment hearings
    and, 898
  reapportionment and, 869
Houses of Congress. *See* Congress
  (U.S.); House of
  Representatives; Senate
House Un-American Activities
  Committee (HUAC), 842
Housing
  in cities, 551, 742

discrimination in, 743
New Deal and, 743, 750
for poor, 551, 630
progressive reforms and, 637
Reagan and, 926
sod, 511, 512, 519
in suburbs, 552–553
after World War II, 788–789, 796, 804, 806
Housing and Urban Development, Department of, 865
Howard, O. O., 495
Howard University, 500
Howe, Frederic C., 646
Howells, William Dean, 631, 952
"Howl" (Ginsberg), 803
How the Other Half Lives (Riis), 634, 637
HUAC. *See* House Un-American Activities Committee (HUAC)
Huerta, Victoriano, 668
Hughes, Charles Evans, 646, 669, 713
Hughes, Langston, 706
Hull, Cordell, 755
Hull House (Chicago), 554, 581, 646
Kelley, Florence and, 632–633
racism and, 651
Human resources, Reagan and, 926
Humphrey, Hubert, 879
Hungary, 940
"freedom fighters" in, 830
Soviet control of, 828
Versailles Peace Conference and, 686
Huns, Germans as, 665, 671
Hunt, E. Howard, 895
Hunter, Robert, 631
Hurricane Katrina, 973
Hurston, Zora Neale, 706
Huston, John, 769
Hutus, Tutsi fighting with, 976
Hydroelectricity, TVA and, 732–733
Hydrogen bomb, 838

"I Am Woman" (Reddy), 904
Iberia. *See* Spain
ICBM. *See* Intercontinental ballistic missile (ICBM)
Ickes, Harold, 729, 739
Idaho, 636
"I have a dream" speech (King), 861
Illegal immigrants, 814, 931
Illinois
child labor law in, 633
law aiding mothers with dependent children, 646

Illness. *See* Disease; Health and health care
Immigrants and immigration
Americanization programs for, 584
backlash against, 954
child labor and, 559
Chinese, 568, 620
in cities, 644–645
economy and, 948–949
election of 1896 and, 594–595
Great Plains farming and, 517, 518
Japanese, 622
labor and, 556, 567–568, 640
new immigration and, 548–550, 588, 950–954
in 1920s, 702–704
after 1970, 951
political participation and, 577
progressivism and, 629
quotas on, 703, 816
restriction of, 702–703
settlement houses and, 580–582
after World War II, 799
Immigration Acts
in 1920s, 702–703
of 1965, 865, 951
of 1990, 951
Immigration and Nationality Act (1952), 815–816
Immigration and Naturalization Service (INS), 954
Immigration Reform and Control Act (1986), 951
Impeachment
of Clinton, 493, 968–969
of Johnson, Andrew, 492–493, 969
Nixon and, 493, 898
Imperialism, 600–604
anti-imperialism and, 611–612
British, 624
in Caribbean region, 618–620
European, 603–604
Lenin on, 670
political cartoons against, 617
social Darwinism and, 579
Imports
to Latin America, 713
of oil (1973-1980), 891
Inauguration, date of, 727
Income. *See also* Wealth
disparities in, 558
distribution of, 723, 737
family, 558
of Native Americans, 932
in New South, 530

after World War II, 788
Income gap. *See also* Wealth gap
between white and black women, 802
Income tax, 537, 653, 656, 711
Independence
in Africa, 810 (map)
of Baltic states, 940
for Cuba, 610, 619
of Philippines, 599
Vietnam and, 834
of women, 553
India, Americans from, 739, 765
Indiana, Klan in, 694
Indian Claims Commission, 815
Indian policy. *See also* Native Americans
Dawes Severalty Act and, 527–528, 740
in Great Depression, 740
in 1950s, 815
reservations, 523
Indian Reorganization Act (1934), 740
Indians. *See* Native Americans
Indian schools, 528
Indian Self-Determination Act (1975), 912
Indigenous peoples. *See* Native Americans
Individualism
American frontier and, 516
Christianity and, 579
Indochina, 791, 834. *See also* Cambodia; Vietnam
Industrialization. *See also* Labor; Strikes
cities and, 550–553
after Civil War, 541–547
class conflict and, 561
labor and, 640–644
natural resources and, 521
pollution and, 547
South and, 529–530
working class and, 556–561
worldwide, 545–546
Industrial Relations Commission, 643
Industrial Revolution, 545
Industrial wealth, 558
Industrial Workers of the World (IWW), 644
Industry
blacks in, 533, 561
cutbacks in, 937–938
electricity and, 697

Industry *(continued)*
  German postwar, 828
  Great Depression and, 731
  in New South, 529–530
  power for, 543
  productivity decline in, 934
  World War II and, 761, 767,
    791–792
  worldwide, 545–546
Infant mortality, 547
Infections. *See* Disease
Inflation
  Carter and, 901
  decline in, 956–957
  in Great Depression, 729
  1940-1980, 890
  in 1980s, 937
  Nixon and, 887, 889
  during World War I, 680
  after World War II, 790
Influenza pandemic, 679–680
In His Steps (Sheldon), 582
Initiative, 646
Inness, George, 514
In Re Debs, 567
Installment plans, 798
Institute of Defense Analysis, 876
Insular cases, 613
Insurance
  for bank deposits, 728
  health, 658
  Social Security and, 735
  unemployment, 658
Insurrections. *See* Resistance;
    Revolts and rebellions
Integration. *See also* Civil rights
    movement; Desegregation
  of baseball, 810, 812
  of public schools, 812–813, 858,
    860
  of University of Mississippi, 859
Intellectual thought. *See also* Art(s);
    Literature
  Harlem Renaissance and, 705–706
  Lost Generation and, 706–707
  in 1960s, 851–852
Intelligence agencies, 819
Intercontinental ballistic missile
    (ICBM), 838
Interest rates, 956
Interior tribes. *See* Native
    Americans
Intermediate Range Nuclear Forces
    Treaty, 939–940
International affairs. *See* Foreign
    policy

International Association for Labor
    Legislation, 630
International Court of Justice. *See*
    World Court
International Ladies' Garment
    Workers Union (ILGWU), 565,
    643, 738
International Migration Society,
    534
International Monetary Fund, 779
International Suffrage Alliance,
    636
Interstate commerce
  child labor prohibited in, 743
  minimum wage and, 743
Interstate Commerce Act (1887), 536
Interstate Commerce Commission
    (ICC), 536, 649, 658
Interstate Highway Act (1956), 788,
    789 (map)
Inventions, industrial, 542–543
Investment, 545
  expansion and, 606
  in New South, 529
  in 1980s and 1990s, 934
  overseas, 713
Investment banking, 545
Iran, CIA and revolution in, 836
Iran-*contra* affair, 943
Iraq
  Persian Gulf War and, 944–945
  World War I and, 665
Iraq war (2003–), 973, 978
Ireland
  immigrants from, 540–541, 549,
    551, 569
  World War I and, 665
Iron and iron industry, 529
  Bessemer converter and, 542
"Iron curtain" speech (Churchill),
    824
Irrigation, 520, 650, 936
Islam. *See also* Muslims
  fundamentalist, 920
Israel
  creation of, 835–836
  Egyptian recognition of, 901
  peace talks in, 945
  Six Day War and, 872–873, 887
  Yom Kippur War and, 887, 888
    (map)
Issei, 763
Italy
  Ethiopia and, 603, 756
  fascism in, 712, 756
  immigrants from, 703

  Mussolini in, 756
  World War I and, 664
It Happened One Night (film), 746,
    747
Iwo Jima, 781
IWW. *See* Industrial Workers of the
    World (IWW)

Jackson, Jesse, 928
Jagger, Mick, 906
James, William, 580, 630
Japan. *See also* Russo-Japanese War
  atomic bombing of, 780, 781–782,
    791
  automobiles from, 888–889
  British treaty with, 624
  China and, 603, 622, 623
  economic competition from,
    936–937
  economy in, 934, 956
  Great White Fleet in, 623
  immigrants from, 622
  imperialism by, 603
  Korea and, 603, 623, 831
  Manchuria and, 603, 623, 759
  Pearl Harbor attack and, 759–760
  Perry in, 601
  Russia and, 614, 623
  student protests in, 876
  treaty with, 833
  United States and, 622–623
  Vietnam and, 834
  World War I and, 686
  World War II and, 759–760, 772,
    778–779
Japanese Americans
  citizenship for, 816
  during Great Depression,
    739–740
  internment of, 762–765
Jazz. *See also* Music
  in Harlem Renaissance, 706
Jazz Singer, The (film), 700
Jeffords, James, 971
Jerusalem, 872, 887
Jet magazine, 810
Jews and Judaism. *See also* Anti-
    Semitism; Holocaust
  Brandeis and, 669
  communities for, 551
  discrimination in housing and,
    743
  fundamentalist, 920
  immigration and, 548, 549, 703
  Israel and, 835–836
  Klan and, 694

Nazis and, 756, 757
  prejudice against, 695
  after World War II, 800
Jiang Jieshi (Chiang Kai-shek), 830, 831, 894
Jim Crow, 533, 675
Job Corps, 864
Jobs. See Employment
John XXIII (Pope), 800
Johns, Jasper, 878
Johns Hopkins University, 555
Johnson, Andrew, 483, 484, 574
  impeachment of, 492–493, 969
  Reconstruction policy of, 488
Johnson, Billy Don, 753
Johnson, Lady Bird, 865
Johnson, Lyndon B., 852, 861–863
  black voting rights and, 813–814
  civil rights and, 863, 865–868
  containment and, 872–873
  environment and, 913
  Great Society and, 863–869
  legislative program of, 863–865
  National Youth Administration and, 735
  Vietnam War and, 875, 898
Johnson, Tom, 645, 646
Joint Committee on Reconstruction, 489
Jones, "Mother," 585, 644
Jones, Samuel ("Golden Rule"), 584
Jordan, Israel and, 974
Journalism, muckraking, 631
Journals (periodicals). See Magazines
Judaism. See Jews and Judaism
Judiciary. See Courts; Supreme Court (U.S.)
Judiciary Committee (House), 897
Jungle, The (Sinclair), 631, 649–650, 733
Juveniles, progressive reformers and, 633

Kamikazes, Japanese, 781
Kansas, 519, 736
Kansas City, 516
Karenga, Maulana Ron, 868
Kasserine Pass, 773
Katrina (Hurricane), 973
Keating-Owen Child Labor Bill (1916), 669
Kelley, Florence, 632–633, 655
Kelley, Oliver, 535
Kellogg, Frank B., 714
Kellogg-Briand pact, 714

Kellor, Frances, 628–630, 658
Kennan, George F., 824–826
Kennedy, Jacqueline, 855
Kennedy, John F., 851, 852, 853–861
  assassination of, 856, 861, 878
  Bay of Pigs fiasco and, 870–871
  civil rights and, 858–861
  New Frontier and, 855–858
  presidential debate and, 854, 856, 857
  Vietnam and, 873
Kennedy, Robert F., 857, 872, 879
Kenya, Mau Mau revolt in, 810
Kerensky, Alexander, 670
Kerouac, Jack, 803
Kesey, Ken, 878
Kettle Hill, 611
Keynes, John Maynard, 742, 804, 863
Khrushchev, Nikita, 822, 871–872
Kim Il Sung, 831
Kindergartens, 581
King, Martin Luther, Jr., 813, 858
  assassination of, 857, 879
  challenges to, 866, 868
  March on Washington (1963) and, 860–861
King, Rodney, 929, 962
King Cotton, 530
Kingston, Maxine Hong, 952
Kinsey, Alfred C., 801
Kiowa Indians, 526
  Momaday and, 753–754
Kissinger, Henry A., 886, 895
Klamath Indians, 815
Klan. See Ku Klux Klan
Klir, John, "Lost Bet" painting by, 574
Knights of Labor, 533, 563–565
  Chinese Exclusion Act and, 568
  WCTU and, 578
Knox, Philander, 618
Korea, Japanese control of, 604, 623
Korean Americans, 739, 765
Korean War, 789, 831–833, 832 (map)
Kremlin. See Soviet Union
Kroc, Ray, 785–787, 791, 816
Ku Klux Klan, 490, 498–499, 503, 505
  violence by, 504
  after World War I, 694
Ku Klux Klan Act (1871), 504
Kurdish people, 978
Kuwait, 944–945
Ky, Nguyen Cao, 875

Labor. See also Labor unions; Strikes; Workers; Working class
  African American, 556–557
  Asian, 932
  capital and, 540–541
  of freedpeople, 486, 487
  in Great Depression, 731
  immigrant, 540, 549, 550, 556
  Latino, 814
  Ludlow Massacre and, 643
  mining and, 520–521
  New Deal and, 737–738
  in New South, 529
  organizing by, 563
  progressivism and, 640–644
  radical, 643–644
  women as, 558, 559–561, 633–636
  work patterns and, 792–793
  World War I and, 681–683, 696
  World War II and, 761, 793–794, 804–805
Labor Department
  Children's Bureau of, 633
  creation of, 565
Labor unions, 563. See also Strikes; Trade unions; specific unions
  African Americans and, 533
  Chinese workers and, 568
  Danbury Hatters case and, 641
  decline of, 935
  injunctions against, 567
  IWW and, 644
  National Industrial Recovery Act and, 731
  in New Deal, 737–738
  in progressive era, 641–642
  Taft-Hartley Act and, 804–805
  World War II and, 761, 793–794
Lackawanna Valley (Inness), 514
LaDuke, Winona, 964
Lady Chatterley's Lover (Lawrence), 878
Lafayette Escadrille, 664
La Follette, Robert, 646
  election of 1924 and, 711
  Taft administration and, 653
  World War I and, 672
La Guardia, Fiorello, 643
Laissez-faire, 580
Lakota Indians, 523
Land. See also Environment; Public lands
  city growth and, 699
  for freedpeople, 486, 494, 495, 496, 498
  homesteading on, 518

Land (continued)
  impact of ranching and farming on, 519
  Indians and, 528, 964
  for railroads, 506
  Southern Homestead Act and, 494
Land-grant colleges, 513
Landon, Alfred, 741
Language(s), Spanish, 931
Lansing, Robert, 666, 667, 685
Lapp, Ralph, 838
Lathrop, Julia, 658
Latin America
  dominance in, 602
  immigrants from, 951
  refugees from, 865
  revolt in, 836–837
  United States and, 619 (map), 667–668, 713–714, 755–756, 942–943
Latinos
  anti-Communist fears and, 848
  in cities, 938
  employment of, 569
  mobilization of, 905–909
  in 1990s-2000, 963–964
  in population, 955–956
  rights of, 814, 931
  in Vietnam War, 894
Latvia, 686, 940
Law(s). See also Legislation
  child labor, 633
  immigration, 702
"Law and order," Nixon on, 889
Lawlor, David, 556
Lawrence, D. H., 878
Lawrence, David, 790
Layoffs, 935, 957
Leadership
  in Cold War, 822
  conservative, 921–923
League of Nations, 686, 688, 712, 714
  Article 10 of, 687–688
  Italian invasion of Ethiopia and, 756
League of United Latin American Citizens, 814
Leary, Timothy, 878
Lease, Mary E., 586
Leeper family, 511, 538
Left-wing politics, 819, 842
  New Left and, 875
Legislation. See also Law(s); New Deal
  child labor, 633
  environmental, 913

in Gilded Age, 587
  muckraking, 628–629
  settlement house movement and, 581
  social, 630, 669
Legislature. See Congress (U.S.)
Leisure, 553
  in 1920s, 696, 708
  in 1930s, 745–748
Lend-lease, 758–759, 774, 823
Lend-Lease Act (1941), 759
Lenin, V. I., 670, 678
Lesbians. See Gays and lesbians; Homosexuals
Letter from Bataan (movie), 769
Levenger, Sam, 757
Leviathan (ship), 661
Levitt, William J., 796
Levittowns, 796
Lewinsky, Monica, 969
Lewis, Fulton, Jr., 847
Lewis, John L., 710, 738
Lewis, Sinclair, 707
Leyte Gulf, Battle of, 778
Liberalism
  Carter and, 901
  decline of, 885–892
  in 1960s, 851–852, 855–858, 863–869
"Liberal" Republicans, 506
Liberia, 534, 603
Liberty, in World War I, 672–673
Liberty bonds, 680
"Liberty Halts American Butchery in the Philippines," 617
Liberty League, 733
Lichtenstein, Roy, 878
Liddy, G. Gordon, 895, 897
Life expectancy, 955, 960
  in 1920s, 696
  after World War II, 795
  in Zimbabwe, 960
Lifestyle
  automobiles and, 698–699
  in cities and towns, 550–553
  corporations and, 791–792
  of freedpeople, 494–498, 499–501
  during Great Depression, 743–750
  on Great Plains, 511–512
  of immigrant workers, 540
  middle-class, 553–556
  in 1920s, 708
Light in August (Faulkner), 748
Liliuokalani, 603
Limited Test Ban Treaty (1963), 872
Lincoln, Abraham, 482
Lindbergh, Charles, 700, 758

Literacy, in World War II, 770
Literacy tests
  for immigrants, 702
  for voting, 532
Literature. See also Poets and poetry
  of Beat Generation, 803
  Harlem Renaissance and, 705–706
  of muckrakers, 631
  in 1920s, 706–707
  of 1930s, 748
  Populist, 593
  Reconstruction novels, 490–491
  utopian, 572
Lithuania, 686, 940
Little, Malcolm. See Malcolm X
Little Big Horn, Battle of, 526
Little Big Horn College, 931
Loan, Nguyen Ngoc, 877
Loans
  Depression of 1893 and, 591
  to Soviets, 823–824
Local politics, 577–578
Locke, Alain, 706
Lodge, Henry Cabot
  African American voting and, 588
  expansion and, 606
  League of Nations and, 687–688
  Versailles Peace Conference and, 685
Loewy, Raymond, 744
Long, Huey P., 734, 737
Long, John, 608
Longhorns, 516
Looking Backward (Bellamy), 572, 579, 630
Lorwin, Val, 819–820, 841, 848
Los Alamos, New Mexico, 779, 840
Los Angeles
  growth of, 939
  population of, 644, 795
  race riot in (1992), 929, 962
  zoot-suit riots and, 766–767
"Lost Bet" painting (Klir), 574
Lost Generation, 706–707
Louisiana, Klan in, 694
Loyalists (Spain), 757
Loyalty issues
  in Cold War, 819–820
  congressional program and, 842
  Truman's program and, 841–842
Loyalty Review Board, 841
LSD, 878
Luce, Henry, 772
Ludlow Massacre, 643
Lumber industry, 521, 529
  public domain and, 521
Lusitania (ship), 666, 667

Lynching
  of African Americans, 532, 533,
    651, 738
  of German, 672

MacArthur, Douglas, 726, 791, 833
Machinery
  for farming, 513, 515, 518–519
  in Germany, 546
Maeby, Leslie, 917–918, 927
Magazines, 524–525
  muckrakers and, 631
Maginot line, 758
Magon, Ricardo Flores, 672
Mahan, Alfred Thayer, 606
Maine (ship), 608, 610
Making of an Un-American, The
  (Cowan), 852
Malaya, World War II and, 760
Malcolm X, 867
  autobiography of, 952, 953
Management
  vs. operations, 544
  after World War I, 697
Manchu dynasty (China), 607
Manchuria, 603, 621, 623, 759
Mandela, Nelson, 944, 976
Manhattan Project, 758, 779–780,
  840
Manifest Destiny, 601
Man in the Gray Flannel Suit, The,
  792
Mann-Elkins Act (1910), 653
Man Nobody Knows, The (Barton), 710
Manufacturing, 505, 541
  overseas markets for, 604–606
  regional, 542
  in urban areas, 548
  world production and, 545, 546
Mao Zedong (Mao Tse-tung), 830,
  831, 894
March for Life, 926
March on Washington
  civil rights (1963), 860–861
  by Coxey (1894), 592
  by Randolph (1941), 765–766
Marijuana, 878
Marines. *See also* Armed forces
  in Latin America, 667–668, 713
Marine Signal Corps, 770
Market(s). *See also* Stock market
  for American agriculture, 513,
    514–515
  Depression of 1893 and, 590
  foreign, 604–606
  for southern agricultural crops,
    496

U.S. loss of, 934–935
  after World War II, 826–827
  worldwide, 546
Marriage. *See also* Divorce
  of freedpeople, 484–485
  between gays, 965–966
  women avoiding, 584–585
  after World War II, 800–801
Marshall, George C., 827, 846
Marshall, Thurgood, 930
Marshall Plan, 825, 826–829
Marx, Karl, 670
Maryland, workers' compensation
  in, 646
Massive retaliation program, 840
Mass production, 543
Material culture. *See* Culture(s)
Materialism, 816
Mau Mau revolt (Kenya), 810
Mayor-council form of city
  government, 645
McAdoo, William, 680
McCallum, Daniel, 544
McCarran-Walter Act. *See*
  Immigration and Nationality
  Act (1952)
McCarthy, Joseph, 843
  McCarthyism and, 820, 843–847
McCormick Reaper Works,
  Haymarket Riot and, 564
McDonald's, 785–787, 791, 816
McGovern, George, 897
McKay, Claude, 706
McKinley, William, 588, 611, 613
  assassination of, 614, 647
  election of 1896 and, 593–594
  Spanish-American War and, 608,
    610
McKinley Tariff, 588, 589
McNamara, Robert S., 855
McNary-Haugen Farm Relief Bill,
  709
McPherson, Aimee Semple, 701
Meany, George, 793
Meat Inspection Act (1906), 650
Meatpacking industry, 631, 649–650
Mechanization, 557, 798
Media
  on Asian immigrants, 932
  Nixon and, 886, 889–890
Medicaid, 865
Medicare, 865, 945
Medicine. *See also* Disease; Health
  and health care
  aging and, 960
  socialized, 790
  in World War II, 770

Mellon, Andrew, 711
"Memorial Day Massacre," 738
Memphis, 489, 529
Men. *See also* Gender
  mobility and success ethic of,
    555–556
  roles of, 800–801
Mencken, H. L., 701, 707
Meredith, James, 859
Mergers, 934, 957
Mesopotamia, World War I and,
  665
Meuse-Argonne offensive, 661, 679
Mexicans and Mexican Americans,
  905. *See also* Chicanos; Latinos
  California farming and, 520
  as cowboys, 516
  during Great Depression, 739
  immigration of, 703, 704 (map),
    814
  protests by, 908–909
  World War II and, 766–767
  zoot-suit riots and, 766–767
Mexico
  immigrants from, 549, 814, 931,
    951
  NAFTA and, 966–967
  nationalization of industries in,
    755
  in 1920s, 713–714
  U.S. intervention in, 667–668
  Wilson and, 668
  Zimmermann telegram and, 670
Miami, Florida, 954
Michiko, Yamaoka, 780
Middle class
  Asian Americans in, 816
  in cities, 551
  in Great Depression, 723, 742–743
  lifestyle of, 553–556, 937
  in New South, 529
  Reagan and, 926
  reforms by, 578–585, 631
  urban, 550, 553
  women and, 553–555, 584–585
Middle East. *See also* Arab-Israeli
  wars
  Carter and, 901, 902
  Clinton and, 974–975
  Iran-*contra* and, 943
  Israel and, 835–836, 887, 974–975
  in 1920s, 712–713
  Nixon and, 887, 895
  Persian Gulf War and, 923,
    944–945
  Saddam Hussein and, 944
  violence in, 975

Middlemen
in agriculture, 514, 535
labor hiring through, 556
Midway Island, 601, 760
Midwest
industry in, 542
woman suffrage in, 636
Migrant farm labor. *See*
Farmworkers
Migration. *See also* Immigrants and
immigration; Westward
movement
by African Americans, 534, 548,
588, 681–682, 691–692,
703–704, 739, 766, 810
from 1860 to 1910, 549 (map)
in 1920s, 701–703
from rural to urban areas, 548
to West, 795
in World War II, 767
Migratory Labor Agreement, 814
Military. *See also* Armed forces;
Draft (military); Soldiers;
Veterans
African Americans in, 675
desegregation of, 806, 811–812
Reagan and, 926
segregation in, 765
technology of, 664–665
women in, 771
in World War I, 673–680
Military draft. *See* Draft (military)
Miller, David, 599, 600
Mills, immigrant labor in, 540
Mills, C. Wright, 793
Milosevic, Slobodan, 973–974
Mines and mining, 505. *See also*
United Mine Workers
strike in, 565–566, 649
in West, 520–521
Mineta, Norman Y., 965
Minimum wage, 743, 804, 806
Mining camps, 520
Minorities. *See also* specific groups
in cities, 938
in Great Depression, 738–740
in 1930s, 738–740
in 1990s-2000s, 962–965
poverty of, 959
in World War II, 765–767
Miracle drugs, 795
Miranda v. *Arizona,* 868
Missiles. *See* Cuban missile crisis;
specific types
Missions and missionaries. *See also*
Catholicism

expansionism and, 606–607
in Reconstruction South, 499
Mississippi, 894
integration of University of, 859
Mississippi Freedom Summer
Project (1964), 851, 866
Mississippi Plan, 503, 504
Mississippi River region, floods
and, 709
Mitchell, George, 910
Mitchell, John (attorney general),
886–887, 889, 896–897
Mitchell, Margaret, 748
Mobile, Alabama, 767
Mobility
economic and social, 555–556
of ethnic groups, 569–570
Mobilization
for World War I, 680–681
for World War II, 761–762
Model T Ford, 698
"Modern Republicanism,"
808–809
Molders' Union, 568
Moley, Raymond, 727
Molotov, Vyacheslav, 823
Momaday, N. Scott, 753, 782, 910
Mondale, Walter, 922
Money. *See also* Paper money
in Gilded Age, 576–577
silverites and, 588
Money supply, 537, 590
Monopolies. *See also* Trusts
Taft and, 653
Monroe, Marilyn, 801, 802, 878
Monroe Doctrine, 601, 602
Cuba and, 870
Panama Canal and, 618
Roosevelt Corollary to, 620
Venezuela-British Guiana dispute
and, 604
Moody, Anne, 859
Moody, Dwight, 582
Moon landing, 858
Morality, progressive reforms and,
638–640
Moral Majority, 920–921
Morehouse University, 500
Morgan, J. Pierpont, 545, 649
Morgan, Marabel, 905
Morgan & Co., 545
Moroccan crisis (1905, 1906), 624
Mortality rate
from AIDS, 961
urban, 547, 551
Mortgages, 742, 789, 796

Mossadegh, Mohammed, 836
Mother Earth, 585
Mothers. *See* Families; Women
Motown Records, 906–907
Movies
HUAC and, 842
in 1920s, 700, 707, 713
in 1930s, 746–747, 750
in progressive era, 639
during World War II, 769
Moynihan, Daniel Patrick, 886
Mr. X, 824
Ms. magazine, 904, 905
Muir, John, 521, 650–651
Mulattos, in Republican state
governments, 502
Multiculturalism, 954
Multiracial identifications, 956
Municipal reform, 644–646
Munn v. *Illinois,* 536
Murphy, Edgar Gardner, 633
Murrow, Edward R., 768–769
Music
counterculture and, 878
cultural rebellion in, 803
jazz, 706
in 1960s and 1970s, 906–907
in World War II, 769
Muslims. *See also* Islam
in Bosnia, 941
fears of, 978
fundamentalist, 920
Mussolini, Benito, 756
Mutual-protection treaty, England-
Japan, 624
My Lai massacre, 893

NAACP. *See* National Association
for the Advancement of Colored
People (NAACP)
Nader, Ralph, 914, 964
NAFTA. *See* North American Free
Trade Agreement (NAFTA)
Nagasaki, Japan, 782
Napalm, 875
Nasdaq Composite index, 957
Nasser, Gamal Abdel, 836
Nast, Thomas, 507, 524, 616
Nation, The, 524
National Aeronautics and Space
Administration (NASA), 858
National Alliance, 536–537
Ocala Platform of, 537–538
National American Woman
Suffrage Association (NAWSA),
585, 684

National and International
  Conferences on Black Power
  (1967 and 1968), 868
National Association for the
  Advancement of Colored
  People (NAACP), 534, 651, 652,
  812
National Association of
  Manufacturers (NAM), 641,
  730
National Association Opposed to
  Woman Suffrage, 684
National banking system, 537
National Chicano Moratorium
  Committee, 909
National Committee for Immigrants
  in America, 629
National Conservation
  Commission, 650
National Consumers League, 633
National Council of Negro Women,
  739
National Credit Corporation, 723
National currency, 536
National debt, 761, 957
  in 1970-1992, 925
National Endowment for the Arts,
  968
National Endowment for the
  Humanities, 968
National Farmers Alliance, 589
National forests, 650–651. *See also*
  Forest(s)
National government. *See*
  Government (U.S.)
National Grange. *See* Grange
National Guard
  at Kent State, 893
  labor unrest and, 505
  in Little Rock, 813
  World War I and, 667
National Housing Act (1937), 742
National Housing Association, 637
National Industrial Recovery Act
  (NIRA), 731
National Institutes of Health, 797
Nationalism. *See also* New
  Nationalism
  Black Power movement and, 868
  expansion and, 606
  of freedpeople, 500–501
  in Latin America, 836–837
  World War I and, 663
Nationalist China, 831
National Labor Relations Act
  (1935), 731, 737–738, 741

National Labor Union (NLU), 505,
  563
National Liberation Front, 873
National Magazine, 524
National Manufacturing
  Association, 710
National Organization for Women
  (NOW), 903
National Outdoor Recreation
  Review Commission, 797
National Recovery Administration
  (NRA), 731
National Science Foundation, 797
National Security Act (1947), 789,
  829
National Security Council (NSC)
  Cuban missile crisis and, 872
  Iran-*contra* and, 943
  Kissinger and, 886
  NSC-68 of, 829, 833
National War Labor Board (NWLB),
  761
National Wilderness Preservation
  Act (1964), 865
National Woman's Party (NWP),
  684, 708
National Youth Administration
  (NYA), 735
Nation of Islam, 867
Native American Graves Protection
  and Repatriation Act (1990), 964
Native Americans, 506, 931–932
  Black Hills gold strike and, 526
  buffalo and, 522, 527
  characterizations of, 525
  citizenship rights of, 754
  Civil War and, 522
  Dawes Act and, 527–528
  from 1850 to 1896, 527 (map)
  gambling industry and, 931
  Ghost Dance movement of, 527
    (map), 528
  in Great Depression, 740
  Indian Reorganization Act and,
    740
  in 1990s-2000, 964–965
  protests by, 909–912
  Red Cloud and, 523
  rights of, 814–815
  second great removal of, 586
  transcontinental railroad and, 526
  in West, 522–528
  whites and, 522–526
  World War II and, 767, 770
  Wounded Knee massacre of, 528
Native Son (Wright), 703

NATO. *See* North Atlantic Treaty
  Organization (NATO)
Naturalists, 650
Natural resources, 512, 521–522,
  542, 650–651, 913
Natural selection, 579
Navajo Indians, 740, 847
  as code talkers, 770
Naval bases. *See also* Pearl Harbor
  in Cuba, 619, 755
  in World War II, 758
Navy. *See also* Navy (U.S.); Royal
  Navy (England)
  Germany, 624
  Mahan on, 606
  Washington Conference and, 713
Navy (U.S.). *See also* Pacific Ocean
  region
  Great White Fleet of, 623
  in Spanish American War, 619
  women in, 771
Nazi Germany, 756, 762. *See also*
  Germany
  Allied bombings of, 777
  Holocaust and, 757, 775
  Rome-Berlin Axis and, 756
  Spanish Civil War and, 757
  World War II and, 771–772, 775
Nazi-Soviet pact, 757–758
Near East. *See also* Middle East
  after World War I, 685 (map)
Negro Baptist Church, 499
Negro leagues, 810
Neighborhoods, 551–553
Nelson, Donald, 761
Netherlands
  World War I and, 664
  World War II and, 758
Neutrality, 624
  toward Europe, 756
  in World War I, 664, 665–667
Neutrality Acts, World War II and,
  756–757, 758
Nevada Test Site 65, 840
New Deal
  "black cabinet" and, 739
  critics of, 733–734
  first, 726–734
  labor in, 737–738
  legacy of, 750–751
  minorities and, 738–740
  second, 734–740
  third, 741, 742–743
  welfare state and, 735
  West and, 736
  women and, 740

New England, industry in, 542
New Freedom, 654, 669
New Frontier, 853, 855–858
New immigration, 548–550, 588, 950–954
    in labor force, 556
Newlands Act (1902), 650
New Left, 875
New Mexico, 931
    atomic tests in, 779, 823
    Mexican American protests in, 909
New Nationalism, 656–658
New Negro, The (Locke), 706
New Orleans, Hurricane Katrina in, 973
New Right, 921
Newsboys, 632
New South, 512, 528–529
    African Americans in, 530, 531–533
    agriculture in, 530–531
    cities in, 529
    industrialization in, 529–530
    investment in, 529
Newspapers. *See* Media
Newton, Huey P., 868
"New woman," Gibson girl as, 553
New York (city)
    Harlem Renaissance in, 705–706
    Lower East Side of, 552
    population of, 644
    Puerto Ricans in, 814
    riots in, 868
New York (state), 795
New York Consumers League, 727
New York Times, Pentagon Papers and, 894
New York World's Fair (1939), 744
New Zealand, 665
    woman suffrage in, 636
Niagara movement, 652
Nicaragua, 602
    intervention in, 618, 620, 667–668, 713, 755, 943
    Somoza rule in, 713, 943
Niebuhr, Reinhold, 770
1984 (Orwell), 822
Nineteenth Amendment, 636 (map), 684
92nd Division, 679
Nisei, 763, 765
Nixon, Richard, 493, 885–887
    China and, 894–895
    election of 1960 and, 854
    election of 1968 and, 879
    election of 1972 and, 887, 894, 897

environment and, 913
Hiss-Chambers case and, 842
Latinos and, 909
National Youth Administration and, 735
nuclear testing and, 841
pardon of, 899
presidential debate and, 854, 856, 857
resignation of, 897
Watergate affair and, 895–900
Nixon Doctrine, 893
Nonaggression pact, Nazi-Soviet, 757, 759
Nonviolence. *See also* Civil rights movement
    challenges to, 866
    King and, 858, 866
Noriega, Manuel, 943
Normandy invasion, 777
Norris, Frank, 631
Norris, George, 671, 732
North
    African American migration to, 681–682, 691–692, 703–704, 739, 766, 794
    African Americans in, 810
    investment in New South, 529
North, Oliver, 943
North Africa, World War II and, 772, 773–774
North American Free Trade Agreement (NAFTA), 966–967
North Atlantic Treaty Organization (NATO), 808, 828, 973
North Carolina
    reconstructed government of, 488
    terror campaign in, 503
Northeast, immigrants in, 595
Northern Securities Company, 649
North Korea, 831–833. *See also* Korea; Korean War
North Vietnam, 834, 873, 893, 894. *See also* Vietnam; Vietnam War
Norway, 664
    woman suffrage in, 636
Novels. *See also* Literature
    in Harlem Renaissance, 706
    Reconstruction, 490–491
NSC. *See* National Security Council (NSC)
Nuclear weapons. *See also* Arms race; Atomic bomb
    atomic shield for, 840
    in Cold War, 837–841
    proliferation of, 838–839
    protests against, 840–841

rockets for, 798
Soviets and, 829, 837–839
testing of, 840–841
Nurses, in World War II, 771
Nye, Gerald P., 756

Obrycki family, 917
Ocala platform, 537–538, 589–590
O'Connor, Sandra Day, 929, 930
Octopus, The (Norris), 631
O'Donnell, Thomas, 540–541, 570
Officeholders
    former Confederate, 492
    Latino, 931
    in Republican state governments, 502
Office of Civil and Defense Mobilization, 839
Office of Economic Opportunity (OEO), 864, 910
Office of Price Administration (OPA), 761
Office of Strategic Services, 819
Office of War Information, 762
Oglala Lakota College, 911
Oglala Sioux Indians, 522
Oil and oil industry, 934
    Carter and, 901
    imports of (1973-1980), 891
    Mexico and, 755
    Middle East and, 836
    muckrakers on, 631
    OPEC embargo and, 887, 923
    overexpansion in, 937
    Rockefeller and, 544–545
"Okies," 743, 748
Okinawa, 781
Oklahoma
    blacks in, 534
    dust bowl in, 736
    Klan in, 694
Oklahombie, Joseph, 679
Old-age pensions, 658, 735, 809
Old Horn, Dale, 931
Old immigrants, 548
Old Person, Earl, 815
Oligopoly, 696
Olney, Richard, 567, 604, 606
Olson, Floyd, 733
Omaha, Populist convention in, 589
Omnibus (vehicle), 550
One-crop farming, 496
One Flew Over the Cuckoo's Nest (Kesey), 878
Oneida Indians, 964
Ong, Paul M., 965
On the Beach (Shute), 839

On the Road (Kerouac), 803
OPEC. *See* Organization of
    Petroleum Exporting Countries
    (OPEC)
Operation Desert Storm, 945
Operation Overlord, 776–777
Operation Wetback, 814
Oppenheimer, J. Robert, 780
Oral contraceptives, 877
Oregon
    Klan in, 694
    woman suffrage in, 636
    women's workday in, 646
Organization of Petroleum
    Exporting Countries (OPEC),
    887
Organized crime, 715
Organized labor, 563. *See also* Labor;
    Labor unions
    in New Deal, 737–738
    in 1920s, 710
Origin of Species (Darwin), 579
Orthodox Judaism, 800
Orwell, George, 822
Oswald, Lee Harvey, 861
Other America, The (Harrington),
    809
Ottoman Empire, World War I and,
    664
Our Bodies, Ourselves, 904
Out of Work (Kellor), 628
Overseas issues
    investment as, 713, 934
    U.S. overseas involvement and,
    941–945

Pacific Coast, 938
Pacific Ocean region
    acquisitions in, 612
    expansion in, 601–602, 603–604
    United States in, 603, 621 (map)
    World War I and, 664, 686
    World War II in, 773 (map), 778,
    779
Pacifism
    of Jones, Samuel, 584
    World War I and, 673
Packinghouses, 516
Padrone, 556
Painting, rebellion in, 803
Paiute Indians, 815
Palestine, Israel and, 834, 974–975
Palestine Liberation Organization
    (PLO), 901, 974–975
Palmer, A. Mitchell, 693
Palmer raids, 693–694
Pan-African Conference, 534

Panama, 602, 615
    Colombia and, 618, 667
    independence of, 618
    U.S. invasion of, 943
Panama Canal, 618
Pan-American conferences
    of 1889, 602
    of 1938, 755–756
Panics. *See also* Depression
    (economic); Great Depression
    of 1873, 506
Paper money, 537, 576
Pardons, of Nixon, 899
Paris
    student protests in, 876
    Versailles Peace Conference and,
    684–686
Parity prices, 730
Parker, John and Lizzie, 691–692,
    703
Parks, Rosa, 813
Parochial schools, 578
Partial birth abortion, 963
Partisan politics, Clinton's
    impeachment and, 968–969
PATCO. *See* Professional Air Traffic
    Controllers Organization
    (PATCO)
Patent medicines, 650
Patriotism
    expansion and, 606
    in World War I, 672, 682
    in World War II, 762
Patronage, 575
Patton, George, 777
Paul, Alice, 684, 708–709
Payne-Aldrich Tariff (1909), 653
Peabody Museum (Harvard),
    Indian grave repatriation and,
    964
Peace. *See also* Pacifism
    trade and, 714
Peace Corps, 851–852, 858
Peace movements. *See* Pacifism;
    Peace
Pearl Harbor, 603
    attack on, 759–760
Peking (Beijing), Boxer Rebellion in,
    621–622
Peña, Federico, 931, 963
Pendleton Act (1883), 577
Pensions. *See also* Old-age pensions
    for Civil War veterans, 588, 589
    in Great Depression, 733, 735
Pentagon Papers, 894
Peonage, 498
People's Party. *See* Populism

People's Republic of China. *See*
    China
Perestroika, 939
Periodicals. *See* Magazines
Perkins, Frances
    garment workers and, 643
    labor and, 737
    as Roosevelt adviser, 727
Perot, H. Ross
    election of 1992 and, 966
    election of 1996 and, 968
Perry, Matthew (Commodore), 601
Pershing, John "Black Jack"
    in Mexico, 668
    in World War I, 671, 678
Persian Gulf War, 923, 944–945
Pesticides, 865, 936
Peurifoy, John, 842–843
Philadelphia, 795
Philippines, 599–600, 609
    annexation of, 611–612, 617, 621
    Dewey in, 608
    World War II and, 759, 760, 772,
    778
Phillips, David Graham, 631
Photography, documentary, 634,
    635, 637
Piecework, 560, 561
Pinchot, Gifford, 520–521, 650–651,
    653
Pine Ridge Reservation, 911
Pioneers. *See* Settlement(s); Trans-
    Mississippi West; West;
    Westward movement
Pittsburgh
    Homestead Steel Works near, 543
    Homestead Strike and, 566
Plains Indians, 522
    buffalo and, 527
Planned Parenthood Federation,
    637
Planned Parenthood v. *Casey*, 929–930
Planters and plantations, at end of
    Civil War, 481, 482, 484, 486, 496
Platform. *See* Political parties
Platt Amendment, 619, 755
Playboy magazine, 801, 904
Playgrounds, 646
Pledge of Allegiance, "under God"
    in, 800
Plessy v. *Ferguson*, 533, 812
Plunkitt, George Washington, 577
Plutonium, 840
Poets and poetry
    Beat Generation and, 803
    in Harlem Renaissance, 706
    of Lost Generation, 706

Poland
immigrants from, 703
Solidarity movement in, 940
Versailles Peace Conference and, 686
after World War II, 823
World War II and, 758
Yalta conference and, 779, 823
Polio vaccine, 795
Polish Americans, 518, 766
Political cartoons, 616–617
Political parties. See also specific parties
affiliations with, 575, 578
excitement generated by, 578
in Gilded Age, 574–576
patronage and, 575
realignment in, 573
Politics
business of, 710–716
conservative, 917–946
after election of 1896, 595
at end of Civil War, 483–484
in Gilded Age, 573–578, 586–595
immigration and, 703
Latinos in, 963–964
local, 577–578
in 1980s and 1990s, 919–927
public opinion and, 607
self-interest in, 506
shift in national priorities, 505–506
urban reform and, 584
Polk, Leonidas, 589
Pollock, Jackson, 803
Polls. See Public and public opinion
Poll tax, 532, 739
Pollution, 547, 865, 912
Pollution Act (1924), 712
Population
of cities, 644, 699, 795
of farmers, 513
growth of, 547–548
Latino, 963
of Mexican Americans (1930), 704 (map)
Native American, 964
shifts in, 938–939
in South, 529
state, 795
in 2000, 954–956, 955 (map)
in West, 516, 795
after World War II, 794–795
Populism, 565, 586, 588, 589–590
election of 1896 and, 592–595
Pornography, 869

Port Huron Statement, 875
Portsmouth, Treaty of, 623
Potsdam Conference (1945), 823
Poverty, 540, 948–949. See also Great Depression; Wealth
antipoverty program and, 864–865, 973
in Depression of 1893, 592
in 1980s, 937–938
in 1990s-2000s, 958–959
Reagan and, 924
settlement house movement and, 580–582
after World War II, 809–810
Poverty (Hunter), 631
Powderley, Terence V., 563, 564, 565
Powell, Adam Clayton, 810
Powell, Colin, 978
Powell, Lewis F., Jr., 889
Power (energy). See Energy
Power (political). See also Balance of power
of Congress, 574–575
Pragmatism, 580, 630
Prague, 940
Preachers. See Revivalism
Prejudice. See Discrimination; Segregation
Prescription drugs
costs of, 960
regulation of, 650
Preservation of nature, 521, 650–651
Presidency. See also President
as bully pulpit, 658
after election of 1896, 595
executive power of, 492
President. See also Presidency; specific presidents
inauguration date for, 727
terms of, 576
Presidential Reconstruction, 488
Presley, Elvis, 803, 906
Press. See Media
Price(s), in World War II, 761
Price, J. C., 534
Private property. See also Property
Indians and, 528
Production
expansion and, 605
in World War II, 761
Productivity, 956
agricultural, 515
declines in, 934
worker control of, 572
Profession(s)
Asians in, 932

women in, 554–555, 628–629, 802, 963
Professional Air Traffic Controllers Organization (PATCO), 935
Professional organizations, 555
Profit(s)
expansion for new markets and, 604–605
in World War I, 680
Progress, Spencer on, 579
Progress and Poverty (George), 580, 630, 645
Progressive party
in 1912, 629, 654
in 1924, 711
Progressivism. See also Progressive party
climax of, 683
global context of, 630–631
housing and, 637
immigration and, 628–629
labor and, 640–641
as middle-class movement, 658
morality uplift and, 640–644
municipal reform and, 644–646
in 1920s, 714–715
schools and, 630, 638
state reform and, 644–646
Taft and, 653
woman suffrage and, 636–637, 636 (map)
women and children and, 632–637
World War I and, 688–689
Prohibition, 715
Eighteenth Amendment and, 639, 715
end of, 728
local politics and, 578
progressivism and, 638–639
Propaganda
on Great Plains farming, 517
World War I and, 676, 677
Property, women and, 553
Proposition 187 (California), 954
Proposition 209 (California), 962
Prosperity
McKinley and, 594, 595
in 1920s, 716–718, 722
in 1990s-2000s, 979
stock market and, 716
workers and, 709–710
after World War I, 696
after World War II, 787
Prostitution, 555, 560, 583
Chinese, 550

progressive reforms and, 639–640
World War I and, 683
Protectionism, 576
Protest(s). *See also* Civil rights
  movement; Revolts and
  rebellions; Strikes
  farm, 535–538
  by Latinos, 905–909
  by Native Americans, 909–912
  of 1960s, 816
  against nuclear weapons, 840–841
  against Vietnam War, 875–876,
    879–880, 893–894
  by Weathermen, 879–880
  by workers, 561–562
Protestants and Protestantism
  fundamentalism and, 701–702
  revivalism and, 582
Public and public opinion
  on expansionism, 607
  polls of, 844, 845
Public Broadcasting System, 968
Public education. *See* Education;
  Public schools; Schools
Public health, 967
Public lands. *See also* Land
  as forest reserves, 521, 650–651
  timber companies and, 521
Public schools, in South, 502
Public Utility Holding Company
  Act (1935), 736–737
Public Works Administration
  (PWA), 729
Publishing, 524
Puddler, 556
Pueblo Indians, return of bones of,
  964
Puerto Ricans, 613, 814, 905
Puerto Rico, U.S. acquisition of, 610
Pulitzer, Joseph, 607, 616
Pullman Palace Car Company
  (Chicago)
  Brotherhood of Sleeping Car
    Porters and, 765
  strike against, 566–567, 586, 647
Pure Food and Drug Act (1906),
  653
Putin, Vladimir, 976
Puzo, Mario, 770
Pyle, Ernie, 770

Quotas
  on car exports by Japan, 937
  on immigration, 703, 816
  on races in schools, 892
Qur'an, 920, 977

Rabin, Yitzhak, 945, 974, 975
Race and racism. *See also* African
  Americans; Ku Klux Klan; Race
  riots; Slaves and slavery
  anti-Communist crusade and,
    847–848
  toward Filipinos, 611–612
  toward Japan, 760
  toward Japanese Americans,
    763–765
  progressivism and, 651–653
  Proposition 209 (California) and,
    962
  social Darwinism and, 579
  World War I and, 675, 686
  after World War II, 810–814
Race riots
  anti-Japanese, 622
  in Brownsville, Texas, 651
  in Chicago, 703–704
  in Detroit, 766
  in East St. Louis, 675
  after King's assassination, 879
  in Los Angeles (1992), 929, 962
  in Watts (1965), 868
Racial integration. *See* Integration;
  Segregation
Radical feminists, 903–905
Radical Republicans, 488, 493
Radicals and radicalism. *See also*
  Activism; Protest(s)
  in civil rights movement, 867–868
  in labor, 643–644
  of miners, 521
  Red Scare and, 693
Radio
  households with, 792
  in 1920s, 699–700, 701–702
  in 1930s, 748–750
  during World War II, 768–769
Radioactive fallout, 838–839, 841
Railroad commissions, 536
Railroads, 546. *See also*
  Transcontinental railroad
  agriculture and, 514
  big business and, 543
  cattle ranching and, 516
  in cities, 550
  costs of building, 545
  Depression of 1893 and, 590
  at end of Civil War, 484
  Granger laws and, 536
  Great Plains farming and, 517
  land grants to, 506
  muckrakers on, 631
  natural resources and, 521

in 1930s, 744
  progressivism and, 646–647
  Pullman strike and, 566–567
  rates and rebates of, 535, 536, 544
  refrigerated cars and, 520
  regulation of, 536, 576
  strikes against, 505, 562, 564, 565
  subsidies to, 506
  in World War I, 681
Rainbow Coalition, 928
Ranching, 516–517, 519
Randolph, A. Philip, 1941 march on
  Washington and, 765–766
Rankin, Jeannette, 686
Rauschenbusch, Walter, 582
Reading. *See* Literacy
Reagan, Ronald, 769. *See also* Iran-
  contra affair
  Alzheimer's disease of, 960
  civil rights and, 928
  conservatism and, 921–923
  deregulation under, 925
  economy and, 923–925, 936
  Iran-*contra* affair and, 943
  labor unions and, 935
  Latin America and, 620, 942–943
  New Federalism of, 926
  presidency under, 923–925
  Soviet Union and, 939
Reaganomics, 924
Real estate appraisal, 742–743
Realism
  in arts, 631
  Christian, 770
Reapportionment, 869
Rebellions. *See* Revolts and
  rebellions
Recessions
  in 1950s, 808
  in 1960s, 855
  in 1969-1970, 887
  of 1980s, 936–937
  in 2000s, 971
  elderly and, 960
Reconcentration camps, 608
Reconstruction, 481–509
  congressional, 488–492
  congressional actions during,
    493–494
  end of, 506–508
  freedpeople and, 484–486,
    494–498, 499–501
  novels of, 490–491
  presidential, 488
  redemption during, 503–505
  in states, 501–505

Reconstruction *(continued)*
  violence during, 503–504
  white farmers and, 498–499
  white South and, 486–487
Reconstruction Acts (1867), 492,
  501
Reconstruction Amendments. *See*
  Fifteenth Amendment;
  Fourteenth Amendment;
  Thirteenth Amendment
Reconstruction Finance
  Corporation (RFC), 725
Red China. *See* China
Red Cloud, 512, 523
Red Cloud War, 523
Red Cross, World War II and, 762
Reddy, Helen, 904
Redlining, 743
Reds. *See* China; Communism;
  Soviet Union
Reed, John, 693
Referendum, 646
Reform(s). *See also* Progressivism
  of cities, 582–584, 644–646
  of civil service, 577
  end of social reform, 927–933
  Great Society programs and,
    863–865
  labor, 640–644
  middle-class, 578–585
  in 1960s, 851–881
  philosophical basis for, 580
  photography and, 634, 635
  progressive, 630–659
  schools and, 638
  settlement house movement and,
    580–582
  Sheldon and, 582
  social justice movement and,
    628–640
  in states, 646–647
  tariff and banking, 655–656
  Wilson and, 669
  of women's rights, 641–642,
    902–905
Reform Darwinism, 579–580
Reform Judaism, 800
Refrigerated railroad cars, 520
Refugees, 865
  after Civil War, 495
  Jewish, 775
Regional planning, TVA and,
  732–733
Regions
  industrialization in, 542
  Populist support by, 590

Regulation. *See also* Progressivism
  by business, 649
  of food and drug sales, 650
  of railroads, 536, 576
  of working conditions, 557
Rehnquist, William, 889
Reisner, Marc, 913
Relief measures. *See also* New Deal;
  Welfare and welfare programs
  in Great Depression, 734–735
Religion(s). *See also* Evangelicalism;
  Revivalism
  Christian fundamentalism in,
    701–702
  education and, 578
  Gospel of Wealth and, 579
  of immigrants, 703
  intolerance and, 695
  labor organization and, 568
  Moody and, 582
  on radio, 701–702
  Social Gospel movement and,
    582
  after World War II, 800
  World War II and, 769–770
Removal, Indian, 586
Reparations
  after World War I, 714
  after World War II, 791
Republican party, 917–919. *See also*
  Conservatism; Election(s)
  changes in, 506
  Eisenhower and, 808–809
  at end of Civil War, 483
  in Gilded Age, 575
  immigrants and, 703
  legislation in 1890s, 588–589
  in 1990s and 2000s, 967–968
  Nixon's domestic policy and,
    887–890
  Reagan and, 923–925
  in Reconstruction South, 501–503,
    501 (map), 504, 505
Republicans (Spain), 757
Republic Steel, 738
Research
  agricultural, 513
  Cold War R&D, 797–798
  by Edison, 543
  post-World War I technology and,
    797–798
  universities for, 555
Reservations (Indian), 523, 526, 527,
  753, 814, 910
Reserve Officer Training Corps
  (ROTC), 756

Resettlement Administration (RA),
  735
Resistance. *See also* Protest(s);
  Revolts and rebellions
  by African Americans, 534
  to apartheid, 943–944
  to gay marriage, 965–966
  Native American, 526–527
Resource Recovery Act, 913
Resources. *See* Natural resources
Retailing, 553
Retirement accounts, 972
Revenue Act, of 1942, 761
Reverse discrimination, 892, 920
Revivalism
  Moody and, 582
  after World War II, 800
Revolts and rebellions. *See also*
  Protest(s); Revolution(s)
  Boxer Rebellion, 621–622
  in Latin America, 836–837
  in 1960s, 851–881
Revolution(s), in Russia, 670, 686,
  693
Reynolds, George, 494
Rhodes, James, 893
Richardson, Bill, 964
Richmond, 529
Rights. *See also* Civil rights
  movement; Voting and voting
  rights; Women's rights
  of African Americans, 489, 492
  civil liberties and, 868
  gay and lesbian, 912, 965
  of Latinos, 814, 931
  of Native Americans, 814–815
  Nixon and, 889
  of women, 494, 585
  during World War I, 672–673
Right wing. *See* Conservatism
Riis, Jacob
  municipal reform and, 646
  writings and photography by,
    634, 637
Rio de Janeiro, Earth Summit in, 933
Riots. *See* Race riots
Roads and highways, 698, 699
  beautification of, 865
  interstate highway system and,
    788, 789 (map)
  after World War II, 788
Robeson, Paul, 848
Robinson, Jackie, 810, 812
Rock and roll music, 803, 878
Rockefeller, John D., 544–545, 546,
  555

Ludlow Massacre and, 643
wealth of, 558
Rockefeller, John D., Jr., 579
Rockets
space exploration and, 798
in World War II, 777
Rockwell, Norman, 763
Roe v. *Wade,* 890
Rolling Stones, 878, 906
Roman Catholicism. *See*
Catholicism
Romania, 940
Rome-Berlin Axis, 756
Rommel, Erwin, 772
Roosevelt, Eleanor
as adviser, 727
African Americans and, 739
as first lady, 727–728
Roosevelt, Franklin D. *See also* Great
Depression; World War II
advisers of, 727–728
African Americans and, 739
election of 1920 and, 710
election of 1932 and, 726–727
election of 1936 and, 741
election of 1940 and, 758–759
factory regulation and, 643
first New Deal and, 726–734
foreign policy of, 755–758
Holocaust and, 775
"Hundred Days" of, 728–734
march on Washington and, 766
Pearl Harbor attack and, 759–760
second New Deal and, 734–740
Stalin and, 772, 779
Supreme Court and, 741–742
television use by, 856
welfare state and, 735, 803
Yalta conference and, 778–779
Roosevelt, Theodore, 594, 610–611,
614–624
big stick policy of, 614, 623
conservation and, 650–651
election of 1900 and, 613, 614
election of 1912 and, 653, 654–655
European policy of, 623–624
expansion and, 606
food and drug safety and, 650
Germany and, 624
on *Maine* sinking, 608
navy and, 608–609
Nobel Prize to, 614
on presidency as bully pulpit,
658
Progressive Party (1912) and, 629
racism and, 651–652

Square Deal and, 647–655
Taft and, 653
trust busting and, 648–649
World War I and, 673
Root, Elihu, 614
Root-Takahira Agreement (1908),
623
Roper, Elmo, 844
Rosenberg, Julius and Ethel, 846
"Rosie the Riveter," 768
Ross, Diana, 907
ROTC. *See* Reserve Officer Training
Corps (ROTC)
Royal Navy (England), 624
RU-486, 963
Rumsfeld, Donald, 978
Rural areas. *See also* Agriculture;
Farms and farming
electrification and, 735–736
migration to cities from, 548
in 19th century, 511–538
in 1920s, 709
protest in, 535–538
Rural Electrification Administration
(REA), 735
Rusk, Dean, 854–855
Russia, 940. *See also* Soviet Union;
World War I; World War II
Alaskan purchase from, 601
Allied effort against bolshevism
in, 687
imperialism by, 603
Manchuria and, 621, 623
Russian Revolution, 670, 686, 693
Russo-Japanese War, 614, 623
Ruth, Babe, 700
Rwanda, Tutsi-Hutu fighting in,
976

Saar region (Germany), 686
Sacco-Vanzetti case, 694–695
al-Sadat, Anwar, 901, 902
Saddam Hussein, 978
Safety
industrial, 557
workplace, 643
Saigon, 876
Sakhalin Island, 779
Salinger, J. D., 802
SALT treaties. *See* Strategic Arms
Limitation Treaty (SALT I and
SALT II)
Salvation (religious), Social Gospel
movement and, 582
Same-sex relationships. *See* Gays
and lesbians; Homosexuals

Samoa, U.S. acquisition in, 604
San Antonio, 931
Sanborn, Franklin, 580
Sanchez, Loretta, 964
Sanctuary (Faulkner), 748
Sand Creek massacre, 522–523
Sandia National Laboratory, 840
Sandino, Augusto, 713
Sandino, César, 943
SANE (National Committee for a
Sane Nuclear Policy), 841
San Francisco
counterculture in, 878
exclusion of Japanese in, 622
gay marriage in, 965
United Nations charter and, 779
Sanger, Margaret, 637, 708
San Joaquin Valley, 520
Sansei, 763
Santo Domingo, 602. *See also*
Hispaniola
Sarajevo, World War I and, 664
Satellites. *See also* Rockets
Sputnik as, 838
Saturday Evening Post, 763
Saudi Arabia, 887
Savings and loan crisis, 927
Savings banks, 545
Scab labor, 557, 566
Schine, G. David, 846
Schlafly, Phyllis, 905
Schneiderman, Rose, 642
School prayer, 869, 926
Schools. *See also* Education
Brown case and, 812–813
busing and, 891–892
expansion of, 555
Freedmen's Bureau, 500
for freedpeople, 495, 499–500
Indian, 528
integration of, 812–813, 858, 860
Mexican-American protests in,
908–909
parochial, 578
progressivism and, 630, 638
public, 502
segregation in, 812–813, 858,
891–892
in South, 530
Schwerner, Michael, 866
Science. *See also* Research;
Technology
evolution and, 701
in Germany, 545
social Darwinism and, 579
Scientific management, 641

Scopes trial, 701
Scottsboro Boys, 738
Scribner's, 524
Scudder, Vida, 580–581, 584
Seabrook nuclear plant, 913
Sea Islands, 486, 496
Seattle, Washington, Red Scare and,
  693
Second New Deal, 734–740
Second World War. *See* World
  War II
Security
  intelligence agencies and, 819
  nuclear weapons and, 838
Security Council (UN), 779, 832, 944
Sedition Act, of 1917, 672
Seeger, Pete, 906
Segregation, 550. *See also* African
  Americans; Civil rights
  movement; Integration; Race and
  racism
  apartheid as, 943–944
  bus boycott and, 813, 858
  civil rights movement and,
    866–868
  by gender, 633
  of Japanese, 622
  in military, 765–766, 770
  in northern cities, 551
  in progressive era, 651
  in public places, 860
  in schools, 812–813, 858, 891–892
  in southern public facilities, 533
  during World War II, 765–766
Selective Service Acts
  World War I and, 673, 675
  World War II and, 758
Self-government, Indian, 815
Self-interest, in Spanish-American
  War, 608
Seminole Indians, 910
Senate
  election to, 537
  McCarthy and, 846, 847
  Nixon investigation by, 897
Seneca Falls Convention (1848), 585
Seneca Indians, Allegany
  reservation of, 910
Separate but equal doctrine, 533,
  813
Serbia, 941, 973–974
  World War I and, 664
Servants, for middle class, 553
Service economy, 934–935
Settlement, changing patterns of,
  950–951

Settlement house movement, 554,
  580–582, 628, 637
Seward, William, expansion and,
  601–602
Sewing machine, 546
Sex and sexuality. *See also* Gays and
  lesbians; Homosexuals
  arts and, 878
  birth control movement and, 637
  counterculture exploration of, 877
  in 1920s, 708
  progressive reformers and,
    639–640
  Viagra and, 960
  after World War II, 801
Sexual Behavior in the Human Female
  (Kinsey), 801
Sexual Behavior in the Human Male
  (Kinsey), 801
Sexual harassment, Hill-Thomas
  issue and, 930
Shah of Iran, 836
Shaker Heights, Ohio, 699
Shame of the Cities, The (Steffens),
  631
Shannon, William, 799
Shantytowns, 720
Sharecropping, 496, 497 (map), 531,
  691
  Agricultural Adjustment Acts
    and, 731, 742
"Share the Wealth" program
  (Long), 734, 737
Sheldon, Charles, 582
Shepherd, Matthew, 965
Sheppard-Towner Maternity Act
  (1921), 714–715
Sheridan, Philip, 526
Sherman, John, 588
Sherman, William Tecumseh, 523,
  526
Sherman Anti-Trust Act, 588, 589,
  659
Sherman Silver Purchase Act, 588,
  592
Ships and shipping. *See also*
  Railroads; Transportation
  strike in, 693
  Washington Conference and, 713
  in World War I, 666–667, 670
  in World War II, 759, 772
Shopping centers, 797
Shute, Nevil, 839
Siberia, Soviet labor camps in, 822
Sierra Club, 521, 650
Silent majority, 879, 886

Silent Spring (Carson), 865, 912
Silver, 520, 588
  coinage of, 576–577
  election of 1896 and, 592–593
  as specie, 576
Simmons, William J., 694
Simpson, Jerry ("Sockless"), 586
Sinai Peninsula, 873, 901
Sinclair, Upton, 631, 649–650, 733
Singer Sewing Machine, 546
Singleton, Benjamin "Pap," 500, 501
Sinte Gleska College, 911
Sioux Indians, 512, 523, 526
  Wounded Knee massacre and,
    528, 910
  Wounded Knee takeover by,
    910–911
Sit-down strike, 738
Sit-ins, during civil rights
  movement, 858, 860
Sitting Bull, 526, 528
Six Day War (1967), 872–873, 887
Sixteenth Amendment, 653, 656
Skilled workers, 558
Skyscrapers, 699
Slaves and slavery
  after Civil War, 481
  Thirteenth Amendment and, 488
Slepian, Barnet, 963
Sloan, Alfred P., Jr., 697
Sloan, John, 631
Slovak republic, 940
Slums, 550, 551, 635, 637, 742
Smith, Alfred, 715–716, 733
Smith, Hoke, 646
Smith, Jacob H., 612
Smoking. *See* Tobacco and tobacco
  industry
SNCC. *See* Student Nonviolent
  Coordinating Committee
  (SNCC)
Social classes. *See* Classes
Social Darwinism, 579
Social Gospel movement, 582, 630
Social hygiene progressives, 639
Socialism, 572
  Cold War and, 819
  election of 1912 and, 655
Socialized medicine, 790
Social justice movement, 629,
  630–640, 645–646. *See also*
  Progressivism
Social mobility. *See* Mobility
Social sciences, 579–580
Social security, 735, 806, 945, 972
  solvency of, 957, 960

Social Security Act (1935), 735
Social welfare. *See* Welfare and welfare programs
Society
    African Americans in, 706
    in cities, 553
    computers and, 798
    consensus and conformity in, 799–803
    in 1960s, 851–881
    Nixon and, 889
    postwar women in, 883–884
    Reagan and, 926
    values in 1920s, 701
    after World War I, 692–718
    after World War II, 787
Sociology, 580
    progressivism and, 630
Sod house, 511, 512, 519
Soft-money advocates, 576–577
Soldiers. *See also* Armed forces; Military; Wars and warfare
    black, 675, 766, 770
    segregation of, 765
    in World War I, 658, 673–680
    in World War II, 770–773
Solidarity movement, 940
Somalia, 944, 976
Somoza family (Nicaragua), 943
    Anastasio, 713
Souls of Black Folks, The (Du Bois), 535
Sound and the Fury, The (Faulkner), 748
South. *See also* Civil War (U.S.); Confederate States of America; New South; Reconstruction; Slaves and slavery
    African American migration from, 794
    African Americans in, 588
    agricultural changes in, 496–498, 498–499
    Black Codes in, 486–487
    financial and physical reconstruction of, 502
    military districts in, 492
    Reconstruction and, 501–505, 508
    redemption in, 501 (map) 503–505
    Republican party in, 501–503, 501 (map), 505
    school desegregation in, 813
    segregation in, 651–652
    violence in, 503–505
South Africa, 943–945, 976

South America. *See also* Latin America
    U.S. influence in, 602
South Carolina, violence in, 504
Southeast Asia, 834
Southern Christian Leadership Conference (SCLC), 858
Southern Farmers' Alliance, 536–537
Southern Homestead Act (1866), 494
South Korea, 831–833. *See also* Korea; Korean War
South Vietnam, 834, 873, 877, 893. *See also* Vietnam; Vietnam War
Southwest. *See also* West
    Mexicans in, 703
Soviet Union. *See also* Russia
    atomic weapons of, 829, 837–839
    Bay of Pigs fiasco and, 870
    Berlin and, 828, 871–872
    breakup of, 940–941, 942 (map)
    Cold War with, 787, 821–848
    containment policy toward, 824–833
    Cuba and, 870–872
    disillusionment with, 822–823
    eastern European control by, 779
    economy in, 791, 823–824
    Egypt and, 836, 901
    goals of, 821–822
    Korea and, 831
    lend-lease to, 759, 774
    Nazi-Soviet pact and, 757, 759
    Poland and, 758
    Reagan and, 939
    revolts against, 830
    U.S. recognition of, 755
    Versailles Peace Conference and, 686
    World War II and, 778
Soyer, Isaac, 724
Space exploration, 798, 858
Spain
    Cuba and, 607–608, 609, 610
    fascism in, 712, 756–757
    Franco in, 756–757
    World War I and, 664
    World War II and, 774
Spanish-American War, 600, 607–610, 616–617
Spanish Civil War, 757
Specie (gold or silver), 576
Specie Resumption Act (1875), 576
Speculation, 934
    in land, 520, 528

Spencer, Herbert, 579
    "Americans, The" speech of, 555
Spending. *See also* Defense spending
    consumer, 788, 956
    deficit, 808
    in Great Depression, 742
    for social welfare, 926
    in World War II, 767
Spies and spying
    CIA and, 829
    Rosenberg case and, 846
Spock, Benjamin, 801
Sports
    in 1930s, 745–748
    for women, 904
Sputnik, 838, 858
Stalin, Joseph. *See also* Soviet Union
    Cold War and, 822, 824
    at Potsdam, 823
    Soviet purges and, 772
    World War II and, 776, 777, 778
    Yalta conference and, 778–779, 823
Standard of living, 553
    of Indians, 910–911
    after World War I, 696
Standard Oil Company, 544–545, 546
    muckrakers and, 631
    trust busting and, 649
Stanford University, 555, 921
Stanton, Edwin, 492
Stanton, Elizabeth Cady, 493, 580, 585
    autobiography of, 953
START treaty. *See* Strategic Arms Reduction Treaty (START)
"Star Wars." *See* Strategic Defense Initiative ("Star Wars")
State(s)
    child labor laws in, 633
    governments in Reconstruction South, 501–503
    populations of, 795
    progressive reforms and, 646–647
    railroad land and, 543
    readmittance to Union, 492, 493
    woman suffrage in, 636–637
State Department, Loyalty-Security Board of, 820
States' Rights (Dixiecrat) party, 805
Stead, W. T., 592
Steam engine, 543
Steam power, industrialization and, 543

Steamships, 514
Steel industry, 529
  Bethlehem Steel strike and, 693
  Carnegie and, 542, 544
  Homestead strike in, 566
Stegner, Wallace, 939
Steinbeck, John, 736, 748
Steinem, Gloria, 904, 905
Stereotypes, of blacks, 531–532
Stevens, John Paul, 971
Stevens, Thaddeus, 488, 494
Stimson, Henry L., 837
Stock market
  crash of 1893, 590
  crash of 1929, 716, 722–723
  growth of, 545
  in 1960s, 855
  in 1980s, 937
  in 1990s, 957
Stonewall Inn riot, 912, 965
Strategic Arms Limitation Treaty
    (SALT I and SALT II), 895, 939
Strategic Arms Reduction Treaty
    (START), 940
Strategic Defense Initiative ("Star
    Wars"), 939
Strauss, Lewis, 838
Streamliners (trains), 744
Streets. See Roads and highways;
    Transportation
Strikes. See also Labor; Labor
    unions
  by black cotton pickers, 537
  Depression-era, 738
  after 1876, 562–563
  between 1881 and 1905, 562, 563
  by freedmen in South Carolina,
    505
  Gompers and, 565
  Homestead, 566
  by miners, 565–566, 649
  by northern railroad workers, 505
  PATCO, 935
  in progressive era, 641
  Pullman strike (1894), 566–567,
    647
  against railroads, 505, 562, 564,
    565
  by women garment workers, 643
  after World War I, 692, 693
  after World War II, 793
  in World War II, 761
Strong, Josiah, 606–607
Student Nonviolent Coordinating
    Committee (SNCC), 858, 859,
    866, 868

Students
  antiwar protests by, 756, 875–876,
    893–894
  sit-ins in, 858, 860
Students for a Democratic Society
    (SDS), 875, 876
Submarines
  in World War I, 665, 666, 670
  in World War II, 759, 772
Sub-Saharan Africa, 829, 960
Subsidies
  to housing, 750
  to railroads, 506
Subtreasuries (federal warehouses),
    537
Suburbs, 550, 698, 699
  commuting to, 551–552
  economy and, 938
  environmental impact of, 797
  housing in, 552–553
  after World War II, 795–797, 800
Subways, 546, 550
Sudetenland, 757
Suez Canal, 772, 836
Suffrage. See also Voting and voting
    rights
  black male, 492, 493
  universal male, 502
  for women, 493–494, 584–585,
    636–637, 636 (map), 708
Sugar and sugar industry
  in Cuba, 608
  Hawaiian annexation and, 603
Sullivan, Ed, 856
Summit meetings
  Bush-Gorbachev, 940
  Reagan-Gorbachev, 939–940
Sumner, Charles, 488
Sumner, William Graham, 579
Sun Also Rises, The (Hemingway),
    706–707
Sun Belt, 795
  economy in, 889, 937
Sunday, Billy, 701
Superpatriot organizations, 693
Supply-side economics, 924
Supreme Court (U.S.)
  affirmative action and, 962
  big business and, 588
  Brown decision and, 812–813
  on bus segregation, 813
  on citizenship in territories, 613
  civil rights and, 507, 531, 533, 868
  discriminatory voting laws and,
    533
  on labor rights, 641

  in 1960s, 868–869
  Nixon and, 889
  railroads and, 536, 567
  2000 election and, 970–971
  violence against blacks and, 505
  women on, 929, 930
  on women workers, 633
Supremes (singing group), 907
Surplus
  agricultural, 709, 742
  budget, 957, 972
  tariff protection of, 576
Survival of the fittest, 579, 580
Swanson, Gloria, 707
Sweden, World War I and, 664
Switzerland, World War I and, 664
Symmonds, Robert, 720–721

Taft, Robert, 759
Taft, William Howard, 653
  dollar diplomacy of, 623
  election of 1912 and, 653–655
  Latin American intervention by,
    620
  as Philippines governor, 613, 653
Taft-Hartley Act (1947), 804–805,
    935
Taiwan (Formosa), 603, 831
Taliban, 977–978
Tammany Hall, 616
Tanks
  in World War I, 665
  in World War II, 777
Tarbell, Ida, 631
Tariffs, 537, 655–656
  of 1890, 588
  in Gilded Age, 576
  in 1920s, 714, 723
  in 1930s, 755
  protectionism and, 576
Taxation
  budget surplus and, 957
  excess profits, 711
  Hoover and, 723
  income, 537, 653, 656, 711
  in 1960s, 855
  in 1990s and 2000s, 968
  Reagan and, 924–925
  wealthy and, 957–958
  in World War I, 680
  in World War II, 761
Taylor, Frederick, 641
Taylor Grazing Act (1934), 736
Teachers
  in Reconstruction South, 499–500
  women as, 554

Teach-ins, 876
Teapot Dome scandal, 711
Technology. *See also* Science
  for agriculture, 514, 515, 709, 794
  consumer culture and, 798
  in Germany, 545–546
  in iron industry, 542
  labor force and, 557
  military, 664–665
  nationalism and, 663
  power sources and, 543
  workplace and, 933–934
  after World War II, 787, 797–798
Telegraph, 544
Telephone, 699
Television, 798, 856–857
  evangelists on, 920–921
  households with, 792
  presidential debates on (1960),
    854, 856, 857
  Reagan and, 922–923, 925
Teller Amendment, 610
Temperance
  Eighteenth Amendment and, 715
  support for, 578
Tenant farming, 496–498, 497
  (map), 518, 531. *See also*
  Sharecropping
Ten Days that Shook the World
  (Reed), 693
Tenements, 551, 635, 637. *See also*
  Riis, Jacob
Ten-hour workday, 633
Tennessee Valley Authority (TVA),
  732–733, 732 (map), 808
Tenure of Office Act, 492
Termination program, 815
Territories, of United States,
  612–613
Terrorism, 979
  against African Americans,
    503–504
  deaths from, 978
  in Reconstruction South, 503–504
  of September 11, 2001, 601, 971,
    976–978
Tet offensive, 874 (map), 876
Texas
  affirmative action in, 962
  cattle ranching in, 516
  Klan in, 694
Textile industry, 529, 544
Thatcher, Margaret, 920
Thermal pollution, 912
Thermonuclear bombs, 840
Thieu, Nguyen Van, 875

Third New Deal, 741, 742–743
Third parties, 506
Thirteenth Amendment, 488, 489
This Side of Paradise (Fitzgerald), 707
Thomas, Clarence, 930
Thomas, Piri, 952
Thurmond, J. Strom, 805, 891
Tijerina, Reies López ("El Tigre"),
  909
Tilden, Samuel J., 507
Timber and Stone Act (1878), 521
Times They Are A-Changin', The
  (Dylan), 906
Title VII (Civil Rights Act, 1964), 903
Title IX (Education Amendments,
  1972), 904
Tito, Josip Broz, 774
Tobacco and tobacco industry, 530
  suits against, 969
Tojo, Hideki, 764
Toledo, Jones in, 584
Tortilla Flat (Steinbeck), 748
Totalitarianism, Soviet, 791, 822–823
Total Woman, The (Morgan), 905
Tourgée, Albion, 490, 491
Towns. *See* Cities and towns
Townsend, Francis E., 733
Townsend Pension Clubs, 733
Toxic waste, 912
Toynbee Hall, 630
Trade. *See also* Commerce;
  Transportation
  with China, 620, 621
  expansion and, 604–605
  free trade, 965
  with Japan, 759
  Latin America policy and, 755
  in 1920s, 713, 723
  Open Door policy and, 621
  peace and, 714
  World War I and, 666–667
Trade Agreements Act (1934), 755
Trade unions, 505, 935. *See also*
  Labor unions
Trading with the Enemy Act, 672
Tranquilizers, 816
Transcontinental railroad, 505, 544
  Native Americans and, 526
Transistors, 798
Trans-Mississippi West, movement
  to, 515
Transportation
  in cities, 550
  farming and, 514
Treason of the Senate, The (Phillips),
  631

Treaties. *See also* Alliance(s); specific
  treaties
  Indians and, 526
  Moroccan crisis and, 624
  Native Americans and, 910, 911
  outlawing war, 714
Treaty of Versailles. *See* Versailles
  Peace Conference
Trench warfare, 665, 674
Triangle Shirtwaist Company fire,
  642–643
Trickle-down economic theory, 809
Trolleys, 550
Trudeau, Garry, 898
Truman, Harry S, 778
  atomic bomb and, 780–781
  Atomic Energy Act and, 838
  civil rights and, 811–812
  Cold War and, 822
  Congress and, 804–805
  election of 1948 and, 805, 806
  Fair Deal of, 803, 805–807
  Israel and, 835
  Korean War and, 831–833
  at Potsdam, 823
  Soviets and, 823
Truman Doctrine, 826
Trusts
  after Sherman Act, 589
  Taft and, 653
Tugwell, Rexford, 727
Tunisia, 773
Turkey
  Cuban missile crisis and, 872
  Soviet Union and, 826
  World War I and, 664, 665
Turner, Frederick Jackson, 515, 516,
  604
Turner, Henry, 534
Tuskegee Institute, 534, 652
Tutsis, Hutu fighting with, 976
TVA. *See* Tennessee Valley
  Authority (TVA)
Twain, Mark, 573, 611
Tweed, William "Boss," 506, 616
Tweed ring, 507
Twentieth Amendment, 727
Twenty-first Amendment, 728
24th Infantry Division, 675
Two-party system, 595
Typewriters, 546

U-boats. *See* Submarines
Ulyanov, Vladimir Ilyich. *See* Lenin,
  V. I.
UN. *See* United Nations (UN)

Underwood Tariff (1913), 656
Unemployment, 506, 546, 724, 927
  African Americans and, 739
  conference on, 711, 712
  Coxey's march and, 592
  decline in, 957
  Depression of 1893 and, 591, 592
  Great Depression and, 722, 723,
    731–732, 742
  growth of, 936, 938
  among Latinos, 931
  1940-1980, 890
Unemployment benefits, 804
Unemployment insurance, 558, 658
Union (Civil War). *See* Civil War
  (U.S.); North
Union Pacific Railroad, 505, 506, 564
Unions. *See* Labor unions
United Automobile Workers
  (UAW), 738, 793, 935
United Farm Workers, 905
United Fruit Company, 606
United Kingdom. *See* England
  (Britain)
United Mine Workers, 649, 710, 738
United Nations (UN)
  establishment of, 779
  Korean War and, 832–833, 832
    (map)
  Persian Gulf War and, 944–945
  Rio Earth Summit and, 933
  Yom Kippur War and, 888 (map)
United Railway Administration,
  681
United States, migration to (1860-
  1910), 549 (map)
U.S. Steel
  labor and, 738
  trust busting and, 649
United States v. *E. C. Knight*, 588
Universal Negro Improvement
  Association, 704–705
Universities and colleges. *See also*
  specific schools
  African Americans and, 500
  enrollments in, 555
  Native Americans in, 911
  women in, 554, 801, 902–903
  after World War I, 696
Unsafe at Any Speed:.... (Nader), 914
Unskilled labor, 558
  in New Deal, 737–738
Upper class, 550, 553, 937. *See also*
  Elites and elitism
Urban areas. *See also* Cities and
  towns
  black lifestyles in, 810

  housing in, 742
  poverty in, 958
  Social Gospel movement and, 582
Urbanization. *See also* Cities and
  towns; Urban areas
  in industrial age, 547–550,
    550–553
  by 1990s, 938
Urban planning, 582–583
Ushijima, Kinji, 622
USSR. *See* Soviet Union
Utah, 636
Ute Indians, 964
Utilities
  in Great Depression, 736–737
  TVA and, 732–733
Utopianism, 572

Vagrancy laws, 487
Vallezo, California, 767
Values
  immigration and, 702–704
  Ku Klux Klan and, 694
  Native American, 910
  in 1920s, 701
Vandenberg, Arthur, 826
Vanzetti, Bartolomeo, 694–695
Vatican Ecumenical Council (1962),
  800
Venezuela
  boundary dispute and, 604, 624
  debt dispute and, 618
Versailles Peace Conference,
  684–686
Veterans
  Bonus Army and, 725–726
  Confederate, 589
  GI Bill and, 788–789
  pensions for, 588
Veterans of Future Wars, 756
Viagra, 960
Viet Cong, 873, 877, 893
Vietnam, 834
  division of, 834
  immigrants from, 932
  U.S. involvement in, 834, 892–895
Vietnamization policy, 893
Vietnam War, 873–878, 874 (map),
  879–880
  African Americans in, 894
  consequences of, 894
  economy and, 934
  end of, 894
  French and German posters on,
    896
  Great Society programs and, 869

  Latinos and, 894, 909
  Nixon and, 892–895
  student protests against, 875–876,
    879–880, 893–894
Viguerie, Richard, 921
Villa, Francisco "Pancho," 668
Villard, Oswald Garrison, 652
Violence. *See also* Race riots
  anti-Asian, 568, 932
  after King's death, 878
  in Middle East, 975
  at Pullman strike, 567
  racial, 489, 532, 533
  in Reconstruction South, 499,
    503–504
Virgin Islands, 609
VISTA program, 864
Volstead Act (1919), 715
Vorhees, Daniel, 576
Voting and voting rights, 577. *See
  also* Woman suffrage
  African Americans and, 532–533,
    588–589, 739, 813–814, 866
  in election of 1896, 594, 595
  for freedmen, 492, 493
  initiative and referendum in, 646
  for Native Americans, 754
  in Reconstruction South, 492, 503,
    504
  for women, 493–494, 585, 636–637,
    636 (map)
Voting Rights Act (1965), 866, 891,
  928
Wabash v. *Illinois*, 536

WACS (Women's Army Corps), 771
Wade, Benjamin, 493
Wade-Giles system, 831n
Wages
  minimum, 743
  in New South, 530
  in 1920s, 710
  for skilled labor, 558
  for women, 768, 929
  for workers, 590
  World War II and, 761, 793
Wage slavery, 561
Wagner, Robert, 737
Wagner Act (1935), 737–738
Wainwright, Jonathan, 772
Wake Island, 772
Wald, Lillian, 646
Walesa, Lech, 940
Walker, Francis Amasa, 526
Walking cities, 550
Wallace, George C., 859, 879
Wallace, Henry A.

election of 1940 and, 758
election of 1944 and, 778
on Marshall Plan, 828
as Progressive party candidate, 805
as Roosevelt adviser, 727
Ward, Lester Frank, 580
Warhol, Andy, 878
War industries. *See* Defense industries
War Industries Board, 681
"War of the Worlds, The" (radio broadcast), 748
War Production Board (WPB), 761
Warren, Earl, 868
War Revenue Act (1917), 680
Wars and warfare. *See also* specific wars
between whites and Plains Indians, 522–523, 526
Washington (state), 636
Washington, Booker T., 534–535, 652
Du Bois, W. E. B. and, 535
Tuskegee Institute and, 534, 652
Washington Conference on Naval Disarmament (1921), 713
Washington Post, Watergate affair and, 897
Water
irrigation of California farms, 520
New Deal projects for, 736
in West, 650, 913
Watergate affair, 895–900
Water power, 543
Water Quality Improvement Act, 913
Water rights, 520
Watson, Tom, 538, 594, 613–614
Watt, James, 933
Watts riot (1965), 868
WAVES (women's branch of the Navy), 771
WCTU. *See* Woman's Christian Temperance Union
Wealth
concentration of, 558
corporate, 696
in Depression of 1893, 591–592
distribution of, 643, 762
in Great Depression, 722–723, 736–737
inequality of, 573, 709–710
in 1980s, 927
poverty and, 586
in South, 496
Wealth gap, 946, 958

Wealthy
in 1920s, 711–712
tax cut for, 957–958
Weapons. *See also* Atomic bomb; Nuclear weapons
in Cold War, 837–841
naval armaments and, 712, 713
in World War I, 664–665
Weary Blues (Hughes), 706
Weaver, James B., 589, 590
Weavers (singing group), 906
Webster v. *Reproductive Health Services,* 929
Welch, Joseph, 846–847
Welfare and welfare programs
Clinton and, 949
end of commitment to, 968
Great Depression and, 735
Nixon and, 889
Reagan and, 926
Sheppard-Towner Act and, 714–715
Social Security and, 735
"Welfare capitalism," 697
Welfare state, 851–852
origins of, 803–809
Welles, Orson, 748
"We Shall Overcome" (song), 906
West. *See also* Far West; Trans-Mississippi West; Westward movement
African American migration to, 766
agriculture in, 512
cattle raising in, 516–517
Chinese in, 568
environment and, 517 (map), 913
frontier thesis and, 515, 516
Great Plains farmers and, 517–519
mining in, 520–521
Native Americans in, 522–528
natural resources in, 521–522
New Deal and, 736
nuclear weapons in, 839–840
preservation and conservation in, 521–522
water in, 650, 913
woman suffrage in, 636
World War II and, 767
West Bank, 872, 887, 974, 975
West Coast
Asian immigration to, 549–550
Japanese Americans and, 763–764
Western Europe, Marshall Plan and, 828
Western Federation of Miners (WFM), 566

Western Hemisphere
immigration within, 703
U.S. rights in, 618, 620
U.S. role in, 601, 755–756
West Germany, 791, 825, 828, 870–871. *See also* Germany
Westmoreland, William, 875
Westward movement, 515. *See also* Trans-Mississippi West
of freedpeople, 500
in global context, 516
after World War II, 795
Weyler, Valeriano, 607–608
Wheat, 515
"Whip Inflation Now" program, 900
Whiskey Ring affair, 506
White City. *See* Columbian Exposition (Chicago)
White-collar jobs, 559, 792–793, 802, 816, 935
White Earth Land Recovery Project, 964
White man's burden, 612, 615
Whites
anti-Japanese attitudes of, 622
black soldiers and, 675
in civil rights movement, 859
after Civil War, 486
Native Americans and, 522–526
net worth of, 958–959
in population, 955
southern poor whites, 498–499
White supremacy, 498
Why America Fights Germany (pamphlet), 676
Wilhelm II (Germany), 610, 624, 679
Willard, Frances, 578, 579, 585
Wills, Garry, 885
Wilson, Charles E., 808
Wilson, Woodrow, 624, 646
collapse of, 688
election of 1912 and, 653–655
election of 1916 and, 668–669
Latin America and, 620, 667–668
neutrality and, 664, 665–666
New Freedom and, 654, 655–658
New Nationalism and, 656–658
on politics, 575
progressivism and, 653–655, 683
racism and, 656
tariff and banking reform and, 655–656
Versailles Peace Conference and, 684–686
World War I and, 664, 666–667
Windmills, 519

Winesburg, Ohio (Anderson), 707
Winthrop, John, 601
Wisconsin, progressivism in, 646
"Wobblies." *See* Industrial Workers
    of the World (IWW)
Wolfe, Thomas, 748
Wolfe, Tom, 927
Woman Rebel, The (Sanger), 637
Woman's Christian Temperance
    Union, 578, 638
Woman suffrage, 493–494, 584–585,
    636–637, 684
    Nineteenth Amendment and, 636
        (map)
    in states, 585
Women. *See also* Feminism; Gender;
    Woman suffrage; Workers;
    Workforce
    abortion rights of, 637
    AFL and, 565
    education for, 902–903
    employment of, 558, 633–636
    in factories, 530, 557
    feminism and, 905–905
    Fourteenth and Fifteenth
        Amendments and, 493–494
    as garment workers, 642–643
    Great Depression and, 724
    Illinois aid to mothers with
        dependent children, 646
    in Klan, 695
    labor law and, 633
    in labor unions, 641, 738
    Latina, 908, 931
    marriage and, 485, 561
    middle-class, 553–555
    in military, 771
    Native American, 964
    New Deal and, 740
    in 1920s, 707–709
    in 1990s-2000s, 963
    in post-World War I society,
        883–884
    poverty of, 959
    in professions, 963
    progressivism and, 632–637, 658,
        659
    prostitution by, 560
    return to college by, 801
    roles of, 800–801
    settlement house movement and,
        580–582
    sexual preferences of, 912
    Sheppard-Towner Maternity Act
        and, 714–715
    stereotypes of, 801

on Supreme Court, 929, 930
voting by, 711
work and home responsibilities
    of, 934
in workforce, 558, 559–561
in World War I, 675, 682
in World War II, 768
Women's Army Corps (WACS),
    771
Women's health collective, 904
Women's International League for
    Peace and Freedom, 686
Women's liberation, 903–904
Women's rights, 506, 902–905
    conservatives and, 929–930
    movement in 1890s, 585
    Seneca Falls and, 585
Women's sphere, 555
    Gilman on, 637
Women's Trade Union League, 642,
    643
Wonderful Wizard of Oz, The (Baum),
    593
Woodward, Bob, 897
Work. *See also* Labor
    changes in, 557
    changes in patterns of, 792–793,
        933–934
    New Deal relief and, 734–735
Work, Robert, 551–552
Work contracts, 487, 495, 505, 509
Workday, 557
    eight-hour, 563, 653
    ten-hour, 633
    of women, 633, 646
Workers. *See also* Labor; Labor
    unions; Women; Workforce
    benefits for, 557, 558
    changing conditions of, 935–936
    computers and, 934
    in factories, 544
    living conditions for, 551
    in New South, 530
    1920s prosperity and, 709–710
    in progressive era, 640–644
    protests by, 561–562
    rights to organize, 643
    World War I and, 681–683
Workers' compensation, 646
Work ethic, 555–556
Workforce. *See also* Women;
    Workers
    changes in, 557
    Civil War and, 541
    farming, 935–936
    in service economy, 934

women in, 682–683, 707, 708, 768,
    801, 802, 904, 935
young people in, 935
Working class
    alcohol use by, 553
    city neighborhoods of, 550, 551,
        553
    family economy of, 558–559
    industrialization and, 556–561
    labor benefits for, 558
    living standards of, 551, 552,
        568–570, 793
    setbacks for, 565–566
    urban, 550
Workmen's Compensation Bill
    (1916), 669
Workplace, 557, 643, 933–934. *See
    also* Industrialization; Industry;
    Workers
Works Progress Administration
    (WPA), 734–735
Workweek
    maximum, 743
    for women, 643
    after World War I, 696
World Christian Fundamentalist
    Association, 701
WorldCom, 958
World Court, 662–663, 712, 974
World markets, 546
World power, United States as, 599
World's Columbian Exposition, 515,
    591, 592
World's Fair (New York, 1939), 744
World War I, 624, 661–662
    African Americans in, 674, 675,
        679, 681–682
    Allies in, 663, 665–666, 678–680,
        686
    casualties in, 678–679
    causes of, 662–664
    debt after, 714
    domestic impact of, 680–684
    economy after, 696–700
    Europe and Near East after, 685
        (map)
    financing of, 680–681
    legacy of, 688–689
    military technology in, 664–665
    problems after, 692–695
    propaganda and, 676, 677
    Russian/German separate peace
        in, 678
    trade in, 666–667
    trench warfare in, 678
    U.S. entry into, 670, 671–673

U.S. neutrality in, 664, 665
woman suffrage and, 684
women in, 675, 682
workers in, 681–683
World War II
  aims of, 772
  Allies in, 772–779
  Asian Americans in, 753
  bracero program during, 814
  causes of Cold War and, 848
  defeated nations after, 791
  diplomacy in, 771–775
  Dresden bombing and, 777
  economy after, 786–794
  end of, 776–779
  in Europe, 757–758
  events leading to, 754–757
  home front in, 761–767

mobilization for, 761–762
Pacific theater of, 773 (map)
Pearl Harbor attack and, 759–760
politics of victory after, 778
social impact of, 767–771
women after, 883–884
Worship. *See* Freedom(s);
  Religion(s)
Wounded Knee
  Indian takeover of, 910–911
  massacre at, 528, 586, 910
Wovoka, 528
Wright, Nathan, Jr., 868
Wright, Richard, 703
Writers. *See* Literature

Yalta Conference, 778–779, 823
"Yellow Peril," 622

Yeltsin, Boris, 940, 941, 976
Yom Kippur War (1973), 887, 888
  (map), 895
York, Alvin, 679
Yosemite National Park, 521,
  650–651
Youth movement, 876
  counterculture and, 877–878
Yugoslavia
  breakup of, 940–941, 942 (map)
  fighting in former, 973–974
  Versailles Peace Conference and,
  686

Zhou Enlai, 894
Zimmermann, Arthur, 670
Zionism, 835

The World

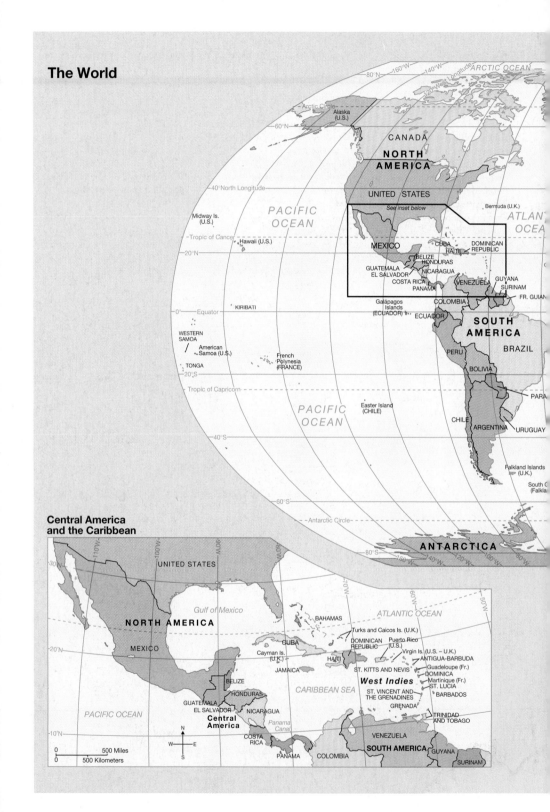

Central America and the Caribbean

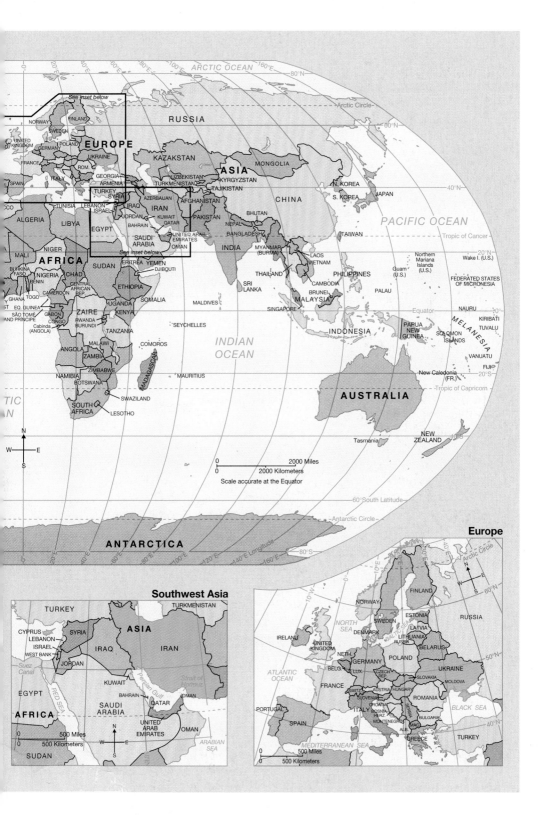